HISTORICAL DICTIONARY

The historical dictionaries present essential information on a broad range of subjects, including American and world history, art, business, cities, countries, cultures, customs, film, global conflicts, international relations, literature, music, philosophy, religion, sports, and theater. Written by experts, all contain highly informative introductory essays of the topic and detailed chronologies that, in some cases, cover vast historical time periods but still manage to heavily feature more recent events.

Brief A–Z entries describe the main people, events, politics, social issues, institutions, and policies that make the topic unique, and entries are cross-referenced for ease of browsing. Extensive bibliographies are divided into several general subject areas, providing excellent access points for students, researchers, and anyone wanting to know more. Additionally, maps, photographs, and appendixes of supplemental information aid high school and college students doing term papers or introductory research projects. In short, the historical dictionaries are the perfect starting point for anyone looking to research in these fields.

HISTORICAL DICTIONARIES OF LITERATURE AND THE ARTS

Jon Woronoff, Series Editor

Science Fiction Literature, by Brian Stableford, 2004.

Hong Kong Cinema, by Lisa Odham Stokes, 2007.

American Radio Soap Operas, by Jim Cox, 2005.

Japanese Traditional Theatre, by Samuel L. Leiter, 2006.

Fantasy Literature, by Brian Stableford, 2005.

Australian and New Zealand Cinema, by Albert Moran and Errol Vieth, 2006.

African-American Television, by Kathleen Fearn-Banks, 2006.

Lesbian Literature, by Meredith Miller, 2006.

Scandinavian Literature and Theater, by Jan Sjåvik, 2006.

British Radio, by Seán Street, 2006.

German Theater, by William Grange, 2006.

African American Cinema, by S. Torriano Berry and Venise Berry, 2006.

Sacred Music, by Joseph P. Swain, 2006.

Russian Theater, by Laurence Senelick, 2007.

French Cinema, by Dayna Oscherwitz and MaryEllen Higgins, 2007.

Postmodernist Literature and Theater, by Fran Mason, 2007.

Irish Cinema, by Roderick Flynn and Pat Brereton, 2007.

Australian Radio and Television, by Albert Moran and Chris Keating, 2007.

Polish Cinema, by Marek Haltof, 2007.

Old Time Radio, by Robert C. Reinehr and Jon D. Swartz, 2008.

Renaissance Art, by Lilian H. Zirpolo, 2008.

Broadway Musical, by William A. Everett and Paul R. Laird, 2008.

American Theater: Modernism, by James Fisher and Felicia Hardison Londré, 2008.

German Cinema, by Robert C. Reimer and Carol J. Reimer, 2008.

Horror Cinema, by Peter Hutchings, 2008.

Westerns in Cinema, by Paul Varner, 2008.

Chinese Theater, by Tan Ye, 2008.

Italian Cinema, by Gino Moliterno, 2008.

Architecture, by Allison Lee Palmer, 2008.

Russian and Soviet Cinema, by Peter Rollberg, 2008.

African American Theater, by Anthony D. Hill, 2009.

Postwar German Literature, by William Grange, 2009.

Modern Japanese Literature and Theater, by J. Scott Miller, 2009.

Animation and Cartoons, by Nichola Dobson, 2009.

Modern Chinese Literature, by Li-hua Ying, 2010.

Middle Eastern Cinema, by Terri Ginsberg and Chris Lippard, 2010.

Spanish Cinema, by Alberto Mira, 2010.

Film Noir, by Andrew Spicer, 2010.

French Theater, by Edward Forman, 2010.

Choral Music, by Melvin P. Unger, 2010.

Westerns in Literature, by Paul Varner, 2010.

Baroque Art and Architecture, by Lilian H. Zirpolo, 2010.

Surrealism, by Keith Aspley, 2010.

Science Fiction Cinema, by M. Keith Booker, 2010.

Latin American Literature and Theater, by Richard A. Young and Odile Cisneros, 2011.

Children's Literature, by Emer O'Sullivan, 2010.

German Literature to 1945, by William Grange, 2011.

Neoclassical Art and Architecture, by Allison Lee Palmer, 2011.

American Cinema, by M. Keith Booker, 2011.

American Theater: Contemporary, by James Fisher, 2011.

English Music: ca. 1400–1958, by Charles Edward McGuire and Steven E. Plank, 2011.

Rococo Art, by Jennifer D. Milam, 2011.

Romantic Art and Architecture, by Allison Lee Palmer, 2011.

Japanese Cinema, by Jasper Sharp, 2011.

Modern and Contemporary Classical Music, by Nicole V. Gagné, 2012.

Russian Music, by Daniel Jaffé, 2012.

Music of the Classical Period, by Bertil van Boer, 2012.

Holocaust Cinema, by Robert C. Reimer and Carol J. Reimer, 2012.

Asian American Literature and Theater, by Wenjing Xu, 2012.

Beat Movement, by Paul Varner, 2012.

Jazz, by John S. Davis, 2012.

Crime Films, by Geoff Mayer, 2013.

Scandinavian Cinema, by John Sundholm, Isak Thorsen, Lars Gustaf Andersson, Olof Hedling, Gunnar Iversen, and Birgir Thor Møller, 2013.

Chinese Cinema, by Tan Ye and Yun Zhu, 2013.

Taiwan Cinema, by Daw-Ming Lee, 2013.

Russian Literature, by Jonathan Stone, 2013.

Gothic Literature, by William Hughes, 2013.

French Literature, by John Flower, 2013.

Baroque Music, by Joseph P. Swain, 2013.

Opera, by Scott L. Balthazar, 2013.

British Cinema, by Alan Burton and Steve Chibnall, 2013.

Romantic Music, by John Michael Cooper with Randy Kinnett, 2013.

British Theatre: Early Period, by Darryll Grantley, 2013.

South American Cinema, by Peter H. Rist, 2014.

African American Television, Second Edition, by Kathleen Fearn-Banks and Anne Burford-Johnson, 2014.

Japanese Traditional Theatre, Second Edition, by Samuel L. Leiter, 2014.
Science Fiction in Literature, by M. Keith Booker, 2015.
Romanticism in Literature, by Paul Varner, 2015.
American Theater: Beginnings, by James Fisher, 2016.

Historical Dictionary of American Theater

Beginnings

James Fisher

ROWMAN & LITTLEFIELD
Lanham • Boulder • New York • London

Published by Rowman & Littlefield
A wholly owned subsidiary of The Rowman & Littlefield Publishing Group, Inc.
4501 Forbes Boulevard, Suite 200, Lanham, Maryland 20706
www.rowman.com

Unit A, Whitacre Mews, 26-34 Stannary Street, London SE11 4AB

British Library Cataloguing in Publication Information Available

Library of Congress Cataloging-in-Publication Data

Fisher, James, 1950–
Historical dictionary of American theater : beginnings / James Fisher.
pages cm. — (Historical dictionaries of literature and the arts)
Includes bibliographical references.
ISBN 978-0-8108-7832-7 (hardcover : alk. paper) — ISBN 978-0-8108-7833-4 (ebook)
1. Theater—United States—History—Dictionaries. 2. American drama—Dictionaries. I. Title.
PN2266.F57 2015
792'.097303—dc23
2014043282

Contents

Editor's Foreword ix

Acknowledgments xi

Reader's Notes xiii

Chronology xv

Introduction 1

THE DICTIONARY 21

Bibliography 487

About the Author 525

Editor's Foreword

Given the scope of American theater, the Literature and the Arts series is approaching the topic through different periods, with the volumes "Modernism," from about 1880 to 1930, and "Contemporary," from 1930 on. The current volume, "Beginnings," is last in order of writing but first chronologically—from the start of American theater until 1880. This early period was quite different from the others, with some of it occurring while the colonies were still under British rule. It was a time of strong religious feelings and patriotism, and some of the plays were primitive and the actors untrained. But there were also remarkable advances as the theater gained a foothold around the country, with Broadway as its anchor.

The stage is set by the chronology, which recounts the earliest steps taken, year by year. The introduction provides an overview of the inception and advances of American theater during this formative period. Details are then provided in the dictionary section, with a multitude of entries on actors and actresses, directors and others on the production side, and playwrights, to say nothing of the various genres and more notable plays and venues. The volume encompasses both Bernhardt and Barnum; tragedy, comedy, and melodrama; and minstrel shows and dog dramas. Finally, the extensive bibliography lists other sources of information.

This *Historical Dictionary of American Theater: Beginnings* was written by James Fisher, who was the sole author of the *Historical Dictionary of American Theater: Contemporary* and coauthor of the *Historical Dictionary of American Theater: Modernism*. All three books are rooted in his background and experience. He has been at the University of North Carolina, Greensboro, for almost a decade, following nearly three decades at Wabash College, nearly half of this as department chair. In addition to teaching on American theater, he has written numerous papers and articles. And unlike most academics, he has also worked as a director and written two plays of his own, which provides rather special insight into the trade. This now completed series of books is quite an accomplishment, one that fills a large gap in available reference material. It will be appreciated by scholars, students, and anyone with a love of the theater.

Jon Woronoff
Series Editor

Acknowledgments

I am most grateful to the staff of Rowman & Littlefield for their patience and support, with particular and sincere thanks to editor Jon Woronoff for his impressive grasp of the big picture as well as his attention to details. Jon's prompt and insightful responses to numerous queries were invaluable throughout the entire process, and his patience when an extended illness significantly delayed my timely completion of the manuscript is deeply appreciated. Jon's astute eye makes him the most effective of editors.

I would also like to express my gratitude to my theater colleagues and students at the University of North Carolina at Greensboro, as well as several teachers whose encouragement led me toward theater both as a practitioner and a scholar, especially Kathryn England, Herman Middleton, Andreas Nomikos, and Lauren K. "Woody" Woods, all of whom enhanced my love of theater and its rich history.

My occasional collaborator, Felicia Hardison Londré, invited me to work with her on *The Historical Dictionary of American Theater: Modernism* over a decade ago, and aside from the delight of working with her and the privilege of learning from her vast knowledge of American theater, she has been a loyal, thoughtful, and generous friend. We wrote the modernism book together and that led to the opportunity for me to do this book on early American theater and a prior two-volume work covering the contemporary era. I have too much to be grateful to her for to put in a few simple words.

My family, especially my children, Daniel and Anna, and Daniel's wife, Stephanie Lyn, offered their love and support, adding to the happiness they provide me for being the remarkable individuals they are. Among the rest of my family, I also appreciate the concern and support of my brothers, Daniel R. Fisher, Judge Clarkson S. Fisher Jr., and the late Scott L. Fisher; my nephew and nieces; my late parents Clarkson and Mae Fisher; and my in-laws, Daniel and Kathleen Warner. Among friends and coworkers, past and present, I wish to acknowledge Michael Abbott, Douglas Calisch, Fredric Enenbach, Peter Frederick, Ken Kloth, Erminie Leonardis, Diane and Jamey Norton, my beloved Penland family, Warren Rosenberg, Bert Stern, and John Swan, all of whom gave me so much over many years. I would also like to thank colleagues in the American Theater and Drama Society for the high standard they set and the generosity of spirit they exude.

Finally, this book is dedicated to my wife and best friend, Dana Warner Fisher, whose loving concern and practical assistance with matters small and large have helped all the way along. During the time I researched and wrote this volume, more than a year was lost to a serious illness. While I went through the doctor's appointments, hospital stays, tests, procedures, and the attendant frustrations and fears, Dana was there for me totally as she has been for the nearly 40 years we have been together. When I began to feel better, I was able to work on this book again and Dana continued to be consistently supportive while I dealt with mobility issues, helping me to devote as much well time to my job and to this project as possible. For all of that, and much more, this book and everything else I am and do is for Dana.

Reader's Notes

The plan of this volume follows the format established for Rowman & Littlefield's series of Historical Dictionaries of Literature and the Arts. The focus of the volume is on legitimate theater while leaving aside musical and variety entertainment forms (except as these directly impact the evolution of legitimate theater). For those knowledgeable about theater in the Americas, the amazing richness of its history from the first performances by Europeans in North America to the slow rise of modernism in the decades following the American Civil War, as the United States became a world power, necessitate selective coverage. To attempt to list every performer, manager, designer, or critic who made a mark on the theater during three centuries, or every play staged in major venues leading to the rise of Broadway, would require far more than a single volume.

The difficult choices between inclusion and exclusion were made with the probable needs of the reader or researcher in mind. It has thus necessitated a weighing of relative influences, and yet much of the value of a work of this nature lies in the rescue of reputations and works that were common currency in their day, but in danger of being lost to obscurity. Some pointedly obscure works of a unique variety are included, as are lesser-known artists, if the author considered them a useful reflection of the range of entertainments and personalities at work during the centuries covered by the volume. There is much evidence lost or only partially in existence, a problem particular to American theater between 1538 and 1880, a long period with many decades prior to the 19th century offering little reliable evidence and comparatively little scholarship on some periods, persons, movements, and plays.

The vastness of the subject may be seen in the length of this volume's bibliography, which is divided into numerous subcategories. Other approaches to the material are offered in the introduction, which attempts to provide an overview history; in the chronology, which points out particular events year by year as they occurred in relation to other events; and in occasional catchall entries in the dictionary itself on such broad topics as African American theater, censorship, the circus, critics/criticism, female/male impersonation, foreign plays adapted to the American stage, frontier theater and drama, the Irish in American theater and drama, lighting, magic/magicians, medicine shows, melodrama, minstrels and minstrel shows, musical theater, Native Americans, photographers, playwrights, religious drama, scene design and scenery, sexuality and gender, Shakespeare in America, stock companies and stock characters, technological developments, theater fires, and so on. These overview entries make reference to the most important names related to that category (and may appear in separate individual entries based on their relative importance), and those names are boldfaced to indicate cross-referencing to these individual entries.

Individual entries cover the noteworthy dramatists, actors, directors, designers, and critics of the era, as well as individual plays, terminology, theatrical publications, theater facilities, companies, clubs, producing organizations, genres, and sundry other areas. Some of the plays merit plot summary in their individual entries. Other plays are notable more for the artists involved or the unusual nature of the material or the audience response or, perhaps, for the work as a harbinger of things to come. In any case, rather than adhere to a rigid formula, the author has endeavored to offer what is likely to be most useful in understanding the importance of the individual work within the context of American and international theater history and of the era. In some cases, lost plays are included with what information exists if the work is deemed to have been influential in some way.

In many instances, the influence or accomplishment of an individual extends beyond 1880, the year established as the demarcation between early and modernist theater. Such entries in this volume stress an entrant's activity *before* 1880, but include reference to the direction of later work. Those entrants will also be found in *Historical Dictionary of American Theater: Modernism* (which covers the period from 1880 to 1929) stressing post-1880 achievements. Names, titles, terms, etc., included in the "Modernism" volume will be identified with a dagger (†); those included in the "Contemporary" volume will be identified with an asterisk (*); and cross-references of names, titles, terms, etc., within this volume will be indicated by **bold** type (**Edwin Booth**, for example).

Chronology

1538 It is believed that this year soldiers at a Spanish settlement in the Southwest gave performances of plays for their own amusement.

1567 24 June: According to some evidence, two comedies were performed at a Spanish mission at Tequesta, Florida, but little else is known except that these were apparently performed for Spanish soldiers. These were possibly church-related plays, but evidence is slim.

1598 30 April: A performance of a Spanish *comedia* on the banks of the Rio Grande, near what is now El Paso, Texas, is presented by Spanish soldiers. **10 July:** The same Spanish soldiers give a performance of *Moros y Los Cristianos* (*Moors and Christians*), author unknown.

1665 27 August: William Darby's *Ye Bare and Ye Cubb*, believed to be the first English-language play staged in the American colonies, is performed in Accomack County, Virginia, featuring Cornelius Watkinson and Philip Howard as performers—and possibly co-authors—of the play. Only Darby was arrested by local authorities and, with Watkinson and Howard, compelled to perform the play before a local judge to determine if any fault was to be found—it was not, and Darby was acquitted.

1703–04 Strolling player Anthony Aston performs in Charleston, South Carolina, and in other places in the colonies, including New York.

1714 Robert Hunter's farce *Androboros* is the first play published in America.

1716 The first American theater building is constructed in Williamsburg, Virginia, under the proprietorship of William Livingston (the building may not have been completed until 1718), and the first recorded performances of a play in the theater are believed to have occurred in 1718 in honor of the birthday of King George I (the theater is demolished in 1745).

1723 A band of strolling players intends to perform in Philadelphia, but bow to Quaker pressures and perform outside city limits.

1730 William Shakespeare's *Romeo and Juliet*, believed to be the first of Shakespeare's plays produced in the American colonies, is performed in New York.

1732 6 December: George Farquhar's *The Recruiting Officer*, believed to be the earliest performance of a play by a professional company in the American colonies, is presented at the New Theatre in New York; little is known about this performance or the theater itself, although it is believed that the building belonged to Rip Van Dam, acting governor of the city, with Thomas Heady acting the lead.

1735 English impresario Henry Holt presents the first production of a ballet in the American colonies at Charleston, with John Hippisley's opera *Flora* as the first work of that genre staged in the colonies at Charleston; Thomas Otway's *The Orphan* is also performed in Charleston.

1736 12 February: The Dock Street Theatre, Charleston, opens.

1747 Mercy Otis Warren publishes a collection of plays and poetry.

1750 The first playhouse in New York opens. Following a minor riot at a performance in Boston, local authorities ban theatrical activity, a ban that held until 1793, though when British forces hold Boston during the American Revolution, they perform plays at Faneuil Hall. Actor and manager Thomas Kean appears in *Richard III* at the Theatre on Nassau Street in New York, followed by other plays, though puritanical attitudes ultimately end his work in New York.

1752 June: The newly formed American Company presents its first production, *The Merchant of Venice*, in Williamsburg, Virginia. **15 September:** The first professional theater company in the colonies, the Virginia Company of Comedians, performs *The Merchant of Venice* in a temporary wooden playhouse at Williamsburg, Virginia.

1753 The first brick playhouse constructed in the American colonies opens in Annapolis, Maryland, with a production of George Farquhar's *The Beaux' Stratagem*. **June:** Lewis Hallam Sr. and company leave Williamsburg to perform in other areas, where they frequently meet with resistance from religious or civic leaders, including in New York, Philadelphia, and South Carolina—Hallam subsequently leaves the colonies for Jamaica, where he dies. **17 September:** British author Richard Steele's comedy *The Conscious Lovers* is performed at New York's Nassau Street Theatre by Lewis Hallam's company—some historians, including William Dunlap, consider this to be the first play acted by a professional company in North America, but other evidence suggests the first was *The Recruiting Officer* in 1732.

1754 April: A temporary theater in a warehouse presents *The Fair Penitent*; the French and Indian War begins, continuing until 1763.

1756 Students at the College of Philadelphia stage *The Masque of Alfred*, and the performance is defended by the college's provost over local protests, only the first of such controversies over the subsequent 100 years or more as colleges and universities struggle with the appropriateness of theatrical activities for students. John Home's blank verse tragedy *Douglas*, which premiered in Scotland in an amateur production, becomes popular on both sides of the Atlantic Ocean and one of the most frequently produced plays in America, first with Lewis Hallam Sr. in the leading role of Young Norval, a character often seen as the first test of a new male talent.

1758 David Douglass marries Lewis Hallam's widow in the West Indies and reconstitutes Hallam's company with his wife and stepson, Lewis Hallam Jr., as leading actors. **28 December:** Despite local resistance, Douglass and the company perform Nicholas Rowe's *Jane Shore*.

1759 7 February: David Douglass's company performs in a temporary theater on Cruger's Wharf before departing for Philadelphia where, despite local resistance, he opens a theater on Society Hill.

1761 Summer: David Douglass and company perform in various locations in New England.

1764 An anonymous author writes *The Paxton Boys*, a farce satirizing local events in western Pennsylvania involving an uprising of frontier settlers against Native Americans.

1766 Robert Roberts's *Ponteach; or, The Savages of America* is written, but not produced until after the American Revolution as the first American play to deal seriously with Native American subjects. **14 November:** The Southwark Theatre, the first permanent theater building constructed in the American colonies, is built and opens in Philadelphia.

1767 The John Street Theatre, the first permanent playhouse in New York (inspired by the Southwark Theatre in Philadelphia), opens and becomes the home of the American Company. **24 April:** David Douglass's and Lewis Hallam Jr.'s American Company perform the first professional production of an American play, Thomas Godfrey's tragedy *The Prince of Parthia*, in New York. **April:** Thomas Forrest's *The Disappointment; or, The Force of Credulity* is written, but withdrawn before being performed.

1768 Isaac Bickerstaff's two-act comic opera with music by Charles Dibdin, *The Padlock*, opens in London followed by great success in America with Dibdin performing in blackface as a West Indies servant in a role later played by Lewis Hallam Jr. and African American actor Ira Aldridge.

1769 3 July: The first theater in Albany, New York, opens with a production of *Venice Preserved*.

1770 Colonel Robert Munford writes *The Candidates; or, The Humours of a Virginia Election* lightly satirizing a local election process for two burgesses. **5 March:** The Boston Massacre heightens tensions between American colonists and the British.

1771 An anonymous play, *The Trial of Atticus before Justice Beau, for a Rape*, is published but not produced. Philip Freneau's *The Rising Glory of America* is produced by students of the College of New Jersey.

1772 Mercy Otis Warren's satire assailing Massachusetts royal governor Thomas Hutchinson, *The Adulateur*, is published in portions in the *Massachusetts Spy* newspaper.

1773 Mercy Otis Warren writes a satiric play *The Defeat*. George Cockings's *The Conquest of Canada; or, The Siege of Quebec*, a tragedy on the British conquest of French Canada, is presented by the American Company at the Southwark Theatre featuring Lewis Hallam Jr. and David Douglass. **16 December:** Rebellious colonists, many dressed as Native Americans, board ships in Boston Harbor and hurl stores of tea into the harbor, increasing hostilities between the colonies and the British in what becomes known as the Boston Tea Party.

1774 David Douglass builds the first playhouse in Charleston. **5 September:** The First Continental Congress meets in Philadelphia. The Congress passes a resolution discouraging theatrical "entertainments" and following the issuing of the Declaration of Independence in 1776, individual states pass laws forbidding theatrical activity—these actions force professional companies to disband or depart from the colonies until after the Revolution, when many anti-theater laws remain in effect until the 1780s (in some states, including Massachusetts and Rhode Island, these strictures remain in place until 1793).

1775 Mercy Otis Warren writes her satire *The Group*, imagining King George III repealing the Massachusetts charter of rights. **23 March:** Patrick Henry delivers his fiery "Give me liberty or give me death" speech as tensions between colonists and England increase. **15 June:** George Washington is named commander in chief of the Continental Army. **17 June:** The Battle of Bunker Hill takes place, with British and the Continental Army locking horns in the first important battle of the Revolution, with the British prevailing.

1776 Hugh H. Brackenridge writes *The Battle of Bunkers-Hill* celebrating the courage of the participants and the American leaders and it is produced within months after the actual events. John Leacock's *The Fall of British Tyranny; or, American Liberty Triumphant, the First Campaign* is published and is probably performed in Philadelphia. *The Battle of Brooklyn*, by an unknown author, appears as one of several loyalist works published and staged during the Revolution. Between 1767 and this year, playwrights regularly feature a number of stock characters in plays, most based on minority ethnic groups in the country, including African Americans, Native Americans, Irish, and the Yankee. **8 January:** British General John Burgoyne's play *The Blockade of Boston* is performed in Boston's Faneuil Hall while the British hold the city—and an anonymous play, probably written by Mercy Otis Warren called *The Blockheads; or, The Affrighted Officers*, is a satiric answer to the Burgoyne's play. **15 January:** Thomas Paine's *Common Sense* is published. **4 July:** The Continental Congress declares independence from Great Britain by adopting the Declaration of Independence, written by Thomas Jefferson. **26 December:** General George Washington and his forces cross the Delaware River and capture Trenton, New Jersey, from Hessian forces holding the town.

1777 A British garrison requisitions New York's John Street Theatre and performs amateur theatricals there. Hugh H. Brackenridge's blank verse tragedy, *The Death of General Montgomery at the Siege of Quebec*, is performed by Brackenridge's students at Maryland's Somerset Academy. Colonel Robert Munford's *The Patriots*, set during the American Revolution, is written, probably this year, but not published until after his death. **19 December:** General George Washington and the Continental Army dig in at winter quarters in Valley Forge, Pennsylvania, and endure difficult hardships including freezing temperatures, lack of food, and proper clothing.

1778 19 June: General George Washington's Continental Army leaves Valley Forge, Pennsylvania, and reengages with the British at the Battle of Monmouth.

1779 Mercy Otis Warren writes a one-act farce, *The Motley Assembly*, in which she promotes the then-radical idea of votes for women.

1780 23 September: Major John André is arrested as a spy, leading to the revelation of General Benedict Arnold's plans to cede West Point to the British and switch sides from the American to the British.

1781 Adam Lindsay and Thomas Wall establish the Maryland Company of Comedians, the first company of players in residence in Baltimore. **2 March:** The Articles of Confederation are adopted by the Continental Congress. **19 October:** British general Cornwallis surrenders at Yorktown, Virginia.

1782 John Henry returns from Jamaica, where the Old American Company, David Douglass, and Lewis Hallam Jr. have spent the American Revolution while the ban on theatrical activity has been in full force.

1783 3 September: The United States of America and Great Britain sign the Treaty of Paris.

1784 Barnabas Bidwell's play, *The Mercenary Match*, is staged by students at Yale College. Lewis Hallam Jr. returns to America from Jamaica, where he has spent the years of the American Revolution. Mercy Otis Warren's *The Ladies of Castile*, a five-act blank verse tragedy, is completed, but not published in 1790 due to Warren's wish that it not be produced.

1785 John Henry and Lewis Hallam Jr. join forces with Thomas Wignell, and reassemble the Old American Company at the John Street Theatre, where they become dominant forces in post-Revolutionary American theater. *Sans Souci, Alias, Free and Easy, or, An Evening's Peep into a Political Circle*, possibly authored by Mercy Otis Warren, is written and though she denies writing it, scholars believe it is her work.

1786 16 August: Baltimore's first theater is built by Lewis Hallam Jr. and John Henry.

1787 William Dunlap's first play, *The Modest Soldier; or, Love in New York*, is written, very likely inspired by Tyler's *The Contrast*. **16 April:** Royall Tyler's five-act comedy, *The Contrast*, written in the style of English comedy of manners plays, is the first written by an American citizen performed professionally and is well-received by its audience. **17 September:** The United States Constitution is signed.

1788 Samuel Low's *The Politician Out-Witted*, an early topical and politically driven work fiercely defending the US Constitution, is a harbinger of many political works focused on current events seen over the early decades of the United States, and Low's play also features an early example of the Yankee character type, which would be seen prevalently in comedies and melodramas well into the 19th century.

1789 William Hill Brown's *The Better Sort; or, A Girl of Spirit*, a satire of social fashions, is published in Boston. Samuel Low's *The Politician Out-Witted*, dealing in a lighthearted fashion with contemporary politics, opens and is published. **7 September:** William Dunlap's comedy, *The Father; or, American Shandyism*, is produced at the John Street Theatre. **24 November:** William Dunlap's *Darby's Return*, opens at the New York Theatre as a benefit for Thomas Wignell in a comedy about an Irishman's involvement in the American Revolution and his return to his Irish home to tell of his experiences.

1790 Mercy Otis Warren publishes *Poems, Dramatic and Miscellaneous*, which contains two of her plays *The Sack of Rome* and *The Ladies of Castile*.

1792 16 August: The "New Exhibition Room," the first theater in Boston, is built and opens, causing a riot when local authorities arrest the actors during performances of *Douglas* and *The Poor Soldier*, which had been billed as "Moral Lectures" to get around antitheatrical attitudes.

1794 Yale College president Timothy Dwight condemns theatrical activity in his "Essay on the Stage," suggesting that indulging theatrical tastes means risking "the immortal soul" of the playgoer. American sailors face problems with Barbary pirates in this period, and a number of playwrights address the issues, including Susanna Haswell Rowson in *Slaves in Algiers; or, A Struggle for Freedom*, which is staged by the Federal Street Theatre that year. **February:** Philadelphia's Chestnut Street Theatre opens with a double-bill of *The Castle of Andulasia* and *Who's the Dupe?* **3 March:** Anne Kemble Hatton contributes the libretto for the musical drama, *Tammany; or, The Indian Chief*, with music by James Hewitt, which opens at the John Street Theatre. **24 April:** William Dunlap's *The Fatal Deception; or, The Progress of Guilt*, a tragedy compared to Shakespeare's *Macbeth*, opens at the John Street Theatre.

1795 Harvard students found the Hasty Pudding Club. Susanna Haswell Rowson's *The Female Patriot; or, Nature's Rights* is performed at Philadelphia's New Theatre. William Dunlap's *Fontainville Abbey*, inspired by Ann Radcliffe's 1791 Gothic novel *The Romance of the Forest*, opens at the New York Theatre, a true departure from romantic tragedy in its Gothic trappings. **22 May:** John Murdock's *The Triumphs of Love; or, Happy Reconciliation*, satirizing the ways of the Quakers, the Whiskey Rebellion, and America's tensions with Algiers over piracy, opens at the New Theatre. **25 September:** Baltimore's Holliday Street Theatre opens.

1796 Royall Tyler writes *The Farm House; or, The Female Duellists*, probably performed that year (the play is considered lost). **18 April:** William Dunlap's adaptation of Friedrich von Schiller's *William Tell, The Archers; or, The Mountaineers of Switzerland* opens at the John Street Theatre in an Old American Company production.

1797 As American nationalism grows in the years following the American Revolution, dramatists celebrate its heroes and events in such plays as William Hill Brown's *West Point Preserved; or, The Treason of Arnold*, recounting in tragic form the story of Major John André. **January:** William Dunlap's farce, *Tell the Truth and Shame the Devil*, opens in New York in an Old American Company production. **17 February:** John Daly Burk's *Bunker-Hill; or, The Death of General Warren* opens at Boston's Haymarket Theatre. **12 April:** Susanna Haswell Rowson's comedy *Americans in England; or, Lessons for Daughters* is presented at Boston's Federal Street Theatre. **20 December:** Royall Tyler's *The Georgia Spec; or, Land in the Moon* opens at New York's John Street Theatre satirizing land speculation and the Yazoo Purchase.

1798 *The Thespian Oracle*, a periodical largely devoted to theatrical matters (and the first of its kind in America), begins publication. Colonel Robert Munford's plays, *The Candidates; or, The Humours of a Virginia Election* and *The Patriots*, are published this year, though both were written in the 1770s, when Munford served in the American Revolution. **29 January:** The first Park Theatre opens in New York under the management of William Dunlap and John Hodgkinson. **30 March:** William Dunlap's popular drama *André*, offering a sympathetic portrait of the British spy executed during the American Revolution, opens at the Park Theatre. **13 April:** *Female Patriotism; or, The Death of Joan D'Arc*, John Daly Burk's verse tragedy, opens at the Park Theatre, a play using the broad facts of Joan D'Arc's life as a case for the triumph of democracy over tyranny. **27 April:** William Dunlap takes over management of the Old American Company at the Park Theatre (first known as the New Theatre), which is built that year by Lewis Hallam Jr. and John Hodgkinson to rival the John Street Theatre. **10 December:** William Dunlap stages his own adaptation of August von Kotzebue's *The Stranger* starring Thomas Abthorpe Cooper at the Park Theatre and scores a major success.

1799 William Dunlap's *The Italian Father*, inspired by Thomas Dekker's *The Honest Whore, Part II*, is first performed, and Dunlap regards it as one of his best works. **11 December:** William Dunlap's comedy *False Shame; or, The American Orphan in Germany*, adapted from an August von Kotzebue play, opens at the Park Theatre.

1800 Thomas Wignell builds and opens the United States Theatre, the first in Washington, DC. **12 March:** William Dunlap's *The Virgin of the Sun*, adapted from a play by August von Kotzebue, opens at the Park Theatre, followed mere weeks later by Dunlap's *Pizarro in Peru*, both plays scoring success with the New York audience. **26 March:** William Dunlap's adaptation of Richard Brinsley Sheridan's *Pizarro*, called *Pizarro in Peru*, opens at the Park Theatre.

1802 *The Essex Junto; or, Quixotic Guardian* by J. Horatio Nicholas is produced and published, satirizing President John Adams as the "Duke of Braintree." *A New World Planted; or, The Adventures of the Forefathers of New England Who Landed in Plymouth, December 22nd 1620* by Joseph Croswell opens in Boston, borrowing on the myth of Pocahontas.

1803 William Dunlap's musical extravaganza, *The Glory of Columbia, Her Yeomanry*, intended for holiday celebrations, borrows elements from Dunlap's 1798 blank verse play, *André: A Tragedy*.

1804 4 April: James Workman's comedy *Liberty in Louisiana*, celebrating the Louisiana Purchase, opens at the Charleston Theatre with John Hodgkinson.

1805 Mercy Otis Warren publishes her three-volume *History of the Rise, Progress, and Termination of the American Revolution*. **January:** John Minshull's opéra bouffe, *Rural Felicity: With the Humor of Patrick, and Marriage of Shelty*, opens at the Grove Theatre with Irish characters reflecting the growing influx of Irish immigrants to the United States.

1806 John Blake White's blank verse tragedy, *Foscari; or, The Venetian Exile*, opens at the Charleston Theatre.

1807 Sarah Pogson Smith's dramatization of Charlotte Corday's murder of Jean Paul Marat during France's Reign of Terror, *The Female Enthusiast*, is probably performed at the Charleston Theatre. A. B. Lindsley's *Love and Friendship; or, Yankee Notions* opens at the Park Theatre featuring Brother Jonathan, a Yankee character. **4 March:** James Nelson Barker's three-act comedy, *Tears and Smiles*, inspired by Royall Tyler's *The Contrast*, opens at the Chestnut Street Theatre.

1808 The St. Philip Street Theatre in New Orleans is built and opens and eventually operates under the management of James H. Caldwell. **16 March:** The Embargo Act of 1807 causes controversy explored in James Nelson Barker's *The Embargo; or, What News?* which opens at the Chestnut Street Theatre. **6 April:** James Nelson Barker's *The Indian Princess; or, La Belle Sauvage* opens at the Chestnut Street Theatre, a fictionalized account, starring William Burke Wood, of the Pocahontas myth.

1809 The Walnut Street Theatre in Philadelphia is founded and opens its first production, Richard Brinsley Sheridan's *The Rivals*, in 1812 with ex–US president Thomas Jefferson and the Marquis de Lafayette in attendance at the first performance.

1810 Isaac Harby's second play, written in 1807, *The Gordian Knot*, is finally produced by Alexandre Placide and William Warren and becomes a popular melodramatic revenge drama.

1812 John Blake White's tragedy, *Modern Honor; or, The Victim of Revenge*, about the tragic ramifications of the prevalent practice of dueling, opens at the Charleston Theatre. **18 June:** Hostilities between the United States and Great Britain explode into armed conflict, the War of 1812, when the United States declares war to, among other things, end the British policy of capturing American sailors and pressing them into English naval service. **7 September:** William Dunlap's *Yankee Chronology; or, Huzza for the Constitution!* opens at the Park Theatre, celebrating the sea battle between the USS *Constitution* and the HMS *Guerriere* only a week before. **11 December:** The anonymous play, *The Return from a Cruise*, opens at the Chestnut Street Theatre only three days after the victory of the USS United States of the HMS *Macedonian*.

1813 18 January: The Green Street Theatre in Albany, New York, opens as the first permanent theater in that city.

1814 24 August: The British capture and burn Washington, DC. **13 September:** Francis Scott Key writes "The Star-Spangled Banner" while watching the bombardment of Fort McHenry. **24 December:** The Treaty of Ghent is signed, ending the War of 1812.

1815 1 January: Richard Penn Smith's play, *The Eighth of January*, receives mixed reviews when it opens at the Chestnut Street Theatre, but finds an audience for its story of a British loyalist trying to hold his family together during the War of 1812. **8 January:** General Andrew Jackson triumphs leading American forces in the Battle of New Orleans, unaware that the War of 1812 has ended two weeks previously.

1816 Gas lighting is used for the first time in a theater in the United States in Philadelphia's Chestnut Street Theatre. Thomas Drummond invents the limelight, widely employed in American theaters for the subsequent 100 years. William Henry Brown founds the African Company, the first known African American theater troupe in the United States. **4 July:** C. E. Grice's *The Battle of New Orleans; or, Glory, Love and Loyalty* opens at the Park Theatre recounting General Andrew Jackson's triumphant victory at the end of the War of 1812.

1818 Sarah Pogson Smith's drama, *The Young Carolinians; or, Americans in Algiers*, depicting the true events of a 1785 capture of American sailors by Barbary pirates, is first performed.

1819 Feminist writer Frances "Fanny" Wright's play *Altorf* is produced in New York starring James W. Wallack. James Ellison's patriotic drama, *The American Captive; or, The Siege of Tripoli*, opens and is published. Edwin Forrest makes his debut as Young Norval in *Douglas* at the Walnut Street Theatre. English actor Edmund Kean makes his first New York appearance as Richard III, winning acclaim though the American press increasingly reports on his controversial behaviors dallying with a married woman and drinking. John Neal's poetic tragedy, *Otho: A Tragedy in Five Acts*, intended as a vehicle for Thomas Abthorpe Cooper, is published, though not performed, despite the influence of Shakespeare, Lord Byron, and others on

Neal. **15 March:** John Howard Payne's *Brutus; or, The Fall of Tarquin* opens at the Park Theatre, following an earlier run in London starring Edmund Kean, who would be succeeded in the role by such actors as Edwin Forrest, Junius Brutus Booth, Edwin Booth, and James W. Wallack. **27 April:** Isaac Harby's last play, *Alberti*, opens at the Charleston Theatre, a work based on Vittorio Alfieri's tragedy *The Conspiracy of Pazzi.* **21 June:** *She Would Be a Soldier; or, The Plains of Chippewa* by Mordecai M. Noah opens at the Park Theatre, a play reflecting on the War of 1812.

1820 1 March: Samuel B. H. Judah's melodrama, *The Mountain Torrent*, opens at the Park Theatre with a plot involving a young woman compelled to marry a man she does not love in order to help her father. **15 May:** Mordecai M. Noah's *The Siege of Tripoli* opens at the Park Theatre, followed by a production in Philadelphia, dramatizing the problem of Barbary Coast pirates.

1821 *Logan, The Last of the Race of Shikellemus, Chief of the Cayuga Nation* by Joseph Doddridge, opens, a rare play depicting a Native American as a sympathetic figure. **2 February:** John Howard Payne's *Thérèse, The Orphan of Geneva* opens in London, followed by a New York production at the Anthony Street Theatre later in the year. **1 September:** The second Park Theatre opens in New York. **21 September:** William Henry Brown opens his African Grove Theatre in New York with a production of Shakespeare's *Richard III* and also stages other works by Shakespeare and the first play written by an African American, *The Drama of King Shotaway* (1823), written by Brown (the theater is believed to have closed in 1823, though later dates have been posited).

1822 Samuel B. H. Judah's *A Tale of Lexington: A National Comedy Founded on the Opening of the Revolution* opens in New York, one of the better of many plays reflecting on Revolutionary times presented in the first three decades of the 19th century. **1 March:** Charles Powell Clinch's *The Spy: A Tale of the Neutral Ground* opens at the Park Theatre, a play of intrigue set during the American Revolution.

1823 The African Grove Theatre presents William Henry Brown's *The Drama of King Shotaway*, the first full-length play by an African American produced in the United States. William Niblo opens his Niblo's Garden for a range of entertainments and exhibitions continuing until 1872, when a fire destroys the theater, but it is rebuilt and operates until 1895. Jonathan S. Smith's *The Siege of Algiers; or, The Downfall of Hadgi-Ali-Bashaw, A Political, Historical and Sentimental Tragi-Comedy* is published and possibly produced. **21 November:** John Howard Payne's operetta, with music by Henry Rowley Bishop, *Clari, The Maid of Milan*, opens at the Park Theatre.

1824 W. T. Moncrieff's equestrian melodrama, *The Cataract of the Ganges; or, The Rajah's Daughter*, which premiered in London in 1823, wins popularity at the Park Theatre when it opens in 1824. **12 March:** James Nelson Barker's *Superstition; or, The Fanatic Father* is produced by William Burke Wood at the Chestnut Street Theatre, a play attacking the excesses of Puritanism. **17 May:** The Chatham Garden Theatre opens in lower Manhattan. **25 October:** *Charles the Second; or, The Merry Monarch* by John Howard Payne and Washington Irving opens at the Park Theatre. **29 November:** *The Saw-Mill; or, A Yankee Trick* by Micah Hawkins, an opera with orchestra arrangements by James Hewitt, opens at the Chatham Garden Theatre.

1825 7 October: Samuel Woodworth's *The Forest Rose; or, American Farmers*, a musical play with music by John Davies, opens at the Chatham Garden Theatre featuring among its characters the Yankee Jonathan Ploughboy. **25 November:** Samuel Woodworth's *The Widow's Son; or, Which Is the Traitor?* opens at the Park Theatre, offering a tragedy set during the American Revolution. **25 December:** Richard Penn Smith's *William Penn; or, The Elm Tree* opens at the Walnut Street Theatre billed as an "historical play," set in colonial times and focused on the central events in Penn's life, including saving the life of the Indian chief Tammany.

1826 The Bowery Theatre opens on New York's Lower East Side. **February:** John Howard Payne's *The French Libertine*, originally named *Richelieu*, overcame objections to its content in England through some revision and was also produced in the United States with little success. **March:** James H. Hackett makes his stage debut. **15 June:** *Briar Cliff; or, Scenes of the Revolution*, a tragedy depicting political tensions during the American Revolution, opens at the Chatham Garden Theatre. **23 June:** Edwin Forrest, who will become America's leading tragedian prior to the Civil War, makes his New York stage debut in *Othello* at the Park Theatre. **October:** The 3,000-seat Bowery Theatre opens, with gas lighting, and is the first to employ a full-time press agent—the theater becomes the center of theater for working-class audiences.

1827 26 December: James McHenry's *The Usurper* opens at the Chestnut Street Theatre, one of the earliest American plays to draw on Irish mythology.

1828 Thomas Dartmouth "Daddy" Rice appears in his "Jump Jim Crow" act for the first time, inaugurating a century of blackface minstrelsy in the United States (though white actors in blackface playing African American roles predates Rice's performance by at least 50 years). William Dunlap's *A Trip to Niagara; or, Travelers in America*, a patriotic work in which a scoffing Englishman becomes enamored of America's wonders, opens and becomes the most popular play of Dunlap's long career. **22 February:** William Dunlap's melodrama, *Thirty Years; or, The Life of a Gamester*, is produced at the Bowery Theatre. **21 October:** Philadelphia's Arch Street Theatre opens with a production of *The Honeymoon*. **3 December:** James H. Hackett's adaptation of George Colman's *Who Wants a Guinea?*, which he called *Jonathan in England*, a Yankee comedy, opens with Hackett in the lead at the Park Theatre.

1829 Following experience in provincial theater, Edwin Forrest makes his New York debut at the Park Theatre. The General Theatrical Fund is established in Philadelphia to benefit stage workers who have fallen on hard times. **10 December:** *The Times; or, Life in New York*, an anonymous comedy created for James H. Hackett, opens at the Park Theatre. **15 December:** John Augustus Stone's drama, *Metamora; or, The Last of the Wampanoags*, wins Edwin Forrest's $500 prize for a play with a Native American as the major character and Forrest scores a great personal success in the role.

1830 6 January: Stephen E. Glover's adaptation of James Fenimore Cooper's novel, *The Last of the Mohicans*, opens under that title in Charleston, followed in rapid succession by productions in New Orleans and New York, winning great popularity. **8 January:** Richard Penn Smith's comedy-drama set during the War of 1812, *The Triumph of Plattsburg*, opens at the Chestnut Street Theatre. **4 February:** Richard Penn Smith's *The Deformed; or, Woman's Trial*, a tragedy inspired by Thomas Dekker, opens at Philadelphia's Chestnut Street Theatre. **March or April:** James H. Kennicott wins $300 for his blank verse tragedy, *Irma; or, The Prediction*, staged at James H. Caldwell's American Theatre in New Orleans. **14 December:** *Sertorius; or, The Roman Patriot* by David Paul Brown and inspired by Shakespeare opens at the Chestnut Street Theatre starring Junius Brutus Booth in the title role.

1831 Nathaniel Deering's *Carabasset; or, The Last of the Norridgewocks*, a tragedy offering stereotypical views of Algonquin Indians as savages, is produced. H. M. Milner's adaptation of Lord Byron's poem, *Mazeppa; or, The Wild Horse of Tartary*, is first performed with little success, but when revived 30 years later, starring Adah Isaacs Menken in the title role, and with the illusion of stage nudity, this equestrian sensation melodrama becomes a runaway success, much produced with Menken and many other actresses taking the leading role for the rest of the 19th century. William T. Porter and his brothers establish the weekly periodical *The Spirit of the Times*, which covers a range of cultural activities, including theater. **12 January:** Richard Penn Smith's tragedy, *Caius Marius*, starring Edwin Forrest, opens at the Arch Street Theatre. **25 April:** James Kirke Paulding's *The Lion of the West; or, A Trip to Washington* premieres at the Park Theatre starring James H. Hackett as frontiersman Nimrod Wildfire, whom some consider a comic parody of Davy Crockett—the play is a major success and Hackett commissions some other Wildfire plays, making the character a familiar American type. **July:** William Chapman and his theatrical company are the first to set sail on a showboat from Pittsburgh headed south down the Mississippi River. **26 September:** Robert Montgomery Bird's *The Gladiator* opens at the Park Theatre, becoming a major vehicle for Edwin Forrest and remaining popular on the 19th-century stage for decades.

1832 William Dunlap publishes his *History of the American Theatre*, a seminal work recording the history of the stage in the United States from its beginnings to 1832 (later historians have identified many errors, but Dunlap's work remains significant). Stephen E. Glover adapts James Fenimore Cooper's *Lionel Lincoln; or, The Leaguer of Boston* as *The Cradle of Liberty; or, Boston in 1775*, and it opens at the Bowery Theatre following runs in New Orleans and Boston. James Sheridan Knowles's *The Hunchback*, about a young country woman dazzled by big city decadence, opens first in London, followed by a New York premiere, scoring a success and leading many major actresses, including Viola Allen, Mary Anderson, Charlotte Cushman, Julia Marlowe, and Clara Morris to play the role at various times. **22 September:** Louisa Medina's *Guy Rivers; or, The Gold Hunters*, examining life in rural Georgia, opens at the Bowery Theatre. **10 October:** Robert Montgomery Bird's *Oraloosa; or, The Last of the Incas* opens at Philadelphia's Arch Street Theatre starring Edwin Forrest.

1833 George Washington Parke Custis, adopted son of George Washington, writes *North Point; or, Baltimore Defended*, a drama about the War of 1812, which opens in Baltimore. **30 December:** Louisa Medina's adaptation of John Richardson's Gothic novel called *Wacousta; or, The Curse*, opens at the Bowery Theatre, a rare play in that period featuring a major Native American character.

1834 Richard Emmons's *Tecumseh; or, The Battle of the Thames*, opens in New York, dramatizing Richard M. Johnson's purported killing of the Shawnee chief. **12 February:** Robert Montgomery Bird's *The Broker of Bogota*, a tragedy starring Edwin Forrest, opens at the Bowery Theatre. **10 May:** James H. Hackett plays the title role in *Major Jack Downing; or, The Retired Politician*, which opens at the Park Theatre based by an anonymous adaptor on the writings of humorist Seba Smith. **7 June:** Fanny Kemble becomes the first American actress to marry a wealthy man, Pierce Butler, but the marriage is unhappy as Kemble develops abolitionist sentiments while residing on Butler's plantation, which functions on slave labor—she later writes a memoir of her life there, taking a strong stance against slavery. **18 October:** *Beulah Spa; or, The Two B'Hoys*, a "burletta" by Charles Dance, opens at the Bowery Theatre.

1835 9 February: Louisa Medina's stage adaptation of Edward Bulwer-Lytton's novel, *The Last Days of Pompeii*, opens at the Bowery Theatre featuring Thomas Hamblin in the leading role. **7 September:** President Andrew Jackson's fierce battle with the United States Bank is dramatized in farcical manner in *Removing the Deposits*, a play by Henry J. Finn in which he appears at the Bowery Theatre. **30 November:** The St. Charles Theatre in New Orleans is built and opens with James H. Caldwell as manager. **30 November:** The St. Emanuel Street Theatre opens in Mobile, Alabama, under the management of Noah Ludlow and Sol Smith. **9 December:** Robert T. Conrad's blank verse tragedy, *Jack Cade; or, Captain of the Commons*, opens at the Walnut Street Theatre where it was popular, but it becomes a major success when Edwin Forrest plays the lead in 1840.

1836 The National Theatre is built in Boston with a design by William Washburn. Nathaniel H. Bannister's tragedy, *Gaulantus the Gaul*, opens in Cincinnati, set in ancient times dealing with the romance of a Gaul and his Roman wife.

1837 Macauley's Theatre is built by actor Bernard "Barney" Macauley and opens on Walnut Street in Louisville, Kentucky. *Pocahontas*, Robert Dale Owen's "historical drama," dramatizes the myth of Pocahontas and Captain John Smith. **13 February:** Josephine Clifton opens in Epes Sargent's *The Bride of Genoa* at Boston's Tremont Theatre. **1 May:** E. H. Thompson's *Sam Patch; or, The Daring Yankee*, starring Dan Marble, premieres at the Bowery Theatre, dramatizing the life of daredevil Sam Patch. **24 August:** Nathaniel Parker Willis's *Bianca Visconti; or, The Heart Overtasked* opens at the Park Theatre featuring Josephine Clifton. **8 November:** Charlotte Mary Sanford Barnes's tragedy *Octavia Bragaldi; or, The Confession* opens at the National Theatre with Barnes and her husband, E. S. Connor, among the cast. **20 November:** Epes Sargent's *Velasco*, a tragedy set in 11th-century Spain, opens at the Tremont Theatre.

1838 Cornelius A. Logan's *The Vermont Wool Dealer*, which centers on a Yankee character, one of many seen across the 19th century, opens. **28 March:** Louisa Medina's *Ernest Maltravers*, an adaptation of Edward Bulwer-Lytton's novel of the same name, opens at Wallack's Theatre to positive reviews. **14 May:** Edward Bulwer-Lytton's *The Lady of Lyons; or, Love and Pride*, opens at the Park Theatre starring Edwin Forrest, Charlotte Cushman, Peter Richings, and Mrs. Richings, scoring a major success and becoming a perennial favorite of the 19th century in the United States and England.

1839 *Whigs and Democrats; or, Love of No Politics*, probably written by J. E. Heath, opens this year as a satire of the frictions between the major political parties. An anonymous play, *Crockett in Texas*, about the legendary Davy Crockett at the Alamo, opens. Joseph S. Jones's comedy is first performed in Boston as *The People's Lawyer*, but is ultimately revised and performed in 1842 at the Park Theatre starring George H. Hill as the Yankee character Solon Shingle, which becomes the play's title. **19 February:** Nathaniel H. Bannister's *The Maine Question*, concerning northeastern boundary disputes, opens at the Franklin Theatre. **8 April:** Nathaniel Parker Willis's tragedy *Tortesa, the Usurer*, premieres at the National Theatre starring James W. Wallack. **6 May:** Louisa Medina's adaptation of Robert Montgomery Bird's novel, *Nick of the Woods; or, The Jibbenainosay*, opens at the New Bowery Theatre. **4 September:** Edward Bulwer-Lytton's *Richelieu; or, The Conspiracy* stars Edwin Forrest at the National Theatre and the play continues its success when Edwin Booth plays it in 1866. **December:** William Mitchell commences a 10-year run of productions at the Olympic Theatre, which is built this year, staging musical and burlesque entertainments.

1840 Cornelius Mathew's *The Politicians* opens in New York, depicting a corrupt electoral battle between two candidates.

1841 The Boston Museum is opened by Moses Kimball, and serves as a facility to present the leading actors of the mid-19th century. **11 October:** Dion Boucicault's *London Assurance*, which had opened with great success in London the previous March, opens at New York's Park Theatre starring Charlotte Cushman and Henry Placide, becoming one of the enduringly popular comedies of the 19th century.

1842 William Charles Macready plays the title role in James Sheridan Knowles's *Virginius* at the Park Theatre, appearing opposite Charlotte Cushman. E. P. Christy claims to have founded his Christy's Minstrels this year, though historians believe it did not occur until after the Virginia Minstrels were established the following year. John Brougham's *The Irish Yankee; or, The Birthday of Freedom* opens at New Orleans's St. Charles Theatre featuring a fictional Irish hero during the American Revolution.

1843 The Howard Athenaeum is built, first as a church and later as a theater, in Boston. Henry Wadsworth Longfellow's *The Spanish Student* opens and finds receptive audiences that appreciate its sentimental moralizing. **31 January:** The Virginia Minstrels, Dan Emmett, Frank Brower, R. W. Pelham, and Billy Whitlock, make their first major appearance in New York at the Chatham Garden Theatre, becoming one of the archetypal minstrel troupes of the mid-19th century and significantly popularizing the form of blackface minstrelsy.

1844 Nathaniel H. Bannister's *Putnam, The Iron Son of '76*, a patriotic melodrama based on the life of General Israel Putnam of American Revolutionary fame, opens at the Bowery Theatre for a long run. William H.

Smith's enduringly popular temperance melodrama, *The Drunkard; or, The Fallen Saved*, premieres at the Boston Museum, followed by a successful run at P. T. Barnum's American Museum. Thomas D. English's *Handy Andy: A Tale of Irish Life*, adapted from Samuel Lover's 1842 novel, opens at the Chatham Garden Theatre with William J. Ferguson in the lead.

1845 March: Oliver E. Durivage's *The Stage-Struck Yankee* opens at Boston's Eagle Theatre, a popular play spoofing theatrical practices. **1 March:** President John Tyler signs a proposal of statehood for Texas as Mexico warns against the attempt of the United States to annex Texas. **24 March:** Anna Cora Mowatt's *Fashion* opens at the Park Theatre in New York for a record run of 20 performances (Mowatt's first work, *The Gypsy Wanderer; or, The Stolen Child*, was written in the early 1840s, but was only performed privately). **25 July:** General Zachary Taylor and the US Army arrive in Corpus Christi, Texas, as a show of force against Mexico.

1846 Joseph M. Field's *Oregon; or, The Disputed Territory*, an allegory about the conflicts over the disputed northwestern territories, opens. **23 April:** Mexico declares defensive war against the United States, beginning the Mexican-American War.

1847 The Broadway Theatre is built and opens for a 12-year run. **17 May:** Cornelius Mathew's blank verse tragedy, *Witchcraft; or, The Martyrs of Salem*, opens at the Bowery Theatre, with a dark story set against the background of the famous Salem, Massachusetts, witch hunt. **19 November:** John Brougham's burlesque of John Augustus Stone's 1829 melodrama, *Metamora; or, The Last of the Wampanoags*, comically titled *Met-a-mora; or, The Last of the Pollywogs*, opens at Boston's Adelphi Theatre.

1848 James W. Wallack appears in a stage adaptation of the Alexandre Dumas 1844 novel, *The Count of Monte Cristo*, though several other adaptations followed, including one starring James O'Neill, which wins him great popularity. **2 February:** The Treaty of Guadalupe Hidalgo essentially ends the Mexican War. **2 February:** Benjamin A. Baker's *A Glance at New York*, originally titled *New York in 1848*, opens at William Mitchell's Olympic Theatre, becoming one of the most popular comedies of the era with its tale of a country bumpkin visiting New York where, among others, he encounters Mose, a "fire laddie," played memorably by Frank S. Chanfrau—his character becomes an iconic figure of the Bowery "b'hoy." **13 April:** Cornelius Mathews's *Jacob Leisler, The Patriot Hero; or, New York in 1690* opens at the Bowery Theatre starring James E. Murdoch. **24 July:** John Brougham's adaptation of Charles Dickens's *Dombey and Son* opens at Burton's Theatre. **2 October:** William E. Burton stars in his own two-act comedy, *The Toodles*, his most popular vehicle as a mild-mannered man with an eccentric wife, which opens at Burton's Chambers Street Theatre.

1849 The fraternal society, The Actors' Order of Friendship, is founded in Philadelphia. John B. Ordway founds his blackface minstrel troupe, Ordway's Aeolians, eventually establishing residence in Boston at Ordway Hall. Morris Barnett's adaptation of a French play, *The Serious Family*, opens at William Burton's Theatre, with Burton scoring a major personal success in the lead, followed by William Davidge, who also has a success with it. **10 May:** The Astor Place Opera House riot breaks out between partisans of American actor Edwin Forrest and English actor William Charles Macready—at least 22 people are killed and scores of others injured. **24 May:** Cornelius A. Logan's *Chloroform; or, New York a Hundred Years Hence*, his last Yankee comedy, opens at Burton's Chamber Street Theatre. **September:** Sacramento, California's Eagle Theatre opens in the midst of the Gold Rush, offering a minstrel show. **10 September:** Edwin Booth makes his stage debut as Tressel in *Richard III* in Boston, appearing with his father, Junius Brutus Booth. **October:** San Francisco's Bella Union opens, becoming the city's rowdiest performance space presenting minstrel shows, vaudeville, and burlesque.

1850s The San Francisco Minstrels are founded in this period and become one of the most beloved of blackface minstrel troupes for decades.

1850 Edward Sherman Gould's *The Very Age!*, mocking the fashions of New York society in the period, opens. John Brougham writes the comedy *The Irish Fortune Hunter* for actor John Collins. W. R. Derr's Western melodrama *Kit Carson, The Hero of the Prairie* opens, creating a template for many Western plays, in this case mythologizing Carson's adventures. James Pilgrim's *Paddy the Piper*, an Irish-themed one-act, opens at the Broadway Theatre, one of several plays establishing Pilgrim as one of the most popular Irish American dramatists after Dion Boucicault. **10 June:** Oliver Bell Bunce's *Marco Bozzaris; The Grecian Hero* opens at the Bowery Theatre starring James W. Wallack Jr.; Wallack's wife, Ann Duff Sefton; and John Gilbert. **23 December:** John Brougham opens Brougham's Lyceum Theatre in New York.

1851 James Pilgrim's melodrama, *Ireland and America; or, Scenes in Both: A Drama in Two Acts*, opens starring Barney Williams at the Broadway Theatre. **20 January:** George Henry Boker's tragedy, *Calaynos*, opens at the Walnut Street Theatre starring James E. Murdoch, following its 1849 debut in London. **10 March:** James Pilgrim's *Harry Burnham* opens at the National Theatre depicting a Yale student rabble-rousing his peers to fight the British during the American Revolution. **26 April:** John Brougham's unique *A Row at the Lyceum; or, Green Room Secrets*, which pretended to show a fight among cast members of a play rehearsing at the Lyceum, premieres at the Lyceum Theatre with Brougham, his wife, and W. J. Florence in the cast.

15 August: James Pilgrim's two-act Irish romantic drama, *Shandy Maguire; or, The Bould Boy of the Mountain,* opens at the Arch Street Theatre starring Barney Williams. **1 December:** F. B. Conway and Madame Ponisi appear in the turgid melodrama, *Ingomar, The Barbarian.*

1852 2 February: Adapted from the Alexandre Dumas fils novel, *The Lady of the Camellias,* often billed simply as *Camille,* premieres at the Theatre du Vaudeville in Paris, before becoming extraordinarily popular in the United States and throughout Europe with the title role taken on by many of the greatest actresses of the age, including Sarah Bernhardt. **26 February:** Joseph Stevens Jones's *The Silver Spoon,* a four-act comedy, opens at the Boston Museum featuring William Warren and W. H. Smith. **September:** George L. Aiken dramatizes and stages portions of Harriet Beecher Stowe's popular abolitionist novel, *Uncle Tom's Cabin; or, Life among the Lowly,* in Troy, New York, and the popularity of Aiken's stage adaptation achieves unparalleled success, with numerous productions in the United States over the subsequent half century, sometimes in variant adaptations. **8 November:** Joseph Stirling Coyne's *One Thousand Milliners Wanted for the Gold Diggins in California* opens at Burton's Theatre, with William Burton in the cast, though the play only becomes a major success when Ben De Bar plays the role and it becomes one of his most popular vehicles.

1853 *The New York Clipper,* a publication covering theater and other entertainments, begins publication. James Pilgrim's *Robert Emmet, The Martyr of Irish Liberty,* opens at the St. Charles Theatre in New Orleans, followed by productions in Philadelphia and New York and elsewhere, celebrating the life of the Irish patriot. **18 July:** George L. Aiken's production of *Uncle Tom's Cabin* opens at Purdy's National Theatre in New York (C. W. Tayleure's adaptation had played at Purdy's the year before), and it is the first production to feature Wednesday and Saturday matinees, as becomes a longstanding practice. **3 October:** George H. Boker's *Leonor de Guzman,* a five-act tragedy, opens at the Walnut Street Theatre featuring Kate Wemyss. **5 December:** C. W. Tayleure's *Little Katy; or, The Hot Corn Girl,* based on Solon Robinson's *Hot Corn* stories, opens at the National Theatre starring Cordelia Howard. **6 December:** Another version of Solon Robinson's *Hot Corn* stories, *Hot Corn; or, Little Katy,* opens at Barnum's American Museum (another version opens at the Bowery Theatre the next year).

1854 Thomas Maguire builds Maguire's Opera House in San Francisco. **20 October:** The Stadt Theatre opens to produce German-language theater. **10 November:** Summerfield Barry's one-act farce, *The Persecuted Dutchman; or, The Original John Schmidt,* opens at the Bowery Theatre featuring S. W.

Glenn, who specialized in German/Dutch roles. **16 November:** Thomas Blades de Walden's temperance melodrama *The Upper Ten and the Lower Twenty* premieres at Burton's Theatre starring William E. Burton.

1855 26 March: William Gilmore Simms's *Michael Bonham; or, The Fall of Bexar: A Tale of Texas* opens at the New Charleston Theatre dramatizing the siege of the Alamo and Texas's fight for independence and other aspects of the Mexican-American War. **12 September:** John Brougham's *The Game of Love*, inspired by Charles Dickens's *Bleak House*, opens under James W. Wallack's direction at Wallack's Theatre with a cast including Mrs. John Hoey, Lester Wallack, and Henry Placide. **26 September:** George H. Boker's tragedy *Francesca da Rimini* premieres at the Broadway Theatre starring Elizabeth Ponisi. **3 December:** Cornelius Mathews's satire, *False Pretenses; or, Both Sides of Good Society*, opens at Burton's Theatre, lampooning contemporary society in a similar vein as Anna Cora Mowatt's *Fashion*. **24 December:** John Brougham's burlesque with music (James G. Maeger), *Po-ca-hon-tas; or, The Gentle Savage*, opens at Wallack's Theatre for a popular run.

1856 John Brougham's *The Irish Emigrant*, starring Brougham in the lead, opens a successful run, but John Drew later took on the role and made a personal success as Paddy O'Bryan. **5 May:** Clifton W. Tayleure's *Horseshoe Robinson*, about intrigue during the American Revolution, opens at Baltimore's Holliday Street Theatre. **27 October:** Mrs. Sidney Bateman's three-act comedy, *Self*, is staged at William Burton's Chamber Theatre, with a cast including Burton and Charles Fisher. **18 November:** Charles Selby's drama *The Marble Heart; or, The Sculptor's Dream: A Romance of Real Life* premieres at Laura Keene's Theatre starring Keene and, in later productions, John Wilkes Booth, who scores a success in this play. **25 December:** *Hi-a-wa-tha; or, Ardent Spirits and Laughing Water*, Charles Melton Walcot Sr.'s parody of Henry Wadsworth Longfellow's epic poem, *Hiawatha*, opens at Wallack's Theatre.

1857 Thomas Blades de Walden's *Wall Street*, a satire of the stock exchange and those working in it, opens at Burton's Old Chamber Street Theatre starring Lawrence Barrett. Alonzo Delano's *A Live Woman in the Mines; or, Pike County Ahead!*, written and published under the pseudonym "Old Block," is first performed, helping to gain Delano a reputation as a humorist nearly equal to Mark Twain and Bret Harte. James H. McVicker opens McVicker's Theatre in Chicago, where he serves as actor and manager, and the theater thrives until it is destroyed in the great Chicago Fire of 1871. Thaddeus Mehan's *Modern Insanity; or, Fashion and Forgery*, starring E. L. Davenport, opens at the American Theatre. Oliver S. Leland's *The Rights of Man* premieres at Wallack's Theatre, a two-act comedy that also scores a success at the Howard Athenaeum, featuring advanced ideas about rights for women. **27 February:** Oliver Bell Bunce's *Love in '76: An Incident of the Revolution* opens at Laura Keene's Theatre, a romantic comedy set during the American Revolution. **16 March:** Julia Ward Howe's *Leonora; or, The World's Own*, begins a run at Wallack's Theatre. **16 March:** J. T. Trowbridge's dramatization of his abolitionist novel, *Neighbor Jackwood*, opens at the Boston Museum with the innovation of dropping blackface for black characters and, instead, using Yankee characters for comedy, avoiding demeaning racial humor. **10 April:** E. L. Davenport appears as the famed Spanish explorer in George H. Miles's flop, *DeSoto, The Hero of Mississippi*, at the Broadway Theatre along with his wife, Fanny Vining Davenport. **November:** A. D'Ennery and F. Dugue's *Sea of Ice; or, A Mother's Prayer* is produced by Laura Keene during New York's economic panic of 1857 and its success saves Keene's company's finances. **December:** John Brougham's burlesque *Columbus el Filibustero!!* opens at Burton's Theatre. **8 December:** Dion Boucicault's *The Poor of New York* (also known as *The Streets of New York*) premieres at Wallack's Theatre, becoming one of the most iconic and popular melodramas of the 19th century.

1858 William Wells Brown, an ex-slave, writes a melodrama, *The Escape; or, A Leap for Freedom*, the first play by an African American published in the United States, and Brown's previous play, *Experience; or, How to Give a Northern Man a Backbone* (1856), was not published and is now considered lost. The anonymous play, *The Battle of Buena Vista*, opens and recounts the pivotal 1847 battle of the Mexican War. The Hanlon-Lees troupe debuts at Niblo's Garden after a few years honing their act in England and wins great popularity. An anonymous play, *Life in Brooklyn, Its Lights and Shades— Vices and Virtues*, opens and though it is a melodramatic play with spectacle, it is also a harbinger of greater realism in drama. J. Burdette Howe's *The Mysteries and Crimes of New York and Brooklyn* begins a run making a melodramatic case against foreign influences. Charles Pfaff establishes Pfaff's, a "trysting place" for literary and theatrical personages. **15 March:** Harry Seymour's *Jessie Brown; or, Havelock's Last Victory*, competing with Dion Boucicault's *Jessie Brown; or, The Relief of Lucknow* playing at Wallack's Theatre where it opened a month earlier, premieres at Purdy's National Theatre—both plays fictionalized the Sepoy Rebellion. **17 March:** *The Mormons; or, Life at Salt Lake City* by Thomas Dunn English opens at William Burton's Theatre, with Charles Fisher playing Brigham Young and a supporting cast including Burton, E. L. Davenport, and Fanny Vining. **16 May:** C. W. Tayleure's *Clam-eel*, a burlesque inspired by *Camille*, opens at the Chatham Garden Theatre. **24 May:** *Deseret Deserted; or, The Last Days of Brigham Young Being a Strictly Business Transaction in Four Acts and Several Deeds, Involving Both Profit and Loss*, an anonymous work, begins a run at Wallack's Theatre satirizing Brigham Young. **1 July:** Joseph A. Nunes's five-act comedy *Fast Folks; or, Early Days of California* opens at San Francisco's American Theatre starring James W. Wallack. **23 August:** William W. Pratt's temperance melodrama *Ten Nights in a Bar-Room* opens at the National Theatre and despite a short run becomes a perennial favorite for decades. **15 October:** Tom Taylor's *Our American Cousin* premieres at Laura Keene's Theatre with Keene and Joseph Jefferson in the cast of the farcical piece about the social collisions of crude Americans with stuffy English relatives. **25 November:** John Brougham's *Take Care of Little Charley*, a one-act Irish farce, opens at Wallack's Theatre.

1859 The French Opera House, the first major opera house constructed in America, is built and opens in New Orleans. John Brougham's *The Ruling Passion*, a six-act comedy, opens at Wallack's Theatre with an "all-star" cast including Lester Wallack, W. R. Walcot, John Dyott, Mrs. Hoey, Mary Gannon, Mrs. Vernon, and Mrs. Walcot. **14 September:** Dion Boucicault's *Dot*, adapted from Charles Dickens's *The Cricket on the Hearth*, opens at the Winter Garden Theatre with Agnes Robertson as the title character. **6 December:** Dion Boucicault's sensation melodrama, *The Octoroon; or, Life in Louisiana*, premieres at the Winter Garden Theatre and though only subtly polemical, the play deals with attitudes about race and fuels abolitionist sentiments as the Civil War approaches. **16 December:** Mrs. J. C. Swayze's *Ossawattomie Brown; or, The Insurrection at Harper's Ferry* opens at the Bowery Theatre, starring G. C. Boniface in a freely fictionalized drama of John Brown's family, opens.

1860–1880 Theatrical activity spreads across the United States and its territories, while New York City maintains its well-established dominance as the center of the American entertainment industry. The Civil War (1861–1865) puts a damper on some theatrical activity, and yet theater continues to be available in cities in both the United States and the Confederate States (some actors are able to cross borders with relative ease). Rivers are the main highways into the interior of America until the 1870s, and from this era into the mid-20th century, showboats provide access to theater for those residing in river towns—during the 1870s, a transition from trouping by horse-drawn wagon and riverboat to train travel occurs. With the rapid expansion of railroads during the 1880s, touring companies enter a golden era as "the road" becomes a lucrative source for producers and actors, with a network of towns and cities across the country providing a seemingly endless audience for theater, vaudeville, burlesque, and other forms of entertainment. Though theatrical stock companies established across the country continue to flourish into the mid-20th century, touring troupes provide stiff competition for local companies.

1860 9 January: Dion Boucicault's *Jeanie Deans*, inspired by Sir Walter Scott's *The Heart of Midlothian*, opens at Laura Keene's Theatre starring Boucicault and his wife, Agnes Robertson. **16 January:** Edwin Booth appears in *Henry II; or, The Death of Thomas à Beckett* at the St. Charles Theatre in New Orleans. **29 March:** Dion Boucicault's *The Colleen Bawn; or, The Brides of Garryowen*, one of his most popular Irish-themed melodramas, premieres at Laura Keene's Theatre, starring Keene, Boucicault, Agnes Robertson, Charles Fisher, and Mme. Ponisi.

1861 The Brooklyn Academy of Music opens. Brigham Young donates more than half the cost of the Salt Lake Theatre, and construction begins in 1861 and continues into 1862. John Hill Hewitt, manager of the Richmond Theatre, known as the "Bard of the Stars and Bars," signifying sympathy with the Confederate States of America, writes *The Scouts; or, The Plains of Manassas*, celebrating the first great Confederate victory. New York's Star Theatre is built by James W. Wallack Sr. and managed by his son, Lester Wallack. **January:** Actress Maggie Mitchell, triumphant in her signature role in *Fanchon, the Cricket*, adapted by Charlotte Birch-Pfeiffer from August Waldauer's original, opens at Benedict De Bar's St. Charles Theatre followed by a run at Laura Keene's Theatre in New York the following year. **January:** South Carolina, followed by other Southern states, secedes from the United States following the election to the presidency of Abraham Lincoln, a known opponent of slavery. **4 March:** Abraham Lincoln is inaugurated as the 16th president of the United States. **12 April:** The Civil War commences when rebels fire shots at Fort Sumter. **6 June:** Adah Isaacs Menken scores a major success playing the title role, a male character, in the H. M. Milner melodrama, *Mazeppa; or, The Wild Horse of Tartary*, based on Lord Byron's 1819 poem, for the first time in Albany, New York—in the play's famous climactic scene, wearing flesh-colored tights, Menken creates the illusion of nudity while strapped to the back of a horse sent galloping up a ramp decked in canvas painted to represent a mountain. **15 August:** Charles Gayler's drama *Bull Run; or, The Sacking of Fairfax Courthouse* opens at the Bowery Theatre a mere three weeks after the actual Civil War battle it depicts.

1862 *The Guerillas; or, The War in Virginia* by James D. McCabe opens presenting a sympathetic view of the Confederacy and melodramatically depicting the impact of strife among neighbors and in families during the Civil War. **11 July:** John Brougham's *The Duke's Motto; or, I am Here!*, a play with music and a ballet, opens at Niblo's Garden.

1863 The Fifth Avenue Theatre, originally known as the Madison Square Theatre, is built, becoming the Fifth Avenue Theatre in 1868 under Augustin Daly's management. Ford's Theatre, in Washington, DC, opens under the management of John T. Ford. **1 January:** President Abraham Lincoln issues his Emancipation Proclamation, declaring all slaves held in rebellious states are free. **19 January:** Augustin Daly's melodrama, *Leah, the Forsaken*, opens at Niblo's Garden starring Kate Bateman under the management of her father, H. L. Bateman, and a supporting cast including Edwin Adams and James W. Wallack. **26 January:** Clifton W. Tayleure adapted Mrs. Ellen Wood's popular novel *East Lynne* and it premieres in Brooklyn, becoming one of the most frequently staged melodramas of the 19th century. **27 March:** Tom Taylor's sensation melodrama, *The Ticket-of-Leave Man*, opens at the Olympic Theatre prior to a 30 November production at the Winter Garden Theatre and becomes one of the popular comedies of the era. **June–July:** Gettysburg, Pennsylvania, becomes the central battle of the Civil War as the ultimate defeat of the Confederate Army under the command of General Robert E. Lee is driven out of Pennsylvania. **30 September:** Lester Wallack's *Rosedale; or, The Rifle Ball*, a complex five-act melodrama, opens at Wallack's Theatre with a cast including Mrs. Hoey, John Gilbert, Charles Fisher, and Wallack. **19 November:** President Abraham Lincoln delivers his "Gettysburg Address" at the battlefield in Gettysburg, Pennsylvania, where the decisive battle of the Civil War took place the previous summer.

1864 November: President Abraham Lincoln is reelected. **26 November:** Edwin Booth opens his record 100-performance run in the title role in *Hamlet* at the Winter Garden Theatre in New York (this record number of performances stands until John Barrymore's production in 1923).

1865 Joseph Jefferson performs the title role in Dion Boucicault's adaptation of Washington Irving's *Rip Van Winkle* in London for the first time and Jefferson becomes associated with the role and plays it frequently throughout the remainder of his career. Tony Pastor establishes his Opera House, where he initiates the trend toward making variety entertainment appropriate for women and families. **4 March:** President Abraham Lincoln is inaugurated for a second term, delivering a speech calling for the rejoining of the country and appealing to all Americans to consult "the better angels of our nature" in national reconciliation. **9 April:** Confederate general Robert E. Lee surrenders to Union general Ulysses S. Grant at Appomattox Court House, Virginia, essentially ending the Civil War. **14 April:** Actor John Wilkes Booth, brother of Edwin Booth, assassinates President Abraham Lincoln at Ford's Theatre in Washington, DC, during a performance of Tom Taylor's comedy *Our American Cousin* by Laura Keene's company. **26 April:** Lincoln's assassin, John Wilkes Booth, is shot to death when tracked to Port Royal, Virginia, by Union soldiers. **21 July:** Dion Boucicault's Irish romance, *Arrah-na-Pogue; or, The Wicklow Wedding*, set during the Irish Rebellion in 1798, opens at Niblo's Garden.

1866 The Thalian Dramatic Association, one of the first academic theater groups, is established at Brown University. New York's Fourteenth Street Theatre is established under its original name, Theatre Francais, and is later known as Haverly's Fourteenth Street Theatre. Photographer Napoleon Sarony founds a photographic studio on Broadway where, for over 30 years he captures images of the leading actors and actresses to work in New York, as well as other celebrities. **January:** Edwin Booth leaves the stage for several months following his brother's murder of President Abraham Lincoln, but returns to acting as Hamlet and audiences welcome his return. **3 September:** Joseph Jefferson stars in Dion Boucicault's adaptation of Washington Irving's *Rip Van Winkle* for the first time in the United States (he had previewed the play in London the previous year) at the Olympic Theatre, beginning a long association for Jefferson and what was likely his most emblematic role. **12 September:** *The Black Crook*, a fantasy-melodrama with spectacular effects and ballet sequences, premieres to acclaim at Niblo's Garden, and is later regarded a milestone in the development of American musical theater. **25 September:** Benjamin E. Woolf's *The Doctor of Alcantara* opens at the French Theatre following an 1862 run in Boston.

1867 7 August: African American actor Ira Aldridge dies while touring Poland. **13 August:** Augustin Daly's classic melodrama, *Under the Gaslight; or, Life and Love in These Times*, opens at the New York Theatre starring Rose Eytinge—it becomes one of the best-known, most frequently produced melodramas of the 19th century. **14 August:** John Brougham's adaptation of Charles Dickens's *The Old Curiosity Shop*, named *Little Nell and the Marchioness*, opens at Wallack's Theatre starring Lotta Crabtree, incorporating Crabtree's special musical skills, dancing, and banjo playing.

1868 Lydia Thompson and her British Blondes introduce burlesque in the United States. **10 March:** Pantomimist/clown G. L. Fox's most popular vehicle, *Humpty Dumpty*, opens at the Olympic Theatre. **10 June:** Augustin Daly's *A Flash of Lightning* premieres at the Broadway Theatre, inspired by a Victorien Sardou play, and starring McKee Rankin and Kitty Blanchard. The same day, Daly's *The Red Scarf* opens at the Bowery Theatre, a play containing one of the great melodrama clichés in a scene in which the hero is tied to a log in a sawmill headed for the cutting blade.

1869 Augustin Daly opens his Fifth Avenue Theatre, home to his acclaimed ensemble for a decade. **18 January:** The California Theatre opens in San Francisco. **25 January:** John Brougham's *The Drama Review for 1868* opens at the Fifth Avenue Theatre, a precursor to musical revues. **3 February:** Edwin Booth builds the Booth Theatre in New York, starring in his production of *Romeo and Juliet* playing opposite Mary McVicker, his second wife, whom he married that year.

1870 The Lotos Club opens as a "gentleman's club" for writers, newspapermen, and critics, eventually expanding to include artists and stage celebrities. Michael B. Leavitt establishes the Rentz-Santley Novelty and Burlesque Company, the first burlesque show featuring women and using elements of blackface minstrelsy and inspired by Lydia Thompson and her British Blondes. **15 February:** Augustin Daly's *Frou-Frou* premieres at the Fifth Avenue Theatre starring Agnes Ethel in a role later played by Sarah Bernhardt. **17 June:** *The Red Mazeppa; or, The Madman of the Plains* by Albert W. Aiken opens in New York billed as a "Grand Romantic Drama." **11 July:** Charles Gayler's melodrama, *Fritz, Our Cousin German*, is staged at Wallack's Theatre, followed by a run at Niblo's Garden, starring Joseph K. Emmet as the title character. **28 November:** Oliver Doud Byron's revision of James J. McCloskey's melodrama *Across the Continent; or, Scenes from New York Life and the Pacific Railroad*, opens at Brooklyn's Park Theatre prior to runs at Wood's Museum and the Metropolitan Theatre. **21 December:** The first play by Bronson Howard, *Saratoga; or, Pistols for Seven*, premieres at the Fifth Avenue Theatre, starring Fanny Davenport and produced by Augustin Daly, a production of his company including such players as John Drew, Ada Rehan, and Otis Skinner.

1871 L. W. Osgood's *The Union Spy; or, The Battle of Weldon Railroad* opens, mixing together fictional and historical characters from the Civil War. Sheridan Shook and A. M. Palmer open the Union Square Theatre. **21 March:** Augustin Daly's *Horizon*, adapted from a Bret Harte story, premieres at the Olympic Theatre with a cast including Agnes Ethel and legendary pantomimist G. L. Fox. **8 May:** Thomas Blades de Walden's and Edward Spencer's *Kit, The Arkansas Traveler*, opens at Niblo's Garden starring Frank S. Chanfrau, George C. Boniface, Rose Evans, and six-year-old Minnie Maddern. **5 September:** Augustin Daly's *Divorce* is staged at the Fifth Avenue Theatre starring Fanny Davenport, Clara Morris, William Davidge, and Louis James. **23 October:** Bartley Campbell's *Peril; or, Love at Long Branch*, is written for E. L. Davenport, who stars his daughter, Fanny Davenport.

1872 A trio of brothers, the Gormans, form their own minstrel troupe and debut successfully at the Bowery Theatre. Alfred Ford's *Jael and Sisera: A Woman's Rights Drama*, draws inspiration from the biblical book of Judges and is staged. **8 September:** The Germania Theatre opens at Eighth Street and Fourth Avenue in New York, but mostly with lackluster productions for the first two decades, changing the theater's name, leasing it to a Yiddish company, and finally restoring it and reopening in 1892. **26 September:** Bronson Howard's *Diamonds*, a "comedy of contemporaneous manners," opens at the Fifth Avenue Theatre with William Davidge, James Lewis, Fanny Davenport, Fanny Morant, and Mrs. G. H. Gilbert.

1873 Tommaso Salvini begins his first American tour performing with Edwin Booth in a polyglot production. **21 February:** Dan Selby produces *Oroloso; or, Dead Shot of the Sierra Nevadas* at St. James Hall featuring the acrobatic troupe the Zitella Family. **17 March:** Dion Boucicault's Irish play *Daddy O'Dowd; or, The Turn About Is Fair Play* opens at Booth's Theatre on St. Patrick's Day. **2 June:** Frank Murdoch's melodrama, *Davy Crockett; or, Be Sure You're Right, Then Go Ahead*, celebrating the legend of Davy Crockett, opens at Wood's Museum. **4 June:** Equestrian actress Leo Hudson, in the title role in the play *Mazeppa*, is fatally injured onstage in St. Louis when the horse bearing her up a ramp falls and is also killed. **10 November:** Wilkie Collins's *The New Magdalen* is produced by Augustin Daly at the Broadway Theatre, following a hit run at London's Olympic Theatre and a number of European productions. **6 December:** Dion Boucicault's play, *Led Astray*, opens at the Union Square Theatre starring Rose Eytinge, C. R. Thorne, Kate Claxton, and McKee Rankin.

1874 Thomas F. Power's play, *The Virginia Veteran*, written and published for the benefit of veterans of both the Mexican War and the Civil War, appears offering a plea for peace. The Lambs Club is founded by cast members of Dion Boucicault's *The Shaughraun*. The Gerry Society, originally known as the New York Society for the Prevention of Cruelty to Children, is established to provide protective services for abused or overworked children, including in the theatrical profession. William Dean Howells's first play, *Samson*, opens on tour starring Tommaso Salvini, but it is not produced in New York until October 1889. **20 March:** Fred Marsden's *Zip; or, Point Lynne Light* opens at the Booth Theatre, making an enduring star of Lotta Crabtree in one of her best vehicles. **April:** George Densmore's adaptation of Mark Twain and Charles Dudley Warner's *The Gilded Age*, titled *Colonel Sellers*, premieres in San Francisco, followed by a successful run at the Park Theatre later in the year. **10 August:** Dion Boucicault's Civil War drama, *Belle Lamar: An Episode of the Civil War*, opens at the Booth Theatre. **14 November:** Dion Boucicault's most iconic Irish play, *The Shaughraun*, opens at Wallack's Theatre with Boucicault playing the lead. **21 December:** A. M. Palmer opens N. Hart Jackson's drama of the French Revolution, *The Two Orphans*, at the Union Square Theatre with a cast including Kitty Blanchard, Kate Claxton, Rose Eytinge, and Charles R. Thorne Jr., becoming one of the most popular melodramas of the 19th century.

1875 After some unsuccessful attempts to adapt Jules Verne's *Around the World in 80 Days* to the stage, the Kiralfy Brothers open a much-revived version at the Academy of Music. Denman Thompson writes and performs a vaudeville sketch, *Joshua Whitcomb*, which ultimately grows into the play *The Old Homestead* and is performed in 1886. **17 February:** Augustin Daly's Wall Street satire, *The Big Bonanza: A Comedy of Our Time*, scores a hit at the Fifth Avenue Theatre with a stellar cast including Fanny Davenport, Charles Fisher, James Lewis, and John Drew—a rival play on the same subject, Bartley Campbell's *Bulls and Bears*, opens at San Francisco's Dickinson's Grand Opera House and is also successful. **6 September:** Benjamin E. Woolf's Wall Street comedy, *The Mighty Dollar*, opens at the Park Theatre starring W. J. and Malvena Florence and Maude Granger. **23 November:** Steele MacKaye's *Rose Michel* opens at the Union Square Theatre starring Rose Eytinge, Charles Thorne, Stuart Robson, and Fanny Morant. **14 December:** Augustin Daly's popular drama *Pique* opens at the Fifth Avenue Theatre with Fanny Davenport as Mabel Renfrew supported by a strong cast featuring John Drew, John Brougham, James Lewis, and Maurice Barrymore.

1876 The Goodspeed Opera House is founded on the banks of the Connecticut River. Polish actress Helena Modjeska makes her first tour of the United States. William Dean Howells's one-act romantic comedy, *The Parlor Car*, is written and praised by Mark Twain. **17 July:** Bret Harte's three-act romantic tale, *Two Men of Sandy Bar*, set in old California, stars Charles R. Thorne Jr. and J. H. Stoddart at the Union Square Theatre Company.

1877 The burlesque *Evangeline; or, The Belle of Acadia*, based on Henry Wadsworth Longfellow's epic 1847 poem, premieres at Niblo's Garden and becomes a major success. J. H. Haverly founds the United Mastodon Minstrel Company. Thomas Stewart Denison's *The Sparkling Cup*, a five-act temperance drama, opens in Washington, DC. **29 January:** Leonard Grover's comedy *Our Boarding House* opens at the Park Theatre, becoming a popular vehicle for comedians Stuart Robson and W. H. Crane. **4 June:** African American actor Paul Molyneaux Hewlett makes his stage debut as Othello at the Union Hall in Boston, supported by a white cast. **2 July:** African American playwright John S. Ladue's *Under the Yoke; or, Bound and Free* opens at the Third Avenue Theatre in a production by the Louisiana Colored Troupe. **31 July:** *Ah Sin*, a comedy by Mark Twain and Bret Harte, opens in an Augustin Daly production at the Fifth Avenue Theatre, running for 35 performances. **20 August:** Joaquin Miller's melodrama *The Danites; or, The Heart of the Sierras*, set among the Mormons, opens at the Broadway Theatre. **11 October:** William Dean Howells's *Yorick's Love*, written for Lawrence Barrett, premieres at Cincinnati's Grand Opera House. **10 December:** Steele MacKaye's comedy, *Won at Last*, opens at the Wallack Theatre, with Rose Coghlan and John Gilbert in the leads. **22 December:** Polish actress Helena Modjeska makes her English-speaking debut at the Fifth Avenue Theatre in Eugène Scribe's *Adrienne Lecouvreur*.

1878 L. D. Shear's temperance drama, *The Wife's Appeal*, another potboiler on the subject of the evils of drink, premieres. Edwin Booth produces Tom Taylor's 1868 drama, *The Fool's Revenge*, at Niblo's Garden, playing a witty court fool in 15th-century Italy. Bayard Taylor's *Prince Deukalion*, written in verse and with allegorical characters and considerable symbolism, opens. **23 January:** *A Celebrated Case* by Eugène Corman and Adolphe D'Ennery opens at the Union Square Theatre in an A. M. Palmer production featuring Charles Coghlan, Mrs. Gilbert, and Agnes Booth. **1 April:** Victorien Sardou's *Diplomacy* opens at Lester Wallack's Theatre, with Wallack in the lead, along with Maude Granger, H. J. Montague, Rose Coghlan, and Madame Ponisi. **8 April:** Benjamin Ford and J. A. Arneaux establish an all-black company and perform *Richard III* at the Lyceum Theatre—by 1884, the company is known as the Astor Place Company of Colored Tragedians. **31 August:** Bronson Howard's sentimental romance *Old Love Letters*, starring Agnes Booth in one of her most popular roles as a widow reliving her romances through her love letters, is staged at Abbey's Theatre. **1 September:** Bronson Howard's comic-drama *Hurricanes* opens at the Park Theatre, depicting three young husbands who attend a masquerade ball without their wives, causing turmoil in their households. **23 September:** Clay M. Greene's play, based on Bret Harte's story, *M'Liss*, opens at Niblo's Garden, providing a star part for Annie Pixley. **30 November:** Bronson Howard's play, *The Banker's Daughter*, a popular melodrama, opens at the Union Square Theatre.

1879 Steele MacKaye opens his state-of-the-art Madison Square Theatre, with an elevator stage, on West 24th Street. David Belasco collaborates with James A. Herne to write *Hearts of Oak*, a popular success. Harrison Grey Fiske establishes the *New York Dramatic Mirror*, an important trade newspaper. Augustin Daly opens Daly's Theatre at 1221 Broadway. The Boston Ideal Opera Company is founded by Effie H. Ober to present the first American productions of Gilbert and Sullivan's operettas, as well as new American operettas. Salmi Morse's *The Passion Play*, based on the New Testament, opens at Tom Maguire's Theatre in San Francisco, staged by David Belasco and starring James O'Neill as Christ, but local censors resist stage depictions of Christ, as reoccurs in New York when the play is performed there in 1883. **4 January:** Harrison Grey Fiske's *New York Dramatic Mirror* begins publication. **13 January:** Edward Harrigan and David Braham's *The Mulligan Guards' Ball* opens at the Theatre Comique starring Harrigan and Tony Hart and scores a major success and begins a series of Mulligan Guard plays starring Harrigan and Hart, works that are a prototype for the evolving form of musical comedy. **17 February:** James A. Herne and David Belasco collaborate on the melodrama *Within an Inch of His Life*, which opens at San Francisco's Grand Opera House, followed by a New

York run, marking a debut for both Belasco and Herne, and starring James O'Neill. **12 May:** Nate Salsbury's *The Brook; or, A Jolly Day at the Picnic*, a lightweight farce little more than an excuse for musical acts, opens at the San Francisco Minstrels Hall. **August:** *The Mulligan Guard's Chowder* by Edward Harrigan premieres at the Theatre Comique (followed in December by *The Mulligan Guard's Christmas*, launching the popular Mulligan Guard series of plays with music and ethnic characters, set in New York's Lower East Side, an American alternative to Gilbert and Sullivan and other European-style operettas). **16 September:** Bartley Campbell's melodrama *My Partner*, featuring Maude Granger, opens at the Union Square Theatre. **17 September:** Augustin Daly's Theatre is built at Broadway and 13th Street. **1 December:** Bartley Campbell's romantic melodrama *The Galley Slave*, with Emily Rigl, opens at Haverly's Theatre for a long run.

1880 *Uncle Tom's Cabin* is performed with an integrated cast for the first time at the Gaiety Theatre (Boston). George H. Jessop's *Sam'l of Posen; or, The Commercial Drummer* begins its long life as a stock and touring vehicle. Steele MacKaye presents his play, *Hazel Kirke*, starring Effie Ellsler, at Madison Square Theatre. Tony Pastor introduces Lillian Russell as a star attraction at his Music Hall. Sol Smith Russell becomes a star in *Edgewood Folks*, a four-act musical by J. E. Brown first performed in Buffalo, New York. English's Theatre is built in Indianapolis, Indiana. By this year, "Broadway" becomes a generic term to describe the grouping of legitimate theaters offering plays, musicals, and other entertainments in New York. **4 February:** Steele MacKaye's melodrama, *Hazel Kirke*, starring Effie Ellsler, opens at the Madison Square Theatre. **15 March:** Adapted from humorist Frances M. Whitcher's stories, David Ross Locke's *Widow Bedott; or, A Hunt for a Husband*, opens at Haverly's Fourteenth Street Theatre starring Neil Burgess in his most famous drag vehicle. **29 March:** David Belasco's and James A. Herne's collaboration, *Hearts of Oak*, the first New York production for both of them, opens. **8 November:** Sarah Bernhardt makes her American debut at Booth's Theatre on the first of her nine American tours. **8 November:** Clay Meredith Greene and Slauson Thompson's *Sharps and Flats*, a four-act farce, begins a run at the Standard Theatre with the comedy team of Stuart Robson and W. H. Crane.

Introduction

The more than 1,000 entries included in the *Historical Dictionary of American Theater: Beginnings* reflect the long formative era of the stage in the American colonies and, ultimately, the United States of America. By 1880, with the rise of modernism and its profound influence on American artists, and the emergence of Broadway as the center of American theater (especially during a golden age of American theater between 1918 and 1960), the stage in the United States came into its own. Two generations of dramatists, from Eugene O'Neill to Edward Albee, crafted important dramas reflecting the remarkable changes in American life across the 20th century. In this era, the United States emerged as a world power and progress on various levels moved America closer to a realization of the high ideals set down by the "Founding Fathers" in the period of the American Revolution.

The history of America can be seen in the work of its playwrights and in the achievements of the performing artists who brought it to life, as those denied their equal place (women, LGBT Americans, African Americans, and other ethnic and racial minorities) spoke out in many ways, not least through the theater. It was a long journey from the arrival of the first white Europeans in North America to the revolution that led to the founding of the United States in the late 18th century, but it seems clear that American drama was truly born in the aftermath of the American Revolution. Prior to the late 18th century, theater in America was essentially European theater.

BEGINNINGS TO THE AMERICAN REVOLUTION

Native American rituals long preceded any European-style theater, which did not arrive until the 16th century, but what would come to be understood as American theater in this period was simply the transplanting of English (mostly) plays and theatrical traditions to the New World. The influence of European theater on the American stage literally began before any of the colonies were formed. In 1567, two comic plays were performed at a Spanish mission near Tequesta, Florida, probably acted by Spanish soldiers for their own amusement (such performances may have taken place in the New World as early as 1538). Other early documented Spanish performances were given near what is now El Paso, Texas, in 1598. Such events had no influence on the development of a truly American stage, because such a thing did not exist and would not for at least a century.

There are several moments during the 17th century that might be considered the beginning of American theater, such as William Darby's *Ye Bare and Ye Cubb*, considered the first English-language play staged in the colonies, in August 1665 in Accomack County, Virginia, leading to the arrest of Darby and his actors. This event established the love-hate dynamic between the stage and its potential audience, which included a strong Puritan element who found theatrical activity licentious and, as such, undesirable. Darby was acquitted, but theater in the colonies was slow to get off the ground in the more than a century prior to the outbreak of the American Revolution. The deeply felt resistance to theater, dancing, music, and other entertainments was rooted in puritanical resistance, which had simply arrived in the colonies in the attitudes of many colonists.

There was theatrical activity, however, imported to America (much as the resistance to it was) by English immigrants, including strolling players like Anthony Aston, who, in the early years of the 18th century, attempted with little success to find an audience. Legitimacy for the theater may have been born in the involvement of the privileged few and public officials dabbling in theater, such as in the case of Robert Hunter, whose farce *Androboros* was the first play published in America. At one time the royal governor of New York and New Jersey, Hunter was only an occasional participant in theater—and, in fact, no playwright could hope to make a living on a stage in the Americas before the late 19th century. Most playwrights either had another career within the theater (actor, manager, etc.) or away from the stage until a growing volume of demand and, more importantly, copyright protections made it possible for dramatists to survive exclusively on their writing.

As an increasing number of European settlers established themselves along the eastern seaboard of the North American continent, theatrical activity slowly expanded. Construction began on the first permanent playhouse in Williamsburg, Virginia, in 1716 under the management of William Livingston (or Levingston). Resistance remained, however, in some eastern cities. For example, a band of strolling players set up to perform in Philadelphia in 1723 but were driven from the city to its outskirts by Quakers, whose values did not incorporate theatrical activities. Yet inroads were slowly made despite resistance; life in the colonies was hard, and few had time or resources for recreation. The first-known production of a Shakespearean play in the colonies, *Romeo and Juliet*, was given in 1730 in New York, and a professional company of actors from England also appeared in New York in 1732 in a performance of George Farquhar's *The Recruiting Officer*. The first operas and ballets followed during that same decade, and in 1736, Charleston's Dock Street Theatre opened. In the next few decades, permanent playhouses were constructed in major cities of the 13 original colonies, and theater slowly became, for some, an enjoyable and acceptable pastime.

There were many firsts in the early 18th century, but theatrical activity prior to the American Revolution was sporadic at best and except in the largest cities—New York, Boston (though theater was banned there for a few decades until after the Revolution), Philadelphia, Baltimore, Charleston—any sense of permanence for the stage as a solid enterprise was virtually nonexistent. Even in the larger cities, players struggled for an audience and seemed to be awaiting the arrival of great American plays and not those from English and other European stages. Some began to recognize the power of plays to agitate as part of the mounting resistance to British rule in the colonies. Mercy Otis Warren, a rare woman writer in the era, had no involvement in theater per se, though she used the dramatic form to satirize English policies and politicians as the inevitability of revolution became clear. At this time, intrepid stage artists continued to gain a foothold. Lewis Hallam Sr. formed the appropriately named American Company and produced Shakespeare's plays in Williamsburg, Virginia, though performers were often compelled to present their work in temporary or borrowed spaces, as most communities were resistant to the construction of permanent theaters.

Hallam and his troupe met with resistance in several regions, though they toured the colonies, winning support for a lively American stage. In 1753, the American Company toured to Jamaica, but Hallam's death there threatened the troupe's survival. One of his actors, David Douglass, stepped up to manage the company and, eventually, in 1758, to marry Hallam's widow. Douglass and Hallam's son, Lewis Hallam Jr., acted in significant roles, bringing greater success to the company. The American Company returned to the colonies and performed Richard Steele's *The Conscious Lovers* at New York's Nassau Street Theatre. In this era, academic theater also made its first appearance in the colonies when students at the College of Philadelphia staged *The Masque of Alfred*, even though the college's provost was compelled to defend the students from local protests.

The American Company under Douglass's management, with Lewis Hallam and his mother playing major roles, appeared at various times in the 1750s and 1760s throughout the colonies. In the same era, other firsts for the American stage led to progress for the profession in general. In 1766, *Ponteach; or, The Savages of America* was probably the first play to deal with Native Americans seriously and centrally in dramatic form, though *The Paxton Boys* (1764), whose author is unknown, dealt with a frontier uprising of settlers against Indians. The Southwark Theatre, the first permanent theater structure in the colonies, opened in Philadelphia in 1766, despite the objections of the Quaker majority residing there. The following year, New York's John Street Theatre, another permanent space, was constructed, and the

American Company made it their home. In 1767, they performed the first professional production of an American play, Thomas Godfrey's tragedy *The Prince of Parthia*.

In 1770, the Boston Massacre inflamed sentiments against British rule in the colonies, and Mercy Otis Warren's satires of English policies and the royal governor of Massachusetts, among others, contributed to inflamed divisions. In 1773, the Boston Tea Party and similar acts of defiance led to the American Revolution, with colonists seeking independence from what many considered oppressive British rule and unfair taxation.

REVOLUTIONARY THEATER

During the American Revolution, theatrical activity more or less disappeared. In 1774, the Continental Congress categorized theatrics with "gaming, cock fighting, and other expensive shows and entertainments," and forbade theater despite the fact that permanent playhouses stood and, that very year, David Douglass built another in Charleston, that city's first. As a result of the ban, the American Company left the colonies for Jamaica, where they would remain during the war. However, despite the ban on theatrical activity, the events of the Revolution would provide dramatists with much material in both the events and persons that commanded attention during the war years. In 1776, the Declaration of Independence gave meaning to the conflict, and playwright Hugh H. Brackenridge wrote *The Battle of Bunkers-Hill*, the title of which makes clear his focus, with celebratory speeches about the courage of the American colonists in standing up to overwhelming British forces. Also that year, John Leacock's *The Fall of British Tyranny; or, American Liberty Triumphant, the First Campaign* was published in support of the American efforts. At the same time, *The Battle of Brooklyn*, by an unknown author, offers a view of loyalist sentiments, as did British general John Burgoyne's *The Blockade of Boston*, performed at Boston's Faneuil Hall while his forces held that city. However, the British did not have the last word when a satiric response came in *The Blockheads; or, The Affrighted Officers*, probably written by Mercy Otis Warren, a play directly mocking Burgoyne's play. In 1777, Brackenridge also wrote the blank verse tragedy, *The Death of General Montgomery at the Siege of Quebec*, and it was performed by his students at Maryland's Somerset Academy.

The deprivations, fears, and human suffering engendered by the Revolution did not stop sometime playwrights, like Mercy Otis Warren, from approaching other issues. In her one-act farce *The Motley Assembly* she made a case for the then-radical notion of votes for women even as the country was as yet unformed. Her call would be unheeded for more than a century, but when British general George Cornwallis surrendered to American general George Washington at Yorktown, Virginia, a new nation was truly born, and the concerns of the citizens of this new nation would be expressed in many ways, not least in theatrical terms as stage activity returned to the former colonies and the new United States of America.

THE DRAMA OF A NEW NATION

Within a short time after the end of the American Revolution, John Henry, who had thrown in his lot with the American Company (now referred to as the Old American Company) as one of its managers, returned from Jamaica. David Douglass and Lewis Hallam Jr., along with other members of the company, followed, reigniting interest in theater in the new nation. By 1784–1785, Henry and Hallam, with the involvement of Thomas Wignell, reassembled the American Company at New York's John Street Theatre, emerging as the major post-Revolutionary theater and establishing New York as the center of theatrical life, though they also built Baltimore's first theater in 1786.

In 1787, Royall Tyler scored a success with the five-act comedy *The Contrast*, the first work written by a citizen of the United States professionally mounted. Written in the style of British comedy of manners plays, indicating the continued dependence on English culture, the success of *The Contrast* encouraged others, and even more than before the war, theater activity grew rapidly in the major East Coast cities. Other important forces emerged, including William Dunlap, a playwright and manager (and, ultimately, the first historian of the American stage), whose first play, *The Modest Soldier; or, Love in New York*, was written in the same year as Tyler's comedy. While these and other dramatists delved into American subjects, various theaters were more often inclined to produce European (especially English) plays, if for no other reason than that there was an existing body of work. Writers including Samuel Low, William Hill Brown, Susanna Haswell Rowson, and Dunlap, among others, wrote new works beginning to reflect the influence of the influx of immigrants coming to America's shores and other national problems. From Barbary pirates interrupting trade (as in Rowson's 1794 play *Slaves in Algiers; or, A Struggle for Freedom*) to Native Americans (as in Ann Kemble Hatton's 1794 libretto *Tammany; or, The Indian Chief*), corrupt schemes and land speculations like the Yazoo Purchase (dramatized in Tyler's 1797 play *The Georgia Spec; or, Land in the Moon*) to continued conflicts with England, American plays—while using English models—were filled with American issues and attitudes. Some plays in this era revisited the events of the Revolution, as in Brown's *West Point Preserved; or, The Trea-*

son of Arnold (1797) and John Daly Burk's *Bunker-Hill; or, The Death of General Warren* (1797), but the best of these last was Dunlap's *André* (1798), a somewhat sympathetic portrayal of Major John André, who had been executed by American forces as a spy for his involvement in Benedict Arnold's betrayal of the Continental Army at West Point. It opened at New York's newly constructed Park Theatre to a positive reception, as audiences continued to confront the toll and the triumph of the American Revolution.

The Park Theatre (originally called the New Theatre) under Dunlap's management served as a home to the Old American Company; it had, in fact, been built by Lewis Hallam Jr. and John Hodgkinson with the expressed intention of rivaling the well-established John Street Theatre. The Park featured productions of numerous Dunlap plays, many adapted from European sources, and he demonstrated an impressive range in his choice of topics and inspirations. The Park featured such leading actors as Thomas Abthorpe Cooper, as well as Hallam, and staged a few early American classics, albeit inspired by foreign works. Among these, Dunlap's *The Stranger* (1798), adapted from August von Kotzebue's original, became an oft-performed work, while his other adaptations in this era, including other works by Kotzebue and Richard Brinsley Sheridan, consistently drew audiences to the theater.

As the New York stage began to thrive through the efforts of Dunlap and the Old American Company and as the new century dawned, other cities confirmed their commitment to theatrical culture, including Washington, DC, the new nation's new capital, where Thomas Wignell opened the United States Theatre in 1800. New Orleans's St. Philip Street Theatre opened in 1808, but the following year, in 1809, one of America's most historic theaters, the Walnut Street Theatre in Philadelphia, opened its doors with a production of Sheridan's *The Rivals*, an auspicious performance with ex-president Thomas Jefferson and the Marquis de Lafayette in the audience. And 205 years later, the Walnut Street Theatre continues to operate without interruption since that night in 1809. A lively American stage became a significant part of life in the United States in the 19th century, and despite periodic highs and lows, it continues to be so into the 21st century.

Despite Dunlap's successes, and those of a few other dramatists, the American stage had, as the 19th century began, arrived at a crossroads. To move to the next level, a playwright of surpassing quality was required, though none would truly be found before the early 20th century, despite the efforts of many proficient craftsmen to achieve works of immediate import and lasting significance. Through the 19th century, the most vital energy on American stages was supplied by the country's first great actors, Edwin Forrest and Edwin Booth. Both were tragedians, most often appearing in the plays of Shakespeare, but a growing diversity of entertainments including everything from tragedy to comedy, farce to burlesque, variety acts to Shakespeare, equestrian plays to opéra bouffe, and the arrival of melodrama, a form already popularized in Europe, flourished on American stages. However, melodrama, above all, would dominate in legitimate theater and become the major conduit of a nation's sensibilities and tempo.

FINDING A VOICE

As the American stage found its footing in the early 19th century, the nation's tenuous security was threatened from the outside when the British navy's habit of capturing American sailors and pressing them into their service became a problem of national concern. In response, the United States declared war on Great Britain and what became known as the War of 1812 (which actually lasted until 1815) began. Though this tragic conflict had an impact on America's security, as demonstrated when the British captured and burned much of Washington, DC, including the White House, forcing President James Madison and his wife, Dolley, to flee, theatrical activity continued without an official ban or interruption. Though the war officially ended in the last week of 1814, word did not reach General Andrew Jackson, who led American forces against the British in the Battle of New Orleans, winning what proved to be a Pyrrhic victory for the United States and the source of several celebratory dramas enshrining Jackson, including C. E. Grice's *The Battle of New Orleans; or, Glory, Love and Loyalty* at the Park Theatre, which ultimately carried him to the White House.

During the decade immediate following the War of 1812, the emergence of actors of note continued to aid the growth and development of the American stage. Among such figures as Junius Brutus Booth, James W. Wallack, James H. Hackett, and others, the aforementioned Edwin Forrest stood out in his command of the two most popular forms with American audiences: contemporary melodramas and the plays of Shakespeare. In 1819, the same year that English actor Edmund Kean made his first appearance in the United States in *Richard III*, Forrest made his debut in British playwright John Home's *Douglas*, in the role of Young Norval, a part that would serve as a debut role for a number of America's leading actors over the subsequent decades. Forrest's mastery of a bombastic style of acting won him a large following over the subsequent years, and he used his growing fame to encourage American playwrights to create new works. He believed that for the US theater to predominate and excel, it would have to develop a canon of outstanding plays on American subjects. Forrest ultimately had many successes and 19th-century works associated with his name, but in 1829 he offered a cash prize of $500 and a production of the best play with a Native American hero, leading to the selection of John Augustus Stone's *Metamora;*

or, The Last of the Wampanoags. Offering a sympathetic portrait of a Wampanoag Indian chief fighting in vain to save his diminishing tribe, *Metamora* became, among other works of the first half of the 19th century, an oft-revived play until well after the Civil War.

Another significant development was the establishment, in 1821, of the African Grove Theatre, the first all-black company in New York, founded by William Henry Brown. This pioneering company produced Shakespeare, contemporary plays, and the first-known drama by a black author, Brown's *The Drama of King Shotaway* (1823). White managers are believed to have harassed the company until, in 1823, the African Grove disbanded. This was an unfortunate turn of events, as a leading actor with the African Grove, Ira Aldridge, chose to leave the United States to perform on European stages for audiences friendlier to accepting an African American actor in Shakespeare's plays. The end of the African Grove blocked opportunities for black artists to work in the realms of serious drama, and, as such, they were left only the variety stage and minstrel shows for decades.

The rise of minstrelsy in the early 19th century provided a conduit for popular music, but also established a range of odious racial stereotypes as white actors donned blackface makeup to portray exaggerated images of African Americans in comic sketches and songs. The popularity of minstrels was undeniable and pervasive during the 19th and into the 20th centuries, but within a short time, African Americans also participated. All-black companies and mixed companies emerged and toured throughout the United States and to Europe, finding enthusiastic audiences. The form evolved over time, but essentially began in the late 1820s when actor Thomas Dartmouth "Daddy" Rice offered his "Jump Jim Crow" routine, an eccentric song and dance with Rice in blackface. The astonishing popularity of this simple act inspired large-scale variety bills with the performers in blackface offering songs, dances, and comedy, including drag acts. Seen as a major development in a movement toward musical theater, minstrelsy helped create a venue for variety acts of various sorts, creating a branch of American theater aimed at delivering pure entertainment, albeit depending on racial stereotypes. In this period, the construction of grand "museums," which offered a variety of exhibits and amusements along with legitimate theater, began, and one dominant figure, P. T. Barnum, became legendary through his American Museum, his promotion of a range of celebrities from Jenny Lind to Tom Thumb, and his ultimate involvement in making the circus a cherished American tradition. At about the same time, another important name, E. P. Christy, appeared to establish his Christy's Minstrels, which, along with the Virginia Minstrels, were minstrel shows created as elaborate entertainments and whose names became synonymous with the form.

The depiction of African Americans in exaggerated stereotypes continued for well over a century and found its way into virtually all kinds of plays in which white actors portrayed black characters in comedies and even in dramatic roles, from Shakespeare's *Othello* to a range of melodramatic works. Across the 19th century, white performers also co-opted virtually all racial and ethnic characters as the arrival of immigrant populations encouraged depictions of the lives of these transplanted peoples. Such stereotypes became ingrained in popular culture, and it would take more than a century to destroy them as African Americans, Asians, the Irish, Germans, Italians, and Eastern Europeans, not to mention Native Americans and all ethnic groups, fought to depict the reality of their lives in plays, but generally only began to succeed in this after World War I.

In 1828, the same year that Rice's "Jump Jim Crow" became popular, Philadelphia's Arch Street Theatre opened and in short order established itself as one of the premiere theaters in the northeastern United States. Playwrights including John Howard Payne, Richard Penn Smith, James M. Kennicott, Nathaniel Deering, James Kirke Paulding, and Robert Montgomery Bird filled stages with new works in the decades prior to the Civil War, some adapting plays from literary works, both American and European, by a range of authors, including Lord Byron and James Fenimore Cooper, among many others. William Dunlap, who had provided the American stage with a consistent flow of new plays (many adaptations), published his *History of the American Theatre*, providing an invaluable record (though not without errors) of the development of theater in the United States from its beginnings until 1832. That year, playwright James Sheridan Knowles's *The Hunchback*, which first appeared in London, scored a major success in the United States and became a perennial success for a score of leading actresses, including Viola Allen, Mary Anderson, Charlotte Cushman, Julia Marlowe, and Clara Morris.

Women on the American stage increasingly asserted themselves as actresses, but also in what were considered male occupations, including dramatists like Louisa Medina, Josephine Clifton, and Charlotte Mary Sanford Barnes. Women took on activist roles, including Fanny Kemble, an English actress who became popular on American stages, but proved herself an important voice for change. When Kemble married a wealthy Southerner and lived for a time on his large Georgia plantation, she increasingly spoke out against slavery and wrote of her observance of the abuses inherent in slavery in a memoir, an early example of an artist using her celebrity to encourage the abolitionist movement that ultimately led the nation to the Civil War.

THE NATION DIVIDED

The year 1841 began auspiciously for the American theater with the opening of the Boston Museum, a center of that city's entertainment world, and when Dion Boucicault's first play, *London Assurance*, scored a success in London and New York and established him as a playwright, actor, and manager whose significance between the 1840s and the 1870s was singular. Few playwrights could rival Boucicault in the quality and quantity of his work, as he emerged as a prolific dramatist capable of bringing great variety to the melodramatic form. Boucicault wrote a series of Irish-themed plays (as did others, including John Brougham and James Pilgrim), drawing attention to the growing Irish population in America as immigrants crowded into New York and other major eastern cities. Boucicault also adapted many European works and composed original plays. His *London Assurance* premiered in the United States at the Park Theatre, with Charlotte Cushman and Henry Placide in major roles, and during the subsequent four decades Boucicault's name was featured on billboards as both star actor and playwright in New York and London.

Boucicault was not the only writer to find success in the antebellum theater, as the volume and variety of plays on the American stage grew in quality and diversity. A long series of temperance melodramas found popularity, including William H. Smith's *The Drunkard; or, The Fallen Saved* (1844), and plays with comic "Yankee" characters, dating back to Royall Tyler's *The Contrast*, were consistently well received, including Oliver E. Durivage's *The Stage-Struck Yankee*, and the Bowery "b'hoy" (played by Frank S. Chanfrau) made his first significant appearance in Benjamin A. Baker's hit, *A Glance at New York* (1848). Also in this period, the first important play by a woman playwright, Anna Cora Mowatt's *Fashion*, appeared successfully in 1845 with Mowatt in the cast. Her promise as a playwright went mostly unfulfilled, as she preferred acting, but others supplied stages in the major cities with a steady flow of works. As the nation moved westward, the "road," a network of theaters in cities and town across the United States and the territories, became a lucrative option for actors and playwrights, as even settlers on the frontier sought entertainments of various kinds. Touring became something most actors did, though it was not without its hazards, as demonstrated when tragedian Junius Brutus Booth died on a steamship while touring, apparently after drinking contaminated water. There were other hazards in pre–Civil War American theater. The friction between British and American culture found its peak in the rivalry between America's leading tragedian, Edwin Forrest, and England's foremost Shakespearean, William Charles Macready. On 10 May 1849, admirers of both actors collided in a riot in New York's Astor Place, ending in the deaths of at least 22 participants with scores of others injured, including militiamen called up to end the riot.

That same year, Edwin Booth, who would inherit Forrest's laurels as America's finest actor, and one who would bring a less bombastic and more natural style to the acting of Shakespeare and contemporary melodramas, made his stage debut opposite his father, Junius Brutus Booth, in *Richard III*. Booth would win great respect from audiences, most particularly after his record-setting 100-performance run in *Hamlet* in 1864–1865. The high standards of his productions and his predominance would only be temporarily shaken in 1865, when his brother John Wilkes Booth, also an actor, assassinated President Abraham Lincoln in Washington, DC's Ford's Theatre.

Lincoln's assassination, only days after the end of the catastrophic Civil War separating the American North from South over issues of the abolition of slavery and states' rights, was the culminating event of decades of tensions that became inflamed in the 1850s, in part as a result of Harriet Beecher Stowe's wildly popular abolitionist novel, *Uncle Tom's Cabin* (1852), which, the same year as its publication, became equally successful on stage, most particularly in an adaptation of the first half of the novel by actor George L. Aiken, which played consistently in theaters across the United States for over 75 years. The profound seriousness surrounding the moral and economic questions of the slavery issue did not find much attention on the stage, although William Wells Brown, an ex-slave, wrote a melodrama, *The Escape; or, A Leap for Freedom*, which was published in 1858, and Dion Boucicault's tragic melodrama, *The Octoroon* (1859), raised the issues with emphasis on the explosive subject of mixed-race relations between the play's leading characters. In the run-up to the Civil War, other plays also tracked current events, as in Mrs. J. C. Swayze's *Ossawattomie Brown; or, The Insurrection at Harper's Ferry* (1859), her highly fictionalized depiction of John Brown's radical abolitionist views.

The Civil War inevitably slowed the progress of theater as attentions were focused on the war and its deprivations, and, particularly, it interfered with touring actors who, depending on their political sentiments, were uncertain of their reception on either side of the Mason-Dixon Line. However, some actors found it possible to perform in both North and South, keeping their loyalties hidden. Aside from war, other changes were afoot. Women, who had gained fame as actresses, slowly began to move into management. Laura Keene, for example, ran her own company and for a time had her own theater in New York. Other women followed suit in the postwar decades, with Louisa Lane, better known as Mrs. John Drew, successfully managing the Arch Street Theatre in Philadelphia for decades. The spread of American theater westward is exemplified by the building of the Salt Lake Theatre, largely funded by Brigham Young, and other midwestern and western cities eventually had theaters in order to welcome touring actors and, ultimately, local actors who gained popularity in their region even if New York success eluded them. Traditional values were also tested on stages as, for example, with a revival of H. M. Milner's old melodrama, *Mazeppa; or, The Wild Horse of Tartary* (based on a poem by Lord Byron), in which the title character, a male, was played by actress Adah Isaacs Menken, who shocked and titillated audiences in this breeches role, appearing in fleshings to simulate nudity and lashed to a horse for a spectacular ride up a mountain at the play's climax.

Lacking full equality in all quarters, women in theater demonstrated their obvious equality with men—and, it should be noted, their frequent superiority. Such actor/managers as Keene, Mrs. Drew, Mrs. D. P. Bowers, Susan Denin, Kate Claxton, Rosina Vokes, and others; playwrights from Mercy Otis Warren, Sarah Pogson Smith, and Louisa Medina to Sidney Frances Cowell Bateman and Anna Cora Mowatt; and scores of major actresses, including Keene, Mrs. Drew, Lotta Crabtree, and Charlotte Cushman to Mrs. Gilbert, Menken, and Ada Rehan, and even international women stars who spent much of their time on American stages, including Sarah Bernhardt, Fanny Kemble, Fanny Janauschek, and Helena Modjeska, brought women closer to full equality, at least in the theater. Women eventually moved into design, directing, and dramatic criticism as well, particularly after 1890.

In this period, as women rose in the ranks of theater, plays by authors supporting the Confederate States of America, such as James D. McCabe's *The Guerillas; or, The War in Virginia* (1862), were produced in the Southern theaters, while a range of melodramatic plays depicting the tragic aspects of the war on personal lives were also staged. However, much theater remained escapist entertainment, and the New York theater scene continued to expand. The Fifth Avenue Theatre, first known as the Madison Square Theatre, opened under Augustin Daly's management, and Daly won popularity for his theater with a range of melodramatic works he wrote or adapted, including his first success, staged at New York's Niblo's Garden, the popular *Leah, The Forsaken* (1863) starring Kate Bateman. Daly, like Boucicault, would become a manager and playwright of quality, and his company at the Fifth Avenue Theatre was notable for the quality of its ensemble acting in diverse works. As the war drew to a close, Joseph Jefferson, from a theatrical family reaching back several generations to England, found enduring popularity in the title role of Boucicault's adaptation of *Rip Van Winkle* (1865) in London (and the following year in the United States for the first time). Jefferson played the role for decades despite his popularity in flavorful character roles in other works, including Boucicault's *Dot* (1859), adapted from Charles Dickens's *The Cricket on the Hearth*, and *The Octoroon* (1859).

As previously noted, the catastrophe of the Civil War ended with one final tragedy that had a profound impact on the newly reunited nation. President Abraham Lincoln was assassinated at Washington, DC's Ford's Theatre while watching a performance of Laura Keene's company in one of their most popular productions, British playwright Tom Taylor's *Our American Cousin*. Confederate sympathizer and theatrical matinee idol John Wilkes Booth assumed he would be hailed a hero in the Southern states for his murder of Lincoln, which he incorrectly presumed would revive the Confederacy's chances of reversing the end of the conflict. For a time after the assassination, the normal antitheatrical prejudices dating back to Puritan resistance of theater in the 17th century were inflamed by Booth's horrific act taking place in a theater. Booth's brother, Edwin, a star actor via his recent and unprecedented 100-performance run in *Hamlet*, felt obliged to withdraw from the stage in the aftermath of Lincoln's murder, but within months he was encouraged to return. With his successful comeback, the theatrical community as a whole was able to return to business as usual.

BROADWAY

Sometime in the post Civil War decades, the conglomeration of theaters in Manhattan began to be referred to as "Broadway," in part because this major artery in the city cut through neighborhoods within which most theaters were located. More importantly, this catchall name identified the New York stage as the center of theatrical America. Despite the continued influence of English and other European plays, playwrights, and visiting actors, and the volume of activity on the road, Broadway suggested that theater in America was a unified entity. It was not, but it is clear that for a century Broadway was the center of new innovations in dramatic art. The theaters themselves steadily moved from downtown to midtown, but Broadway was more an idea than geography, and more than anything, it was the place where playwrights, designers, and performers could gain critical success and lasting fame. Broadway became the pinnacle.

In the immediate aftermath of the Civil War, the diversity and innovation of the American stage became increasingly evident. Tony Pastor, for example, opened his Opera House and sought to elevate variety amusements, which he referred to as vaudeville, into family-friendly entertainment. *The Black Crook*, a melodramatic work with sequences of ballet and music, was a runaway hit and a harbinger of the musical theater, which would fully flower after World War I. In 1867, Augustin Daly continued his run of successful productions with one of the classic melodramas of the mid-19th century, *Under the Gaslight; or, Life and Love in These Times*. And, in 1868, Lydia

Thompson, with her "British Blondes" in tow (followed by the Rentz-Santley Novelty and Burlesque Company in 1870), took the New York stage by storm with her own particular brand of burlesque, creating the template for the form as a mixture of sexual innuendo, scantily clad women, music, and comedy that would gain popularity that continued into the mid-20th century. That same year, G. L. Fox appeared for the first time as an anarchic clown in his most popular production, *Humpty Dumpty*, spawning a series of sequels. In 1869, Edwin Booth opened his own theater and produced lavish and carefully planned and detailed productions of Shakespeare's plays, and in 1870, Daly, having firmly established himself in New York, offered another hit, *Frou-Frou*, starring Agnes Ethel. This began a long string of successes for his Fifth Avenue Theatre company and provided, in this case, a popular vehicle for leading actresses, including Sarah Bernhardt, who commenced her first of many American tours in 1880. Other European actors, such as Italy's Tommaso Salvini, who appeared in a polyglot production of *Othello* with Edwin Booth, and England's Henry Irving, who toured the United States with his costar, Ellen Terry, found fertile fields on the road in America.

During the 1870s, a generation of proficient American dramatists, including Daly, Boucicault, Bronson Howard, Bartley Campbell, James J. McCloskey Jr., Clay M. Greene, Thomas Blades de Walden, and others, provided the New York stage (and ultimately the road) with a range of popular melodramas and comedies. Leading actors, like Booth, Wallack, Lotta Crabtree, John Drew, E. L. Davenport, McKee Rankin, Rose Eytinge, Fanny Davenport, James O'Neill, Emily Rigl, Kate Claxton, Maude Granger, Kitty Blanchard, and many others, dominated stages in New York and, at times, on tour. Economic uncertainties in this decade led playwrights, like Daly with *The Big Bonanza* and Benjamin E. Woolf with *The Mighty Dollar*, to both dramatize and satirize Wall Street excesses in 1875, as did Bronson Howard's *The Banker's Daughter* in 1878 and, more memorably, his 1887 comedy *The Henrietta*. In this decade, such literary figures as William Dean Howells and Mark Twain dabbled in theater, but the real innovations came in facilities, as larger and more technologically advanced theaters were built, from Booth's Theatre to Steele MacKaye's extraordinary Madison Square Theatre, erected in 1879 with an elevator stage and all of the latest advances in technology. In the 1870s, the next generation of playwrights, including David Belasco and James A. Herne, established themselves; in the case of Belasco and Herne, their first New York productions, *Hearts of Oak* and *Within an Inch of His Life*, were collaborative efforts, but individually they would prove influential on late 19th- and early 20th-century stages. Belasco, in fact, would remain a force into the 1920s.

A range of popular entertainments flourished and became a showcase not only for diverse talents, but diverse cultures as the immigrants finding their way to the United States offered images of themselves and their views of America's melting pot. The runaway popularity of *The Mulligan Guards' Ball* (1879), which starred author Edward Harrigan and his comic partner Tony Hart, gave Irish Americans a glimpse of themselves in a popular entertainment, while other ethnicities began to assert their presence, with German, Italian, Eastern European, Asian, and other characters seen, often in stereotypical ways, in a range of amusements. African Americans still found theater essentially a closed shop except in minstrel entertainments, but in 1878 J. A. Arneaux and Benjamin Ford established the Astor Place Company of Colored Tragedians, which within a few years won praise for performances of Shakespeare's plays. Blacks slowly found occasional opportunities to play black characters, often demeaning stereotypes, in mainstream theater. In 1880, a revival of *Uncle Tom's Cabin* featured an integrated cast for the first time, a sign of changes to come. The English stage continued to have influence on the American stage, not only in touring actors, like Bernhardt, Salvini, Irving, and Terry, but also in operetta. Gilbert and Sullivan's works found popularity in the United States beginning in 1879 and beyond as American composers, lyricists, and librettists experimented with the forms of operetta, opéra bouffe, burlesque and travesty, and a range of hybrid entertainments mixing drama and music in search of the American musical theater as it emerged at the dawn of the 20th century.

THE THEATER AS A PROFESSION

Particularly between the American Revolution and 1880, changes in the functioning of theater as a profession were significant in all of the key areas. As the American stage became more and more a part of everyday American life, with permanent theaters springing up in most towns and the "road" for touring productions, everything relating to changes in management, acting, playwriting, and design and technology led, over 100 years, to a much-changed theater by the end of the 19th century.

In acting, progress from English acting styles brought from Great Britain to the colonies in the 18th century led to a highly technical, larger-than-life, and bombastic style for most American actors, to the point that lines of business (leading man, leading woman, heavy or villain, juvenile, eccentric, walking, utility, etc.) were codified to make the art of acting a technical matter to be learned and, at its best, to be enlivened by the individual qualities that often translated into star power. But star quality is ineffable. As Eleonora Duse often noted, the art of the actor is "writ on water." The stylishness and beauty of various leading ladies or the charm of a Lotta Crabtree could hold their interest or the hypnotic effect of Edwin Forrest's chesty manliness or Edwin Booth's liquid vowels and piercingly expressive dark eyes and melancholic countenance could heighten their acting in ways that thrilled audiences. Booth was an important transitional figure as well, moving toward a more natural acting style that not only employed his individual gifts, but led the taste of audiences toward a greater reality ultimately adopted by other actors and eventually enhanced by plays, even of the melodramatic variety, that provided opportunities for a realistic approach to flourish in the years before the plays of Henrik Ibsen led to the triumph of realism in late 19th-century Europe and early 20th-century America.

The progression from both English (and other European) dramatic traditions and the melodramatic theater as it was practiced in America to the rise of realism in the Ibsenite mode, was slow and, at times during the 19th century, hard to discern. Ever since 1820, when Scottish clergyman Sydney Smith posed his famous question: "In the four quarters of the globe, who reads an American book? or goes to an American play? or looks at an American picture or statue?," the subsequent decades before and after the Civil War saw vast changes in the quality and quantity of American arts. Literature flourished, and the best authors rivaled their European peers, but theater still mostly lagged behind, dogged by sentimentalized values deemed necessary by most actor-managers eager not to offend audiences with challenges to those values in a public setting, the sort of challenges that literary figures throughout the 19th century, from Nathaniel Hawthorne to Mark Twain, could offer.

Smith's remark certainly challenged Americans to find and promote theater artists who could gain international recognition and fueled the resistance to foreign influences, which, by the 1840s, exploded into violence in several instances, most lethally in the Astor Place Opera House riot in 1849. Ultimately, American actors like Charlotte Cushman and Edwin Booth, and many others included in this dictionary, won over European audiences when they dared, for example, to play Shakespeare or other popular British plays in London. But the American playwright who could win a nod from abroad proved more elusive, though a prolific writer (and actor) like Dion Boucicault could win popularity with English audiences, and African American actor Ira Aldridge found approving audiences throughout Europe. Expectations that proprieties be carefully observed, and an affection for sentimentality and sensation melodramas by American audiences, held dramatists in check, so the greatness that had arrived in acting via a Forrest or a Booth often came through non-American plays, from Shakespeare to a range of British and continental dramas and comedies. However, some dramatists, including European-born figures like Boucicault, brought to the burgeoning American stage a range of genres and plays, many of which found appreciative audiences for generations.

Perhaps no changes in the profession of theater were as significant as in the areas of theater architecture, technology, and design during the period covered in this volume. Stage decorations tended to be minimal prior to the early 19th century, in part because permanent theater spaces were few and far between. Actors and playwrights did their work in borrowed or converted spaces in which the possibilities of stage effects and elaborate scenery, costuming, and lighting were minimal. However, in the wake of the Industrial Revolution, as materials became more available and were significantly cheaper, and as permanent theater spaces were constructed in major cities, managers sought to attract audiences with elaborately painted realism scenery, not to mention increasingly elaborate theater buildings. One-dimensional, the painted realism scenery could create an effective stage picture as a backdrop. However, as the 19th century moved forward, scenery became increasingly three-dimensional. Madame Vestris pioneered the box set for interior scenes, and as stage technology permitted increasingly extraordinary effects, theaters could offer their patrons a visual excitement to equal anything a melodramatic playwright could concoct, including fires, train wrecks, waterfalls, etc.

Following the Civil War, traveling companies still relied on basic one-dimensional stock settings to cover all scenic needs: a street with houses or shops, a forest, a grand or humble interior, a prison. If a company did not carry its own roll drops for those scenes, most opera houses could provide wings and backdrops for that range of locales, if not more. With the increasing ease of rail transportation during the late 19th century, the best touring ensembles tended increasingly to travel with their own more specialized settings created for specific plays. Still, most first-class theaters employed a scenic artist who could paint a backdrop as needed when the occasion arose. The ten, twent', thirt' melodramas required very specific scenic effects for their cheap thrills, and they would carry their own mechanical devices easily adapted to the trap and fly systems of various sizes of theaters on the road. Whereas the touring repertory companies of the 1880s carried scenery for as many as four or five plays, the combinations sent out from New York in the 1890s and after each formed a single-play package that was much easier to tour. In New York, the major theaters offered the latest scenic effects and topped in scenic spectacle anything one could see on the road. Some producers, like David Belasco, would go to extreme lengths in capturing the realism of a scene; however, the plays for which these scenes were often created remained within the realm of melodrama, an inherently artificial and highly sentimentalized form.

Throughout the 19th century, audiences continued to enjoy racist, ethnically stereotyped, or dialect comedy and cliché-ridden sentimental and/or sensational melodramas, though across the 19th century evidence can be found of a slow progression toward greater sophistication. The vast majority of playwrights avoided controversy or serious challenges to mainstream values in their plays even late in the century as European theaters embraced modernist concepts and challenged long-accepted values.

The cataclysm of the Civil War marked a violent end of a decades-long cultural debate over slavery and its place in American society, though a difficult Reconstruction for the South and over a century of racial friction lay ahead. With the war over, many Americans could turn their attention to other concerns, as did the theater, which, after 1865, only featured the war in nostalgic and increasingly romanticized dramas about what was also known as "The War between the States." The long struggle for racial equality for African Americans continued into the 21st century; for much of the 20th century, blacks living in the Southern states found themselves struggling with a separate and unequal society. The strictures African Americans experienced were known as "Jim Crow" laws, a caustic reference to the era of minstrelsy and the stereotyping of blacks as inferior beings. Little would occur in the last decades of the 19th century to change the Jim Crow South—such changes waited until well into the 20th century.

As the 19th century wore on, the role of women in American life came to the forefront as both a subject and within the theater profession. Women dramatists dating from the time of the American Revolution often led the way in challenging the accepted societal wisdom on the place of women in surprising ways, and of course, women working in theater in a variety of tasks, from acting to management, brought vast changes to attitudes about the professional capabilities of women within the profession (or any profession) as they conquered jobs typically belonging to men.

After the Civil War, America's renewed and ever-increasing optimism led record numbers of people from all walks of life to theaters. The New York stage—Broadway—is often described as the center of American theater from the mid-19th to the mid-20th century, but as this volume demonstrates, American theater was a truly national phenomenon. The aforementioned "road," a network of theaters served by an improving railway transportation system, meant that even small towns on the frontier and in the territories could expect visits by stars as well as journeyman actors. The road brought performances of every kind for audiences in cities, towns, and even the smallest rural communities, as the nation moved westward. The hurly-burly activity included not only plays ranging from Shakespeare and other classics to contemporary melodramas, but also operettas, minstrel shows, dime museums, Wild West shows, vaudeville, burlesque, medicine shows, and essentially all manner of popular entertainments. There was something for every

American social and economic level. Ethnic and racial stereotypes abounded in plays as well as on variety stages, nowhere more prominently than in minstrel shows, which continued to offer demeaning portrayals of African Americans in which both white and black performers wore blackface.

By the 19th century, European influences were relatively minor on American stagecraft and were not to have a significant impact until after the 1880s. Changes in the drama itself, resulting from Henrik Ibsen's social problem plays beginning in the 1870s in Europe and the inherent greater frankness in subject matter formerly taboo (certainly in the United States), was largely ignored by American dramatists until James A. Herne's *Margaret Fleming* (1890), which was the first fully identifiable American play influenced by Ibsen. After the Civil War, melodrama continued unabated, even though occasionally addressing social problems, as a few before the war had done. Leading playwrights took on increasingly important subject matter, sometimes political, but more often in regard to the general terrain of human behavior; however, it was usually treated in a sentimentalized and melodramatic manner.

Needless to say, during the 19th century, theater became big business, rivaling railroads, steel and textile manufacturing, and other industries in terms of numbers of people employed in the profession and in its impact on the American economy at large. This would continue to the birth of motion pictures in the 1890s, when a panoply of electronic forms of entertainment increasingly distracted Americans from live theater and significantly changed the way theater worked. Prior to 1880, however, a burgeoning New York stage and a growing network of legitimate and vaudeville theaters on the road allowed the stage to thrive. Theater managers were public personalities in their own cities (and often nationally) and frequently involved themselves in charitable or social causes. Some, like P. T. Barnum, even ran for political offices, and his name became synonymous with the circus, which he developed from a small entertainment to an elaborate American tradition.

After the Civil War, and toward the end of each summer, managers from all across America flocked to New York City to book attractions for the coming season. From the late 1870s to the 1890s, managers of 5,000 or so theaters would annually visit the booking agencies clustered around Union Square with the goal of getting the best shows they could afford to cover every week of the theater season, leaving no dark nights. Many theaters in smaller towns could not support a company for more than one performance, a fact even when the company was led by a major star like Edwin Booth or Sarah Bernhardt.

By the 1870s and beyond, the theater in America had tremendous vitality and variety. A remarkable range of entertainment options were available, including notably minstrelsy, burlesque, circus, vaudeville, the evolving musical theater, Wild West shows, dime museum exhibitions, and, of course, the legitimate stage. What became known as "Broadway" in the late 19th century led, in the 20th century, to a golden age of American theater between the World Wars. *The Historical Dictionary of American Theater: Beginnings* aims to provide a reference for access to the diverse range of plays, dramatists, actors, managers, directors, designers, theaters, terminology, and genres, some of all of these famous and others largely forgotten, to emerge between the first European performances in North America in the 16th century to the rise of the modernist era around 1880. It is from these early American theatrical activities that the golden age of American theater would evolve, mirroring in its greatness that of the increasingly powerful nation that inspired it.

†ABBEY, HENRY EUGENE (1846–1896). Son of clockmaker-jeweler Henry Stephen Abbey and Elizabeth Smith, Henry Eugene Abbey was born in Akron, Ohio, and rose to prominence as a theater **manager**.*† As one of the most respected impresarios in the United States between the 1870s and 1890s, Abbey managed theaters, attaining the **Park Theatre** in New York in 1876, followed by **Booth**'s,† **Wallack**'s, and the Metropolitan Opera House. He managed the **tours***† of such international theatrical luminaries as **Sarah Bernhardt**,† Hortense Rhéa,† and Adelina Patti and won renown for arranging tours of elaborate productions. **William H. Crane**'s† memoir *Footprints and Echoes* recounts how Abbey brought him together with **Stuart Robson†** for their highly successful 12-year partnership in comedy.

*†ACADEMIC THEATER. Exploration of dramatic literature by colleges and universities in the United States dates to well before the **American Revolution**, but prior to the middle of the 19th century little evidence suggests that performances of plays were frequent on campuses or that theatrical techniques were studied. The first pseudotheater college organization, **The Hasty Pudding Club**, was founded in 1795 at Harvard as a social club before it indulged in theatrical mock trials. The Hasty Pudding Club began staging plays in 1844 with the **burlesque***† *Bombastes Furioso*, but the gulf between studying plays as literature and giving performances remained distinct, with many academics viewing theatrical activities as a distraction from serious study and, in some cases, as morally unsound.

Theatrical performances were strictly limited to the extracurricular activities of literary societies, many of which sprang up at colleges after the **Civil War**. Some actual dramatic societies sprang up on college campuses throughout the 19th century. In 1881, Harvard students spent six months rehearsing *Oedipus Rex* in Greek for a performance considered to be the first of its kind in the United States. William O. Partridge, a Columbia University professor, called for the creation of drama classes and departments of theater as early as 1886, but the first formalized instruction in theatrical techniques appears to have been George Pierce Baker's† English 47 course at Harvard, first offered in 1905, where he essentially taught **playwriting***† to a couple of generations of the **dramatists***† who transformed American drama after World War I.†

†ACCIDENTS. Theater accidents causing serious injury were all too common prior to the era of union regulations. **Scenery***† and **lighting***† equipment sometimes fell onto performers, trapdoors† malfunctioned, prop pistols misfired, electric lights on costumes could short-circuit, hems of dresses might swish over the **footlights**† and ignite, and so on. In Louisville, on 20 October 1877, the leading **actress***† in Spalding's Dramatic Company production of **Dion Boucicault**'s† *The Shaughraun* was wounded by the paper wad and powder from a pistol shot. The popular **equestrian**† **Leo Hudson** died in St. Louis on 4 June 1873, about three weeks after a performance of *Mazeppa*† in which her horse, Black Bess, lost its footing during the dramatic ascent up a zigzag runway; she and the horse fell 14 feet.

The *Sacramento Bee* reported in December 1885 that the operator of the thunder effects in *Rip Van Winkle*† stood on a small platform in the theater's loft and became so engrossed in his work that he stepped off the platform and one leg went through the ceiling, causing a rain of plaster on the orchestra. The audience started to panic, but when they looked up and saw the limb with a foot that was "not of Cinderella like proportions," the terror turned to uproarious laughter.

"Happy accidents" also proliferated, like those recounted in Claude Bragdon's† memoir, *More Lives Than One*. For example, an audience member appreciated the "marvelous illusion of a twinkling star in the sky," which turned out to have been created by the shiny head of a safety pin used to repair a tear in the sky cloth. More serious accidents resulted from **theater fires**,† especially from the beginnings of theater in America into the early 20th century. The tragic Iroquois Theatre† fire in Chicago in 1903 sped the elimination of gas lighting, after which theater fires became relatively rare.

ACROSS THE CONTINENT; OR, SCENES FROM NEW YORK LIFE AND THE PACIFIC RAILROAD. **Actor***† **Oliver Doud Byron** revised **James J. McCloskey**'s **melodrama**,*† which premiered at Brooklyn's **Park Theatre** on 28 November 1870 before moving to Wood's Museum and Metropolitan Theatre, where it opened on 13 March 1871 for 42 performances.

A talented cast (including **Ada Rehan**'s† sister Kate in a small role) enlivened a grim tale of life in New York's notorious Five Points slum, where a penniless widow (played by Lizzie Safford) with children puts a curse on a heartless saloonkeeper, John Adderly (played by Charles Waverly), who refuses to help her despite the fact that her wastrel husband has expended all of their resources in the bar. The play leaps ahead 20 years, finding Adderly in the act of framing a gambler, Joe "The Ferrit" Ferris (played by Byron), and ruining a wealthy merchant, Thomas Goodwin (played by Joseph Sefton), whose daughter, Louise (played by Annie Firmin), is the object of his nefarious affections. "The Ferrit" escapes prison and sees to it that Adderly is jailed.

Another five years elapses, during which Ferris has become a stationmaster for the new Union Pacific railroad in hostile Indian territory. Goodwin and Louise are on a train heading for Ferris's station when Adderly, who has escaped prison, leads an Indian attack on a train while Ferris manages to telegraph for US troops to save the day. The train arrives safely, and the curtain falls on Ferris and Louise in an embrace.

Just another melodrama to most **critics**,*† *Across the Continent* was uncommonly popular with audiences, especially for Byron's acclaimed performance, and it helped popularize plays set in the western territories, which proliferated in the last decades of the 19th century as many of the once uncivilized territories grew larger populations and became states. The production's sensational effects, including the use of the Union Pacific Railroad and the telegraph, pleased audiences, who kept the play on stages for over 30 years.

*†ACTING/ACTOR/ACTRESS. Before the long-running play became economically feasible in the mid to late 19th century, the fundamental qualification for a career on the stage was the ability to memorize a lot of lines on short notice, for only a **star***† knew the luxury of the limited **repertory**.*† **Stock***† company actors were cast according to **lines of business**,† but might be called upon to play a different role every night for months on end. Vocal projection skills were essential, including the ability to adapt to a variety of acoustic environments.

For actors, periodic unemployment was to be expected, and there were few **economic**† protections for actors, especially in **touring***† circumstances. A failed tour might leave actors stranded in the hinterlands. Even actors who enjoyed long association with a single company based in a large city found themselves obliged to travel. Acting styles from the 18th century to the modernist era were patterned on the techniques of English stage stars (not surprising, given that much of the dramatic canon was drawn from British theater before the late 19th century), and in the early 19th century, actors adapted to the demands of **melodrama**:† making **points**† in vocal interpretation, using grand gestures, and striking attractive poses both in terms of individual physicalization of the text and in **tableaux vivants**† by the ensemble.

This romantic school of acting, with the climactic unleashing of a storm of passion, was the foundation for the careers of many tragedians who performed the **Shakespearean***† repertoire;† for example, **Edwin Forrest, Junius Brutus Booth, Fanny Janauschek,**† **Thomas W. Keene,**† Robert Mantell,† and **John McCullough**.† At the same time, however, other actors gradually introduced greater **realism***† into their performances. As early as the 1850s, **Edwin Booth**† was turning away from the romantic style of his father, Junius Brutus Booth, adopting an economy of gesture, while eschewing points. His natural manner of delivery and immersion in his character proved highly influential on such actors as **Lawrence Barrett,**† **Mary Anderson,**† and **Otis Skinner,**† and his approach began a steady movement toward increasingly natural acting into the 20th century.

The handsome actor-**playwright***† **William Gillette,**† a **matinee idol,**† has been signaled as another leader in the move away from elocutionary artifice of line interpretation; his biographer Doris E. Cook described him as "one of the first American actors to speak rather than declaim his roles." She quotes his recollection of his early days of acting in the earlier style: "I began very humbly indeed, in **stock,***† and if I had tried to be natural, I'd have lost my position. My business then was to learn the tricks of the stage. We had our tragic walk, our proper comedy face, our correct and dreadful laugh, our carefully learned gestures, our shrieks and outcries and our stilted voices. We were to hope for success in so far as we mastered these rules and tricks and put force and personal 'vigor' into our execution of them." In 1936, several **critics***† analyzed Gillette's contribution to the art and mentioned his detailed handling of properties, his "under-acting," and "the illusively effective naturalness of his acting."

Comic acting was largely realistic while allowing for exaggerations to heighten character or get the laugh. **Rube**† or **Yankee**† characters, or racial and ethnic stereotypes, appeared frequently in **legitimate**† drama as well as on the variety stage. **William H. Crane**† and **Stuart Robson**† figured prominently among actors specializing in comedy. For polished light romantic comedy, **John Drew**† reigned supreme and established a model followed by many others into the era of commercial films.

*†ACTOR/MANAGER. The tradition of the **leading actor***† also serving as **manager***† of the **touring***† company was long-standing in England, though less prevalent in the United States. **Star***† actors certainly preferred to retain control over casting, rehearsal discipline, bookings, and salaries rather than leaving those decisions entirely to **agents**† and company managers. From the time of **Lewis Hallam** and **David Douglass** to the early 20th century, name actors often managed their own companies in seasons in New York and major cities, as well as on tour. Star **actresses***† also managed their own companies often as frequently as male actors, with figures like

Laura Keene providing models, and European stars, including **Sarah Bernhardt**,† proving to be skillful managers who amassed great wealth through lucrative tours and clever self-promotion.

Broadly used, the term "manager" could encompass the activities of the **producer**,*† the entrepreneur, and the local theater lessee. By the mid-19th century, aspects of the role of manager were often divided among more than one individual. A company manager would need to interact with a theater's manager, and both might deal with the management of a circuit of theaters. Alfred L. Bernheim quotes two comments about managers made in 1883: "Most of our managers are thick-skulled people and few of them are gentlemen. They seem to have been born on the **road**,*† and how they got to New York and succeeded is only to be accounted for on the principle of ignorance and the almighty dollar." "As a general thing they are financiers and brokers, who, like their Wall Street brethren, watch the market and go as that goes." And an observation from 1879, also quoted by Bernheim: "The manager, if he would succeed, must cater to the taste of his patrons, both in the selection of his company and of his plays. He must give the public what they want, not what he thinks they ought to want."

Actor-managers of note of the 19th century include nearly every star actor or, by midcentury, actress of the era, including **William Dunlap, Thomas Abthorpe Cooper, Thomas Hamblin, Edwin Forrest, Edwin Booth,† J. W. Wallack, Lester Wallack,** Laura Keene, **Dion Boucicault,† John McCullough, P. T. Barnum, Lydia Thompson, David Belasco,† James A. Herne,† Joseph Jefferson,† Steele MacKaye, John Sleeper Clarke, Augustin Daly, E. L. Davenport, Mrs. John Drew,† Minnie Maddern Fiske,† William Gillette,†** Richard Mansfield,† and Robert B. Mantell,† among many others.

ACTORS' ORDER OF FRIENDSHIP. A fraternal society for **actors**,*† it was founded in Philadelphia in 1849 in the **Shakespeare***† Lodge, where it continued for 50-plus years, providing charitable support for members of the theatrical profession. A 25 June 1886 meeting at New York's **Madison Square Theatre**† was covered by the *New York Times*, which remarked on the large turnout of notable theater personages, led by speakers **Stuart Robson** and F. F. Mackay. The participants in the meeting passed resolutions "that the dramatic profession should take care of its sick and distressed members" and established some performances to serve as benefits to support the effort. A New York branch was formally founded in 1888, called the **Edwin Forrest** Lodge, by several name actors, including **Louis Aldrich,† John Drew,†** and **Otis Skinner**,*† before the organization vanished to be replaced by the Actors Fund of America.†

ADAMS, EDWIN (1834–1877). This popular **actor*†** was born in Medford, Massachusetts, and after apprenticeships with **Joseph Jefferson†** and **E. A. Sothern**, he scored his first success in 1853 in *The Hunchback* with **Kate Bateman** at the **National Theatre** in Boston before appearing in *Hamlet* opposite **James W. Wallack** and Bateman in 1860. **Touring*†** as a **star*†** after 1863, he had a stretch of bad luck, such as being booked to appear at Washington, DC's **Ford's Theatre** two nights after President **Abraham Lincoln**'s assassination there.

After a long series of roles in various popular plays of the era, including *The Serf, The Dead Heart, Wild Oats, The Lady of Lyons, Narcisse,* and *The Marble Heart,* Adams joined **Edwin Booth**'s† company in 1867, appearing in *Romeo and Juliet* (as Mercutio) and *Othello* (as Iago) with Booth, among others. He toured through the early 1870s in roles he had popularized, most notably a dramatization of Alfred Tennyson's poem *Enoch Arden,* beginning in 1869, before ill health while on a tour in Australia caused him to leave the stage, followed by his death shortly thereafter. Adams was praised in both drama and comedy, described in the *New York Times* at the time of his death as "a picturesque and scholarly player" who, in comedy, exuded "rollicking humor and manliness."

ADAMS, JOHN JAY (1798?–1839). An **actor*†** who began his working life as a merchant, John Jay Adams made his debut in 1822 as Hamlet, winning acclaim. He appeared in other **Shakespearean*†** roles, including *Othello,* and in popular plays of the early 19th century, but bouts of alcoholism ended his career prematurely.

THE ADULATEUR. **Mercy Otis Warren**'s five-act satire labeled "a Tragedy, As it is now acted in Upper Servia," was apparently never staged, but portions of it appeared in the *Massachusetts Spy* newspaper in 1772, before it was published in its entirety in 1773. Its publication meant that the play, widely disseminated in print and popular with readers, was better known than it might have been if performed. Using thinly veiled portraits of public personages, Warren mocked the actions of Massachusetts royal governor Thomas Hutchinson, who, as the play has it, pretends to be in sympathy with independence-minded colonists while working against their interests.

In the play, which seems prescient about the coming **American Revolution**, Rapatio (based on Hutchinson) works against the goals of freedom led by Brutus (John Adams), Cassius (Samuel Adams), Junius (John Hancock), and Portius (James Otis, Warren's brother).

Warren was a close friend of Abigail Adams; when she wrote *The Adulateur,* Warren wrote to John Adams asking if she was "deficient" in femininity for writing a satiric political play, but Adams encouraged her in her efforts.

However, Adams subsequently became less supportive of her pronouncements on history and politics when, in 1805, her three-volume *History of the Rise, Progress and Termination of the American Revolution* was published and criticized some of Adams's positions.

†**ADVANCE AGENT/ADVANCE MAN.** Traveling ahead of a **touring***† company, the advance agent or "working agent," later called *press agent*, would oversee any special arrangements contracted with the theater **manager**,*† consult with the local billposting business on the design of posters and on getting them posted in advantageous locations, and develop relationships with local news organizations to attract favorable coverage. In the 1870s, before the rise of booking agencies,† the advance man functioned as a booking agent, arranging dates, negotiating contracts, and tending to the advertising, often even posting the bills himself.

Although legendarily underpaid, advance agents had to be gregarious personalities with long memories, for it might be a year between visits to a given city. By the dawn of the 20th century, centralized booking of **combinations**† out of New York City contributed to the decline of the advance agent, while the later term *press agent* referred to more circumscribed public relations responsibilities.

*†**ADVERTISING.** Prior to the 20th century, theatrical advertising consisted largely of newspaper notices and broadsides or large bills posted on walls of buildings. By the 1870s, advertisements tended to be simple notices of the title of the work and the time and place of performance, but in that same period, more text (and occasionally some artwork) was added, often describing the scenic thrills, emphasizing the **stars**,*† and providing a schedule of performances of the plays in **repertory**.*† Curiously, the name of the **playwright***† virtually never appeared. Newspapers were also full of paid **puffs**,† little snippets of promotional material disguised as reporting.

*†**AFRICAN AMERICAN THEATER.** Black **playwrights***† and **managers***† were precious few in the United States prior to 1880, despite the appearance of the **African Grove Theatre** in New York in 1821, a rare oasis for serious black artists at which every sort of work from **Shakespeare***† to new plays by black writers provided African American actors with opportunities. For blacks, there were few roles available in white theaters in a time when demeaning depictions of black characters performed by white actors in **blackface**† predominated.

Serious African American actors such as **Ira Aldridge**, **Morgan Smith**, and **Paul Molyneaux** found it necessary to cross the Atlantic to build careers abroad on friendlier stages. The first decades after the **Civil War** in America brought some opportunities for professional black performers, primarily in **minstrel**† shows or minor servile roles. Only gradually did African American performers move into **legitimate**† theater, the way paved by **amateur**† groups associated with schools and churches, and by solo platform readers like Emma Hatcher and Henrietta Vinton Davis,† both in the 1880s.

AFRICAN GROVE THEATRE. Believed to be the third of four attempts to establish a theater for **African Americans***† in New York in the years prior to the complete abolition of slavery in New York, which occurred in 1827, the African Grove Theatre began in 1821 (some sources believe it may have started in 1820) and performed for predominantly black audiences with an all-black company and **managers.***† Founded by free African Americans **William Henry Brown** and **James Hewlett**, who had both worked as ship stewards, it is generally believed that **Ira Aldridge** performed with the company prior to leaving the United States to become a celebrated **Shakespearean***† **actor***† **touring***† European cities.

First established in Brown's backyard, where food and drink were served, the performances of the African Grove Theatre were mostly poetry and short plays. In an ironic turnabout, white audience members were seated in a separate section of seats because, as the African Grove's management wittily noted, "whites do not know how to conduct themselves at entertainments for ladies and gentlemen of color." In fact, working-class audiences of both races were known to be boisterous, which, in the case of the African Grove, provided police an excuse for harassing the company, which was seen as threatening the prosperity of theaters run by whites.

Shakespearean plays (*Richard III* and *Othello* were most popular), accompanied by comic prologues, were ultimately the theater's fare, though the company was small and actors played multiple roles. The theater also produced Brown's original play, *The Drama of King Shotaway* (1823), which is considered the first full-length play by an African American produced in the United States and is, unfortunately, lost.

White theater managers and audiences were often hostile to the African Grove, which led to several changes of location in the city and, finally, a more rural environment believed to be somewhere north of 14th Street. When **Junius Brutus Booth** appeared in *Richard III* at the **Park Theatre**, the African Grove company rented a space nearby and performed their own version of the play. It is believed that the Park's manager, **Stephen Price**, orchestrated a disturbance of the African Grove's performance, which he believed was hurting his business.

References to the African Grove Theatre's operations ceased after 1823 when, presumably, the theater was shut down (either for financial reasons or for charges of disturbing the peace), but one account refers to a **fire**† destroying the theater in 1826, though most scholars believe the theater had shuttered permanently in 1823. The next significant attempt to establish an African American company came in 1878 with the formation of the **Astor Place Company of Colored Tragedians**. In 2011, an Atlanta, Georgia–based company called the New African Grove Theatre Company chose its name, in part, to honor work begun in 1821.

*†AGENTS. An agent represented the business interests of another party, whether individual **actors*†** or a **manager*†** or a company on the **road**.*† Agents might specialize in areas like drawing up contracts, handling theater and railroad† bookings, or generating publicity.

AH SIN. Two of the more celebrated nondramatic writers of the 19th century, **Bret Harte** and **Mark Twain**, teamed to write this seriocomic play, which was produced by **Augustin Daly†** and opened at the **Fifth Avenue Theatre** for 35 performances on 31 July 1877. The title character of the play, taken from Harte's poem, "Plain Language from Truthful James" (also known as "The Heathen Chinee"), was inspired by the rapid growth of the Chinese population of the United States.

Twain and Harte sought to build a play around the clever Chinese character, Ah Sin (played notably by **Charles T. Parsloe**), who solves a murder in time to prevent a lynch mob from hanging the wrong man. Twain made a curtain speech that seemed an attempt at preempting **criticism**,*† explaining that the play was more a lesson than an **amusement**.† Some critics found his speech better than the play, though most praised Parsloe's performance and the novelty of a major Chinese character in an era when racial stereotypes (as well as multiple ethnicities) proliferated on the American stage, although they were exclusively played by white actors and usually in secondary comic roles. Otherwise, at best, it was considered "diverting" by the *New York Sun*, if also ultimately tiresome.

AIKEN, GEORGE L. (1830–1876). A journeyman **actor*†** who otherwise would be little remembered, George L. Aiken won a place in American theatrical history with his stage adaptation of the most popular and controversial novel of the mid-19th century, Harriet Beecher Stowe's *Uncle Tom's Cabin; or, Life Among the Lowly†* (1852). Aiken was born in Boston and left school in his early teens to work in a carpet warehouse and perform in amateur† theatricals. He made his professional acting debut in *Six Degrees of Crime* in 1849 in Providence, Rhode Island, before joining the company of his cousin, **George C. Howard**, as a **utility man**.†

Howard subsequently produced Aiken's adaptation of *Uncle Tom's Cabin* with phenomenal success from its premiere on 27 September 1852 at the Troy Museum in Troy, New York, before an astonishing 325-performance run at **Purdy's National Theatre** in New York, with Aiken playing the dual roles of George Selby and George Harris. Others adapted the novel, but few found anything approaching the success of Aiken's version, which ultimately was accepted as the dominant text widely produced until well into the 20th century.

Following the runaway success of *Uncle Tom's Cabin*, Aiken adapted Ann S. Stephens's novel, *The Old Homestead*† (1856) to the stage, playing the lead role himself (the play was revised in 1887 by **Denman Thompson,**† who made it a perennial success). He also adapted Sylvanus Cobb's *The Gun Maker of Moscow* (1856). Aiken was the resident **dramatist***† at **Barnum's Museum** for a time, associate **manager***† of the Troy Theatre in Troy, New York, and as an actor appeared in New York in the **burlesque***† *King Cotton* (1862) and *The Firefly* (1869) with **Lotta Crabtree**. After retiring from the stage in 1869, Aiken wrote novels under the pseudonym Bernard Clyde.

ALBAUGH, JOHN W., SR. (1837–1909). A native of Baltimore, John William Albaugh began an acting career as a teenager in **stock***† at the **Holliday Street Theatre**. His first success, in 1855, was the title role of **John Howard Payne**'s *Brutus, or The Fall of Tarquin*, and among his most celebrated performances, he won acclaim as Louis XI. Albaugh married Mary Lomax Mitchell, sister of **Maggie Mitchell**, and they **toured***† the United States before Albaugh became a theater **manager***† in St. Louis, Albany, and Washington, DC, in the 1860s, although he continued to act. By the late 1870s, he added the Holliday Street Theatre and Washington's **National Theatre** to his holdings, among others, continuing successfully until shortly before his death. His son, John Albaugh Jr. (1867–1910), was a successful **actor**.*†

ALBERTI. This popular romantic history play in five acts by **Isaac Harby** was his last (and best known) and opened at the **Charleston Theatre** on 27 April 1819. Set in Florence, Italy, in 1480, the play centered on issues of patriotism and freedom, seen through the bitter rivalry of Alberti, a general, and his jealous brother, Ridolpho. Romantic entanglements past and present prevent, for a time, an ultimate reconciliation between the brothers. President James Monroe attended the second performance.

American **critics***† appreciated the play, which was inspired by Vittorio Alfieri's tragedy *The Conspiracy of Pazzi* (although Harby's play ends happily), as did audiences in the United States and Europe, though European critics were dismissive. When one wrote that the play was well done for an "American production," Harby replied in the published preface to the play, writing, "I plead guilty" and expressing his pleasure in "the accident of birth, which has placed me under the protection of laws that I revere, and in the bosom of a country that I love."

†**ALDRICH, LOUIS (1843–1901).** Born Salma Lyons (or Lyon) while his mother traveled from Germany to Ohio, Louis Aldrich performed under various names, including Master Moses and Master McCarthy. He **toured***† with the March **Juvenile**† troupe for five years (1858–1863) playing **Shakespearean***† tragic roles and joined the **stock***† company of the **Boston Theatre** in 1866. At the peak of his career, he was **leading man**† at Philadelphia's **Arch Street Theatre** under **Mrs. John Drew**.† He appeared with **McKee Rankin**† in *The Danites* during the 1878–79 New York season and then, in 1879, in his great vehicle as Joe Saunders in *My Partner* by **Bartley Campbell**.† Aldrich's career continued through the 1890s, and he became president of the Actors Fund of America† in 1897, continuing in that job until his death.

ALDRIDGE, IRA (1807–1867). The son of Daniel Aldridge, a minister, and his wife, Lurona, both free blacks, Ira Frederick Aldridge was born in New York and studied at New York's African Free School. He turned to stage work in his youth with the **African Grove Theatre** in the early 1820s, though this company devoted to productions populated with **African American***† **actors***† was treated with hostility, at times, from audiences and white **managers**.*†

To a significant extent, Aldridge has become the most representative example of the problems facing aspiring black talents in 19th-century American theater. Denied access to challenging roles in theaters run by whites—and given the virtual nonexistence of black theaters in the first half of the 19th century—an actor with Aldridge's promise had little recourse but to leave the United States and perform in Europe, where there was hope of finding less resistance.

Aldridge also tested social barriers by playing opposite white **actresses***† in *Othello*, arguably his greatest role, but such mixed-race casting would have been unacceptable in American theaters in this era. In 1824, within a year of the end of the African Grove Theatre, Aldridge took work as a ship's steward and sailed to Liverpool. He studied at the University of Glasgow and prepared a repertoire of plays, mostly **Shakespeare's**,*† with the aim of **touring***† Europe. In 1825, he appeared at the Royal Coburg Theatre as Oroonoko in *A Slave's Revenge* and was generally well received, though some white **critics***† were not disposed to applaud his work.

Billed as "Tragedian of Colour, From the African Theatre, New York," Aldridge impressed audiences with a series of appearances in *The Ethiopian, or The Quadroon of the Mango Grove, The Libertine Defeated or African Ingratitude, The Negro's Curse, or The Foulah Son* (an original work written for him), and *The Death of Christophe, King of Hayti* within that year. Over the next few years, Aldridge appeared with success throughout the United Kingdom, excelling in a range of Shakespearean roles, including the aforementioned *Othello*, as Shylock in *The Merchant of Venice*, and in *Macbeth* and *Richard III.*

When Edmund Kean collapsed and died in 1833 during a run of *Othello*, Aldridge took the opportunity to appear in his place. However, he was attacked in print for appearing opposite noted white actress Ellen Tree, with critics objecting to Aldridge's "pawing" of the **leading lady**.† London theaters were disinclined to book him, but Aldridge gained popularity in the provinces and then toured European capitals to considerable acclaim, particularly in Russia, and became one of the highest-paid actors of his day. An activist abolitionist, Aldridge aided the cause with money, including buying African Americans out of slavery. He died while on tour in Poland and planning a post–**Civil War** return to the United States.

ALTORF. Celebrating Swiss independence, this 1819 play by Scottish-born feminist writer **Frances "Fanny" Wright** was produced in New York by **James W. Wallack**, but closed after a mere three performances. Wright, who became an American citizen in 1825, published the play that same year and subsequently became a vocal advocate for women's equality, abolition of slavery, and worker rights.

*†AMATEUR. Theater in the colonies and in the early United States during the 18th century was largely an amateur activity and comparatively few made their living in the profession. By the early 19th century, in towns where long dark periods interspersed appearances by professional players on **tour**,*† locals formed amateur dramatic societies and rehearsed a play one or two nights a week for a few months, then performed it at an **opera house** or some other suitable and available space for a paying audience. Any profit after expenses would often go to charity. The widespread enjoyment of amateur theatricals grew in the mid to late 19th century and underlay the Little Theatre*† movement of the 1910s, which in turn became the foundation for a vast network of community theaters*† to appear in the 1920s and beyond.

†**AMBERG, GUSTAV (1844–1921).** A naturalized citizen of the United States born in Prague, Gustav Amberg settled in Detroit in his early twenties. Shortly after the **Civil War**, Amberg became **manager***† of German-lan-

guage theaters in Detroit and Cincinnati. Moving to New York, he managed the **Germania Theatre** and then renovated the old **Bowery Theatre**, which he reopened as the Thalia, headquarters for his presentation of the top attractions† from Germany, including **musical*† stars*†** like Marie Geistinger and tragedians like **Ludwig Barnay**.

Amberg's efforts on behalf of the German theater in America secured his place in theatrical history and, as *New York Globe* **critic*†** Louis Sherwin wrote in 1912, "At a time when the American stage was the despair of all intelligent people, the German theater in New York . . . was their only refuge from cheap sentimentality and vulgarity." He was among the first managers to stage the plays of Henrik Ibsen† in America, and he ultimately built the Amberg Theatre, which opened in 1889.

THE AMERICAN CAPTIVE; OR, THE SIEGE OF TRIPOLI. James Ellison's five-act drama, first produced in Boston in 1819 (and published that year), emphasizes patriotic American fervor during the Tripolitan War (1801–1805), as it came to be known. The plot revolves around a group of American captives in Tripoli, and their leader, Anderson, a fictional **Yankee†** figure based on real-life Army Office and Tripolitan War diplomat, William Eaton.

In the play, Anderson struggles to outsmart a tyrannical bashaw who has cruelly banished his own brother, the rightful bashaw. Immolina, the daughter of the deposed bashaw, aids Anderson, while Ellison's dialogue makes his abolitionist sentiments known in the play's dialogue, as when Anderson acknowledges owning slaves. A North African character ruminates on this and replies, "Go where the Senegal winds its course, and ask the wretched mothers for their husbands and their sons! What will be their answer? *Doom'd to slavery, and in thy boasted country too!*" Some scholars view the play as more about what were then current American issues regarding slavery than those of the past Tripolitan War.

THE AMERICAN COMPANY. Considered the first completely professional theatrical company in North America, the American Company was founded initially as the Hallam Company when set up by **William Hallam** in London. He put his brother, **Lewis Hallam**, in charge of a company of 12 adults and three children and they sailed for America. The little troupe arrived in Yorktown, Virginia, on a ship called *Charming Sally*, and gave their first performance, **Shakespeare**'s*† *The Merchant of Venice*, in June 1752 in Williamsburg, Virginia. This is believed to be the first professional production of Shakespeare in North America.

During 1753, the company performed in New York, followed by stints in Philadelphia and Charleston, during 1754, after which they moved to the West Indies in 1755, where they merged with the company of **David Douglass**. Hallam died there and Douglass subsequently married Hallam's widow before the company **toured***† America again in 1758, then under the banner of the American Company, a name reflecting growing anti-British sentiments within both the company and the colonies. Hallam's son, **Lewis Hallam Jr.**, took on major roles in the company, along with Douglass, who was a more effective **manager***† than **actor**.*† The company ran afoul of puritanical resistance to theater in some areas; for example, in 1761 the company billed its production of *Othello* as a "series of moral dialogues" to avoid constraints in areas populated with a majority of Quakers and Puritans. Ultimately, the American Company is believed to have given over 180 performances and performed 14 of Shakespeare's plays.

The company also staged **Thomas Godfrey**'s original tragedy, *The Prince of Parthia*, the first by an American-born writer, on 24 April 1767 in Philadelphia. In 1774, the Continental Congress banned all theater for the duration of the **American Revolution** and the American Company decamped for Jamaica, where they spent the duration of the war. In 1783, the company returned and established itself in New York with Lewis Hallam Jr. as the **leading**† actor and **John Henry** as manager. Henry was replaced by **John Hodgkinson**, who, in 1796, sold his share to **William Dunlap**. In 1798, Dunlap took over the company, which was known as the Old American Company until 1805, when **Thomas Abthorpe Cooper** took over, after Dunlap fell into bankruptcy, and established the troupe in residence at the **Park Theatre**.

AMERICAN DRAMATIC FUND ASSOCIATION. Following in the footsteps of Philadelphia's **General Theatrical Fund**, established in 1829, the American Dramatic Fund Association, incorporated on 10 April 1848, was an attempt to provide a safety net for members of the theatrical profession who were subscribers to the association. Benefits included support for elderly members, widows, and orphans, and providing funeral expenses for indigent **actors**,*† although the problem arose that members forced by financial setbacks might allow their subscriptions to elapse and thus lose their benefits. Ultimately, calls were heeded for a stronger organization, which emerged as the Actors Fund of America,† set up in 1881.

AMERICAN MUSEUM. Founded in 1810 by John Scudder, the American Museum ultimately became closely associated with the legendary entrepreneur **P. T. Barnum** when he bought the operation, then housed at **Broadway***† and Ann Street in New York, and reopened it with great fanfare on 1

January 1842. Known more often to the public as Barnum's Museum, the American Museum presented both theatrical entertainments† of a wide variety, from **vaudeville†** and **minstrel†** shows to popular **melodramas†** and classic works, all performed in a lecture room. Along with these performances, the museum featured a range of **amusements,†** including a zoo, wax museum, and freak show.

Barnum attempted to present the public with every sort of curiosity—human and inanimate, from famous individuals, including the little person **Tom Thumb**, to the latest inventions, dioramas, scientific innovations, modern appliances, and animal acts, among others. A number of acts, including the supposed corpse of a mermaid, were fakes, but the public accepted such shams as part of the fun Barnum supplied.

In 1850, Barnum remodeled the space into a theater seating nearly 3,000 patrons, with the opening production being an 1844 **melodrama,†** William **H. Smith**'s *The Drunkard*, which ran for an astonishing 100 performances. An estimated 38 million people visited the American Museum during Barnum's tenure, an amazing number given that the population of the United States in this period was estimated at 35 million. A **fire†** destroyed the American Museum in 1865, a spectacular disaster during which police were compelled to shoot numerous animals escaping the burning building. Barnum built a bigger theater and museum, but fire again destroyed the American Museum in 1868, after which Barnum turned his attentions to **circus.*†**

AMERICAN REVOLUTION. The **war*†** known as the American Revolution was a defining event for North America and, in fact, Europe, as American colonists increasingly resisted what many considered English tyrannies over the liberties of American colonists who, increasingly, sought to manage their own affairs. Thirteen colonies along the eastern seaboard banded together to break with the British Empire, first through negotiation, but ultimately only succeeded through armed conflict. By 1774, the colonies had rejected the rule of the Parliament of Great Britain and expelled royal officials, setting up a provincial congress to begin self-government, although remaining within the British Empire. King George III responded with combat troops to restore British rule, but the colonists resisted this hostile act, and war broke out in 1775 and continued through 1783, when the British forces surrendered.

The Second Continental Congress, with elected representatives from the 13 colonies, governed the war, with **George Washington** established as commander of the Continental Army. Washington's army was generally outnumbered and undersupplied, but pressed on against superior British and mercenary forces as the Continental Congress, including such luminaries as

Benjamin Franklin and John Adams, ultimately adopted Thomas Jefferson's Declaration of Independence, explaining the reasoning behind the rebellion, in July 1776.

The war was rife with dramatic circumstances, as families and neighbors found themselves at odds over the establishment of a new nation or a return to British rule. Of enduring significance is that many of the guiding ideals of American life were born in this era, as the so-called founding fathers were compelled to debate the question of what sort of nation would emerge should the colonists win victory.

Though the Declaration of Independence stated that "all men are created equal," enslaved **African Americans***† remained in bondage for almost another 100 years and **women***† were provided second-class status (including being denied the right to vote or own property) for at least another century as well. The war's end in 1783 led to the establishment of the United States of America and the writing of a constitution. Washington, regarded as the hero of the American Revolution, became the first US president, serving two four-year terms before retiring from office to be succeeded by John Adams.

Adams was succeeded by Jefferson, who defeated him as Adams tried for reelection. Jefferson's two-term administration greatly increased the territories of the United States via the Louisiana Purchase, which more than doubled the size of the country, but this ultimately led to the displacement and slaughter of **Native Americans**,*† particularly during the administration of President Andrew Jackson. Hostilities with Great Britain did not end entirely after the American Revolution, with war breaking out again in 1812 and continuing to 1815, ending in a negotiated peace. Known as the **War of 1812**, this conflict led to the destruction of federal buildings, including serious damage to the White House, in Washington, DC, but over the course of subsequent decades, relations between Great Britain and the United States became more cordial, and the two nations ultimately became permanent allies in many subsequent world conflicts.

AMERICA'S LOST PLAYS. This 20-volume series of anthologies, edited by Barrett H. Clark and published in the early 1940s, provides readers of early American plays access to a range of otherwise rarely published pre-20th-century works by such diverse writers as **William Dunlap**, **John Howard Payne**, **Robert Montgomery Bird**, **Dion Boucicault**,† **George Henry Boker**, **James A. Herne**,† **Steele MacKaye**,† Charles H. Hoyt,† **Bronson Howard**,† and others.

AMERICANS IN ENGLAND; OR, LESSONS FOR DAUGHTERS. **Susanna Haswell Rowson**'s 1796 three-act comedy, in which she made her last appearance as an **actress**,* was retitled *Columbian Daughters* for an 1800 production. *Americans in England* opened on 12 April 1797 at Boston's **Federal Street Theatre** and was well received for three performances. In this play with **melodramatic†** flourishes, Rowson played her heroine, Jemima Winthrop, a young woman involved with the unscrupulous Englishman, Courtland, who flees his debts in the United States, taking Jemima to England, where he attempts to establish her in a bordello while he pursues another woman. Courtland attempts to seduce Jemima, who vigorously resists and is aided by Rhymer, a writer whom she ultimately marries after Courtland's machinations are foiled.

This social comedy's text is lost and was apparently never published, despite its original popularity, acknowledged in 1797 by the *Massachusetts Mercury* **critic*†** who wrote to report "the reiterated and unequivocal bursts of applause with which [the comedy] was received."

†**AMUSEMENTS.** In the mid-19th century and before, the word "entertainment"† conveyed a sense of wasteful self-indulgence. The term "recreation," while respectable, encompassed activities beyond the scope of **legitimate†** theater. In the 18th century, the promoting of plays and other theatrical entertainments required careful wording to get around local restrictions on amusements, especially where Quakers and Puritans held significant local authority.

As theatrical endeavors became more widely acceptable by the early 19th century, the word "amusements" often served both as the header for the theater column in newspapers and as the category under which **opera houses†** were listed in city directories. Meanwhile, theater **managers*†** took up the term "**attractions.**"† Amusements were regarded as wholesome distractions from the cares of everyday life.

†**ANDERSON, MARY (1859–1940).** A native of Sacramento, California, Mary Antoinette Anderson moved with her parents to Louisville, where her father joined the **Confederate Army** during the **Civil War** and was subsequently killed in combat. Despite the brevity of her career as an **actress,*†** Anderson was vividly remembered and beloved for the fresh beauty of her face and stature as well as the charm of her portrayals. "Our Mary," as she became known, made her professional debut as Juliet at **Macauley's Theatre** in 1875.

She impressed to the point that she was cast in **leading†** roles at Macauley's in *The Hunchback*, *Fazio*, and *Evadne*. Anderson also worked under **actor*†-manager*†** John McCullough† and manager **John T. Ford**, playing Lady Macbeth for the latter. Anderson **toured*†** in the standard **repertory*†** of romantic **melodramas†**—*The Lady of Lyons*, *Ingomar*, and others—reaching New York's **Fifth Avenue Theatre** in 1877. She honed her vocal skills for a rich, pleasing delivery. Her plasticity of form made her especially good as Galatea in *Pygmalion and Galatea,* beginning in 1881. Her 1883 London debut was followed by several other engagements† in England. Following her 1890 marriage, she retired from the stage. Despite calls for her return, she performed only rarely for charity events.

ANDRÉ: A TRAGEDY. **William Dunlap** wrote this fictionalized account of Major John André (1751–1780), the British officer executed as a spy for assisting notorious American traitor, Benedict Arnold, which opened at the **Park Theatre** on 30 March 1798 in an Old **American Company** production. The five-act blank verse tragedy, which covers a period of 10 hours leading up to André's execution in 1780, places its emphasis on the unresolved American debate over the fate of André, who is depicted by Dunlap as intelligent and charming, yet duplicitous.

Though the play was a moderate success, it met with controversy, including reports of audience members rising in outrage when one character, an American soldier named Bland, reacts angrily, throwing his cockade (a knot of decorative ribbons worn on the hat) to the ground when learning of André's impending execution. Dunlap's pointed use of the cockade, which was worn by American soldiers (and later by French Revolutionaries), suggested to audiences disrespect on Dunlap's part for the triumph of the **American Revolution**.

Dunlap had acknowledged in his preface to the published version of the play that "recent events are unfit subjects for tragedy" in the prevailing opinion of his countrymen. In fact, **George Washington** was alive at the time of the play's first production, and *André* may be the first dramatic depiction of an American president during his lifetime. Washington is seen lamenting André's execution, which he attempts, unsuccessfully, to prevent. Dunlap's feelings are made similarly clear as Bland reacts to André's death, saying,

> Farewell, farewell, brave spirit! O, let my countrymen,
> Henceforward, when the cruelties of war
> Arise in their remembrance; when their ready
> Speech would pour forth torrents in their foe's dispraise,
> Think on this act accurst, and lock compliant in silence.

Most of the play's characters are fictional other than André, his romantic interest, Honora Sneyd (though the real Honora died some time before André's execution), and Washington (called only "The General"). **Lewis Hallam Jr.** played the Washington character with **John Hodgkinson** as André. **Critics***† over the centuries have regarded *André* as Dunlap's best play (and among the best of the proliferation of historical dramas of the era) and the author used portions of it for a later work, a **musical*†** pageant called *The Glory of Columbia, Her Yeomanry* (1803), which remained popular for the first half of the 19th century.

ANDROBOROS. Written in 1714 by the royal governor of New York and New Jersey, **Robert Hunter**, this "Bographical [sic] Farce in Three Acts," as it was described in its published form (and its city of publication was listed as "Moronopolis"), is a political satire considered the first play published in the North American British colonies, though it may not have been performed. In the play, Hunter mocks his political enemies through thinly veiled caricatures (including Hunter's archnemesis, colonial administrator Francis Nicholson, as well as Lewis Morris, Rev. William Vesey, Thomas Smithfield, and Adolphe Philipse). Led by Androboros ("Man Eater"), the character based on Nicholson, they are seen as a secret fraternity hiding in a basement room of the governor's mansion plotting to go to **war*†** with "Mulomachians" (the French) and take over leadership of the colony. Some are coaxed into female **drag*†** in an attempt to kidnap the governor; however, they are unmasked and driven from the colony.

†ANIMALS/ANIMAL IMPERSONATION. The use of performing animals in theater was infrequent on stages in the 18th century, but by the mid-19th century the use of animals was frequent in **melodrama.†** For example, dogs and horses are integral to the action in *Uncle Tom's Cabin*, which held the stage for over half a century. Companies that carried their own **scenery*†** also had dogs trained to chase Eliza as she crossed the Ohio River on ice floes, but small troupes of **Tommers†** would borrow a local dog in each town and lure it after Eliza by the scent of meat hidden in the blanket she carried.

Victorien Sardou's† *Theodora* called for a lion in a cage; **Sarah Bernhardt†** traveled with a real lion, but rising **stars*†** like Lillian Olcott† made do with a *papier-mâché* beast. Horses added to the thrill of plays like *Mazeppa†* or *Ben-Hur*,† and to the atmospheric spectacle of plantation melodramas. Animal impersonation dates back to ancient theater, but was rarely seen in the United States until the advent of **children's theater,*†** and animal acts were frequent in theatrical entertainments† such as **circus,*† vaudeville,†** and **burlesque,*†** where animal impersonations were also seen. Animals were also prevalent in such entertainment venues as the **American Museum**, which, when run by **P. T. Barnum**, had along with a theater, its own zoo.

ARCH STREET THEATRE. Constructed from designs based on those by America's leading architect, John Haviland, in 1828, the Arch Street Theatre was an intended rival to Philadelphia's major theaters, the **Chestnut Street**

Theatre and the **Walnut Street Theatre**. It was funded by New York interests, but **William Burke Wood** was the local **manager**.*† The theater officially opened on 21 October 1828 with a production of *The Honeymoon*. **Edwin Forrest**'s brother, William Forrest, took over as manager in 1830, leading the Arch Street Theatre to predominance among Philadelphia theaters. Forrest appeared there with regularity at the height of his fame and in his greatest vehicles, which helped the theater sustain success.

When **William Burton** became manager in the 1840s, the theater presented some of its most popular productions, including *A Glance at Philadelphia*, a local revision of **Benjamin A. Baker**'s popular *A Glance at New York*. **William Wheatley** took over for a time, but was not fully engaged, often leaving Philadelphia for extended **tours**.*† He was partnered with **John Drew**, who, until his early death, was a more hands-on manager. **John Wilkes Booth**† was a member of the Arch Street Theatre company in 1857—and performed there occasionally in the early 1860s, including an appearance in *The Marble Heart* in 1863, the same year the theater was renovated and its amenities made grander.

The theater's greatest era began in 1861 when **Mrs. John Drew**† assumed management, setting up a **stock***† company ultimately considered the finest in the United States. She led the company for a remarkable 31-year run during which time generations of leading American **actors***† performed there, including her own grandchildren, Ethel,*† Lionel,† and John Barrymore.*† After Mrs. Drew stepped down in 1892, appearing for the last time in *The Love Chase* on 7 May 1892, the theater fell on hard times. In 1894, it was reported in the *New York Times* that the theater would be demolished. However, another stock company moved in and failed before Charles E. Blaney,† assuming management, produced a series of popular **melodramas***† there. During the early 20th century, the theater was used for **musicals**,*† **Yiddish theater**,*† and **burlesque***† before being torn down in 1936.

THE ARCHERS; OR, THE MOUNTAINEERS OF SWITZERLAND. **William Dunlap** adapted Friedrich von Schiller's *William Tell* and transformed it into a popular three-act opera (with music by **Benjamin Carr**) examining the contrasting concepts of liberty and anarchy within the legend of Tell. Produced by the Old **American Company**, it opened at the **John Street Theatre** on 18 April 1796 for three performances, with **John Hodgkinson** as Tell and **Charlotte Melmoth** as his wife, with support from **Joseph Jefferson** and **Lewis Hallam Jr.** Settings for the production were created by **Charles Ciceri**, with **James Hewitt** as conductor for the first performances.

†**ARCHITECT, ARCHITECTURE.** In the earliest days of American theater in the 17th century, theater spaces tended to be any existing building that could serve the necessary purpose. Over time, wooden structures with crude bench-like seats were built in various cities on the eastern seaboard, including New York, Boston, Philadelphia, Baltimore, and Charleston. The wooden structures were frequently destroyed by fire, and over time, audiences grew and began to demand more comforts. Brick structures resisted **fires,**† though **gas lighting***† and flammable stage materials for **scenery***† were a continual hazard. The larger cities had multiple theaters and featured visually appealing decoration on both the exterior and interior of the buildings and became familiar landmarks to locals. Successful theaters grew in size and stage technology and, when destroyed by fire, were often rebuilt on a grander scale.

The decades after the **Civil War** saw the rise of the **opera house**† style as a venue to attract more fashionable people than those who would attend traditional theater spaces. While a theater could be anything from a barn to a third-floor hall above a commercial space, the opera house was purpose-built for respectable entertainments.† The seating for up to 2,000 people in different sections at various prices created social (and racial) segregation. Often there was a separate box office and side entrance for the cheap gallery seats above the more fashionable balconies. Early opera houses had flat auditorium floors (so that the facility could also be rented for balls) and raked stages. The opera houses built in towns across the nation devoted more space to amenities—lobbies, refreshment rooms, ladies' parlors, smoking rooms—than did those in New York, where square footage was more costly.

Each decade brought refinements in ventilation, lighting, fire-prevention devices (sprinklers or "inundators," asbestos curtain, additional exits), **actor***† dressing rooms† (eventually with fixed washstands), and equipment to support and operate **scenery.***† Few theaters, either in New York or elsewhere, contained their own scene shops; exceptions were **Booth's Theatre**† (1869–1883) and **Daniel Frohman**'s† Lyceum Theatre. A number of innovations may be credited to **Steele MacKaye**† at his spectacular **Madison Square Theatre,**† which he remodeled in 1879.

†**ARNEAUX, J. A. (b. 1855).** The son of a white Frenchman and a black woman, John A. Arneaux was born in Savannah, educated in America and Paris, and worked in Paris for a time as a journalist. As an **actor,***† he debuted in 1876 in *Under the Yoke; or, Bound and Free*, a play by **African American***† writer **John S. Ladue**. Arneaux performed in **vaudeville**† for **Tony Pastor**† and established the **Astor Place Company of Colored Tragedians** in 1878, an all–African American company devoted to productions of classics, particularly **Shakespeare.***† Established in New York, Arneaux's troupe also **toured***† to Philadelphia and Providence, Rhode Island.

As an actor, Arneaux was the logical successor of **Ira Aldridge** and was praised as Macbeth, Iago, and particularly in his favorite role, Richard III, which was favorably compared to major actors of the 19th century. He sported a wide handlebar mustache for characterizations in portraits from the time. Arneaux also wrote songs, including "Jumbo; The Elephant King!," published in 1883. He returned to Paris in 1888 for further study, but after the early 1890s he disappeared completely from the historical record.

AROUND THE WORLD IN 80 DAYS. Jules Verne's 1873 adventure novel *Around the World in 80 Days,* in which Londoner Phileas Fogg and his French valet, Passepartout, attempt an 80-day around-the-world trip to win a bet, has been a perennial source of stage and film† adaptations. Verne began working on the story as a play with Edoard Cadol in 1872, but after several failed attempts to interest theatrical **producers,***† Cadol withdrew and Verne published it as a novel, after which it opened as a stage spectacle in Paris in 1874, with Verne collaborating with celebrated French dramatist and adaptor, **Adolphe-Philippe D'Ennery**.

Two competing extravaganza† versions of *Around the World in 80 Days* appeared in New York in 1875, one mounted at the Academy of Music in a production by the **Kiralfy Brothers**. The Kiralfy version, the more popular, was revived frequently into the 1890s, but subsequent American versions, including a **musical***† adaptation staged by Orson Welles,* with music by Cole Porter, appeared in 1946.

ARRAH-NA-POGUE; OR, THE WICKLOW WEDDING. **Dion Boucicault's**† **Irish** romance premiered at **Niblo's Garden** on 21 July 1865 for 68 performances. The three-act comedy-drama set in Ireland in 1798 during the Irish Rebellion centers on good-hearted Arrah Meelish, a poor Irish girl (Arrah-na-Pogue, or Arrah of the Kiss), who helps a desperate fugitive. When an unscrupulous informant for the British—who also harbors feelings for Arrah—learns of this, he attempts to ruin her planned marriage to Shaun the Post, but the intrepid Shaun is not fooled and takes the blame with authorities for harboring the fugitive in order to protect Arrah. Matters are subsequently cleared up, and Arrah and Shaun marry.

Boucicault himself played Shaun in the London debut of the play in 1864, and frequently throughout the remainder of his career. *Arrah-na-Pogue* became one of his most enduringly popular works, despite carping from **critics***† who admired Boucicault's sensational effects and lyrical language, but found it inferior to some of his earlier plays and objected to the patriotic Irish fervor, as when one character proclaims, "My own land! Bless every blade of grass upon your green cheeks!"

†**ASIAN AMERICAN THEATER.** While Chinese and Japanese **stock*†** characters abounded in plays of the early American theater alongside other ethnic stereotypes as more and more immigrants from various countries arrived in significant number, there was little that could be called Asian American **legitimate*†** drama. More often than not, prior to the late 20th century, Asian characters were played by white **actors.*†** To provide opportunity, **amateur*†** groups sprang up in Asian communities, but only in cities like New York and San Francisco were there professional troupes performing traditional music-based theater or plays with Asian casts—or cities that could boast large Asian communities.

ASTON, ANTHONY (d. 1731). Comparatively little is known about this English **playwright*†** and vagabond **actor*†** except that he is considered to be the first professional actor on the American stage. Historians believe he appeared in North America in 1703 and 1704, but little is known about either his repertoire† or itinerary. An autobiographical preface for his play *The Fool's Opera, or, The Taste of the Age* describes him as "a Gentleman, Lawyer, Poet, Actor, Soldier, Sailor, Exciseman, Publican; in England, Scotland, Ireland, New York, East and West Jersey, Maryland, Virginia (on both side Chesapeek), North and South Carolina, South Florida, Bahamas, Jamaica, Hispaniola, and often a Coaster by all the same."

Aston's preface also gives a hint about the quality of life for a **touring*†** actor in the early 18th century: "Well, we arriv'd in Charlestown, full of Lice, Shame, Poverty, Nakedness and Hunger:—I turned Player and Poet, and wrote one Play on the Subject of the Country." As far as can be determined, this son of a lawyer spent most of his career in the British Isles touring widely with his wife and son. Aston's other plays include the comedy *Love in a Hurry* (c. 1709) and an opera, *Pastora, or The Coy Shepherdess* (1712).

ASTOR PLACE COMPANY OF COLORED TRAGEDIANS. Benjamin Ford and **J. A. Arneaux** founded this company, also known as the Astor Place (Colored) Tragedy Company, which emphasized the plays of **Shakespeare*†** and gave its first performance under that name on 17 June 1884, when it performed *Othello*, with Ford in the title role and Arneaux as Iago. However, Ford seems to have begun a troupe of **African American*† actors*†** as early as 8 April 1878, when he played the lead in a production of *Richard III* at New York's Lyric Theatre. Following success with *Othello*, the group presented John Banim's *Damon and Pythias* in late 1884, *Richard III* in 1885, and *Romeo and Juliet* in 1886, which were performed in New England, Philadelphia, and New York until 1888.

ASTOR PLACE OPERA HOUSE RIOTS. The major event took place on 10 May 1849 at the Astor Place Opera House, though a series of outbursts lasting over two decades surrounded a rivalry between admirers of British actor*† **William Charles Macready** and America's leading tragedian, **Edwin Forrest**. The problems dated back to 1826, when the two actors debuted in New York, with Forrest perceiving them as rivals for the respect and affection of American audiences. Macready's major crime, in Forrest's view (and that of many among the American theatergoing audience of the time), was that he was an Englishman.

Forrest shared a cultural resentment of the British dating back to the **American Revolution**, and it was exacerbated by the renewed hostilities between Great Britain and the United States during the **War of 1812**. Macready was thus seen as a cultural usurper, though the early rivalry manifested itself mainly in a class division, with the more educated, well-to-do audiences preferring Macready's intellectual, formal acting to Forrest's bombastic, larger-than-life approach and appeal to the working class.

By 1845, when Forrest appeared in London to a tepid response from critics,*† he held Macready personally responsible; the following year, Forrest attended a Macready appearance in Edinburgh, pointedly sitting in a visible box and hissing at his rival. When Macready **toured***† to America in 1849, he was scheduled to perform *Macbeth* at the Astor Place Opera House on 7 May 1849. Renewed hostilities began when Forrest immediately announced his appearance in the same play on the same night at the nearby **Bowery Theatre**.

Forrest's rowdy fans attended Macready's performance and disrupted it not only vocally, but by hurling food and chairs at the stage. At Forrest's performance that evening, the **gallery**† rose in cheers when he spoke Macbeth's line, "What rhubarb, senna, or what purgative drug, Would scour these English hence?" The disturbances led Macready to announce his intention to cancel the rest of his engagement,† but important New York citizens, including Herman Melville and **Washington Irving**, lobbied him to continue. A petition was circulated, and Macready agreed to appear again on 10 May 1849.

By performance time, it was estimated that over 10,000 people had assembled in the vicinity of the theater. A mob of thugs made up of denizens of the notorious Five Points area, and led by E. Z. C. Judson, a known agitator and founder of the Know-Nothing political party, headed for the theater, as well as to homes of prominent New Yorkers who had signed the petition. Upon the arrival of the mob at the Astor Place Opera House, they were met by a force of police and militia, but refused to stand down and instead hurled rocks and wielded clubs against the authorities. The resulting riot, which lasted for hours, led to the deaths of at least 22 (and perhaps as many as 31), with many more injured (including over 140 militiamen), and only added to decades of bitterness between the English and Americans. Judson was jailed for a year for instigating the riot, but many were convinced that Forrest had hired Judson and was, as such, the true culprit.

On the night following the riot, a crowd assembled at City Hall Park to hear speakers condemn authorities for their handling of the situation (and a child was killed in the melee at this event), but despite the casualties, New York authorities were mostly praised for taking a hard line against the rioters. The career of Forrest began a decline, Macready never returned to the United States, and the Astor Place Opera House, subsequently referred to as the "Massacre Opera House" or "DisAster Place," fell on hard times.

†**ATTRACTION.** Because of the great variety of entertainments† on the **road***† from the early 19th century into the early 20th century, theater **managers***† used the umbrella term "attractions" to cover all kinds of bookings: **legitimate***† plays, operas, **musical***† **revues***† and **burlesque,***† lectures, and **minstrel**† shows.

AUDIN [or ODIN], MONSIEUR (late 18th century). Little is known about the life of this **scene designer***† who created scenery mostly in Charleston in the late 18th century. Credited by Edwin Duerr in a 1932 *Theatre Arts Monthly**† article with "bringing to his southern stages some of the most varied and opulent of eighteenth century American theatrical scenes," Audin was rivaled in achievement only by **Charles Ciceri** and was noted for re-creating scenes from well-known paintings on the stage. An Audin worked under Ciceri at the **Park Theatre** in 1798, but whether this was Audin himself or possibly his son cannot be verified.

AUGUSTA, MLLE. (1806–1901). Born in Munich, Germany, Caroline Augusta Josephine Thérèse Fuchs studied with F. Taglioni and Albert prior to her London debut at the Drury Lane Theatre in 1833, after which she appeared at the Paris Opera in 1835. **Touring***† the United States, she scored triumphant successes in *La Bayadère* in 1836 and *La Sylphide* in 1838. In New York, she succeeded again as the city's first Giselle in 1846. A contemporary **critic***† writing in *Knickerbocker* magazine in January 1838 described her as a "graceful, brilliant and fascinating" danseuse, whose "magnificent dancing" was supported by her "graceful agility, united with ladylike modesty and good taste in every movement."

AYLMERE. See JACK CADE; OR, CAPTAIN OF THE COMMONS.

B

BACKUS, CHARLIE (1831–1883). Born in Rochester, New York, Charles Backus was the son of a doctor and grandson of the first president of Hamilton College. He studied literature, but ultimately turned to the stage in 1851 in Cleveland, where he appeared in *The Widow's Victim*. Winning his first acclaim as a mimic of celebrated **actors*†** in their signature roles, Backus ultimately turned to **blackface†** and founded the Backus **Minstrels†** in 1854, **toured*†** Australia, and worked as a clown in Burton's **Circus.*†** He returned to minstrelsy in 1865 when he established the **San Francisco Minstrels**. A year later, the troupe moved to New York and made extended world **tours.*†** Much beloved by audiences, Backus performed until shortly before his death. **Critics*†** considered his talents beyond those typical of minstrels, arguing that he would have succeeded in **legitimate*†** theater, though this theory was never tested.

BAKER, BENJAMIN A. (1818–1890). A native of Natchez, Mississippi, Benjamin A. Baker would be little remembered despite a long career as an **actor,*† playwright,*†** and **manager*†** were it not for a play he wrote to be performed as a **benefit†** for himself, *A Glance at New York* (1848). This highly successful comedy of a **rube†** in the big city was much imitated and set off a slew of imitators with localized comedies featuring familiar **stock*†** types. In the case of *A Glance at New York*, the character of "Mose," a volunteer fireman who speaks in Bowery vernacular, became an iconic type, frequently evident in stage comedies and **films†** until well into the 20th century.

Baker wrote sequels, including *New York As It Is* (1848), *Three Years After* (1849), and *Mose in China* (1850), with some success, and from 1856, he managed **Edwin Booth**'s† company. He had begun his career in 1837 in small roles in the company of Booth's father, **Junius Brutus Booth**, and subsequently worked as an actor and prompter for **William Mitchell** at the **Olympic Theatre**, also writing **burlesque*†** sketches.

BAKER, GEORGE MELVILLE (1832–1890). A **playwright*†** and publisher in Boston, he established George M. Baker & Co. and published his own plays, and those by others, during the 19th century until 1885, when his company was supplanted by his brother's, Walter H. Baker & Co. He appeared as an **actor*†** in Lyceum entertainments† in New England in his own sketch *Too Late for the Train*, performing with **Henry Clay Barnabee**. His first comedy, *Wanted, a Male Cook*, was performed by **amateurs,*†** as were dozens of plays, including *Above the Clouds, Among the Breakers, The Flowing Bowl, Our Folks, Past Redemption, A Close Shave, Better Than Gold, The Freedom of the Press, Rebecca's Triumph, The Tempter*, and *We're All Teetotalers*, among many others.

BALDWIN THEATRE. Well-known San Francisco gambler and businessman Elias Jackson "Lucky" Baldwin hired **architect†** Sumner Bugbee to build this theater (also known as Baldwin's Academy of Music) on Market Street in 1875, and it became the San Francisco theater most likely to present **touring*†** productions. Rivaling the **California Theatre**, which focused on productions by its resident company, the Baldwin Theatre was soon incorporated into a large hotel, also built by Baldwin. The theater provided **managers*† Thomas Maguire** and Charles Frohman† their first important opportunities. A **fire†** on 25 November 1898 destroyed the hotel and theater, with at least 20 deaths resulting.

BALLET IN AMERICAN THEATER. Ballet on theater stages in the United States was comparatively rare prior to the mid-19th century, though ballet troupes, usually European, were frequently seen as separate entities. As ballad operas became popular in the late 18th century, ballet was often a featured embellishment and this led ultimately to the inclusion of dancers and ballet segments in popular plays.

The most notable example appeared in 1866 with ***The Black Crook***, a **melodramatic†** work that featured a corps of ballet dancers scandalously (or enticingly, for some) clad in pink **fleshings.†** This merging of story and dance is considered by some scholars to be the first example of **musical*†** theater in the United States, and *The Black Crook* inspired many imitators during the second half of the 19th century. In the mid-19th century, **star*†** ballerinas such as **Fanny Elssler** and **Mlle. Celeste**, among others, commanded popular attention, but the true merging of ballet and theater in America came in the 1920s–1930s as musical theater evolved as a singular art form and often featured ballet as a means of revealing character and story elements in a uniquely visual way.

†**BANDMANN, DANIEL (1840–1905).** Born in Cassel, Hesse, Germany, Daniel Bandmann arrived in New York to perform in German-language theater in the 1860s. Later, he formed a company and **toured*†** the western United States, gaining repute as a pioneer. Lewis C. Strang described him in an essay on Julia Arthur† as "an eccentric German tragedian, who probably played **Shakespeare*†** in more outlandish places than any actor that ever lived." At the end of his life, Bandmann settled on a ranch near Missoula, Montana, where the University of Montana's players eventually honored his memory by naming an award for him. Bandmann's memoir, *An Actor's Tour; or, 70,000 Miles with Shakespeare*, was published in 1886.

THE BANKER'S DAUGHTER. This early **Bronson Howard†** play, first called *Lilian's Last Love* (1873), was produced at **Hooley's Theatre** in Chicago. Howard significantly revised it in 1878 as the five-act *The Banker's Daughter*, the creation of which Howard subsequently chronicled in his book, *The Autobiography of a Play* (1886). *The Banker's Daughter* opened on 30 November 1878 at the **Union Square Theatre†** for 137 performances in a **Sheridan Shook** and **A. M. Palmer†** production.

In this **melodramatic†** play, which won **critical*†** favor and was popular with audiences for decades, Lilian Westbrook, who is in love with Harold Routledge (and also courted by a count), marries a rich older man, Strebelow, to spare her father the humiliation of bankruptcy. She has a daughter with Strebelow, though she pines for Routledge. When the former rivalry between Routledge and the count comes to a head, a duel is fought and Routledge is killed, prompting an emotional outburst from Lilian, who confesses to Strebelow that she loved Routledge. Strebelow leaves Lilian, but she comes to realize over time that she truly cares for Strebelow. Howard had written his first play in the 1860s, and *The Banker's Daughter* was his first major work as he emerged as perhaps **Broadway's*†** leading **playwright*†** of the 1880s.

BANNISTER, NATHANIEL H. (1813–1847). Born in Baltimore, Nathaniel Harrington Bannister made his stage debut as an **actor*†** in 1830 as Young Norval in *Douglas* at the Front Street Theatre in Baltimore. In New York, he acted at the **Bowery Theatre** and the **Chatham Garden Theatre** and wrote numerous plays. His patriotic **melodrama†** *Putnam, The Iron Son of '76* (1844), a popular drama set during the **American Revolution**, was his only true success as a **playwright.*†** He adapted **Shakespeare's*†** *Titus Andronicus* for an 1839 production at the **Walnut Street Theatre** where, as actor **John Durang** noted, Bannister "excluded the horrors with infinite skill, yet preserved the interest of the drama." Despite his prolific output, Bannister died a pauper.

BARKER, JAMES NELSON (1784–1858). Born the son of the mayor of Philadelphia, and subsequently becoming mayor himself, James Nelson Barker went into the United States Army at the start of the **War of 1812**, rising to captain of artillery and commanding Fort Mifflin. He devoted much of his life to public service, but also wrote ten plays, of which five survive. The best known of these, the tragedy *Superstition: or, The Frantic Father* (1824), was also his last produced work. His other plays include *The Indian Princess; or, La Belle Sauvage* (1808), a comedy with music about Pocahontas, which is also believed to be the first American play about a **Native American***† character performed in the United States and the first American play staged in England (at the Drury Lane Theatre in 1820 under the title *Pocahontas; or, The Indian Princess*).

Barker's other plays include the comedy *Tears and Smiles* (1807), the topical drama *The Embargo; or, What News?* (1808), the blank verse drama *Marmion; or, The Battle of Flodden Field* (1812), the drama *How to Try a Lover* (1817), the drama *The Armourer's Escape; or, Three Years at Nootka Sound* (1817), and two early unpublished and unproduced works, *The Spanish Rover* (1804) and *America* (1805), the latter a masque. John W. Crowley writes that Barker "shared the characteristic faith of his generation in America's literary and cultural destiny. Yet his hopes for a native, democratic theater were qualified by his own career, and between *The Indian Princess* and *Superstition* Barker's strident nationalism was muted by an increasing awareness of threats to his American pastoral ideal."

†BARNABEE, HENRY CLAY (1833–1917). An **actor***† and singer sometimes called "the Dean of the comic opera stage," Henry Clay Barnabee was born in Jamaica Plains, Massachusetts, and debuted in 1866 as Toby Winkle in *All That Glitters Is Not Gold* at the **Boston Museum**. He subsequently enjoyed his greatest renown in *Robin Hood* as the Sheriff of Nottingham, a role he played nearly 1,900 times. He estimated that he had sung the popular song "The Cork Leg" 5,000 times. Barnabee was also a proprietor of the celebrated **Boston Ideal Opera Company**, or "The Bostonians," the leading **touring***† company for light opera. He appeared in several **William S. Gilbert** and **Arthur Sullivan operettas**† as well as American **musicals.***† It was Barnabee who gave Alice Nielsen† her big break, when he hired her for the Bostonians.

BARNES, CHARLOTTE MARY SANFORD (1818–1863). New York-born Charlotte Mary Sanford Barnes was the daughter of **actors***† **John** and **Mary Barnes** of the **Park Theatre**, where she began walking on as a **child**† in 1822. She appeared at Boston's **Tremont Theatre** in 1833, playing Juliet to her mother's Romeo, and in 1834 also appeared there in *The Castle Spec-*

tre. Also a **playwright**,*† she wrote and played the title role in *Octavia Bragaldi; or, The Confession* (1837). Barnes also adapted novels and French **melodramas**† to the American stage, including the plays *La Fitte* (1840) and *The Forest Princess* (1844). **Critics***† praised her performances in several **Shakespearean***† roles, as well as contemporary American and English works. She married actor Edmond S. Connor, and while he was **manager***† of the **Arch Street Theatre** in Philadelphia, she acted with him.

BARNES, JOHN (1761–1841) and MARY BARNES (1780?–1864). English-born **actors**,*† they made their first stage appearances in London before journeying to America to debut in 1816 at the **Park Theatre**. Though the Barneses returned to England for a time in the early 1820s, they ultimately became fixtures at the Park, most frequently seen in **Shakespearean***† or other English plays. Mary was generally the more acclaimed of the two in major roles, including Tullia in the American premiere of **John Howard Payne**'s *Brutus; or, The Fall of Tarquin*† (1819), with John often taking secondary roles and winning approval in comic parts. She retired in 1833. They were the parents of **actress***† and **playwright***† **Charlotte Mary Sanford Barnes**.

†**BARNSTORMERS.** Theatrical troupers who traveled in areas where there were no established theaters and made use of found spaces like hotel dining rooms, dance halls, warehouses, and barns. Barnstormers, according to Alfred L. Bernheim, were distinguished by "their lack of association with a specific theatre." The term "barnstormer" was sometimes applied to overacting performers (**hams**)† given to crude and elaborate gestures, presumably the style of **actor***† popular with provincial audiences.

BARNUM, PHINEAS TAYLOR (1810–1891). This legendary showman, one of the iconic figures of American popular culture, was born in Bethel, Connecticut, where he began as an entrepreneur in local businesses and published a newspaper. In 1834, he moved to New York and began a career as **manager***† of a variety act called "Barnum's Grand Scientific and **Musical***† Theatre," before buying Scudder's **American Museum**. Barnum combined theater and **attractions**† of various sorts in the museum, some impressive and some pure hokum. Whether a fraudulent "mermaid" from Fiji (spelled *Fee-Jee*) or an elderly **African American***† woman he claimed was **George Washington**'s childhood nurse, Barnum's attractions also included European singer Jenny Lind, who, through his management, became the toast of New York (she appeared for 150 performances at $1,000 per, at the time an unprecedented salary), and the beloved little person General **Tom Thumb**, among many others.

Barnum arranged for Thumb to meet President **Abraham Lincoln** and England's Queen Victoria while on a world **tour***† managed by Barnum, who promoted Thumb into one of America's major attractions, enhanced by Thumb's much-hyped marriage to female midget, Lavinia Warren, in 1863. The American Museum under Barnum's management reflected a famous statement attributed to him (although unverifiable)—"there's a sucker born every minute"—in its bizarre combination of genuine scientific rarities and inventions with a carnivalesque freak show atmosphere and outright fraudulent exhibits.

The American Museum presented **melodramas**,† musical entertainments, and variety attractions, including **minstrel**† shows that, in Barnum's hands, not only exploited racial stereotypes, but mocked white attitudes about **African Americans**.*† American and tourist patrons, estimated in the millions, could not get enough of Barnum's brand of show business. Extravagance, bad debts, and other problems led to financial ruin for Barnum in the 1850s, but he reinvented himself as a **temperance** lecturer on **tour***† and recouped his finances. Also a sometime politician, Barnum served two terms in the state legislature of Connecticut and as mayor of Bridgeport, Connecticut, where he made his home.

Comparatively late in his career, Barnum went into the **circus***† business, establishing "P. T. Barnum's Grand Traveling Museum, Menagerie, Caravan & Hippodrome" in 1871, ultimately merging his interests with those of James Bailey and James L. Hutchinson to form "P. T. Barnum's Greatest Show on Earth, And the Great London Circus, Sanger's Royal British Menagerie and The Grand International Allied Shows United," an unwieldy moniker ultimately shortened to "Barnum & Bailey's Circus." The first circus to feature three rings, it was also the largest circus in the world at the time. Seeking major attractions, Barnum purchased an African elephant known as Jumbo from the London Zoo, and other Barnum acts, including Thumb and the various performers and freaks associated with the American Museum, also appeared. The circus was popular with audiences, but railroad† accidents (one ultimately killed Jumbo), **fires**,† and other problems hampered the circus.

Barnum evolved into a master of marketing—always inviting the public to his attractions with unbridled bombastic hype and the intriguing promise of seeing something previously unknown, or at least very special, should the "sucker" only buy a ticket. Barnum's style of advertising would be much imitated by other show business impresarios in all media well into the 21st century. Barnum and Bailey dissolved their partnership in 1885, but reteamed in 1888 to present "Barnum & Bailey's Greatest Show on Earth," with the goal of making the circus a permanent American tradition guided by his philosophy, "The noblest art is that of making other people happy."

Barnum authored several books about his life and adventures, only confirming his status as "The Prince of Humbug," an image he encouraged and wore proudly. In a sense, Barnum himself was his greatest attraction.

BARNUM'S AMERICAN MUSEUM. *See* AMERICAN MUSEUM.

BARRETT, GEORGE (1794–1860). George Hooker Barrett made his debut as a **child†** in *The Stranger* in 1798, appearing with his parents, who were members of **William Dunlap**'s company. He appeared in Boston, but made his adult New York debut as Young Norval in *Douglas* in 1806 in New York. He ultimately found great popularity as a comic **actor*†** at the **Chatham Garden Theatre** in both **Shakespearean*†** and more contemporary works.

Known as "Gentleman George" for his sartorial splendor and genial manner offstage, as well as his onstage popularity, Barrett became a **manager*†** at the **Bowery Theatre** in 1826 and later at other theaters in New York and Boston. Barrett's wife, Anne Jane Henry (1801–1857), began as a dancer at the **Federal Street Theatre**, but despite some success, alcoholism marred her career, although she was much admired by **Fanny Kemble** and others at the height of her popularity.

†BARRETT, LAWRENCE (1838–1891). Paterson, New Jersey, was the birthplace of **actor*†** Lawrence Patrick Barrett, who was born to **Irish** immigrant parents and worked his way through an apprenticeship at Detroit's Metropolitan Theatre to an acting debut there in 1853 in *The French Spy*. His New York debut came in the 1856–1857 season in *The Hunchback*, and he quickly moved into **leading man†** roles.

During 1858, Barrett appeared for a season at the **Boston Museum**. After serving as a captain in Company B of the 28th Massachusetts Regiment in the Union Army during the **Civil War**, he resumed his career as actor-**manager*†** of the **California Theatre** in San Francisco, partnered with **John McCullough.†** In this period, Barrett's repertoire† placed an emphasis on **Shakespearean*†** roles—Richard III, Hamlet, Othello, King Lear, and Shylock—although he also appeared in *Money*, *Francesca da Rimini*, and *The Man of Airlie*, among others. He scored success in **William Dean Howells's†** plays, *A Counterfeit Presentment* and *Yorick's Love*, during the 1877–1878 season.

Slight of build with sunken eyes and a reserved manner, Barrett seemed ill-equipped for tragic roles. Yet he was capable of unleashing a burst of passion for dramatic effect in the style of the era. His approach to acting could be seen as intellectualized or coldly calculated, yet his status as a **star*†** was never questioned. By all **critical*†** accounts, his great role was

Cassius in *Julius Caesar*. After two decades of **touring*†** as a star, he joined forces with **Edwin Booth†** for two seasons, 1887–1889, serving as tour manager while performing opposite Booth. Barrett encouraged new **playwrights*†** and worked for the betterment of the theatrical profession in the United States; he also exhibited a strong sense of theatrical history, reviving worthy past plays and, as in the case of *Francesca da Rimini*, restoring their luster.

Barrett subsequently wrote books about **Edwin Forrest** and Booth, arguably the two finest American actors of the 19th century. Though most **critics*†** felt he did not quite equal their artistry, he was much admired. Confirming this, theater historian George Odell wrote that Barrett was "the most farsighted and ambitious, if not our greatest tragedian." He was unable to complete a performance as De Mauprat in **Edward Bulwer-Lytton**'s *Richelieu* and died of pneumonia, with the *New York Times* concluding that he was an actor of "unfailing zeal."

BARRIÈRE, HENRY P. (1783?–1826). Little is known about his early life beyond his work as a confectioner, but Henry P. Barrière became **manager*†** of the **Chatham Garden Theatre** in 1819, providing modest entertainments† and sweets, including ice cream. He opened a theater, which became a popular location for summer entertainments with a bill of fare including **musical,*†** comic, and dramatic works, but his death led to the theater's decline.

BARROW, JULIA BENNETT (1824?–1903). British-born Julia Bennett was the daughter of William Bennett, secretary of the Drury Lane Theatrical Fund. She debuted in her teens in a provincial production of *The Soldier's Daughter* prior to joining the company of the Haymarket Theatre. As Mrs. Barrow, she made her American stage debut in 1851 (she had married Jacob Barrow in 1848) playing Lady Teazle in **Richard Brinsley Sheridan**'s *The School for Scandal* at the **Broadway*† Theatre**, with **critics*†** noting her beauty and grace, though pointing out her high-pitched voice.

Barrow appeared in Philadelphia in 1851 in *The Love Chase* at the **Walnut Street Theatre**, and won praise as Viola in *Twelfth Night* and in contemporary comedies. Despite her expertise in comedy, she appeared successfully in serious roles in *Richard III* and *The Marble Heart*, playing opposite **John Wilkes Booth†** in the latter. She ultimately moved to Boston and ran the **Howard Athenaeum** with her husband, but presumably returned to England at some point or left the stage.

BARRY, THOMAS (1798–1876). English-born **actor*†** and stage **manager*†** Thomas Barry made his name playing opposite **William Charles Macready** as Hotspur to Macready's Henry IV. He made his first appearance in America in the title role of *The Stranger* at the **Park Theatre** in 1826, but was generally unsuccessful in dramatic roles. However, he did attain popularity as a comic actor, though his greatest gifts were as a stage manager, a task he carried out much as a contemporary stage **director*†** works, emphasizing preparation, working closely with the actors, and making necessary changes to the script. He produced seasons at an array of American theaters, including the Park Theatre, **Bowery Theatre, Tremont Theatre, Purdy's National Theatre, Broadway Theatre**, and **Boston Theatre**. Barry also wrote **melodramas,†** including *The Battle of Mexico*.

†BARRYMORE, GEORGIANA DREW (1856–1893). The daughter of **John†** and **Louisa Lane (Mrs. John) Drew,†** Georgiana Emma Drew spent her formative years as an **actress*†** at her mother's **Arch Street Theatre** in Philadelphia. She made her stage debut in 1872 in *The Ladies' Rattle*, and when she made her New York debut at the **Fifth Avenue Theatre** in 1876 in **Arnold Daly**'s† *Pique*, she **costarred*†** with **Maurice Barrymore,†** whom she married later that year. She also appeared with success that season in *As You Like It*.

Following her marriage, motherhood slowed Barrymore's career, but provided the American stage with a theatrical dynasty: Lionel,† Ethel,*† and John Barrymore*† were all born between 1878 and 1882. Following the birth of John, the youngest, Barrymore returned to the stage. Admired most for her charm in comic roles, she played opposite **William H. Crane†** in *The Senator†* (1889) and also scored successes in *Mr. Wilkinson's Widows†* (1891), *Settled Out of Court* (1892), and *The Sportsman* (1893). Barrymore also acted in her husband's play, *Nadjezda* (1884). Her early death ended a promising career.

†BARRYMORE, MAURICE (1849–1905). Born in Fort Agra, India, Herbert Arthur Chamberlayne Blythe changed his name to Maurice Barrymore when he left Oxford University to go on the stage. He became the **amateur*†** middleweight boxing champion of England before his 1872 stage debut at the Theatre Royal, Windsor. After serving an apprenticeship for three years on provincial English stages, Barrymore moved to the United States, appearing for several **managers,*†** including **Augustin Daly,† Lester Wallack,†** and **A. M. Palmer.†**

Barrymore's good looks and witty charm made him a favorite with audiences, and he was considered a **matinee idol.†** His American debut in Boston in *Under the Gaslight* established him, after which he replaced **John**

Drew† in *The Big Bonanza* and appeared with his future wife, **Georgiana Drew**,† in *Pique* (1875). Barrymore's most noted stage successes were in **Shakespeare***† opposite **Helena Modjeska**,† beginning in 1882, and in major roles in the **melodramas**† *Alabama*† and *Captain Swift*, both in 1888. The latter was a significant popular success that Barrymore failed to fully exploit, as was the case with the eight plays he wrote, including *Nadjezda* (1884), *The Robber of the Rhine* (1892), and *Roaring Dick & Co.* (1896). He unsuccessfully sued **Victorien Sardou**, claiming that the French playwright plagiarized the plot of *Nadjezda* for *Tosca*.

Barrymore appeared with Mrs. Leslie Carter† and Minnie Maddern Fiske† in later successes. He fathered Lionel,† Ethel,*† and John Barrymore,*† among the most celebrated stage and film† **actors***† of the first half of the 20th century. After his wife died in 1893, however, Barrymore's profligate ways spun out of control, and his career was cut short when he died of paresis.

BATEMAN, ELLEN (1844–1936). Daughter of **H. L. Bateman** and **Sidney Frances Cowell Bateman**, Ellen Bateman went on the stage as a **child**,† appearing with her parents and sister, **Kate Bateman**. For a time, she specialized in male roles, appearing as Richard III, Shylock in *The Merchant of Venice*, and Macbeth, opposite her sister playing the major female roles. When she married Claude Greppo in 1860, Bateman retired from the stage.

BATEMAN, H. L. (1812–1875). Born in Baltimore, Hezekiah Linthicum Bateman studied to be an engineer, but at age 20, in 1832, he became an **actor**,*† performing with Ellen Tree. He married **actress***† and **playwright***† **Sidney Frances Cowell**, and they produced daughters, **Kate**, **Ellen**, **Virginia**, and **Isabel**, all of whom became actresses. In 1855, he became **manager***† of the St. Louis Theatre, but moved to New York four years later.

When his daughters Kate and Ellen became **child**† prodigies, he began guiding their careers and acted only infrequently. Kate became a particular favorite, and he wrote plays for her, including *Rose Gregorio; or, The Corsican Vendetta* (1862). Bateman produced **Augustin Daly's**† *Leah, the Forsaken* in 1863, with Kate in the title role scoring one of her most notable successes. In 1867, Bateman staged the **opéra bouffe** *La Grande Duchesse de Gérolstein*, which popularized the form with the American public. Ultimately, in 1871, he moved to London and managed the Lyceum Theatre, guiding a young Henry Irving to one of his most legendary successes in *The Bells*.

BATEMAN, ISABEL (1854–1934). Daughter of **H. L. Bateman** and **Sidney Frances Cowell Bateman**, she went on the stage like her sisters **Kate**, **Ellen**, and **Virginia**. To ensure her success, Bateman's father leased London's Lyceum Theatre and hired Henry Irving as leading man opposite her. Bateman played opposite Irving in *Hamlet*, *Richelieu*, and *Othello*, among other roles. She herself managed the Lyceum for a time, but it was ultimately taken over by Irving. Bateman retired from acting in 1898 to become an Anglican nun, fulfilling at least one **critic**'s*† view that she was "refined and spirituelle."

BATEMAN, KATE (1842–1917). The eldest daughter of **H. L. Bateman** and **Sidney Frances Cowell Bateman**, Kate Josephine Bateman was born in Baltimore, and went on the stage in **childhood***† as a prodigy, acting until 1856, when she and her sisters, **Ellen**, **Isabel**, and **Virginia**, all ceased child acting. Bateman made her adult debut in 1860 in her mother's adaptation of **Henry Wadsworth Longfellow**'s *Evangeline*, which made her a **star**.*† She subsequently won further popularity as a **Shakespearean***† romantic lead, most notably as Juliet, and in popular **melodramas**,† including *The Lady of Lyons* and *The Hunchback*.

Bateman won her greatest acclaim in the title role of **Augustin Daly**'s† *Leah, the Forsaken*, which opened at **Niblo's Garden** in late 1862, following the next year in London in the same role for a remarkable 211 performances. **Critics***† found her "admirably suited" to the role of a tragic Jewish woman abandoned by her Christian lover, and *Leah, the Forsaken* became the play and role most associated with Bateman. When she married George Crowe in 1866, Bateman retired from the stage, but returned as Leah again in 1868 at London's Haymarket Theatre. Illness forced another retirement, but much later she appeared in London in Henry James's *The American* in 1892. In 1907, Bateman appeared as Euripides's *Medea* and operated an acting school in London.

BATEMAN, SIDNEY FRANCES COWELL (1823–1881). Born in New York, Sidney Frances Cowell began her career performing opposite her husband, **H. L. Bateman**, but ultimately found success as a **playwright**,*† most notably with *Self* (1856), *Geraldine; or, Love's Victory* (1858), and *Evangeline* (1860), the latter **starring***† her daughter, **Kate Bateman**. Her children also included **actresses***† **Ellen**, **Isabel**, and **Virginia Bateman**.

BATEMAN, VIRGINIA (1853–1940). Born in Cincinnati, she was the youngest daughter of **H. L. Bateman** and **Sidney Frances Cowell Bateman**, and, as such, a stage career was inevitable for Virginia Bateman, who, like her sisters **Kate**, **Isabel**, and **Ellen**, debuted as a **child**.† She made her adult debut in London in her mother's play *Fanchetle* in 1871 and spent most of her career in England, where she married **actor*†** Edward Compton. Following Compton's death in 1918, Bateman served as **manager*†** of his theater company for a time. Her children included actress Fay Compton.

THE BATTLE OF BROOKLYN. The first major battle of the **American Revolution** in August 1776 shortly after the Continental Congress issued the Declaration of Independence is dramatized in this anonymous 1776 play. It was also the largest battle of the **war*†** and, following blunders on both sides, ended with General **George Washington** and his forces escaping the considerably larger and better-armed British forces. The play reflected Tory sentiments and was obviously written by a British loyalist.

THE BATTLE OF BUENA VISTA. An anonymous 1858 play, *The Battle of Buena Vista* recounts the events of the 23 February 1847 battle, also known as the Battle of Angostura, one of the decisive conflicts of the **Mexican War** and the greatest military triumph of General Zachary Taylor, which led to his election to the presidency of the United States shortly thereafter.

THE BATTLE OF BUNKERS-HILL. **Hugh H. Brackenridge** wrote this 1776 blank verse drama in five short acts celebrating the courageous response of Americans in the face of the overwhelming opposing English forces at this **critical*†** battle of the **American Revolution**. The acts feature the leaders of both sides exhorting their men and reacting to events, ending with the victorious British praising the daring Americans. An epilogue for the play honored **George Washington**.

THE BATTLE OF NEW ORLEANS; OR, GLORY, LOVE AND LOYALTY. **C. E. Grice** wrote and published this five-act drama produced at the **Park Theatre** on 4 July 1816, not long after the events of the last battle of the **War of 1812**, which is depicted in the play. Despite the fact that its heroics all came after a peace treaty had been signed in 1815 ending the conflict, theaters featured many dramatic works celebrating the American victory. With characters including General Andrew Jackson, the hero of the battle, the multiscene patriotic play was intended as a tribute to Jackson and his troops, with Jackson concluding with a stirring speech celebrating "the daring of the patriot band, that foiled the invader and redeemed the land."

BEACH, BOBBY (1855–1905). Born in Rome, New York, Bobby Beach went onstage in his teens as a contortionist and dancer. He found his way into **minstrels†** in the company of **Primrose and West's Minstrels** in 1881, and with Otis Bowers (1870–1908) he formed Beach and Bowers Famous Minstrels, an all-white company, a year later and **toured***† for several seasons. He was ultimately injured in a pedestal act, and his career ended.

THE BEAR AND THE CUB. _See YE BARE AND YE CUBB [YE BEAR AND YE CUBB]._

†BELASCO, DAVID (1859–1931). Born David Valasco in San Francisco, he learned theater as a **child,**† frequenting **Maguire's** and other theaters there. When the **stars***† **toured***† to San Francisco, young Belasco would find a spot in the company. At age 11 he played the Duke of York to **Charles Kean**'s _Richard III_, followed by stints with **Edwin Booth,**† **John McCullough,**† and other notables. Belasco moved up from callboy† to prompter† to assistant stage **manager,***† while performing at every opportunity, including imitations of the stars before audiences of gold miners. However, two **playwrights***†—**Dion Boucicault**† and **James A. Herne**†—provided Belasco with his breakthrough opportunities.

Belasco worked as a secretary for Boucicault, who encouraged his playwriting aspirations. With Herne, Belasco co-authored _Hearts of Oak_† (1879) and staged it, which led to his move to New York in 1882. Belasco became stage manager and resident playwright of the **Madison Square Theatre**† for a time in 1882. Two years later, he took over similar duties at **Daniel Frohman**'s† Lyceum Theatre, where he was **director***† of many productions and collaborated on writing as many as 35 plays before his first solo success, _May Blossom_ (1884). Between the 1880s and the 1920s, Belasco was recognized as one of the most influential and prolific **producers,***† directors, and playwrights of the American stage. He relished being dubbed the "Bishop of **Broadway**"*† (due, in part, to his habit of wearing clerical garb). Known for flashes of temperament, Belasco frequently threw his watch to the ground and crushed it to make a point, but associates later revealed that he kept a cache of inexpensive watches solely for this purpose.

Belasco was both admired and **criticized***† for the visual **ultra-realism***† of his productions, which, in one case, included brewing real coffee and making pancakes onstage in a restaurant scene. He continued producing plays until his retirement in 1930, although his influence waned after the First World **War.***† Most of Belasco's major plays were collaborations with Henry C. DeMille,† including _The Wife_† (1887), _Lord Chumley_ (1888), _The Charity Ball_† (1889), and _Men and Women_† (1890). In 1888, Belasco directed Sophocles's _Electra_ for the American Academy of Dramatic Arts,† a production noted for its trailblazing use of a simple, stark setting. His career continued well into the 20th century.

BELLE LAMAR: AN EPISODE OF THE CIVIL WAR. Dion Bouci-
cault's† **Civil War** play was first staged at **Booth's Theatre**, where it
opened on 10 August 1874, though it was only mildly successful. Some
critics*† felt Boucicault strived too much to avoid offending either side of
the conflict that had ended a mere nine years before. Inspired by various
legends of spies during the **war*†** (most notably Belle Boyd), the play is set
early in the war in 1862 in the Shenandoah Valley, where a Confederate
woman has divided loyalties between her beloved South and her husband
(played by **John McCullough**), who is a Union officer forced, ultimately, to
arrest her as a spy. **Frederick Warde** made his American debut in the role of
another Union officer.

After a disappointingly short four-week run in New York, *Belle Lamar*
closed. Boucicault, who made use of historic figures for some of his characters (including Stonewall Jackson, played by Frank Mackay in the original
production), presented the play in 1887 in Boston under the title *Fin Mac
Cool* with no better results, and a *New York Times* **critic*†** reported that it
"lacks coherence and dramatic significance" despite its subject matter.
Though not essentially one of Boucicault's **Irish** plays, it featured Irish characters as heroic figures during the Civil War, conveniently reinventing the
Irish role in the New York Draft riots in 1863.

BELLA UNION. Built in 1849 and opened in October of that year as a
performance venue in San Francisco, Bella Union was built on the site of the
Colonnade Hotel (on Portsmouth Square). Initially best known as a gambling
hall and saloon, it also offered a variety of entertainments,† including **min-
strel†** and **burlesque*†** shows. In 1856, when gambling was outlawed, it
became a melodeon (**vaudeville†** house) and, in its later days (after 1893 and
until the 1906 earthquake), was a waxworks and penny arcade.

The Bella Union, in its heyday prior to the **Civil War**, drew rough crowds
(on its opening night, a performer was shot and killed in a fight following the
performance). The original building was destroyed in an 1868 **fire,*†** but
rebuilt by **manager*†** Samuel Tetlow. At various times, major performers,
often at the beginning of their careers, appeared at Bella Union, including
Edward Harrigan† and **Lotta Crabtree.†** Though Bella Union was rebuilt
after other fires, the 1906 earthquake and fire ended its turbulent existence.

†BENEFIT. The practice of designating a specific performance as a benefit
for a particular **actor*†** has been traced back to Restoration England. In the
19th century, the benefit had become part of the fabric of the theater throughout Europe and the United States. When the **manager*†** of a resident
stock*† company allotted benefit evenings to certain company members, the
date could be fixed well in advance, allowing the beneficiary to choose a

work to her/his advantage and attract the fans who might even pay inflated prices as a show of respect. After deduction of the house share,† the entire proceeds of a benefit went to the announced beneficiary.

The terms of a benefit were often part of a performer's contract negotiations. Benefit performances in a resident stock company often occurred at the end of a season. While a **leading**† actor and **actress***† each got an individual benefit, other benefit evenings could be announced for several lesser actors collectively. Among **touring***† companies of the latter half of the 19th century, a benefit might be announced for the end of an engagement, however short, before the troupe moved on to the next town. Occasionally a local group of male citizens would together tender a benefit to a **woman***† performer who had captivated them. To tender a complimentary benefit, the locals might publish a card in the newspaper with the offer to pay all the expenses of a performance of a play on a date of the beneficiary's choosing.

BENNETT, JAMES GORDON (1795–1872). Of Scottish heritage, James Gordon Bennett studied for the priesthood in an Aberdeen seminary before leaving his homeland for the United States in 1819, where he became a newspaperman. He worked for several publications along the eastern seaboard before founding the *New York Herald* in 1835 and serving as its editor. His innovations shaped American journalism permanently, beginning with the first interviews, including an exclusive with President Martin Van Buren.

Despite this auspicious development, the *Herald* was often sensationalizing in style, offering front-page coverage of lurid murders. One controversy came in 1865, when the *Herald,* by then New York's most influential paper, refused to accept advertisements from **P. T. Barnum** after they fell into a disagreement over a property deal. In retaliation, Barnum, with the particular support of opera **producer***† Max Maretzek, who was annoyed by the negative coverage the *Herald* consistently gave his company, persuaded other theatrical producers to remove their advertisements from the *Herald*. After months of stalemate, Barnum and the producers relented with the realization that all sides were hurt by the disagreement.

BERNARD, JOHN (1756–1828). A popular English-born comic **actor***† who reigned supreme at the Covent Garden Theatre in the late 18th century, John Bernard made his American debut in Philadelphia in 1797 with **Thomas Wignell**'s company at the **Chestnut Street Theatre**. He remained a popular **attraction**† in English comedies, including **Shakespeare**,*† in Philadelphia for over five years, after which he joined Boston's **Federal Street Theatre** company in 1803, becoming its **manager***† in 1806. After a few years, he **toured***† the United States beginning in 1810, after which he returned to Boston in 1816 for farewell performances before returning to

England in 1819. His memoir, *Retrospections of America, 1797–1811*, was published in two volumes in 1830 after his death by his son, English **playwright*†** and **critic*† William Bayle Bernard**.

BERNARD, WILLIAM BAYLE (1807–1875). Son of English comedian **John Bernard**, William Bayle Bernard was born in Boston, but spent most of his career in England writing popular plays (often with American settings), including *Casco Bay* (1832), *The Kentuckian* (1833), *The Nervous Man* (1833), and an early adaptation of *Rip Van Winkle* (1834) for **actor*† James H. Hackett.**

†BERNHARDT, SARAH (1844–1923). Born in Paris, France, as Rosine Bernard, this legendary French **actress*†** frequently performed in the United States, where she made her American debut on 8 November 1880 at **Booth's Theatre** in one of her greatest vehicles, *Adrienne Lecouvreur.* She won **critical*†** acclaim and was guaranteed $1,000 per performance, at the time an astronomical sum. The subsequent **tour*†** of the country, under the **management*†** of **Henry E. Abbey,** was so lucrative that she toured America eight more times, the last in 1916. She performed in French, and during her 1905–1906 tour she joined American performers in defying the monopolizing Theatrical Syndicate,† choosing to perform in tents rather than pay the high theater rentals levied by the Syndicate. Bernhardt was, perhaps, the first truly **international*† star*†** due, in part, to her skill in manipulating the press, and was better known in the United States than some American stars.

THE BETTER SORT; OR, A GIRL OF SPIRIT. Written by **William Hill Brown**, this "operatical, comical" farce was published in Boston by Isaiah Thomas in 1789 and performed that same year. Focused on a social-climbing woman, Mrs. Sententious, the play's antics involve her attempts to ingratiate herself with society's "better sort." The farce owes much to British comedy of manners and much of the humor derives from the many malapropisms spouted by Mrs. Sententious, a popular comic device.

BEULAH SPA; OR, THE TWO B'HOYS. This two-act burletta sometimes called *The Two B'Hoys; or, The Beulah Spa*, was written by English **dramatist*†** Charles Dance in 1833 and first produced in the United States at the **Bowery Theatre** on 18 October 1834. A popular success, it led to "b'hoy" becoming common slang for a rowdy young man fond of fisticuffs. Such characters grew in popularity prior to the **Civil War**, especially following the runaway success of **Benjamin A. Baker**'s *A Glance at New York*, in which a Bowery b'hoy fireman, Mose, played notably by **Frank S. Chanfrau**, fully established the character. **Madame Vestris** presented the play in November 1833 at London's **Olympic Theatre**.

BIANCA VISCONTI; OR, THE HEART OVERTASKED. This five-act tragedy by **Nathaniel Parker Willis** was first staged at the **Park Theatre** under **manager*†** **Edmund Simpson**, where it opened on 24 August 1837. **Josephine Clifton** appeared in the title role as the long-suffering wife of the cold Duke of Milan. When she learns of an assassination plan against her husband, she conspires to substitute her loyal aide, Giulio. Following Giulio's death, Bianca discovers that he was her brother, which drives her insane. The play received awards encouraging new American plays, and a **critic*†** writing in the *Knickerbocker* at the time of the first performance praised Willis, asserting that the play "deserves the place of honor" among other contemporary works and that it was "well-received and attracted large audiences."

BIDWELL, BARNABAS (1763–1833). A Massachusetts politician who late in his career had to flee his home state after embezzling funds from a bank, Barnabas Bidwell was educated at Yale and made one foray into **playwriting*†** with a tragedy, *The Mercenary Match* (1784), described by **William Dunlap** as a "very pleasant and laughter-provoking tragedy." The play was staged by Yale students and published in 1785 in New Haven.

THE BIG BONANZA, A COMEDY OF OUR TIME. **Augustin Daly**'s five-act Wall Street comedy was first performed at Daly's New **Fifth Avenue Theatre** on 17 February 1875. The play, adapted from Gustav von Moser's German comedy *Ultimo*, was also adapted that same year by **Bartley Campbell** as *Bulls and Bears*. The snobbish Lucretia Cawallader is outraged when she hears that her marriageable daughter, Eugenia, played by **Fanny Davenport**,† was seen with a tattered-looking young man. Her annoyance extends to her investor husband, Jonathan (**Charles Fisher**),† who argues about their professions with his visiting cousin, Agassiz (**James Lewis**),† a professor. In an attempt to settle their dispute, Jonathan gives Agassiz $30,000 as part of a wager that Agassiz cannot invest it with positive returns in a month. Agassiz fails, although it turns out that Jonathan's clerk had disobeyed his instructions about the investments, and when his nephew, Bob Ruggles (**John Drew**, in his debut performance), arrives, it is revealed that Bob was the tattered-looking young man. After reconciliations, the Cawalladers allow Eugenia to marry Bob.

BIRCH, WILLIAM [BILLY] (1831–1897). Minstrel† comedian William "Billy" Birch began his career in 1844 near his birthplace, Utica, New York, before performing in California during the gold rush and with the Raymond Minstrels in Connecticut. In 1864, he founded Billy Birch's **San Francisco Minstrels**, performing with **Charles Backus**, W. H. Bernard, and David Wambold. He was a rotund, much-loved comic and performed until 1890 in troupes he often headed. Late in his career, he performed for a time with Lew Dockstader's† Minstrels, long after **blackface†** minstrelsy had begun its decline in popularity. At the time of his death, the *New York Times* reported that Birch, "an old time negro minstrel" was "penniless, although he had made a fortune by making others laugh."

BIRD, ROBERT MONTGOMERY (1806–1854). New Castle, Delaware, was the birthplace of **Robert Montgomery Bird**, who attended the University of Pennsylvania to study medicine. During that time, he began to write fiction for the *Philadelphia Monthly Magazine*. Bird gave up his medical practice shortly after beginning it to pursue **playwriting,*†** including works inspired by ancient classics and Elizabethan plays, such as *The Cowled Lover* (1827), *Caridorf; or, The Avenger* (1827), *News of the Night; or, a Trip to Niagara* (1828), and the unfinished *'Twas All for the Best; or, 'Tis a Notion* (1827) and *The City Looking Glass: A Philadelphia Comedy* (1828).

Bird was significantly encouraged about his playwriting when he won $1,000 from **Edwin Forrest** for his play *Pelopidas; or, The Fall of the Polemarchs* (1830), a work inspired by Plutarch. Forrest did not stage it, but he subsequently appeared in Bird's *The Gladiator* (1831), scoring one of his most enduring successes. Forrest also appeared in Bird's *Oraloosa* (1832) and *The Broker of Bogota* (1834), and at Forrest's request, Bird revised **John Augustus Stone**'s *Metamora; or, The Last of the Wampanoags* in 1836. However, a disagreement over finances caused Bird to abandon the stage, and he turned his attention to writing novels, including *Calavar* (1834), *The Infidel* (1845), *The Hawks of Hawk-Hollow* (1835), *Sheppard Lee* (1836), *Nick of the Woods* (1837)—which was adapted to the stage by **Louisa Medina** to great success—and *The Adventures of Robin Day* (1839). He also worked as a journalist.

THE BLACK CROOK. Considered by many scholars to be the first American **musical*†** theater piece, *The Black Crook* featured a book by Charles M. Barras, lyrics by Theodore Kennick, and original music by Giuseppe Operti (with interpolations). Bearing a resemblance to 20th-century book musicals, *The Black Crook* seems to have created not only a template for musicals, but its runaway success helped to popularize the form and led others to imitate its style. The style was created by necessity when **producers*†** **Henry C. Jarrett** and Harry Palmer hired a Parisian ballet company to perform at the New York Academy of Music.

When a **fire†** devastated the Academy, Jarrett and Palmer made a deal with **William Wheatley** at **Niblo's Garden** for the ballet troupe to appear as part of a musical spectacle to be made up of the ballerinas as part of Barras's **melodramatic†** play. Operti's "March of the Amazons" was a standout musical segment making good use of the ballerinas, as was "You Naughty, Naughty Men," an interpolation with music by George Bickwell and lyrics by Theodore Kennick. The cast included **Marie Bonfanti** and **George C. Boniface**. *The Black Crook* opened at Niblo's Garden on 12 September 1866 for an astonishing 474 performances prior to **touring*†** the country. The first of its many revivals occurred in 1870 and it remained a perennial entertainment† until the end of the 19th century, by which time the musical theater form it had been instrumental in creating had progressed from its style.

†BLACKFACE. This term refers to performers "blacking up" with burned cork, typically to perform exaggerated images of **African Americans,*†** usually in **minstrel†** shows and early **musicals,*†** though white **actors*†** in blackface typically played African American characters in straight plays as well during the 18th and 19th centuries. The minstrel show, one of the most durable entertainments† from the early 19th into the early 20th century, ostensibly began in the 1820s when entertainer **Thomas Dartmouth "Daddy" Rice** adopted the practice in a performance in Baltimore after supposedly witnessing an elderly black man doing an eccentric dance. The "**Jump Jim Crow**" routine Rice perfected was widely imitated by other performers when minstrel shows, which were essentially variety entertainments featuring songs, dances, and comedy, sprang up around the United States.

By the 1840s, **Dan Emmett** founded the **Virginia Minstrels**, an early prototype of the tradition continued by **E. P. Christy** and innumerable others. Blackface was dropped for a time in all-white, all-black, and mixed troupes, but by the 1880s audiences who had seen it for generations demanded its return. Simultaneously, the popularity of minstrel troupes began a slow decline in the late 19th century, and blackface moved from the **legitimate†** stage to **vaudeville†** and musicals, used notably by white entertainers Al Jolson,† Eddie Leonard, Eddie Cantor, and by *Ziegfeld Follies†* star Bert Williams, an African American, the last generation of major stage **stars*†** to rise via the use of blackface. By the 1930s, performers had mostly abandoned blackface as an outmoded and demeaning stereotype.

BLAKE, WILLIAM RUFUS (1805–1863). A native of Halifax, Nova Scotia, but of **Irish** descent, William Rufus Blake began acting in his teens in Canada, appearing there with Thomas Placide's company in *Richard III*. Blake made his New York debut at the **Chatham Garden Theatre** in 1824 in *The Poor Gentleman*, followed by *The Three Singles*. Legend has it that when he appeared at Boston's **Tremont Theatre** in 1827, he became the first **actor*†** in American history to be called before the curtain to acknowledge applause from the audience.

At the height of his career, Blake was believed to be the highest-paid actor in America. Blake also acted periodically in England beginning in 1839. Cast as **leading men†** in his early career, he demonstrated skill in comedy and increasingly played such roles in **Shakespeare,*†** British comedy of manners, and contemporary American plays. At various times, he was the lead comedian in several notable companies, including **William Burton**'s and **James W. Wallack**'s, and was a **manager*†** of several New York theaters, including the **Bowery**, Philadelphia's **Walnut Street Theatre**, and Boston's Tremont. Blake also wrote a few plays, including *Nero, The Turned Head, Norman Leslie,* and *The Buggs*, and is believed to be the author of *Fitzallan* (1833), the first play by a Canadian-born writer.

BLANCHARD, KITTY (1847–1911). Daughter of a Bowdoin College professor, Kitty Blanchard went on the stage in **childhood†** as a dancer in 1857. Her father's early death compelled her to pursue a theatrical career to support her family. She worked in Louisville for **manager*† John Albaugh**, becoming popular there and in other western cities. She married **actor*† McKee Rankin,†** with whom she frequently acted, usually under the name Mrs. McKee Rankin. Among her New York credits are *The Two Orphans* in 1874, *At Piney Ridge* (1897), *The Ghetto* (1899), *Mam'selle 'Awkins* (1900), *The Girl and the Judge* (1901), and *The Girl with the Green Eyes†* (1902), but along with Rankin she scored one of her greatest successes in **Joaquin Miller**'s *The Danites; or, The Heart of the Sierras* (1877). In 1907, Alla Nazimova,*† Ethel Barrymore,*† and other major **actresses*†** gave a benefit performance in Blanchard's honor. Stricken while bathing in her home, Blanchard drowned in her bathtub.

THE BLOCKADE OF BOSTON. Written in 1775 by British general John Burgoyne, this satiric play produced in Boston at Faneuil Hall on 8 January 1776, while English troops held the city, mocked American soldiers. General **George Washington** was a target of satire in the play, and legend has it that the performance was interrupted when a British soldier came onstage to report that American troops were raiding a British outpost in nearby Charlestown. The audience presumed this was part of the play, but General William

Howe, who was present, ordered his soldiers to their posts. Later that year, with the British driven out of Boston, a satiric **burlesque*†** *The Blockheads*, attributed to **Mercy Otis Warren**, turned the tables.

THE BLOCKHEADS; OR, THE AFFRIGHTED OFFICERS. Generally believed to have been written by **Mercy Otis Warren**, *The Blockheads* was an otherwise anonymous **burlesque*†** of British general John Burgoyne's satire of the American military, *The Blockade of Boston*.

BLONDIN, CHARLES (1824–1897). French-born Jean François Gravelet-Blondin became tightrope walker and acrobat Charles Blondin in **childhood†** as "The Boy Wonder." In 1855, he first performed in the United States, where he was employed by **William Niblo** to appear with the **Ravel Family**, gaining fame for his famous stunt of crossing Niagara Falls on a tightrope on 30 June 1859. He repeated the stunt several times thereafter. Much of the remainder of Blondin's career was spent in England and Ireland.

BOKER, GEORGE HENRY (1823–1890). The scion of a wealthy banking family, George Henry Boker was born in Philadelphia and attended Princeton University to study law. Instead, he founded the university's literary magazine, the *Nassau Monthly*, and embarked on a career as a writer. Boker published his own book of poetry, *The Lessons of Life, and Other Poems*, in 1848, the same year he wrote his first play, *Calaynos*, a tragedy, which had its first production in London that year and was produced at Philadelphia's **Walnut Street Theatre** by **James Murdoch** in 1851. Boker followed this with a comedy, *The Betrothal* (1850), as well as additional tragedies, *Anne Boleyn* (1850) and *Leonor de Guzman* (1853).

Other Boker plays include the comedies *The World a Mask* (1851) and *The Widow's Marriage* (1852), a **melodrama,†** *The Bankrupt* (1855), and an unproduced tragedy, *Königsmark* (1857). Based on the fifth canto of Dante's *Inferno*, Boker's 1853 play *Francesca da Rimini*, a romantic verse tragedy, became his most acclaimed and produced work. With the coming of the **Civil War**, Boker was instrumental in defining the goals of the Republican Party. From that time, he turned his attentions to politics and diplomacy, though he continued to write poetry. However, in 1883, when **Lawrence Barrett** successfully revived *Francesca da Rimini*, Boker wrote two additional plays, *Nydia* and *Glaucus*, both inspired by **Edward Bulwer-Lytton**'s novel, *The Last Days of Pompeii*, though they were never produced.

BONFANTI, MARIE (1845–1921). Remembered mostly as the prima ballerina of the original production of *The Black Crook* (1866), widely considered the first example of American **musical*†** theater, Marie Bonfanti had made her dancing debut at **Niblo's Garden** on 10 September 1866, a mere two days before *The Black Crook* opened. Bonfanti appeared in it for its entire long run. Born in Milan, Italy, Bonfanti began dancing in her early teens. Following *The Black Crook*, she appeared in a production in a similar style, *The White Fawn* (1868), but it failed. In 1876, **Augustin Daly** featured her as a dancer in his play *Life*. She appeared at the Metropolitan Opera House in the first season of ballet offered in New York in 1901.

†BONIFACE, GEORGE C. (1833–1912). Born in New York, George C. Boniface debuted as an **actor***† in Baltimore in 1851, followed by his New York debut in 1857 playing opposite **Charlotte Cushman** for a season. This was followed by a season with **Lester Wallack** at the **National Theatre** before he became **comanager***† of the old **Bowery Theatre**, where he appeared as John Brown in *Ossawattomie Brown; or, The Insurrection at Harper's Ferry* (1859), among other roles. He ultimately moved to the new Bowery Theatre playing heroes in **melodramas**.† In 1866, he played Rudolf in the original production of *The Black Crook* (1866), considered by many to be the first true American **musical***† as the form ultimately evolved in the 20th century.

Boniface was sometimes **criticized***† as a bombastic actor as the modern era dawned and such techniques gave way to a more natural approach. Despite reservations of critics, he appeared with success for many years in such productions as *The Twelve Temptations* in 1870, *The Colleen Bawn* in 1871, *Les Misérables* in 1871, *Pygmalion and Galatea* in 1872, *Kit, The Arkansas Traveler* in 1877, *Under Cover*† in 1888, *Sam'l of Posen*† in 1894, *Trelawny of the Wells* in 1898, and *The Climbers*† in 1901. He made his final appearance in a 1911 revival of *Trelawny of the Wells*, playing James Telfer, the role he had originated in 1898.

†BOOTH, AGNES (1846–1910). The third wife of **Junius Brutus Booth Jr.**† was already an experienced **actress*** before they married in 1867. Marion Agnes Land Rookes was born in Sydney, Australia, and moved with her family to San Francisco in her youth. She acted there at **Maguire's Opera House** under the name Agnes Land and married **actor***† Harry A. Perry (1826–1862). In 1865, she appeared at the **Winter Garden Theatre** and the following year became a member of the **Boston Theatre** company. She married Booth in 1867 and took his name. As an accomplished **emotional actress**,† Booth maintained a solid string of good roles throughout the 1870s and 1880s, most notably in the **Union Square Theatre**† production of *A Celebrated Case* in 1878. From 1881 to 1891, she was a member of the **Madison Square Theatre**† company. Her third husband, John B. Schoeffel, was a theatrical **manager***† in partnership with **Henry Abbey**† and Maurice Grau.† A **critic***† for *Belford Magazine* wrote in 1889 that "Agnes Booth is in the front rank of **leading**† ladies."

BOOTH, ASIA. *See* CLARKE, ASIA BOOTH (1835–1888).

†BOOTH, EDWIN (1833–1893). Generally acknowledged as the greatest **actor***† in American theater history—at least of the 19th century—Edwin Thomas Booth was born on **Junius Brutus Booth**'s Bel Air, Maryland, farm, reportedly on a night of shooting **stars**.*† He was named for America's leading tragedian, **Edwin Forrest**. He was also illegitimate (his mother was Mary Ann Holmes), as were his multiple siblings, and some scholars believe this fact inspired his drive to legitimize himself through unprecedented stage success. In his youth, Booth **toured***† with his erratic, alcoholic father and even on occasion substituted for the elder Booth, although he developed a more restrained and natural style in contrast to the bombastic excesses typical of his father's generation.

Booth's physical attributes contributed to his compelling portrayals: a lithe body, luminous and expressive eyes, and a melodiously caressing voice. In 1858, *New York Herald* **critic***† **Edward G. P. Wilkins** wrote that Booth displayed "the true fire of genius which needs by time, industry, and study to place its possessor in the very rank of living tragedians." The time, industry, and study had already been expended in touring with his father after making his 1849 stage debut in Boston as Tressel in *Richard III*.

Following his father's death, Booth toured widely, with lengthy stints in Hawaii and Australia. In 1854–1855, Booth toured Australia with **Laura Keene**, with whom he apparently had a romantic involvement, and bracketed his career with successful European tours in 1861–1862 and 1881–1882. He was married twice, first in 1860 to **actress***† **Mary Devlin**, with whom he had a daughter, Edwina. Devlin died in 1863, a devastating event in Booth's life as he was away performing (and drinking) and failed to open telegrams calling him to her bedside.

In 1869, Booth married actress **Mary McVicker**, but ultimately this proved to be an unhappy marriage as McVicker suffered increasingly from mental challenges. Booth reached the pinnacle of his career in 1864, famously playing Hamlet at New York's **Winter Garden** for 100 consecutive performances. Booth's natural acting style surely contributed to his success as Hamlet (as did his deep melancholy over the early death of Devlin, as some historians have noted), and, in fact, in other roles in **Shakespeare***†—and his approach had a significant influence on acting techniques during the 1870s and 1880s as **playwrights***† slowly embraced modernist principles and the new **realism***† evolving in European drama.

The glow of Booth's Hamlet triumph was short-lived; on 14 April 1865, Booth's younger brother **John Wilkes Booth†** assassinated President **Abraham Lincoln** at **Ford's Theatre**, coincidentally in Laura Keene's production of **Tom Taylor**'s *Our American Cousin*. Devastated by this national and personal tragedy, Booth left the stage for nearly a year and banned any mention of his brother in his presence. Despite this, a photograph of his brother was displayed on Booth's bedroom wall for the rest of his life. With his return to the stage, Booth's predominance among American actors remained unquestioned. His other great roles, Iago in *Othello*, Benedick in *Much Ado About Nothing*, and the title roles in *Richelieu*, *Macbeth*, and *King Lear*, won critical acclaim nearly equal to that of his Hamlet. Booth built the exquisitely appointed **Booth's Theatre†** in New York, which opened on 3 February 1869, but it proved to be financially draining; he was forced to sell it in 1874.

Booth toured extensively during the 1880s, including two noteworthy "joint star" tours with **Lawrence Barrett**.† In this same era, Booth's voice reading speeches from Shakespeare was recorded by Thomas A. Edison, a first for any major actor. In 1888, Booth founded The Players',† a theatrical **club**,*† which continues to this day in what was his New York home on Gramercy Square, where he died.

Despite his many successes, to theatergoing audiences of his generation Booth did not play Hamlet, he was† Hamlet. The merging of his brilliant characterization with the tragic events of his own life, including his brother's murder of Lincoln and the premature death of his first wife, was, to audiences and critics alike, unforgettable. As **William Winter†** wrote,

> his impersonation of Hamlet was vital with all the old fire, and beautiful with new beauties of elaboration. Surely the stage, at least in our time, has never offered a more impressive and affecting combination than Mr. Booth's Hamlet of princely dignity, intellectual stateliness, glowing imagination, fine sensitiveness to all that is most sacred in human life and all that is most thrilling and sublime in the weird atmosphere of 'supernatural solicitings,' which enwraps the highest mood of the man's genius.

†BOOTH, JOHN WILKES (1839–1865). The darkly attractive tragedian, son of **Junius Brutus Booth**, was born on his father's farm near Bel Air, Maryland. His mother, Mary Ann Holmes, was not married to his father; it is believed by some scholars that his illegitimacy was a driving force in his pursuit of fame at all costs. Scholars also debate his merits as an **actor**,*† though most concur that he was not the equal of his celebrated brother, **Edwin Booth**.†

Many historians describe Booth as an exceedingly handsome **matinee idol**,† a view supported by numerous photographs. He made up in intensity and physicality what he lacked in technical skill and intellectual capacity. Some contemporaries, including his sister-in-law **actress*† Mary Devlin Booth**, considered him a poor actor. Booth made his debut in 1855 at Baltimore's Charles Street Theatre as the Earl of Richmond in *Richard III* and also worked for **John T. Ford** at Baltimore's **Holliday Street Theatre**. In 1857, Booth joined the **stock*†** company of Philadelphia's **Arch Street Theatre**, billing himself as J. B. Wilkes, presumably to avoid comparisons with his father and brother. In 1858, Booth played Horatio to his brother's Hamlet. That year, Booth appeared in numerous plays and he continued a hectic pace of performances, perhaps intending to make up in quantity what he lacked in quality.

He **toured*†** widely in the early 1860s and was billed as a **star*†** for his New York debut at **Wallack's Theatre** in 1862, transfixing audiences with his intense portrayal of Richard III, although prophetically he stated that his favorite role was as the assassin Brutus in *Julius Caesar*.

Booth was well known as a Confederate sympathizer and often acted in the South. In the waning days of the **Civil War**, an unhinged Booth plotted to kidnap President **Abraham Lincoln** in hopes of reviving the Confederacy's chances of ultimate victory. Botched attempts were made, and as the war ended Booth's plan shifted to a plot to murder Lincoln and other high officials of the United States government, including Vice President Andrew Johnson and Secretary of State William H. Seward. The plan languished until Booth heard Lincoln give a speech (his last) from a White House window in which he posited the possibility of voting rights for **African American*†** men, infuriating the deeply racist Booth.

Determined to move forward with his murderous plot, Booth made his final stage appearance at **Ford's Theatre** in Washington, DC, performing in a benefit for **John McCullough**,† in March 1865. Tragically, he achieved lasting fame weeks later as the assassin of Lincoln during a performance of **Tom Taylor**'s comedy *Our American Cousin* by **Laura Keene**'s company at Ford's Theatre on 14 April 1865. After slipping in the back of Lincoln's stage box, he fired a derringer, which sent a bullet into the back of Lincoln's head. To escape, Booth leapt over the railing of the stage box, catching his foot in the flag bunting decorating it, and tumbled to the stage floor. He managed to rise and flee the theater, limping with a broken bone in his foot, brushing past actor **Harry Hawk**, the only actor onstage at that exact moment. Booth took flight south into Virginia, where he hoped to be viewed as a national hero of the nearly defunct Confederacy. Instead, Northerners and Southerners alike labeled him a coward and murderer. Tracked by Union troops to a barn in rural Virginia, Booth was shot to death by a soldier less than two weeks after the assassination.

BOOTH, JUNIUS BRUTUS (1796–1852). Born in London to a lawyer father, Junius Brutus Booth attempted a series of professions before turning to the stage after he attended a production of *Othello* at the Covent Garden Theatre. Eventually, at that same theater, he scored a success as Richard III in 1817, following several years as an **actor*†** in the provinces. **Critics*†** and audiences compared him favorably to **Edmund Kean**, leading to a rivalry that resulted in rowdy partisans of both actors fighting at performances. In 1821, Booth married and fathered a son before abandoning his wife and child, and, with his mistress Mary Ann Holmes, traveled to the United States, settling on a farm in Bel Air, Maryland, from which he pursued his acting career in America.

Within a short time, Booth was recognized as a standout tragedian, appearing regularly in Baltimore, New York, and Boston. Leading artistic voices in America acclaimed his talents, including **Walt Whitman**, who described Booth as "the grandest histrion of modern times." Booth fathered several children with Holmes, four of whom died in childhood, but among his surviving children, three became notable actors: **Edwin Booth,† Junius Brutus Booth Jr.,†** and **John Wilkes Booth**.† In **Shakespearean*†** roles, Booth was especially admired as Hamlet, Iago, and Cassius, while also scoring successes in contemporary plays, such as **John Howard Payne**'s *Brutus*. Booth **toured*†** often, and his death on a Mississippi steamboat, following an engagement† in New Orleans, possibly resulted from his having imbibed contaminated water.

†BOOTH, JUNIUS BRUTUS JR. (1821–1883). The eldest of **Junius Brutus Booth Sr.**'s 10 children made a career onstage. He was born in Charleston and debuted in Pittsburgh in 1834 in *Mazeppa*.† He made his 1851 New York debut at the **Bowery Theatre** in the same play. Booth's three wives included Agnes Land Perry, an **actress*†** who achieved fame as **Agnes Booth**.† Booth was not considered the equal of his father, brothers, or wife, and though he worked steadily, he never achieved significant acclaim. On 23 November 1864, he appeared in *Julius Caesar* with his brothers **Edwin Booth†** and **John Wilkes Booth†** (an event recorded in a now-famous photograph) for a benefit performance. Like his brother Edwin, Booth suffered a major career setback in 1865 in the aftermath of his brother John Wilkes's assassination of President **Abraham Lincoln**. In time, he was able to continue his work, but after several seasons in California and as **manager*†** of the **Boston Theatre**, he retired from the stage.

BOOTH, MARY DEVLIN (1840–1863). Born in Sand Lake, New York, to a large **Irish** Catholic family, Mary "Molly" Devlin made her debut in Troy, New York, in 1852 as a dancer. At 16, her angelic looks made her a perfect

Juliet to play opposite **Edwin Booth**'s† Romeo, and they subsequently married in 1860. She is credited with encouraging Booth to challenge himself as an **actor**,*† writing to him, "Dear Edwin, I will never allow you to droop for a single moment; for I know that power that dwells within your eye." They had a daughter, Edwina, who later wrote that her father told her that Mary was "his severest, and therefore his kindest **critic**."*† She found her brother-in-law **John Wilkes Booth** to be a poor actor, but believed her husband could achieve greatness.

Devlin's own stage work is of comparatively little significance, but her surviving letters and notebooks offer an extraordinary view of theatrical life in the 1850s and early 1860s, including her husband's work, not to mention an account of their courtship and marriage. Mary and Edwina accompanied Booth to England in 1861, where he appeared in several cities with little success. They returned to the United States, where his work won increasing appreciation. Mary's 1863 death from pneumonia devastated Booth, who could never forgive himself for performing in a drunken state, which caused him to overlook telegrams urging his return home. Some scholars believe that Booth's despair over Mary's death contributed significantly to his artistry, particularly in melancholic tragic roles, including his most acclaimed performance as Hamlet.

BOOTH, MARY MCVICKER (1849–1881). The stepdaughter of Chicago theater **manager***† **James H. McVicker**, Mary Frances Runnion took her stepfather's surname and went on the stage. At the age of 10, in 1859, she debuted in her father's theater in *Gianetta,* and in a short time emerged as a favorite to Chicago audiences. She repeated her initial success in the company of the **Boston Museum** in the early 1860s. McVicker also scored successes as a singer, beginning in 1862, which led to a **tour***† of Southern cities. She appeared in Chicago as Juliet opposite **Edwin Booth**'s† Romeo in 1867, a role he had played opposite his first wife, **Mary Devlin Booth**, who had died in 1863, a mere three years after their marriage.

Booth married McVicker on 7 June 1869 at Long Branch, New Jersey, but the death shortly after the birth of their child, Edgar, in 1870, caused her to sink into a deep depression, leading to chronic ill health and mental instability. She had given up acting following her marriage to Booth, and the marriage was an unhappy one as a result of her slow descent into insanity, according to contemporary accounts.

†BOOTH'S THEATRE. The lavishly appointed theater at Sixth Avenue and 23rd Street in New York was constructed at a cost of more than a million dollars, while **actor***† **Edwin Booth**† **toured***† strenuously to pay for its construction, which began in 1867. Among its innovations—which may be credited to his **scene designer***† **Charles W. Witham**†—were a flat-floor stage (as opposed to the raked stages prevalent at the time) and a scene construction shop within the facility, a rarity in the mid-19th century. The theater also featured an ornate design and a statue of Booth's father, **Junius Brutus Booth**, created by sculptor Thomas Ridgeway Gould.

Heavily mortgaged, Booth's Theatre opened to acclaim on 3 February 1869 with a performance of *Romeo and Juliet* **starring***† Booth and his soon-to-be second wife, **Mary McVicker**. However, even capacity audiences could not sustain it, partly as a result of Booth's insistence on the highest production standards, which, as noted of *Romeo and Juliet*, adhered to the strictest "historical propriety." In 1874, Booth succumbed to bankruptcy and lost his theater.

Subsequent **managers***† were similarly unable to run Booth's Theatre at a profit. The final performance at Booth's Theatre, on 30 April 1883, starred **Helena Modjeska**† and **Maurice Barrymore**,† after which the real estate was turned to more lucrative commercial interests. Booth's Theatre (1869–1883) is not to be confused with the Booth Theatre at 222 West 45th Street, which opened in 1913 and is still in operation in 2014. Some years after losing his theater, in December 1878, Booth, showing frustration, wrote an open letter in *The Christian Union*, stating,

> If the management of theatres could be denied to speculators, and placed in the hands of actors who value their reputation and respect their calling, the stage would at least afford healthy recreation, if not, indeed, a wholesome stimulus to the exercise of noble sentiments. But while the theatre is permitted to be a mere shop for gain,—open to every huckster of immoral gimcracks,—there is no way to discriminate between the pure and base than through the experience of others.

BOSTON IDEAL OPERA COMPANY. Founded in 1879 by Effie H. Ober to stage **W. S. Gilbert and Arthur Sullivan**'s *H.M.S. Pinafore*, which they did with significant success, it inspired other **operettas**† to be written and staged. Some productions **toured***† across the United States and Canada. A company was established and ultimately run by its members, and although such European operettas as *Fra Diavolo*, *Martha*, and *The Elixir of Love* were their raison d'être, the company ultimately stressed new American operettas. Among these, the company scored a major success with Reginald De Koven's *Robin Hood* (1891) and some of Victor Herbert's early works, including *Prince Ananias* (1894) and *The Serenade* (1897). Divisions formed in the company, and it disbanded in 1905.

BOSTON MUSEUM. Opened by **Moses Kimball** in 1841 at Tremont and Bromfield Street, and filled with exhibits from the New England Museum, which Kimball had purchased, the Boston Museum established a **stock***† company and began presenting plays in the fall of 1843 in a theater called a lecture hall to avoid objections from the puritanical Boston public. Scores of major theater **stars*** appeared at the Boston Museum, including **Edwin Booth,† Lawrence Barrett,† John Wilkes Booth,† Richard Mansfield,† E. H. Sothern,† Mrs. J. R. Vincent**, and **William Warren**, among others. Kimball also befriended **P. T. Barnum**, with whom he exchanged exhibits, most successfully the supposed corpse of a "Fee-Jee" mermaid, a creature cobbled together from parts of an orangutan and a large fish. Kimball died in 1895, and the Boston Museum continued to operate until 1903.

BOSTON THEATRE. Two Boston theaters bore this name in the 18th and 19th centuries. The first, established in 1794 at Federal and Franklin Streets, and later called the **Federal Street Theatre**, opened with a performance of *Gustavus Vasa* and gained a reputation as one of the finest theaters in the country. It burned down in 1798, but was rebuilt and operated as a theater until 1835, when it became a lecture hall called the Odeon.

In 1846, the Boston Theatre transitioned back to theater performances, and during its history such leading players as **Edwin Forrest** and **Julia Dean** appeared there. In 1852, the building was torn down to make way for the construction of a new larger and more lavish structure, designed by Edward and James Cabot and Jonathan Preston from plans conceived by **architect** Henri Noury. The facility seated 3,000, and such notable stars as Forrest, **Charlotte Cushman, Sarah Bernhardt,† Edwin Booth,†** Henry Irving, Ellen Terry, Lily Langtry,† and **Maurice Barrymore†** appeared there. The theater closed in 1925.

†BOUCICAULT, DION (1820?–1890). Born Dionysius Lardner Boursiquot in Dublin, Ireland, this colorful **actor,***† **manager,***† and prolific **playwright†** launched his career in London. He might be thought of as both an English and American dramatist since he spent considerable time writing, acting, and producing plays in both London and New York, but there is no denying his significant impact on the development of American theater. His first play, *A Legend of the Devil's Dyke*, was staged in Brighton, England, in 1838, but his first true success came with his hit comedy *London Assurance* (1841), first staged at Covent Garden with a distinguished cast including **Charles Mathews**, William Farren, and **Madame Vestris**. It became an enduringly popular work in 19th-century theater and is one of the few from that era still produced in the 21st century.

Boucicault followed *London Assurance* with a string of successes, including *Old Heads and Young Hearts* (1844), *The School for Scheming* (1847), *Confidence* (1848), *The Knight Arva* (1848), **The Corsican Brothers** (1852; written for **Charles Kean)**, *Used Up* (1854), and *Louis XI* (1855).

As an actor, Boucicault debuted in his own play, **The Vampire** (1852), and frequently performed in his own works throughout his career. Boucicault often won approval as an actor, particularly in his **Irish**-themed plays, such as **The Shaughraun** (1874). Of Boucicault's acting, **critic*† William Winter†** wrote that he was "all intellect . . . but he knew the emotions by sight, and he mingled them as a chemist mingles chemicals; generally with success." From 1853, Boucicault spent most of his time in the United States as manager of theaters in New Orleans and New York, and **touring*†** with his own company, which included his common-law wife, **Agnes Robertson,†** who bore him six children. Of these, his son Darley George Boucicault (1859–1929), known onstage as Dion Boucicault Jr., and to his family as Dot, was the most successful and made his debut in 1879 in his father's play *Louis XI.* The senior Boucicault continued to write a steady stream of plays, many of which were adapted, often loosely, from French sources. As he noted himself, "I can spin out these rough-and-tumble dramas as a hen lays eggs. It's a degrading occupation, but more money has been made out of guano than out of poetry."

Following his arrival in America, Boucicault's dramatic output continued unabated, with the emphasis on **melodrama,†** as in **The Poor of New York** (1857), **Jessie Brown; or, The Relief of Lucknow** (1858), **The Octoroon; or, Life in Louisiana** (1859), **Dot** (1859), **The Colleen Bawn; or, The Brides of Garryowen** (1860), **Jeanie Deans** (1860), **Arrah-na-Pogue; or, The Wicklow Wedding** (1864), **Rip Van Winkle** (1866; written as a vehicle for **Joseph Jefferson†**), *The Flying Scud* (1866), *Formosa* (1866), *After Dark: A Tale of London Life* (1868), **The Shaughraun** (1874), *Robert Emmet* (1884), and *The Jilt* (1885).

In 1885, Boucicault embarked on a **tour*†** of Australia, during which time he broke off his longtime relationship with Robertson and married Louise Thorndyke (c. 1864–1956), an actress 44 years his junior. The resulting scandalous tabloid press and alimony payments to Robertson (financed by royalties of his plays) damaged both his reputation and financial security. Boucicault's career essentially ended at this time.

Boucicault possessed a strong instinct for what the theatergoing public wanted in the mid-19th century and the dramatic skills and theatrical flair to create remarkably successful melodramas and sentimental Irish plays. He often used Irish themes and settings, incorporating gripping suspense and dazzling **sensations†** in his melodramas. He is credited with as many as 200 plays, several of which remained central to the canon of the American stage until the early 20th century. Perhaps reflecting on his own legacy, in 1889, the year before his death, Boucicault wrote in the *North American Review*: "There is only one stern question and true test that can be applied to the dramatist or to the actor, if we would determine the quality of his talents: what characters has he left as heirlooms to the stage and to dramatic literature? He can materialize to the future in that way alone."

†**BOWERS, MRS. D. P. (1830–1895).** Born Elizabeth Crocker in Stamford, Connecticut, as the daughter of an Episcopal clergyman, she made her debut at New York's **Park Theatre** in 1846 as Amanthis in *The Child*† *of Nature*. In 1847, she married **actor***† David P. Bowers (1822–1857) and thereafter performed as Mrs. D. P. Bowers. For several seasons, she performed in **stock***† at Philadelphia's **Arch Street Theatre** and subsequently became **actor***†**-manager***† of the city's **Walnut Street Theatre** between 1857 and 1859. She scored notable successes in *Romeo and Juliet*, *The Hunchback*, and *The Lady of Lyons*, among others.

In the years immediately following her husband's death, she **toured***† and had a successful London debut in 1861. Bowers subsequently moved from **leading lady**† roles to **supporting**† roles, most notably as Emilia in the **Edwin Booth**†–**Tommaso Salvini**† productions of *Othello* and as Gertrude in *Hamlet*, both in 1886. She was also well received as the Duchess of Berwick in the 1893 American debut of Oscar Wilde's† *Lady Windermere's Fan*. From the 1870s, she toured extensively in historical **melodramas**† and **Shakespearean***† productions.

BOWERY THEATRE. This theater, built in 1826 on New York's Lower East Side with the intention of rivaling the **Park Theatre**, enjoyed its heyday earlier in the 19th century, particularly under **manager***† **Thomas Hamblin**. The theater stressed its credentials as an American theater, with a strong populist sensibility, and featured light American-made entertainments,† including **blackface**† **minstrels**† **George Washington Dixon** and **Thomas Dartmouth "Daddy" Rice**, **clowns***† such as **George L. Fox**, **animal**† acts, and potboiler **melodramas**,† though such noted dramatic **actors***† as **Junius Brutus Booth**, **Edwin Forrest**, and **Louisa Lane (Mrs. John) Drew**, among others, also appeared there.

Under Hamblin, the Bowery became a working-class theater, dubbed "The Slaughterhouse" for its generally "low class" fare. Contemporary plays staged at the Bowery tended to favor the more popular of American character types, including, along with blackface minstrels, the Bowery **b'hoy**, the **Yankee**,† and frontiersmen. During Hamblin's tenure, **gas lighting***† was installed, among other contemporary innovations. The nativist sentiments of the Bowery audience came to a head in 1834 with what became known as the Farren riots, resulting, in part, from an anti-American comment expressed by

George P. Farren, the theater's British-born stage manager, for whom the theater was presenting a performance of *Metamora; or, The Last of the Wampanoags* **starring*†** **Edwin Forrest** as a benefit. Abolitionist and anti-black sentiments also fueled the situation, leading to violence and destruction of property, extending over a two-day period, which was quelled, ultimately, by military forces.

The theater long retained its reputation for rowdy audiences. In 1879, the fifth theater on the site had its name changed from the Bowery to the Thalia Theatre. By this time, the surrounding neighborhood was populated with immigrants, and the Thalia presented plays in German and **Yiddish**.† This building was destroyed by fire in 1929.

†BOX SET. The first use of a box set is difficult to pinpoint, but the Mann-heim Court Theatre may have employed something like a box set as early as 1804. This practice of enclosing the action of a play in a three-walled room (with the invisible fourth wall separating the play from the audience) was a European convention ultimately adopted in the United States, where it radically influenced developments in **scenery.*†** It slowly gained favor when **Madame Vestris** famously employed it in 1832 and later in a staging of **Dion Boucicault's†** *London Assurance* in 1842.

With the rise of **realism,*†** the use of the box set became commonplace, although at first shifting scenes was more difficult than with the old system of painted wings† and backdrops. In America, box sets were seen frequently in the productions of **David Belasco†** and other **managers*†** who prized greater reality. When the post-realistic New Stagecraft† emerged in Europe after 1900 and powerfully influenced American **scene design,*†** new techniques were explored, but by then the box set had become a standard stage setting for professional and **amateur*†** theaters in America.

BRACKENRIDGE, HUGH HENRY (1748–1816). Born in Kintyre, Scotland, Hugh Henry Brackenridge came to America with his family in 1757 and resided on the frontier of Pennsylvania, near the Maryland border. He attended Princeton University, where he studied divinity and also became involved in politics. With the start of the **American Revolution**, Brackenridge served as a chaplain in General **George Washington**'s army. During the **war,*†** Brackenridge wrote two plays supporting the American cause, *The Battle of Bunkers-Hill* (1776) and *The Death of General Montgomery at the Siege of Quebec* (1777), both of which were blank verse tragedies in the classical tradition. Following the war, Brackenridge wrote novels and became a justice of the Pennsylvania Supreme Court.

BRIAN O'LINN. **Samuel D. Johnson**'s two-act **Irish** farce was written and first performed in 1851 for comic **actor*† Barney Williams**, who played the title character, based on an anonymous poem about a bumptious Irishman. This was one of many such plays inspired by Irish folklore and literature aimed at Irish immigrant audiences in mid-19th-century American theater.

BRIAR CLIFF; OR, SCENES OF THE REVOLUTION. First performed on 15 June 1826, George Pope Morris's five-act tragedy, produced by **Henry Wallack** at the **Chatham Garden Theatre**, was based on the novel *Whig and Tory*. Mary Jansen, the daughter of a loyalist family during the **American Revolution**, is in love with Alfred Leslie, played by **John Duff**, an American soldier fighting for independence. Alfred is captured but cannot be persuaded to return to loyalty to the crown, even for Mary's sake. She helps Alfred escape, and he hides out for a time in the cave residence of Crazy Bet (played by **Mary Ann Duff**). Mary is kidnapped by another of her suitors, an English officer named Waldron, who hides her on a British sloop. She is subsequently rescued by friendly **Native Americans*†** and reunited with Alfred. However, Waldron shoots her in a jealous rage, and she dies in Alfred's arms. The play remained a popular one for decades.

THE BRIDE OF GENOA. **Epes Sargent**'s 1836 five-act historical tragedy was written and first produced under the title *The Genoese* (and published under that title in 1855) for **Josephine Clifton**, who appeared as the play's historical character, Antonio Montaldo. The play opened on 13 February 1837 at Boston's **Tremont Theatre**, followed by a production at New York's **Park Theatre starring*† Charlotte Cushman** in the role of Laura, where it opened on 18 November 1837. Set during the Plebian revolt in Genoa in 1393, it recounts incidents in the life of Montaldo, who ultimately became the Doge of Genoa.

*†BROADWAY. This prominent avenue in New York City runs the length of Manhattan Island from north to south. As early as 1735, a map depicts a playhouse on this street, but not until the late 19th century did Broadway come to represent the New York theater (and, in fact, the American theater) as a whole. As an increasing number of theaters were built in the decades just before the **Civil War**, many were on Broadway or nearby, but closer to the south end of Manhattan Island than would ultimately be the case.

Theaters in the vicinity of 14th Street and Broadway were the center of the theatrical universe in the mid-19th century, but by the mid-20th century, most of the theatrical action had moved up to 40th Street and a dozen blocks north of it, where Broadway stands in the early 21st century. Theater buildings came and went from the 18th through the 20th centuries—and names changed, usually to honor great **stars***† or **playwrights**,*† and, by the late 20th century, **producers***† or corporations—but Broadway remained in essentially the same neighborhood, surrounding Times Square (in earlier times, known as Longacre Square).

Broadway was also known in the early 20th century as "The Great White Way"† because of the electric **lighting***† illuminating theaters and businesses along that street in the late 19th century. Despite the thriving **road***† as well as resident **stock***† theaters established in various regions, a producer, playwright, **actor**,*† or **designer***† was not considered to have succeeded without work on Broadway. Eventually, after the mid-20th century, Off-Broadway* and Off-Off-Broadway* theaters proliferated (most south of the Times Square area) and many were reinvented or found spaces (warehouses, storefronts, etc.), and though Broadway theaters remained proscenium spaces, many Off- and Off-Off-Broadway theaters moved to arena or environmental use of the available space, radically changing the ways in which theater is conceived. However, though Broadway is no longer where the American theater is being made, as it once was, it still symbolically represents theater at its most iconic.

BROADWAY THEATRE. Built in 1847, this 4,500-seat theater, often called "the Old Broadway," situated at 326–328 Broadway, had a relatively short life, housed few successes, and was torn down a mere 12 years after being built. Among its **attractions**,† **Edwin Forrest** appeared in *Macbeth* there in 1849. At various times, other theaters used the name, including Euterpean Hall at 410 Broadway, renamed in 1837, but torn down that same year; a former Unitarian Church at 728 Broadway, opened in 1865 and destroyed by fire in 1884; **Brougham**'s Lyceum at 485 Broadway, built in 1850 and known as "The Broadway" in the late 1860s, but torn down in 1869; a converted museum at 1221 Broadway that was operated by **Augustin Daly**† as "The Broadway Theatre" from 1879 to 1899, after which it was a **vaudeville**† and film† theater until it was demolished in 1920; and the Broadway Theatre at 1445 Broadway at 41st Street, which was built in 1888 and demolished in 1929.

THE BROKER OF BOGOTA. **Robert Montgomery Bird**'s five-act blank verse tragedy, **starring***† **Edwin Forrest**, gave its first performance on 12 February 1834 at the **Bowery Theatre**. Forrest played Batista Febro, who unhappily disinherits his favored son, Ramon, who has fallen in with unsavory friends. Ramon's engagement to Juana, daughter of the viceroy of New Granada, is called off due to the loss of his estate and his father's approval. Ramon is convinced by a wastrel friend to rob and frame his scrupulously honest father, who is convicted of the crime. Juana learns of Ramon's scheme and angrily confronts him, causing the young man to kill himself in remorse. Batista is cleared of the crime, but his son's betrayal and suicide cause his death from grief.

Forrest wrote to Bird following the first performance that *The Broker of Bogota* "was performed and crowned with entire success" and that the play "will live when our vile trunks are rotten." It became one of Forrest's sturdiest vehicles, and he appeared in it frequently for the remainder of his career, even as his popularity waned.

THE BROOK; OR, A JOLLY DAY AT THE PICNIC. This farcical play by **Nate Salsbury**,† who produced it with his troupe, the Salsbury Troubadors, debuted at San Francisco **Minstrels***† Hall on 12 May 1879. Simply depicting friends on a picnic singing, dancing, and performing comic bits, presumably for their own amusement,† this play has been identified as an early prototype of a **musical***† theater structure.

Its timing was fortuitous, appearing when **operetta**,† via **Gilbert and Sullivan**'s *H.M.S. Pinafore*, had premiered in New York, and **Edward Harrigan**† and **Tony Hart**† were scoring their first successes with the Mulligan Guards musicals. These and other works provided varied approaches to combining music and story and encouraged the taste of American audiences for such entertainments.† Previous to presenting *The Brook*, Salsbury had written *Patchwork* (1875), a similar idea that did not achieve the sort of success *The Brook* found. Contemporary **critics***† found *The Brook* devoid of plot and character development, but labeled a "farce-comedy," it was widely praised as amusing despite these deficiencies.

BROOKLYN ACADEMY OF MUSIC. In 1861, the first Brooklyn Academy of Music building opened at 176–194 Montague Street in Brooklyn Heights, with a mission of providing a place for the finest American and **international***† musicians. The larger of the two halls in the facility seated 2,200, with a smaller hall and supporting spaces. Designed by **architect***† Leopold Eidlitz, the building soon provided a venue to outstanding theater artists, including **Edwin Booth**,† Ellen Terry and Henry Irving, and **Tommaso Salvini**,† as well as orators and literary figures such as **Mark Twain** and Booker T. Washington. The building was destroyed by **fire**† on 30 November 1903, but a new facility bearing the same name, with a new location on Lafayette Avenue, opened in 1906 and continues to function in the 21st century with an emphasis on progressive and avant-garde performance while maintaining its original commitment to international artists.

BROUGHAM, JOHN (1814–1880). Born in Dublin, Ireland, John Brougham planned to study medicine at Dublin University, but while there he performed in plays for **amusement**.† A visit to London in 1830, where he became acquainted with **Madame Vestris**, led to his debut in *Tom and Jerry* that year. He wrote his first play, a **burlesque**,*† for Vestris, and worked with **Dion Boucicault**† on *London Assurance*, scoring a success in the role of Dazzle.

For a time, beginning in 1840, Brougham served as **manager***† of London's Lyceum Theatre, but eventually traveled to America, where he made his debut in *His Last Legs* in 1842 at the **Park Theatre** and, subsequently, became a popular comic **actor***† in a range of contemporary plays in the companies of **William E. Burton** and **James W. Wallack**. He also wrote comedies including *Irish Yankee*†*; or, The Birthday of Freedom* (1842) and a burlesque parody of **John Augustus Stone**'s *Metamora; or, The Last of the Wampanoags* called *Met-a-mora; or, The Last of the Pollywogs* (1847). He managed **Niblo's Garden** for a time, after which he opened Brougham's Lyceum in 1850 and managed the **Bowery Theatre**, neither with much success.

Brougham is believed to have written over 120 plays in virtually every genre, from burlesque (*Po-ca-hon-tas; or, The Gentle Savage* [1855] and *Much Ado About the Merchant of Venice* [1869]) and **melodrama**† (*The Duke's Motto; or, I Am Here* [1863]) to sentimental **Irish** plays (*Take Care of Little Charlie* [1858]), literary adaptations (*Dombey and Son* [1848], *Jane Eyre* [1849], and *Vanity Fair* [1849]), and social satires (*The Game of Love* [1856]). During the **Civil War**, he worked in England, after which he devoted himself to acting at the **Winter Garden** and in **Augustin Daly**'s† company, though he never regained the popularity he had prior to the **war**.*† He opened Brougham's Theatre in 1869, but it was a failure, and his final stage appearance came in Boucicault's *Felix O'Reilly* (1879).

BROWN, DAVID PAUL (1795–1872). Born in Philadelphia, David Paul Brown studied medicine, but the death of his mentor led him to law and, ultimately, to the Pennsylvania Supreme Court. Though his life was devoted almost entirely to the law and politics, he wrote on numerous topics, including the law, speeches on contemporary issues, and eulogies, as well as fictional works. He is considered a member of the Philadelphia School of Dramatists, though he seems only to have written four plays, including a historical tragedy, *Sertorius; or, The Roman Patriot* (1830), which provided a vehicle for **Junius Brutus Booth**, and the romantic drama *The Prophet of St. Paul's* (1836), both of which were performed, and a tragedy, *The Trial*, and a farce, *Love and Honor; or, The Generous Soldier*, which were not. Among his varied writings, *Sketches of the Life and Genius of Shakespeare**† (1838) was the only other work with an emphasis on the stage.

BROWN, T. ALLSTON (1836–1918). Born Thomas Allston Brown in Newburyport, Massachusetts, he began his theater career as a **critic*†** in Philadelphia and New York, where he wrote for the *New York Clipper*. He also founded his own theatrical newspaper, *The Tatler*, in 1859, and ultimately became drama editor of *The Clipper*, from 1864 to 1870. In 1860, Brown became tightrope walker and acrobat **Charles Blondin**'s **manager*†** and a well-known theatrical **agent*†** and **advance man†** for **circuses**.*† His long career as a manager continued to shortly before his death, but he also gained recognition as a theater historian for his *History of the American Stage: 1733–1870* (1870) and *History of the New York Stage: From the First Performance in 1732 to 1901* (1903).

BROWN, WILLIAM HENRY (1815–1884). A native of the West Indies, William Henry Brown arrived in New York in the mid-1810s after retiring as a steamship steward. He settled in a free black community in lower Manhattan, where in 1816 he founded the African Company, the first known black theater troupe in the United States. Brown set the theater up at a house on New York's Thomas Street, where he produced a range of light entertainments† in a tea garden and succeeded in attracting large audiences since blacks were otherwise banned from New York theaters.

In 1821, Brown moved operations to a two-story house at Mercer and Bleeker Streets, naming it the **African Grove Theatre**. The theater opened on 21 September 1821 with *Richard III*, followed by a range of plays, including ***Tom and Jerry; or, Life in London***, *The Poor Soldier*, *Othello*, *Don Juan*, and *Obi; or, Three-Finger'd Jack*. Brown is also credited with authoring the first **African American*†** play, ***The Drama of King Shotaway*** (1823), which was based on the 1796 Black Carib insurrection on St. Vincent Island in the West Indies against the English and French (the play is believed lost).

Brown's theater profited from the talents of two **actors*†**—**James Hewlett** and **Ira Aldridge**—who gained skill performing **Shakespearean*†** plays by observing European actors in productions at the **Park Theatre**. Harassed by white **managers**,*† and after the theater burned in 1823 under suspicious circumstances, Brown is believed to have operated a theater in Albany, New York, though little else is known about him.

BROWN, WILLIAM HILL (1765–1793). Born in Boston as the son of a clockmaker, William Hill Brown was educated at a boys' school and suffered from ill health for most of his short life. Brown wrote *The Power of Sympathy; or, The Triumph of Nature Founded in Truth* (1789), considered the first American novel, as well as essays, poetry, and plays. His dramatic works included the tragedy *West Point Preserved* (1797), one of several plays about British spy Major John André, and the comedy of manners, *The Better Sort; or, A Girl of Spirit.*

BROWN, WILLIAM WELLS (1814–1884). Son of an **African American*** mother in slavery and her white owner, George W. Higgins, William Wells Brown was born in Lexington, where his father acknowledged him as his son. However, Brown was sold to various others and in 1833 unsuccessfully attempted escape. The following year he did escape and eventually settled in Buffalo, where he actively participated in aiding the underground railroad,† helping innumerable slaves escape to Canada. Brown lectured on abolition in the United States and England and wrote on the subject as well during the 1840s and 1850s.

In 1847, Brown published *Narrative of William W. Brown, a Fugitive Slave, Written by Himself,* which condemned slavery and indicted the use of violence in master-slave relationships; it was a best seller. He also lectured on **temperance**, and during the 1850s, he wrote novels and two plays. Brown's importance to theater history results from his 1858 play, *The Escape; or, A Leap for Freedom,* which is considered the first published play by an African American. His other known play, *Experience; or, How to Give a Northern Man a Backbone* (1856), was not published and is believed lost. Brown also wrote fiction, including *Clotel; or, The President's Daughter: A Narrative of Slave Life in the United States* (1853), the first novel by an African American published in the United States, and nonfiction works; and he recruited black soldiers to fight in the **Civil War**.

BROWNE, JAMES S. (1791–1869). English-born comedian James S. Browne arrived in America in 1838, settled in New York, and by the 1840s was performing as a popular comic at the **Chatham Garden Theatre**. Browne originated the title role in Charles Selby's *Robert Macaire* in the United States. He gained a reputation for living well—too well, perhaps, since he died penniless.

BRUTUS; OR, THE FALL OF TARQUIN. Contemporary **critics***† consider this **John Howard Payne**'s finest play, and it became a sturdy vehicle for tragic **actors**,*† including England's **Edmund Kean**, as well as **Edwin Forrest**, **Junius Brutus Booth**, **Edwin Booth**,† and **James W. Wallack**. The five-act tragedy premiered on 3 December 1818 at London's Drury Lane Theatre, followed by its American debut on 15 March 1819 at the **Park Theatre**.

James Pritchard appeared in the title role as Lucius Junius, a Roman noble-man whose family has been violently deposed from their prominence by the Tarquins. He manages to escape by pretending to be insane, leading to his becoming court jester for the Tarquins, crowned with the mocking name of Brutus by Tullia (**Mrs. Barnes**), the Tarquin queen. The rape of Lucretia, a senator's wife, by a Tarquin prince, causes Lucius to abandon his disguise to lead a Roman revolt. Sadly, Lucius's son, Titus, in love with a Tarquin princess, finds himself in opposition to his father. When Lucius and the Romans prevail, Lucius, as a defender of justice, must sadly sentence his son to death.

Kean, who had originated the title role in England, played it again in the United States during a **tour**.*† For Americans, the play's popularity, despite predominantly negative critical response to Payne's language and tech-niques, stemmed from Payne's efforts to depict the society moving from monarchy to a kind of freedom as a republic.

BRYANT, DAN (1833–1875). Banjo-playing **blackface**† singer Dan Bryant was born in Troy, New York, as Daniel Webster O'Brien and went on the stage as a dancer. In 1849, he made his adult debut with the **minstrel**† troupe the Sable Harmonists, followed by his first New York appearance with Charles White's Minstrels in 1851. He performed with several minstrel troupes, including Losee's Minstrels and Campbell's Minstrels, partnered with his brothers Jerry (1828–1861) and Neil (1835–1902). The brothers established their own company, **Bryant's Minstrels**, which gave its first performance on 23 February 1857 at New York's Mechanics' Hall, which became their usual venue. In 1859, Bryant's Minstrels introduced **Dan Emmett**'s "Dixie Land"; with its title ultimately shortened to "Dixie," it was soon to become the anthem of the Confederate States of America during the **Civil War**. Throughout the Civil War era, Bryant's Minstrels became known as one of the best and most successful minstrel troupes, only truly challenged by **Christy's Minstrels**.

Bryant was an adept minstrel performer, but was rare among his peers in also appearing successfully in mostly **Irish** plays, such as *Handy Andy* (1863), *The Irish Emigrant* (1864), *Born to Good Luck* (1865), and *Shamus O'Brien* (1866), as well as two by **Dion Boucicault**,† *The Colleen Bawn* (1864) and *Arrah-na-Pogue* (1867). Despite the death of Jerry in 1861, Dan and Neil continued performing until 1875, when Dan's death, along with changing entertainment† tastes, threatened the company's survival. Neil pressed on for seven additional years, but by the early 1880s Bryant's Min-strels shut down, one of several major developments that led to the decline of blackface minstrelsy in America.

BRYANT'S MINSTRELS. *See* BRYANT, DAN (1833–1875).

BUCHANAN, MCKEAN (1823–1872). Born in Philadelphia, son of a Navy paymaster, McKean Buchanan spent three years in the navy before making his stage debut in New Orleans as Hamlet. He was well received, but when he presented himself in the role in New York in 1850, he was not successful. Specializing in **Shakespearean***† tragic roles, including Hamlet, Macbeth, and Othello, Buchanan **toured***† widely with his company, including his daughter, **Virginia Buchanan**, who played Ophelia and Desdemona.

Never successful with New York audiences, Buchanan confined much of his career to touring in the West. For some, Buchanan became the embodiment of a bombastic acting style that was falling out of favor by the mid-19th century. Despite this, Buchanan remained committed to his acting style, which led to the ultimate decline of his career. **Mark Twain** noted Buchanan's problems when he wrote of a Buchanan performance he attended: "The great McKean Buchanan having been driven from all the world's great cities many years ago, still keeps up a pitiless persecution of the provinces, ranting with undiminished fury before audiences composed of one sad **manager**,*† one malignant reporter, and a Sheriff waiting to collect the license, and still pushes his crusade from village to village, strewing his disastrous wake with the corpses of country theatres."

BUCHANAN, VIRGINIA (1846–1931). The daughter of a noted **Shakespearean***† actor,*† **McKean Buchanan**, Virginia Ellen Buchanan was born in Cincinnati. She worked closely with her father, playing Desdemona and Ophelia opposite his Othello and Hamlet, among others. She also appeared in **stock***† for many years in contemporary American and British plays. Buchanan scored a particular success as Margaret Dalrymple in *Our Boarding House* (1877) and appeared with the **Madison Square Theatre** Company. When **Tommaso Salvini**† appeared in America, she performed with him in his established **repertory**,* and she also appeared with such American **actors***† as **Henry E. Dixey**, **John Drew**,† Charles Dickson, Ethel Barrymore,*† and James K. Hackett,† among others.

BUCKLEY'S SERENADERS. Established by George Swayne Buckley, Frederick Buckley, and R. Bishop Buckley in 1853, this **blackface**† **minstrel**† company was the most important in the United States prior to the **Civil War**, though an extended **tour***† in England permitted the troupe of **Edwin P. Christy** to ultimately gain predominance. In residence in New York City as much as half of each year, Buckley's Serenaders performed there at a

theater on **Broadway***† they called Buckley's **Opera House** or the Ethiopian Opera House. When in New York, they performed sans blackface, but
used it on extended tours.

George Swayne Buckley was a gifted musician, and at times while in New
York, the company performed serious religious music, but their reputation
was based on their performance of contemporary popular music typical of the
minstrel canon—and for comedy and **burlesques**.*† Buckley's Serenaders
disbanded during the **Civil War** for several reasons, not least a change in
local laws resulting from the Concert Saloon Bill of 1862, banning a combination of entertainment† with the serving of alcohol by female waitresses.

THE BUCKTAILS; OR, AMERICANS IN ENGLAND. James Kirke
Paulding's comedy, written shortly after the conclusion of the **War of 1812**,
but not published until 1847, focuses on British disdain for the rough and
uncivilized American personality in its plot, simply another example of the
contrast between the Old and New Worlds frequently examined in theater
from the **American Revolution** to the **Civil War**. The plot is a simple one in
which a young American girl visiting England is wooed by English courtiers.
She is initially dazzled by the opulence and pretensions she finds, only to
ultimately realize the hollowness of the decadence and accept the young
American she has loved all along. Paulding, a die-hard nativist, used this
comedy as a vehicle through which to condemn what he viewed as the
overbearing influence of English culture on American life, the subject of
much of his writing. The play appeared in print in an era in which the
tensions he writes about were coming to a head, ending in tragedy in the
Astor Place Opera House riot.

BUFFALO BILL. *See* †CODY, WILLIAM FREDERICK ("BUFFALO
BILL") (1846–1917).

BULL RUN; OR, THE SACKING OF FAIRFAX COURTHOUSE.
Charles Gayler's drama centered on the Battle of Bull Run during the **Civil
War** opened on 15 August 1861 at the New **Bowery Theatre** a mere three
weeks after the actual battle took place. The cast, including **George C. Boniface**, performed the play for a four-week unbroken run, and during the season it was frequently brought back. The prolific Gayler, who is believed to
have written well over 100 plays in every conceivable genre, made a specialty of bringing timely topics to the stage in the immediate wake of the event
itself, as in this case.

BULLS AND BEARS. **Bartley Campbell**'s four-act 1875 comedy based on Gustav von Moser's German comedy *Ultimo* competed with **Augustin Daly**'s *The Big Bonanza* (1875), which made use of the same source. With its references to Wall Street excesses, audiences appreciated the play when it opened at San Francisco's Dickinson's Grand Opera House in 1875, and it made a profit of $16,000 in four weeks. Despite the popularity of Daly's *The Big Bonanza*, Campbell's play was frequently produced for the remainder of the 19th century.

BULWER-LYTTON, EDWARD. *See* LYTTON, EDWARD BULWER- (1803–1873).

BUNCE, OLIVER BELL (1828–1890). New York–born Oliver Bell Bunce found his initial success in theater with a rural comedy, *The Morning of Life* (1848), but his **producer,***† **James W. Wallack**, followed it with Bunce's drama *Marco Bozzaris; or, The Green Hero* (1850), which failed. Bunce won most acclaim for *Love in '76: An Incident of the Revolution* (1857), a comic romance set during the **American Revolution**. He wrote drama **criticism,***† as well as essays, novels, and short stories, and served as editor of *Appleton's Post* beginning in 1872.

BUNKER-HILL; OR, THE DEATH OF GENERAL WARREN. **John Daly Burk**'s five-act historical tragedy was produced in Boston's Haymarket Theatre on 17 February 1797. The intention to depict the 1775 Battle of Bunker Hill met with approval from audiences, and the death of General Joseph Warren in the battle, which had been immortalized in a painting by John Trumbull, was a subject of great interest to Boston audiences 20 years after the fact. When the play was staged in New York, President John Adams was in attendance. At the play's end, Adams was escorted by the theater **managers***† and players to his carriage. When an **actor***† asked Adams for his opinion of the play, Adams replied, "Sir, my friend General Warren was a scholar and a gentleman, but your author has made him a bully and a blackguard."

†**BURGESS, NEIL (1846–1910).** Born in Boston, Neil Burgess began his stage career as a variety performer, but found his niche as a **female impersonator,**† namely essaying old "widders" in **legitimate**† drama. He made his first such appearance in 1865, at the age of 19, covering for an indisposed **actress***† in *The Quiet Family* in a theater in Providence, Rhode Island. His most acclaimed characters were in the title role of *Widow Bedott*† (1880) and Aunt Abby Prue in *The County Fair*† (1889).

BURK, JOHN DALY (1775?–1808). **Irish**-born John Daly Burk attended Dublin's Trinity College. As a newspaperman in Boston, Burk served as editor for the *Polar Star* beginning around 1796. In New York, he wrote for *The Time-Piece*, not long after his play *Bunker-Hill; or, The Death of General Warren* (1797) premiered at Boston's Haymarket Theatre. The play was not well received, though a later work, *Female Patriotism; or, The Death of Joan D'Arc* (1798), was well-regarded. He was arrested on sedition charges in New York, so he settled in Virginia in 1798. Though a few other plays were attributed to him, the only certain Burk work is a Gothic tragedy, *Bethlem Gabor, Lord of Transylvania; or, The Man-Hating Palatine* (1807). Burk himself was a member of the cast in its first production, but his life was cut short when he was killed in a duel.

BURKE, CHARLES (1822–1854). Born Charles Saint Thomas Burke in Philadelphia, he performed as a **child**† prodigy, but as an adult he played comic roles, most frequently in **burlesque**,*† though he also won approval as **Rip Van Winkle** and Solon Shingle in *The People's Lawyer*. In 1848–1849, Burke served as **manager***† of the **Chatham Garden Theatre**. Burke's premature death in his early 30s was much lamented by his contemporaries, and as **William Winter**† wrote in his *Life and Art of Joseph Jefferson*,† Burke "was pre-eminently a man of genius in the dramatic art; his temperament so dream-like and drifting, and his experience so sad, that he neither made a rightfully ample impression on his own period, nor left an adequate memory to ours."

BURKE, JOSEPH (1818–1902). A **child**† prodigy billed as "Master Burke, The **Irish** Roscius," Joseph Burke was born in Ireland and performed a range of adult roles from **Shakespeare***† (Richard III, Shylock) and contemporary plays, as well as demonstrations of his musicianship, playing the violin and conducting orchestras. He first performed in the United States in 1830 and for a time was extremely popular with audiences. Unlike most child prodigies, his career did not end with his childhood, and he continued to play the violin in concert settings.

*†BURLESQUE/TRAVESTIES. Most commonly understood today as a bump-and-grind entertainment† featuring strippers and comics, burlesque in the 19th century derived from 18th-century **travesties** (parodies) of well-known works. This spilled into **minstrel**† shows, which often featured burlesques of other stage forms and popular songs, and into **vaudeville**† and **musicals**.*† Sometime in the mid-19th century, due in part to the runaway

success of *The Black Crook* (1866), which featured a chorus line of ballerinas in revealing pink **fleshings**,† and **Lydia Thompson**'s† British Blondes,
the more recent form of burlesque began to evolve.

When **Tony Pastor**† and B. F. Keith† attempted to rid vaudeville of its
more salacious elements, those entertainments found their way into burlesque theaters, thus creating a clear separation between family-oriented
vaudeville bills and increasingly risqué burlesque shows. Burlesque ultimately became the realm of strippers and low comedians in the early 20th century
until it died out entirely by the 1960s.

BURNETT, ALF (1825–1884). Born Alfred Burnett in Utica, New York,
Alf Burnett worked as a reporter and sometime **actor***† prior to achieving
success in **vaudeville**† as a humorist, comic elocutionist, and mimic.

BURTON, WILLIAM EVANS (1804–1860). London-born **actor**,*† **manager**,*† and **playwright***† William Evans Burton was the son of a publisher
and planned a career in the clergy before joining an **amateur***† theatrical
group with the aim of becoming a tragic actor. However, it became apparent
from the start that his strengths were as a comic. In 1834, and often billed as
Billy Burton, he moved to the United States, making his debut at the **Arch
Street Theatre** in Philadelphia in *The Poor Gentleman*. He made his New
York debut in 1837, but for a decade remained mostly in Philadelphia.

In 1848, Burton opened Burton's Chambers Street Theatre, which specialized in comic plays, **burlesques**,*† and adaptations of novels. Burton frequently appeared, generating particularly positive response for his performances in *Dombey and Son*, adapted by **John Brougham** from **Charles
Dickens**, and his own play, *The Toodles*. Demonstrating versatility, Burton
also staged several **Shakespearean***† plays. He gave up his theater in 1856,
but continued to work in various other theaters. In the late 1830s, Burton
commenced a publishing career with the *Gentleman's Magazine*, followed
by several others, and he wrote plays, including *The Toodles*, and sketches.

BUSH, FRANK (1856?–1927). Born Benjamin Franklin Bush, he began his
career performing a range of ethnic stereotypes, including **Irish** characters,
but it was as a broadly Jewish caricature that Frank Bush found an audience.
He was a longtime **vaudeville**† favorite, with frequent appearances at **Tony
Pastor**'s,† among other venues. Audiences and **critics***† alike appreciated
Bush's skill, as a critic for New York's *Spirit of the Times* wrote in 1896,
when Bush appeared at the **Fourteenth Street Theatre** in *Girl Wanted*. This
vehicle, written to supply Bush ample opportunities to display his versatility,
allowed him to appear "as a **Yankee**† farmer, a German girl, a Bowery
waiter, a Jew, an Irishman and a prima donna." Over time, Bush's ethnic

portrayals, particularly the Jewish character, became offensive in its gross stereotyping, compelling Bush to make changes, although by the 1910s, the audience for ethnic humor was dwindling.

BUSINESS. *See also* †LINES OF BUSINESS.

†BYRON, OLIVER DOUD (1842–1920). Born in Frederick, Maryland, the tragedian Oliver Doud Byron made his debut as a schoolboy in *Nicholas Nickleby* with **Joseph Jefferson**'s† company in Baltimore in 1856. He also performed with **James W. Wallack, John Wilkes Booth,**† and **Edwin Booth,**† alternating in the roles of Othello and Iago with the latter Booth. Byron had his greatest popular success as virtuous Joe Ferris in **James J. McCloskey**'s *Across the Continent* (1871). George Odell recalled Byron's performance in this **melodrama**† as a "manly, wholesome, resourceful characterization that pleased **women***† and men alike." Byron married Kate Crehan, the sister of **Ada Rehan,**† and his son, Arthur Byron,† became a noted **actor.***†

C

CAIUS MARIUS. **Richard Penn Smith**'s five-act blank verse tragedy opened on 12 January 1831 at the **Arch Street Theatre** in Philadelphia with **Edwin Forrest** in the title role. Caius is seen as a Roman general who has risen from the lower class to a position of great power. However, Caius runs afoul of two former friends, Sylla and Metellus, who aided his rise. Ultimately, Caius is compelled to fight both former friends. He kills Metellus and, finally, as Sylla's army is poised to attack at Rome's border, Caius and his adoring slave girl, Martha, drink poison.

The initial production was not a success, and Forrest eventually dropped it from his repertoire. In 1858, **F. B. Conway** led a cast in two performances celebrating the life of Smith, who had died a few years earlier. The play, which had been inspired not only by the historical record of Caius Marius, was also influenced by Thomas Otway's *The History and Fall of Caius Marius* (1680).

CALAYNOS. First staged at London's Sadler's Wells Theatre on 10 May 1849 with Samuel Phelps in the title role, *Calaynos*, a five-act tragedy by **George Henry Boker** (his first play), had a long run there. *Calaynos* made its American debut on 20 January 1851 at the **Walnut Street Theatre starring*†** **James E. Murdoch**. A wealthy Spanish nobleman, Calaynos, receives a summons to Seville by the king of Spain. He goes, leaving his wife, Dona Alda, behind. In Seville, Calaynos befriends the dissolute Don Luis, whom he brings home from Seville. Don Luis falls in love with Dona Alda and attempts to seduce her. When he discovers that Calaynos has Moorish ancestry, Don Luis presents this news to Dona Alda. She faints, and Don Luis carries her off to Seville. She ultimately returns to Calaynos, but dies shortly thereafter, leading Calaynos to duel with Don Luis, whom he kills. Calaynos is also wounded in the duel and dies.

CALDWELL, JAMES H. (1793–1863). An English-born **actor,*†** James H. Caldwell arrived in the United States and made his debut in Charleston in *The West Indian* in 1816. His New York debut came in 1828 in the same play. Despite success as an actor, Caldwell transitioned by the early 1840s into a builder and **manager***† of new theaters in several cities, most notably New Orleans, where he managed the St. Philip Street Theatre and the American Theatre, installing **gas lighting***† in the latter, as well as building the **St. Charles Street Theatre** in 1835. He also built or managed theaters in several other cities, including Cincinnati, Ohio; Nashville, Tennessee; St. Louis, Missouri; Natchez, Mississippi; Petersburg, Virginia; and Mobile, Alabama, among others. After retiring from theater work, Caldwell held several civic positions in New Orleans.

CALIFORNIA THEATRE. Opened in 1869, the California Theatre at 414 Bush Street in San Francisco was built by banker William Ralston, who admired the **actors***† **John McCullough** and **Lawrence Barrett** and wanted to showcase them in a worthy playhouse. The theater officially opened on 18 January 1869 with a production of **Edward Bulwer-Lytton**'s *Money*, a prophetic title for a venture that succeeded beyond Ralston's best hopes. Along with plays, the theater also presented concert artists and opera. The theater operated successfully until it was demolished in 1888 to make way for the new California Theatre, which opened in 1889 and operated until it was destroyed in the San Francisco earthquake and **fire**† of 1906.

CAMILLE. See THE LADY OF THE CAMELLIAS.

†**CAMPBELL, BARTLEY (1843–1888).** The son of **Irish** immigrants, Bartley Thomas Campbell was born in Pittsburgh, where he began his working life as a newspaper reporter for the *Pittsburgh Post*. He moved to the *Pittsburgh Leader* as drama **critic**,*† but quit journalism with the successful production of his 1871 play, *Through Fire*. Campbell developed his skill as a writer of **melodrama**† at **Hooley's Theatre** in Chicago, and some scholars suggest he or **Bronson Howard**† were the first American **playwrights***† to earn a living exclusively writing plays. Campbell discovered his affinity for the West on a **tour***† there, which inspired his best plays, notably *My Partner*† (1879) and *The White Slave*† (1882). His other plays include *Peril; or, Love at Long Branch* (1872), *Risks, or Insure Your Life* (1873; co-authored with **actor***† John Dillon), *The Virginian* (1874), and *Bulls and Bears* (1875), which **Augustin Daly**† produced under the title *The Big Bonanza* and which critic **William Winter**† condemned as "four acts of hopeless commonplace in which there is not one spark of wit, not one bright thought, not even a gleam of smartness." Despite this pan, the play ran a year.

Campbell's later plays included *The Galley Slave* (1879), *Siberia*† (1883), and his last, *Paquita* (1885). Long hailed as a major playwright, Campbell's ventures as a **producer***† were less successful. He was declared insane as a result of paresis in 1886 and died two years later in a Middletown, New York, asylum. **Frances Wilson**† recalled that Campbell's stationery featured busts of **Shakespeare***† and himself adorned with the inscription "A friendly contest for supremacy."

THE CANDIDATES; OR, THE HUMOURS OF A VIRGINIA ELEC-TION. Colonel **Robert Munford**, at various times the sheriff and burgess for Mecklenburg County, Virginia, wrote this three-act comedy, his first play, in 1770. Its plot is a simple one, focused on the efforts of a fictional county selecting its two burgesses. As scholar Jack P. Greene writes of *The Candidates*, "Munford was trying to prescribe how an election should turn out rather than to describe one that actually happened." The play was not published until 1798, 15 years after Munford's death.

CARABASSET; OR, THE LAST OF THE NORRIDGEWOCKS. **Nathaniel Deering**'s five-act tragedy defends the leader of the Maine Norridgewock Indians, a sect of Abenakis, an Algonquin tribe. The play, written in 1830, was staged at the Portland (Maine) Theatre in 1831, and is in most respects a stereotypical depiction of Indian savagery, despite the **playwright**'s*† sympathy for the murdered chief Carabasset.

CARNCROSS, JOHN L. (1834–1911). Born in Philadelphia, John L. Carncross, a highly influential figure in the history of **minstrel***† shows, spent much of his career at the Eleventh Street **Opera House** in his hometown. He made his debut in 1858 with **Sanford's Minstrels**, winning approval for his tenor voice, and he appeared with them until 1860, when he formed a partnership with Sam Sharpley to establish the Carncross and Sharpley Minstrels. Within two years, Carncross and Sharpley parted ways and the troupe became the Carncross and Dixey Minstrels, as a result of a new partnership with E. F. Dixey. Among his minstrel show innovations, a greater emphasis was placed on music, and the elimination of vulgar and suggestive material allowed the troupe to present itself as family oriented. The Carncross and Dixey Minstrels became the most celebrated in Philadelphia until Dixey retired in 1878, after which Carncross continued on his own with Carncross's Minstrels until his retirement in 1896.

CARR, BENJAMIN (1768?–1836). Born in London, Benjamin Carr studied **musical***† composition before leaving England for America in 1793. As an **actor***† in Philadelphia and New York through the rest of the 1790s, he settled in Philadelphia, where he became a leading figure in the music scene.

He wrote ballads and ballet music, but his score for the opera *The Archers* (1796), set to a libretto by **William Dunlap** based on Friedrich Schiller's *William Tell*, is considered the first true opera written in America.

CARR, MARY (c. 1790s–c. 1830s). Born in Philadelphia, Mary Carr lived there and in New York and worked to earn her living as a writer, a near impossible task in her era. After the death of her husband, who was in the military during the **War of 1812**, Carr needed a means of supporting herself and her children. She wrote for periodicals, edited a weekly magazine, ghost-wrote biographies, composed songs and poems, and worked as a theater critic.*† An association with Philadelphia's **Chestnut Street Theatre** led to the production, probably on 6 January 1815, of her comedy *The Return from Camp*, later published (and possibly revised) as *The Fair Americans*. The play depicted two rural families near Lake Erie at the start of the War of 1812. Recruiters come for the available men, so **women***† are left to manage farms, which they do, gaining new strengths and skills in the process. Sophia and Anna, two of the women, are kidnapped by Indians as the men go through similar struggles while the **war***† rages on. Eventually the men return, and the two worlds of the play are reconnected with one major change: the women are now equal partners with the men.

One other Carr play is extant, the **melodrama**† *The Benevolent Lawyers; or, Villainy† Detected*, about a virtuous wife whose sea captain husband is delayed in his return from a voyage, leaving her virtue to be threatened by a villainous figure. Her most successful play, *Sara Maria Cornell; or, The Fall River Murder* (1823), was published in 1833 following a lengthy run at the Richmond Hill Theatre. It deals with the sensational murder of a young woman factory worker.

†**CASTING.** From the 18th century until well into the 19th, casting was a matter handled by the particular theater or **manager**,*† who usually engaged **actors***† to perform a kind of role (i.e., **ingénue**,*† **leading man**,† etc.). As longer runs and the **combination**† system became the norm in the decades following the **Civil War**, the old practice of casting according to **lines of business**† declined. Managers were less inclined to prize the versatility of the **stock***† company actor who could perform a variety of roles in repertory,† nor was possession of a theatrical wardrobe† essential for an actor seeking to join a company. As the repertoire† itself evolved from historical **melodrama**† toward **realism***† during the late 19th century, casting became far more specific to the needs of the individual play than was typical of the stock company model of actors being assigned according to the types of roles they typically played from one play to the next. In any event, casting became more and more specific to a given role in a single play.

THE CATARACT OF THE GANGES; OR, THE RAJAH'S DAUGHTER.
W. T. Moncrieff's **equestrian**† two-act **melodrama**† premiered at London's Drury Lane Theatre on 27 October 1823, a year before its American production at the **Park Theatre** in 1824. The play's success depended on its theatrical spectacle, most notably a scene in which the heroine, Zamine, makes her escape on horseback, leaping over a waterfall in the process. In the plot, Zamine, a female child of the rajah, is raised as a prince. When a war comes, to settle it the opposing Brahmin leader offers the hand of his daughter to the young prince. When the ruse is revealed, the Brahmin insists that Zamine either marry him or face execution. Zamine's escape on horseback, aided by her father, takes her up the cataract of the Ganges to safety. Contemporary **critics***† praised this stunt and the scenic effects over the play's thematic content and stereotypical views of India, but also made clear that its excitements had pleased audiences.

CAZAURAN, AUGUSTUS R. (1820–1889). A native of Bordeaux, France, Augustus R. Cazauran worked as a reporter following his move to the United States, writing for the *New York Herald.* During the **Civil War**, he was jailed as a spy. On his release, Cazauran worked for the *Washington Chronicle* and, while attending **Ford's Theatre**, witnessed and wrote about the assassination of President **Abraham Lincoln** by actor*† **John Wilkes Booth**.† Subsequently, Cazauran became a play reader for **producer***† **A. M. Palmer**,† where he demonstrated his talents adapting plays, particularly from French sources. This ability resulted, in part, from his multilingual education in France and Ireland. His adaptations included *Miss Multon* (1876), *A Celebrated Case* (1878), *The Danicheffs* (1878), *French Flats* (1879), and *The Parisian Romance* (1883). He was also an effective play doctor, and among his achievements in this area was his work on **Bronson Howard**'s *The Banker's Daughter* (1878), which Howard acknowledged as essential to the play's success.

A CELEBRATED CASE. Eugène Cormon and **Adolphe D'Ennery**'s French **melodrama***† featured Sarah Jewett as Adrienne, a young woman whose testimony as a child was instrumental in convicting her father, Jean Renaud (played by **Charles Coghlan**), of murdering her mother. The cast included **Mrs. Gilbert**† and **Agnes Booth**† and won considerable audience favor when it opened in **A. R. Cazauran**'s adaptation at the **Union Square Theatre** on 23 January 1878. Arthur Hornblow describes it as "one of the most successful melodramas ever presented in this country."

A controversy accompanied this production when **producer***† **A. M. Palmer**† discovered that **Dion Boucicault**† was attempting to stage a pirated version of the play under **Lester Wallack**'s producing banner. When Wallack realized the situation, he withdrew Boucicault's version of the play, engendering Boucicault's public attacks against him and Palmer. *A Celebrated Case* was successfully revived at the Empire Theatre by Charles Frohman† and **David Belasco**† in 1915 with a cast including Nat C. Goodwin† and Florence Reed.*†

†**CELESTE, MLLE. (1810–1882).** Paris-born Celeste Keppler was presented as a dancer-**actress***† to New York audiences by **Charles Gilfert** in 1827, but scored little success in appearances in eastern cities. She found approval appearing in a double bill of the **melodrama**† *The French Spy* and a ballet, *La Bayadère*, in 1834, earning a fortune for her demonstration of versatility. At the **Bowery Theatre**, she continued to please audiences, playing multiple roles at the same performance in such vehicles as *The Wizard Skiff*, *The Wept of Wish-ton Wish*, and *The Spirit Bride*. Celeste continued to win favor until 1843, when she returned to France, though she came back for two later stints in America (1851 and 1865). A *New York Herald* **critic***† described her impact at the rough-hewn Bowery Theatre as exhibiting "wonderful tragic power amidst peanuts, cigar smoke, and scenes of the varied kind. We never saw real pathos and peanuts so mixed up before."

*†**CENSORSHIP.** Battles over censorship of various aspects of theatrical entertainments† of all kinds were prevalent in America from colonial times to the present. In the 17th and 18th centuries, this proclivity stemmed from Puritans, as well as the merchant class, who viewed the stage as a den of idleness and iniquity. Plays and players were condemned from church pulpits and in civic discourse, but theatrical troupes often found ways to circumvent all but the most stringent restrictions through the manner in which they advertised their wares. Over time, censorious forces, having lost the battle to stifle theater entirely, focused on what they considered in any era to be controversial content. Over time, these taboo areas included certain forms of human behavior (especially **sexuality***†), language, **race***† and ethnicity, and what were deemed radical political viewpoints, much as remains the case in the 21st century.

In the 19th century, performances featuring scantily clad **women***† both titillated and offended audiences. This culminated in major controversies, such as **Adah Isaacs Menken**'s† appearance in *Mazeppa*† (1861), featuring the illusion of **nudity** (she was actually wearing **fleshings**),† and the **musical***† **melodrama**† *The Black Crook* (1866), decried for its chorus of ballerinas wearing little more than pink tights. Depictions of women (especially when shown out of traditional or sentimentalized roles) and issues of **gen-**

der*† and **sexuality***† often inspired censorious responses, particularly in the late 19th century when these subjects were more frequently featured than had previously been the case as **realism***† came to the fore.

Though the focus of censorship began to shift toward the franker content of social problem plays during the rise of realism, increasingly censorship conflicts came over the content of specific plays and productions or in places outside major cities. Rural Americans were generally less accepting of cutting-edge attitudes expressed in plays, and often **managers**† of **tours***† adapted works to suit local tastes. From the 19th century and well into the 20th century, race posed some dilemmas, with certain scenes and characters excised from performances below the Mason-Dixon Line before, during, and after the **Civil War** and until the breakdown of the Jim Crow South after the Civil Rights movement of the 1950s–1960s.

CENTRAL CITY OPERA HOUSE. Citizens of Central City, Colorado, raised funds to build a grand opera house in 1877, acknowledging the city's wealth in the gold mining era. Many of the miners were of Welsh and Cornish descent and were accustomed to a rich tradition of music. When the opera house opened in 1878, **musical***† events shared the stage with plays and other entertainments,† including **P. T. Barnum**'s **circus***† and **Buffalo Bill**'s† Wild West show. Over time, as the gold mines were played out, Central City fell into hard times and the opera house deteriorated. A drive to renovate and preserve the opera house began in 1929 and by 1932 renovation was complete and the opera house continued as a popular performance venue. Again, in the 1980s and 1990s, significant renovations were required, but the Central City Opera House was declared a National Historic Landmark in 1973 and now houses the Central City Opera company.

CHABERT, DR. JULIEN XAVIER (1792–1859). Entertainer Julien Xavier Chabert, who also used the name Ivan Ivanitz Chabert and was billed as "The Fire King," was born in Avignon, France. In the United States from 1832, Chabert became known for feats such as the one in which he stood in a **fire**† and emerged unscathed while the suit of clothes he wore burned away. Though he might be thought of as a **magician**, his taming of fire bears more of a resemblance to the **vaudeville**† acts prevalent in the late 19th and early 20th centuries.

CHANFRAU, FRANK S. (1824–1884). Of French descent, Francis S. Chanfrau was born in New York and aspired to become an **actor***† after seeing **Edwin Forrest** onstage. Celebrated for his skill doing impressions of ethnic stereotypes and famous personages, including Forrest and other celebrities, Chanfrau was cast as Mose, the fireman and Bowery B'hoy, in **Benja-**

min A. **Baker**'s *A Glance at New York* (1848). His performance and the play itself caused a sensation and drew working-class audiences intrigued to see this familiar contemporary type perform heroic feats.

With Chanfrau as **manager***† of the **Chatham Garden Theatre**, the name of which he changed to Chanfrau's **National Theatre**, working-class audience members were permitted to sit in any seats in the theater and not relegated to the galleries, as had been the prior practice. The Mose character became so popular that Chanfrau **toured***† as the character—and appeared in a number of revivals and a series of sequels. In 1857, Chanfrau took over as manager of the **Bowery Theatre** and began to move away from the Mose character, appearing in parodies of **Shakespeare**,*† the plays associated with Forrest, and **Dan Rice**.

Chanfrau married **actress***† Henrietta Baker in 1858, and though they occasionally performed together, they mostly worked separately. Late in his career, he appeared successfully in two hit plays by **Thomas Blades de Walden**, *Sam* (1865) and *Kit, The Arkansas Traveler* (1871). Chanfrau was acting in Jersey City, New Jersey, in the latter when he collapsed and died of a stroke. **Scene designer***† E. T. Harvey remembered Chanfrau as "unmistakably American. He had a quick manner of speech and sort of bit off his words. He could be very sarcastic when he wished and was a very keen **critic**,*† but he knew what was good when he saw it, and there is always satisfaction in working for a man of that kind."

CHAPMAN, WILLIAM B., SR. (1764–1839). English-born William B. Chapman became an **actor***† in his youth and made his New York debut as Iago playing opposite **Edwin Forrest** in *Othello* at the **Bowery Theatre** in 1828. He spent some years at the **Park Theatre**, after which while **touring***† in the West he conceived the idea of bringing theater to Ohio River and Mississippi River towns with a "floating theater." Chapman's **showboat**† vision created an iconic American tradition.

CHAPMAN, WILLIAM B., JR. (1799–1857). Born in England as the son of an **actor**,*† William B. Chapman Jr. followed his father on the stage. In the United States, he found success as a low comedian at the **Bowery Theatre** following his debut in *Smiles and Tears* in 1827. He ultimately served as **manager***† of the **Walnut Street Theatre** in Philadelphia and spent the latter part of his career on San Francisco stages.

†CHARACTER ACTOR/ACTRESS. This familiar term refers to those **actors***† especially adept at creating varied supporting† characterizations from play to play, moving easily through all genres of dramatic performance. Such actors were particularly valuable to **stock***† companies. Character actors usually played supporting or bit roles, though some became **stars***† as a result of their uncanny skill at developing diverse characterizations or their association with a particularly popular character or type, moving easily from playing young or old as well as every type of persona. Some worked steadily playing one character type (Mrs. Thomas Whiffen,† for example, played old women from virtually the beginning of her long career to its end). Conversely, many stars developed into character actors as they aged.

CHARLES THE SECOND; OR, THE MERRY MONARCH. **John Howard Payne** and **Washington Irving** collaborated on this three-act comedy, though Irving's contributions were not billed. The play opened in New York at the **Park Theatre** on 25 October 1824, following a successful production at London's Covert Garden Theatre in May 1824. The simple plot involved Lady Clara and the Earl of Rochester plotting to reform King Charles II (played by **Edmund Simpson**) by leaving him in a common tavern without money to contend with real life. The king runs afoul of an old sailor, Captain Copp (played by **Thomas Hilson**), who threatens him with arrest when he cannot pay his bill. The king escapes and ultimately forgives the earl and Lady Clara, whom, he understands, were trying to help him.

Inspired by Alexandre Duval's *La Jeunesse de Henri V*, Payne did little more than provide a translation of Duval's manuscript, while Irving added the Copp character and much of the play's humor. Despite Irving's insistence that his involvement remain anonymous, Payne later acknowledged Irving's contributions to this and other of his plays.

CHATHAM GARDEN THEATRE. Situated on Chatham Street in lower Manhattan, the Chatham Garden Theatre opened on 17 May 1824 with the intent of challenging the predominance of the **Park Theatre**. Hippolite Barrière established the theater in a tent at Chatham Gardens in 1823 prior to the completion of a permanent structure. Designed by **architect** George Conklin, the theater was ornate and without a gallery. **African Americans***† were not admitted to the theater, which found its audience by presenting well-known **actors***† at modest ticket prices.

The Chatham Garden Theatre also produced what may have been the first two American operas, *The Saw-Mill* (1824) and *The Forest Rose* (1825). The theater struggled for a time and ultimately shifted away from operas and other high art attractions. In 1829, **James H. Hackett** took over as **manager***† and renamed it the American **Opera House**. Within a year and with changes in management, the theater staged **equestrian**† spectacles and contemporary drama prior to **Thomas S. Hamblin** assuming management duties, though the theater closed in 1832. The building was ultimately leased to a radical abolitionist minister who converted it to a Presbyterian church for a number of years, after which it became a hotel before its demolition.

CHEER, MISS MARGARET (mid-18th century). Popular in the mid- to late 18th century, Margaret Cheer (whose real name may have been Catherine Cameron) made her debut with **David Douglass**'s company in 1764 in Charleston, followed by stints in New York and Philadelphia. She was most admired in **Shakespeare**'s*† *The Merchant of Venice, Hamlet, Romeo and Juliet,* and *King Lear,* but also appeared successfully in *Venice Preserved* and *The Recruiting Officer.* A marriage to Lord Rosehill in 1768 and a move to England curtailed her career for a time, but she returned to the United States in 1793 under the name Mrs. Long, but acted without much success.

CHESTER, SAMUEL KNAPP (1836–1921). Born S. C. Knapp, he debuted as an **actor***† in Baltimore in 1855 and married an **actress,***† Annie S. Hodges, in 1862. Chester's brush with history came when he refused **John Wilkes Booth**'s† offer of $3,000 to shut off the lights and hold open the stage door of **Ford's Theatre** on the night of the assassination of President **Abraham Lincoln**. As Chester later recalled it, Booth "told me that he was in a large conspiracy to capture the heads of the government, including the president, and take them to Richmond. I asked him if that was the speculation that he wished me to go into. He said it was. I told him I could not do it; that it was an impossibility; and asked him to think of my family." In fact, Booth asked Chester on several occasions to join the conspiracy since Chester played Claudius in *Hamlet,* opposite **Edwin Booth**,† Booth's brother. Though Chester managed to stay out of the plot, he feared for his life since Booth threatened to kill him if he revealed the plans to anyone, and after Lincoln's murder and Booth's death, he testified about his near involvement in Booth's plans.

CHESTNUT STREET THEATRE. Built in Philadelphia, the Chestnut Street Theatre resulted from efforts by **managers***† **Thomas Wignell** and **Alexander Reinagle** to involve a group of the city's entrepreneurs in creating a permanent performance venue. Planning began in 1791, and the facility, first called the New Theatre, was the first of its kind in the United States, scheduled to open in 1793. Its plans were modeled on the Theatre Royal in Bath, England, and it is believed that the theater seated 2,000. Just prior to its opening, it was immediately closed due to a yellow fever scare, so its actual opening did not occur until February 1794 with a double bill, *The Castle of Andulasia* and *Who's the Dupe?*

In 1816, the Chestnut Street Theatre became the first US theater lit by **gas**. From its opening until well into the 19th century, the theater was populated with America's leading actors and plays, stressing those by the Philadelphia school of dramatists. **William Warren** and **William Wood** took over management after Wignell retired, but as competition from the **Walnut Street Theatre** and the **Arch Street Theatre** intensified between 1811 and 1828, the Chestnut Street Theatre fell on hard times. The building burned in 1856, and though it was rebuilt in 1863, its glory days were past. The rebuilt theater continued operation until 1933, when it was torn down.

†**CHILD PERFORMERS/CHILDREN'S THEATER.** From the beginnings of theater in North America through the heyday of **touring***† **stock***† companies, when whole families toured and performed together, children grew up filling out crowd scenes. In the mid-19th century, a fad for putting talented child performers into adult roles and presenting them as novelties emerged; for example, the popularity of little sisters **Kate** and **Isabel Bateman** as Richard III and Richmond best exemplify this odd practice. It was more usual to put child performers into plays with strong roles written for children, such as Little Eva in *Uncle Tom's Cabin* and the title character in *Little Lord Fauntleroy*, although child roles were often taken by adults until well into the 20th century, an equally odd practice.

CHLOROFORM; OR, NEW YORK A HUNDRED YEARS HENCE. Cornelius A. **Logan**'s last **Yankee**† comedy, produced at **William Burton**'s Chamber Street Theatre on 24 May 1849 for a run of eight performances, makes use of an amusing conceit apparently inspired by *Rip Van Winkle.*† Aminadab Slocum (played by Logan) is chloroformed for the extraction of a tooth and the dentist believes he is dead and Slocum is buried. He awakes 100 years later to meet his descendants.

CHRISTY, E. P. (1815–1862). Philadelphia-born Edwin Pearce Christy went on the stage as a **blackface**† **minstrel**† in the Buffalo, New York, area in 1843. Christy and his troupe of performers made their first New York appearances at Polmer's **Opera House**, but in 1847 they frequently performed at Mechanics Hall. That same year, Christy appeared at a benefit performance for **Stephen C. Foster** in Cincinnati, after which Christy's troupe specialized in performing Foster's songs, most particularly "Old Folks at Home," which Foster signed over to Christy for exclusive use by **Christy's Minstrels** (Christy published the song as his own in its initial printing). In 1855, Christy retired from performing, but as a **manager***† of Christy's Opera Houses, he established a presence in several cities. The start of the **Civil War** and prospective financial losses for blackface minstrels, and signs of mental instability, led to Christy's suicide. He leapt from a window in his New York home. Christy had frequently claimed that he created the first minstrel troupe, but most evidence suggests that the **Virginia Minstrels** preceded the establishment of his company. He was the stepfather of **George N. Christy**, who performed with Christy's Minstrels.

CHRISTY, GEORGE N. (1827–1868). Born in Palmyra, New York, as George N. Harrington, he changed his name to Christy, the surname of his stepfather, **E. P. Christy**. As a performer, Christy performed in **blackface†** with **Christy's Minstrels.†** Like his stepfather, Christy was something of a minstrel innovator. For example, he is credited with establishing the stage arrangement of the interlocutor in the center, with Mr. Tambo and Mr. Bones at each end of a line of chairs at the front of the stage.

CHRISTY'S MINSTRELS. Though its founder, **E. P. Christy**, claimed to have founded Christy's Minstrels in 1842, evidence suggests his company did not take shape until the following year. As such, the **Virginia Minstrels†** were the first such troupe. Christy's success and innovations in the establishment of a minstrel show are significant, including the use of **burlesque*†** elements to parody popular songs and other cultural manifestations. He also created the olio structure, separating the performance into distinct acts. Christy's stepson, **George N. Christy**, joined the company, but by the mid-1850s, Christy's health issues, the proliferation of other **blackface†** minstrel troupes (some of whom unscrupulously used the Christy name), and George Christy's resignation compelled him to disband the company in 1855. Within a few years, members of the troupe established the Original Christy Minstrels and **toured*†** for two decades.

CICERI, CHARLES (late 18th–early 19th centuries). Born in Milan, Italy, and educated in Paris, Charles Ciceri is considered the first significant **scene designer*†** in the United States. After working in several European theaters, including London's **Opera House**, Ciceri arrived in the United States, where he became scene painter for Philadelphia's **Southwark Theatre**. He ultimately moved to New York, where he designed diverse works, from the opera *Tammany; or, The Indian Chief* to *Hamlet* and **William Dunlap**'s *André*. Credited with being the first designer in America to use transparent scrims, he also caused wonder with ingenious **transformation scenes†** prior to his permanent return to Europe in the early 19th century.

***†CIRCUS.** The rise of the American circus is one of the significant developments in entertainment† in the 19th century. Englishman John Bill Ricketts established an entertainment considered to be the first circus in the United States when he arrived in Philadelphia from London in 1792. As the seminal circus event in the United States, the Ricketts show was actually a demonstration of a range of **equestrian†** skills (Ricketts also ran a riding school). The first performance, at the corner of Market and 12th Streets, on 3 April 1793, featured a single ring. On 26 April 1793, the Ricketts show performed in New York, followed by performances in Charleston and Baltimore, among others. In 1797, Philip Lailson organized the first circus parade and a traveling menagerie appeared in Putnam and Westchester counties in New York. Moving circuses was a particular challenge, but Victor Pepin moved his show by steamboat and constructed a performance arena at each performance site.

J. W. Bancker's New York Circus was the first to identify itself with the word *circus*. In 1825, Joshuah Purdy Brown made use of a large canvas tent ("big top") to enhance the mobility of his show, as did the use of railroad† lines, a means for moving circuses, which grew exponentially between the 1830s and the 1860s. Brown's other innovations include merging his circus with an animal menagerie.

During the first half of the 19th century, several names associated with the circus were significant in transforming circuses into a major entertainment medium. **P. T. Barnum†** is a dominant figure in this period and from 1841, when he purchased New York's **American Museum**. He contributed multiple innovations to circus and popular entertainment in general, developing celebrity **attractions,†** some of which were bogus (Joice Heth, for example, whom Barnum passed off as President **George Washington**'s childhood nanny) and some of whom achieved lasting fame (General **Tom Thumb**). Clowns became popular circus attractions, with some, like **Dan Rice**, billed as "America's Favorite Clown," becoming legendary. Rice made his first appearance in 1844 and mixed political satire into his act, which helped endear him to the American public for the remainder of the century.

The golden age of the American circus began after the **Civil War** as Barnum partnered with W. C. Coup and Dan Castello to establish P. T. Barnum's Great Traveling World's Fair, which used railroads to move the big show on nearly a daily basis. Other major circus **producers,*†** including James A. Bailey, James E. Cooper, W. W. Cole, and others, developed rival circuses, and over time, through various mergers, the modern conception and structure of the circus emerged. By the early 1880s, Barnum's show adopted the now familiar three-ring circus. During the 1880s, **William F. "Buffalo Bill" Cody†** created the first Wild West show, using many circus techniques in both presentation and the practical problems of moving a big show on tour.***†**

The visit of a circus to either a small town or a large city was an eagerly anticipated event by local audiences. The menagerie, sideshows, clowns, exotic and freak exhibitions, and dazzling feats of acrobatics under the big top became an American tradition by the middle of the 19th century. At the turn of the century, nearly 100 individual American circuses toured the United States and Europe.

A number of plays, particularly toward the end of the 19th century, were set behind the scenes at circuses, including *Circus in Town* and *The Circus Rider* (both 1887), *The Circus Girl* (1897), *Polly of the Circus*† (1907), *The Circus Man* (1909), and *The Wisdom Tooth*† (1926). Many performers found fame performing in circuses and remained there, while others, especially those with specialty acts, moved on to **vaudeville**,† **legitimate**† theater, and **musical***† comedy.

CIVIL WAR. The bloody and nation-defining cataclysm of the Civil War (1861–1865) had a profound impact on all aspects of American life in the mid-19th century—and changed the nation's ideals, economics, and culture in the aftermath of the war. In the decades leading up to the **war**,*† particularly the 1850s, theater in America presented plays on the rising frictions between North and South, most especially in regard to the abolition of slavery. Harriet Beecher Stowe's sensationally popular novel, *Uncle Tom's Cabin; or, Life Among the Lowly*, published in 1852, inspired numerous stage adaptations, most notably one by **George L. Aiken** in 1852, which, over time, emerged as the standard version. Presented within the traditions of **melodrama**,† the play is credited, along with Stowe's novel, as increasing abolitionist sentiments.

Dion Boucicault's† *The Octoroon; or, Life in Louisiana* (1859) similarly fanned abolitionist sentiments in the years just before the war. The Civil War itself served as the backdrop to sentimental or melodramatic action, but relatively few plays treated specific issues related to the **war**.*† With the Union having won, the South could be safely romanticized on the stage, and plays depicting antebellum plantation life were popular on the **road**.† Plantation life—or sentimentalized images of it—provided inspiration for **minstrel**† shows and the songs and sketches presented, as well as in the tradition of **blackface**,† which created odious stereotypical images of **African Americans***† as white actors (and some black actors) wore makeup exaggerating black images.

The best and most commercially successful of Civil War plays appeared after the war and tended to be unabashedly romanticized works, including *Shenandoah*† (1889) by **Bronson Howard**,† *Alabama*† (1891) and *The Copperhead*† (1918) by Augustus Thomas,† *May Blossom* (1884) and *The Heart of Maryland*† (1895) by **David Belasco**,† *Secret Service*† (1896) by **William Gillette**,† *A Grand Army Man*† (1907) by Belasco, Pauline Phelps, and Marion Short, and *The Warrens of Virginia*† (1907) by William C. deMille.†

CLAM-EEL. **C. W. Taylor's burlesque*†** inspired by *Camille* premiered on 16 May 1858 at the **Chatham Garden Theatre** and is merely one of many such parodies of familiar plays and works of literature presented there and in other venues during the 19th century. It shared the bill with a Thompson Townsend **melodrama,†** *Mary's Dream.*

†CLAPP, HENRY AUSTIN (1841–1904). Born in Dorchester, Massachusetts, Henry Austin Clapp became a drama **critic*†** and specialist on the plays of **William Shakespeare.*†** He graduated from Harvard University in 1860, after which he taught at the Boston Latin School, practiced law, and served in the Union Army during the **Civil War.** He wrote drama criticism for the *Boston Daily Advertiser* from 1868 to 1902, followed by two years with the *Boston Herald.* Clapp lectured across the country on American theater and literature, gaining a reputation as a witty and erudite critic. In 1902, Clapp published his well-received memoir, *Reminiscences of a Dramatic Critic,* which captured the theater world of his time. At his death in 1904, the *New York Times* described him as "one of the most distinguished dramatic critics in the United States."

CLARI, THE MAID OF MILAN. **John Howard Payne** crafted the libretto for this three-act **operetta†** with music by Henry Rowley Bishop. First staged at the **Park Theatre** on 21 November 1823, *Clari, The Maid of Milan* was frequently performed in the 19th century, and one of its cultural contributions was the song "Home! Sweet Home!," sung by the title character. Clari, a simple farm girl, has been lured to the palace of the jaded Duke Vivaldi with the promise of marriage. He subsequently reneges on the marriage proposal because he believes it might cost him his royal rank. Despite gifts and other pleasures meant to please her, Clari wants to go home. With the aid of some traveling players, she does so, only to be rejected by her father. However, the duke arrives with the news that the king, who has met Clari, approves of their wedding. The operetta was also well received at London's Covent Garden that year.

CLARKE, ASIA BOOTH (1835–1888). The youngest daughter of the 10 children of **Junius Brutus Booth** and his common-law wife, Mary Ann Holmes, Asia Frigga Booth was born in Bel Air, Maryland, and married **actor*† John Sleeper Clarke** in 1859. She was the mother of eight children, two of whom, Creston and Wilfred, became little-known actors, but three of her brothers, **Edwin Booth,† Junius Brutus Booth Jr.,†** and **John Wilkes Booth,†** were successful.

Following John Wilkes Booth's assassination of President **Abraham Lincoln**, Clarke, her husband, and children left the United States for England to avoid the relentless notoriety. Her husband had been imprisoned for a month and interrogated following the assassination, and his ultimate desire to disassociate himself from the Booth family estranged him from his wife. Though she was not a member of the theatrical profession, Clarke provides one-of-a-kind insights about her brother as an actor and a man in *Unlocked Book, John Wilkes Booth, a Sister's Memoir* (the manuscript was untitled at the time of Clarke's death; the editor subsequently supplied one), which she wrote in 1874, though she kept it secret to avoid upsetting her husband. Fifty years after her death, the book was finally published.

CLARKE, CORSON WALTON (1814–1867). From Elizabethtown, New Jersey, Corson Walton Clark made his theatrical debut as an **actor*†** in 1838 in **James W. Wallack**'s company. A few years later, Clarke played Macduff to **William Charles Macready**'s Macbeth at the performance interrupted by the **Astor Place Opera House** riots. Clarke joined the company at **P. T. Barnum**'s **American Museum**, where he scored a notable success as the alcoholic Edward Middleton in **W. H. Smith**'s *The Drunkard* (1850). Through many years and roles in which he demonstrated versatility, Clarke, who also became Barnum's director of **amusements†** in 1852, remained permanently identified with *The Drunkard*, so much so that he became affectionately known as "Drunkard" Clarke.

CLARKE, JOHN SLEEPER (1833–1899). Born in Baltimore, John Sleeper Clarke studied law, but was attracted to the theater in part through **Edwin Booth,†** who was his classmate. Together, they performed in **amateur†** theatricals with the Baltimore Thespian Club. In 1851, Clarke made his professional debut at Boston's **Howard Athenaeum** in a production of *Paul Pry*, and in 1855 he made his first New York appearance at the Metropolitan Theatre (shortly after renamed the **Winter Garden**) in *The Spectre Bridegroom*.

As an **actor,*†** Clarke performed in both serious and comic works, but he was most appreciated as a comedian. He married **Asia Booth** of the theatrical Booth family, and not long after, Clarke and Edwin Booth partnered as **managers*†** of theaters, including the **Winter Garden** and the **Walnut Street Theatre**. The assassination of President **Abraham Lincoln** by Clarke's brother-in-law **John Wilkes Booth†** estranged him from the Booth family (Clarke was imprisoned for a few weeks with other members of the Booth family in the immediate aftermath of the assassination), including his wife, to whom he remained married, but in name only. From 1867, he lived and worked successfully in England, returning to the United States a few times for theatrical engagements.†

CLARKE, MARY CARR. *See* CARR, MARY (c. 1790s–c. 1830s).

†CLAXTON, KATE (1848?–1924). Daughter of a theatrical **manager,***† Kate Claxton was born in Somerville, New Jersey, as Kate Elizabeth Cone, and debuted in Chicago in 1870 in a supporting† role with **Lotta Crabtree.**† Later that year, Claxton joined **Augustin Daly's**† company for several seasons, making her New York debut in *Man and Wife* (1870). In 1872, Claxton also joined **A. M. Palmer's**† **Union Square Theatre**† company, with whom she appeared in *Rose Michel* with **Agnes Ethel**. She made a particular hit in **Dion Boucicault's**† *Led Astray* in 1873.

In 1874, Claxton formed her own company and was acclaimed as one of the outstanding **emotional actresses**† of her time, though she also excelled in comedy. On three occasions she was performing at the time of a **theater fire:**† in St. Louis, Missouri; in La Crosse, Wisconsin; and in Brooklyn, New York, in 1876, the latter resulting in the loss of 278 lives, becoming one of the worst fires in New York City history. The play with which Claxton was most associated in popular memory was *The Two Orphans,*† which she **toured***† widely

CLIFTON, JOSEPHINE (1813?–1847). The early life of Josephine Clifton is shrouded by mystery and, until her debut in 1831 in the **Bowery Theatre** production of *Venice Preserved,* very little is verifiable. Despite lacking training or experience, Clifton had been given this opportunity by **Thomas Chamblin**, with whom she may have been involved romantically. At the Bowery, she also appeared in *Pizarro* and as Lady Macbeth, before moving to the **Park Theatre**, where she played Bianca in *Fazio.*

Hounded by rumors of affairs, Clifton left the United States for England, and when she appeared at London's Drury Lane Theatre, she became the first American **actress***† to **star***† there. On her return to the United States in 1836, she appeared opposite **James W. Wallack** and, at the **Tremont Theatre**, in *The Bride of Genoa*, a play written for her by **Epes Sargent**. **Nathaniel Parker Willis** also wrote a play for Clifton, *Bianca Visconti,* in which she appeared in 1837. After this time, she frequently acted opposite **Edwin Forrest** and, in 1846, married Robert Place, **manager***† of New Orleans's **American Theatre**. Following her death, it was revealed that Clifton and Forrest had been romantically involved, when she was cited as a factor in Forrest's highly publicized divorce.

CLINCH, C. P. (1797–1880). Born Charles Powell Clinch in New York, he was the son of an entrepreneur. He was an associate of the Knickerbocker school of writers and worked as a drama **critic.***† He scored a major success with his first play, *The Spy, A Tale of Neutral Ground* (1822), which was adapted from James Fenimore Cooper's novel only weeks after the novel itself had appeared in print. That same year, Clinch's *The Expelled Collegian*, a farce, was staged at the **Park Theatre**, where his 1824 tragedy, *The Avenger's Vow*, was also produced. Despite demonstrating his versatility and achieving success, Clinch abandoned theater work after his final play, the farce *The First of May in New York* (1830), was completed.

CLINE, MAGGIE (1857–1934). "The **Irish** Queen" of **vaudeville**† was born in Haverhill, Massachusetts, as a daughter of Irish immigrants. In 1879, Cline ran away from home to appear with a **burlesque***† troupe and within two years was successfully performing in New York at **Tony Pastor**'s,† where she became something of a regular, performing rowdy Irish songs crafted to her specific skills, which included a vigorous performing style and a raucous persona. Her specialty number, "Throw Him Down, McCloskey," famously involved stagehands and performers backstage making a racket throwing objects around to create the sound of a fight. Cline also sang such similar specialty songs as "Down Went McGinty" and "McNulty Carved the Duck." By 1914, when she played New York's Palace Theatre, its vaudeville mecca, Cline's ethnic comedy was becoming passé.

THE CLIPPER. This early theatrical newspaper, founded in 1853, chose to define the boundaries broadly, covering theater, music, dance, **circus,***† and sports. As such, it provides a remarkable record of American culture from the time of its founding until it was subsumed by *Variety**† in 1924. Founded by Frank Queen, the *New York Clipper* evolved over the years, moving away from sports coverage (though it had been instrumental in popularizing baseball) to emphasizing **vaudeville.**† To some extent, reflecting developments in theatrical tastes, the *Clipper* published satirical stories making use of dialects, including those of the Bowery b'hoys, **Irish**, and pseudo–**African American***† as heard in **minstrel**† shows.

*†CLUBS. Theatrical clubs in New York date to 1870, with the founding of the Lotos Club, which was not exclusively for members of the theater profession, but sought members who were "lovers of literature and art." Established by request of the mayor of New York City as an appropriate place to entertain foreign dignitaries, the Lotos Club, which began its life at 2 Irving Place, continues in the 21st century. Of the three most important New York City clubs for members of the theatrical profession, The **Lambs**,† founded in

1874 mostly by cast members of **Dion Boucicault's**† *The Shaughraun*, was the first, followed by The Players (1888), which was established by **Edwin Booth,**† and The Friars† (1907). Many *bon mots* have been devised over the years to differentiate among them. As a broad generalization, one might say that most Players came from **legitimate theater,**† Lambs from **musical***† comedy, and Friars from nightclubs and variety entertainment.† It has been quipped that the Lambs are players pretending to be gentlemen, Players are gentlemen pretending to be **actors,***† and Friars are neither, pretending to be both. Another saying is that Players smoke pipes, Lambs smoke cigarettes, and Friars smoke cigars.

†CODY, WILLIAM FREDERICK ("BUFFALO BILL") (1846–1917). Born in Le Claire, Iowa, William Frederick Cody became a popular stage **attraction**† in plays depicting his exploits as a frontiersman and scout (for which he won the Congressional Medal of Honor) before, during, and after the **Civil War**. When Ned Buntline wrote of "Buffalo Bill" Cody's adventures in magazine serial form in 1869, various **actors,***† including **John B. Studley**, played Cody in **melodramatic**† adaptations, leading Buntline to craft a play, *The Scouts of the Prairie* (1872), in which Cody played himself in a Chicago production. Despite his lack of acting experience and the play's pedestrian quality, urban audiences thrilled to see a genuine frontier hero.

Cody subsequently appeared in a series of similar melodramas during the 1870s and early 1880s, continuing to work as a scout for the army between theatrical seasons. Cody partnered with William F. Carver in 1883 to stage an outdoor Wild West show, but disagreements soon ended their collaboration. **Nate Salsbury**† took over to exploit the Wild West show for 34 years, generating considerable publicity with American and European **tours,***† despite occasional financial problems that finally shuttered the show in 1915. Among the many acts to appear in Cody's Wild West show were sharpshooter **Annie Oakley,**† who joined his company in 1885, and Chief Sitting Bull. Cody and his show earned a permanent place in the American imagination, and he has often appeared as a stage and screen character, perhaps most notably in Irving Berlin's 1946 **musical,***† *Annie Get Your Gun*, and in numerous films.†

†COGHLAN, CHARLES FRANCIS (1842–1899). Born in Paris, France, Charles Francis Coghlan began a career as an **actor***† in England with minor roles with Sadler's Wells Theatre. In 1876, he followed his sister **Rose Coghlan**† to New York. Coghlan had a polished manner that worked well in society comedies like **Edward Bulwer-Lytton's** *Money*, in which he made his New York debut in 1876 at the **Fifth Avenue Theatre**. His strong dramatic roles included the title character in *Jim the Penman*,† and he played

Orlando opposite **Fanny Davenport**'s Rosalind in **Shakespeare**'s*† *As You Like It*. Also a writer, Coghlan adapted Alexandre Dumas's play *Kean*, which he retitled *The Royal Box*, in which he also appeared. At various times, Coghlan had played opposite major actresses, including Minnie Maddern Fiske† and Lily Langtry.†

†**COGHLAN, ROSE (1851–1932).** Born in Peterborough, England, Rose Coghlan performed as a **child**† there prior to traveling to the United States with **Lydia Thompson**, after which she made her New York debut in 1872 in the **musical***† *Ixion* at **Wallack's Theatre**. After performing in England again, this time with Barry Sullivan, she returned to Wallack's in 1877 as **leading lady**† for nine years and proved her versatility by playing both intense **melodrama**† and light comedy with equal skill. Her brother **Charles Coghlan**† wrote the romantic drama *Jocelyn* to feature her abilities. She appeared in **Shakespearean***† plays and was also appreciated in *Diplomacy* (1878), *A Woman of No Importance* (1893), *Our Betters* (1917), and *Deburau* (1921), among many others.

THE COLLEEN BAWN; OR, THE BRIDES OF GARRYOWEN. **Dion Boucicault**'s† three-act "domestic drama" became one of the most popular **Irish melodramas**† of the mid-19th century. It opened on 29 March 1860 at **Laura Keene**'s Theatre, with Keene in the cast, as well as Boucicault, **Agnes Robertson,**† **Charles Fisher**, and **Madame Ponisi**. The source material for the play, Gerald Griffin's 1829 novel *The Collegians*, was based on the true story of a girl murdered by her husband and his servant in 1819.

Boucicault's play, the first among many Irish-themed works he wrote, was driven by the upper-class Mrs. Cregan, who, along with her son Hardress, has fallen on financial hard times. The only hope is her possible marriage to a lawyer or his to a wealthy girl, Anne Chute. However, Anne loves Kyrle Daly. Unknown to all is that Hardress is secretly married to Eily O'Connor, an impoverished girl referred to as the Colleen Bawn. When Anne misunderstands a letter from Eily to Hardress, which she believes was meant for Kyrle, she breaks off her relationship with Kyrle. Hardress's servant agrees to kill Eily if the signal (the delivery of a glove) is given. Unknowingly, Mrs. Cregan gives the signal, and Danny pushes Eily off a cliff into the sea, but he is shot by Myles-na-Coppaleen, a bootlegger in love with Eily. Before he dies, Danny admits the involvement of Hardress. As authorities arrive to arrest Hardress, Coppaleen appears with Eily, whom he has rescued. All confusions are finally resolved, and Anne and Kyrle are reunited.

Following its New York success, Boucicault opened the play in London for a phenomenally long run (278 performances), followed by a Dublin production in 1862 and innumerable revivals as late as the early 21st century.

The play has been filmed† no less than three times (1911, 1924, and 1929), and an 1862 opera, *The Lily of Killarney*, composed by Julius Benedict and set to a text based on the play by Boucicault himself, was frequently staged for over 50 years.

COLLINS, JOHN (1811–1874). Irish-born **actor*†**-comedian John Collins made his first American appearance in 1846 and was presumed to be the logical successor to **Tyrone Power**, playing many Irish roles associated with Power, including *The Nervous Man* and *Teddy the Tiler*. **John Brougham** wrote ***The Irish Fortune Hunter*** for Collins in 1850, but he returned to Ireland a few years later. Brougham wrote *The Duke's Motto* (1863) for Collins as well—and Collins returned to the United States to appear in it.

COLONEL SELLERS. George Densmore wrote a five-act play based on **Mark Twain** and Charles Dudley Warner's 1873 novel, *The Gilded Age*, and produced it in San Francisco, in April 1874. However, Twain sued Densmore, and a new version of the play, ultimately called *Colonel Sellers*, by Twain and Warner, featured **John T. Raymond** as the title character. When the play opened at New York's **Park Theatre** on 16 September 1874, audiences were receptive, and it ran for 119 performances.

Colonel Sellers is something of a character study, focusing on ne'er-do-well Sellers, who dreams up inventions and get-rich-quick schemes while the married Colonel Selby attempts to seduce Laura Hawkins, who kills him when she discovers that he is married. With Raymond in mind, Twain and **William Dean Howells** later collaborated on another Sellers play, *Colonel Sellers as a Scientist*, which Raymond turned down. With a new title, *The American Claimant; or, Mulberry Sellers Ten Years Later* (1887), it flopped.

COLUMBUS EL FILIBUSTERO!!. John Brougham's popular **burlesque,*†** subtitled "A new and audaciously original historico-plagiaristic, ante-national, pre-patriotic, and omni-local confusion of circumstances, running through two acts and four centuries," opened at **Burton**'s Theatre in December 1857, followed by a run at **Niblo's Garden** in July 1858 and at Baltimore's **Holliday Street Theatre** that same year. Brougham played Don Christoval Colon, alias Columbus, "a clairvoyant voyager, whose filibustering expedition gave rise at the time to a world of speculation." Filled with **musical*†** parodies, *Columbus el Filibustero!!* transforms the story of America's founding into a fable of national and individual greed and self-interest, with the other characters in the play all hoping to get rich from Columbus's voyage.

COLVILLE, SAMUEL (1825–1886). A native of Castle Avery, County Down, Ireland, Samuel Colville arrived in the United States in 1840 with an interest in a theatrical career. By 1853, he was **manager*†** of California's Sacramento Theatre, after which he managed three theaters in Australia, and in 1865, he took over Cincinnati's **National Theatre**, where he presented **Edwin Forrest**, **Joseph Jefferson,†** and a **touring*†** production of *The Black Crook*. In New York, he partnered with **George Wood** to open Wood's Museum and scored a great commercial success by importing **Lydia Thompson†** and her British Blondes, a **burlesque*†** act that caused a major sensation.

Colville produced **Dion Boucicault's†** *Flying Scud* in 1867, but increasingly focused his energies on **musical*†** theater. He established varied companies to **tour,*†** including Colville's Folly Company, the Henderson and Colville Opera Company, Colville Burlesque Opera Company, and the Colville Opera Company, each with specialized musical entertainments† from burlesques to **operetta**.† Many of the productions staged for these companies were instrumental in the evolution of musical theater and provided experience and opportunity to a range of musical talents.

†COMBINATION SYSTEM. A combination was an entire production—cast and **scenery*†**—assembled in New York to be sent on the **road*†** as a unit. By the 1890s, the combination system largely displaced the **touring*†** repertory*† company, which had displaced the resident **stock*†** company in the 1870s, because it was cheaper to tour a single contemporary play than a repertory of old favorites.

*†COMEDY. Aristotle's articulation of the distinct genres of tragedy and comedy in *Ars Poetica* was largely ignored in the evolution of comedy on American stages from its beginning. Audiences often saw pre-19th century European comedy, from occasional productions of classical Greek and Roman comedies to those of **Shakespeare*†** and English 18th-century writers of comedy of manners, such as **Richard Brinsley Sheridan**, whose plays were popular with audiences and served as a model for early American comic writers, including **Royall Tyler**, whose 1787 comedy *The Contrast* liberally borrows on the techniques of British comedy of manners. Though late 18th-century British comedy of manners plays provided the structural model, the American variations featured the folkways of rural life in the new and expanding nation. Tyler's comedy, and those of his contemporaries, borrowed the English formula, but also praised American values over European mores.

Many comedies made use of broad **stock***† characters and romantic situations vaguely inspired by classical models, from the comedies of Plautus and Terence to archetypal characters inspired by commedia dell'arte and Renaissance comedies. Throughout the first half of the 19th century, purely comedic plays tended to be ramshackle vehicles for dynamic comic actors and the stock characters they created from emerging national stereotypes drawn from **gender,***† **race,***† and ethnic characteristics. Comedy was more effectively employed within other popular genres of this period, including **burlesque***† and **travesties,**† **minstrel**† shows, **vaudeville**† entertainments,† and the emerging **musical***† theater. Significantly, comedy was also a central component of **melodrama,**† with a range of secondary characters supplying comic relief† from the suspenseful main actions of the plays and depending on the established racial, ethnic, and rural stereotypes.

As the 19th century neared its end, comedies of greater wit and style appeared with increasing frequency. **Manager***† **Augustin Daly**† led the way by showcasing his venerable stock company, **John Drew,**† **Ada Rehan,**† **Mrs. G. H. Gilbert,**† and **James Lewis,**† in classical and contemporary comedies for fashionable New York audiences. As a rule, however, the more sophisticated comedies seen on **Broadway***† at the turn of the century were likely to be foreign imports.

New American comedies after the **Civil War** tended, in most cases, to depict middle- and lower-class values and characters and rural settings. Female impersonator† **Neil Burgess**† scored a success in the role of an old lady in *Widow Bedott*† (1880) and *The County Fair*† (1889). Similarly, **Denman Thompson**† scored as the title character of the **rube**† comedy *Joshua Whitcomb* (1878), honing a role he revisited for the hugely successful *The Old Homestead*† (1887). From the mid-19th century, various immigrants—**Irish,** German, Eastern European—influenced comedy in that writers and performers created archetypal characters drawn from the cultural collisions inherent in the arrival of large numbers of immigrants to the American shore.

COMIQUE. *See* †THEATER COMIQUE.

CONNOR, CHARLOTTE BARNES. *See* BARNES, CHARLOTTE MARY SANFORD (1818–1863).

THE CONQUEST OF CANADA; OR, THE SIEGE OF QUEBEC. George Cockings's five-act historical tragedy was staged in 1773 by the **American Company** at the **Southwark Theatre**, with **Lewis Hallam** as General Wolfe and **David Douglass** as Leonatus. It was not well received and is believed to have had only two performances. Completed and published in 1766, the play, as its title suggests, focuses on events surrounding the British conquest of French Canada during the **French and Indian War**.

CONRAD, ROBERT T. (1810–1858). Born in Philadelphia, Robert Taylor Conrad studied law, worked as an editor, wrote poetry, and before his 21st birthday, completed a tragedy, *Conrad, King of Naples*, which was staged in 1832 at the **Arch Street Theatre** with **James E. Murdoch**. He was centrally involved in politics and publishing, but continued his literary involvements with another tragedy, *The Noble Yeoman*, which was a failure in 1836, but after considerable revisions and turned over to **Edwin Forrest** under the title *Aylmere* (1841), it succeeded. Despite this, Forrest changed the title to that of the main character, **Jack Cade**. He completed another tragedy, *The Heretic*, but it was not produced during his lifetime. Conrad ultimately became the first mayor of Philadelphia following the city's consolidation in 1854.

THE CONTRAST. First performed at New York's **John Street Theatre** on 16 April 1787, **Royall Tyler**'s comedy, considered the first by an American-born dramatist, was successful enough to call for additional performances on 18 April, 2 May, and 12 May 1787. Productions of *The Contrast* immediately followed in Philadelphia, Baltimore, and Boston, and it was performed 38 times between 1787 and 1804. The plot and style of the comedy owes much to British comedy of manners plays, most particularly **Richard Brinsley Sheridan**'s *The School for Scandal*, which Tyler had seen performed in New York.

The plot centers on an American, Van Rough, who has arranged the marriage of his daughter, Maria, to wealthy Billy Dimple, a young man obsessed with English ways and manners. Despite the engagement, Dimple keeps up flirtations with Maria's friends, Letitia and Charlotte. The latter's brother, Colonel Manly, an honorable officer and veteran of the **American Revolution**, loves Maria but steps aside because of her engagement to Dimple. Gambling away his fortune, Dimple breaks off his engagement to Maria in hopes of instead marrying the wealthy Letitia. When Van Rough discovers Dimple's plot, he also sees his daughter's unhappy obedience to his wishes is separating her from the man she truly loves, Colonel Manly. Dimple is subsequently foiled by the disclosure that he is simultaneously courting both Letitia and Charlotte to hedge his bets, and Manly and Maria are happily united, with Van Rough's blessing.

A broadly comic subplot concerns Jonathan, Manly's servant, whose rural manner and speech are seen in contrast with the effete wiliness of the popinjay Jessamy, Dimple's manservant. Jessamy educates Jonathan in the ways of the world and coaches him in courting Jenny, a maid, hoping to turn her affections toward himself by her horror at the missteps he is teaching Jonathan. Jenny, however, discovers Jessamy's scheme and rejects both servants.

Jonathan emerges as a prototype of the American **Yankee stock*†** character, a stock character that would be seen in numerous plays during the 19th century. *The Contrast* was frequently performed in the late 18th and early 19th centuries, but rarely afterward, though its title reflects a potent dynamic of early American culture characterized by a growing resistance to European (particularly British) influence as the new nation, and its theater, found its own voice. Contemporary audiences overwhelmingly applauded the play, with one **critic*†** noting that it was "an added specimen in proof that these new climes are particularly favorable to the cultivation of arts and sciences."

CONWAY, FREDERICK B. (1819–1874). Born in England as the son of **actor*† William A. Conway**, Frederick Bartlett Conway made his New York debut in 1850. He worked with **Edwin Forrest**, playing opposite him in *Othello* and *Richelieu*. Conway married Sarah Crocker, an **actress*†** and the sister of **Mrs. D. P. Bowers**, and she billed herself as Mrs. F. B. Conway, acting with him in many productions and with greatest success in classic plays, including *Macbeth*. Despite his ability as an actor, **critics*†** tended to find Mrs. Conway the superior of the duo. They failed as **managers*†** of a theater in Cincinnati in 1859, **toured*†** in England in 1861, and again in the United States upon their return. For some years, beginning in 1864, they were associated with the **Park Theatre**.

CONWAY, H. J. (1800–1860). A **playwright*†** with at least 29 plays to his credit, Henry J. Conway's claim to theater history is his adaptation of Harriet Beecher Stowe's novel *Uncle Tom's Cabin*, produced in Boston in November 1852, only months after **George L. Aiken**'s adaptation of the novel had first appeared. Though Aiken's version has widely been accepted as the definitive adaptation of Stowe's novel, Conway's play was well received at that time and had a successful run at **P. T. Barnum**'s **American Museum**. Conway's emphasis on historical and/or nationalistic drama was evident in *The Battle of Stillwater* (1840), which depicted the 1777 battle of the **American Revolution**, and *Dred: A Tale of the Great Dismal Swamp* (1856), adapted from another Stowe novel. It was produced at **P. T. Barnum**'s **American Museum** with General **Tom Thumb** as a cast member. Conway was a versatile writer, also contributing short farces as afterpieces, including *Hiram Hireout; or, Followed by Fortune* (1851).

CONWAY, WILLIAM AUGUSTUS (1789–1828). A London-born **actor***† who angrily left England when his performance as Hamlet was **criticized**,*† William Augustus Conway arrived in the United States in 1824 and made his debut as Hamlet to greater success than he had achieved in England. He appeared in other **Shakespearean***† roles, including Romeo, Petruchio, and Coriolanus, and acted with **Thomas Abthorpe Cooper** in *Venice Preserved* and *Othello*. He **toured***† Eastern cities with some success and appeared with **William Charles Macready** in several productions. Conway abruptly retired from the stage to devote himself to religious pursuits, but he committed suicide by drowning in Charleston in 1828. He was the father of actor **Frederick B. Conway**.

COOKE, GEORGE FREDERICK (1756–1812). Late in his career, London-born **actor***† George Frederick Cooke, who won fame for his romantic acting style, often in **Shakespearean***† roles, was also known for his eccentricities and alcoholism. When he arrived in the United States in 1810, he was the first major international actor to visit. His fame was such that scholars see his American debut at the **Park Theatre** in the role of Richard III as demonstrating to American **managers***† the lucrative possibilities of **star***† actors, as well as international "name" actors. Though some of Cooke's performances in this and several other roles were undermined by Cooke's drinking, **William Dunlap** managed a **tour***† of American cities until Cooke's declining health brought on his death in New York City.

COOMBS, JANE (b. 1842). Described in 1864 by a contemporary **critic***† in the *New York Times* as "a charming **actress**,"*† Jane Coombs was born in Cincinnati. After training with **Clara Fisher**, Coombs made her New York debut opposite **Edwin Forrest** in *The Lady of Lyons* in 1855. She also scored successes in an 1858 New York revival of *London Assurance*, and performed in London, but truly made her reputation on the **road***† in Chicago and St. Louis in the 1870s and early 1880s. Coombs married **actor***† F. A. Brown in 1864 and retired for a time, but was known to be **touring***† as late as 1900. Little is known about her later life, including when her death took place. In his 1903 *History of the New York Stage*, **T. Allston Brown** described her as a "handsome blonde, with wonderful eyes and excellent elocution."

COOPER, THOMAS ABTHORPE (1776–1849). English-born tragedian Thomas Abthorpe Cooper was the son of an **Irish**-born doctor, and by the mid-1790s, he emerged as a promising young **actor***† in London theaters. In 1796, **Thomas Wignell** convinced Cooper to make his American debut in Baltimore and Philadelphia as Macbeth. For his highly praised New York debut, Cooper appeared in *Venice Preserved* and *Hamlet* in 1797. Eventually, disagreements over roles and finances led Cooper to part with Wignell, and on his own, he developed an impressive range of classic and contemporary roles.

Cooper scored a particular success in **William Dunlap**'s adaptation of Kotzebue's *The Stranger* in 1798 and subsequently took over as **manager*†** of the **Park Theatre**. Cooper played Othello to **Edwin Forrest**'s Iago, but over time his audience diminished, and he made his final New York appearance as Marc Antony in *Julius Caesar* in 1835, though he continued to act on **tour*†** until 1838. Not all **critics*†** appreciated his acting, but because he became an American citizen, he is considered to be America's first great tragedian.

THE CORSICAN BROTHERS; OR, THE FATAL DUEL. Alexandre Dumas's 1844 novel was popularized through several **melodramatic*†** stage adaptations and, in the 20th century, in several films.† The most notable stage version was **Dion Boucicault**'s three-act version written in 1852 for **actor*†** Charles Kean, who first appeared in it in February 1852 at London's Princess's Theatre prior to its debut in the United States. Other adaptations, including one by **Charles Fechter**, only enhanced its popularity.

Produced regularly for over a century, the twin brothers of the play's title are Fabian and Louis Dei Franchi. *The Corsican Brothers* presented the unique device of its first and second acts occurring simultaneously and involving Louis in romantic pursuit of Lady De Lesparre, a married woman with yet another suitor, Chateau Renaud, who kills Louis in a duel. In the final act, Renaud is attempting to flee following Louis's death, but when Fabian arrives, Renaud believes he is seeing Louis's ghost. Fabian, discovering his brother's death, duels with Renaud and kills him, avenging Louis. The play's melodramatic elements were the likely reason for its longevity on 19th-century stages, as well as the frequent presence of **star*†** actors in the cast.

COSTA, DAVID (d. 1873). Born in Italy, David Costa was a dancer in the 1840s before becoming a successful choreographer (though the term was not used at that time) in 1853. He immigrated to the United States in the mid-1860s and staged "The Amazon March" and other dances for the phenomenally successful **musical*†** *The Black Crook* (1866). Costa subsequently staged dances for *The White Fawn* (1868), *Humpty Dumpty* (1868), *Barbe-Bleue* (1868), *Hiccory Diccory Dock* (1869), and *The Twelve Temptations* (1870) in that formative era for the American musical.

†COSTUMES. *See* †WARDROBE.

COTTRELLY, MATHILDE (1851–1933). Born into a **musical***† family as the daughter of an opera conductor in Hamburg, Germany, Mathilde Meyer began as a child **actor***† and in her teens was playing **ingénues**† in **operettas**.† She married **actor***† George Cottrelly in 1866, and they performed together, but his death in 1869 led her to the United States, in 1875. Cottrelly **toured***† with McCaull's Comic Opera in comic roles due to her thick German accent. She also worked as a **director***† and **designer***† of costumes and involved herself in the business aspects of the company. In the 1890s, Cottrelly focused on a career in nonmusical works with roles in *Trilby*† (1895), the popular *Potash and Perlmutter*† plays of the 1920s, and the longest-running **Broadway***† comedy of its time, *Abie's Irish Rose*† (1922).

†COULDOCK, C. W. (1815–1898). Born Charles Walter Couldock in London, England, C. W. Couldock established himself as a **leading man**† there, then made his American debut in 1849 at Philadelphia's **Walnut Street Theatre** in support of **Charlotte Cushman** in *The Stranger*. He appeared in **Dion Boucicault**'s *The Willow Corpse*, in the role of an aging farmer driven to madness by his daughter's behavior. He played this role frequently throughout his career. In New York, Couldock joined **Laura Keene**'s company, playing the title role of *Louis XI* (1859), and he **toured***† extensively as a **star***† in tragedies, including **Shakespearean***† roles, most notably Hamlet and as Iago. In his later years, Couldock had a particular success as a domineering father in the hit *Hazel Kirke*† (1880).

THE COUNT OF MONTE CRISTO. The 1844 novel by Alexandre Dumas, set in the midst of turbulent French historical events between 1815 and 1838, focuses on an innocent young sailor, Edmond Dantès, who learns of a hidden treasure, is jailed, escapes, finds the treasure, and sets out to achieve revenge against those who imprisoned him, making for an exceedingly popular stage **melodrama**† during the 19th century. **James W. Wallack** first played the role in an 1848 adaptation, followed by **Edward Eddy** and **Charles Fechter**, who created his own adaptation in 1882. James O'Neill,† the father of **playwright***† Eugene O'Neill,*† played in early adaptations, first in 1875 at **Hooley's Theatre** in Chicago, but in 1883 he appeared with extraordinary success in Fechter's version, and ultimately performed the role at least 6,000 times throughout the remainder of his career. In his drama *Long Day's Journey into Night** (1939), Eugene O'Neill has the character based on his father lamenting the easy money he made in his popular stage vehicle that may have dimmed his promising talents as a true artist.

COWELL, JOE (1792–1863). Born Joseph Leathley Whitshed in England, he went into the Royal Navy, but deserted rather than face charges of hitting an officer. Turning to the stage, Cowell debuted in 1812 at the Drury Lane Theatre, and nearly a decade later, in 1821, he made his American debut at the **Park Theatre** in *The Turnpike Gate*. Cowell made a name as a **touring*†** **actor,*†** but was also associated with Philadelphia's **Walnut Street Theatre** for several years. He was the father of actor **Sam Cowell**.

COWELL, SAM (1820–1864). The son of **actor*†** **Joe Cowell**, Samuel Houghton Cowell was born in England, but brought to America by his father in 1822. He went on the stage in the United States as a **child*†** in **Shakespearean*†** productions and was educated at a military academy, but around 1840 he returned to England and remained there as a successful music hall performer.

†CRABTREE, LOTTA (1847–1924). The pert, red-haired, banjo-playing, singing **actress,*†** born Charlotte Mignon Crabtree, began her stage career as a **child*†** in the California mining camps of the 1850s, and when she retired at 45, she was beloved as "The Nation's Darling." Crabtree and her mother, Mary Ann, followed her father, John, to the California gold mines in 1851. She met **Lola Montez**, who taught her to sing and dance, and she began performing in mining camps and variety theaters. After winning popularity on the San Francisco stage, billed as "Miss Lotta, the San Francisco Favorite," and in such plays as *The Loan of a Lover*, she worked with **manager*†** J. F. Whitman of Chicago, where she performed **soubrette†** roles in a **stock*†** company. Subsequently, Crabtree's mother, a severe watchdog over her daughter's behavior and reputation, took over management of her career.

As one of the most beloved performers on the **road,*†** Crabtree played to sellout houses in response to posters announcing simply, "Lotta tonight!" She appeared in *Uncle Tom's Cabin* in the 1860s, as well as vehicles such as *Jenny Leatherlungs*, *The Pet of the Petticoats* and *Heart's Ease*, among others. Her sprightly energy, improvisational skills, and winning ways shone through all her roles, and she would usually find a moment to interpolate some banjo playing and clog dancing or an **Irish** jig.

Among Crabtree's perennially popular offerings were both title roles in *Little Nell and the Marchioness*, which **John Brougham** adapted for her from **Charles Dickens**'s *The Old Curiosity Shop*, as well as the title roles in *The Little Detective, Musette*, and *The Firefly*. In 1870, she began **touring*†** with her own company instead of working with local companies to keep the quality high. Though romantically linked with several men, Crabtree never married, perhaps to avoid spoiling the stage illusion she created when playing young romantic roles. When she retired in 1892, she had accumulated a fortune of four million dollars, which she subsequently left to charity, including veteran and **actor***† charities. At the time of her death, the *New York Times* described her as the "eternal child."

THE CRADLE OF LIBERTY; OR, BOSTON IN 1775. Stephen E. Glover adapted this 1832 play from James Fenimore Cooper's 1825 novel *Lionel Lincoln; or, The Leaguer of Boston*. First performed under the title *The Rakehellies* on 24 March 1831 at the Camp Street Theatre in New Orleans, with Glover playing the role of Lord Noodle, the play was subsequently produced at Boston's **Tremont Theatre** and New York's **Bowery Theatre** in 1832 under the title *The Cradle of Liberty*. Set during the **American Revolution**, the novel and play focus on the title character, a Boston-born American with an English noble heritage who goes to England, where he becomes a British soldier sent back to America, forcing him to confront his divided loyalties.

†**CRANE, WILLIAM HENRY (1845–1928).** Born in Leicester, Massachusetts, William Henry Crane made his stage debut in Utica, New York, in 1863 in *The Daughter of the Regiment*. He scored a triumph in the popular **burlesque***† *Evangeline* (1873). From 1877 to 1889, he performed in partnership with **Stuart Robson**† in a long succession of comedies, and they enjoyed notable success as the two Dromios in *The Comedy of Errors*, as well as their great vehicle, **Bronson Howard**'s† *The Henrietta*† (1887). After the amicable dissolution of the partnership, Crane found vehicles for his talent, notably *Fool of Fortune* (1896) and *David Harum*† (1900), becoming one of America's most beloved comedians. Crane's career even extended to the era of silent films,† most notably *David Harum* in 1915 and *Three Wise Fools*† in 1923.

*†**CRITICS/CRITICISM.** Dramatic criticism of early American theater in newspapers or periodicals was often anonymous when a byline was included at all. Comments on plays included in 19th-century publications rarely mention much about the production values of the play until about midcentury and are usually brief and without much opinion on overall quality. In the early 19th century, critics appeared in some newspapers in major cities, including J. W. S. Hows of the *New York Albion*, Stephen Cullen Carpenter of the *Charleston Courier*, and **Washington Irving**, though these and other critics often published their reviews under pseudonyms.

In the mid-19th century, publications devoted to theater (and often the other performing and literary arts) provide richer critical responses to the stage of the day. Periodical critics became significantly more influential after the **Civil War**, led by **William Winter**,† and included such writers as **Thomas Allston Brown, Henry Austin Clapp**,† Edward A. Dithmar,†

William Dean Howells,† **Laurence Hutton**,† **J. Ranken Towse**,† and **Andrew Carpenter Wheeler**,† among others. Some critics, like James Huneker, as frequently reviewed art, music, and literature as they covered theater. Also, major literary figures like Irving, including **Edgar Allan Poe**, **Mark Twain**, and others, occasionally wrote on theater for publication.

By the mid-19th century, the slang term for a theater critic was "aisle sitter," as critics were given aisle seats so that they could rush from the theater to the newspaper office in time to bang out a review for the morning edition. Theater **managers***† had uneasy relationships with critics, and on occasion, a critic might find himself barred from a particular theater if he published some comment at which the theater manager took offense. Alfred L. Bernheim recounts an instance when **Augustin Daly**† attempted to have the critic of the *San Francisco Evening Post* ejected from the theater where his company was performing because a prior review had failed to mention the **star**,*† **Ada Rehan**.†

CROCKETT IN TEXAS. This anonymous 1839 play was one among several works that exploited the life of the legendary frontiersman Davy Crockett, whose adventures ended when he died at the Alamo mission in 1836. In fact, during Crockett's lifetime, he was celebrated in the 1831 play, *The Lion of the West*, which starred **James H. Hackett** as Colonel Nimrod Wildfire, a thinly veiled portrait of a heroic Crockett. *Crockett in Texas*, as its title suggests, emphasized the final heroics of Crockett's life leading up to his death at the Alamo. The same year as the play, Crockett, whose legend has only grown over time, was celebrated in a song, "The Alamo, or the Death of Crockett," which was set to the tune of "The Star-Spangled Banner."

CROSS-DRESSING. This time-honored theatrical tradition dates back to the ancient theater. From that period into the 17th century, most European theaters did not permit **women**† to perform. As a result, women's roles were played by men until into the 17th century, well past the start of theater in the United States. British theater traditions dominated in early America, and, when in England women took to the stage after 1660, women performed in America as well. After 1660, women often played male roles, sometimes as male romantic characters, or **child**† roles. Helping to popularize this convention, several of **Shakespeare**'s*† plays conveniently featured female characters disguised as men (breeches roles), and such works were popular on American stages with certain **actresses**,*† including **Sarah Bernhardt**† and **Charlotte Cushman**, widely admired in male roles. However, Cushman disturbed **critics***† when she played Cardinal Wolsey in Shakespeare's *Henry VIII*, a role that had never been played by a woman before.

During the first half of the 19th century, some male and female **actors***† specialized in cross-dressing. **Neil Burgess**† built his career around playing matronly roles, usually as sharp-tongued New Englanders. In the same era, **blackface**† **minstrel**† shows (most featuring all-male companies) and other **musical***† entertainments† often featured cross-dressing, usually for comic purposes or musical numbers, and farces made use of intentional gender confusions as well. The rise of realism*† in the late 19th century seemed to militate against cross-dressing in serious plays, but during the 20th and 21st centuries, American **playwrights***† and performers challenged **gender** stereotypes in complex ways.

CUSHMAN, CHARLOTTE (1816–1876). Born in Boston, as Charlotte Saunders Cushman, she descended from a *Mayflower* family and aimed for a career as an opera singer. She performed with **Mrs. Joseph Wood** in 1834, who introduced her to James G. Maeder, a **musical***† **director***† who guided her to her initial appearances in the operas *The Marriage of Figaro* and *Guy Mannering*, but her voice ultimately failed while she was performing in New Orleans. There, **manager**† **James H. Caldwell** encouraged her to become an **actress,***† and she scored an initial success as Lady Macbeth. Following her engagement with Caldwell in New Orleans, she debuted in New York at the **Bowery Theatre**, also as Lady Macbeth. She scored another notable success in 1837 playing Romeo opposite her sister, Susan Webb Cushman, as Juliet. Other notable triumphs followed, including her iconic performance as Meg Merrilies in a dramatic adaptation of *Guy Mannering*.

Cushman joined the **Park Theatre** company in 1837, playing several **Shakespearean***† roles, including as Volumnia opposite **Edwin Forrest**'s Coriolanus. By this time, she was widely acclaimed as America's leading tragedienne, as she was frequently billed. In another literary adaptation, Cushman was acclaimed as Nancy Sykes in **Charles Dickens**'s *Oliver Twist* in 1839. Cushman was a lesbian and involved in relationships with several **women,***† which was accepted in her time largely because the relationships of women were believed by bourgeois sentiments to be inherently chaste, with physical desire a solely male trait. For a time, Cushman managed Philadelphia's **Walnut Street Theatre** and acted with **William Charles Macready**, who encouraged her to perform in London. She spent several years in England, returning to the United States in 1852 to play Katherine in *Henry VIII*, for which she won **critical***† approval. Cushman played Claude Melnotte in *The Lady of Lyons* (she also played Pauline at various times), one among several male roles she played, later adding Hamlet and Henry VIII's Wolsey to her repertoire, which also included successes in *Much Ado about Nothing*, *As You Like It*, and *The Taming of the Shrew*, among others.

Late in her career, Cushman won new acclaim giving dramatic readings, and her final performance in New York was, appropriately, as Lady Macbeth, her debut role. Following her death in Boston, **William Winter†** wrote, "When she came upon the stage she filled it with the brilliant vitality of her presence. Every movement that she made was winningly characteristic. Her least gesture was eloquence, her voice was soft or silvery, or deep or mellow, according as emotion affected it, used now and then to tremble, and partly to break, with tones that were pathetic beyond description. These were denotements of the fiery soul that smouldered beneath her grave exterior, and gave iridescence to every form of art that she embodied."

CUSTIS, GEORGE WASHINGTON PARKE (1781–1857). As adopted son of **George Washington**, for whom he was named, George Washington Parke Custis was born into privilege and spent part of his youth living with Washington during his presidency. He was educated at Germantown Academy, the College of New Jersey, and St. John's College, and as he became an adult he inherited significant funds and built the Custis Mansion at Arlington Cemetery as a monument to Washington. He was a successful public orator and writer, whose work included plays, two of which, *The Indian Prophecy; or, Visions of Glory* (1827) and *Pocahontas; or, The Settlers of Virginia* (1830), were published. His other plays include *The Rail Road* (1828), *The Eighth of January; or, Hurra for the Boys of the West* (1830), **North Point; or, Baltimore Defended** (1833), and *Montgomerie; or, The Orphan of a Wreck* (1836).

D

DADDY O'DOWD; OR, THE TURN ABOUT IS FAIR PLAY. **Dion Bou-**
cicault's† **Irish** play opened on 17 March 1873, St. Patrick's Day, at
Booth's Theatre, with Boucicault himself playing the title role. Plot elements were derived from a French play, *Les Crochets du Père Martin* by
Grangé and Cormon, and the play was well received, though Boucicault
substantially rewrote it for its London premiere on 21 October 1880, retitling
it *The O'Dowd; or, Life in Galway.*

In the play, Michael O'Dowd, a young Irishman studying to be a lawyer, is
living on borrowed money and a fake name, Percy Walsingham. Under this
pseudonym, he pretends to be part of English society to be near the girl he
loves, Lady Gwendoline. His debtors are putting the squeeze on him—and
when O'Dowd's father, also named Michael, and sister arrive unexpectedly,
their Old World manners meet with ridicule from Percy's society friends.
Later, back in Galway, "Percy's" father learns that his son's debts have led to
a charge of fraud, and he banishes "Percy" from the family. Lady Gwendoline arrives in Galway still wishing to marry Percy, but he leaves to avoid
causing her further social disgrace. After considerable machinations and the
passage of three years, Percy is thought lost at sea. However, the truth is that
he saves the ship, earns a fortune in salvage (to redeem his debts), and returns
home to restore his good name. Lady Gwendoline is reunited with him, and
Percy makes amends with his father and family.

†DALY, AUGUSTIN (1838–1899). Born in Plymouth, North Carolina, as
John Augustin Daly, he was educated in Norfolk, Virginia, and in New York
City. Son of a sea captain, the **playwright*†** and **manager*†** began his
theatrical career as a drama **critic.*†** His first play, *Leah, the Forsaken*,
adapted from S. H. von Mosenthal's *Deborah*, scored a success in 1862 and
remained in the dramatic canon for the rest of the 19th century. Daly had an
even greater triumph with his sensationally popular **melodrama†** *Under the*
Gaslight (1867), one of the best-known American stage works of the era. He
began producing plays at the **Fifth Avenue Theatre** in 1869, where he
established an innovative **repertory†** company, staging both contemporary

and classic works (frequently adapted by Daly). Daly broke away from the standard **lines of business**,† expecting his performers to play a wide range of characters, a practice that ultimately became the standard.

Daly operated the Fifth Avenue Theatre successfully until the building burned in 1873, but he pressed on in other facilities until he retired briefly in 1877. Back at work in 1879, Daly established an acclaimed company at the Daly Theatre (formerly Wood's Museum) that included the "Big Four," as they became known: **Ada Rehan**,† **Mrs. G. H. Gilbert**,† **James Lewis**,† and **John Drew**,† with **William Davidge** and **Charles Fisher** in strong support. The company performed every manner of play, from works by **Shakespeare***† and Tennyson to new American plays, including works credited to Daly. Even popular **operettas**† and **musicals***† were performed. Daly's company dominated the New York theater in the last two decades of the 19th century. The troupe **toured***† the United States and England frequently, as well as three residencies in France and one in Germany.

Daly is credited with writing as many as 100 plays, though many were adaptations of classics or European plays. It is believed that Daly's brother, Joseph, an attorney, was an uncredited co-author. The most appreciated Daly plays, *A Flash of Lightning* (1868), *Frou-Frou* (1870), *Horizon* (1871), *Divorce* (1871), and *Pique* (1875), were staples of his company's **repertory**.*† Later Daly successes include *Needles and Pins* (1880), *Dollars and Sense* (1883), *Love on Crutches* (1884), and *The Lottery of Love*† (1888). Daly's most successful Shakespearean production, *The Taming of the Shrew*, was performed at Stratford-upon-Avon in 1888, billed as the first production of the play there.

Of Daly, critic **William Winter**† wrote, "He made the Theatre important, and he kept it worthy of the sympathy and support of the most refined taste and the best intellects of his time." One of Daly's **stars**,*† **Clara Morris**, remembered his strict discipline and talent fondly: "Before I came under the management of Mr. Daly, I may say I never really knew what stage-management meant. He was a young man then; he had had, I believe, his own theatre but one season before I joined his forces, yet his judgment was as ripe, his decisions were as swift and sure, his eye for effect as true, his dramatic instinct as keen as well could be."

†DALY, CHARLES PATRICK (1816–1899). Born in New York to **Irish** immigrant parents, Charles Patrick Daly worked various jobs while studying law and was admitted to the bar in 1839. As an eminent and respected jurist, he wrote prolifically on many subjects, as well as serving as president of the American Geographical Society. His love of theater impelled him to offer legal aid without charge to indigent **actors**.*† In regard to theater, Daly's most important case involved the **Astor Place Opera House** riot. In response to the antitheatrical sentiment of his time, he published *First Theatre in America: When Was the Drama First Introduced in America?*

DALY'S THEATRE. *See* FIFTH AVENUE THEATRE.

†*THE DANITES; OR, THE HEART OF THE SIERRAS.* Western poet **Joaquin Miller**'s† 1877 **melodrama**† of Mormon revenge remained popular on the **road,***† especially in the West, throughout the 1880s, and was particularly identified with **actor***† **McKee Rankin,**† who played Alexander "Sandy" McKee, who ultimately takes on the Danites, a secret Mormon group. **Critics***† commented on the similarity of the play's characters to those created by **Bret Harte**.

Among the strong appeals of the play's action was a woman, Nancy Williams (played by **Kitty Blanchard**), who disguises herself in male dress and lives in a crude mining camp in order to escape the Danites, who seek to kill her as they have done other members of her family. Sandy is fooled by her disguise for a time, but ultimately wards off a lynch mob when he learns that Nancy is a woman.

In its original run, *The Danites* played only 30 performances at the **Broadway Theatre**, where it opened on 20 August 1877. One critic called it "obscure and tedious," while others questioned the plausibility of a woman disguised as a man in a mining camp, but the play remained in the repertory† of American drama for many years and through multiple revivals and **tours***† (Rankin played the role for several years). In London, the play was seen under the title *The First Families of the Sierras*. In a 13 May 1878 letter to the *New York Times*, Miller described his play as "a rough stone, but I believe a real one."

DARBY'S RETURN: A COMIC SKETCH. **William Dunlap**'s comic interlude, his second produced work, was first performed on 24 November 1789 at the **New York Theatre** as a benefit for **Thomas Wignell**, who played the title character. The performance was distinguished by the presence in the audience of President **George Washington**. Darby, a naïve, occasionally cowardly **Irish** bungler, a character inspired by John O'Keefe's *The Poor Soldier* (1786) and by aspects of the **Yankee**† Jonathan of **Royall Tyler**'s *The Contrast* (1787), offers comic commentary on current events, including the adoption of the Constitution and the inauguration of the first president of the United States. Darby returns to Ireland following his visits to America and France (although Dunlap removed the references to France in performances, fearing negative responses from those in the audience sympathizing with the French), where he has observed both revolutions.

Dunlap later recalled concern about Washington's response, but he was pleased to note that the president smiled at Darby's commentary on the change in the structure of the government provided by the Constitution:

> There too I saw some mighty pretty shows;
> A revolution, without blood or blows,
> For as I understood, the cunning elves,
> The people all revolted from themselves.

DAVENPORT, E. L. (1815–1877). Born Edward Loomis Davenport in Boston, he debuted as an **actor*†** using the stage name Mr. Dee in 1836 playing opposite **Junius Brutus Booth** in *A New Way to Pay Old Debts* in Providence, Rhode Island. His first New York appearance was in *He's Not A-Miss*, and he **toured*†** for several years before working in England in supporting roles† with **Anna Cora Mowatt, Frederick B. Conway**, and **William Charles Macready** from 1848 to 1854, proving his talents in a range of contemporary plays (*Black-Eyed Susan, Francesca da Rimini, The Lady of Lyons*) and **Shakespearean*†** parts, including Hamlet and Iago.

In 1849, Davenport married English **actress*†** Fanny Vining (1829–1891) and two of their children, **Fanny Davenport** and Harry Davenport (1866–1949), followed them into the acting profession. Upon returning to the United States in 1854, Davenport continued to develop his versatility with the most notable companies, including **Burton**'s, **Wallack**'s, and **Daly's Fifth Avenue Theatre**. He also toured for many years with his own company, playing opposite his wife.

Late in his career, Davenport had two notable successes opposite **Lawrence Barrett** in Shakespeare, playing Brutus to Barrett's Cassius in *Julius Caesar* and as Edgar to Barrett's King Lear in 1875. Davenport retired in 1877, shortly before his death. Henry A. Weaver, a member of Davenport's company in his later years, recalled that Davenport's "kind and amiable disposition endeared him to his associates, while his great ability as an actor won their unbounded admiration."

†DAVENPORT, FANNY (1850–1898). Born in London as Fanny Lily Gipsy Davenport, she was the first **child†** of American **actor*†** and **manager*† E. L. Davenport**, who had come to London as **Anna Cora Mowatt**'s **leading man,†** and English **actress*†** Fanny Vining. Her brother, Harry Davenport (1866–1949), had a long career onstage and as a much-admired **character actor†** in films. The Davenports returned to America in 1854 and settled in Boston, where "Miss Fanny" was educated and where she played the title character's daughter in *Metamora; or, The Last of the Wampanoags* at the **Howard Athenaeum**. Davenport played other child roles at the Howard, which her father managed from 1859.

Davenport's early adult **line of business†** was playing **soubrette†** roles in a **stock*†** company in Louisville, and then at Philadelphia's **Arch Street Theatre**. She also appeared at **Niblo's Garden** in 1862 where, at the age of 12, she played the King of Spain in *Faint Heart Never Won Fair Lady*. On 29 September 1869, she made a very successful debut with **Augustin Daly's†** company at his **Fifth Avenue Theatre** in New York. She remained with Daly until 1877, triumphing notably as Mabel Renfrew in *Pique*, which Daly wrote for her and which achieved a run of 238 performances. She then **toured*†** as a **star*†** with a **repertory*†** of **Shakespeare,*† melodramas,†** and English comedies. In 1883, she began acquiring the American rights to French actress **Sarah Bernhardt's†** vehicles (*Fedora, La Tosca, Cleopatra,* and *Gismonda*), all of which she performed with considerable success. In 1889, she married her second husband, **matinee idol†** Melbourne MacDowell.†

DAVENPORT, JEAN. *See* LANDER, MRS. F. W. (1829–1903).

DAVENPORT BROTHERS. Ira Erastus Davenport (1839–1911) and William Henry Davenport (1841–1877), known as the Davenport Brothers, were popular **magicians** on the **vaudeville†** stages of the mid-19th century. Born in Buffalo, New York, the sons of a police officer, they capitalized on the Spiritualism movement when they went on the stage in 1854. As part of their act, the Davenports employed a minister, Dr. J. B. Ferguson, whose presence was intended to validate the legitimacy of their box illusion (and William Fay, a conjurer, also joined them). The brothers were bound and closed up in a box filled with **musical*†** instruments. Shortly thereafter, sounds emanated from the musical instruments, but when the box was opened, the brothers were revealed still tied up.

The Davenports **toured*†** America for a decade before traveling to England, where Spiritualism had also become popular, and had their tricks investigated by the Ghost Club. For a time, beginning in 1868, magician **Harry Kellar** joined their act, although he ultimately broke away as a solo performer. Though the act continued to tour, attempts were made to expose them as frauds, including by **P. T. Barnum**, a rather ironic turn since Barnum reveled in fraudulent exhibits and acts he managed. The brothers inspired Harry Houdini,† although he never allied himself with Spiritualism and made clear to his audiences that his tricks were a matter of skill.

DAVIDGE, WILLIAM (1814–1888). London-born William Pleater Davidge made his debut as an **amateur†** at the Drury Lane Theatre in *The Miller's Maid* and appeared in the English provinces beginning in 1836, ultimately finding success as a comic **actor.*†** In 1850, Davidge made his

American debut at the **Broadway Theatre** and acted in a number of leading theaters (**Bowery Theatre, Winter Garden**) and supported such notable actors as **Edwin Forrest, Julia Dean, Lola Montez**, and **Fanny Davenport** before joining **Frederick B. Conway**'s company, after which, beginning in 1863, he appeared with **Mrs. John Wood**'s company at the **Olympic Theatre**.

Davidge was a key member of **Augustin Daly**'s† **Fifth Avenue Theatre** company from 1869 to 1877, after which he originated the role of Dick Deadeye in the American premiere production of *H.M.S. Pinafore* (1879). Davidge's last years were spent as a member of the **Madison Square Theatre** company, beginning in 1885 and concluding with his sudden death in Wyoming while on **tour***† with the company. Davidge's son, William Davidge (1847–1899), was also an actor. In 1866, Davidge published an autobiography, *Footlight Flashes*.

DAVIS, L. CLARKE (1835–1904). Born in Sandusky, Ohio, L. Clarke Davis grew up in Maryland, the son of farmers. He studied for a legal career, but his proficiency in writing and deep interest in literature led to a newspaper career. Davis became editor of the *Philadelphia Inquirer* in 1870, and much of his reputation was based on his skill as a drama **critic**,*† winning him the admiration and friendship of such **leading**† **actors***† as **Edwin Booth**† and **Joseph Jefferson**.† He also wrote short stories and essays on drama for a range of periodicals and published one novel, *The Stranded Ship* (1869). In 1863, Davis married Rebecca Blaine Harding (1831–1910), a writer noted as a leader in literary realism*† in American literature whose voluminous writings include commentary on the stage.

DAVY CROCKETT; OR, BE SURE YOU'RE RIGHT, THEN GO AHEAD. **Frank Murdoch**'s five-act **melodrama**† celebrating the legendary life of frontiersman Davy Crockett opened at **Wood's Museum** on 2 June 1873 for 12 performances, following a poorly received initial production in Rochester, New York, the previous year. **Frank Mayo** played Crockett, who, during the course of the action, saves Little Nell, his **childhood**† sweetheart, from the elements, wolves, and **villains**† battling over an estate. In the highly fictional work, Crockett saves the day and marries Little Nell. Mayo scored a particular success as Crockett and played the role throughout the remainder of his career.

DEAN, JULIA (1830–1868). Born to a theatrical family in Pleasant Valley, New York, Julia Dean won acclaim as both a beauty and an **actress***† despite a short life. Her mother died when Dean was a toddler, and she began acting as a **child**† under the auspices of her father, Edwin Dean, with Ludlow's **Stock***† Company. Her adult debut, in Louisville in 1845 in *Lady of the Lake*, led to her New York debut a year later at the **Bowery Theatre** in *The Hunchback*. She was well received in the standard repertory† of the time in such plays as *The Lady of Lyons*, *The Stranger*, and *Pizarro*, but was especially acclaimed as Juliet. She **toured***† widely, for a time billed as Julia Dean Hayne during her first marriage to Arthur P. Hayne, including a highly successful time in California. Hayne was an abusive drunk, compelling Dean to divorce him in 1865. She remarried, but her life was cut short by her death in childbirth. Dean's niece and namesake, Julia Dean† (1880–1952), became a successful actress in the early 20th century.

THE DEATH OF GENERAL MONTGOMERY AT THE SIEGE OF QUEBEC. **Hugh H. Brackenridge** composed this 1777 blank verse tragedy for his students at Maryland's Somerset Academy, where he was headmaster. As a patriotic history-based drama emphasizing the inhumanity of the British Army during General Richard Montgomery's ill-fated siege of Quebec in December 1775 during a blizzard, the play was appreciated when it was published during the **American Revolution** (and possibly performed at Harvard College), when Brackenridge served as chaplain to General **George Washington**'s army.

†**DE BAR, BENEDICT (1812–1877).** The London-born **actor***† and **manager***† known familiarly as "Ben" De Bar is largely associated with mid-19th-century theater in New Orleans and St. Louis. He and his sister, Clementine, who later married **Junius Brutus Booth**, began as actors in **James H. Caldwell**'s **St. Charles Street Theatre** in New Orleans in 1834. De Bar made his official debut in *The School for Scandal* the following year. In 1838, De Bar joined **Noah Ludlow** and **Sol Smith**'s company as a comedian and was also with **James W. Wallack** at the **National Theatre** in New York. His most acclaimed role was Falstaff, but he also excelled at parodies and was known to be very funny offstage as well. De Bar also won acclaim playing Mose, the Bowery b'hoy fireman.

By the 1850s, De Bar was devoting himself largely to management, having leased the **St. Charles** as well as Bates Theatre in St. Louis. For a time he would conduct an autumn season in St. Louis, then rent out that theater during the winter while he took his company to New Orleans. During the **Civil War**, De Bar, who was believed to be a Southern sympathizer, remained in St. Louis. Following the assassination of President **Abraham Lincoln** by **John Wilkes Booth**,† and because of his sister's association with the Booth family, federal authorities searched De Bar's home. In 1873, De Bar bought Field's Varieties in St. Louis and named it De Bar's Opera House, while the Bates became the **Theatre Comique**.† The mildly eccentric

De Bar, frequently heard exclaiming "Egad!" was much loved by all who worked with him. At the time of his death, the *New York Times* hailed De Bar as "a man of the strictest integrity and honor."

DEERING, NATHANIEL (1791–1881). Born in Portland, Maine, Nathaniel Deering studied at Exeter Academy and Harvard, graduating in 1810, before ultimately distinguishing himself as a lawyer, journalist, and writer, though he began his working life in business. He may have written several plays, but the titles of only three are confirmed: a tragedy, *Carabasset; or, The Last of the Norridgewocks* (1831); a comedy, *The Clairvoyants* (1844); and *Bozzaris* (1851), a romantic blank verse drama. He also wrote humor based on life in New England.

THE DEFEAT. **Mercy Otis Warren**'s play, published in 1773 in installments in the *Boston Gazette*, was intended to expose Massachusetts governor Thomas Hutchinson as too closely allied to the British, a traitorous position in the eyes of American patriots. Warren had previously depicted Hutchinson as a hypocrite in her play *The Adulateur* (1772), but the public exposure of Hutchinson's letters to the British, uncovered by Benjamin Franklin in England, inspired *The Defeat.* Hutchinson is seen in the guise of Rapatio, Bashaw of Servia, in Warren's satire.

THE DEFORMED; OR, WOMAN'S TRIAL. **Robert Penn Smith**'s five-act romantic tragedy, inspired by the works of Thomas Dekker, opened on 4 February 1830 for four performances at Philadelphia's **Chestnut Street Theatre**. The title character, Adorni, is consumed with paranoia, unable to comprehend the love of his wife, Eugenia, given his deformities. Adorni enlists a friend, Claudio, to test Eugenia's faithfulness, but is so consumed with jealousy that he betrays Claudio, who is condemned to death. Adorni eventually recognizes his erring ways and decides to take Claudio's place at the execution, but both men are spared by the duke's pardon. The role of the duke was played by **Francis Courtney Wemyss, manager*†** of the Chestnut Street Theatre.

DELANO, ALONZO (1806–1874). Born in Aurora, New York, Alonzo Delano won popularity as an American literary humorist in the same class in his time as **Mark Twain** and **Bret Harte**. Writing under the pseudonym "Old Block," Delano found his subjects in the American West, most particularly as one of the "Forty-Niners" of the California gold rush of 1849. Most of his work was fiction, sometimes in the style known as "California Humor," but he dabbled in theater with his two-act play *A Live Woman in the Mines; or, Pike County Ahead!* (1857), which, as its title suggests, places an "Amazonian" woman, High Betty Martin, in a male-dominated mining town.

DELMONICO'S RESTAURANT. This popular eatery, founded in 1837 near the Battery in New York by the Delmonico brothers, John and Peter, was an extension of the small pastry and wine shop they had begun in 1827 after their arrival in the United States from Italy. Delmonico's became the first fine dining restaurant, especially known for its steaks. By the 1860s, other uniquely original dishes were created and popularized at Delmonico's, including eggs Benedict, baked Alaska, and lobster Newburg. The restaurant's unprecedented luxury, including private dining rooms and outstanding food, brought all manner of celebrities to its door, including esteemed members of the theatrical community. A group of **actors*†** dining at Delmonico's agreed to create the **Lambs' Club†** to make it possible for members of the profession to enjoy the sort of evening available at Delmonico's in the private dining rooms.

DENIN, KATE (1837–1907). Kate Denin's father died when she was an infant, but a few years later her mother married an **actor,*†** John Winans, and the Philadelphia-born Denin went on the stage with him as a **child,†** appearing at the **Chatham Garden Theatre**, the **Bowery Theatre**, and others. In her early teens, she played Romeo to the Juliet of her older sister, **Susan Denin**. She **toured*†** widely and settled for a time in San Francisco in 1854. Denin toured Australia beginning in 1857 and lived there and in England for long periods. Known especially for her flair in comedy, Denin appeared in a range of plays, from **Shakespeare*†** (usually opposite her sister) to contemporary plays, often appearing with **McKee Rankin**. She married actor John Wilson in 1861 and afterward appeared with his company. In 1881, Denin, billed as Kate Denin Wilson, appeared in *Esmeralda†* at the **Madison Square Theatre**, followed by many **character roles**, including her last, shortly before her death, in Israel Zangwill's† *Nurse Marjorie* (1906).

DENIN, SUSAN (1835–1875). Philadelphia-born Susan Denin lost her father in **childhood,†** but her mother's remarriage to an **actor,*†** John Winans, provided entrée to the stage for Denin and her younger sister **Kate Denin**. The sisters began their careers as dancing fairies at Philadelphia's **National Theatre**, and Susan appeared in *Pizarro*, but in their teens the Denin sisters played opposite each other in *Romeo and Juliet*, with Susan as Juliet to Kate's Romeo. They appeared together in other **Shakespeare*†** plays and were particularly successful performing in San Francisco, on **tour,*†** and in London, where Susan first appeared in 1869. Denin appeared with **Junius Brutus Booth**, **Frank S. Chanfrau**, and her stepfather in **Benjamin A. Baker**'s *New York as It Is* (1848), but her career ended prematurely as the result of injuries from a fall onstage in an Indianapolis theater while playing in *Leah, the Forsaken*.

D'ENNERY, ADOLPHE-PHILIPPE (1811–1899). A French **dramatist†** of Jewish descent, Adolphe-Philippe was born in Paris, added D'Ennery (or Dennery) to his name, and pursued a highly successful career as the writer of **melodramas†** popular in Europe and in America, beginning with *Emilie* (1831). Among the most frequently produced plays were *The Two Orphans* (1874) and *A Celebrated Case* (1878). D'Ennery also wrote opera librettos, including Gounod's *Faust* and Massenet's *Le Cid*.

DESERET DESERTED; OR, THE LAST DAYS OF BRIGHAM YOUNG BEING A STRICTLY BUSINESS TRANSACTION IN FOUR ACTS AND SEVERAL DEEDS, INVOLVING BOTH PROFIT AND LOSS. This anonymous four-act farce, supposedly written by members of the Moon Club, opened on 24 May 1858 at **Wallack's Theatre**. Satirizing the Mormon leader, Brigham Young, who is depicted in a drunk scene and meeting Muhammad in a fantasized oriental paradise, the play was among several satiric or outright anti-Mormon works of the time, including two others produced within months of *Deseret Deserted* in 1858: Thomas Dunn English's *The Mormons; or, Life at Salt Lake City*, produced at **Burton's** Theatre, and *Life of the Mormons at Salt Lake*, staged at the **National Theatre**.

DESIGNER. *See* *†SCENE DESIGN/SCENERY.

DESOTO, THE HERO OF MISSISSIPPI. George H. **Miles**'s five-act tragedy debuted on 20 April 1857 with **E. L. Davenport** as the Spanish explorer and conquistador Hernando de Soto (1496–1542) and Fanny Vining Davenport as a **Native American*†** girl, Ulah. It was unsuccessful at the **Broadway Theatre** and withdrawn within a week of its opening.

DEVLIN, MARY. *See* BOOTH, MARY DEVLIN (1840–1863).

DE WALDEN, THOMAS BLADES (1811–1873). Actor,*† playwright,*† and **manager*†** Thomas Blades was born in London and became a regular at **Pfaff**'s. He made his debut in the United States in 1844 in *Is He Jealous?* at the **Park Theatre**, after which he served as business manager for **Frank S. Chanfrau** and wrote plays, including the **melodrama†** *The Upper Ten and the Lower Twenty* (1854), *Manifest Destiny* (1855), *Vice and Virtue; or, A Woman's Heart* (1855), *Wall Street* (1857), *The Monkey Boy*

(1860), *Toodles, a Father* (1860), *The Man of Destiny* (1861), *Luck; or, The Gentleman of Nature* (1862), *Pomp of Cudjo's Cave* (1863), *Sam* (1865)—in which he acted, **Kit, the Arkansas Traveler** (1871), and *The Life and Death of Natty Bumppo* (1873), the last written for actor **Edward Eddy**.

†DIALECT ROLE. Characters requiring ethnic or regional dialects date to the beginning of American drama. Regional dialects increasingly identified not only those living in the Northern or Southern colonies/states, but also defined **race**,*† national background, city, and rural character. Ethnic and national dialects were a popular source of comedy not only on the variety stage, but also in legitimate† plays during the second half of the 19th century as immigrants came to the United States in record numbers.

Before the racial integration of the American stage in the 20th century, **African American***† characters were often played by whites in **blackface**,† using linguistic clichés and stereotypical pronunciations (or mispronunciations). Many of the 19th-century **melodramas**† featuring African American or **Native American***† characters, for example, *Uncle Tom's Cabin* (1853) or *The Octoroon* (1859)—the latter featuring both black and Indian characters—are written in exaggerated dialects and typically for comic relief, a practice that continued well into the 20th century. Similarly, **Irish**, Jewish, German, Scandinavian, and other ethnicities were portrayed largely through exaggerated dialects and vocabularies—and attributed stereotypical characteristics recognized by audiences as belonging to the particular group supposedly depicted.

DIAMOND, JOHN (1823–1857). Sometimes known as Jack or Johnny, and billed as Master Diamond or Master Jack Diamond, John Diamond was an **Irish** American dancer and **minstrel**† performer who won a jig contest in New York, which attracted **P. T. Barnum** as a **manager**.*† Barnum hyped him as the "King of Diamonds," but Diamond and Barnum parted company after a short association. Diamond developed a distinct style of **blackface**† performing, mixing aspects of English, Irish, and African dance. He drew particular attention to himself with challenges to other performers, losing only to **William Henry Lane**, known as Master Juba, an **African American***† performer.

In 1843, Diamond joined the **Virginia Minstrels**, after which he also performed with the **Ethiopian Serenaders**. Of Diamond's style, theater manager **Noah Ludlow** recalled that "He could twist his feet and legs, while dancing, into more fantastic forms than I ever witnessed before or since in any human being." Diamond also performed comic stump speeches in an exaggerated Negro dialect. After his popularity waned, he died penniless, but several minstrel performers arranged a benefit to pay his funeral expenses.

DIAMONDS. **Bronson Howard**'s five-act comedy of manners opened at the **Fifth Avenue Theatre** on 26 September 1872 with a stellar cast including **William Davidge, James Lewis, Fanny Davenport, Fanny Morant**, and **Mrs. G. H. Gilbert**. Brander Matthews† called it "a comedy of contemporaneous manners," but *Diamonds* proved a disappointing opener for **Augustin Daly**'s† company, and **critics***† felt it was uncomfortably similar in plot to English **playwright***† **Tom Taylor**'s 1855 play *Still Waters Run Deep*. Howard did not respond to the implication of plagiarism.

DIPLOMACY. **Victorien Sardou**'s four-act play was first staged in the United States on 1 April 1878 by **Lester Wallack** at his theater in an adaptation by Saville and Bolton Rowe. Set in Monte Carlo, Dora, a poor girl, played by **Maude Granger**, is unwittingly caught between her new husband, Julian Beauclere (**H. J. Montague**), and Countess Zicka (**Rose Coghlan**), who has been jilted by Julian. The countess, seeking revenge, attempts to frame Dora over a stolen document, but her plot fails. The cast also included Wallack and **Madame Ponisi**. Despite its relatively slight content, *Diplomacy* was frequently produced into the 1920s, including New York revivals in 1901, 1910, 1914, and an **all-star***† 1928 George C. Tyler production.

†**DIRECTING.** The rise of the stage director as the dominant force in theatrical production began in the last decades of the 19th century. The **actor***†-**manager***† of the 18th century and first three-quarters of the 19th century slowly evolved into a dominant interpretive force commanding overall responsibility for every facet of a production.

Prior to the rise of the director as the guiding artistic force of a production, the aforementioned actor-manager ran her or his company and repertoire of plays as she or he saw fit, often favoring their own performance over the dramatic requirements of the play. As stage technology developed rapidly in the first decades of the 19th century, large-scale productions, from **sensation**† **melodramas**† to **Shakespeare**,*† increasingly required a force to unify and shape all of the elements created by disparate artists contributing to the production. In short, the job of director created itself out of the increasing demands of theater production as the 19th century progressed. The **star***† actor found it increasingly difficult to manage her or his own performance and see to all of the other production elements growing in size, scope, and complexity.

As pioneered by Georg II, Duke of Saxe-Meningen, in 1870s Europe, the modern director was a force to guide actors, **designers**,*† and technicians to achieve an aesthetically unified production, with an emphasis on the signposts provided by the text of the play. The control of actor-managers, particularly those who were star actors, continued well into the 20th century as the star often remained the strongest presence in a commercial theater production, while artistically inclined **producers*†** such as George M. Cohan*† (who often directed, while also producing, acting, and writing) or Florenz Ziegfeld Jr.† (strictly a producer, albeit one with strong aesthetic sensibilities) employed directors as little more than glorified stage managers while they continued to control all aspects of production.

Indeed, in England, the practice of directing continued to be ascribed to a "producer" for several decades after the term "director" became current in American theater. The abandonment of **lines of business,†** the rise of **realism*†** in US drama influenced by the works of Henrik Ibsen† and other innovative European dramatists in the late 19th century, and in the painstakingly detailed and highly naturalistic stage productions of producer-playwrights like **David Belasco,†** along with significant advances in theatrical technology, increased the need for a strong director to guide actors through the intricacies of challenging plays and to supervise increasingly complex technical productions.

THE DISAPPOINTMENT; OR, THE FORCE OF CREDULITY. This satiric ballad opera by Andrew Barton (believed to be a pseudonym for Colonel Thomas Forrest, later an officer in the **American Revolution** and a politician), was scheduled for a performance in Philadelphia in April 1767 by **David Douglass**'s company, but canceled for reasons that remain unclear. Most likely the play's satirizing of King George III's governance and mocking of prominent Philadelphia personages caused local outrage and led to the cancellation. Despite the fact that it was not performed in its time, *The Disappointment* is notable for several reasons, not least in that it is believed to be the first indigenous American opera and because it contains the first evidence of the tune "Yankee Doodle," which was interpolated with lyrics by Barton/Forrest. In 1976, on the 200th birthday of the United States, the Library of Congress partnered with the University of Rochester's Eastman School of Music to reconstruct *The Disappointment.*

DIVORCE. **Augustin Daly**'s five-act comedy opened at Daly's **Fifth Avenue Theatre** on 5 September 1871 for an impressive 200 performances, making it one of the major successes of its era. Freely borrowing and adapting characters and events from Anthony Trollope's novel *He Knew He Was Right*, Daly set *Divorce*, which he subtitled "A Play of the Period," in present-day America. Centered on the topic of divorce, Daly depicts two couples with troubled marriages. Two sisters, Lu and Fanny Ten Eyck, played by **Fanny Davenport†** and **Clara Morris,†** respectively, marry, but within a short time problems arise. Lu has married a much older man, De Wolf De Witt, played by **William Davidge**, while Fanny's marriage to her longtime love, Alfred, played by D. H. Harkins, is threatened by the fact that he is jealous of her innocent relationship with another man, Captain Lynde, played by **Louis James**.† Alfred kidnaps their young son when Fanny leaves, but she tracks him to Florida, and they are ultimately reunited, as are Lu and De Witt. A **critic***† in the *New York Herald* praised the play's "naturalness in dialogue and action" and, in what became the hallmark of Daly's company, lauded the "perfection of ensemble, even down to the minutest detail."

†**DIXEY, HENRY E. (1859–1943).** Despite the fact that he was largely associated with the **musical***† theater, Henry E. Dixey (born Henry E. Dixon in Boston) also **starred***† in legitimate† plays. He made his debut as a **child**† at the **Howard Athenaeum** in *Under the Gaslight* in Boston in 1869 when he was nine. For his adult debut in 1874, he played eight roles (including half of a dancing cow) in the **burlesque***† *Evangeline*, under **manager***† **Augustin Daly**,† at the **Fifth Avenue Theatre**. Dixey was best remembered in the title role in *Adonis* (1884), as he cut a handsome figure in the form-revealing costume. His nonmusical credits included *Oliver Goldsmith* (1900), *Becky Sharp*† (1911), *Mrs. Bumpstead-Leigh*† (1911), *Twelfth Night* in 1914, *Treasure Island*† (1916), *The School for Scandal* in 1923, and others. Dixey also appeared in silent films† and died after being struck by a bus in Atlantic City, New Jersey.

DIXON, GEORGE WASHINGTON (1801?–1861). An early **blackface**† entertainer† probably born in Richmond, Virginia, George Washington Dixon ran away to work in a **circus***† in his teens. Details about his early life are scarce, including whether he was Caucasian or **African American***† (some period accounts refer to him as a mulatto). He found success as a singer of **minstrel**† songs such as "Coal Black Rose" and "Zip Coon." In the late 1820s and early 1830s, he rivaled **Thomas Dartmouth "Daddy" Rice** in popularity.

In July 1829, he performed "Coal Black Rose" at the **Bowery Theatre**, **Chatham Garden Theatre**, and **Park Theatre**, as well as a comic sketch, *Love in a Cloud*, based on the song, that some scholars deem the first blackface farce. He was especially popular with working-class audiences, but in the early 1830s he started the first of several newspapers for which he served as editor. He also became embroiled in various topical controversies and disagreements with other journalists and in advocating for workers' rights.

By the early 1840s, Dixon made fewer appearances onstage to focus on his journalistic activities. With the outbreak of the **Mexican War**, Dixon again performed "Zip Coon," but with new lyrics emphasizing topical politics about the conflict. He retired to New Orleans in the late 1840s, and it is believed he was penniless at the time of his death.

DOCK STREET THEATRE. Believed to be the first permanent structure in America built with the sole purpose of presenting theater, this Charleston, South Carolina, theater, situated in the French Quarter at the corner of Church Street and Dock Street, opened with a production of *The Recruiting Officer* on 12 February 1736. The theater apparently fell into disuse by 1738 and is believed to have burned in a citywide fire in 1740.

THE DOCTOR OF ALCANTARA. Benjamin E. Woolf's two-act opéra bouffe with music by Julius Eichberg was first produced in Boston in 1862 and opened in New York at the French Theatre on 25 September 1866 for 12 performances. Carlos and Isabella, two young lovers, are compelled by their fathers to acquiesce to arranged marriages. After considerable machinations, they ultimately discover that they are, in fact, each other's intended spouse. A forerunner of **operettas**† like those of **W. S. Gilbert** and **Arthur Sullivan**, *The Doctor of Alcantara* did not equal the popularity of the later works that populated American stages within little more than a decade after its premiere.

DODDRIDGE, JOSEPH (1769–1826). Born in New Bedford, Pennsylvania, Joseph Doddridge moved with his Wesleyan Methodist family to West Virginia in his **childhood**.† He went to school in Maryland, and in his late teens he worked as a traveling Methodist minister. The death of his father necessitated his return to West Virginia to run the family farm, and while there he attended Jefferson Academy, becoming a medical doctor. His sole work for the theater was a play, *Logan, The Last of the Race of Shikellemus, Chief of the Cayuga Nation* (1821), which offered a sympathetic portrait of the half-white son of a **Native American***† chief who led raids on white settlements in retaliation for the murders of his family during the Yellow Creek Massacre. Doddridge also wrote *Notes on the Settlement and Indian Wars of the Western Parts of Virginia and Pennsylvania, from 1763–1783, inclusive; Together with a View of the State of Society, and Manner of the First Settlers of the Western Country* (1824).

DOG DRAMAS. By the 1830s, under **manager***† **Thomas Hamblin**, the **Bowery Theatre** presented a wide variety of entertainments,† from standard plays to **minstrel**† shows. Among the novelties were **melodramas**† in which trained dogs performed significant actions, often at the climactic moments by aiding or rescuing heroic characters or attacking **villains**.† As early as the late 18th century, plays featuring dogs centrally in a play's action were popular in England and Ireland, but the vogue caught on in America, with such plays, including *The Planter and His Dogs* and *The Dogs of the Wreck*, popular until after the **Civil War**.

At the **Bowery Theatre**, British performers Barkham Cony and Edwin Blanchard had been major forces in popularizing such plays—and when they broke up their partnership, each continued, with Cony and his son appearing in *The Cross of Death; or, The Dog Witness* and *The Butcher's Dog of Ghent*, among other such vehicles. Blanchard appeared at the **National Theatre** in plays including *The Watch Dogs* and *The Fisherman and His Dogs*. Among American **actors**,*† **Fanny Herring** exploited the vogue of dog plays when, in the 1860s, she appeared at the Bowery in *The Rag Woman and Her Dogs* **costarring***† with her own pets.

DOMBEY AND SON. **Charles Dickens**'s novel, first published in serial form between 1846 and 1848, was adapted for the stage as a three-act play by **John Brougham**, first called *Bunsby's Wedding* when it was presented on 24 July 1848 at **Burton's** Theatre. The play was not well received and was withdrawn after four days for reworking. The revised version, retitled *Dombey and Son*, reopened on 16 August 1848 to great acclaim. Brougham and his wife were in the cast, as well as **William Burton**, who played Captain Cuttle, in what became one of his most popular roles.

Other adaptations of the novel were produced, some stressing **melodramatic**† elements, while Brougham's version emphasized comedy. *Dombey and Son* is a typically **Dickensian** work, filled with colorful characters and a rich social panorama. The proliferation of various adaptations stressed certain characters or circumstances in the novel. The title character is a wealthy owner of a shipping company and favors his son, but when the boy dies he is for a long time unable to appreciate his daughter, Florence. When he finally recognizes his love for her, they are happily reunited.

DOT. **Dion Boucicault**'s† adaptation of **Charles Dickens**'s *The Cricket on the Hearth* (1845) opened on 14 September 1859 at the **Winter Garden Theatre** featuring **Agnes Robertson**, Boucicault's common-law wife, as the title character. Laurence Hutton, describing Robertson's performance in this sentimental fantasy, recalled her as "the most charming and perfect **actress***† we have ever known." The plot centered on a young couple, Dot and John Perrybingle, who fall victim to a hard-hearted miser, Tackleton, who convinces John that Dot is unfaithful. Tackleton's duplicity is eventually revealed, and the Christmas season inspires his reformation. **Joseph Jefferson**† scored a particular success as Caleb Plummer, a role he played throughout his long career. **John E. Owens** also won appreciation as Plummer in his own production of the play. *Dot* was produced successfully in London, where it opened at the Adelphi Theatre on 14 April 1862.

†**DOUBLING.** It was common practice for **utility**† and even supporting† **actors***† to play two or more roles in the same play, especially in **stock***† or **touring***† companies. **Stars***† occasionally doubled in roles as a tour de force, as when **Mary Anderson**† became the first **actress***† on record to play both Hermione and Perdita in *The Winter's Tale*.

DOUGHERTY, HUGHEY (1844–1918). A **blackface**† **minstrel**† man, Hughey Dougherty was born in Philadelphia, where he began his career as a member of the company of **Sanford's Minstrels** in 1858. Billed as "Young America," he had a long career in which he performed with many of the major minstrel companies in the second half of the 19th century. He was perhaps the finest "stump speech" performer in his era and **toured***† widely, including with a company to Africa.

DOUGLAS. John Home's blank verse tragedy premiered with an **amateur**† cast in Scotland in 1756, which was followed by a production at London's Drury Lane in 1757, **starring***† Peg Woffington. Its first production in America is believed to have been in 1758, though the cast and particulars are unknown. *Douglas* was subsequently staged in Philadelphia with **Lewis Hallam** as Young Norval, a young man who has been raised by an old shepherd, but is in fact the long-lost son of a woman who has since become Lady Randolph. The young man ultimately reclaims his real name, Douglas, but the **villainous**† Glenalvon manipulates events, leading to the murder of Douglas and the tragic ends of Lord and Lady Randolph. The play became one of the most-produced tragedies in America and England between the 1750s and the 1850s—and the role of Young Norval was often the debut role of a talented young **actor**.*†

DOUGLASS, DAVID (d. 1786). Born in England, David Douglass took charge of a theatrical company organized by John Moody in 1754 with plans to perform in Jamaica. With Douglass heading the troupe, they encountered the company of **Lewis Hallam Sr.**, and the two companies subsequently merged. Hallam died shortly thereafter, and Douglass took over as **manager***† of the company and married Hallam's widow. The troupe arrived in New York in 1758, established a theater, and **toured***† along the Eastern seaboard. Though he was not particularly admired as an **actor**,*† Douglass led the troupe, named the **American Company**.

Lewis Hallam Jr. became the company's **leading actor,**† gaining particular acclaim for his declamatory style in **Shakespearean***† roles. Douglass was also instrumental in promoting the construction of playhouses in cities in which the company regularly performed, including Philadelphia's **Southwark Theatre**, New York's **John Street Theatre**, and Charleston's **Dock Street Theatre**. Douglass was apparently an effective diplomat who managed to negotiate the obstacles of puritanical religious leaders and antitheater public officials. The American Company under Douglass's leadership produced an array of classics and contemporary British plays, as well as the first known tragedy by an American author, **Thomas Godfrey**'s *The Prince of Parthia* in 1767. When the **American Revolution** began and the Continental Congress banned theater in the colonies, Douglass and the American Company returned to Jamaica.

D'OYLY CARTE OPERA COMPANY. Formed in England by Richard D'Oyly Carte in 1875 to present the **operettas**† of William S. Gilbert and Arthur Sullivan, the troupe **toured***† to the United States first in 1879 with *H.M.S. Pinafore*—and then occasionally for over a century until the company closed in 1982.

DRAKE, SAMUEL (1768–1854). Born into a theatrical family, Samuel Bryant was born in Barnstable, England, and eventually took the stage name of Drake. He worked as **manager***† of a small provincial theater in England prior to arriving in the United States in 1809, working in theaters in Boston (at the **Federal Theatre**, where he made his 1810 debut) and Albany, New York. The death of his wife in 1815 led to his move into western territories, where he opened a theater in Frankfort, Kentucky, and he ultimately owned theaters in Ohio, Indiana, Tennessee, and Missouri, in many cases giving the first theatrical performances in various river towns along the Ohio, Allegheny, and Mississippi Rivers. Known as the "pioneer of drama in the American West," Drake was also admired as a fine **actor.***†

THE DRAMA OF KING SHOTAWAY. FOUNDED ON FACTS TAKEN FROM THE INSURRECTION OF THE CARAVS ON THE ISLAND OF ST. VINCENT, WRITTEN FROM EXPERIENCE BY MR. BROWN. **William Henry Brown**'s 1823 drama recounts the story of the historical figure Joseph Chatoyer (d. 1795), a Garifuna chief who led a revolution against British government control over St. Vincent Island in 1795. Indigenous caribs embraced runaway African slaves on St. Vincent, developing a unique mixture of African and Amerindian culture. Chatoyer was successful in compelling the British to sign a treaty, but it ultimately became clear that the British were ignoring it. As a result, Chatoyer led a revolt in which Caribs and Africans joined with French radicals whose interests were inspired by the French Revolution. Chatoyer was killed in battle and became a national hero. Brown's play was produced by the **African Grove Theatre company** in 1823 and is considered the first by an **African American*†** author, though the text is lost.

THE DRAMA REVIEW FOR 1868. **John Brougham**'s entertainment opened on 25 January 1869 for 28 performances at the **Fifth Avenue Theatre**. It was a precursor of the **musical*†** revue† with songs and sketches. In this case, Brougham's sketches were mini-**burlesques*†** of recent stage hits and personalities, including the craze for **opéra bouffe** and **G. L. Fox** as Humpty Dumpty.

DRAMATIC CRITICISM. *See* *†CRITICS/CRITICISM.

DRAMATIC MIRROR **(1879).** *See* †*NEW YORK DRAMATIC MIRROR.*

†**DRAMATISTS.** *See* *†PLAYWRIGHTS.

DREW, JOHN, SR. (1827–1862). Born in Dublin, Ireland, as John Henry Drewland, he was brought to the United States as a **child**.† As an **actor,*†** he found success in **Irish** and other comic roles, and by the 1840s he became **manager*†** of Philadelphia's **Arch Street Theatre**, where he established a **stock*†** company including his wife, **Louisa Lane Drew,**† billed as Mrs. John Drew. They had married in 1848 and had three children, including **John Drew Jr.†** and **Georgiana Drew,**† both of whom became noted actors. Drew's early death from injuries sustained in a fall left the fate of Arch Street Theatre to his wife, who for over 30 years managed it with notable success.

†**DREW, JOHN, JR. (1853–1927).** Named for his father, the **manager*†** of the **Arch Street Theatre**, John Drew, born in Philadelphia, initially shied away from a life in the theater, working for a time as a clock salesman in his hometown. Returning to the family profession, Drew made his 1873 stage debut at the **Arch Street Theatre** with his mother, **Louisa Lane (Mrs. John) Drew**.† After two seasons in her company, Drew made his New York debut in *The Big Bonanza* (1875) for producer **Augustin Daly,**† who guided Drew's career for many years. As one of the Daly stars, including **Ada Rehan,**† **James Lewis,**† and **Mrs. G. H. Gilbert,**† Drew won **critical*†** approval as Petruchio in *The Taming of the Shrew* and other **Shakespearean*†** and Restoration comedies. Drew's good looks secured his position as a popular box office **attraction**.† Through his sister, **Georgiana Drew Barrymore,**† he was the uncle of Lionel,† Ethel,*† and John Barrymore.†

†**DREW, LOUISA LANE (MRS. JOHN) (1820–1897).** Daughter of British **actors***† Thomas Frederick and Eliza Trenter Lane, Louisa Lane was born in London, England, and took to the provincial stage as a **child**† following her father's death. She made her adult debut at New York's **Bowery Theatre** in *The Spoiled Child* (1828), impressing audiences by playing five characters in *Twelve Precisely; or, A Night at Dover.* In 1838, she married **Irish** actor Henry Hunt, with whom she acted at the **Walnut Street Theatre**, and played opposite **Junius Brutus Booth** in *Richard III* and other plays (and also with Booth's son **John Wilkes Booth**†). Lane shared the stage with **Edwin Forrest** in *William Tell* and *Macbeth*, as well as the first performance of Edward Bulwer-Lytton's *Richelieu* in 1839.

Lane was married briefly to actor George H. Mossop in 1848, but he died within a year of their marriage. She married for the third time, to **John Drew**, a **Shakespearean***† actor, in 1848. He was actor-**manager***† of the **Arch Street Theatre** in Philadelphia, and, following his death in 1862, Lane, billed as Mrs. John Drew, took over management of the theater for 30 years. She continued to act into the 1890s, most notably in Shakespearean and comedy of manners roles. She scored a particular late success as Mrs. Malaprop in *The Rivals*, costarring with **Joseph Jefferson**.†

Drew was the mother of **Georgiana Drew Barrymore**† and grandmother of Lionel,† Ethel,*† and John Barrymore.† Her *New York Times* obituary reported that "Mrs. John Drew probably had a longer active career than any other actress. She was a remarkably versatile and intelligent actress, and although her efforts late in life were exclusively confined to comedy, yet she had won respect in tragedy as well." She is almost certainly the model for intrepid **actress***† Fanny Cavendish in the George S. Kaufman*†–Edna Ferber*† comedy-drama, *The Royal Family*† (1927).

†**DRUMBEATER.** *See also* †ADVANCE AGENT/ADVANCE MAN.

THE DRUNKARD; OR, THE FALLEN SAVED. **William H. Smith**'s surprisingly enduring five-act **temperance melodrama**† exceeded all other American plays of its day in popularity prior to *Uncle Tom's Cabin*. Smith, a recovering alcoholic, and with the likely collaboration of a Unitarian minister, John Pierpont, wrote the play and staged it at **Moses Kimball**'s **Boston Museum** during the 1844–1845 season.

In the play, Edward Middleton is manipulated by his family's lawyer, Cribbs, after he inherits his father's estate. Cribbs wants Edward to dispossess a poor family from a building he owns, but Edward instead falls in love with the family's daughter, Mary. They marry and have a daughter. Despite his personal happiness, Edward continues to have a weakness for drink, and finally, broke (according to Cribbs) and despairing, he ends up on the street in New York's notorious Five Points district. Cribbs tries unsuccessfully to get Edward to forge documents to Cribbs's advantage, but through the intercession of Edward's half brother and a family friend, Edward is rescued and Cribbs is unmasked as a **villain**† illegally controlling Edward's wealth. Edward, Mary, and their daughter are reunited.

The play also ran for 100 performances at **P. T. Barnum**'s **American Museum**, and it was the most widely seen temperance play prior to the appearance of T. S. Arthur's *Ten Nights in a Bar-Room* in 1858. Frequently revived, and often parodied, *The Drunkard* has near iconic status as a representative American melodrama.

THE DRUNKARD'S WARNING. Written by English-born **playwright***† Charles Western Taylor, this three-act play, performed at **Barnum's Museum** in 1856, was meant to capitalize on the popularity of **temperance melodramas**† and, as was typical of Taylor's work, emphasized spectacle.

DUFF, JOHN (1787–1831). Born in Dublin, Ireland, John Duff became a successful **actor***† in his homeland, but when he married Mary Ann Dyke, billed throughout her career as **Mrs. John Duff**, they decided to pursue their careers in the United States. Duff made his debut in 1810 in Boston, the year of their arrival, and within a few years he demonstrated versatility playing *Macbeth* and the three roles in the comedy, *Three and the Deuce* in 1812. For a time his success was built on his versatility, playing **Shakespeare***† (*Richard III* was a particular success for him), the **melodrama**† *The Stranger*, and a farce, *Raising the Wind*. He frequently performed with his wife, and they were generally successful, but his popularity (and health) declined in comparison to her growing popularity.

DUFF, MRS. JOHN (1794–1857). Irish-born Mary Ann (or Marianna) Dyke made her stage debut as a dancer in Dublin, but very soon after transitioned to acting. She performed for a time with her sister, Elizabeth, but they made their final appearance together in 1809. The following year, she received a marriage proposal from the Irish poet Thomas Moore, but she had already accepted **actor***† **John Duff**. In 1810, they married and he was recommended by **Thomas Abthorpe Cooper** to the **Boston Theatre**, leading the Duffs move to the United States, where they both gained popularity with American audiences.

In 1812, the Duffs appeared together in Philadelphia, but when she ultimately made her New York debut in 1823 in a range of **Shakespearean***† and contemporary plays, including acting opposite **Junius Brutus Booth** in *The Distressed Mother*, her fame began to eclipse her husband's. By 1831, his health had failed and he died. She continued acting for a number of years, married unhappily for a second time, then, ultimately, for a third time, when she married a lawyer and moved to New Orleans, where she retired.

DUFF, MARY (1811?–1852). Born to **actors***† **John** and **Mary Ann (Dyke) Duff**, she went on the stage at age 20, playing Ernestine in *The Somnambulist* in 1831 at Philadelphia's **Arch Street Theatre**. She married A. A. Addams in 1835, but the marriage was brief, and she married again to Joseph Gilbert, but this was also a short-lived marriage. She appeared on **tour***† on the Eastern seaboard for a time, but also performed in the West. Upon her return to the East, **critics***† were less appreciative of her tendency to overact, though she was popular with audiences. She appeared with some success in **Shakespeare***† (most notably as Lady Macbeth), 18th-century British comedies of manners, and a few minor contemporary plays. She married again, to **actor***† J. G. Porter, billing herself thereafter as Mrs. Porter, but her death at 41 cut her career short.

DUFFIELD, MRS. *See* WEMYSS, KATE (b. 1821).

THE DUKE'S MOTTO; OR, I AM HERE!. **John Brougham**'s play with music and a ballet featured a prologue and four acts. Brougham provided lyrics for two songs, "Wine, Bright Wine" and "While There's Life There's Hope," with music by John Collins. *The Duke's Motto* opened on 11 July 1862 at **Niblo's Garden**. After revisions, it was revived beginning 6 July 1863, with Thomas E. Morris and John Collins. On 13 July 1863, the *New York Daily Tribune* noted that the "sweeping success of 'The Duke's Motto' carries it triumphantly along from week to week and threatens to propel it into the heart of the Fall season. . . . It is quite clear that the performance of the one or two principal parts in 'The Duke's Motto' has vastly changed since the opening nights; and that the stiff formality of by-gone dramatic ages has gradually taken the place of the natural and easy freedom which constituted the charm of the early representations." The play was adapted by **Charles Fechter**† in 1870 with the subtitle "a romantic drama," and a few decades later was again adapted, this time with the subtitle "a **melodrama**"† by Justin H. McCarthy and published in 1908 after Lewis Waller† appeared in it.

DUNLAP, WILLIAM (1766–1839). Born in Perth Amboy, New Jersey, William Dunlap was, in many respects, the first renaissance man of the American stage; as a **playwright**,*† **actor**,*† **manager**,*† and theater historian, Dunlap is a dominant figure of the immediate post–**American Revolutionary** era. Though it is believed he had little formal education, he read

Shakespeare's*† plays during his youth and became enamored of theater while watching British soldiers acting in plays. In 1784, he went to London to study art with Benjamin West and completed a portrait of **George Washington** now in the collection of the United States Senate. In England, he regularly attended theater and saw the great British actors of the time, John Philip Kemble and Sarah Siddons, among other major players, in contemporary and classic works. The standards of theatrical production he encountered in England were significant both to his desire to work in theater and to endeavor to elevate the quality of the American stage as he found it upon his return to America in 1787.

Dunlap worked exclusively in American theater for the next 18 years, though he sporadically continued painting to enhance his meager income from stage work. It is believed he wrote in excess of 60 plays, including *The Modest Soldier; or, Love in New York* (1787), which he submitted for production to the **American Company** in New York. They rejected the play, but produced his next work, *The Father; or, American Shandyism* (1789), which was well received.

By 1796, Dunlap was a partner in the American Company with **Lewis Hallam Jr.** and **John Hodgkinson**. Following *The Father; or, American Shandyism*, Dunlap kept up a steady stream of plays in various genres, including *The Fatal Deception; or, The Progress of Guilt* (1794), *Fontainville Abbey* (1795), *The Archers; or, The Mountaineers of Switzerland* (1796), and *André: A Tragedy* (1798), all successful at various levels, with *André* considered perhaps his finest work. In 1798, Dunlap adapted August von Kotzebue's *The Stranger* (1798), which led him to ultimately adapt many of Kotzebue's works. That same year, Hallam, Hodgkinson, and Dunlap opened New York's **Park Theatre**. Something of a reformer, he aimed to raise the quality and tone of theater production. Dunlap, a man with a puritanical nature, succeeded at some reforms, but faced resistance when he attempted to end the practice of seating ladies of dubious character in a special section of the audience.

Subsequently buying out Hallam and Hodgkinson, Dunlap managed the Park, and his subsequent plays included *False Shame* (1799), *The Italian Father* (1799), *The Virgin of the Sun* (1800), and *The Glory of Columbia, Her Yeomanry* (1803). However, he was forced to declare bankruptcy in 1805, though a year later he returned to work as assistant to the Park's new manager, **Thomas Abthorpe Cooper**. Dunlap's later dramatic works include *Yankee Chronology; or, Huzza for the Constitution* (1812) and *A Trip to Niagara; or, Travellers in America* (1828).

Dunlap's most enduring fame results from his two-volume nonfiction work, *The History of the American Theatre* (1832), an essential document of the workings of the 18th- and early 19th-century US stage. Post-1817, Dunlap spent much of his time painting and on his historical writings, which also include his three-volume *History of the Rise and Progress of the Arts of Design in the United States* (1834), and he was a founder of the National Academy of Design in 1825. Dunlap also wrote a novel, *Thirty Years Ago; or, The Memoirs of a Water Drinker* (1836), which promoted **temperance** in its depiction of an alcoholic actor, and biographical works on actor **George Frederick Cooke** (1813) and Charles Brockden Brown (1815). Of Dunlap's significance, Arthur Hobson Quinn wrote that he "had the soul of an artist and the intrepidity of the pioneer, and his place in our dramatic literature will remain secure."

DUPREZ, CHARLES H. (1830–1902). Ultimately one of the leading **managers***† of **minstrel**† shows, Charles H. Duprez was born in Paris, France, but became a naturalized American citizen in 1887, having begun a successful minstrel career as a performer in 1852. He debuted in New Orleans with Carle, Duprez, and Green's Minstrels, which, by 1858, had evolved into Duprez and Green's and later Duprez and Benedict's (Green's share having been bought out by Lew Benedict, who had joined the troupe in 1861). Duprez continued the company until 1885 prior to buying the Washington Tavern Hotel in Lowell, Massachusetts, which he attempted unsuccessfully to restore. He spent his last years running **amusement**† parks in the Lowell area and later ran a "boat merry-go-round" in Providence, Rhode Island.

DURANG, JOHN (1768–1822). Born in Lancaster, Pennsylvania, John Durang became known as the first professional dancer born in the United States to become a major success, mostly as the result of his hornpipe dance. He debuted in 1784 with **Lewis Hallam**'s troupe while they were performing "moral lectures" in a period when plays and dances were officially banned. Durang worked with most of the major **managers***† of the time, including **William Dunlap** and **Thomas Wignell**. He subsequently performed with Ricketts's **Circus**,*† demonstrating a wide range of skills, including acrobatics, acting, pantomime, and as a **blackface**† comedian. Contemporary accounts report that Durang was **George Washington**'s favorite entertainer.† He married dancer Mary McEwen, and most of their six children also became performers.

DURIVAGE, OLIVER E. (1816?–1861). Born Oliver Everett Durivage, he worked at various times as a newspaperman and a storyteller, with his specialty telling **Yankee**† tall tales. By the 1840s he worked at **William Mitchell**'s **Olympic Theatre** as both a performer and a writer of **burlesques**.*† Among his works was the one-act farce *The Stage-Struck Yankee* (1845), billed as an "American comedy" and ultimately a popular vehicle for **Dan Marble**, who, as **Joseph Jefferson**† recalled, dressed like Uncle Sam in the role. Durivage also parodied **Shakespeare***† in *Richard Number 3*.

DYKE, MARY ANN. *See* DUFF, MRS. JOHN (1794–1857).

EAGLE THEATRE. This gold rush–era Sacramento wood-framed theater, the first erected in California, featured canvas siding and a tin roof (partially constructed of materials from derelict ships abandoned on the Sacramento River) and opened in September 1849 with a **minstrel**† show. Located on the eastern bank of the Sacramento River, the theater operated there until 4 January 1850, when it was destroyed in a flood. It was subsequently rebuilt at another location.

EAST LYNNE. **Clifton W. Tayleure** adapted **Mrs. Ellen Wood**'s popular English **sensation**† novel of 1861 into a three-act play for **Lucille Western**, who appeared frequently in the **leading lady**† role of Lady Isabel Carlyle for 10 years. Numerous versions of the novel were adapted for the stage, but Tayleure's **melodramatic**† adaptation was by far the most popular. The plot centers on a young woman who abandons her husband and children to run off with a wealthy suitor who subsequently abandons her. In due course, Isabel gives birth to a **child**† and, in disguise, returns to her former home to serve as a governess for her own children.

In its themes of infidelity, divorce, and illegitimacy, not to mention the inferior position of **women***† in the Victorian era, *East Lynne* proved to be surprisingly popular with audiences for a half century, decades before the first productions of modernist realistic plays that dealt with similar subjects of social significance. *East Lynne* was first performed on 26 January 1863 in Brooklyn. Western appeared in an 1869 revival at **Niblo's Garden** acting with **James A. Herne**.† A short-lived 1926 **Broadway***† revival produced by the Provincetown Players*† featured Mary Blair† as Isabel.

EATON, CHARLES HENRY (1813–1843). The **actor***† son of a well-to-do merchant, Charles Henry Eaton first acted in *The Stranger* at the Warren Street Theatre in Boston, his hometown. Although he **toured***† on occasion, he spent much of his career in Boston, appearing in **Shakespearean***† roles (including Richard III and Hamlet). Easton's New York debut at the **Park**

Theatre playing Richard III was well received. His career was cut short when he was fatally injured in a fall at the Exchange Hotel while performing in Pittsburgh.

†**EBERLE, ROBERT M. (1840–1912).** An **actor*†-manager*†** born in Philadelphia to a family of actors,* Robert M. Eberle made his debut at the **Walnut Street Theatre** when he was two in *The Hunter of the Alps.* By age 19, Eberle was stage manager at the **Boston Museum**. His career included a number of significant management positions: San Francisco's **California Theatre**, the companies of **Edwin Booth**,† **Lawrence Barrett**,† and Olga Nethersole,† and many **road*† attractions**.† Late in his career, he worked as business manager for **William Gillette**.†

†**ECONOMICS OF THE STAGE.** In his seminal work, *The Business of the Theatre: An Economic History of the American Theatre 1750–1932*, Alfred L. Bernheim posits that the economic organization of the American theater changed little from colonial times to the middle of the 19th century, but thereafter "the **star*†** system was the ferment which brought about a new economic order in the theatre."

Actor*†-managers*† led the way from the times of **Lewis Hallam** and **David Douglass** into the mid-19th century, but the proliferation of star actors after the **Civil War** only increased the public's demand for them; this caused managers to bid their salaries up, which necessitated reducing expenses elsewhere. The consequent demise of resident **stock*†** companies coincided with the rise of traveling **combination†** productions, which led to centralized production and booking of **tours*†** out of New York. The entertainment industry ranked among America's big businesses by the mid-19th century, but sending combinations on the **road*†** for a season was complicated, leading eventually to bookings arranged by a relatively few all-powerful managers and, inevitably, to the rise and subsequent demise of the Theatrical Syndicate† in the mid-1890s.

EDDY, EDWARD (1822–1875). Born in Troy, New York, Edward Eddy made his New York debut in a recital in 1839, but after **touring*†** for several years, he made his true theatrical debut in New York in *Othello* in 1846. In 1851, he became the **star*† actor*†** of the boisterous **Bowery Theatre**, where his good looks and vital masculinity made him a natural **leading man†** in such **melodramas†** as *The Lady of Lyons, The Hunchback, The Stranger, The Count of Monte Cristo*, and **Shakespearean*†** roles, though his boldly presentational style ultimately led to a subsequent decline in his popularity as audiences began to prefer a more natural approach. In his last years, he operated a theater company in the West Indies.

EDGEWOOD FOLKS. Though he had been on the stage for many years, **Sol Smith Russell** ascended to **stardom***† in this 1880 four-act **musical***† play by J. E. Brown, written especially for him, which he first performed in Buffalo, New York. The comic role of Tom Dilloway in what was billed as a "pastoral comedy drama" provided Russell with ample opportunity to sing and present his character specialties, in which he imitated various country types.

EDOUIN, WILLIE (1846–1908). Born in England, Willie Edouin **toured***† Australia and England before journeying to the United States in 1869 to appear with **Lydia Thompson**'s **burlesque***† company. He also appeared with **Lawrence Barrett**† and **John McCullough**.† During the latter half of the 19th century, Edouin worked in both England and America, and his versatility as a performer was much admired. In the 1890s, he returned to England to appear in **opéra bouffe**, but in 1906 he was back in the United States performing in **vaudeville**.† Among the works in which he appeared in New York were *Lurline* (1870), *Paris* (1870), *The Forty Thieves* (1871), *St. George and the Dragon!* (1871), *Bluebeard* (1871), *The Princess of Trébizonde!* (1871), *Robin Hood* (1872), *Ixion* (1872), *Kenilworth* (1872), and the highly successful *Florodora* (1900). It is believed that he portrayed over 500 characters in his career, but despite his mastery of the stage, he was not an effective **manager***† and died a relatively poor man.

THE EIGHTH OF JANUARY. First performed in repertory† at the **Chestnut Street Theatre** in Philadelphia, this play by **Robert Penn Smith** received a mixed response from **critics**,*† but was popular with audiences. **William Warren** appeared as John Bull, a father and British loyalist attempting to hold his divided family together during the **War of 1812**. Bull's son, Charles, is fiercely American and serves under General Andrew Jackson at the Battle of New Orleans on 8 January 1815 without realizing that the **war***† has ended. **Joseph Jefferson I** appeared as a comic Cockney character, Billy Bowbell.

THE EIGHTH OF JANUARY; OR, HURRA FOR THE BOYS OF THE WEST!. Written circa 1830 by the adopted son of **George Washington**, **George Washington Parke Custis**, this play focused on Andrew Jackson's military adventures, especially the Battle of New Orleans during the **War of 1812**, and his eventual candidacy for president of the United States. **Thomas Dartmouth "Daddy" Rice** appeared in the comic role of Sambo, a **blackface**† caricature, in productions of this play.

†**ELLSLER, EFFIE (1855–1942).** She was the daughter of John A. Ellsler, a well-known **actor*†-manager*†** who built the Euclid Avenue Opera House in Cleveland, where she was born. Ellsler's mother, Euphemia Murray, had, at one time, played Portia to **Edwin Booth**'s† Shylock. Ellsler acted in **stock*†** throughout her youth and grew up to perform opposite **Edwin Booth**,† **John McCullough**,† **Lawrence Barrett**,† and other **touring*†** **stars*†** during their Cleveland engagements.† She went to New York in 1880 and immediately achieved **stardom*†** when she created the title role in *Hazel Kirke*† (1880) at the **Madison Square Theatre**.† Under **Daniel Frohman**'s† management, she toured extensively, typically in inferior **melodramas**.† She eventually settled in Hollywood and during the 1930s played character roles in **films**.*†

THE EMBARGO; OR, WHAT NEWS?. First performed at the **Chestnut Street Theatre** in Philadelphia on 16 March 1808, this play by **James Nelson Barker** caused a riot over its support of Thomas Jefferson's administration, particularly the Embargo Act. Controversy had emerged over the first Embargo Act, which stated that American ships could only trade in a foreign port with permission of the president of the United States. Punishments for violations were made more severe in the second and third Embargo Acts. The country was divided over the Embargo Acts, though most Americans had concerns about English and French encroachments. No text of the play is known to survive.

EMERSON, BILLY (1846–1902). Born William Redmond, this popular **vaudeville**† performer made his initial mark in **minstrel**† shows as an end man. During his career, he **toured*†** Australia three times between 1873 and 1893. His use of **blackface**† was not relegated to rural characters, as had been typical since the advent of **Jim Crow**; instead, Emerson dressed in dapper (if somewhat exaggerated) clothes and danced to such songs as "I Feel Just as Happy as a Big Sunflower," "Rip-Tearing Johnny," "Nicodemus Johnson," "Josephus Orange Blossom," and many others. Emerson took over as **manager*†** of San Francisco's Standard Theatre, where for many years he was a popular **attraction**,† eventually partnering with Charley Reed.

EMERY, MISS (d. 1832). Also billed at times as Mrs. Burroughs, Miss Emery was born in London and appeared with success at the Surrey Theatre before **actor*†-manager*†** **Francis Courtney Wemyss** introduced her to audiences in the United States. Her debut as Belvidera in *Venice Preserved* in 1827 was also one of her most notable successes, leading to well-received performances in *The Merchant of Venice*, *Fazio*, and others. Unknown circumstances led to the abrupt end of her career, after which she sank into prostitution in New York's notorious Five Points slum, where she was subsequently killed in a brawl.

†EMMET, J. K. (1841–1891). Joseph Kline Emmet was born in St. Louis, where he remained a popular favorite throughout his acting career. Despite **Irish** parentage, he specialized in playing a German **stock*†** character, "Fritz," appearing in a spate of varied vehicles with Fritz as the central figure. The most popular of these, **Charles Gayler**'s *Fritz, Our Cousin German*, appeared in 1870, with **Charles Fisher** and Minnie Maddern† in support. His success in subsequent variations, including *Fritz in Ireland* and *Fritz in a Madhouse*, continued unabated, despite his penchant for alcohol. At the time of his death, the *New York Times* wrote, "He had a host of imitators, but not one of them was ever so popular as he."

EMMETT, DAN (1815–1904). Born Daniel Decatur Emmett in Mount Vernon, Ohio, Dan Emmett learned an appreciation of music from his mother. He worked as a printer's apprentice prior to enlisting in the United States Army in 1834. Discharged from the army the following year, Emmett worked in various **circuses*†** as a **blackface†** banjo player, singer, and songwriter. Among his early compositions, "Bill Crowder" typified the stereotypical images of **African Americans*†** that pervaded **minstrel†** shows in the 19th century. Emmett ultimately found great success when, along with Billy Whitlock, Dick Pelham, and Frank Brower, he formed the **Virginia Minstrels**. They made their debut in 1843 at New York's **Chatham Garden Theatre**, where they triumphed, but a subsequent **tour*†** to London brought a mixed response.

The structure of their act provided a much-imitated prototype, and the Virginia Minstrels are credited with being the first true minstrel show. Though its origins are not completely clear, Emmett is credited with writing the song "Dixie" (originally titled "Dixie's Land"), which found particular success in the South, ultimately becoming the anthem of the Confederate States of America during the **Civil War**. Emmett subsequently joined **Bryant's Minstrels** in 1858 and continued to perform through most of his long life. The 1943 film *Dixie*, **starring*†** Bing Crosby, celebrated (and highly fictionalized) Emmett's life and career.

†EMOTIONAL ACTRESS. **Matilda Heron** was said to have founded the "emotional school" of acting. According to Catherine Reignolds-Winslow, "Matilda Heron was dramatic to the last degree on every occasion." Emotional intensity also characterized performances by **Lucille Western**, but it was **Clara Morris†** who pushed that mode of acting to the heights. For her alternating restraint and release of strong feelings, according to Kansas City critic*† Austin Latchaw,† "Morris was unsurpassed. There was a poignancy in the break of her voice, in the very pauses she prolonged, that touched the most cynical audience." He added that she became "the most moving emotional actress of her time. She could sound the depths of passion, of sorrow, and could compel us to go into the depths with her. There was no embarrassment when we wept at a Clara Morris performance. When we went to see this actress we had tears to shed and prepared to shed them."

ENGLISH'S THEATRE. Built by businessman and politician William Hayden English and originally called English's Hotel and **Opera House**, the theater opened in 1880, the same year English was a candidate for vice president of the United States. When the theater opened on 27 September 1880, **Lawrence Barrett†** appeared as Hamlet. English's became the leading theater in Indianapolis, presenting all manner of entertainments,† from plays to **minstrel†** shows, **musicals,***† opera, ballet, and **vaudeville.†** Most of the major **touring***† **actors***† of the late 19th century appeared at some point on the stage of English's Theatre, including **Sarah Bernhardt,†** John Barrymore,† George M. Cohan,*† and Helen Hayes,*† among many others. The theater and hotel were demolished in 1948.

†EQUESTRIAN DRAMA. Plays that made a spectacle of horsemanship were expensive to **tour,***† but their popularity with audiences seems to have justified the cost. While *Mazeppa†* (1825) required only one horse for its show-stopping seminude ride of the title character, *Ben-Hur†* (1899) multiplied the thrills with many horses; its climactic chariot race was performed with live horses on treadmills, simulating a race. Often **melodramas†** not specifically written as equestrian dramas made use of horses onstage as an element of spectacle, as in *Putnam, Iron Son of '76* (1844) and *Uncle Tom's Cabin* (1852), the latter featuring what audiences considered a thrilling chase of Eliza and her baby across the frozen Ohio River by **villain†** Simon Legree and his henchmen. William A. Brady's† 1901 revival of *Uncle Tom's Cabin* included "horses, carriages, pony carts, donkeys, and dogs," according to the *New York Times.*

ERNEST MALTRAVERS. In 1838, **Louisa Medina** adapted this three-act drama from **Edward Bulwer-Lytton**'s 1837 novel of the same name. The play was first performed at **Wallack's Theatre** on 28 March 1838 and won praise for Medina, with **critics***† applauding the "freshness of thought, novelty of situation, and point of repartee" featured. Ernest Maltravers is a wealthy man who loves a woman of limited means. She saves his life, but leaves him to marry another in an arranged marriage, which proves to be a disaster. Alice finally leaves her husband to return to Maltravers. Considered expert in creating popular **melodramas,**† Medina also adapted Bulwer-Lytton's novel *The Last Days of Pompeii* in 1835, among others.

THE ESCAPE; OR, A LEAP FOR FREEDOM. **William Wells Brown**'s only surviving play, a five-act **melodrama**† with comic elements, is considered the first published play by an **African American*** author. Melinda, the central female character, endures sexual aggression from her master, Gates, who promises her money and freedom if she will abandon her husband. Gates's wife also abuses Melinda, who ultimately escapes to Canada with her husband. *The Escape* emphasizes tensions between North and South over slavery, with attention paid to the inherent moral questions of slavery, not to mention **sexuality.***† The play's gender politics feature a frankness uncommon for its era and debunks stereotypes of the **blackface**† **minstrel**† variety. Brown himself read the play to audiences in lieu of more traditional lectures on abolitionist views.

THE ESSEX JUNTO; OR, QUIXOTIC GUARDIAN. J. Horatio Nichols wrote this four-act comedy in 1802. This play, like most of Nichols's other works, is highly politicized, in this case the satiric humor is directed at the Federalists, whom Nichols portrays, as one **critic***† writes, as "monarchical, avaricious, unethical, and generally **villainous**."*† President John Adams is depicted as a manipulative character called the "Duke of Braintree." The disgruntled members of the Essex Junto were pro-British in their sympathies and opposed Adams's French policy. The play was published in Boston in 1802 and distributed along with other political writings by Nichols.

ETHEL, AGNES (1853–1903). Born in New York, Agnes Ethel went on the stage there in 1868 in a private production of *Camille* and was guided by noted **actress***† Mathilde Heron. The following year, she appeared in a production of T. W. Robertson's *Dream* with **Fanny Davenport**. In 1870, Ethel appeared in the first production of *Frou-Frou* staged by **Augustin Daly** with his **stock***† company at the **Fifth Avenue Theatre**. That same year, she acted in *Fernande*, also with Daly's company, and her beauty and skill attracted **playwright***† **Victorien Sardou**, who wrote a play, *Agnes*, especially for her; the play ran at the **Union Square Theatre** for 100 performances in 1872.

Despite her successes, Ethel retired at the peak of her career to marry a millionaire, Francis W. Tracy. Following Tracy's death, Ethel married again to Clinton DeWitt Roudebush in 1890, subsequently divorcing him in 1901.

She only appeared onstage two times after her retirement, both in support of charitable work, and she made herself available to guide young, struggling members of the acting profession.

ETHIOPIAN SERENADERS. One of the earliest **blackface†** **minstrel†** troupes, the Ethiopian Serenaders made their first appearance in the early 1840s, and by 1844 they performed for President John Tyler at the White House (and later for President James K. Polk). The troupe aimed to appeal to an upper-class audience, a section of society not typically drawn to minstrel shows. As such, their performances boasted a refinement not typical of the more boisterous approach applied by many minstrel companies. Beginning with a **tour*†** in 1846, the troupe spent much of its time performing in England, where eventually they were joined by **William Henry Lane**, known as Master Juba. The term "Ethiopian minstrels" was often used by various troupes to identify themselves as blackface performers specializing in fare typical of the minstrel tradition.

EVANGELINE; OR, THE BELLE OF ACADIA. Based on **Henry Wadsworth Longfellow**'s epic 1847 poem of the same name, this "American **burlesque**"*† was written by J. Cheever Goodwin and featured music by E. E. Rice. Goodwin and Rice were generally disappointed in **operettas†** from Europe and decided to create a particularly American brand, and as such, this work is a landmark in the early **musical*†** theater in the United States. *Evangeline*, which is set during the Expulsion of the Acadians, focuses on the efforts of an Acadian woman, Evangeline, to find her long-lost lover, Gabriel.

First staged in a modest production at **Niblo's Garden**, it was so successful that Goodwin and Rice were able to produce a more lavish production in New York and Boston in 1877. Realizing that "burlesque" typically referred to comic parodies, Rice feared that audiences might misunderstand when he hoped to present the work as a family-friendly entertainment. As such, he rebranded *Evangeline* as an "American **opéra-bouffe**." In explaining this change, he also referred to the piece as a "musical comedy," the first time on record such terminology was applied. *Evangeline* remained popular for the rest of the 19th century via frequent revivals. An 1885 New York revival ran for an astonishing 251 performances prior to a successful **tour**.*†

†EYTINGE, ROSE (1835–1911). The beautiful and temperamental **actress**,*† born in Philadelphia, was one of the favorites of the American stage in the 1860s and 1870s. She appeared with such **actors*†** as **Edwin Booth†** and was invited to the White House by President **Abraham Lincoln**, who attended several of her performances. Among her major successes was creating the role of Laura Courtland in **Augustin Daly's**† **melodrama**† *Under the Gaslight* in 1867. Until 1869, she appeared in several New York theaters before she spent some time overseas with her husband, George H. Butler, the consul general to Egypt.

A divorce from the abusive Butler led to Eytinge's return to the stage in 1871, with her appearance at the **Broadway Theatre** as Cleopatra in *Antony and Cleopatra*, to acclaim. Eytinge joined the **Union Square Theatre**† company in 1873, and for the rest of that decade was well received in notable performances as Nancy in *Oliver Twist*, Gervaise in *Drink*, Ophelia to **E. L. Davenport**'s Hamlet, and Desdemona to **James W. Wallack**'s Othello, with Davenport as Iago. She made fewer appearances after 1880 when she married actor Cyril Searle (they were subsequently divorced), making her final stage appearance in 1907. In 1905, she wrote a play, *Golden Chains*, and published a novel, *It Happened This Way*, as well as her memoirs, *The Memories of Rose Eytinge*, which does not mention the fact that she was Jewish.

THE FALL OF BRITISH TYRANNY; OR, AMERICAN LIBERTY TRI-UMPHANT. A five-act tragic-comedy by **John Leacock**, with the play attributed to his pseudonym, Dick Rifle. Little is known about Leacock other than that this play was published in Philadelphia in 1776, where it was likely performed. The title amply suggests its thematic content.

FALSE PRETENSES; OR, BOTH SIDES OF GOOD SOCIETY. A five-act satire by **Cornelius Mathews**, this play was written in 1855 and produced that same year on 3 December at New York's **Burton's** Theatre. Lampooning hypocrisy in contemporary society and, in particular, mocking the affectations of those rising in class via easy wealth, this play bore some resemblance in theme to **Anna Cora Mowatt's** *Fashion*, though it is generally considered an inferior work.

FALSE SHAME; OR, THE AMERICAN ORPHAN IN GERMANY. This comedy in four acts was adapted by **William Dunlap** from August von Kotzebue's play, *Falsche Scham*, and was first performed on 11 December 1799 at the **Park Theatre**. In the play, a young Hessian military officer rescues an orphan from a **fire†** while a battle at Charleston rages during the **American Revolution**. The officer ultimately adopts the orphan, taking the **child†** with him to Germany. The play was published in 1800.

FANCHON, THE CRICKET. **Maggie Mitchell** appeared with great success in this dramatization of George Sand's *La Petite Fadette*, first performing the play in January 1861 at **Benedict De Bar's** **St. Charles Street Theatre** in New Orleans, followed by a run at **Laura Keene's** Theatre in New York the following year. She subsequently **toured*†** with the play, adapted by Charlotte Birch-Pfeiffer from a translation by August Waldauer. Fanchon, a country girl, is suspected of witchcraft by the local citizenry and, as such, lives an isolated existence with her grandmother, Old Fadet, who is also believed to be a witch. Whether or not Fanchon has supernatural powers never becomes clear, but she endeavors to win over the resistant parents of Landry, the man she loves, and subsequently succeeds. This became an iconic role for Mitchell, who named her daughter Fanchon, and when she died, her obituary mentioned the play in the *New York Times* headline, noting that she was "inseparably linked" with the character.

THE FARM HOUSE; OR, THE FEMALE DUELLISTS. This farcical play written by **Royall Tyler** in 1796 is believed to be lost. The play is thought to have been adapted from John Philip Kemble's *The Farm House* (1789).

FARREN RIOTS. A complex intersection of nationalism, abolitionist sentiments, and racism, along with simple mischief caused what became known as the Farren riots, allegedly set off by an anti-American statement made by the **Bowery Theatre**'s stage **manager,***† George P. Farren. Presumably, Farren, for whom the theater was staging a benefit performance of *Metamora; or, The Last of the Wampanoags* starring*† **Edwin Forrest**, said, "Damn the **Yankees**;† they are a damn set of jackasses and fit to be gulled." The Bowery's manager, **Thomas S. Hamblin**, and Forrest attempted to placate an outraged mob demanding an apology from Farren, who obliged by appearing onstage and displaying an American flag to calm passions. However, over the subsequent two days, the situation was exacerbated by the distribution of handbills with opposing views on abolition. Ultimately, the mayor of New York called up the New York First Division to parade through the Bowery district to restore order.

FASHION; OR, LIFE IN NEW YORK. **Anna Cora Mowatt**'s first successful play, *Fashion*, opened in New York on 24 March 1845 at the **Park Theatre**. A comedy of manners with a sharply satiric edge, *Fashion* centers on the social ambitions of Mrs. Tiffany, a former milliner, who is besotted with French fashions, providing malapropisms in her failed efforts to master the French language.

The play's good-natured humor is also evident in Mowatt's depictions of the pretensions, hypocrisy, and shallowness of social climbers, all presented by a set of stereotypical character types, including a phony French count, a saucy maid, and a nosy spinster, all of whom are caught up in the false accusations made against a young governess who is ultimately saved by the play's hero, Adam Trueman, who states the play's theme, declaiming that "Fashion is an agreement between certain persons to live without using their souls! To substitute etiquette for virtue—decorum for purity—manners for morals!" Mowatt, who began acting shortly after the initial success of *Fashion*, wrote other plays, but she subsequently devoted herself more fully to acting. That tension in her work can be found in her own comments about *Fashion* during an early rehearsal when she wrote, "There were no attempts in *Fashion* at fine writing. I designed the play wholly as an acting comedy. A dramatic, not a literary, success was what I desired to achieve. Caution suggested my not aiming at both at once."

As a writer, Mowatt is chiefly remembered for this farce, a rare American play from this period to endure in the theatrical canon, and her memoirs. In 1924, the Provincetown Players† revived *Fashion* in New York for 152 performances, with a cast including Clare Eames and Walter Abel,† and professional and **amateur**† productions have been frequent. **Edgar Allan Poe** twice reviewed the original production of *Fashion*, calling it "superior to any American play."

FAST FOLKS; OR, EARLY DAYS OF CALIFORNIA. This five-act comedy by **Joseph A. Nunes** opened on 1 July 1858 at San Francisco's American Theatre with **James W. Wallack** and was produced again on 20 January 1859 at Philadelphia's **Arch Street Theatre** with **Mrs. John Drew** among the cast. A lighthearted depiction of the early history of California, Nunes dedicated his play to William H. Seward, soon to become President **Abraham Lincoln**'s secretary of state, for his efforts in bringing California to statehood. The play was published in 1861.

THE FATAL DECEPTION; OR, THE PROGRESS OF GUILT. **William Dunlap**'s five-act tragedy was produced at the **John Street Theatre** on 24 April 1794 under the title *Leicester* and subsequently renamed *The Fatal Deception* by the time it was published in 1806. The plot involves Lord Leicester returning from **war***† and anxious to be with his wife, Matilda. He is not aware that she has installed her lover, Henry Cecil, in her household in the guise of her brother. When she receives word that her actual brother will soon arrive, she persuades Cecil to kill her husband. Believing he is murdering Leicester, he stabs a man sleeping in a darkened room; but it is soon revealed that he has killed his own brother. When Leicester learns of Matilda's adulterous relationship, she attempts to poison him, but fails and commits suicide. Cecil is confronted by Leicester and runs on the lord's sword, killing himself. Writing about Dunlap's work, **critic***† Oral Sumner Coad has favorably compared this play to **Shakespeare**'s *Macbeth* despite the fact that it had a short stage life.

THE FATHER; OR, AMERICAN SHANDYISM. **William Dunlap**'s comedy of manners, his first to be produced, was a popular success when staged by the **American Company** on 7 September 1789 at the **John Street Theatre** for four performances prior to productions in Philadelphia and Baltimore. The play depicted the contrasting romantic values of masters and their servants in contemporary America. The cast included **Lewis Hallam** in the leading role of Mr. Racket and **Thomas Wignell** as Doctor Quiescent. Dunlap borrowed elements of plot and characters from Lawrence Stern's *Tristram Shandy*, as acknowledged by the subtitle.

The play was popular and almost immediately printed in *Massachusetts Magazine* in October and November 1789. *American Quarterly Review* praised *The Father*, noting that its "plot is sufficiently dramatic to carry an interest throughout; the characters are well drawn, and well employed; and the dialogue possesses, what is indispensible to genuine comedy, a brief terseness and unstudied ease, which few of the productions of the present afford." Dunlap later revised *The Father*, changed the title to *Father of an Only Child*,† and published it in 1807. Dunlap referred to this play as the second American comedy following **Royall Tyler**'s *The Contrast* as the first.

FECHTER, CHARLES (1824–1879). Born in London as Charles Albert Fechter, he made a name for himself as an **actor*†** in romantic **melodramas†** and **Shakespeare*†** in London, Paris, and Berlin. In 1869, he traveled to the United States, appearing at **Niblo's Garden** in *The Duke's Motto* and *Hamlet*, the latter causing great controversy. His Hamlet differed so significantly from **Edwin Booth**'s† interpretation, which in America had come to be accepted as definitive, that audiences and **critics*†** were polarized over it. Except for a brief stint in England, Fechter remained in the United States until his death. He was **manager*†** of his own company, but his explosive temperament militated against success. He spent the last years of his life in seclusion on a farm in Pennsylvania.

FEDERAL STREET THEATRE. *See* BOSTON THEATRE.

†FEMALE/MALE IMPERSONATION. In England, pantomime performances routinely featured cross-dressing (usually men dressed as women), but such entertainments were comparatively unpopular in the United States, though drag was employed in **minstrel†** shows during the 19th century. Before the 20th century, men who donned dresses and adopted the movements and manners of women were mostly seen in minstrel or **burlesque.*†** Francis Leon† ("The Only Leon") achieved renown in the latter. Leon also appeared in **musicals*†** and **vaudeville,†** which also made occasional use of female impersonators.

Tony Hart,† who became **Edward Harrigan**'s† stage partner, carried over his female impersonations from minstrelsy to the **legitimate†** stage. **Neil Burgess†** had been a **blackface†** entertainer† at **Tony Pastor**'s† theater, but turned to female impersonation in 1877 at Harrigan and Hart's **Theatre Comique†** and found his true niche. In 1879, he **starred*†** in *Widow*

Bedott,† playing the title role and finding a character he would perform throughout the remainder of his career. A sign of the growing acceptance of female impersonation came in 1891 when Burgess played Lady Teazle in the first **Lambs' Club**† Gambol.

Women playing male roles had long been accepted and popular in American theater, partly due to the demands of **Shakespeare**'s*† comedies *As You Like It* and *Twelfth Night*, which required women to perform "breeches" roles, but contemporary plays also provided opportunities, and some **actresses**,*† most notably **Adah Isaacs Menken, Clara Fisher, Leo Hudson, Charlotte Cushman**, and **Mrs. Henry Lewis**, among many others in the 19th century, frequently indulged in such characterizations. Cushman and Menken were perhaps the greatest of these for different reasons. Cushman seemed to have a more powerful impact on an audience playing a male role than a female character due to her strong presence and commanding manner. **Critics***† were approving, and the only controversy she faced was when she played Cardinal Wolsey in *Henry VIII* simply because that particular Shakespearean role had never been played by a woman before. In Menken's case, her playing of the title (and male) role in *Mazeppa* made her perhaps the first American sex symbol. Her seminude ride lashed to a real horse onstage made her a legend. After the **Civil War**, performers in burlesque, **travesties**, and musicals, not to mention **circus**,*† drew comedy from reversing gender roles, but serious exploration of the complexities of **gender***† and **sexuality***† would wait until after World **War** I.*†

THE FEMALE ENTHUSIAST. In 1807, **Sarah Pogson Smith** dramatized Charlotte Corday's murder of Jean Paul Marat during France's Reign of Terror. This romantic tragedy in blank verse is highly fictionalized, and Smith uses only the broad outlines of the historical events to offer a sympathetic portrait of Corday. The play explores ideas of patriotism and democracy, which were of immediate pertinence to audiences in the aftermath of the **American Revolution**. As Corday awaits her execution, she explains that she committed the murder of Marat for her country and humanitarian principles. Smith's first known play, *The Female Enthusiast*, was published anonymously in 1807, and some scholars believe the play was produced at the **Charleston Theatre**, though this cannot be verified.

THE FEMALE PATRIOT; OR, NATURE'S RIGHTS. **Susanna Haswell Rowson**'s 1795 farce, adapted from Philip Massinger's *The Bondsman*, was first performed at the **New Theatre** in Philadelphia in 1795. Believed to have explored issues of women's rights, no known copy of the play survives.

FEMALE PATRIOTISM; OR, THE DEATH OF JOAN D'ARC. **John Daly Burk**'s five-act verse tragedy opened at the **Park Theatre** on 13 April 1798. The play recounted the general facts of Joan D'Arc's life to make a strong case for the ultimate triumph of democracy and reason over tyranny, a popular post–**American Revolution** subject. The play did find favor with its audiences, though **William Dunlap** attributed its failure to a poor production, not the play itself.

FENNELL, JAMES (1766–1816). The handsome English-born **actor***† James Fennell gained a reputation as unreliable. He began his career in Edinburgh, before playing Othello at the Covent Garden Theatre in London in 1787. Gambling debts and disagreements with **managers***† hampered his ability to make a steady living acting, though he was successful in England for several years before accepting an offer from **Thomas Wignell** to appear at the Philadelphia Theatre. For several years he acted in New York, Boston, and Philadelphia, but his fecklessness about money led to the decline of his career, and despite an attempt at a comeback playing King Lear at the **Chestnut Street Theatre** in 1815, he failed to regain **stardom**.*†

FENNO, AUGUSTUS W. (1815–1873). Born William Augustus Fenno in Boston, where he spent his **childhood**,† he left Boston in his teens to seek adventure. He signed on as a sailor and sailed around the world. At 17, he became an **actor***† with his debut at the **Bowery Theatre** in *The School for Scandal*. He appeared in an early (1853) Philadelphia production of *Uncle Tom's Cabin*, playing George Harris. He played Romeo at the **Arch Street Theatre** in 1848, and his penchant for adventure took him to California during the gold rush. He began **touring***† in England in 1864, but returned to the United States where he played the Second Actor in **Edwin Booth**'s† 1870 production of *Hamlet*. He had been a close friend of Booth's father, **Junius Brutus Booth**.

†**FERGUSON, WILLIAM J. (1845–1930).** Born William Jason Ferguson in Baltimore, he began his career as a callboy† at **Ford's Theatre** in Washington, DC, where, on the evening of 14 April 1865, he was called upon to fill in for an ailing **actor***† in *Our American Cousin*, starring*† **Laura Keene**. President **Abraham Lincoln**, who was in attendance, was assassinated by **John Wilkes Booth**† midway through the performance. Ferguson, who later wrote a book about the events of that tragic night, claimed to have escorted Keene to the stage box where Lincoln lay dying. During his six decades as an actor, Ferguson performed with numerous **stars**,*† including Richard Mansfield,† Robert Mantell,† and **Helena Modjeska**.† At the time of his death, he was the oldest living member of the **Lambs' Club**† and the

last surviving member of the 1865 *Our American Cousin* cast. He also appeared in more than a dozen silent films,† coincidentally portraying Lincoln in *The Battle Cry of Peace* (1915), a film now lost.

FIELD, JOSEPH M. (1810–1856). Part of the Southwestern Humor movement, which emphasized Wild West adventures or broad farces, satires, and **burlesques**,*† Joseph M. Field was born of English parentage in Dublin and brought to America as an infant. He debuted in his teens at Boston's **Tremont Theatre** in 1827. As an **actor**,*† he worked the circuit of major theaters in the Eastern states and wrote a popular comic afterpiece, *Down South; or, A Militia Training* (c. 1830). Field appeared in comic roles with distinction, but also scored successes in **Shakespearean***† plays and contemporary drama. Under the guidance of **Noah Ludlow**, Field moved to the American West, where he developed as an actor and **playwright**,*† settling in St. Louis, though he performed throughout the country.

Field spent a year in Europe as an international reporter for the *New Orleans Picayune* in 1841–1842, after which he returned to the United States to work with **William Mitchell** at the **Olympic Theatre**. He wrote many broad comedies, but also a variety of works including *Victoria; or, The Lion and the Kiss* (1839), *Tourists in America* (1840), ***Oregon; or, The Disputed Territory*** (1846), and the winning entry in **Dan Marble**'s contest seeking a **Yankee**† play, *Family Ties; or, The Will of Uncle Josh* (1846), which he co-authored with J. S. Robb. Field also wrote a **critical***† response in dramatic terms to Harriet Beecher Stowe's ***Uncle Tom's Cabin***, staged in New Orleans, and became a **manager***† of Field's Varieties in St. Louis and elsewhere. Field was the father of **actress***† and antislavery activist **Kate Field**.†

†FIELD, KATE (1838–1896). The multitalented activist **actress***† was born Mary Katherine Keemle Field in St. Louis, the daughter of well-known **Shakespearean***† **actors***† **Joseph M. Field** and Eliza Riddle. Like her father, who built the Field's Varieties Theatre and founded the *St. Louis Daily Reveille*, she devoted herself to both theater and journalism. After her father's death, Field's millionaire uncle Milton L. Sanford financed her education and took her to Italy. However, Sanford disinherited her when she began sending abolitionist-themed travel articles to the *Boston Courier*, so she found a surrogate family in Anthony Trollope and other noted writers living in Florence. Beautiful and outspoken, she became a model for several of the intelligent women characters in Trollope's novels.

Field supported herself by writing for newspapers and magazines, lecturing on the Lyceum circuit, and writing plays in which she performed. She made her acting debut at **Booth's Theatre**† on 14 November 1874 in the title role of *Peg Woffington*. Despite harsh response from **critics**,*† she continued to perform on **tour***† for three seasons, including a stint as **John T. Raymond**'s† **leading lady**† in *The Gilded Age*. Under the name Mary Keemle, she performed her own "brilliant little comedy," *Extremes Meet*, in London and on tour in England in 1877. She also acted before Queen Victoria.

In 1880, Field performed her own **musical***† monologue *Eyes and Ears in London*, which included a **burlesque***† of Italian opera. According to the *New York Times*, the "wittily and charmingly elaborated" monologue was "full of sharp hits at persons and things" and "flavored with a delicate, yet incisive, humor." For five years, she published her own newspaper, *Kate Field's Washington*, which included theatrical news as well as her own short plays.

FIFTH AVENUE THEATRE. Two New York theaters had this name in the years following the **Civil War**, and both were most associated with **manager***† and **playwright***† **Augustin Daly**. The first, originally called the **Madison Square Theatre**, on the south side of 24th Street between Sixth Avenue and **Broadway**,*† was built in 1863. Daly became the theater's manager in 1868, after which the theater was sometimes called Daly's Fifth Avenue Theatre or just Daly's Theatre. It was outfitted with mirrored walls and **gas lighting***† and seated 1,000 patrons. When the theater was destroyed by fire in 1873, Daly moved his company to the St. James Theatre (previously known as Gilsey's Apollo Hall), renaming it the New Fifth Avenue Theatre. This theater, located at 31 West 28th Street and Broadway, had been built in 1868.

FINN, HENRY J. (1787–1840). Born in New York City, Henry J. Finn was educated at Princeton University, after which he studied law. He went on the stage beginning in small roles at the **Park Theatre**. After his father's death, Finn and his mother left the United States for England, where Finn worked as a teacher, became interested in the fine arts, renewed his involvement in theater, and joined a company of itinerant **actors**.*† He acted in England and the United States after 1811, but settled in Boston around 1822, where he focused on character parts and performing monologues. He wrote and published poetry and humorous prose, but subsequently **toured***† for a decade before he was killed in a steamer accident on Long Island Sound.

†**FIRES.** *See* †THEATER FIRES.

FISHER, CHARLES (1816–1891). Born in Suffolk, England, to a family of **actors**,*† Charles Fisher made his stage debut in London in 1844 prior to leaving England for the United States when **William E. Burton** recruited him for his company. In America, Fisher became a popular stage comedian in 18th- and 19th-century plays, including *Masks and Faces, Money*, and *The School for Scandal*, and in **Shakespeare**'s*† *As You Like It, The Merry Wives of Windsor* (in which he was acclaimed a memorable Falstaff), and *The Taming of the Shrew*. However, he was also adept at darker characters, as when he played the **villainous†** jester Pepe in the first production of *Francesca da Rimini* in 1855. He again played the villain as Colonel Crafton in the **melodrama†** *Fritz, Our Cousin German*. At various times, he was a member of the companies of Burton, **Laura Keene, James W. Wallack**, and **Augustin Daly**.

FISHER, CLARA (1811–1898). A London-born **child†** prodigy who began her career at age six, Clara Fisher debuted in 1817 in David Garrick's *Lilliput* and by her teens had played major male roles in **Shakespeare*†** and in contemporary plays. Despite her popularity and being known as a "child wonder," Fisher and her parents moved to the United States in 1827, where she first performed at the **Park Theatre** to an enthusiastic response. **Touring*†** the country, she scored a major success wherever she played and became one of the most popular **stars*†** of her time, both in Shakespearean and contemporary roles.

Fisher married James Gaspard Maeder in 1834, and he ultimately composed an opera, *Peri; or, The Enchanted Fountain* (1852), for her. They also partnered as **managers*†** of a theater in New Orleans. Despite devoting considerable time to motherhood, giving birth to seven children, Fisher performed opposite most of the major **actors*†** of her time, including **William Charles Macready, Edmund Kean, Edwin Booth,† John Brougham, Joseph Jefferson,† Laura Keene**, and **Edwin Forrest**. Her phenomenal success brought her wealth, and she retired in 1844, but some bad investments forced her back on the stage in 1850, and she graduated into older roles with **Mrs. John Drew**'s **Arch Street Theatre** and **Augustin Daly**'s company prior to her second retirement in 1889. In her last years, Fisher wrote her memoirs and taught elocution.

†FISKE, STEPHEN RYDER (1840–1916). Born in New Brunswick, New Jersey, and educated at Rutgers University, Stephen Ryder Fiske took a job writing for the *New York Herald*, replacing **Edward G. P. Wilkins** as drama **critic.*†** He also practiced law prior to serving as a **war*†** correspondent during the **Civil War**. Fiske spent some time in London following the war, but returned in 1874 to pursue a career as a theater **manager,*†** collaborating with **Augustin Daly,†** whom he succeeded at the **Fifth Avenue Theatre**. Fiske worked closely with **Edwin Booth†** and **Joseph Jefferson†** while with the theater. He also worked as a critic for *The Spirit of the Times* (1879–1902) and was a founder of the *New York Dramatic Mirror*† and of The Actors Fund of America.†

A FLASH OF LIGHTNING. **Augustin Daly**'s play opened on 10 June 1868 at the **Broadway Theatre** for 52 performances. Daly borrowed the plot from **Victorien Sardou**'s *Le Perle noire*, adding a spectacular steamboat **fire**† and other sensational embellishments. The play centers on the daughters of Garry Fallon, who has oppressed his wife and favors his daughter Rose, played by **Kitty Blanchard**, over her sister, Bessie. Bessie's suitor, Chauncey, played by **McKee Rankin**, has given her some valuable gold jewelry, but Bessie's former beau, Jack, steals the jewelry. Fallon blames Bessie for the loss of the jewelry, and she runs away, followed by Chauncey and Jack, who save her from a steamboat fire. Jack manages to put the jewelry back and improbably convinces the family that it was moved by electricity from a flash of lightning. Converted to a sensation† **melodrama,**† Daly found success with this play, and along with several other hits he was able to establish his own company.

†**FLESHINGS.** Flesh-colored tights or body stockings revealed the female form and provided the illusion of nudity.† The term has a somewhat scandalous connotation in 19th-century theater, with fleshings used for the latter purpose in such plays as *Mazeppa*, in which **Adah Isaacs Menken** scored a scandalous international success clad in little more than fleshings, and in **musical***† entertainments† like *The Black Crook* (1866), and later, in innumerable musicals, **revues,***† **burlesque***† shows, etc.

†**FLORENCE, W. J. (1831–1891).** William Jermyn Florence was born Bernard Conlin in Albany, New York. This versatile comic **character actor**† was said to equal **Joseph Jefferson**† when they performed together in *The Rivals*, beginning in 1889: Jefferson as Bob Acres and Florence as Sir Lucius O'Trigger. "Billy" Florence also excelled in **Irish** roles, but above all found lasting fame as Honorable Bardwell Slote, a part written for him by **Benjamin E. Woolf**, in *The Mighty Dollar* (1875). He played Slote frequently for the remainder of his career. Malvina Pray Littell (1834–1906), Mrs. Florence, played Mrs. Gilflory opposite him in Woolf's play, and they enjoyed a successful **Broadway***† revival of the play in 1884, which the audience appreciated with, as the *New York Times* reported, "as much zest as if the rollicking humor of the play was new and fresh."

FONTAINVILLE ABBEY. **William Dunlap**'s Gothic tragedy, inspired by Ann Radcliffe's 1791 novel *The Romance of the Forest*, depicted seemingly supernatural occurrences ultimately shown to be natural events and not mysterious incidents. Seen as a departure from traditional romantic tragedy, *Fontainville Abbey* is complete with all of the trappings of a Gothic mystery, featuring evil **villains**,† skeletons, and secret passageways, not to mention the inevitable stormy night. It was a popular success when produced at the New York Theatre in 1795 and published in 1807. Scholar Oral Sumner Coad writes that *Fontainville Abbey* "was more thoroughly Gothic than any of its dramatic precursors in England," claiming for Dunlap the mantle of a forerunner.

THE FOOL'S REVENGE. English **playwright***† **Tom Taylor** wrote this 1868 drama, which was produced by **Edwin Booth**† at **Niblo's Garden** in 1878, years after its 1859 London premiere. Booth's cast included **Rose Eytinge**, Mary Wells, and Ada Clifton. Taylor's authorship was questioned for this dramatization of *Rigoletto*, which he defended by claiming it was "in no sense a *translation*, and ought not, I think, in fairness, to be called even an *adaptation* of Victor Hugo's fine play, *Le Roi's Amuse.*" Set in 15th-century Italy, *The Fool's Revenge* dramatized the murder of Galeotto Manfredi. Booth played the witty court fool Bertuccio and revived the play in 1884, with **critics***† calling his performance "splendid" in merging the "anguish beneath the antics of the fool," in this role, which was also considered a significant departure for Booth from his predominance as a tragedian in **Shakespeare**'s*† plays.

†**FOOTLIGHTS.** Few **lighting***† techniques were as synonymous with the stage as footlights. For example, **Olive Logan**'s† 1870 memoir was titled *Before the Footlights and Behind the Scenes* and **Otis Skinner**'s† in 1923 was *Footlights and Spotlights.* The row of lights usually set into a trough across the front of the stage complemented lighting from above the stage so that **actors***† would not have harsh shadows beneath the brow and chin. Footlights can be traced back to the 17th century when candles would have supplied the source light. By the 19th century, many actors believed that footlights erased wrinkles and brightened the eyes.

The type of footlights described in *The Autobiography of Joseph Jefferson*† could still be found in rural areas during the early 20th century: "The footlights of the best theaters in the western country were composed of lamps set in a 'float' with the counter-weights. When a dark stage was required, or the lamps needed trimming or refilling, this mechanical contrivance was made to sink under the stage." Like other lighting components, footlights progressed from candles to oil lamps to **gas**† to electricity. When an actor objected to being "in the trough," it meant that she/he was forced to play a scene so far downstage that they were compelled to face upstage to exchange dialogue with fellow players—in short, the actor was upstaged by getting too close to the footlights.

FORD, JOHN T. (1829–1894). Born in Baltimore, John Thomson Ford's name might be lost in obscurity were it not for the fact that he was owner and **manager*†** of Washington, DC's **Ford's Theatre** when President **Abraham Lincoln** was assassinated there while attending a performance by **Laura Keene, starring*†** in *Our American Cousin*. Prior to this catastrophic event, Ford worked as a book salesman and wrote a farcical play, *Richmond As It Is*, which was staged by a **minstrel†** troupe. From 1854, Ford managed the **Holliday Street Theatre** in Baltimore, and he opened his first Washington theater in 1861. It burned down the following year, and Ford rebuilt it as Ford's Theatre. Briefly detained by police in the aftermath of the assassination of Lincoln, Ford continued his career as a theater manager for the remainder of his life. The government seized Ford's Theatre, and Ford was paid $100,000 for it by Congress. Ford was a close friend of both **Edwin†** and **John Wilkes Booth†** and was noted for his integrity as a manager. In 1871, he built the Grand **Opera House** in Baltimore.

FORD'S THEATRE. Theater **manager*†** **John T. Ford** built and became manager of this Washington, DC, theater at 511 10th Street NW in 1862, and it officially opened in 1863. The busy theater fell into infamy when **actor*†** **John Wilkes Booth,†** a friend of Ford's, assassinated President **Abraham Lincoln** there on 14 April 1865. The United States government seized possession of the theater, and Congress paid Ford $100,000 for the property. For the remainder of the 19th century, it was used as office space and a warehouse by the government, but a collapse of part of the building killed 22 people in 1893. Ultimately, it was refurbished as a historic site and reopened in 1968 for performances. Ford's Theatre was again renovated in 2009 and, along with the Peterson House (a boardinghouse across the street from the theater where Lincoln died the morning following the shooting), is preserved as a National Historical Site administered by the National Park Service.

†FOREIGN PLAYS ADAPTED TO THE AMERICAN STAGE. In essence, the drama in the United States prior to the decades just before the **Civil War** was foreign—**actors*†** and **managers*†** were dependent on European (mostly British) theater for much of the working **repertory†** of the stage, and in the case of plays written by American **playwrights,*†** international plays provided models for structure and genre, not to mention plot and characters. Eighteenth and 19th-century American playwrights freely adapted many European plays (English, French, and German most particularly), often with little regard to acknowledging the source play or its author.

The first American comedy, for example, **Royall Tyler**'s *The Contrast* (1787), was essentially an English comedy of manners play in style, but "Americanized" in its themes and content. As dramatists introduced their own particular native innovations during the early 19th century, they continued to frequently turn to European plays and novels for source material. In fact, most historical **melodramas**† in the standard repertory† of **touring***† companies in the 19th century were of foreign origin, and every genre from romantic tragedy to farce owed a debt to European works. For example, plays like the English *The Lady of Lyons* by **Edward Bulwer-Lytton**, the German *Ingomar, the Barbarian* by Bellinghausen, the French *The Count of Monte Cristo* by Charles Fechter from Alexandre Dumas père, and *The Lady of the Camellias (Camille)* by Alexandre Dumas fils were staples of the 19th-century American stage and were imitated by US authors.

Adaptations of lesser-known novels and plays—and translations—often went uncredited when produced, and **stars***† freely adapted plot and dialogue to suit their own needs. While **Shakespeare***† was somewhat immune to excessive adaptation because players often performed the same roles with different companies, there were endless parodistic variations on his plays. The **Irish**-born **Dion Boucicault**,† a prolific dramatist and manager, drew from many French and English sources for the numerous plays that flowed from his pen and rarely acknowledged the source, and other writers emulated the practice through much of the 19th century. Even after the US joined the International Copyright Agreement in 1891, it could be difficult to trace the origin of a foreign play whose title and character names had been changed and the action Americanized.

†FOREIGN STARS AND COMPANIES ON THE AMERICAN STAGE. Dating back to the era of **David Douglass** and **Lewis Hallam Sr.**, and continuing well into the 19th century, many European **actors***† and companies made lucrative **tours***† in the colonies prior to the **American Revolution**, a practice many continued after the birth of the United States to the present day. In the formative years of theater in America, international **playwrights***† and actors would have a pervasive influence in the works produced and acting styles. So pervasive, in fact, that by the time of the American Revolution, nationalistic feelings began to resist the presence of foreign actors—particularly the English—on US stages.

Many early American actors were of English birth, and some were classically trained in England—often establishing reputations there before arriving in America. **George Frederick Cooke**'s arrival in 1810, when he debuted as Richard III at the **Park Theatre**, demonstrated the value of international star*† actors to American **managers**.*† In short order, others arrived, including **James W. Wallack** and **Edmund Kean**, widely regarded as England's greatest interpreter of **Shakespeare**.*† Kean **toured***† the United States twice, in 1820–1821 and again in 1825–1826. Whether the European actors ultimately remained in the United States was a variable, but prior to 1880 (and continuing to the present), many toured, including such notables as **Charles Mathews**, **Charles** and **Fanny Kemble**, **Tyrone Power**, **Madame Vestris**, **Charles Fisher**, **Lydia Thompson**,† **Charles Fechter**, **Charles Wyndham**, and **Adelaide Neilson**.

Resistance to British actors grew in this period and came to a head when American star **Edwin Forrest** made a fierce rival of English star **William Charles Macready**. Forrest's supporters depicted Macready as a cultural usurper, though the early rivalry manifested itself mainly in a class division, with the more educated, well-to-do audiences preferring Macready's intellectual, formal acting to Forrest's bombastic, larger-than-life approach, which appealed to the working class. When Forrest appeared in London in 1845 to a lukewarm response, he held Macready personally responsible. When Macready toured to America in 1849, he was scheduled to perform *Macbeth* at the **Astor Place Opera House** on 7 May 1849. Renewed hostilities began when Forrest immediately announced his appearance in the same play on the same night at the nearby **Bowery Theatre**. Loud disturbances in both theaters led Macready to announce his intention to cancel his engagement.† A petition to prevent this was circulated, and Macready agreed to appear again on 10 May 1849. By performance time, it was estimated that over 10,000 people had assembled in the vicinity of the theater. A mob of thugs made up of denizens of New York's notorious Five Points area arrived at the Astor Place Opera House to be met by a force of police and militia. The resulting riot, which lasted for hours, led to the deaths of at least 22 (and as many as 31), with many more injured (including over 140 militiamen), and only adding to decades of bitterness between the English and Americans.

Despite pockets of nationalistic resistance to foreign performers and companies, after the middle of the 19th century, international performers usually found receptive audiences in the United States, especially **Sarah Bernhardt**,† Henry Irving, and Ellen Terry, all of whom toured America regularly. Some, particularly those who stayed in the United States either for extended stays or permanently, were influential in raising the quality of theatrical production by demonstrating a superior level of craftsmanship. British music hall, **vaudeville**,† and **musical***† entertainers also crossed the Atlantic. **Richard D'Oyly Carte's Opera Company**, in productions of Gilbert and Sullivan **operettas**,† first appeared in 1879 and often enlisted American performers to supplement its company.

Among non-English-speaking stars and companies, the most notable included Italians (Eleonora Duse,† **Tommaso Salvini**† and his son Alexander Salvini,† Ermete Novelli, Ernesto Rossi, **Adelaide Ristori**†), Germans (Emma Carus, **Ludwig Barnay**†), Czechs (**Francesca Janauschek**†), Poles (**Helena Modjeska,**† Bogomil Dawison), Russians (Alla Nazimova,*† Moscow Art Theatre), and French (Bernhardt, Constant-Benoît Coquelin,† Gabrielle Réjane†).

FOREPAUGH, ADAM (1831–1890). A Philadelphia-born **child**† of poverty, Adam Forepaugh began working at age nine for a butcher. Ultimately, he started a livestock business in New York, which subsequently made him rich selling horses to the Union Army during the **Civil War**. When John V. "Pogey" O'Brien, a **circus***† owner, could not pay for the horses purchased from Forepaugh, he took over as **comanager***† of the circus. In partnership with O'Brien, he managed the Tom King Excelsior Circus, the Jerry Mabie Menagerie, The Great National Circus, and the **Dan Rice** Circus. Unlike his peers in the circus world, Forepaugh was more businessman than entertainer†—like his main rival, **P. T. Barnum**. After disagreements with Barnum about territory, they signed agreements dividing up the United States to avoid future problems. Forepaugh sold his circus in 1889 and died the following year.

THE FOREST ROSE; OR, AMERICAN FARMERS. **Samuel Woodworth**'s two-act **musical***† play, with music by John Davies, opened at the **Chatham Garden Theatre** on 7 October 1825. In a bucolic setting, two pairs of lovers go through various machinations to be together, but one of the women, Harriet, is also courted by a nefarious Englishman, Bellamy, who attempts to enlist the aid of a **Yankee**† farmer, Jonathan Ploughboy, in the task of kidnapping Harriet. However, Jonathan does not trust Bellamy and instead tricks him by replacing Harriet with a maid. *The Forest Rose* was one of the most popular of the Yankee plays of the late 18th and early 19th century, and most of the outstanding comic **actors***† of the day at some point took on the role of Jonathan, a character inspired by the Jonathan of **Royall Tyler**'s *The Contrast*. Prior to *Uncle Tom's Cabin*, *The Forest Rose* was one of the most popular entertainments† of the first half of the 19th century.

FORREST, EDWIN (1806–1872). Few American **actors***† could be said to rival the talent and accomplishments of Edwin Forrest—certainly not in his time—but a bitter offstage rivalry with English actor **William Charles Macready** diminished Forrest's accomplishments as an actor and his efforts to elevate the quality of American drama in the first half of the 19th century. Though Forrest's Scottish-born father, William, a merchant, originally settled in Trenton, New Jersey, business reversals necessitated a move to Philadelphia, where Edwin was born. Along with his brother, William, Edwin began performing with a local theatrical **club,**† which led to his first professional appearance, at age 11, at the South Street Theatre in *Rudolf; or, The Robbers of Calabria.*

The death of Forrest's father in 1819 sidetracked theatrical pursuits as Forrest worked briefly as an apprentice in various fields. Attending a lecture where he volunteered to participate in an experiment with nitrous oxide, Forrest surprised even himself when he recited a speech from *Richard III* while under the influence. The result was impressive, and he was given the opportunity to audition for the **Walnut Street Theatre**, where he subsequently made his true professional debut as Young Norval in *Douglas* in 1820.

He chose to launch his career with an arduous **tour***† of the southern and western states and scored his first successes performing in **blackface.**† His convincing impersonations of **African Americans***† led to an opportunity to play Othello at New York's **Bowery Theatre** in 1826, which he did to great acclaim. He **toured*** in the role and repeated his success in all venues. Forrest attended many performances by notable actors of the time, including **Junius Brutus Booth**, **Thomas Abthorpe Cooper**, and **Edmund Kean**, attempting to analyze their technical skills. His success also led him to establish a contest to encourage the writing of a play with a **Native American***† as the central character. The winning play, **John Augustus Stone**'s *Metamora; or, The Last of the Wampanoags* (1829), provided him with a strong role, as did **Robert Montgomery Bird**'s *The Gladiator*, in which Forrest played Spartacus (one of his most popular characterizations), and Robert T. Conrad's *Jack Cade*, in which he appeared in the title role. Throughout the remainder of his career, Forrest devoted much of his attention to encouraging American-born **dramatists***† with frequent competitions, often to his financial advantage. Throughout the 1830s and 1840s, Forrest built a reputation that encompassed both contemporary plays, including *Damon and Pythias*, *Venice Preserved, William Tell*, and *She Would Be a Soldier*, and success in **Shakespearean***† roles, with many **critics***† regarding him as the first American actor to equal English greats in Shakespeare's plays.

Forrest's popularity with American audiences was significant, providing him with a lucrative income that he parlayed into a large fortune, but also led to a tragic incident that undermined his popularity. By 1849, some theatergoing audiences in the United States had developed a nationalistic fervor that favored American actors over foreign **stars**,*† most particularly the English. Forrest had developed an antagonistic relationship with British Shakespearean **William Charles Macready**, culminating in a bitter rivalry that climaxed in a riot at New York's **Astor Place** when the two actors were appearing in productions of *Macbeth*. The riot caused the deaths of 22 participants, and injured countless persons, including many police and military personnel called up to quell the riot. The publicity surrounding the Astor Place tragedy did little to help the images of either actor, and in Forrest's case, although he continued to act to admiring audiences, his fiery temperament and other scandals, including a messy divorce fueled by sensationalized newspaper coverage in 1850, damaged his popularity. However, his wealth allowed him to build a spectacular castle on the Hudson River he named Fonthill, which was later turned into a convent. He also had homes in Philadelphia and New York. The Philadelphia home was converted into the Edwin Forrest Home for poor or ailing actors after Forrest's death.

Despite the aforementioned setbacks, Forrest had a notable success with a four-week run of *Macbeth* at the **Broadway Theatre** in 1853, an unprecedentedly long run during which he announced his retirement from the stage. He had developed an interest in politics and considered a run for Congress, but by 1860, he was back onstage reprising his most famous roles, acting in a production of *Hamlet* at **Niblo's Garden**, the standout critical success of his career, though **Edwin Booth**'s† Hamlet eclipsed Forrest's only a few years later. Also at this time, Forrest commissioned noted photographer Matthew Brady to photograph him in costume in his greatest roles.

By the late 1860s, health issues undermined Forrest's performances, and the next generation of actors, led by Edwin Booth, moved toward a more natural acting style; in comparison, Forrest's work seemed dated. He died of a stroke in 1872 while appearing in *Richelieu* and *King Lear*. As the *New York Times* wrote at the time of his death,

> In the life of Mr. Forrest is found much of the history of the American stage. Before his time no American actor had appeared whose delineations of Shakespearean characters equaled those of the best actors on the English boards. With his début as *Othello*, in the Summer of 1826, the previously undisputed superiority of the English actors ceased. . . . With him the American stage loses one of its brightest ornaments and principal supporters.

FOSCARI; OR, THE VENETIAN EXILE. **John Blake White**'s five-act blank verse tragedy written in 1805 was first performed at the **Charleston Theatre** in 1806. The play, centered on the tragic relationship of a father and son, preceded Lord Byron's more famous account, *The Two Foscaris*, by 15 years. The historically based plot is based on the life of Francesco Foscari (1373–1457), doge of Venice from 1423 to 1457, and Jacopo Foscari (d. 1457), his only son, who was tried by the Council of Ten on charges including bribery and corruption, which led to his imprisonment on Crete and ultimate death. His father withdrew from his public role under fire from the

Council of Ten, but his death shortly thereafter led to a public outcry that resulted in a state funeral. Many dramatizations have been based on the Foscaris, including Giuseppe Verdi's opera *I due Foscari* (1844).

FOSTER, STEPHEN C. (1826–1864). Despite the fact that most of his songs reflected the American South, Stephen Collins Foster was born in Lawrenceville, Pennsylvania. His direct involvement in theater was minimal, though many of Foster's songs were popularized by **minstrel**† companies, especially that of **E. P. Christy**. Despite the minstrel association and stereotypical depictions of **African Americans**,*† Foster's compositions are perhaps the most enduring popular songs of the 19th century, including "Beautiful Dreamer," "Jeanie with the Light Brown Hair" (written for his wife, Jane McDowell), "Oh! Susanna," "Swanee River," "Camptown Races," "My Old Kentucky Home," "Hard Times Come Again No More," "Old Black Joe," and nearly 200 others.

In his youth, Foster attended Jefferson College and received some classical music training from Henry Kleber. Foster also befriended entertainer **Dan Rice**,† who performed many of the popular songs of the era, leading Foster to blend elements from classical music with popular rhythms with great success. However, his triumph was popularity, not financial; it was impossible in times before copyright protections for songwriters to make a living writing popular songs. In 1863, Foster partnered with lyricist George Cooper to write songs for **musical***† theater, but he died in poverty the following year, even as minstrel troupes and **vaudevillians**† performed his songs. Foster's songs continue to be performed in the 21st century and for many exemplify the sounds of the years leading up to the **Civil War**.

FOULE, WILLIAM B. (1795–1865). William Beatley Foule wrote *Women's Rights* (1856), a play published in *Parlour Dramas; or, Dramatic Scenes for Home Amusement*, a collection of plays of social significance, in Foule's case dealing with feminism. Foule's play centers on a woman's refusal to include "to obey" in the marriage vows, a radical notion at the time.

FOURTEENTH STREET THEATRE. Opened in 1866 at 107 West 14th Street in New York, the Fourteenth Street Theatre, initially called the Theatre Francais since it specialized in French language works, was designed by Alexander Saeltzer. The theater was renamed the Lyceum in 1871, but when **J. H. Haverly** took over as **manager**,*† he renamed it Haverly's Fourteenth Street Theatre. By the 1880s, it became known as the Fourteenth Street Theatre. Under various managements over the years, it fell on hard times and became a movie theater in the 1910s. However, in 1926, Eva Le Gallienne*

took over the facility for her Civic Repertory Theatre,* but when it folded in 1934 due to the Great Depression, the theater essentially closed and was razed in 1938.

FOX, GEORGE L. (1825–1877). Born **George Washington** Lafayette Fox in Cambridge, Massachusetts, the son of **actors*†** at Boston's **Tremont Theatre**, he became an actor as a **child**,† along with his siblings and parents. His parents did not recognize his particular talents and arranged for him to be an apprentice to a businessman. He eventually returned to the stage, working with his brother-in-law, **George C. Howard**, who, in 1852, commissioned a stage adaptation of Harriet Beecher Stowe's novel, *Uncle Tom's Cabin*. Fox, however, found himself as a comedian beginning in 1850 at the **Bowery Theatre**. He became a favorite with working-class audiences, and in 1852 he staged and played the role of Phineas Fletcher in **George L. Aiken**'s version of *Uncle Tom's Cabin*. Aiken was Fox's cousin, and the play was staged at Peal's Museum in Troy, New York, and became the definitive stage version of Stowe's novel.

The pantomimist **Ravel** Brothers inspired Fox in that direction, and he took over the **National Theatre** (and later the Bowery Theatre) to stage **burlesque*†** entertainments employing pantomime. With the outbreak of the **Civil War**, Fox joined the Union Army as a lieutenant and was a major by the time he completed his service in 1861. He returned to the stage in pantomime, but a fire destroyed the Bowery Theatre. In 1866, Fox took over the **Olympic Theatre**, where he played Bottom in **Shakespeare**'s*† *A Midsummer Night's Dream* and created his signature character, *Humpty Dumpty*, the first pantomime to be extended to two acts.

The white-faced clown Humpty Dumpty became Fox's stage persona, and he appeared in numerous sequels to the original play with great success. Fox also lampooned **Edwin Booth**'s† *Hamlet* and other iconic works of stage notables. Financial problems detracted from his considerable artistic and popular successes, but following a fall onstage in 1875, Fox displayed increasingly erratic behavior, suffered a series of strokes, and died in 1877. Remembered by audiences for the wild antics of his Humpty Dumpty character, Fox joined a relatively small number of clowns who achieved **star*†** status. As scholar Yvonne Shafer has written, "The nineteenth-century American theatre had numerous great comic actors, and to many George L. Fox was the funniest."

FRANCESCA DA RIMINI. **George H. Boker**'s six-act tragedy opened at the **Broadway Theatre** on 26 September 1855 for eight performances, but contemporary **critics*†** and scholars considered it one of the finest American plays of the era. Based on a historical tale from the 13th century that was shaped by Dante Alighieri, who devoted his fifth canto in the *Divine Comedy* to it, Boker's plot centers on the Francesca (played by **Elizabeth Ponisi** in the 1855 production) and Paolo story as written by Dante, though Boker chose to take significant liberties by emphasizing the character of Lanciotto (originally played by **E. L. Davenport**), creating a role suited to a **leading†** **actor**,*† in addition to the title character and Paolo.

Numerous plays have been based on *Francesca da Rimini*, including works by Silvio Pellico, Jan Neruda, Gabriele D'Annunzio, and others, while no fewer than 20 operas and numerous fine arts works have been inspired by the character. Boker's version of the story radically departed from familiar versions, as he wrote to Richard H. Stoddard on 3 March 1853: "You will laugh at this, but the thing is so. *Francesca da Rimini* is the title. Of course you know the story—everybody does; but you, nor anyone else, do not know it as I have created it." Though the play was rarely produced for three decades after its initial production, an 1882 revival by **Lawrence Barrett** popularized the play. Another **Broadway***† revival in 1901 featured Marcia Van Dresser as Francesca, **Otis Skinner** as Lanciotto, and Aubrey Boucicault as Paolo.

†FRENCH, SAMUEL (1821–1898). Born in Randolph, Massachusetts, Samuel French became a publisher of inexpensive editions of various literary works by the 1830s. In 1854, French, who also published plays via his French's American Drama series, made enough capital to buy out his major competitor, William Taylor and Company. French opened a branch of his growing organization in London in 1872, and during the late 19th century his company provided all manner of theatrical services, but ultimately settled on the publication of acting editions of plays and the licensing of those plays for professional and **amateur†** performances, just as the company bearing his name continues to do today.

FRENCH AND INDIAN WAR. In the North American part of the Seven Years' War, the combatants were essentially British American colonies and New France, both sides armed and supported by their parent countries, England and France, respectively. The French were significantly outnumbered, so they turned to Native Americans to enhance their forces (including Wabanaki, Algonquin, Caughnawaga Mohawk, Lenape, Ojibwa, Ottawa, Shawnee, Wyandot tribes), though the British Americans also had allies among Indian tribes (particularly Iroquois, Catawba, and Cherokee). The fighting began in 1754 and continued for nine years, until 1763.

The incitement for the French and Indian War began with fighting over control of the Allegheny and Monongahela Rivers. Fighting for territory spread from Nova Scotia to Virginia along the borders of the colonies and in many unsettled or lightly settled territories. There were significant battles, but much of the skirmishing during the years of the war and in the early years the French seemed to be winning. **George Washington** emerged as a force on the British American side, and although he was not the major force, he gained much military experience that would help him during the **American Revolution**. The Treaty of Paris, signed in 1763, officially ended the conflict, but the fighting declined significantly after 1760.

The French and Indian War was fought in an era of American theater that can only be described as formative—most dramas performed were English plays or translations of other western European works. As such, few plays feature either a factual or fictional depiction of the war—or specific events related to the war.

THE FRENCH LIBERTINE. **John Howard Payne**'s historical drama *Richelieu* met with **critical***† objections over content in England from the lord chamberlain, requiring changes be made, including its title to *The French Libertine*. When the drama opened in February 1826, it met with much negative criticism due to the portrayal of Richelieu as the seducer of a good-hearted wife of a merchant. Payne, who had debuted this play and a number of his other works in England, often found success, but *The French Libertine* was a failure.

FRITZ, OUR COUSIN GERMAN. **Charles Gayler**'s four-act **melodrama**† opened on 11 July 1870 at **Wallack's Theatre** for 63 performances. It moved to **Niblo's Garden** on 21 August 1871, where it played 30 performances. The play begins with Fritz arriving from Germany to find his long-lost sister and money her father left for them. While traveling, Fritz falls in love with a young woman, Katharina, who is kidnapped by the **villainous**† Crafton (played by **Charles Fisher**), but Fritz saves her. Fritz discovers that his sister is the ward of Crafton, but he wins her over by singing an old lullaby from their youth. Fritz and Katharina wed and have a baby, but Crafton kidnaps the **child**,† Little Fritz. Fritz rescues the child, killing Crafton in the process.

Joseph K. Emmet scored a major personal success as the heroic Fritz and appeared in subsequent tailor-made vehicles, including *Carl, the Fiddler* (1871) and *Max, the Magic Swiss Boy* (1873), with Fritz as the central character. The supporting† cast featured Minnie Maddern (later Mrs. Fiske)† as Little Fritz. As was the fashion at the time, the play featured a couple of songs, with Fritz's lullaby serving as a major plot element. The talented Emmet was an alcoholic, and periodically it had an impact on his performances and caused adverse publicity, which, it should be noted, did not seem to have an impact on his popularity.

THE FRONTIER MAID. Mordecai Noah, along with several **playwriting*†** contemporaries, found inspiration in rising nationalistic sentiments in the United States during the 1830s and 1840s. Many plays written in this period, including Noah's 1840 *The Frontier Maid*, presented such views and moved their settings to the western frontier territories.

The popular **Yankee†** character seen in multiple plays set in the eastern states morphed from a Bowery b'hoy fireman into a frontiersman as a means of extending the scope of a beloved national character type. Set during the **American Revolution**, the play reflected the expansion of the nation that would follow the **war*†** by a playwright who had built a reputation as a politician, journalist, and essayist. The play was also known as *Natalie; or, The Frontier Maid*.

FRONTIER THEATER AND DRAMA. Prior to the **Civil War**, performances in the western territories were, at best, primitive in production values. Though the occasional big-name talent might **tour*†** in the growing western portion of the United States (west of the Mississippi River), with the exception of large West Coast cities like San Francisco, performances were given in town halls, tents, saloons, and other makeshift temporary theaters, and audiences were often unruly. However, notable **actors*†** such as **Junius Brutus Booth Sr**. toured successfully, though he died as a result of drinking contaminated river water while touring in the West. Dangers included the general lawlessness of certain towns and territories as well as hostilities between **Native Americans*†** and the US military and settlers.

In literature, James Fenimore Cooper was a significant force in creating a memorable figure that undoubtedly inspired many theatrical manifestations of the character Cooper called Nathaniel "Natty" Bumppo (also known as Leatherstocking), who first appeared in Cooper's *Pioneers: The Sources of the Susquehanna: A Descriptive Tale* (1823) and continued in what ultimately became known as *The Leatherstocking Tales*, a collection of Cooper's novels featuring Bumppo and including *The Last of the Mohicans* (1826), *The Prairie* (1827), *The Pathfinder* (1840), and *The Deerslayer* (1841). Bumppo appeared under his own name in stage adaptations of Cooper's works, or under other names in many popular culture works throughout the 19th century, as fascination with the frontier continued until the frontier was gone. In the theater, this type of character—a bold frontiersman in the Bumppo image—also drew on nonfictional figures, such as Davy Crockett, to works of adventure and danger in the untamed western territories, usually in the **melodramatic†** form.

Both in the plays themselves and in reality for theatrical personnel touring, the dangers were real and modes of travel were primitive as the settled territories moved farther west from the mid-19th century. Covered wagons, boats (where possible), trains (where available), and horseback provided means of moving about sparsely populated territories, but in the last decades of the 19th century, transportation improved significantly, hostilities with Native Americans abated, and lawlessness was quelled in most sizeable towns and cities; as the West became more populated and civilized, it began to prove a lucrative means of income for actors and **managers**.*†

In the years after the **Civil War**, the American frontier depicted in drama was a romanticized version of the West. There were plays about Jesse James and his gang even while the originals were still at large, but most of these were the fare of the ten twent' thirt'† circuits. Aiming higher, **Joaquin Miller**'s† *The Danites*† (1877) remained popular well into the modernist period. Other plays of Western life include **Bartley Campbell**'s† *My Partner*† (1879), **David Belasco**'s† *The Girl I Left Behind Me*† (with Franklin Fyles,† 1893) and *Rose of the Rancho*† (1906), Augustus Thomas's† *In Mizzoura*† (1893) and *Arizona*† (1900), the dramatization of Owen Wister's *The Virginian*† (1904), and Porter Emerson Browne's† *The Bad Man*† (1920).

The great classics of the genre came early in the 20th century: Belasco's *Girl of the Golden West*† (1905), Edwin Milton Royle's† *The Squaw Man*† (1905), and William Vaughn Moody's† *The Great Divide*† (1906). As the frontier pushed westward, touring companies quickly followed. California scarcely qualified as frontier by the 1880s, but many towns between Chicago and San Francisco still had the volatile populations craving lively entertainment.† Performances in frontier towns were usually presented in a second- or third-floor hall above commercial space; often performers and spectators used the same exterior staircase. Audiences in such venues tended to be almost entirely men. **Legitimate**† plays were presented with **musical***† or specialty numbers between the acts. Not until a town built its first **opera house** could it hope to offer a better class of attractions,† but by then it probably could no longer be called a frontier town.

FROU-FROU. **Augustin Daly**'s "Comedy of Powerful Human Interest," was adapted into a five-act work adapted from a sentimental French drama by Henri Meilhac and Ludovic Halévy. *Frou-Frou* opened on 15 February 1870 for 103 performances at Daly's **Fifth Avenue Theatre**. Agnes Ethel won approval in the role of Gilberte, a flirtatious and **childish***† young wife who invites her straitlaced sister to live with her and her husband to cover up her flirtatious behaviors. Gilberte takes up an affair with a former lover, who is subsequently killed in a duel by her husband. Shocked by this turn of events, Gilberte is awakened to the damage her behavior has caused and repents by nursing poverty-stricken patients, catching a fatal disease in the process. She returns to her family to beg forgiveness and dies as the curtain falls. **Sarah Bernhardt**† added the play to her repertoire and played it in French in the United States on her frequent **tours**.*† The play appeared in **Broadway***† revivals in 1902 (**starring***† Grace George†) and 1912.

†FURNESS, HORACE HOWARD (1833–1912). The Philadelphia-born lawyer is remembered as the editor of variorum editions of **Shakespeare**'s*† plays and was widely considered the leading Shakespearean scholar of 19th-century America. He left his vast collection of Shakespearean materials to the University of Pennsylvania for the use of future scholars and **critics**.*†

G

†GALLERY. The upper level of a theater auditorium, usually a tier above the balcony, held the cheapest seats, sometimes referred to as "the heavens." In many cases, a theatergoer paid general admission to the gallery for unreserved seating, leading to considerable jockeying for position among gallery patrons.

†GALLERY GODS. Although the cheap admission price attracted some rowdies to the gallery seating, particularly in locations in which the working class resided, the majority of theatergoers who bought gallery seats were low-salaried people who spent their minimal discretionary income to attend performances several times a week. Thus they were, in a sense, theater literate and developed strong opinions about performers, plays, and production values. Unfortunately for the performers onstage, they did not hesitate to express their pleasure or derision during a performance. They were called "gallery gods" partly because their seats were the closest to the "heavens" and partly because of their power to advance or destroy stage careers.

THE GALLEY SLAVE. **Bartley Campbell**'s five-act play opened 1 December 1879 at **Haverly's Theatre** for 101 performances. The **melodramatic†** plot depicts two lovers, Cicely and Sidney, who are manipulated by Baron Le Bois, who convinces Sidney that Cicely has been unfaithful. The amoral Le Bois has married and abandoned Francesca. When Sidney is caught visiting Cicely, he pretends to be a thief to spare her reputation and is, in due course, jailed. Francesca meets him there, and Cicely, yearning for Sidney, discovers his location, which leads to unmasking the **villainy†** of Le Bois and reuniting the lovers. The original cast featured **Emily Rigl** as Francesca, with Maude Evans, Frank Granger, and J. J. Sullivan in support.

THE GAME OF LOVE. **John Brougham**'s five-act play inspired by **Charles Dickens**'s *Bleak House* premiered under **James W. Wallack**'s direction at **Wallack's Theatre** on 12 September 1855 for 23 performances. **Mrs. John Hoey** played a jilted woman, Alice Devereaux, who impetuously determines to marry the first man who comes along. The man, Paul Weldon, played by **Lester Wallack**, agrees to marry Alice because of her wealth, but learns that the marriage contract renders him little more than an employee. Friction arises, leading Councillor Foxglove, played by **Henry Placide**, to make use of all of his estimable advisory skills to bring Alice and Paul together with the realization they are in love.

GANNON, MARY (1829–1868). Born in New York of **Irish** heritage, Mary Gannon became a celebrated comedienne in her adulthood following experience as a **child†** **actress*†** beginning sometime between 1832 and 1835. Little is known of her early life, but some scholars believe she made her stage debut at the Richmond Hill Theatre in *The Daughters of the Regiment* (others believe her debut was at the **Bowery Theatre** in 1835). She gained early experience as an actress and dancer in provincial theaters.

Gannon spent most of her career working in New York and Philadelphia, where she became a great favorite with audiences, usually in popular contemporary comedies and **vaudeville**.† She scored her first great successes beginning in 1855 when she joined **Wallack's Theatre**, becoming an increasingly important part of an expert ensemble† of comic performers. Appearing in *The Love Chase*, *The Romance of the Poor Young Man*, *Knights of the Round Table*, *To Marry or Not to Marry*, *The Little Treasure*, **Rosedale**, and many of the 18th-century comic matron roles, she became regarded as a major comedienne, though her career was cut short by an early death. Shortly before her death, **critic*†** **Joseph N. Ireland** wrote that she "is now universally acknowledged to be the best general comic actress in the city."

†GAS LIGHTING. Theatrical lighting was significantly advanced by the time gas lighting came into prevalent use in theaters in the early 1800s. European theaters, particularly larger ones such as the Paris Opera, made use of gas lighting well before American theaters began converting to gas. Gas lighting found mostly advocates among theater **managers**,*† who found it cheaper than candlelights, and from an artistic point of view, it allowed for more interesting effects. Gas lighting predominated for approximately one hundred years, with newer and prosperous theaters converting to electric lights during the 1890s. Electric lighting virtually eliminated the danger of **theater fires**,† which had been prevalent during the 19th century. When Chicago's Iroquois Theatre† burned on 30 December 1903, tragically killing at least 605 people, the temporary closing of theaters and a national dialogue over safety led to theaters converting to electricity, which remains the norm after over a hundred years.

GATES, WILLIAM F. (d. 1843). Little is known about the early life of William F. Gates, an **actor***† who is believed to have initiated his career working in a **circus**.*† His debut in the **legitimate**† theater in 1828 came at the **Chatham Garden Theatre** in *Valentine and Orson*. In 1830, he joined the **Bowery Theatre**, where he remained for the rest of his career, playing both serious and comic roles. It was in comedy, including such **Shakespearean***† characters as Trinculo in *The Tempest* and the First Gravedigger in *Hamlet*, that he won great affection from the Bowery audience. He also appeared in such contemporary plays as *The Cannibals*, *Blue Laws*, and *Loan of a Lover*. **Noah Ludlow** wrote of Gates that "he was a quiet, unpretending man, of sound mind and manly nature, genial and well-disposed to all mankind. He lived beloved, and died in New York City, deeply regretted, of a lingering disease, September 17, 1843."

GAULANTUS THE GAUL. **Nathaniel H. Bannister**'s 1836 five-act tragedy had its first production in Cincinnati, with Bannister playing a Gaul, Baranicus, and his wife in the role of the Roman Leonida. C. B. Parsons played the title character, with Bannister as his brother. The play was **melodramatic**† in nature, suiting the tastes of the time, but it was not much produced, though published by Flash, Ryder and Company in 1836.

GAYLER, CHARLES (1820–1892). Born in New York to a working-class family of merchants, Charles Gayler moved to Ohio to become a teacher. He became interested in local and national politics and wrote a song in 1844 supporting Henry Clay for president. Gayler married two years later to Grace Christian, who was the mother of his eight children.† He worked as a journalist, but found life in the theater as having greater appeal. Gayler acted in **Shakespeare***† and wrote **melodramatic**† plays, including *The Buckeye Gold Hunters* (1849), first staged in Cincinnati. The play's success encouraged him to move to New York, where he became a **manager***† and a prolific author of stage works in multiple genres, including melodramas, comedies, **operettas**,† and tragedies.

In the immediate aftermath of the actual **Civil War** battle, Gayler scored a success with *Bull Run, or the Sacking of Fairfax Courthouse* (1861). Charmed by New York life, Gayler used New York as the setting of many of his most popular works, including *Lights and Shadows of New York* (1872), and he also wrote novels with a New York background. One of his most popular works, *Fritz, Our Cousin German* (1870) was a hit at **Wallack's Theatre**, and in 1879 he adapted **Washington Irving**'s "comic pastoral novel," *Sleepy Hollow; or, The Headless Horseman*, for the stage. Gayler's obituary credited him with writing more than 400 dramatic works, an astonishing output, although it acknowledged that most of these works were long forgotten by the theatergoing public.

GENDER. *See* *†SEXUALITY.

GENERAL THEATRICAL FUND. Founded in Philadelphia in 1829, the General Theatrical Fund was established, like several similar organizations, including the Actors'*† Order of Friendship and the Actors Fund of America,† to benefit actors who have fallen on hard times either through illness, chronic unemployment, or age.

THE GEORGIA SPEC; OR, LAND IN THE MOON. **Royall Tyler**'s three-act comedy, at first named *A Good Spec*, was first performed in Boston on 30 October 1797, followed by a 20 December 1797 performance in New York at the **John Street Theatre** (a repeat performance was given on 12 February 1798). The comedy satirized anger over speculation on land in Georgia as part of the Yazoo Purchase. Tyler wrote three other plays (*The Farm House*, *The Doctor in Spite of Himself*, and *The Island of Barrataria*) in 1797, but it appears that none of these were ever performed.

GERMANIA THEATRE. Built in 1872 at Eighth Street and Fourth Avenue, the Germania Theatre was actually intended for other purposes. However, on 8 September 1879, it opened as a theater, and its **attractions**† were often weak and unappreciated. For a time, a **Yiddish**† theater company performed there, and it changed names on occasion, but in 1892, following some restoration, it reopened as the Germania Theatre.

GERMON, EFFIE (1845–1914). Born Euphemia Germon in Augusta, Georgia, Effie Germon was the daughter of **actors***† Greene and Jane (Anderson) Germon, her father being a celebrated interpreter of the title character in *Uncle Tom's Cabin*. She made her stage debut at the **Holliday Street Theatre** in Baltimore in *Sketches in India* in 1857. Germon became a popular soubrette† in **stock***† in Baltimore and Philadelphia. After establishing herself, she retired from the stage to marry Carlo Patti in 1859, but she returned to acting in 1863.

In 1869, Germon joined the **manager***†/actor/**playwright***† **John Brougham** at **Wallack's Theatre** and appeared opposite Richard Mansfield† in the original production of *Little Lord Fauntleroy*. After her divorce from Patti, she married comic Nelse Seymour. She had a brush with history when she appeared in *Aladdin!; or The Wonderful Lamp* at **Grover's Theatre** in Washington, DC, on the night of President **Abraham Lincoln**'s assassination. Germon had also been present a week earlier in the office of Grover's manager, C. D. Hess, when **John Wilkes Booth**† appeared to ask if Lincoln would be attending the performance of *Aladdin* at Grover's, to which he had been invited. The Lincolns decided instead to attend *Our American Cousin* at **Ford's Theatre**, but their young son Thomas "Tad" Lincoln did attend *Aladdin*, where he heard the news that his father was shot from an announcement onstage. When Booth was caught and killed weeks after the assassination, a photo of Germon was found on his person.

GERRY SOCIETY. The 18th- and 19th-century American theater often featured **child**† performers in all kinds of entertainments.† Founded in 1874 and known initially as the New York Society for the Prevention of Cruelty to Children, the Gerry Society was named for one of its founders, Elbridge Thomas Gerry, who concerned himself with the rights of children and with providing protective services to support abused or overworked children. The society was not restricted solely to theatrical children (though theater was regarded as immoral by Gerry), but their power was such that child **actors***† were often prevented from performing in the city or their appearances met with stringent regulations. Ultimately, the society took on the legal enforcement of regulations about children, but did not provide services, instead directing abused children to the appropriate social organization established to care for them.

†**GHOST LIGHT.** This term typically describes a single light on a freestanding pole that is illuminated and remains onstage as a safety precaution when a theater's **lighting***† system is dark. "Ghost light" comes from the days of **gas-lit**† theaters and refers to dimly lit gaslights used to relieve pressure on gas valves as well as the popular myth that a light in a theater kept ghosts away.

†**GILBERT, MRS. GEORGE HENRY (1821–1904).** Born Anne Hartley in London, England, this beloved **character**† **actress***† began as a dancer in the *corps de ballet* at Her Majesty's and Drury Lane Theatres. In 1846, she married dancer George Henry Gilbert, and three years later they left England for America. By 1851, they were performing with a Chicago **stock***† company. In 1861, Mrs. Gilbert played Lady Macbeth opposite **Edwin Booth**† during his brief engagement in Louisville.

After her New York debut in 1864, Mrs. Gilbert's career as a performer of eccentric† roles became well established, marred only by the death of her husband in 1867. That same year, she appeared in one of her greatest successes, the New York premiere of T. W. Robertson's *Caste*. From 1869 until her death, with only a three-year hiatus (1877–1880), she acted in **Augustin**

Daly's† **Fifth Avenue Theatre** company in New York, becoming familiarly known and beloved as "Grandma Gilbert," specializing in older woman characters in comedies. Her memoir, *The Stage Reminiscences of Mrs. Gilbert*, was published in 1901, but despite her advanced years, she still acted occasionally and made her last appearance only one day before her death.

GILBERT, JOHN (1810–1889). Born John Gibbs in Boston, John Gilbert made his debut at Boston's **Tremont Theatre** in 1828 in *Venice Preserved*. He worked toward becoming a major tragedian, but while **touring*†** he found himself consistently praised in classic and contemporary comic roles, including *The Rivals* and *The Hunchback*. As such, he increasingly took comedy parts, particularly those of old men. He scored a success in 1834 at the Tremont in *The Road to Ruin*, a benefit performance for **George Barrett**, his predecessor among comic favorites. Gilbert's appearance was so well received that he worked at the Tremont for five years, acting in all manner of new or classical comedies, including as **Shakespeare's*†** buffoons. He subsequently joined **Wallack's Theatre** company in New York in 1862, assaying a range of comedy parts, and he had a major success opposite **Elsie Germon** in *Brother Sam* in 1872. Audiences favored him in many roles, but many **critics*†** appreciated him most as Sir Peter Teazle in *The School for Scandal*.

GILBERT, WILLIAM SCHWENCK (1836–1911) AND SULLIVAN, ARTHUR SEYMOUR (1842–1900). Gilbert and Sullivan were partners in the late Victorian era and collaborated on 14 comic **operettas†** starting in 1871 and continuing through 1896, just a few short years before Sullivan's death. Gilbert, the lyricist and librettist, created comic absurdity from the notion of the world turned "topsy-turvy" and their operettas essentially turned the social order and Victorian class system upside down (regardless of the time period or exotic setting of some of their works), to the great amusement† of audiences of the era, first in England and, by the mid-1870s, in the United States.

Richard D'Oyly Carte had nurtured the Gilbert and Sullivan partnership, and his company kept up a continual run of Gilbert and Sullivan works, providing them with unparalleled success, including great popularity in America, where **musical*†** theater was evolving. Gilbert and Sullivan were among the many influences on that evolution. Among their best-known and most successful works are *Trial by Jury* (1875), *H.M.S. Pinafore* (1878), *The Pirates of Penzance* (1879), *Patience* (1881), *The Mikado* (1885), and *The Yeoman of the Guard* (1888). A production of *H.M.S. Pinafore* in 1879 was the first appearance of a Gilbert and Sullivan work in America.

THE GILDED AGE. See COLONEL SELLERS.

GILFERT, CHARLES A. (1784–1829). German-born **manager*†** of New York's **Bowery Theatre**, Charles Antonio Gilfert ran the theater from its opening performance in 1826 through a catastrophic **fire†** in 1828 and the theater's reconstruction. The owners terminated their relationship with him when he fell behind in the rent in 1829, and he went on to manage theaters in Charleston, Richmond, and Albany. Various contemporaries found him either a risk-taking manager or a shady figure. Some scholars credit him with introducing the role of the press **agent,†** and his death came supposedly as the result of the loss of the theater he was operating.

GILL, WILLIAM B. (1842–1919). Born William Bain Gill in Newfoundland, William B. Gill spent much of his time as an **actor*†** working in Australia, entertaining workers in the gold fields, and India. Ultimately, he moved to the United States, where he continued acting, but only with minor success at first, though he eventually grew into a popular **Broadway*†** comedian. Turning to writing, he wrote in a variety of forms, from comedy to **melodrama,†** but is most remembered for writing the libretto of the first hit Broadway **musical,*†** *Adonis* (1884), a "**burlesque*†** nightmare" satirizing the Pygmalion-Galatea myth and the traditions of contemporary drama. It ran over 600 performances and earned a fortune. His later works included *The Alderman* (1897), *The Honest Blacksmith* (1901), and *Mrs. "Mac": The Mayor* (1905).

†GILLETTE, WILLIAM (1855–1937). One of the major stage **stars*†** of the late 19th century, William Gillette, a native of Hartford, Connecticut, was the son of a US senator and received his education at Yale, Harvard, and the Massachusetts Fine Arts Institute before making his theatrical debut in *Faint Heart Ne'er Won Fair Lady* in 1875. He played secondary roles in several productions at the **Boston Museum†** before making his New York debut in George Densmore's adaptation of **Mark Twain**'s *The Gilded Age* (1877).

Gillette's greatest period of work as an **actor*†** ran parallel with a career as a dramatist and adaptor; while Gillette **toured*†** in **Bronson Howard**'s† *Young Mrs. Winthrop,†* he began to write plays as vehicles for himself, notably *The Professor†* (1881) and *Digby's Secretary* (1884). His other early plays include *Esmeralda†* (1881), which he adapted with Frances Hodgson Burnett,† *Held by the Enemy†* (1886), *Mr. Wilkinson's Widows†* (1891), *Settled Out of Court* (1892), *Too Much Johnson†* (1894), *Secret Service†* (1896), and his major triumph as an actor in *Sherlock Holmes†* (1899).

THE GLADIATOR. **Robert Montgomery Bird**'s tragedy was first performed in April 1831, though it drew more attention in **repertory*†** at the **Park Theatre** beginning on 26 September 1831. Its earliest performance was five months before an actual slave rebellion in the United States; **African American*** slave Nat Turner led a revolt in Virginia resulting in the deaths of 55 whites and over 200 blacks, leading ultimately to Turner's capture, conviction, and hanging.

How much audiences related the events of the story of Spartacus to current events is unclear, but theatrically speaking, **Edwin Forrest** had one of his greatest non-**Shakespearean*†** roles (he is believed to have performed it more than 1,000 times) as Spartacus in this grim tale of an imprisoned gladiator who acquiesces to fight in a Roman gladiatorial contest with the promise it will free his wife and young son from captivity if he prevails. However, Spartacus discovers that his opponent is his own brother, Phasarius, and they are required to fight to the death. Instead, the brothers agree to rebel, but Phasarius's **attraction†** to Julia and his impatience undercuts their strategy. Spartacus endures the death of his brother, wife, and son, but refuses to give up until he himself is killed.

After Forrest's death, **John McCullough** successfully acted the part, and it was also played by a number of lesser lights. Noting the contemporary relevance of *The Gladiator*, **Walt Whitman** wrote, "Running o'er with sentiments of liberty—with eloquent disclaimers of the right of the Romans to hold human beings in bondage—it is a play, this 'Gladiator,' calculated to make the hearts of the masses swell responsively to all those nobler manlier aspirations in behalf of mortal freedom."

A GLANCE AT NEW YORK. **Benjamin A. Baker**'s hit comedy of a country bumpkin's visit to the big city was widely imitated, especially one of its characters, Mose, a Bowery b'hoy **stock*†** character whose language was riddled with contemporary slang, at that time a novelty on mid-19th-century stages. It opened at **William Mitchell**'s **Olympic Theatre** on 2 February 1848 as *New York in 1848*. The title was changed almost immediately, and it was a runaway hit for a four-month run.

The play is little more than an extended sketch centered on the misadventures of George Parsells, a rube in the big city, who is wised up after losing his watch and wallet to some city slickers. Among the characters, Mose was the standout as famously played by **Frank S. Chanfrau**. A volunteer "fire laddie," Mose delighted audiences and boldly represented class differences in the big city. He is pure working class, and **gallery†** audiences made him their hero. Mose, the play's major legacy, was a Bowery "b'hoy," in this case a fireman, but the character (sometimes with other names) appeared in other jobs in other farces.

The play established a vogue for localized plays and characters—and there were versions of the play set in other cities and usually written by other authors, though Baker crafted some successful sequels himself, including *New York as It Is* (1848), *Three Years After* (1849), and *Mose in China* (1850). Though the play was seldom revived after the 19th century, New York's Axis Theatre Company provided a rare contemporary staging in 2007.

THE GLORY OF COLUMBIA, HER YEOMANRY. **William Dunlap** crafted this 1803 **musical***† extravaganza,† intended for festive holiday performances, from scenes and characters borrowed from his controversial blank verse play, *André: A Tragedy* (1798). Heavy on stage spectacle, music, comedy, and episodes of pathos, *The Glory of Columbia* was popular for a time in the early 19th century, but ultimately faded from view.

GLOVER, STEPHEN E. (1778–1843). Born in Dorchester, Massachusetts, Captain Stephen E. Glover became a merchant ship captain and ship builder who dabbled in theater. He is credited with two plays based on novels by James Fenimore Cooper: *The Last of the Mohicans*, first performed on 6 January 1830 in Charleston, South Carolina, and *The Cradle of Liberty*, based on Cooper's *Lionel Lincoln; or, The Leaguer of Boston*, presented for the first time at the Camp Street Theatre in New Orleans on 24 March 1831. It is believed that he wrote other plays, but no evidence survives.

GODFREY, THOMAS (1736–1763). Born in Philadelphia, Thomas Godfrey worked as a glazier. He won some attention writing poetry and became a member of Benjamin Franklin's Junto Club. Godfrey wrote a lengthy poem, *The Court of Fancy*, but his next major work was a five-act tragedy (the only play he wrote) called *The Prince of Parthia*, which was neither published nor produced during his short lifetime. *The Prince of Parthia*, first staged at the **Southwark Theatre** by the **American Company** on 24 April 1767, attained the distinction of being the first play by an American author to be produced.

GOODALE, GEORGE POMEROY (1843–1919). At the time of his death in 1919, George Pomeroy Goodale was praised as the "Dean of American Dramatic **Critics**."*† A native of Orleans, New York, Goodale began a journalistic career at the bottom, working in a printing office and as a reporter. With the outbreak of the **Civil War**, Goodale served with the Union Army, after which he became city and drama editor for the *Detroit Free*

Press, beginning in 1865 and continuing until his death. Historians favorably compare his moralizing tone and scholarly approach to such peers as **William Winter†** and **John Ranken Towse**.

GOODSPEED OPERA HOUSE. Founded in 1876 by William H. Goodspeed beside the Connecticut River, this facility originally served multiple purposes for Goodspeed, a banker and shipping **manager**.*† Goodspeed, also a theater lover, included a theater, offices, a terminal for steamboat passengers coming and going, and a general store. The first performance in the theater occurred on 24 October 1877 with a **repertory***† company staging a comedy, *Charles II*, and two short farces, *Box and Cox* and *Turn Him Out*. The building needed renovation by the 1960s and was restored and reopened for performances continuing to present times. Its present-day incarnation has stressed celebrating **musical***† theater, with revivals of great or neglected musicals and development of new musicals, including *Man of La Mancha* and *Shenandoah*, both of which moved to **Broadway**.*†

GOODWIN, J. CHEEVER (1850–1912). Born John Cheever Goodwin in Boston, he was educated at Harvard. After a time working as an **actor***† with **E. A. Sothern**, Goodwin partnered with **E. E. Rice** to write the **musical*** **burlesque*** *Evangeline* (1874), a major success that, despite his continuing acting career, led him to continue working as a librettist, including for such works as *The Merry Monarch* (1890), *Wang* (1891), *Dr. Syntax* (1894), *Fleur-De-Lis* (1895), *Lost, Strayed or Stolen* (1896), and *An Arabian Girl and Forty Thieves* (1899).

GOODWIN, NAT (1857–1919). Born Nathaniel Carl Goodwin in Boston, he attended school at the Little Blue Academy in Farmington, Maine, where he acted in school dramatics. This led to a career as an **actor***† beginning with the role of a shoeshine boy in **manager***† **John B. Stetson**'s production of *Law in New York* (1874) at Boston's **Howard Athenaeum**. Goodwin worked in **vaudeville†** for **Tony Pastor†** in 1875 and **starred***† in **E. E. Rice**'s **musicals***† for a few seasons before setting up his own comedy troupe, the Froliques, where he was applauded for his imitations of famous actors and for his eccentric comedic style.

Goodwin was successful in a series of light comedies during the 1880s and 1890s. He gradually added dramatic roles to his repertoire, including Sheriff Jim Radburn in **Augustus Thomas**'s *In Mizzoura* (1893). He found great successes opposite his wife, **Maxine Elliott**, in *Nathan Hale* (1899) and *When We Were Twenty-One* (1900). He continued to act until shortly before his death, scoring one final hit in Jesse Lynch Williams's*† Pulitzer Prize*†–winning comedy, *Why Marry?**† (1917).

THE GORDIAN KNOT. Jewish American playwright **Isaac Harby**'s† second play, written in 1807 in five acts, *The Gordian Knot* had a difficult path to the stage. It was submitted by Harby to **actor*†-managers*† Alexandre Placide†** and **William Warren,**† both of whom first accepted, but then rejected the play. In 1810, Placide finally staged it with many changes. Harby was apparently displeased with the changes and restored his original text for its publication that year. The plot, borrowed from William Henry Ireland's novel *The Abbess* (which Ireland had borrowed from an Italian novella, *Secreto Maligno*), is a **melodramatic*†** revenge drama. Quinn praised the play for its general realism,*† making a convoluted plot more believable and depicting the play's two sets of lovers with fuller characterizations than typical at the time. The characters' ruminations on their circumstances provide witty interludes, such as this speech by Clara, cousin of one of the heartsick lovers.

> Love! 'tis a non-descript, head-ach, heart-ach;
> A painful pleasure and a pleasing pain;
> A something, nothing, that torments, delights us;
> Shot, like a basilisk, on the spell-bound eye,
> It heats the blood, and melts the hearts away,
> In sighing out—heighho!

Though the play's central plot focused on Italian noblemen standing between the mating of true lovers has the makings of a tragedy, Harby ends the play happily and in melodramatic fashion, with the lovers united and **villains†** punished.

GORMAN BROTHERS MINSTRELS. James (b. 1852), John (b. 1855), and George (b. 1864) Gorman, a trio of brothers, all began their careers as **minstrel†** entertainers. James was the first to succeed when he joined **Hooley's Minstrels** in 1869. By 1872, the brothers joined to form Gorman Brothers Minstrels, debuting at the **Bowery Theatre**. They **toured*†** for a number of years and at times were associated with other troupes, including **Haverly's Mastodon Minstrels**, Gorton Minstrels, **Primrose and West**, and others. The Gormans toured England and played at the Drury Lane Theatre for 10 weeks in 1884, prior to touring the provinces. Back in the United States, they appeared at Cincinnati's Heuck's Opera House in early 1885 and continued to perform, together and separately, until the 1910s. Known as the "Gentlemanly Gormans," the brothers were admired for their versatility as comedians, singers, and dancers. James also wrote plays and sketches for the act and was a **producer.***†

GOULD, EDWARD SHERMAN (1805–1885). New York–born writer, Edward Sherman Gould, who wrote a comedy, sketches, and a novel, among other things, did not make much of a mark as a writer. In 1836, Gould wrote *American Criticism of American Literature* in which, among other things, he controversially posited that American writers and journalists, including **dramatists,***† were inherently inferior to their British counterparts. This reactionary argument appeared at the height of overheated American nationalistic feelings and anti-British sentiments that led to considerable friction, including the tragic occurrences of the **Astor Place Opera House** riot, in which at least 22 people were killed and scores of others injured when American **actor***† **Edwin Forrest** became embroiled in a feud with English **star***† **William Charles Macready**.

GRAIN, PETER (1785?–1857). The head of a family of French American **scene**† **designers***† celebrated in the early to mid-19th century, the Grains are believed to have arrived in America on **tour***† in 1807 and honed their skills and built their reputations working in theaters in Southern cities (Richmond, Charleston, Savannah, and others). Their first known New York credits were advertised in 1823. Among Peter's best-known productions were **Henry Barrière**'s *The Lady of the Lake* in 1826 and *The Battle of Algiers* in 1829. Much of Peter's career was spent at **Niblo's Garden**, the **Bowery Theatre**, and in the mid-1840s, the Floating Theatre, but at various times he designed single productions for some of New York's and Philadelphia's finest theaters. New York's Lafayette **Circus***† was redesigned and rebuilt as the Lafayette Theatre in 1827; for a time it was known as the largest theater in the United States and Great Britain. Frederick Grain, Peter's brother, was also a much-admired scene designer. And Grain's son Peter Grain Jr. spent much of his career at Philadelphia's **Walnut Street Theatre**. Grain's other sons George and Urban were also respected designers. Grains worked at various times at the **Chatham Garden Theatre**, the **Park Theatre**, the **Arch Street Theatre**, and Welch's Olympic Circus.

GRANGER, MAUDE (1851?–1928). Born Anna Brainerd Follen in Middletown, Connecticut, she had a long and successful career in which she initially found fame as an uncommonly beautiful **ingénue**,† and as she aged developed into an admired character **actress**.*† Though seldom thought of as a **star*** in the manner of many of her contemporaries, she was well-known and much-photographed. Her performances were usually **critically***† acclaimed, but the dominant comments focused on her physical beauty.

Granger debuted in New York in *Without a Heart* (1873). She had a stretch of successes, including *The Mighty Dollar* (1875) and *Fifth Avenue* (1877). She spent a season playing opposite **John McCullough** in revivals of

Virginius, The Gladiator, Richelieu, and *Othello.* The following season, Granger scored again in **Lester Wallack**'s company in *Diplomacy* and with **Augustin Daly** in *L'Assommoir* (1879). That same year she appeared in **Bartley Campbell**'s plays *My Partner* and *The Galley Slave.*

Despite her long string of successes, including *Two Nights in Rome* (1880), Granger's acting talents were increasingly challenged by critics. However, she continued to pursue a first-rank career, becoming **James O'Neill**'s† leading lady, but ultimately spent her later years, continuing to 1924, playing **character**† roles in **touring***† companies.

GRATTAN, H. P. (1808–1889). Born Henry Willoughby Grattan Plunkett in Dublin, Ireland, his writing included contributing to *Punch* under the pseudonym "Fusbos." Though he wrote for English publications at times, he lived in the United States for 23 years and wrote under his pseudonym, H. P. Grattan. His plays, mostly farcical potboilers and romantic **melodramas**,† some aiming for the **Irish** audience, included *The Dumb Conscript; or, a Brother's Love and a Sister's Honour* (1835), *The Corsair's Revenge; or, Love and Vengeance* (1835), *The White Boys* (1836), *The Gold Seekers; or, The Outcasts of Anzasca* (1839), *Norah O'Donnell; or, The Sybil of the Camp* (1840), *My Uncle's Card, or the First of April* (1840), *Faust; or, The Demon of Drachelfels* (1842), *The Fairy Circle, or Con O'Callaghan's Dream* (1842), and *Judy* (1846). He also wrote poetry and published *The Bottle* (1848). He eventually returned to Great Britain and died in London.

GRAU, MAURICE (1849–1917). A native of Brüun, Austria, Maurice Grau came to America as a **child**† and was educated to practice law at Columbia University. He gave up the law to work with Jacob Grau, his uncle, who was **manager***† of New York's French Theatre. He went into management on his own to bring French **opéra bouffe**† legend Marie Aimée to the United States. Not only was her appearance a success, it solidified the growing popularity of opéra bouffe and the development of **musical***† theater. Grau also managed **tours**† of Jacques Offenbach and **Tommaso Salvini** and ran several New York theaters, including an acclaimed period as manager of the Metropolitan Opera.

GREEN STREET THEATRE. In 1812, construction began on a theater on Green Street in Albany, New York. The theater opened on 18 January 1813 as the first permanent theater in Albany. It did not remain a theater for long, becoming instead a church. However, a few decades later, on 5 July 1852, the building returned to its theatrical roots as both a theater and a concert hall, with **Adah Isaacs Menken** appearing there for the first time as Mazep-pa. Later, the theater became a **vaudeville†** house with a new name, the Gaiety, but was destroyed by fire in 1913.

†GREENE, CLAY MEREDITH (1850–1933). Clay Meredith Greene was, according to his *Variety**† obituary, the first American born in San Francis-co. He presided as Shepherd of the **Lambs' Club***† for 12 years before returning to San Francisco, where he was the oldest member of the Bohemian Club. Among his 80 or so plays and **musical***† librettos were such successes as *M'liss* (1878, based upon a **Bret Harte** story), *Forgiven* (1886), *Blue-beard, Jr.* (1889), *Under the Polar Star* (1896), *A Man from the West* (1900), and *The Silver Slipper* (1902).

GRICE, C. E. (early 19th century). This New Orleans native authored a drama celebrating the city's greatest event to date, *The Battle of New Or-leans; or, Glory, Love and Loyalty* (1815), glorifying General Andrew Jack-son's victory in the last battle of the **War of 1812**. The five-act drama premiered at New York's **Park Theatre**, which, in that period, presented numerous nationalistic works celebrating great American events or charac-ters. Originally intended as a tribute to Jackson, Grice's play had a long life as it became associated with acknowledging American patriotic holidays in the first half of the 19th century. **William Dunlap** had written a play with the same title in 1815.

***THE GROUP.* Mercy Otis Warren** published this 1775 satire in which she ponders life in the colonies if George III repealed the Massachusetts charter of rights. It should be noted that all of Warren's plays were published anony-mously until 1790—and *The Group* was the sole dramatic work that she admitted authoring. Like her other plays of the period, *The Adulateur* (1772) and *The Defeat* (1773), Warren's satire was razor sharp and aimed squarely at the moral ills of the Tory leadership of Massachusetts.

GROVER, LEONARD (1835–1926). Born in Livingston County, New York, to a farm family, Leonard Grover began his stage career as an **actor**,*† but minimal success led him into the jobs of **producer***† and **manager**.* Among the theaters Grover managed were Philadelphia's **Chestnut Street Theatre**, New York's **Olympic Theatre**, and Washington, DC's **National Theatre**.

Famously, President and Mrs. **Abraham Lincoln** had considered attend-ing a performance of *Aladdin! or, The Wonderful Lamp* at Grover's Theatre on Good Friday, 14 April 1865. They changed their minds and went to **Ford's Theatre** to see **star***† **Laura Keene** in the farce *Our American*

Cousin. During the performance, actor and Confederate sympathizer **John Wilkes Booth**† assassinated Lincoln. A Lincoln was present at Grover's on that tragic evening, however; Thomas "Tad" Lincoln, the president's youngest son, then 12 years old, was in attendance and learned of the shooting of his father from an announcement from the stage when the performance was interrupted.

Grover also wrote plays, but only one succeeded and was, in fact, a substantial hit. A four-act comedy, *Our Boarding House* (1877) ran for 104 performances at New York's **Park Theatre** featuring **W. H. Crane** and **Stuart Robson**. However, Grover was unable to repeat its success with other works.

THE GUERILLAS; OR, THE WAR IN VIRGINIA. **James D. McCabe**'s 1862 domestic drama in three acts was written, like many of his works during the **Civil War**, under a pseudonym. This **melodramatic**,† action-heavy play took a sympathetic view of the Confederacy set against the violence, the conflict among neighbors and within families, and the significant differences over the issue of slavery and states' rights. *The Guerillas* was considered the first original drama staged in the Confederacy at the New Richmond Theatre.

†**GUNTER, A. C. (1847–1907).** Born in Liverpool, England, Archibald Clavering Gunter arrived in New York with his parents at age six before moving to San Francisco shortly thereafter, where his father, Henry Gunter, managed the **National Theatre**. From his teens, Gunter worked in a variety of technical theater positions, attended the University of California, and began writing plays, including *Found a True Vein* (1872), a **melodrama**† about life in a mining camp, before moving to New York in 1879, becoming a celebrated novelist and playwright,*† as well as a successful engineer, stockbroker, and publisher.

Gunter set up his own publishing house, Home Publishing Company, and published, among other things, *Gunter's Magazine*. He wrote mostly in the dramatic form from the 1870s to the mid-1880s, when he turned almost exclusively to the writing of novels. Among his plays, he had moderate success with *Ada* (1879), *Two Nights in Rome* (1880), *Fresh, the American* (1881), *A Dime Novel* (1883), *The Deacon's Daughter* (1886), and *Prince Karl*† (1886). He is perhaps best remembered today for spotting the baseball poem "Casey at the Bat" in the *San Francisco Examiner* and giving it to **DeWolf Hopper**,† who scored a popular success performing it.

GUY RIVERS; OR, THE GOLD HUNTERS. Louisa Medina's 1834 adaptation of W. G. Simms's novel of the same year focused on life in rural Georgia. It was first performed at the **Bowery Theatre** on 22 September 1834. Only three plays of Medina's possibly 20–30 works were published, and thus survive. *Guy Rivers* does not survive.

THE GYPSY WANDERER; OR, THE STOLEN CHILD. In her first play (labeled an **operetta†**), written by the early 1840s, **Anna Cora Mowatt** explored the little-known lives of gypsies and the fad for Spiritualism in a verse drama. The plot centers on an unhappy **child†** (played in the original production by the author's daughter, Julia Mowatt) kidnapped by gypsies, who is ultimately saved and reunited with her distraught mother, played by Mowatt. Mowatt dedicated the play to her sister, and it is believed that the play was only produced privately at Mowatt's home.

H

HACKETT, JAMES HENRY (1800–1871). New York–born **actor*†** James Henry Hackett began studies at Columbia College in 1815, but dropped out to study for the bar privately. Instead, by 1818 he was working in a grocery company. Hackett's other efforts in business were failures, but the tide turned when in 1819 he married an **actress,*†** Catherine Leesugg (1797–1848), which eventually led him to becoming an **actor.*†** In March 1826, he made his New York stage debut in *Love of a Village*, playing opposite his wife. Over time, Hackett found a niche as a **character†** actor of eccentric roles.

Hackett **toured*†** England successfully, and much of his career was spent going back and forth on tours to England and the United States. He scored a particular success in both countries in **Shakespeare,*†** most notably as Falstaff. He had some success as a **manager*†** as well, engaging a troupe of Italian opera singers as the core of a company for the first season of the Academy of Music in 1854–1855. His acting work diminished after the mid-1850s while he wrote the book *Notes and Comments on Shakespeare* (1863). Hackett was the father of actor James Keteltas Hackett† (1869–1926), who found success on both stage and the early film† screen.

HALLAM, LEWIS, SR. (1714–1756). English-born **actor*†** and **manager*†** Lewis Hallam had attempted to establish a theatrical reputation in Great Britain with a company for which he served as **comanager*†** with his brother **William Hallam**. The company was not successful, so they sailed to North America in 1752, disembarking at Yorktown, Virginia. They established themselves in Williamsburg, Virginia, the colony's capital. In a rented wooden structure adapted somewhat for theatrical purposes, they offered **Shakespeare**'s***†** *The Merchant of Venice* as their initial offering and as the first professionally produced play in the New World. Well-received, the Hallam company **toured*†** to Annapolis and Philadelphia prior to moving to New York, where Hallam built a theater on Nassau Street in 1754. The company toured with regularity, and it is believed that at some point they performed in all 13 of the original American colonies. Through Lewis Hallam, the Hallam name became perhaps the best-known name associated with theater in America in the mid- to late 18th century, and he is regarded as a singular pioneer of early American theater.

HALLAM, LEWIS, JR. (1740–1808). Born in England as Lewis Hallam Jr. the son of **actor*†** and theater **manager*† Lewis Hallam Sr.**, Lewis Hallam Jr. stepped onto American soil with his parents, and they performed *The Merchant of Venice* and *The Anatomist* in Williamsburg, Virginia, and **toured*†** the colonies. Following his father's death in 1756, he assisted his mother and stepfather, **David Douglass**, in running their company, appropriately named the **American Company**, playing Hamlet in the first known performance of the character in America. Hallam also played the protagonist, Arsaces, in **Thomas Godfrey**'s *The Prince of Parthia*, the first professionally staged American play.

Among other roles, Hallam played Romeo to his mother's Juliet, and was well received in contemporary British comedies. He is credited with performing "Dear Heart! What a Terrible Life I Am Led," the first performance by a white man of a song constructed from **African American*†** rhythms, a harbinger of both American popular music and **minstrelsy.†** Hallam was a major figure in American theater for the rest of his life, though during the **American Revolution**, when the Continental Congress banned theatrical performances, he resided in the West Indies.

Following the war, Hallam returned to America and reopened Philadelphia's **Southwark Theatre** and New York's **John Street Theatre**, both of which became the leading theaters of the immediate post-Revolutionary period. He led the revitalization of the **American Company** with **John Henry** and, after Henry's departure, continued with **William Dunlap** and **John Hodgkinson**. As he aged, Hallam continued to play young roles he had popularized during his youth, and some **criticized*†** this practice, though it became something of a tradition for over 100 years for actors to continue playing their most famous roles well beyond the appropriate age. Hallam's contemporaries thought more of his acting skills than his **managerial*†** style, but he had a significant impact on the development of theater in the early United States.

HALLAM, MRS. LEWIS (d. 1773). Employed as an **actress*†** in London, she married **Lewis Hallam Sr.**, and gave birth to a son, **Lewis Hallam Jr.**, sometime around 1740, and they all traveled to the American colonies in 1752, where they first performed *The Merchant of Venice* in Williamsburg, Virginia, and **toured*†** the colonies. Contemporary accounts describe her as a beauty with a manner and looks well-suited to **ingénues†** in tragic and comic plays. Accounts also suggest she was much admired by audiences of the day, especially appreciated in contemporary comedy, but also in the roles of **Shakespeare**'s*† heroines in *Othello, Romeo and Juliet*, and *King Lear*. Following Hallam's demise, she married **actor***†-**manager***† **David Douglass**, continued her career for several years as part of the **American Company** she formed with Douglass and her son, Lewis Hallam Jr., and retired in 1769.

HALLAM, WILLIAM (c. 1712–c. 1758). Born in England, William Hallam was **manager***† of the Goodman's Fields Theatre in London, though fierce competition from David Garrick's Drury Lane Theatre led him to bankruptcy in 1750. With his brother, **Lewis Hallam Sr.**, Hallam served as comanager of an unsuccessful theatrical company in mid-18th-century England. The brothers decided to bring the company to the American colonies, and to prepare for this they studied 24 plays before departing for North America, rehearsing under Hallam's direction on the ship. Hallam landed in Philadelphia in June 1754 and remained with the company for a year, during which time he did not perform, and he sold his share in the company to his brother and returned to England, dying there not long after his return.

THE HALLAM COMPANY. *See* THE AMERICAN COMPANY.

†**HAM/HAMMING IT/HAMFATTER.** These terms imply overacting as a product of egotism or lack of talent. Sometimes ham acting is intentional in farces or parodies of **melodramatic**† plays, but usually it is undesirable, increasingly so since the rise of realism.*† The term seems to have been born as a result of the habit of **blackface**† entertainers† in **minstrel**† shows smearing their faces with ham fat (used something like cold cream) before blacking up with burned cork when playing in "Tom Shows"† (often referred to as "Tommers") via the innumerable productions of *Uncle Tom's Cabin*† **touring***† the United States from the mid-19th to early 20th centuries, as well as minstrel shows and scores of other plays featuring **African American***† characters.

HAMBLIN, THOMAS (1800–1853). Born in London, England, and studying in school to prepare for a business career, Thomas Hamblin's mind was changed by his appearance in a school production of *Hamlet*. In his teens, he worked as a ballet dancer at the Adelphi Theatre in 1815 and spent nearly a decade **touring***† the British provinces and appearing in London's leading theaters, though **critics***† were not supportive.

Hamblin married Elizabeth Blanchard; they had two children; and in 1825, they left England for the United States. In November of that year, Hamblin displayed his abilities at the **Park Theatre** in an array of roles, both **Shake-**

spearean*† (*Hamlet, Macbeth, Othello, The Taming of the Shrew*) and as contemporary heroes in *William Tell, Virginius,* and others. A mere month later, Hamblin won praise from critics for excellence when he acted opposite **Edwin Forrest**. In partnership with **James H. Hackett**, Hamblin took over as **manager***† of the **Bowery Theatre**. The partnership with Hackett did not work out, and he left within weeks, prompting Hamblin to rebuild the Bowery following a fire and increasingly aim to please the tastes of the Bowery working-class audience. This meant a range of variety entertainments, including **circus***† acts and **blackface**† **minstrels,**† as well as **melodramas,**† Shakespeare, and contemporary British and American comedy.

Like Forrest, Hamblin encouraged new American **actors,***† plays, and theaters; the Bowery stage was also frequently populated with leading talents and the greatest names of the day, from Forrest to **Thomas Dartmouth "Daddy" Rice, Junius Brutus Booth, Frank S. Chanfrau, Louisa Lane (Mrs. John) Drew**, and scores of others. Following an anti-British riot set off by an audience at the Park Theatre, Hamblin renamed the Bowery to make his allegiances crystal clear. The new name was the American Theatre Bowery. He was gifted as a marketer—currying favor with local agencies and organizations he permitted to use the theater facility for events, advertising in all major publications, and permitting extended runs of successful shows at the Bowery.

Hamblin successfully rebuilt the Bowery following **fires**† two times, in 1836 and 1839 (and the 1836 fire allowed him to make the wise move of buying out his co-owners), and acted at other theaters to pay off standing debts. Yet one more fire in 1845 damaged the theater, and Hamblin wanted to build a new one on **Broadway,***† but met with considerable opposition, so he rebuilt the Bowery. As he aged and suffered various health issues, Hamblin passed daily management of the theater to A. W. Jackson. The theater increasingly presented minstrel shows, variety acts, and circuses, all which, it must be presumed, were of less interest to Hamblin, who viewed himself as a serious actor. He was, at the very least, a remarkable manager in succeeding with innovations adopted by other theaters.

HANDY ANDY: A TALE OF IRISH LIFE. Thomas D. English based this play on Samuel Lover's popular 1842 novel *Handy Andy: A Tale of **Irish** Life*; it was produced at the **Chatham Garden Theatre** in 1844 as a comedy with music. The production **starred***† **William J. Ferguson,**† and as Walter J. Meserve describes it, the play was lacking in plot, but was filled with "good Irish dialect, farcical stupidity and a few interesting observations, such as, 'If a gintleman drinks till he can't see a hole in a ladder, he's only fresh—fresh mind ye's—but drunk as a baste is the word for a poor man.'"

THE HANLON-LEES. A legendary **vaudeville†** troupe of acrobats whose fame led them to call their style "entotillation," a bastardization of a French word *entortillage*, roughly meaning *coiling* or *twisting*. The Hanlons led the way to 20th-century film† comedians and **circus*†** entertainers.† The Hanlon-Lees extended their style to include virtually every form of physical movement, including juggling, tumbling, and all manner of slapstick. The Hanlons were six brothers (George, William, Alfred, Thomas, Edward, and Frederick), and their mentor was John Lees, an esteemed acrobatic artist.

They debuted at the Theatre Royal, Adelphi, in London in 1846 as The Hanlons, with only the three eldest brothers, George, William, and Alfred, performing with Lees. Following Lees's death in 1855, the three younger Hanlon brothers, Thomas, Edward, and Frederick, joined the troupe. They honed their reconstituted act in England for a time before making their debut at **Niblo's Garden** in New York in 1858. In 1859, a trapeze was added to the act and expanded physical possibilities. Additional business of aerial juggling was added to their next production, *La Voyage en Suisse*, thrilling audiences with multiple flying objects and humans.

The troupe patented various performing devices, an aerial safety net, and a wooden brace used scenically that is called a *hanlon*. Thomas Hanlon died in 1868, but the troupe pressed on without him until well into the 20th century, appearing in vaudeville, circus, and even a Thomas Edison–produced film† called *Fantasma* (1914), based on one of their celebrated stage acts. In recent years, a group of young performers tracked down Hanlon descendants and received permission to call themselves Hanlon-Lees, with an act featuring the latest in aerial and acrobatic techniques.

HARBY, ISAAC (1788–1828). A descendant of Sephardic Jews from Spain, Isaac Harby was born in Charleston. He became a major figure in the Reform Society of Israelites, founded in 1825, which introduced English and other reforms into traditional Jewish rites and social conventions. Following the study of law, Harby opened a school on Edisto Island, South Carolina, and wrote for and edited several publications, including *The Quiver*, *The Investigator* (later known as *The Southern Patriot*), the *City Gazette*, and the *Charleston Mercury*.

Harby wrote three plays, *Alexander Severus* (1807), **The Gordian Knot** (1807), and *Alberti* (1819), the last also the most popular and **critically*†** acclaimed. President James Monroe attended the second performance of *Alberti*, and Harby counted Thomas Jefferson, Edward Livingston, and Sir Walter Scott among his friends. His later years were spent in New York, where he wrote for the *Evening Post* and involved himself in the advancement of Jewish life in America.

†**HARP.** An **actor***† who specialized in playing **Irish** characters onstage was referred to as a harp.

HARPER, JOSEPH (1759–1811). A native of Norwich, England, Joseph Harper left Great Britain for the American colonies and ultimately became **manager***† of the Theatre, Providence, Rhode Island. He had managed the Old **American Company**, but Harper took on the difficult task of battling Puritan attitudes against theater and, for a time, worked closely with Charles Tubbs. They became comanagers of the Assembly Room, a performance space in Portsmouth where Tubbs's wife, Eliza Poe, and Harper's wife performed. Harper had been the first American Falstaff, a role he played at the **John Street Theatre**, New York, 5 October 1788, and he acted for a season in Montreal, most notably appearing in *Macbeth* opposite his wife. Though he spent much of his career as a manager, he was often flirting with bankruptcy. His tombstone reads, "He preserved through the life the Character of a mild, temperate, and truly Honest Man."

†**HARRIGAN, EDWARD (1845–1911).** Born in New York City, Edward Harrigan began as a **minstrel**† performer and eventually tried writing his own material. He made his professional debut as an **actor***† in San Francisco in 1867. In Chicago, "Ned" Harrigan met **Tony Hart,**† and in 1872 they began to perform together using comic sketches Harrigan had written. Continuing the partnership in New York, they leased a theater and created a series of light and lively comedies featuring the city's late-19th-century ethnic types. Harrigan and Hart's "Mulligan Guard" series between 1879 and 1883 included *The Mulligan Guard Ball*, *The Mulligan Guard's Picnic*, *The Mulligan Guard's Chowder*, *The Mulligan Guard Nominee*, *The Mulligan Guard's Christmas*, *The Mulligan Guard's Surprise*, and *The Mulligans' Silver Wedding*. Other successes in that time were *Squatter Sovereignty* (1882), *Cordelia's Aspirations* (1883), and *The Last of the Hogans* (1891). Harrigan was married to his leading lady, Annie T. Braham.

†**HARRIS, WILLIAM, SR. (1844–1916).** The Prussian-born **manager***† was brought to America when he was six. Starting as a jig dancer, he worked his way up in show business, performing as a **blackface**† comic in **vaudeville**† with John Bowman from 1866 to 1873 and with William Carroll from 1873 to 1879, eventually acquiring and managing several theaters, including the **Howard Athenaeum** in the 1880s. Through his producing partnerships in various enterprises with Charles Frohman,† Al Hayman,† and Klaw & Erlanger,† he was involved in the formation of the Theatrical Syndicate.† According to M. B. Leavitt,† "Billy" Harris was always popular with his

colleagues and had not a single enemy in the entire business of theatrical management. His sons, William Harris Jr.† and Henry B. Harris,† both became theater managers.

HARRY BURNHAM. **James Pilgrim**'s four-act play opened at the **National Theatre** on 10 March 1851 for 18 performances. Many of Pilgrim's plays emphasized **Irish** American life, but in this case **actor*†** **Harry Watkins** appeared in the title role of a Yale student who rabble-rouses his fellow students against the British during the **American Revolution**. His idealism is powerfully tested as he is wounded and captured by the British before he manages to escape. In a highlight of the play, Burnham is at the Battle of Trenton and replaces the English flag with the American stars and stripes, achieving heroic status. During the time of the **Mexican War**, plays like Pilgrim's offered audiences an opportunity to show their patriotism.

†**HART, TONY (1855–1891).** Born Anthony J. Cannon in Worcester, Massachusetts, Tony Hart made his professional debut as "Master Antonio" with the **Howard Athenaeum** in Boston. At 16, he met **Edward "Ned" Harrigan,†** and the two discovered complementary personae and skills. When they settled in New York to present **legitimate†** comedies, Harrigan wrote major roles for Hart, who often performed in drag in their "Mulligan Guards" series of rambunctious **musicals.*†** Their partnership ended in the mid-1880s, not long before Hart's premature death from syphilis.

HARWOOD, JOHN EDMUND (1771–1809). English-born comic **actor*†** John Edmund Harwood signed on with **Thomas Wignell**'s company in 1793 to perform in Philadelphia, where he debuted at the **Southwark Theatre** in 1794 in a comic afterpiece, *Who's the Dupe?* He had successes in *The Critic, The Tempest,* and others. Harwood ultimately retired from the stage to operate a bookstore and establish a circulating library, but it was not successful, so when **William Dunlap** hired Harwood as a member of the **Park Theatre** company in New York in 1803, he readily accepted. Despite a considerable gain of weight, Harwood was welcomed back by audiences and scored notable triumphs in *John Bull; or, An Englishman's Fireside* and as the most admired Falstaff of his era. He also wrote and published a collection of poetry in 1809, but he died later that same year at the age of 39 and at the peak of his stage success.

HASTY PUDDING CLUB. In 1795, several Harvard undergraduates established a student society, the Hasty Pudding Theatricals (known simply as the Pudding). The name comes from an 18th-century porridge made of cornmeal, molasses, and honey, very similar to polenta. The artistic interests of the involved students were explored in various ways, but on 13 December 1844, the club began staging annual **burlesques,*†** in this case the well-known *Bombastes Furioso*. Performances in drag were the tradition (female roles performed by males). This continued for decades, and other traditions developed over time, including honoring a famous **actor*†** annually. Student members of Hasty Pudding over the centuries included many famed Harvard graduates, including Theodore Roosevelt, Oliver Wendell Holmes, Franklin D. Roosevelt, William Randolph Hearst, Jack Lemmon, and many others. It might well be considered that the Hasty Pudding Club was the beginning of college theatricals in the United States.

HATTON, ANNE KEMBLE (1757?–1796?). Worcester, England–born daughter of strolling player Roger Kemble, and sister of John Philip Kemble and Sarah Siddons, Anne Kemble Hatton was the official poet of New York's Tammany Society. She wrote the libretto for *Tammany; or, The Indian Chief* (1794), the first known libretto by a **woman*†** in America and the first major libretto written on an American topic in America.

HAVERLY, COLONEL JOHN H. (1837–1901). Born Christopher Haverly in Bellefonte, Pennsylvania, John H. Haverly purchased a theater in Toledo, Ohio, in 1864 and offered variety entertainments.† The first performance of **Haverly's Minstrels** was given in Adrian, Michigan, on 1 August 1864. During the 1860s and 1870s, "Jack" Haverly, as he was known to his peers, **toured*†** the United States with the company, often in tandem with other small troupes that he either purchased in their entirety or bought an interest in. In the aftermath of the great Chicago **fire,†** Haverly refurbished the remains of the old post office building on the northwest corner of Dearborn and Monroe Streets and christened it the New Adelphi Theatre. Opening on 11 January 1875, it was known, among other things, as Chicago's largest theater.

In October 1878, Haverly established Haverly's Mastodons in Chicago, but embarked on a tour of Great Britain, playing the major cities and the provinces. He introduced a large number of major entertainers in his troupe, but went bankrupt in 1898, dying three years later. Haverly's *New York Times* obituary quoted his philosophy: "The pack-mule luck, is too slippery footed a steed for me. I've a better nag to take me across the black pool of adversity to the shining shore of success. Common sense, saddled with judgment is the horse I ride."

†HAVLIN JOHN H. (1847–1924). Born in Covington, Kentucky, "Johnny" Havlin grew up in Cincinnati, where he would hang around the theaters as a boy. He rose in the ranks to **manager*†** locally and borrowed the capital to build the Havlin Theatre (later called the Lyceum) in Cincinnati. Soon he expanded to building theaters in St. Louis and managing concessions for the St. Louis World's Fair. He underwrote several **circus*†** ventures and backed the first lucrative Hagenbeck circus. He joined with E. D. Stair† to form Stair and Havlin,† a pioneering organization for booking popular-priced† **melodramas†** into their circuit† of theaters, which extended from the East Coast to Kansas City. Havelin eventually returned to Cincinnati to build its **Walnut Street Theatre** and manage the Grand **Opera House**.

HAWK, HARRY (1837–1916). Born William Henry Hawk, the stage name of Harry Hawk would most certainly be forgotten except for the fact that he was the **actor*†** standing alone onstage at **Ford's Theatre** in Washington, DC, on the night of 14 April 1865 as **John Wilkes Booth†** fired a bullet into the head of President **Abraham Lincoln**. Lincoln was seated in a box at the theater watching **Tom Taylor**'s comedy *Our American Cousin*, in which Hawk, playing the **Yankee†** character Asa Trenchard, was appearing with **star*† Laura Keene**. In order to obscure the sound of the fatal shot, Booth had timed it to coincide with one of Hawk's laugh lines, "Don't know the manners of good society, eh? Well, I guess I know enough to turn you inside out, old gal—you sockdologizing old man-trap." Booth leapt from the stage box and rushed past Hawk as he escaped into the wings and out into the alley, where his horse awaited him.

The following day, Hawk composed a letter to his parents in England recounting events as he experienced them. His description of the "assassination of our dear President" is very probably the most reliable eyewitness account:

> The "old lady" of the theatre had just gone off the stage, and I was answering her exit speech when I heard the shot fired. I turned, looked up at the President's box, heard the man exclaim, "Sic semper tyrannis," saw him jump from the box, seize the flag on the staff and drop to the stage; he slipped when he gained the stage, but got upon his feet in a moment, brandishing a large knife, saying, "The South shall be free!" turns his face in the direction I stood, and I recognized him as John Wilkes Booth. He ran toward me, and I, seeing the knife, thought I was the one he was after, ran off the stage and up a flight of stairs. He made his escape out of a door, directly in the rear of the theatre, mounted a horse and rode off.

Following this tragic night, Hawk continued to act in relative obscurity until moving back to his native England, to the town of Grouville, where he died and was buried on the Isle of Jersey.

HAWKINS, MICAH (1777–1825). Born in Head of the Harbor, New York, Micah Hawkins became a poet, **dramatist,***† and composer, gaining his greatest successes writing theater music. He worked odd jobs in New York City beginning in 1798, running a grocery market, building carriages, and playing various musical instruments. He gained notoriety with a **blackface**† song (to be sung in the guise of a comic **African American***† sailor) composed during the **War of 1812,** "Backside Albany," in which he satirized the English. He topped the song's fame by authoring the first opera by an American-born composer on American subjects in *The Saw-Mill; or, A Yankee*† *Trick* (1824) for six performances at **Chatham Garden Theatre**. In late 1834, it was performed there again.

†*HAZEL KIRKE.* **Steele MacKaye**'s four-act **melodrama,**† which opened on 4 February 1880 for a remarkable 486 performances at the **Madison Square Theatre,**† became the longest-running **nonmusical***† play of its era. Its innovations included the omission of an obvious **villain**† and the use of uncommonly subtle and complex characterizations. Disowned by her morally rigid Scotsman father, Dunstan Kirke, Hazel marries Arthur Carrington instead of the man her father has chosen for her. Hazel's troubles are compounded when Arthur's mother, Emily, considers her beneath their social status since Arthur is actually Lord Travers. When Emily convinces Hazel that the marriage to Arthur is illegal, the despondent Hazel attempts suicide by drowning, but has a change of heart and calls for help. Her father, Dunstan, who is now blind, is unable to assist Hazel, but Arthur arrives in time to save her.

The success of *Hazel Kirke*, hinting at the rise of the independent or New **Woman,***† was so significant that five **road***† companies played it while the original continued on **Broadway.***† Among the first plays to spawn road **tours***† (14 were on the road by 1882), it also provided a **star**-making*† role for **Effie Ellsler,**† the original Hazel, who established her own company and continued to play the part until 1905. Other **actresses***† scored successes as Hazel Kirke, including **Georgia Cayvan,**† **Annie Russell,**† and Phoebe Davis. Since Lottie Blair Parker† had acted in a *Hazel Kirke* company, it is perhaps not surprising that her own hit play, *Way Down East*† (1898), bore resemblances to this earlier work.

†*HEARTS OF OAK.* **James A. Herne**'s earliest major play, *Hearts of Oak*, featured a plot and characters suggested by **David Belasco,**† who encouraged Herne's **playwriting***† aspirations. Originally titled *Chums*, the "six **tableaux**"† play was written and first performed under that title on 17 November 1879 at Hamlin's Theatre in Chicago. Reworked, it had successful

performances in several cities and opened at New York's **Fifth Avenue Theatre** on 29 March 1880, but achieved only a short run. Its more lasting significance is that it was the first New York play by Belasco and Herne.

Hearts of Oak deals with a sailor raising two orphans, a boy, and a girl called Little Chrystal, a name Herne subsequently gave his own daughter, Chrystal Herne,† who became a successful **actress**.*† Another sailor, Terry Dennison, ultimately falls in love with Chrystal, but loses her despite his self-sacrificing love. Herne was accused of plagiarizing aspects of *Hearts of Oak*, and in turn, he later sued a troupe performing a play called *Oaken Hearts*. Herne later reused elements of this play in his last dramatic work, *Sag Harbor†* (1899). Director John Ford made *Hearts of Oak* into a 1924 film,† but it is considered lost.

HEATH, J. E. (1792–1862). James Ewell Heath began a writing career and was the editor of the *Southern Literary Messenger*. He wrote an early plantation novel, *Edge-Hill* (1828), set in the Southern colonies during the **American Revolution**. Focused on the Fitzroy family as they contended with the impact of the **war**,*† it was appreciated by older audiences who recalled the era of the war. Heath married Elizabeth Macon in 1820, and he audited the accounts of the state of Virginia. His political interests tended to overshadow his artistic endeavors, but he retains a reputation as a major Virginia literary figure. His sole play was political, but of little lasting value. ***Whigs and Democrats; or, Love of No Politics*** (1839) touched on political hypocrisy, the growing diversity of the American population, and the ways in which politicians market themselves to voters.

HEAVENS. *See* †GALLERY.

†**HEAVY.** The "heavy" was the **villain**† in theatrical parlance.

HEISTER, GEORGE (c. 1822–c. 1892). Almost certainly born in New York, the **scene designer***† George Heister's name first appears as early as 1840 in a program for the Franklin Theatre's *Gamblers of the Mississippi*, and within the year he had become resident designer for the **Bowery Theatre**. When the new state-of-the-art **Broadway Theatre** opened in 1847, Heister was named principal designer, and for the next 10 or more years he designed his most acclaimed productions there, including *Faustus* (1851), *The Vision of the Sun* (1851), ***The Cataract of the Ganges*** (1853), and *A Midsummer Night's Dream* (1854), among others. Heister spent much of the 1860s designing scenes for Philadelphia-area theaters, but after 1870, his output slowed. He designed *Le Roi Carotte* (1872); another version of *A*

Midsummer Night's Dream (1873); *Antony and Cleopatra* (1877), staged at **Niblo's Garden**; *Around the World in Eighty Days* (1878); and *Wolfert's Roost* (1879).

HENRY, JOHN (1738–1794). Born in Ireland, John Henry made his mark as an **actor*†** in Dublin and London before making his debut in the American colonies at New York's **John Street Theatre** in 1767 under **David Douglass**'s management as Aimwell in *The Beaux' Stratagem*. Though he possessed the requisite talent and masculine appeal, Henry appears not to have been particularly ambitious, so for a period of time he was given secondary roles.

Henry joined with **Lewis Hallam Jr.** at the end of the **American Revolution** to run the **American Company**. Scholars believe Henry was the force behind the first production of one of **William Dunlap**'s plays and that he was the first actor to play Peter Teazle in *The School for Scandal* in the United States. In 1792, Henry brought **John Hodgkinson** to the United States, but serious disagreements between the two ultimately forced Henry to sell Hodgkinson his share of the American Company.

Subsequently, Henry drowned while sailing to New England where, scholars believe, he hoped to set up a new company. Henry's personal life was marred by scandals. He was mocked for riding in a coach, something most actors could not afford, and a scandal surrounded the fact that he married Helen Storer and, after her death, had an affair (and a **child†**) with Storer's younger sister, who is believed to have become mentally unhinged at the time of Henry's drowning.

HENRY II; OR, THE DEATH OF THOMAS À BECKET. The original work that emerged as *Thomas À Becket* was written by two lawyers, John Denison Champlin and his son-in-law G. H. Hollister. They took the five-act play to **Edwin Booth**,† who purchased it, but insisted on significant changes. Friends and his wife thought the play a poor choice, but Booth wanted to play Henry II, and the play would provide the desired opportunity. *Thomas À Becket; A Tragedy* was transformed into *Henry II; or, the Death of Thomas À Becket*, cut to four acts, and opened in New Orleans at the **St. Charles Street Theatre** on 16 January 1860. Booth played four performances, but felt the audience's sympathies were with Becket and advised the **playwrights*†** accordingly. He owned the rights to the play, but rarely performed it.

†HERNE, JAMES A. (1839–1901). Born in Cohoes, New York, son of a poverty-stricken **Irish** immigrant family, James Aherne left school in early adolescence to work in a brush factory. His family's Dutch Reformed religious beliefs forbade theater, but when he saw **actor*†** **Edwin Forrest** onstage, he determined to pursue a theatrical career, changing his name slightly to James A. Herne. His first acting experience was in a **stock***† company **melodrama**,† *The Dog Montagris*, in West Troy, New York, after which he worked with **John T. Ford** in Washington, DC, and Baltimore.

Herne also acted at Philadelphia's **Walnut Street Theatre** and in both Montreal and New York, appearing in **Mrs. Henry Wood**'s *East Lynne* (1869) at **Niblo's Garden**. Herne was married briefly to **actress***† Helen Western and later to actress Katharine Corcoran.† He worked for a season as **manager***† of the Grand Opera House in New York before embarking for California, where he encountered **David Belasco**,† who encouraged his budding interests as a **playwright**.*†

Collaborating with Belasco, Herne wrote his first significant work, *Hearts of Oak*† (1880), which veered from the typical melodramas of the day in its heightened **realism**.*† A breach with Belasco led Herne to writing solo for a **panoramic**† historical drama, *The Minute Men of 1774–75*† (1886), which failed. In *Drifting Apart*† (1888), Herne gained some **critical***† approval for embracing the new realism*† inspired by the plays of Norwegian dramatist Henrik Ibsen.†

Herne's major dramatic accomplishment, *Margaret Fleming*† (1891), which depicts an upper-class woman's response to her faithless husband, also won acclaim from critics, but was only performed once since the subject matter and elements of its content were considered taboo, and some found the similarity to Ibsen's controversial plays unsettling. Herne's subsequent plays moved back to his melodramatic roots in content, while retaining a surface realism. These plays include *Shore Acres*† (1893), *The Reverend Griffith Davenport*,† and *Sag Harbor*† (1900). Frequently described as "The American Ibsen," the residue of Herne's fame rests mostly on his enlightened interest in new trends in drama.

HERON, MATILDA (1830–1877). **Irish**-born **actress***† Matilda Agnes Heron arrived in the United States in early adolescence and lived with her family in Philadelphia. Her career as an **actress***† began in 1851, and she gained experience **touring***† California before she went to Paris in 1855, where she attended a performance of the popular Alexandre Dumas fils play, *La Dame aux camellias*. Heron was so taken with the play, and particularly its title character, that she decided to produce an American version. She scored a particular success in *Camille* (as the play was titled in the United States), which debuted in New York in January 1857 at **Wallack's Theatre**, with **E. A. Sothern** as her **leading man**.†

Camille certainly encouraged it, but Heron developed a reputation as an **emotional actress**,† as demonstrated in the 1851 tragedy *Fazio*. She wrote a follow-up vehicle for herself, *The Belle of the Season*, in 1861. Heron gave birth to a daughter, Helen, by her second husband, Robert Stoepel, in 1857

(Helen became widely known by the name "Bijou" when she went onstage). In 1860, Heron played Nancy in a stage adaptation of **Charles Dickens**'s *Oliver Twist* and a series of Irish farces. Her health declined by the late 1860s, and she generally gave up acting to teach instead.

A mammoth benefit was held in Heron's honor in January 1872, with such **stars***† of the time as **Edwin Booth**,† **John Brougham**, and **Laura Keene**, among others, appearing to support Heron, who was well-liked in her profession. Of her approach to acting, **critic***† **William Winter**† wrote, "In her time of success she had everything her own way, and, more than probably, at all times she considered herself to be in the right. When she stated her own case she spoke as she felt, and she was facile in the use of striking figures of speech. [. . .] A more original, lawless, interesting woman, among the luminaries of the Stage, I have not known,—or, unless it be Ellen Terry, one so elusive of complete comprehension and competent portrayal."

HERRING, FANNY (1832–1906). A **child**† of English **actors**,*† Fanny Herring was born in London and brought to the United States in childhood. She worked in numerous theaters during her adolescence, but finally scored some success when she worked at the **Bowery Theatre** in the late 1850s, appealing to working-class audiences in **Shakespearean*** roles, including Ophelia and Juliet, as well as contemporary characters in *The Female Detective* and *The Dumb Girl of Genoa*. Popular in virtually any role, she was appreciated most in breeches† roles, including the Bowery b'hoy Mose in *A Glance at New York* and the leads in *Sinbad the Sailor* and *Jack Sheppard*. By her 40s and beyond, Herring spent increasing time performing in **vaudeville**,† usually in the same sort of youthful roles she played at the beginning of her career.

HERRMANN, ALEXANDER (1844–1896). French-born Alexander Herrmann—eventually known as "Herrmann the Great"—won great **critical***† and commercial acclaim in Europe as a **magician**, at first in partnership with his uncle "Professor" Carl Herrmann (Carl Herrmann may have been Herrmann's brother, not uncle, a fact that has yet to be resolved). From 1861, the Herrmanns made occasional **tours***† of the United States, but by the mid-1870s Alexander Herrmann, with his American wife, Adelaide, were highly popular. In order to clear up complex legal and contractual matters, Herrmann became a naturalized American citizen. Herrmann specialized in dangerous stunts like catching a bullet in his teeth, but had a lighthearted style. He typically performed entire evenings of magic, but also offered a shortened version of his program for **vaudeville**.† He made several attempts as a **man-**

ager*† to run his own theaters, but usually unsuccessfully. Eventually, he took over the San Francisco **Minstrel's†** Theatre, which he renamed Herrmann's Theatre.

HEWITT, JAMES (1770–1827). English-born conductor and composer James Hewitt arrived in America in 1792 and worked for the **John Street Theatre** and, later, the **Park Theatre**. Hewitt composed music for such works as *Tammany; or, The Indian Chief* (1794), the first American theatrical work focused on **Native Americans**.*† Notably, he also composed the music for "The Star-Spangled Banner."

HEWITT, JOHN H. (1801–1890). New York–born journalist, composer, **playwright**,*† and poet, John Hill Hewitt was the son of composer **James Hewitt**, who, in the early 1820s, operated a theatrical company in Augusta, Georgia. Hewitt joined his father's company, but a fire destroyed the theater, and Hewitt instead opened a music business, selling sheet music and instruments, and giving lessons in various instruments, as well as composing. In 1824, Hewitt began teaching at the Baptist Female Academy in Greensville, South Carolina, where local rivals accused him of being a mulatto. Senator John C. Calhoun cleared the matter up with a letter vouching for Hewitt.

Hewitt acclimated to the South, and in 1825 he composed a song, "The **Minstrels†** Return from the War," which became successful in the United States and Europe, making him the first American composer to win success on both sides of the Atlantic. Hewitt married Estelle Mangin in 1827, and they moved several times with Hewitt in search of a satisfying career. He finally took a position teaching at the Chesapeake Female College, where he taught for nine years until his wife's death.

With the outbreak of the **Civil War**, Hewitt attempted to join the Confederate Army, but at age 60 he could only hope to be a drillmaster. He decided instead to become **manager*†** of the Richmond Theatre, where he produced his own works and those of others. His tenure lasted a mere two years due to his dictatorial management style, so he focused on writing, including the song "All Quiet Along the Potomac Tonight," and ballad operas such as *King Linkum the First* and *The Vivandiere*. The content of his writings became increasingly pro-Confederate, even as the **war*†** drew to a close. Once the war ended, Hewitt reinvented himself as a patriotic American, but billing himself as "Bard of the Stars and Bars" retained his Southern sympathies, though he more frequently used the more neutral moniker "Father of the American Ballad."

HEWLETT, JAMES (early 19th century). Considered by many scholars to be the first professional **African American actor*†** in the United States, controversy surrounds James Hewlett's abilities, with some suggesting he only possessed modest gifts, while others thought the fierce force of anti-black prejudice directed at Hewlett and his peers obscured individual and group talents from being appropriately recognized. Surviving evidence points to performances by Hewlett being interrupted by white audience members, making his work especially challenging and his levels of genuine ability difficult to determine.

In 1821, Hewlett played Richard III with an all–**African American*†** company at the **African Grove Theatre**. It is believed that he also appeared with the company in *Othello*, but whether he played the title character or Iago is unclear. In 1823, Hewlett did play the title character of ***The Drama of King Shotaway***, based on an actual insurrection of slaves in the West Indies. The play, viewed by many as the first about an African American subject by a black author, does not survive. Following *The Drama of King Shotaway*, Hewlett was more inclined to give dramatic recitals than full performances of particular roles or plays. He was billed as "**Shakespeare**'s*† Proud Representative," and following an 1831 farewell benefit performance, Hewlett vanishes from the historical record.

HEWLETT, PAUL MOLYNEAUX (1856–1891). The son of Aaron Molyneaux Hewlett, who ran the gymnasium and affiliated departments of Harvard from 1859–1871, Paul Molyneaux Hewlett was born in Cambridge, Massachusetts. He eventually dropped Hewlett from his name, and he became an **actor*†** in Europe, where theaters and audiences were more accepting of **African Americans.*†** He eventually returned to America, with Othello as his specialty role. On 4 June 1877, he made his debut, still billed as Paul Molyneaux Hewlett, as Othello at the Union Hall in Boston, supported by a white cast (which was typical of his appearances in the role). A writer for the *Old Cambridge Chronicle* on 23 June 1877 felt that "Mr. Hewlett's text, gestures and movements were excellent," but offered some **criticism,*†** most notably "closer attention to distinctness of tone, parts of passages being lost to the audience." Hewlett's sister, Virginia, married Frederick Douglass.

HI-A-WA-THA; OR, ARDENT SPIRITS AND LAUGHING WATER. **Charles Melton Walcot Sr.**'s two-act **musical*†** extravaganza† parody of **Henry Wadsworth Longfellow**'s poem *Hiawatha* was written and published by **Samuel French†** in 1856. That same year, *Hi-A-Wa-Tha* was first performed on 25 December 1856 at **Wallack's Theatre**. In his dedicatory letter to **manager*†** W. Stuart, Walcot claimed to have written the play in a

34-hour period during an eight-day bout of rheumatism, pleading as such that the satiric play is a "poor offering." Despite these problems, the play is not without wit and was popular for this reason. In the cast list, for example, Hiawatha is described as "a character strikingly more in the style of a Short-Boy than a Long-Fellow."

THE HIDDEN HAND (OR CAPITOLA THE MADCAP). Southern writer **E. D. E. N. Southworth**, prolific writer of adventure novels in the mid- to late 19th century, serialized what became her most popular novel, *The Hidden Hand*, in the *New York Ledger* in 1859. It was satirized and published in book form in 1888, reportedly selling two million copies. It was also adapted to the stage in an astonishing 40 or more different versions and performed in many American theaters and in London as well, rivaling the era's most popular play inspired by a novel, *Uncle Tom's Cabin*† (1852).

The popular Southworth wrote over 80 novels, most first published in serial form in periodicals. The hoydenish main character of *The Hidden Hand*, Capitola, inspired a sequel title, *Capitola's Peril*, by Southworth. A notable stage production appeared in February–March 1860 at Mrs. Charles Howard's **Broadway*†** Boudoir, and **John Wilkes Booth†** played the male lead in one British version at the Grecian Theatre. Robert Jones's five-act version was frequently produced in the 1880s.

HIELGE, GEORGE (mid-19th century). American-born designer George Hielge (or Heilge), labeled a "native artist," began his theatrical career in 1837 when he painted murals and **scene designs*†** for the Franklin Theatre. He formed a close bond with **William E. Burton** and, following a move to Philadelphia, became a well-respected scene painter at the **Walnut Street Theatre** and **Arch Street Theatre**. Hielge and Burton became such close collaborators that Hielge worked with Burton for the balance of his career. He was celebrated most particularly for Burton's acclaimed productions of *The Merry Wives of Windsor* and *A Midsummer Night's Dream* in 1853 and 1854, respectively. He also won plaudits designing **panoramas** and landscape paintings. Hielge became **P. T. Barnum**'s chief scene designer after Burton retired, but little evidence of him exists after the end of the **Civil War**.

HILL, GEORGE H. (1809–1849). Boston-born son and sibling of acclaimed **musical*†** performers, George Handel Hill began his career as an **actor*†** in secondary roles and performing New England character types in recital form. This led to his becoming one of the most famed **Yankee†** actors of his time, a fact undoubtedly enhanced by his offstage eccentricities. In various productions he made use of what became typical Yankee names, including Jonathan Ploughboy, Jedediah Homebred, Hiram Dodge, Solom Swop, Nathan Tucker, and Major Enoch Wheeler. He made a habit of retiring frequently from acting, though the retirements never lasted long, and he wrote a popular autobiography, *Scenes from the Life of an Actor* (1853). At the height of his career in the 1840s, he was acknowledged as "the Yankee of them all." His peers noted his preeminence by calling him "Yankee" Hill.

HILSON, THOMAS (1784–1834). English-born by the name Thomas Hill, Thomas Hilson left England and debuted as an **actor*†** in 1811 at the **Park Theatre** in a production of *The Children of the Wood*. He won considerable popularity with the Park's audience from nearly the start of his career and was especially popular in comic roles in **Shakespeare,*†** 18th-century comedies, and contemporary plays. Though well-liked in comedy, Hilson also won plaudits in tragic roles and romantic leads, and as historical figures. On occasion, he acted with his wife, Ellen Augusta Johnson (1801–1837).

HIPPOLYTUS. Julia Ward Howe, the poetess, feminist activist, and author of "The Battle Hymn of the Republic" (1857), adapted Euripides's and Jean Racine's *Hippolytus* (1864) to be performed in Boston by theatrical luminaries **Edwin Booth†** (Booth had suggested to Howe that she write the adaptation) and **Charlotte Cushman**. Shortly before the scheduled performance, it was abruptly canceled, and the play was not publicly performed until 1911; it was another 30 years before Howe's play was published. When Margaret Anglin† presented and appeared in the first production of the play in 1911, the **critic*†** for the *New York Times* wrote that "Although the audience was appreciative, classic tragedy—especially declamatory tragedy—is not often played nowadays and does not appeal to modern theatergoers. And the **critics*†** do not warm to Mrs. Howe's."

A HISTORY OF THE AMERICAN THEATRE. **William Dunlap**'s essential two-volume history of the American stage, completed by Dunlap and published in 1832, provides the first major history of American theater with Dunlap himself, as a **manager,*† actor,*†** and **playwright,*†** depicted as an artist aiming to raise the quality of theater production in the United States. His history is not without inaccuracies, but is otherwise a rich compendium of the workaday aspects of theatrical life in the late 18th and early 19th centuries, with anecdotes and observations about the stage and its challenges, as well as the great and forgotten personages of the American theater of his time.

In his history, Dunlap focuses on the rise of theater in certain cities (New York, Philadelphia, Charleston) and chronicles the first attempts by the US Congress to censor elements of theater. *A History of the American Theatre* has remained in print for over 185 years, and a recent edition (2005), with a new introduction by Tice L. Miller, is the first fully indexed version available.

HODGKINSON, JOHN (1767–1805). Manchester, England–born **actor*†** John Meadowcroft built a solid reputation for himself under the name John Hodgkinson in the English provinces before writing to **Lewis Hallam Jr.** and **John Henry** about the possibility of joining the **American Company** in 1792. He debuted that same year at the **Southwark Theatre** in *The West Indian*. Like many of his contemporaries, Hodgkinson appeared in works by **Shakespeare*†** and other Renaissance, Restoration, and 18th-century **playwrights.*†** Hodgkinson had major successes in the title role of **William Dunlap**'s *André* and as Rolla in Dunlap's *Pizarro*, and was an adept **manager.*†** In tandem with Hallam, he had some acclaimed seasons at the **John Street Theatre**. In 1797, Hodgkinson published *Narrative of His Connection with the Old America Company, From the Fifth September, 1792, to the Thirty-First of March, 1797.*

HOEY, MRS. JOHN (1824?–1896). Born Josephine Shaw in Liverpool, England, she was brought by her parents to the United States, where her musician father developed his career and she went on the stage at the Museum in Baltimore in 1839, although she rarely received positive responses from **critics.*†** After her marriage, she worked as Mrs. John Hoey under the **manager*† William E. Burton**, but she retired when she married for a second time, to a wealthy shipping tycoon. Her retirement was short-lived when **James W. Wallack** convinced her to work for him beginning in 1854 to appear in *The Irish Heiress* and *London Assurance*. The critical response was no more favorable even though the general public appreciated her. She usually played women of fashionable tastes, but her career ended again—and permanently—in the mid-1860s when she and Wallack had an irreparable dispute.

HOLLAND, GEORGE (1791–1870). Born the son of a merchant in London, England, George Holland attended boarding school, but did not excel as a student. His father removed him from school to an apprentice job in a ribbon factory and later with a printer. Holland later established himself in the lace business in Dublin on Crow Street in a building directly across from an inn frequented by theatrical persons and near the Crow Street Theatre. Holland was drawn to these individuals, and in a relatively short amount of time he returned to England to learn to be an **actor.*†**

During the late 1810s, Holland played provincial engagements and, within just a few years, became an actor respected in his field. In late 1826, **Junius Brutus Booth**, then **manager*†** of the **Chatham Garden Theatre**, offered Holland an American engagement,† which led to another at the **Bowery Theatre**. At the Bowery, he proved himself an adept farceur in *A Day after the Fair* in 1827, a popular farce of the period, but even more so in an act in which he used ventriloquism, monologues, short sketches, and song. He became much sought after in this entertainment,† which he had fully developed within a short amount of time and which carried him through several years of **touring*†** in the late 1820s and beyond in the eastern and southern areas of the United States.

Holland worked at New Orleans's **St. Charles Street Theatre**, acting with **Charlotte Cushman** and other notable **stars*†** of the time. After the St. Charles burned to the ground in 1842, Holland went to work for the **Wallacks** at the **Olympic Theatre**, scoring a hit in **John Brougham**'s *Game of Love*. Holland worked with **Christy's Minstrels** from the late 1850s to the late 1860s, and his farewell engagement in 1870 was with manager **Augustin Daly** in **Olive Logan**'s comedy *Surf* at the **Fifth Avenue Theatre**.

HOLLAND, JOHN JOSEPH (1776?–1820). English-born John Joseph Holland worked as a theatrical scene painter prominently in Philadelphia's theater community, after being brought there by **Thomas Wignell** to work at the **Chestnut Street Theatre**, from 1796 to 1807. In 1807, he moved to New York and became a notable **scene designer*†** there at the New Theatre, and as his career drew to a close, Holland designed scenery for the **Park Theatre** and was centrally involved in the redesign of the theater itself. In 1809, Holland designed *De Montfort*, which has come to be considered the first attempt at scenic **realism*†** in America. His contemporaries praised his taste and skill.

HOLLIDAY STREET THEATRE. Built in Baltimore, in 1794, this theater, which formally opened on 25 September 1795, had a host of names, including the New Theatre, the New Holliday, the Old Holliday, the Baltimore Theatre, and the Old Drury, though it is most often remembered as the Holliday Street Theatre. One of its major claims to fame is that the first performance of Francis Scott Key's "Star-Spangled Banner" was given there on 19 October 1814 and cheered by an enthusiastic and loudly patriotic audience in the midst of the **War of 1812**.

From its inception, the Holliday Street Theatre featured **musical*†** and variety entertainments† ranging from strictly musical and dance performances to opera. Originally a wooden structure, the successful venue was demolished in 1812 to be replaced by a new brick edifice. The theater was closed in 1842, but got a second life when in 1854 it was purchased by **manager*†** **John T. Ford**, ultimately the owner of **Ford's Theatre** in Washington, DC, where President **Abraham Lincoln** was assassinated by **actor*†** **John Wilkes Booth†** on 14 April 1865. The theater was damaged by **fire†** in 1873, but Ford rebuilt it, and under other managements it remained in operation into the 20th century, ending its days as a silent film† theater.

HOOLEY, RICHARD M. (1822–1893). Born in Ballina, County Mayo, Ireland, Richard M. Hooley was born into a well-to-do merchant-class family, which permitted him a good education in England. An 1844 vacation to the United States won him over to the pleasures of New York City, where he signed on as assistant **manager*†** of a **blackface†** **minstrel†** troupe under the wing of legendary minstrel man **E. P. Christy**, who admired Hooley's skill as a violinist.

After a couple of years, Hooley decided to go into management on his own. He established his own minstrel troupe, and in 1848, the troupe performed at Her Majesty's Concert Rooms in Hanover Square, London. Their performances were successful, and they returned to the United States in 1853. Hooley **toured*†** California in 1855 and took on management of **Thomas Maguire**'s **Opera House** in San Francisco. In 1859, Hooley opened in **Niblo's Garden** in New York, and with Christy, he put together a company first called Hooley & Campbell's Minstrels. When Sherwood Campbell, who was a celebrated singer, died unexpectedly, Hooley informally adopted Campbell's son, Thomas P., and trained the boy for a successful career in management.

In late 1862, Hooley's Minstrels opened in a new venue in Brooklyn, which he operated for several years. He also established what became his flagship theater, Hooley's Opera House on Clark Street in Chicago, which ran successfully until the building was destroyed in the great Chicago fire of 1871. Through an effective business deal, Hooley traded the Clark Street site for space on Randolph Street, where he built a new Hooley's Theatre, which opened in 1872 with the **Kiralfy** Brothers's production of what many consider the first **musical*†** in the modern tradition, *The Black Crook*.

In addition to the theaters and minstrel companies, Hooley set up a **stock*†** company operation with such notables as **William H. Crane, James O'Neill,†** **Nate Salsbury, Sidney Cowell**, etc.; Hooley also produced a number of **Bartley Campbell**'s plays. His *New York Times* obituary indicated he was beloved in Chicago, known as Uncle Dick Hooley, and that Hooley's troupe was an "excellent company of its kind and its performances were of the simple, old-fashioned sort, with a long 'first part' and plenty of tuneful ballads."

HORIZON. **Augustin Daly**'s five-act drama opened on 21 March 1871 at the **Olympic Theatre** in a **John A. Duff** production for a disappointing 63 performances. The disappointment resulted from the positive **critical*†** response the play received, which only grew over time to the point that many scholars consider *Horizon* Daly's finest play. However, at the time of its opening, audiences for the play were scarce. The cast included **Agnes Ethel** and the legendary pantomimist **G. L. Fox** in a rare speaking role as Sundown Rouse, both welcome presences to regular theatergoing audiences.

Adapted from a story by Bret Harte, its focus was strictly American, eliminating the nearly mandatory presence of European types of dramas usual in the period, but held firmly to the traditions of **melodrama.†** Hart Conway played a recent West Point graduate, Alleyn Van Dorp, who is sent to the western territory, but in his free time searches for the daughter and husband of his foster mother. Ethel played Med, a girl the Indians refer to as "the White Flower of the Plains," who looks after her alcoholic father, Wolf. Van Dorp eventually realizes that Med and Wolf are the targets of his search. Wolf is murdered, and in the aftermath, Med is looked after by a **villainous†** figure, Loder, known as the White Panther, who, despite his nefarious activities, truly cares for her. Subsequently kidnapped by an Indian chief, Wannamucka, Med is saved by Van Dorp while Loder kills Wannamucka. Though he loves Med, Loder recognizes that she will be happier with Van Dorp and steps aside, allowing Med and Van Dorp to find happiness.

HORN, "EPH" (1823–1877). Born in Philadelphia as Evan Horn, he became interested in and expert at performing in the **blackface† minstrel†** tradition, then in the first flush of its popularity in the United States. As Uncle "Eph" Horn, he made his professional debut in Philadelphia in 1845, and his success was immediate. He **toured*†** widely in the East and South, frequently in a standout position delivering **burlesque*†**-style pieces of business. One of his most famous was a speech in which he explained, with considerable absurdity, "Woman's Rights."

In 1851, Horn finally gave his first New York performance with Pierce's Minstrels at **Burton's** Theatre. He spent much of the rest of his career as a New York favorite, though he **toured*†** as well, spending two long engagements† in California, as well as most major cities across the country. In the minstrel realm, he was a recognized innovator, including being the first minstrel clown in performance with Slote and Shephard's **Circus.*†**

In 1866, Horn partnered with **Dan Bryant** for a tour of England, though they only played one performance. Horn signed on with Moore & Burgess's Minstrels at St. James's Hall in London in 1871 and drew large, appreciative audiences. He followed this with a successful tour of the English provinces prior to his return to the United States. Despite aging, he performed frequently until shortly before his death, making his last appearances in **vaudeville†** at **Tony Pastor**'s† Opera House. Horn had a son who, under the name Eph Horn Jr., had a moderately successful career after his father's passing. Horn's *New York Times* obituary described him as "one of the oldest and most celebrated negro minstrel performers in the country."

HORSESHOE ROBINSON. **Clifton W. Tayleure**'s three-act play opened on 5 May 1856 at Baltimore's **Holliday Street Theatre** in **repertory**.*† A backwoodsman and Indian fighter, Horseshoe Robinson is involved in providing dangerous help to a friend, Major Arthur Butler (played by **George C. Boniface**), to make his way through the British lines during the **American Revolution**. Butler wants to get to the home of a British loyalist, Lindsay, because he is secretly married to Lindsay's daughter, Mildred, who also supports the American side. Butler is captured and sentenced to death, and Horseshoe Robinson is arrested, too. Robinson manages to escape and goes through several clever ruses to free Butler and foil the English, which he does, and the lovers are reunited.

An earlier version of the play based on John P. Kennedy's novel *Horseshoe Robinson: A Tale of the Tory Ascendency* was adapted by Charles Dance as a vehicle for **James K. Hackett**, who played it for several years. How much Tayleure did or did not make use of the Dance version in creating his adaptation is unknown, as Tayleure's version is the only surviving evidence.

HOT CORN: LIFE SCENES IN NEW YORK ILLUSTRATED. Solon Robinson's stories recount the seamy life of the decadent citizens of Five Points, the notorious crime-ridden section of New York City populated by various (and often rival) immigrants frequently in conflict as the result of alcohol and poverty. Robinson's stories were first serialized in 1853 in the *New York Tribune* before becoming a best-selling book. The *Hot Corn* stories inspired no fewer than three different adaptations during its first year. These and subsequent versions throughout the 1850s were bested only by *Uncle Tom's Cabin* in popularity. The first version to open was *Little Katy; or, The Hot Corn Girl*. Adapted by **C. W. Taylor** and **starring***† **Cordelia Howard** as Katy, it opened at the **National Theatre** on 5 December 1853. The very next day, 6 December 1853, brought the opening of *Hot Corn; or, Little Katy* at **Barnum's American Museum**. The third version to appear in New York, *The Hot Corn Girl*, opened at the **Bowery Theatre** on 3 April 1854. The three versions varied greatly, and audiences seemed to enjoy debating the relative merits of each version, but all reflected the grim overtones of Robinson's stories, which dealt with the tragedies of those, particularly **women***† and **children**,† trapped in lives mired in poverty, alcohol, violence, and other ills.

HOW TO TRY A LOVER. **James Nelson Barker** adapted a French pica-resque novel, *La folie espagnole,* by Charles Pigault-Lebrun (1753–1835) in 1817. It was not produced until 1836 under a different title, *The Court of Love,* a plot involving two lovers whose love is tested by their fathers. Barker stated that the play "is the only drama I have written with which I was satisfied."

HOW WOMEN LOVE: A DRAMA IN SEVEN ACTS. **Bartley Campbell**'s drama written in 1876 was reworked by Campbell the following year and renamed *The Vigilantes; or, The Heart of the Sierras* (1877) while he revised it in England. This Western play, under its later title, was a **melodramatic†** work and not well received by **critics,*** with the *New York Herald* describing it as "entirely devoid of the interest with which an intelligent playwright may invest both dialogue and action, *even in this department.*" Despite the critics, the general public applauded the play, and it helped inspire future Western-themed works.

HOWARD ATHENAEUM. Initially built in 1843 as a church by the Mil-lerite religious sect, the site was quickly abandoned after the congregation was faced with the reality that the world was not coming to an end in 1844 as their minister predicted. Converted to a theater in 1845–1846, it ultimately rivaled the **Boston Museum** as the city's leading performance space. The Museum operated with a strong **stock*** company while the Howard opted to depend on **touring*† stars,*†** including such notables as **Edwin Booth†** and **Charlotte Cushman**, who appeared there frequently.

By the 1870s, as numerous performance spaces were built in Boston, the Howard turned to **vaudeville†** to foil the competition and continued in that vein into the 1920s, when, as vaudeville died with the rise of sound films,† the theater became a **burlesque*†** house, replete with strippers, baggy-pants comics, and the other typical attributes of that form. The city of Boston, hoping to discourage burlesque, would not renew the Howard's license in 1953, and the building sat vacant for seven years, until 1960, when the Howard National Theatre and Museum Committee was formed to save the building and return it to a viable performance space. Tragically, while the committee attempted to raise $1,500,000 for renovations, the building was destroyed by fire in 1961.

†HOWARD, BRONSON (1842–1908). Born in Detroit, Bronson Crocker Howard is often described as the first professional **playwright*†** in the Unit-ed States; that is, he is considered the first to make his living as a dramatist. His more significant "firsts" include his manifesto, "The Laws of Dramatic Composition," as well as a pioneering depiction of Wall Street businessmen in several works, including his most important play, *The Henrietta*† (1887). Howard also fought to bring major and serious American themes to the forefront on US stages. Following schooling at Yale and while working as a newspaperman, Howard wrote his first significant play, *Fantine* (1864), based on Victor Hugo's *Les Misérables.*

Other Howard plays include *Saratoga* (1870), a study of social classes staged by **Augustin Daly**† and later adapted for English audiences as *Brighton* (1874); the comedy *Hurricanes* (1872), renamed *Truth* for its British production; a comedy of manners called *Diamonds* (1872); the **melodramatic**† *Moorcroft; or, The Double Wedding* (1874); **The Banker's Daughter** (1878; adapted from his 1873 play *Lilian's Last Love*) about a woman falling in love with an older man she married for money; *Old Love Letters* (1878), a one-act comedy about the return of a packet of intimate letters between two old lovers; and *Young Mrs. Winthrop*† (1882), a character study of a neglected wife.

Howard contrasted American and French women in *One of Our Girls*† (1885), but this play's success paled in comparison with *Shenandoah*† (1888), a melodrama depicting two friends fighting for the opposing armies during the American **Civil War**. Howard is credited with elevating the quality and status of American playwrights, as exemplified by his founding of the American Dramatists Club in 1891. At the time of his death, playwright Augustus Thomas† opined that Howard "laid the cornerstone of American drama."

HOWARD, CORDELIA (1848–1941). Born in Providence, Rhode Island, daughter of **actor***† **George C. Howard**, Cordelia Howard was also the niece of legendary pantomimist **G. L. Fox**. When she was four years old, she created the role of Little Eva in the original 1852 Troy, New York, production of **George L. Aiken**'s adaptation of *Uncle Tom's Cabin*, a role that became permanently associated with her. She played Little Eva for the remainder of her career, which was relatively brief since she retired from the stage in her teens and married Edmund J. MacDonald, a Scottish bookbinder, in 1871.

HOWELL, ALFRED (1809–1862). English-born **actor***† turned **costume designer***† Alfred Howell settled in Boston, where he spent most of his career. He became surprisingly famous as a costumer at a time when actors were commonly expected to supply their own costumes. As such, Howell demonstrated the importance of carefully designed costumes that were more than merely attractive, but reflected aspects of character, social status, taste, etc.

†**HOWELLS, WILLIAM DEAN (1837–1920).** The eminent **critic,***† novelist, poet, and **playwright***† William Dean Howells was born in Martin's Ferry, Ohio, and was contributing to Ohio newspapers by age 15. In 1871, he became editor of the *Atlantic Monthly*. His close friendship with **Mark Twain** was a source of inspiration and material for several works. He was an early proponent of **realism***† in the arts, stressing his view that the form is "nothing more and nothing less than the truthful treatment of material." Though he was known better for his criticism, novels, and poetry, he wrote some 35 plays, including *A Day's Pleasure* (1876), *A Counterfeit Presentment* (1877), and *A Likely Story* (1885), most of them charming one-act "parlor farces" like *The Mousetrap* (1886) and *The Unexpected Guests* (1893). He also wrote full-length plays, notably *Yorick's Love* (1877) and *A Foregone Conclusion* (1886).

HUDSON, LEO (1839–1873). Born Julia Lee Hodgen, but known by the stage name Leo Hudson, she became a celebrated **equestrian**† and trick rider who distinguished herself in *Mazeppa*,† following in the footsteps of **Adah Isaacs Menken,**† who had been a sensation in that famous equestrian role. Hudson, who was regarded as attractive and a fine **actress,***† appeared in theaters across the United States, Europe, and Australia in the role and other plays. As her equestrian career slowed, she distinguished herself playing male roles. But popular demand brought her back to *Mazeppa* on occasion and, unfortunately, tragically. During a May 1873 performance of the play, Hudson's horse, Black Bess, stumbled while mounting a platform, and the horse and Hudson fell 14 feet. Injuries from the incident brought on Hudson's death, as well as that of the horse, in early June. She had briefly been married to the celebrated **minstrel**† **Charles Backus**.

HUMMEL, ABRAHAM HENRY (1850–1926). Born in Boston and the son of a Jewish peddler, Abraham Henry Hummel was raised in New York, where he worked as an office boy for noted lawyer William F. Howe. Howe served as Hummel's mentor, and six years later, Howe arranged for Hummel's admission to the bar. The two men worked well together as celebrated criminal lawyers. Hummel was drawn to celebrity clients, particularly theater personages, and he handled front-page cases for such noted figures as **Edwin Booth,**† **Maurice Barrymore**, Henry Irving, **Lillie Langtry**, **Abe Erlanger**, and **Lester Wallack**. Despite his fame, he was accused of ethical lapses and disbarred in 1905.

HUMPHREYS, DAVID (1752–1818). Born in Darby, Connecticut, and educated at Yale, David Humphreys was an aide-de-camp to General **George Washington** during the **American Revolution** and eventually American minister to Portugal and Spain. He authored a romantic drama, *The Widow of Malabar* (1790), and a comedy, ***The Yankey in England*** (1814), the only dramatic works among his other writings, which included essays and poems, identifying him as one of the "Hartford Wits."

HUMPTY DUMPTY. A popular **musical***† pantomime in 17 scenes written by A. Oakey Hall and **G. L. Fox**, with music by A. Reiff Jr. (frequently revised and changed in the custom of the time) opened at the **Olympic Theatre** on 10 March 1868 for an impressive 483 performances. Fox, a popular **actor**,*† became a legendary figure as a result of his anarchic performance in the title role. The lunatic comedy focused on the adventures of several comic figures played by **Emily Rigl** (Goody Two Shoes), G. K. Fox (Dan Tucker), and F. Lacy (One Two Button My Shoe) as they enjoy the sights and sounds of New York, both real (City Hall, for example) and imaginative (Enchanted Garden). All manner of mayhem generates humor, and in the long tradition of pantomime, the main characters are transformed into the figures of Clown, Columbine, Pantaloon, and Harlequin.

THE HUNCHBACK. **James Sheridan Knowles** wrote this romantic drama for **Fanny Kemble**, and she debuted in the role in London in 1832, playing the central figure, Julia, a country girl dazzled by the social mores and decadence of the big city. She nearly terminates her relationship with the young man she really loves for an older wealthy man. Julia ultimately comes to her senses, and the lovers are reunited. *The Hunchback* had its New York premiere in 1832 as well, with **Mrs. Sharpe** as Julia. American **actresses***† were drawn to the role, and most of the greats of the 19th century played it, including **Viola Allen, Mary Anderson, Charlotte Cushman, Julia Marlowe,**† and **Clara Morris**. *The Hunchback*'s astonishing popularity was uninterrupted until the modernist era brought significant changes in **critical***† and audience tastes.

HUNTER, RICHARD (17th–18th centuries). Sometime in the three-year period between May 1699 and May 1702, Richard Hunter petitioned John Nanfan, the governor of New York, for a permit to present a play, noting that he had gone to some expense to prepare to do so, although there is no record to suggest that he actually did produce a play. There is no evidence as to whether Hunter, who was probably either an **actor***† or **manager***† (or both), did or did not produce the play, but the permit was the first known for a theatrical production in New York.

HUNTER, ROBERT (1664–1734). The author of *Androboros* (1714), the first play written and published in the North American colonies, Robert Hunter was, at the time, royal governor of New York and New Jersey. Born in Edinburgh, Scotland, Hunter had been an apprentice apothecary before joining the British army, becoming an officer and marrying into a prominent family. He was named lieutenant governor of Virginia in 1707, but was captured by the French, taken as a prisoner to France, and ultimately exchanged for a British prisoner, the French bishop of Quebec. In 1710, Hunter began serving as governor of New York and New Jersey, serving in New York until 1719 and in New Jersey until 1720. Hunter was later appointed governor of Jamaica in 1727, a post he held until his death. Though he devoted much of his energy to politics and other activities, his writings were widely admired by such noted figures as Jonathan Swift.

HURRICANES. **Bronson Howard**'s comic-drama in three acts opened on 1 September 1878 at the **Park Theatre**; it had previously played **Hooley's Theatre** in Chicago in May of that year. For its subsequent London production, Howard renamed the play *Truth*, and it ran over 300 performances at the Criterion Theatre. A group of vivacious young men, some married and some not, attend a masquerade ball with unattached women and other inappropriate activities. They have explained their individual absences from home to their wives and lovers by claiming the demands of business. However, the mother-in-law of one overhears the plotting and tips off the wives and lovers. Several schemes are tried by the men to get them off the hook, but they finally opt for the truth, and there are multiple happy reconciliations.

HUTTON, JOSEPH (1787–1828). Born and educated in Philadelphia, Joseph Hutton became a merchant's apprentice following his schooling. This work clearly did not hold his attention, and he began writing verses and romantic stories. He tried theater for a time, beginning around 1808 with a comedy called *The School for Prodigals*, staged at the **Chestnut Street Theatre**, followed by a Gothic **melodrama,**† *The Orphan of Prague* (1808). The next year led to a **musical***† afterpiece, *The Wounded Hussar, or the Rightful Heir*, followed by a social satire, *Fashionable Follies* (c. 1810). The reasons for his abandonment of stage work are not clear, though it is thought that he might have taken up farming or journalism.

HYDE, RICHARD (1856–1912) AND BEHMAN, LOUIS C. (1855–1902). Partners and theater **managers***† Richard Hyde and Louis C. Behman got to know each other as schoolboys in their hometown of Brooklyn. They quickly became highly regarded as innovators in **vaudeville**† and **burlesque***† and began their partnership opening theaters in Philadelphia in

1876 and Baltimore in 1877. They also set up a **touring***† show, Hyde and Behman's Combination. They operated four vaudeville and burlesque theaters in Brooklyn at their peak, including the **Star Theatre**, the Grand **Opera House**, the Folly Theatre, and Hyde and Behman's Theatre. Following Behman's death, Hyde continued as a successful manager on the burlesque circuit.

I

THE INDIAN PRINCESS; OR, LA BELLE SAUVAGE. James Nelson Barker's play with music (by John Bray, billed as an "operatic **melo-dra-ma**"†) is based on the life and legend of Pocahontas and was first performed on 6 April 1808 at Philadelphia's **Chestnut Street Theatre**, with subsequent performances in Baltimore. Barker had originally intended to write the story in blank verse, but the addition of music helped popularize the play. The story centers on the capture of part of Captain John Smith's expeditionary force to Virginia, but trouble arises when Lieutenant Wolfe, played by **William Wood** in the original production, and Pocahontas fall in love, rais-ing the anger of the Indian prince, Miami, who also loves Pocahontas. She warns the settlers of Miami's planned attack on them, and the lovers are reunited. Considered the first American play about **Native Americans**,*† and the first American play to be staged in London (in a production at the Drury Lane Theatre in 1820 retitled *Pocahontas; or, The Indian Princess*), it was the first of many subsequent theatrical works about Pocahontas.

INDIANS. *See* *†NATIVE AMERICANS.

INGÉNUE. This term is typically applied to the character of an attractive, virtuous young **woman***† who is often the object of romantic interest in the play. The ingénue differs from a **soubrette**,† who is also a young woman, but typically a saucy, comic character.

†*INGOMAR, THE BARBARIAN.* Adapted by Maria Lovell from the turgid German **melodrama**† of the same name by Friedrich Halm, the five-act *Ingomar* opened simultaneously at the **Broadway Theatre (Madame Ponisi** and **F. B. Conway starred***†) and the **Bowery Theatre** (with Amelia Parker and **Edward Eddy**) on 1 December 1851. Across the decades of the 19th century, **critics***† were increasingly unimpressed with the play (in 1863, **Mark Twain** even wrote a mocking review breaking down the play's action scene-by-scene to set up his comic commentary). The action centers on a young maiden, Parthenia, who improbably wins the heart of the invading

233

barbarian, Ingomar. *Ingomar* continued to be popular with American audiences until past the end of the 19th century, particularly with a charming Parthenia; **Mary Anderson†** and Julia Marlowe† both won popularity as Parthenia.

INTERNATIONAL STARS AND COMPANIES. *See* †FOREIGN STARS AND COMPANIES ON THE AMERICAN STAGE.

IRELAND, JOSEPH N. (1817–1898). Born in New York, Joseph Norton Ireland worked in business with his father until 1855, after which he became an early theater historian of the stage in the United States. His two-volume *Records of the New York Stage from 1750–1860* (1866–1867) is an important work in providing biographical portraits of significant American theater personages, though marred by errors corrected by later historians, particularly **George Odell**. He also wrote biographies of **Mrs. John Duff** (1882) and **Thomas Abthorpe Cooper** (1888).

IRELAND AND AMERICA; OR, SCENES IN BOTH: A DRAMA IN TWO ACTS. The prolific **James Pilgrim**'s two-act **melodrama†** contrasting **Irish** and American values, was written for **actor*† Barney Williams** and first performed at the **Broadway Theatre** in 1851. The play centers on the Irish character, Jimmy Finnegan, a rascally Irish peasant who, over the course of the action, is transformed into a successful New York businessman, James Finnegan. Though many stereotypical elements of the boisterous Irishman clung to Pilgrim's plays, he clearly endeavored to introduce a greater level of realism*† to the character in order to make him more accessible to American audiences and laced his dialogue with much humor.

IRISH ASSURANCE AND YANKEE† MODESTY. In this two-act farce and his most successful play, **James Pilgrim** presents his recurring "Paddy" character, an **Irish**-born peasant in the New World, in this case working with a New York businessman to their mutual advantage. It was first performed on 3 July 1854 at the **Broadway Theatre**, one of a number of such works he wrote for **actor*† Barney Williams**. Pilgrim's Irish plays in this period have a **melodramatic†** style, but the Paddy character is more purely comic.

The frequently comically inebriated Irish character(s) in these plays are broadly stereotypical, much in the way that **African Americans*†** were demeaned by **blackface† minstrelsy,†** though the proliferation of such plays and characters provide evidence of a stimulating multicultural environment in New York in the mid-19th century. Pilgrim can be credited with humanizing Paddy, depicting the figure as more industrious and honest than the stage Irishman was often depicted in the 19th century.

THE IRISH EMIGRANT. **John Brougham**'s two-act comedy, originally titled *Temptation; or, The Price of Happiness* when he completed it in 1849, ultimately had its title changed to *Temptation; or, The Irish Emigrant* when performed with Brougham himself in the lead in 1856, after which the title changed again to *The Irish Emigrant.* As with most of his **Irish** plays, Brougham stresses the basic goodness in the Irish character, whether in comic or **melodramatic†** circumstances. In this case, Brougham played O'Bryan, the title character, who goes to work for Tom Bobalink, who refers to O'Bryan as "Paddy," a dismissive generic name for an Irishman. He faces a moral dilemma over a found wallet, but is aided by O'Bryan in making the right decision. **John Drew** eventually played the role, eschewing much of the broad comedy, and Brougham liked Drew's unique interpretation, as did **Joseph Jefferson,†** who praised Drew's "sincerity" in the role.

THE IRISH FORTUNE HUNTER. **Irish** American **actor*†** and **playwright*† John Brougham** wrote this 1850 three-act comedy for Irish comic actor and singer **John Collins**, who appeared in other Brougham plays throughout the mid-1850s.

THE IRISH IN AMERICAN THEATER AND DRAMA. **Playwrights*†** of Irish heritage were numerous in the American theater from its beginning, but increasingly so until the middle of the 19th century when Irish immigrants arrived in greater numbers, many settling in New York City where, like subsequent ethnic groups flocking into the United States, they created their own communities in sections of the city. Maintaining many of their traditions while also steadily assimilating to American life, the maintenance of traditional aspects of Irish life was important to them. The numbers of Irish coming to America increased extraordinarily after 1845 when the Great Famine, known more commonly as the Irish Potato Famine, occurred, leading to tragic disease and starvation of over one million people and as many leaving Ireland, most for the United States.

The impact on the American theater was significant, and across the 19th century, some Irish-born dramatists in the United States became distinguished, including **Dion Boucicault†** and **James A. Herne,†** both of whom often wrote Irish-themed plays or included Irish characters in their plays (often for comic or nostalgic purposes), while also assimilating to the point that many of their plays would not be categorized as Irish and, in fact, were quite diverse. Irish American audiences had a strong appetite for theater of all kinds, particularly plays that provided either serious or romantic images of the Old Country.

Other dramatists found great success and popularity by offering light commercial entertainments, mostly farces, sometimes with music, and often providing affectionately stereotypical images of the Irish. These included **James Pilgrim**, **John Brougham**, **Barney Williams**, **Samuel D. Johnson**, and others, most of whom wrote prolifically, and many, including Boucicault and Herne, were also successful as **actors**.*†

As the 19th century reached its final decades, the taste for Irish-themed entertainments did not abate, continuing well into the 1920s and, in a diminished way, after that time. Slight plays were written as vehicles for Irish singer-comedians like Joe Murphy, William J. Scanlan,† and Chauncey Olcott.† The "stage Irishman" was by then an ethnic type popularized to the point of cliché, though often triumphantly as in the case of **Edward Harrigan**'s† series of Mulligan Guard plays, **costarring***† **Tony Hart**,† beginning in the late 1870s. The characterizations built upon a Hibernian accent, considerable physical action, and references to the "auld sod," as well as vagrancy, fisticuffs, drinking, singing, and Irish myths, from leprechauns to banshees, predominating, particularly in the lighter or more satiric fare. Irish characters have continued into the 20th and 21st century, but more often without the comic clichés and stereotypical behaviors. In 1922, as the taste for Irish-themed works seemed to be declining, Anne Nichols's† *Abie's Irish Rose*,† about a romance between a Jewish boy and an Irish girl, became **Broadway**'s*† longest-running comedy. On the more serious side, Eugene O'Neill*† became America's most celebrated dramatist after **World War I**, and his Irish Catholic heritage often found its way into his dense dramas and troubled characters.

THE IRISH YANKEE; OR, THE BIRTHDAY OF FREEDOM. **John Brougham**'s 1842 three-act comedy merged the stage characters of the bumptious **Irish** hero with the American **Yankee**† to potent results, first performed at the **St. Charles Street Theatre** in New Orleans, and published in 1856. The play is set during the **American Revolution**, and its humor centers on Ebenezer O'Donahoo, whose father is an Irishman and whose mother is a Yankee. Ebenezer's Irish way of speaking and manners require him to explain himself to his Yankee friends. The character of Ebenezer appears in other Brougham plays of the 1840s–1850s, but it could be argued that the heroes of most of the overtly Irish plays by Brougham, regardless of their name, were essentially the same character type.

IRMA; OR, THE PREDICTION. This five-act blank verse tragedy by **James H. Kennicott** was the winner of the $300 prize in a competition for a new tragedy to be offered at **James H. Caldwell**'s American Theatre in New Orleans, where it premiered in March or April 1830. A romantic work set during the **American Revolution**, it was repeated on 15 February 1831 with **Jane Placide** winning **critical*†** approval as the rebellious Irma and Caldwell playing Remington, a loyal but duplicitous British subject.

IRVING, WASHINGTON (1783–1859). The New York–born American writer and historian—one of the major literary figures of the early United States—Washington Irving was a disinterested student who skipped school to attend theater performances. He became friends with **James Kirke Paulding**, who lived in Tarrytown, New York, where nearby Sleepy Hollow and the Catskill Mountains, which would provide sources for Irving's writings, were located.

In his teens, when Irving submitted letters to the New York *Morning Chronicle*, commenting on theater and social events, he became more committed to writing. He **toured*†** Europe from 1804 to 1806 and studied law when he returned to the United States. His first important work, *A History of New York* (1806), written under the pseudonym Diedrich Knickerbocker, was a major success. He wrote biographies, edited, and when the **War of 1812** broke out, he enlisted in the military, though he had initially opposed the conflict. His family's finances were harmed by the **war**,*† so after the war he spent some time in England attempting to improve their situation.

Irving continued to write, and his collection of stories, *The Sketch Book of Geoffrey Crayon, Gent* (1819), was successful. This book included *Rip Van Winkle*,† which, in a dramatization by **Dion Boucicault†** (although there were less popular versions by others) became an enduring stage vehicle in the second half of the 19th century for **Joseph Jefferson**.† He continued to write without abatement until his death. Other than his early critiques and commentaries on theatergoing, Irving wrote plays in collaboration with **John Howard Payne**, most successfully *Charles the Second; or, The Merry Monarch* (1824). Its popularity did not extend to his other plays, including *Richelieu, A Domestic Tragedy* (1826), and Irving gave up writing for the stage. However, his stories, including *Rip Van Winkle*, were frequently adapted and dramatized for the stage—and later, in films.† *Rip Van Winkle*, in fact, was among the most-produced plays of the late 19th century—and Joseph Jefferson's Rip became an iconic American stage character.

ISHERWOOD, HENRY (1803–1885). New York–born son of a famous family of confectioners, Henry Isherwood began his theatrical career as a supernumerary† and **scene designer*†** at the **Park Theatre** in 1817. He won more admiration for his scene painting than as an **actor*†** (though he played in Chicago and throughout the Midwest), providing spectacular scenery at **Niblo's Garden** and for **manager*† James W. Wallack**. Isherwood continued with Wallack for the remainder of his career, which peaked a year before his retirement with his scene designs for the original production of **Dion Boucicault**'s† *The Shaughraun* in 1874. He was an eclectic artist, winning kudos for his designs of the classics as well as contemporary works. Actor **Walter Moore Leman**, Isherwood's contemporary, wrote that Isherwood was "a fine scenic artist, with a craze for acting. Nothing could be much worse than his acting; anything better than his scene painting was rarely seen."

THE ITALIAN FATHER. Inspired by Thomas Dekker's *The Honest Whore, Part II*, **William Dunlap** crafted this 1799 contemporary drama about a father who disguises himself in order to follow the actions of his errant daughter. Dunlap himself thought this play the finest of his dramatic works, an opinion shared by some **critics***† and stage historians.

J

JACK CADE; OR, CAPTAIN OF THE COMMONS. **Robert T. Conrad**'s blank verse four-act tragedy, first produced on 9 December 1835 at the **Walnut Street Theatre** under **manager*† F. C. Wemyss**, was based on the Kentish Rebellion of 1450 in its account of an evil nobleman, Lord Say, who has murdered Jack Cade's father (originally played by C. J. Ingersoll). Cade intends to avenge his father and manages to lead rebel forces to capture London, before killing Say, who mortally wounds him. Cade's wife, Mariamne, is also fatally wounded avenging herself against an attacker, and the play ends with the deaths of the Cades. The play was successful, but became a long-running favorite when **Edwin Forrest** first performed it on 24 May 1840 at the **Park Theatre** under the title *Aylmere; or, The Bondman of Kent.* **John McCullough** also scored a success appearing in it, and the play held the stage for 50 years, until the late 1880s. The character of Jack Cade appears in **Shakespeare**'s*† *Henry VI, Part 2.*

JACOB LEISLER, THE PATRIOT HERO; OR, NEW YORK IN 1690. **Cornelius Mathews**'s historical drama set in 17th-century New York focuses on a governor who is executed for defying the will of his successor. It was staged at the **Bowery Theatre** on 13 April 1848, and as reported in the *Old Fellows' Daily Companion*, it was "a tolerable success" **starring*† James E. Murdoch**, but the **critic*†** also felt that it failed to "arrest the feelings and secure the attention of the spectator." Despite this, the play ran for nine consecutive performances and was deemed a success.

JAEL AND SISERA: A WOMAN'S RIGHTS DRAMA. Alfred Ford's 1872 pageant† drama was based on biblical history, specifically drawn from the book of Judges, in which the heroine Jael kills Sisera to save Israel from the army of King Jabin.

†**JAMES, LOUIS (1842–1910).** This versatile, respected **actor*†** found his greatest success on the **road.*†** Born in Tremont, Illinois, he made his debut in 1863 at **Macauley's Theatre** in Louisville. He joined a succession of

excellent **stock*†** companies: **Mrs. John Drew**'s† at Philadelphia's **Arch Street Theatre**, **McVicker's** in Chicago, and **Maguire's** in San Francisco. In 1872, James joined **Augustin Daly**'s† **Fifth Avenue Theatre** in New York. For five years he **toured*†** in support† to **Lawrence Barrett**,† but a quarrel led him to form his own company and tour as a **star*†** with his second wife, **Marie Wainwright**.† It was said that James performed in nearly every **Shakespeare*†** play, beginning in the early 1880s, both comedies and tragedies, including such roles as Hamlet, Macbeth, Othello, Caliban, Bottom, Falstaff, and Benedick. James was renowned in the profession as an inveterate practical joker. For example, as Brutus to Barrett's Cassius in *Julius Caesar*, James spoke the line "Till then, my noble friend, chew upon this," and slipped a raw oyster into the palm of Cassius's hand.

†JANAUSCHEK, FANNY (1830–1904). Born in Prague as Francesca Romana Magdalena Janauschek, Fanny Janauschek first acted in the United States in German (as Medea in 1867) and was afterward often mistakenly thought to be German. For a time, she performed in **polyglot† productions,†** speaking German while the rest of her cast spoke English. As an internationally lauded tragedienne in the grand manner, Janauschek impressed American audiences favorably enough that she decided to learn English and develop a stage career in the United States. Despite her thick foreign accent and short stature, Janauschek was admired for her interpretation of the title roles in *Mary Stuart* and *Deborah*. Her eruptions of temperament may have hampered her ability to attract good **supporting†** players, and by the turn of the century her style was regarded as old-fashioned.

JARRETT, HENRY C. (1828–1903). Born in Baltimore, Henry C. Jarrett was an **actor*†** before becoming a **manager*†** in 1851 when he bought the **Baltimore Museum**, after which he took over management of Washington, DC's **National Theatre** in 1855. He conceived the idea of a company of America's greatest actors who would perform American plays for English audiences, but the project never came to fruition. Among other theaters Jarrett subsequently managed were the **Brooklyn Academy of Music** and the **Boston Theatre**. Jarrett engaged the Parisienne Ballet Troupe to perform at the Manhattan Academy of Music, but when the theater burned, he added the troupe to a **melodrama,†** *The Black Crook* (1866), in the process of opening at **Niblo's Garden**. This merged entertainment† has been deemed by some scholars as the prototype American **musical,*†** and Jarrett took over the management of Niblo's. In the 1870s, only a few years before he retired to England, Jarrett produced a hit revival of *Uncle Tom's Cabin* at the **Booth Theatre**, which he managed with **A. M. Palmer**.

†JAY TOWN. The relatively small cities and towns on a **tour*†** were jay towns that might support only a one-night stand.† Jays were the inhabitants of these towns, a term used interchangeably with **rube**.†

JEANIE DEANS. **Dion Boucicault†** based this **melodramatic†** three-act play on Sir Walter Scott's novel *The Heart of Midlothian*, which opened on 9 January 1860 at **Laura Keene**'s Theatre. The title character, a religious and upright **woman**,*† was an ideal of female perfection due both to Scott's novel and Boucicault's play, but the driving force of the play's plot was romantic betrayal and illegitimacy. Keene (playing the tragic Effie, an out-of-wedlock mother) performed with Boucicault and his wife, **Agnes Robertson†** (who played the self-sacrificing, noble title character). The play was a success, running until March 1860, after which it appeared in other cities with a different company, while Keene and Boucicault presented Boucicault's *The Colleen Bawn* (1860), which was a triumph.

JEFFERSON, JOSEPH, I (1774–1832). Born in Plymouth, England, the son of Thomas Jefferson, an **actor*†** in the Drury Lane Theatre company, Joseph Jefferson came to the United States in 1795 to appear with **John Hodgkinson**'s company in Boston. Subsequently, in New York, Jefferson made his first appearance at the **John Street Theatre** in *The Provok'd Husband* in 1796. In Philadelphia from 1803, Jefferson was a member of the **Chestnut Street Theatre** company with his brother-in-law, **William Warren**. He also managed the **Park Theatre** for a time where, according to **William Winter**,† Jefferson played "low-comedy parts and old men." Most appreciated as a comedian in contemporary plays, he left Philadelphia in 1830 to **tour**,*† finding little success. He had eight sons, seven of whom became actors, including **Joseph Jefferson II**, an actor and **scene designer**.*† His grandson **Joseph Jefferson III†** became one of the most beloved actors of the second half of the 19th century and won legendary status in the role of **Rip Van Winkle**.†

JEFFERSON, JOSEPH, II (1804–1842). One of eight sons of **Joseph Jefferson I**, Joseph Jefferson II was born in Philadelphia and began his work in theater early, though he did not equal his father's success as an **actor*†** (like his father, he played old men, even in his youth). Jefferson worked more consistently as a **scene designer**,*† winning more appreciation for his accomplishments in that job. Remembered by peers as a kindly, unassertive man, all spoke to his industriousness in all tasks of the stage, though it seems he did not excel in much. He was the father of **Joseph Jefferson III**,† one of America's most celebrated **star*†** actors of the second half of the 19th century.

†**JEFFERSON, JOSEPH, III (1829–1905).** Born in Philadelphia, the son of **scene designer*†** and **actor*†** **Joseph Jefferson II** (and grandson of **Joseph Jefferson I**, a Philadelphia actor in the early 18th century), Joseph Jefferson III made his first stage appearance as a toddler and appeared with **minstrel†** **Thomas Dartmouth "Daddy" Rice** singing "**Jump Jim Crow**." He **toured*†** the United States and Europe with his family before joining **Laura Keene**'s company in the 1850s, where he scored personal successes in productions of *Heir-at-Law* and *Our American Cousin*. He acted at the **Winter Garden Theatre** and toured Australia for four years.

In the 1850s, Jefferson appeared successfully as Caleb Plummer in **Dion Boucicault**'s† *Dot* and won further approval as the comic **rube†** Salem Scudder in Boucicault's mildly antislavery **melodrama,†** *The Octoroon; or, Life in Louisiana*. In 1859, Jefferson's production of a stage adaptation of **Washington Irving**'s *Rip Van Winkle†* failed in the United States, but he subsequently had a triumph in a Boucicault adaptation of Irving's story in London in 1865. The role of the laconic Dutchman of old New York who sleeps for 20 years made Jefferson a major **star,*†** and he played the role frequently (some said incessantly) over the next 40 years. Jefferson's career was dominated by this role, but he also had a significant success playing Bob Acres to **Mrs. John Drew**'s† Mrs. Malaprop in his own 1880 version of *The Rivals*.

In 1890, Jefferson published his autobiography, a vivid account of 19th-century theatrical life with many observations of the work and personalities of his peers. He succeeded **Edwin Booth†** as president of the Players' Club† in 1893. Among his children, four went into theatrical work and one son, Charles Burke Jefferson (1851–1908), worked as his stage **manager.*†** Jefferson continued to play Rip Van Winkle frequently, but chose to reprise the role of Caleb Plummer in *Dot* for his farewell stage appearance in 1904. When his friend Oliver Wendell Holmes pressed **critic*† William Winter†** to name the greatest American actor, Winter stated that he "thought Comedy more exacting than Tragedy" and named the comedian Jefferson, then "at the zenith of his wonderful career."

JEFFERSON, THOMAS (1743–1826). Born in Shadwell, Virginia, and educated at the College of William and Mary, this American Founding Father, author of the Declaration of Independence, and third president of the United States was clearly a signal figure in early American life, though compared with contemporaries like **George Washington**, Thomas Jefferson was rarely depicted in stage works. In satiric works, he was called "Monticello" (the name of Jefferson's Charlottesville, Virginia, estate) in two J. Horatio Nichols political satires, *Jefferson and Liberty; or, Celebration of the Fourth of March* (1801) and *The Essex Junto* (1802), written in the politically charged times when John Adams and Jefferson vied for the presidency, but otherwise Jefferson was not often personified onstage until the 20th century. Jefferson, perhaps the most intellectual of the Founding Fathers, attended theater with regularity, including during his time in Paris in the 1780s. He is not to be confused with **Joseph Jefferson III**'s great-grandfather, also named Thomas Jefferson.

JESSIE BROWN; OR, HAVELOCK'S LAST VICTORY. **Harry Seymour**'s play, billed as a "beautiful drama," was performed on 15 March 1858 at **Purdy's National Theatre**, with advertisements declaring that the title was used with permission of **Dion Boucicault**,† whose *Jessie Brown; or, The Relief of Lucknow* was also playing in theaters at that time. **Fanny Herring**, in the title role of the Scottish wife of a soldier, and J. H. Allen acted in this dramatization of recent real-life events surrounding the Sepoy Rebellion, in which Indians trained to be soldiers by the occupying British in India revolted.

JESSIE BROWN; OR, THE RELIEF OF LUCKNOW. **Dion Boucicault**'s† three-act **melodrama**† of recent events in India opened at **Wallack's Theatre** on 22 February 1858 for 42 performances, with Boucicault playing Nena Sahib, the leader of the rebellion of sepoys (Indians trained as soldiers by their English occupiers) and **Agnes Robertson**† as the title character, a young Scottish wife of a British soldier who is the first to hear Scottish bagpipers in the distance bringing relief to the besieged outpost of Lucknow. Boucicault's play proved popular with audiences, and it was frequently performed during the mid-19th century, including in London in 1862.

JIM CROW. *See* JUMP JIM CROW.

†**JOE JEFFERSON.** This phrase was used interchangeably with "**Rip Van Winkle**"† to mean a good long sleep. To "do a Joe Jefferson," that is, to have a satisfying rest, refers to actor **Joseph Jefferson**'s† signature role in *Rip Van Winkle*, in which the title character slept for 20 years.

JOHN STREET THEATRE. Built at 15–21 John Street through the efforts of **David Douglass**, the John Street Theatre was the first permanent playhouse in New York City, where it opened in late 1767. It remained the center of New York theatrical activity (and home of the **American Company** from 1767 to 1774) until the end of the 18th century, when the **Park Theatre** was built. Inspired by the architecture of Philadelphia's **Southwark Theatre**, it was a wood structure painted red. Most of the plays performed during its 30-year run were British comedies and dramas, including the first New York productions of *As You Like It, Much Ado about Nothing, The Critic*, and *The School for Scandal*, all of which were regularly performed, and during the **American Revolution**, when British forces held New York, its name was changed to Theatre Royal (switching back to its original name after the British were defeated at the **war's*†** end).

Royall Tyler's *The Contrast* (1787), the first comedy written by an American, was performed there and, amusingly, included a scene in which the **Yankee†** character, Jonathan, attends the John Street Theatre believing that the action onstage is a party. **George Washington** is known to have attended at least three performances at the John Street Theatre in 1789. That same year, **William Dunlap**'s *The Father; or, American Shandyism* (1789) was staged there, as was Dunlap's collaboration with **Benjamin Carr**, *The Archers; or, The Mountaineers of Switzerland* (1796), based on Friedrich von Schiller's *William Tell*, considered by some scholars to be the first American **musical.*†** The American Company returned to the John Street Theatre after the Revolution and performed under **managers*†** **Lewis Hallam Jr.** and **John Henry**, later replaced by **John Hodgkinson**. The theater closed its doors on 13 January 1798, after which it was torn down. The John Street Theatre has been referred to as the "Birthplace of American Drama."

†JOHNNY. Any callow youth who made a practice of hanging around the stage door in the alley to catch a glimpse of the **women*† stars*†** (or bring them gifts) was referred to as a "Johnny" or a "Stage-Door Johnny."

JOHNSON, SAMUEL D. (1813–1863). A New York–born **playwright*†** and **actor,*†** Samuel D. Johnson's modest career began with the one-act drama *The Shaker Lovers*, first produced at the **National Theatre** in Boston in 1849 with Johnson in the cast. His other plays include *Our Gal* (1860), a popular one-act farce written as a vehicle for Mrs. **Barney Williams**, and the one-act *In and Out of Place* (1856). He also authored a three-act drama, *The Fireman* (1856), and a two-act **Irish** farce, *Brian O'Linn* (1855).

JONATHAN IN ENGLAND. **James H. Hackett** adapted this three-act **Yankee†** comedy from George Colman's play, *Who Wants a Guinea?* It opened at the **Park Theatre** on 3 December 1828 with Hackett himself playing the character Solomon Swap, a Yankee trader from New Hampshire, shanghaied to England by the British Navy. Not the first Yankee play, it was an early popular one and gave Hackett one of his signature roles for a decade, after which he abandoned it for other ethnic characterizations.

JONATHAN POSTFREE; OR, THE HONEST YANKEE. This three-act musical*† farce by Lazarus Beach, written in 1806 and intended for production, was apparently never staged, but is an early example of the Yankee† character, Jonathan, in this case seen as an old countryman from Connecticut. It is also an early play featuring an **African American***† character, and it was first published in 1807 and again in 1827.

JONES, JOSEPH STEVENS (1809–1877). Playwright,*† actor,*† and manager*† Joseph Stevens Jones, known as Dr. Jones due to his early medical training from Harvard, Joseph Stevens Jones debuted as an actor in 1827, after which he managed the **National** and **Tremont** Theatres in Boston, where he had been born. He is credited with writing as many as 200 plays, including his most popular, *The People's Lawyer* (1839), later retitled *Solon Shingle*, which provided **John E. Owens** with a major success in the title role. Other works include the **Yankee**† comedies *The Liberty Tree; or, Boston Boys in '76* (1832) and *The Green Mountain Boy* (1833), a triumph for **George H. Hill**; however, Jones also wrote **melodramas,**† including *The Usurper; or, Americans in Tripoli* (1835?), *The Surgeon of Paris; or, The Massacre of the Huguenots* (1838), and *The Carpenter of Rouen; or, The Massacre of St. Bartholomew* (1840). He gave up theater work to return to medicine in 1843, when the Tremont Theatre, which he managed, was forced to close. However, he wrote additional plays, including one of his most successful, *The Silver Spoon* (1852).

JOSHUA WHITCOMB. **Denman Thompson**† wrote this short **vaudeville**† sketch in 1875 centered on a rube† from New Hampshire on a visit to the big city. First performed by Thompson in Pittsburgh, it proved so popular over a period of years that he expanded it as a four-act play, *The Old Homestead.*† In that form it opened in April 1886 at the **Boston Theatre**, followed by **Broadway***† revivals in 1887, 1899, 1904, 1907, and 1908. Thompson played Whitcomb over 10,000 times during a 35-year period, and it is believed he made a fortune of $3,000,000 playing the character. At the time of Thompson's death in 1911, the *New York Times* referred to *The Old Homestead* as "not a great play in its plot or construction, but it is clean and wholesome."

JUDAH, MRS. (1812?–1883). Born in New York as Marietta Starfield, she married Emmanuel Judah, though their marriage was short-lived because the couple were in the 1839 shipwreck of the *George Washington*. Judah died after lashing Marietta to a spar, which saved her life. In the United States, she concluded that she could make a living onstage, beginning in 1840 at Russel's Theatre in New Orleans. Despite a second marriage to John Torrence, she continued to act as Mrs. Judah and established herself in San Francisco under **manager***† **Thomas Maguire**. Mrs. Judah won great popularity in a range of roles from contemporary works to **Shakespeare**.*† As the Nurse in *Romeo and Juliet* in 1855, she won her greatest acclaim and performed the role frequently until her retirement in 1878, by which time she was billed as "San Francisco's Favorite **Actress**."*†

JUDAH, SAMUEL B. H. (1804–1876). Born in New York (some sources give his birth year as 1799) to a Jewish family as Samuel Benjamin Helbert Judah, he received a college degree before writing his first play, a **melodrama**† called *The Mountain Torrent* (1820), which was produced at the **Park Theatre** on 1 March 1820, after which he wrote another melodrama, *The Rose of Arragon* (1822) and a historical comedy, *A Tale of Lexington* (1822), both also produced at the Park. Despite these successes, he left the theater to become a lawyer.

JUMP JIM CROW. Comedian **Thomas Dartmouth "Daddy" Rice** performed this song and dance in **blackface**† the first time around 1828. The song was published in the early 1830s by E. Riley and became highly popular. Rice's routine, which involved the song and an eccentric dance, was supposedly inspired by a song and dance performed by a handicapped **African American***† slave supposedly named either Jim Cuff or Jim Crow and seen somewhere in the Midwest by Rice. The song was an important step toward the evolution of popular music in the United States, but its racist content unfortunately helped spread racial division and friction. As post–**Civil War** Reconstruction conflicts permitted laws of racial segregation to proliferate, either genuine laws or accepted social conventions separating the races (and consistently denying rights to blacks) became known as Jim Crow laws, and the term has remained as part of the American lexicon ever since.

†**JUVENILE/JUVENILE COMPANY.** Any **actor***† who could play simple, appealing, youthful roles was a juvenile. The juvenile lead was the male version of the **ingénue**.† **Child***† performers who grew a bit long in the tooth might become juveniles, and many actors continued in juvenile roles even as they aged, as long as they could secure jobs. Before child labor laws put an end to the practice, there were **touring***† companies in which all roles were performed by children. The appeal was largely of the novelty variety, but economics must also have been a management incentive.

K

KEAN, EDMUND (1787–1833). Born in London, England, Edmund Kean was the son of an architect's clerk and an **actress**.*† He went on the stage as a **child***† **actor***† and rose to great fame under the guidance of actress Charlotte Tidwell. As a youth, he studied **Shakespeare***† and offered interpretations far different from the commonly accepted visions of the characters performed by England's leading tragic actor, John Philip Kemble. Kean acted for a time with Sarah Siddons before winning acclaim at the Drury Lane Theatre in his 1814 performance of Shylock in *The Merchant of Venice*, followed by a string of major successes in *Richard III*, *Hamlet*, *Othello*, *Macbeth*, and *King Lear* (to which he controversially restored Shakespeare's tragic ending).

Kean's highly impassioned, earthy, and physical performances differed significantly from Kemble's cerebral and dignified interpretations of Shakespeare, dividing audiences over the quality of both actors and leading to questions of which approach was appropriate. Kean was resistant to some contemporary roles, and his mercurial behavior damaged his popularity with audiences. In 1820, he won great acclaim in a New York appearance in *Richard III*, but battled with the American press and increasingly was depicted as a problematic, if colorful, figure. He appeared opposite **Mary Ann Duff** in *The Distressed Mother* in 1821 in Boston before returning to Great Britain. Kean's drinking and an affair with a married woman became public via a scandal-mongering press, causing audiences to turn against him.

In 1825, Kean again appeared in the United States, but news of his English scandal further diminished his popularity. He continued to act, but was increasingly weakened by alcoholism, leading to a collapse during an 1833 performance in *Othello*. Kean's attributed last words, "dying is easy, comedy is hard," are almost certainly apocryphal (and have at times been attributed to other actors). However, his acting style, which was well received in the United States, inspired America's first great tragedian, **Edwin Forrest**, who appeared in supporting roles opposite Kean in his New York appearances prior to achieving his own fame.

KEAN, THOMAS (18th century). Little is known of the early life of this mid-18th-century **actor*† and manager*†** other than that in partnership with Walter Murray he offered English plays (**Shakespearean*†** and Restoration works, as well as contemporary plays) in Philadelphia in 1749. In New York the following year, Kean and Murray presented *Richard III* at the Theatre on Nassau Street on 5 March 1750, followed by performances of *The Beggar's Opera*, *Love for Love*, and *Cato*, perhaps among others. These appearances were met with controversy on religious grounds, and dogged with other problems, Kean left for Virginia, where he headed a company of actors.

KEENE, LAURA (1826–1873). Remembered less for her theatrical achievements than her appearance in **Tom Taylor**'s *Our American Cousin* at Washington, DC's **Ford's Theatre** on 14 April 1865 when fellow **actor*† John Wilkes Booth†** assassinated President **Abraham Lincoln**, this noted mid-19th-century **actress*†** and **manager*†** was otherwise an estimable figure on the American stage. Though her career never fully recovered from the tragic events of 1865, Keene trouped on until shortly before her death eight years later.

Born Mary Frances Moss in Winchester, England, Keene was the niece of English actress Elizabeth Yates. She began her career in 1851 in **Shakespeare*†** and under the management of **Madame Vestris**. However, within a year, she was in New York performing with **James W. Wallack**, and within another year, she set herself up in Baltimore managing the **Charles Street Theatre**. She **toured*†** widely, including through the American West and in Australia (acting with **Edwin Booth,†** with whom she reputedly had a romantic affair) before returning to New York, where at the Metropolitan Theatre (renamed the Laura Keene Varieties) she appeared for a season in 1856. When she lost the theater to a rival manager, **William Burton**, she built her own, the Laura Keene Theatre, which she operated for seven years. The theater boasted several successes, including the premiere of **Dion Boucicault's†** *The Colleen Bawn* (1857) and *Our American Cousin* (1858). During these times, Boucicault, **Joseph Jefferson,† Edward H. Sothern**, and other notable actors appeared with her.

Lincoln's murder had a damaging impact on Keene's career and was a shattering personal experience. She attempted to calm distraught audience members immediately following the shooting and Booth's escape across the stage (he brushed by her as he escaped through the wings and out the stage door), after which she made her way through the chaos to the stage box and comforted First Lady Mary Todd Lincoln and cradled the dying president's head in her lap until he could be removed from Ford's Theatre.

Historians also believe she was the first to realize that Booth was Lincoln's assassin, though **actor*†** **Harry Hawk**, who was actually onstage when the assassination occurred and Booth escaped, wrote to his family two days after the shooting and informed his parents that Booth was the culprit. It is not known for certain if Keene was briefly arrested in Washington with other *Our American Cousin* cast members and theater owner **John T. Ford** in the wake of the assassination, but newspapers reported that she was briefly held in Harrisburg, Pennsylvania, a few days after the tragic events when local officials seemed confused about her involvement. Keene mostly toured after 1865, although she also served for a time as manager of Philadelphia's **Chestnut Street Theatre**, after which she died of tuberculosis shortly after giving her final performances on tour in Pennsylvania. **William Winter†** described her as "tempestuous and violent" in temperament, but Keene succeeded against significant odds in becoming perhaps the first major female manager in the history of American theater.

†KEENE, THOMAS W. (1840–1898). Born Thomas R. Eagleson in New York City, he changed his name to Thomas Wallace Keene and made his debut as Lucius in *Julius Caesar* in 1856. He joined **John Brougham**'s company at the **Bowery Theatre** prior to **touring.*†** He enjoyed considerable acclaim on the **road*†** as a **star*†** at the head of his own company. Keene presented the standard contemporary **melodramas†** with historical settings and **Shakespearean*†** tragedies in rotating **repertory.*†** His *Richard III* was a popular favorite, a role he played more than 3,000 times. Keene worked with the **leading†** **actors*†** of the mid-19th-century American stage, including **Edwin Booth,† John McCullough,† E. L. Davenport, Mrs. G. H. Gilbert,† William Davidge, Lucille Western, Frank S. Chanfrau,** and others, while never quite attaining their eminence. He died following appendicitis surgery, and the *New York Times* referred to him as "a competent impersonator" of complex characters but a "diligent and ambitious" man.

KELLAR, HARRY (1849–1922). Born in Erie, Pennsylvania, as Heinrich Keller, Harry Kellar became known as the leading **magician*** in the United States after some time as part of the act of the **Davenport Brothers,** embellishing the popularity of his profession and paving the way for such later magicians as Harry Houdini,† whom he befriended. Of his many tricks and illusions, Kellar's audiences especially appreciated his levitation of a girl known only as Princess Karnack and his "self-decapitation" stunt. He **toured*†** America and Europe for many years, but was subsequently eclipsed by other magicians, including Houdini. Though retired, Kellar made his final appearance at a Society of American Magicians benefit for victims of a **World War I**† ship sinking in 1917, after which his fellow magicians carried him from the theater in tribute.

KEMBLE, CHARLES (1775–1854). British **actor***† and youngest sibling of John Philip Kemble, Stephen Kemble, and Sarah Siddons, and son of strolling player Roger Kemble, Charles Kemble was regarded by his contemporary, **William Charles Macready**, as "a first-rate actor of second-rate parts." He made his London debut in 1794, playing Malcolm to his brother John's Macbeth, following a few years acting in the provinces. He ultimately scored a series of successes in contemporary comedies and in secondary roles in **Shakespeare***† in the first decades of the 19th century. A **tour***† of the United States (1832–1834) with his daughter, **Fanny Kemble**, was a triumph (especially for her), but financial difficulties beset the last years of his career.

KEMBLE, FANNY (1809–1893). Born Frances Anne Kemble in London, the youngest child of **Charles Kemble**, Fanny Kemble was educated in France before making her stage debut in London in 1829 as Juliet. Her beauty and charming persona won much praise, and her popularity with audiences in **Shakespearean***† and contemporary romantic roles helped her father succeed as a **manager**.*† Acclaimed in major roles, she scored a major and enduring success in a secondary part, as Julia in **James Sheridan Knowles**'s *The Hunchback*, a character Knowles wrote for her and which she played frequently. She **toured***† the United States with her father, beginning in 1832, but retired from the stage to marry Pierce Mease, who took his grandfather's surname, Butler, in order to inherit the family fortune in cotton, tobacco, and rice.

Kemble lived with Butler on his Sea Island, Georgia, plantation, where she chronicled her feelings about slavery and the times in her journal, published in England in 1839 as *Journal of a Residence on a Georgian Plantation in 1838–39*. Appalled by the institution of slavery in its entirety, she appealed to her husband to improve conditions for his hundreds of slaves, leading to marital tensions causing her departure from Georgia in 1839. Kemble had given birth to two daughters, and Butler threatened to keep her from them if she went public with conditions for slaves on his plantation.

Following public scandal and a protracted custody battle, Kemble and Butler were divorced in 1849, with Butler retaining custody of the daughters, whom Kemble did not see again until they were adults. Butler ultimately squandered his family's fortune through gambling and dubious stock speculations, which forced him to hold a slave auction in 1859, one of the largest public sales of human beings in the history of the United States. At that particular moment, shortly before the start of the **Civil War**, the horrors of the auction, described as "the weeping time" in the press of the day, generated considerable controversy and inspired abolitionist fervor. Butler later went broke when attempting to run his plantation with paid workers after the Civil War.

Following her divorce from Butler, Kemble returned to the stage, playing opposite **William Charles Macready** for a time, and toured the United States, although she shortly abandoned acting to instead offer readings from Shakespeare. Her plantation journal was in continual publication and read by abolitionists, ultimately winning an even wider readership during the Civil War as the **war**'s*† moral purpose became clearer. Kemble published other journals and moved back to England in 1877, where she was popular in society and literary circles, befriending such figures as Henry James, who described her journals as "one of the most animated autobiographies in the language." Kemble also wrote poetry, two plays, *Francis the First* (1832) and *The Star of Seville* (1837); and *Notes on Some of Shakespeare's Plays* (1882), a study drawing on her stage experiences.

Kemble was the grandmother of the writer Owen Wister, author of *The Virginian* (1902). Despite her estimable stage achievements, Kemble is most remembered for her impassioned writing against slavery, especially the plight of **women***† in bondage, and it is believed her journal contributed to causing English authorities to resist recognizing the Confederate States of America during the Civil War. Catherine Clinton, editor of Kemble's journals, notes that those who knew Kemble considered her "witty and engaging," and Clinton posits that reading Kemble's letters and journals is like "being offered a ringside view of the nineteenth century."

KENNICOTT, JAMES H. (1805–1838). James H. Kennicott, a native of New Orleans, was working as a teacher in western New York when he heard of **Edwin Forrest**'s offer of $500 for a play tailored to his style. Kennicott wrote and submitted a five-act tragedy, *Irma; or, The Prediction*, which was admired but deemed too long for Forrest's purposes. However, it was ultimately produced at the American Theatre in New Orleans in March 1830 (and repeated in February 1831) featuring **James H. Caldwell** (who awarded Kennicott $300) and **Jane Placide**. It was the first play written by an American staged in New Orleans. Kennicott also authored *Metacomet*, a play about King Philip's War, which he intended to offer to Forrest, but instead was offered to Caldwell.

THE KENTUCKIAN; OR, A TRIP TO NEW YORK. Following the extraordinary success of ***The Lion of the West; or, A Trip to Washington*** by **James Kirke Paulding** (with revisions by **John Augustus Stone**), featuring the character of bumptious **frontiersman** Nimrod Wildfire in 1831, **James H.**

Hackett, who played the role, persuaded **William Bayle Bernard** to revise the play under this title. The success of Hackett's production led to this two-act comedy, also known by the title *A Kentuckian's Trip to New York in 1815.* The comedy here centered around a society dinner party at which one of the guests, an aristocratic Englishwoman named Mrs. Wollope, sets her sights on teaching manners to what she considers hopelessly vulgar Americans, a plan upset by Wildfire's view of things.

†**KEROSENE CIRCUIT.** Low-budget **touring***† companies of no more than eight **actors***† might be relegated to performing in country towns so small that kerosene lamps were used for **lighting***† the halls even well after the emergence of electric lights. "Playing the kerosene circuit" meant making the best of a long succession of one-night stands† in ill-equipped second-story halls over commercial spaces in towns of perhaps 300 to 1,000 inhabitants.

KERSANDS, BILLY (1842?–1915). Confusion abounds over the early life of **African American***† comedian and dancer William Kersands, who may have been born in Louisiana, Kentucky, or New York, as given in various sources. What is not in doubt is the fact that Kersands became the most popular black comic in the United States in the second half of the 19th century. He began working in **minstrel**† companies in the 1860s, and by the late 1870s, Kersands was highly popular and paid nearly as well as white performers.

Kersands appeared most often with black troupes, including Sam Hague's Georgia Minstrels, a troupe renamed for its post-1872 manager, **Charles Callender**, whom Kersands and other performers attempted to break away from over pay issues. Kersands's popularity became so great that he formed his own troupe, Kersands's Minstrels, in 1885, while also performing when possible with other companies.

Like many talented black performers in his time, Kersands almost certainly struggled to strike a balance between the stereotypes perpetuated in minstrel traditions and using the form to satirize white attitudes. Kersands made use of his enormous mouth (always featured prominently in poster caricatures), which, as he explained on a European **tour***† to an amused Queen Victoria, was so big he might have to have his ears moved. He was a gifted acrobat and also adept musically. His songs and dances were typical of the era, featuring a range of stereotypical concepts associated with minstrelsy—and carried on in **vaudeville**† and **musical theater***† well into the 20th century. Kersands was a forerunner of other early black entertainers, including the legendary Bert Williams.†

†**KIDDER, EDWARD E. (1846–1927). Playwright*†** and **manager*†** Edward E. Kidder was born in Charleston, Massachusetts. Among the **actors*†** he managed were John T. Raymond,† Julia Marlowe,† Joseph Murphy,† and, most notably, **Lotta Crabtree,†** with whom he traveled to England. From the 1880s, he focused on playwriting and had many works produced for such performers as **Nate Salsbury,†** Raymond Hitchcock,† and **Sol Smith**.

KILNER, THOMAS (1777–1862). English-born **actor*†** and **manager*†** Thomas Kilner made his first American appearance in 1818 at the **Park Theatre**. During his long time as **manager*†** of the **Federal Street Theatre** in Boston, Kilner won praise for the high quality of productions under his leadership and for his own character performances in **Shakespearean*†** and contemporary British and American plays.

KIMBALL, MOSES (1810–1895). A native of Newburyport, Massachusetts, and a descendant of colonial forebears, Moses Kimball ultimately became a leading citizen of Boston following some time in land speculating and as a newspaperman. He opened the New England Museum in 1838 and the **Boston Museum** in 1840. In 1842, he met with **P. T. Barnum**, his principal competitor, with whom he went into partnership on the exploitation of a supposed corpse of a mermaid that had come into Kimball's possession. Kimball and Barnum also partnered to purchase and operate Charles Willson Peale's Museum in Philadelphia. In 1843, Kimball added a theater to the Boston Museum, though it was advertised as a lecture hall to avoid Puritan resistance and traditional attitudes regarding the immorality of the stage. Kimball presented his own production and adaptation of *Uncle Tom's Cabin* during the 1850s. Much of his later career was spent in political and civic activities in Boston.

KIRALFY, BOLOSSY (1847–1932) and IMRE KIRALFY (1845–1919). Born in Pest, Hungary, Bolossy and Imre, along with their sister Haniola (1849–1889), debuted on the American stage as dancers and acrobats in the **George L. Fox** vehicle *Hiccory Diccory Dock* (1869), a follow-up to Fox's triumph in *Humpty Dumpty*, with two other siblings, Katherine (1850–1924) and Emilie (1851–1917), and were featured dancing Magyar czardas. They were also in an 1871 revival of Fox's *Humpty Dumpty*, both productions at the **Olympic Theatre**. There were two other Kiralfy brothers, Arnold and Ronald.

These works emerged from the traditions of pantomime, and Bolossy and Imre drew on this resource as they gained significant popularity in a series of spectacular productions at **Niblo's Garden** before staging their own spectacles, beginning with *The Deluge* (1874). Some historians regard this as the first New York stage show to make use of electric **lighting**,*† while others believe the Kiralfys's production *Enchantment* (1879) was the first. Their numerous successes included *Azurine* (1877), *Excelsior* (1893), *Sieba and the Seven Ravens* (1884), and *The Water Queen* (1889), as well as **touring***† productions of ***The Black Crook*** and ***Around the World in 80 Days*** in the 1870s, which were also presented for several seasons in New York. The Kiralfy brothers also worked with **Barnum and Bailey**'s **circus**,*† staging spectacular panoramic sequences, most famously *Nero, or the Destruction of Rome* (1889), which was performed as part of Barnum's circus in London.

KIRBY, J. HUDSON (1810–1848). Born in London, J. Hudson Kirby went on the stage in England before his arrival in America, where he made his first known appearance in 1837 at the **Walnut Street Theatre**. After appearing as Antonio in *The Merchant of Venice* with **James W. Wallack** at the **National Theatre**, Kirby moved from **Shakespeare***† to appearing in second-rate **melodramas**† for the remainder of his career, particularly between 1840 and 1845 at the **Chatham Garden Theatre**. Kirby had the dubious distinction of having a booming voice that permitted him to be heard over the rowdy audiences at the Chatham. The quality of his vehicles inspired the wisecrack "Wake me up when Kirby dies" voiced by audience members. After 1845, Kirby appeared at the Surry Theatre in London, also in melodramas.

KIT, THE ARKANSAS TRAVELER. **Thomas Blades de Walden** and Edward Spencer crafted this sweeping five-act **melodrama**† for **Frank S. Chanfrau** in 1868. Its subtitle was taken from a traditional humorous story and fiddle tune of the same name, in which a rural citizen of Arkansas encounters a big-city type. Chanfrau ultimately produced it at **Niblo's Garden** on 8 May 1871 for 40 performances, following a yearlong **tour***† of the United States.

The happy family of Kit Redding, a farmer in Arkansas played by Chanfrau, is destroyed when his wife, Mary, and daughter Alice are kidnapped by Mary's former beau, Manuel Bond. Kit falls into despair and drink, despite his success in business, and after the passage of many years, he finally encounters Bond traveling under the alias Hastings on a steamboat. Bond hatches a plan to start a fire on the boat in order to commit a robbery, but is foiled by Kit. He discovers that Mary has died, but he is reunited with Alice. The cast was stellar, with Rose Evans doubling as Mary and the adult Alice. The child Alice was played by six-year-old Minnie Maddern† (later Mrs. Fiske), and **George C. Boniface** was the **villain**† Bond/Hastings.

The play had a long stage life, with Chanfrau performing it often. When Chanfrau appeared in an 1880 New York revival of the play, the *New York Times* **critic*** described the play as "an extravagant knife-and-ball melodrama, full of rough life and picturesque story; lively enough as an entertainment† and valueless as a play—if a play is supposed to include something else than mere variety of action."

KIT CARSON, THE HERO OF THE PRAIRIE. **W. R. Derr**'s popular 1850 Western **melodrama**† was one of many stage works inspired, in part, by the character Nimrod Wildfire from **James Kirke Paulding**'s enduringly popular 1831 play, *The Lion of the West.* Like Wildfire, Carson is depicted in this play as a pioneering man of action embodying, as Brenda Murphy writes, "the American virtues of independence, self-sufficiency, rebelliousness to authority, and antipathy to civilization." Fictionalizing adventures from the life of Christopher Houston "Kit" Carson (1809–1868), a famed **frontiersman**, the play was enjoyed by theater audiences hungry for depictions of Western life and the culture of **Native Americans**.*†

KNOWLES, JAMES SHERIDAN (1784–1862). Born in Cork, Ireland, the son of a lexicographer and cousin of **playwright***† **Richard Brinsley Sheridan**, James Sheridan Knowles began publishing his writing in 1798, at the age of 14, after his family moved to London. Encouraged by such literary giants as William Hazlitt, Charles Lamb, and Samuel Taylor Coleridge, Knowles continued to write even during service in the military and studying medicine. His plays, most notably *The Hunchback* (1832), were popular in America. *The Hunchback* was especially so after its English debut, as were other Knowles plays including *Leo* (1810), written for **Edmund Kean**, *Brian Boroihme* (1811), *Caius Gracchus* (1815), *Virginius* (1820), and *William Tell* (1825), written for **William Charles Macready**. He was also an **actor***† and appeared in his own plays in England and continued to write, including *The Wife* (1833) and *The Love Chase* (1837), before giving up the theater to become a preacher.

KOSTER AND BIAL'S MUSIC HALL. This venue, which opened as a concert hall in 1879, resulted from a partnership between John Koster (1844–1895) and Albert Bial (1842–1897), with the partners taking over a structure on 23rd Street and Sixth Avenue that had formerly housed **Dan Bryant**'s **Minstrels**.† Within two years, and after abandoning the concert format, Koster and Bial's rivaled **Tony Pastor's**† **vaudeville**† bills, emphasizing international artists while Pastor sought the family trade. Subsequently, Koster and Bial's moved to Herald Square's Metropolitan Theatre in 1893, partnering with Oscar Hammerstein I.† Along with vaudeville acts, Koster and Bial's presented the first public exhibition of Thomas A. Edison's films† in the Vitascope process on 23 April 1896, signaling the arrival of the film industry. Disputes with Hammerstein led Koster and Bial to buy him out, and the theater continued until 1901, when it was torn down in favor of R. H. Macy's Store, which was built on the site.

KURZ STADT THEATRE. Built in Milwaukee by Austrian-born Henry "Papa" Kurz (1826–1906), the Kurz Stadt Theatre opened on 21 October 1868 and became a fixture in Milwaukee, where it housed the German **Stock***† Company and presented German-language plays under the stewardship of Kurz for nearly 40 years, continuing beyond his death until 1935. The theater itself was situated on Third Street, between Walnut and Wells Streets, and seated over 1,000 patrons. Kurz himself was a popular comedian with the company.

L

THE LADIES OF CASTILE. **Mercy Otis Warren** wrote this blank verse five-act tragedy in 1784, making its heroic depiction of 16th-century Spain in the era of Charles V an analogy to the **American Revolution** and **critical***† of what she viewed as aristocratic tendencies she feared would undermine American liberty. Writing that at the Revolution's end, "America stands alone: May she long stand, independent of every foreign power; superior to the spirit of intrigue, or the corrupt principles of usurpation," Warren dealt with just that subject in her play about Don Velasco, Spanish regent in the era of Charles V. Warren did not wish the play to be staged, though it was published in 1790. Feminist scholars have been less intrigued with the Spanish court historical element than by the play's depiction of politically conscious **women***† characters living with freedoms denied most actual colonial women in late 18th-century America.

LADUE, JOHN S. (b. 1842). Born in New York, John S. Ladue, an **African American***† **actor***† and **playwright,***† attended public schools and, as legend has it, appeared as a **child**† in a production of *Uncle Tom's Cabin.* He performed in both drama and comedy, but was considered superior in the latter. Among his plays were *Under the Yoke; or, Bound and Free* (1876) and *Deceived; or, All Alone* (1884), the former being a plantation drama providing the first important role for black actor **J. A. Arneaux.**† Ladue also appeared in **Shakespearean***† tragedies, but received poor reviews in those works.

THE LADY OF LYONS; OR, LOVE AND PRIDE. British **playwright***† and novelist **Edward Bulwer-Lytton**'s five-act romantic **melodrama**† had its first production at New York's **Park Theatre** on 14 May 1838, featuring **Edwin Forrest** as the play's hero, Claude Melnotte, with **Charlotte Cushman**, **Peter Richings**, and Mrs. Richardson (Elizabeth Jefferson) in support. In the play, Pauline Deschapelles is tricked by a nefarious suitor, Marquis Beauséant, into marriage with the gardener's son, Melnotte, who has been persuaded to pose as a prince. Melnotte, who is truly in love with Pauline, is distraught when the deception is revealed and the marriage abruptly annulled. Melnotte joins the army, and in his absence, Beauséant pressures her to marry him in order to aid her father, who has lost his fortune. In the meantime, Melnotte has become a **war***† hero and Pauline finally realizes she loves him.

Forrest and Cushman were particularly acclaimed and both produced the play with regularity. *The Lady of Lyons* was frequently staged in the United States and England (after its 1841 premiere) throughout most of the 19th century, and it served as the inspiration for William Henry Fry's opera *Leonora* (1845), believed to be the first grand opera written by an American composer.

THE LADY OF THE CAMELLIAS. Adapted to the stage in 1852 from the 1848 Alexandre Dumas fils novel, the play version premiered on 2 February 1852 at the Théâtre du **Vaudeville**† in Paris before being widely produced through Europe and the United States. The following year, Giuseppe Verdi adapted it as an opera, *La Traviata*. As a play, *The Lady of the Camellias*, known most often as *Camille* in its more than a dozen **Broadway***† productions during the second half of the 19th century, won the favor of tragic **actresses***† who found its title character, Marguerite Gautier (based on Marie Duplessis, a French courtesan and mistress of Dumas), a rich role. As late as 1936 celebrated film† **star***† Greta Garbo played the role on-screen and was nominated for a Best Actress Academy Award.

On American and European stages, such actresses as **Sarah Bernhardt**,† Eleonora Duse,† Gabrielle Réjane, Ethel Barrymore,*† Eva Le Gallienne,*† Tallulah Bankhead,*† Lillian Gish, and others scored notable successes in the part. In the 20th century, the play was frequently adapted to the screen, first with Bernhardt re-creating her stage success in a silent version, and others including Theda Bara, Yvonne Printemps, and Alla Nazimova*† as Marguerite, but few to greater effect than Garbo in the aforementioned film. **Musical***† versions, operas, ballets inspired by the novel and play, parodies (including Charles Ludlam's* drag version), and various other international adaptations have been continuous for this enduring work depicting the doomed love affair of Marguerite, a French courtesan, and Armand Duval, an earnest young man who attempts to draw her away from the decadent life that is destroying her.

In America, the play (subtitled *The Fate of a Coquette*) was first seen at New York's **Broadway*** **Theatre**, where it opened on 9 December 1853 starring Jean Davenport (aka **Mrs. Lander**) and **Frederick B. Conway**. Subsequent Broadway productions and the **stars***† involved were in 1857 (**Matilda Heron**), 1900 (Bernhardt and Constant Coquelin), 1904 (three different productions starring Virginia Harned, Margaret Anglin, and Réjane), 1905 (Bernhardt), 1908 (Olga Nethersole†), 1910 (Bernhardt), 1911 (Mildred Holland and, improbably, the movie comic Franklin Pangborn as Armand), 1916 (Bernhardt), 1917 (Bernhardt), 1931 (Eva Le Gallienne), 1932 (Lillian Gish), 1935 (Le Gallienne), and 1963 (Susan Strasberg, in an adaptation by Terrence McNally* directed by Franco Zeffirelli). In 1953, Tennessee Williams* featured Marguerite Gautier among the literary characters in his experimental drama *Camino Real*,* only one of many theatrical and literary manifestations of the character.

THE LAMBS. The origin of the Lambs' Club of New York City could be said to result from a Christmas dinner at **Delmonico's Restaurant** in 1874, when some members of **Lester Wallack**'s company, then appearing in **Dion Boucicault**'s† popular **Irish** play *The Shaughraun*, socialized with their host, George H. McLean, and other cultured gentlemen, and conceived of forming a supper club to repeat such pleasant and instructive gatherings. **Actor*† Henry Montague** had belonged to the Lambs of London, which was then adopted as a model for the organization. Montague was elected the first Shepherd, with Harry Beckett as Boy (treasurer).

After a few years of informal gatherings, the Lambs incorporated in 1877 as a New York institution with a charter membership of 60. During the early decades of the organization, the membership comprised three theater professionals to every nonprofessional. As a precaution against conflicts of interest, no **critic*†** or booking **agent*†** could be a Lamb. After several moves, the clubhouse settled at 34 West 26th Street in 1880, and it was there that the Lambs began presenting their in-house monthly entertainment,† *The Gambols*, in 1888.

Eventually, in the *Gambols* it became customary for **stars*†** to play walk-on roles while major parts went to relatively unknown performers. First-year members, called Lambkins, played the "dame" parts. No **woman*†** ever became a Lamb or was allowed inside the Fold (the clubhouse) until 1952. Several women became devoted members in the 1950s, including Joyce Randolph, "Trixie" Norton of television's classic *The Honeymooners*.

LANDER, MRS. F. W. (1829–1903). Born Jean Margaret Davenport in Wolverhampton, England, she debuted in 1837 as a **child†** at the Richmond Theatre in *The Manager's Daughter*, an apt title since her father ran the theater. She appeared throughout Europe and the United States as a prodigy before taking on adult roles by the 1840s, billed as a tragedienne. She won acclaim in **Shakespearean*†** plays, most notably *Romeo and Juliet*, and popular contemporary works including *The Lady of Lyons*, *The Hunchback*, and *Ingomar*.

In 1853, she became the first **actress***† to play Marguerite Gautier in *The Lady of the Camellias* (under the title *Camille*) and the title role in *Adrienne Lecouvreur* in English on American stages. She retired in 1860 to marry Frederick West Lander, who became a Union General during the **Civil War**, while she worked as a nurse, but his death two years later and the end of the **war***† led her back to the stage at **Niblo's Garden** in 1865 as Mrs. F. W. Lander, appearing in her earlier successes, as well as such plays as *Medea*, *Colombe's Birthday*, *Masks and Faces*, and *The Scarlet Letter*, in which she made her farewell appearance in 1877.

Mrs. Lander lived quietly in Washington, DC, until her death in 1903. In 1867, a biographical sketch described her as possessing "all the elements of character which fit her for the adornment of society or the delight of home. In personating the cultured, graceful, and beautiful heroines of the Drama, she acts no alien part; she has simply to be herself; her pure, natural self in whom beauty of form, feature and mind are exquisitely blended and combined."

LANE, LOUISA. *See* †DREW, LOUISA LANE (MRS. JOHN) (1820–1897).

LANE, WILLIAM HENRY (1825?–1852). Believed to have been free born, possibly in Providence, Rhode Island, William Henry Lane, an **African American***† dancer known onstage as Master Juba (or Boz's Juba), was among the first black performers popular with white audiences in the United States. In his teens, Lane danced in bars in New York's notorious Five Points district before appearing with **minstrel**† troupes in the 1840s. It is believed that Lane is the dancer **Charles Dickens** saw in performance when he visited Five Points and about whom he wrote admiringly in his *American Notes*. It is also believed that Lane may have worked for **P. T. Barnum** for a time and that, supposedly, Barnum had Lane appear as an **Irish** dancer but in **blackface**.†

In 1845, Lane began performing with the four **Ethiopian Minstrels**, and often with billing above the white performers, a first for a black entertainer. He also performed with Pell's Serenaders and White's Serenaders, and in England with the Ethiopian Minstrels in 1848, where he received much acclaim for his early brand of tap dancing. He was known to have been adept at imitating the styles and eccentricities of other dancers, but his own style was most likely drawn from a mixture of African American, Irish, and other European folk styles. Back in America in the 1850s, Lane dropped from sight after a time and is believed to have died impoverished.

THE LAST DAYS OF POMPEII. **Louisa Medina** adapted **Edward Bulwer-Lytton**'s 1834 novel of the same name into a popular three-act **melodrama**† subtitled *A Dramatic Spectacle*. Medina had a notable success with this play, which ran for 29 consecutive performances at the **Bowery Theatre** beginning on 9 February 1835 and featuring **Thomas Hamblin** in the lead. **Walt Whitman** remembered the production as a "capital melodrama" when recalling his youthful theatergoing. Glaucus, the hero of the story, is an oppressed Athenian in decadent Roman Pompeii representing the ill-used artisans, craftsman, and other enslaved workers of the city. The Romans meet justice only, finally, in the eruption of Mount Vesuvius, which, in Medina's play, was depicted visually onstage for a powerful climax.

Some scholars find Medina's play, set in ancient times, a strong analogy for American-style capitalism and the plight of the working class. Bulwer-Lytton's novel—and this and other theatrical adaptations—remained popular well into the 20th century as the result of multiple silent and sound film† versions. Describing Medina as an "unequalled **dramatist**,"*† **Edgar Allan Poe** remarked on the "splendor" of the Bowery production of the play. *The Last Days of Pompeii* was revived numerous times throughout the first half of the 19th century and remained in the American dramatic canon well into the 20th century.

THE LAST OF THE MOHICANS. Stephen E. Glover adapted James Fenimore Cooper's 1826 novel of the same name, which was first performed in Charleston, on 6 January 1830, followed by a production at New Orleans Camp Street Theatre on 19 March 1831 and on 27 December 1832 for a long run in New York with **Charles Thorne** as Magua. Set in 1757 during the **French and Indian War**, *The Last of the Mohicans* was based, to some extent, on historical events, but emphasizes an intense battle of wits between Hawkeye (Natty Bumppo) and Magua, a Huron scout allied with the French, who leads Hawkeye and two daughters of British Colonel Munro into an ambush. Which of the multiple events, characters, and plot twists in Cooper's novel used by Glover for the stage is not clear, since Glover's script was apparently never published and is considered lost.

LEACOCK, JOHN (1729–1802). An early American patriot, poet, and silversmith, John (or possibly Joseph) Leacock lived in Philadelphia during the **American Revolution**. His satire *The Fall of British Tyranny: American Liberty Triumphant*, published in 1776, may not have been produced. Leacock, a member of the Patriotic Society of the Sons of St. Tammany, hoped to arouse revolutionary fervor with this work. He also authored a widely published biblical satire, *The First Book of the American Chronicles of the*

Times, and kept a common book, including his poetry and reflections on the years between 1768 and 1781. Leacock spent the post-Revolution years as Philadelphia's coroner.

†LEADING MAN/LEADING WOMAN. In a **stock*†** company, the parts played by the leading man and leading woman were the major roles in the play and were cast according to those **lines of business**.† However, if a **star*†** performed with the stock company, the star would take that role while the leading man or leading lady would either step down to a **supporting†** role or be at rest during the star's engagement.†

LEAH, THE FORSAKEN. **Augustin Daly**'s* five-act **melodrama,†** adapted from S. H. von Mosenthal's *Deborah*, opened at **Niblo's Garden** on 19 January 1863 for 35 performances under **manager*† H. L. Bateman**. **Kate Bateman** won **critical*†** approval in her signature role as a young Jewish woman in 17th-century Germany secretly in love with a young Christian, Rudolf, played by **Edwin Adams**. Betrayed to local authorities by the duplicitous Nathan, played by **James W. Wallack**, Leah's Jewish community, fearing banishment, attempts to pressure her to end her association with Rudolf. However, she remains loyal to him, unaware that Rudolf has been told that she has given him up. Despairing at this news, Rudolf hastily marries a Christian girl, Madelena, played by Mrs. **Frank S. Chanfrau**, before he discovers that Leah has remained loyal to their pledge of love and is dying of heartbreak at the news of his marriage. Rudolf rushes to Leah's bedside, seeking her forgiveness as she dies.

The emotionally potent play held the stage for the remainder of the 19th century, established Daly as a major force, and was filmed† twice, in 1908 and 1912. Bateman appeared in a London production, which opened at the Adelphi Theatre on 1 October 1863, with critic Clement Scott exclaiming that she "became the talk of all literary and playgoing London."

†LEAVITT, MICHAEL BENNETT (1843–1935). Born in Posen, Prussia, Michael Bennett Leavitt came to America before his second birthday and made his debut with the Mrs. W. B. English Company in Bangor, Maine, performing alongside Mrs. English's two daughters, Helen and **Lucille Western**. By age 14, he was performing in **minstrel†** shows, playing banjo, bones, tambourine, and piano as well as acting in a **burlesque*†** sketch and serving as **advance man**.† As impresario of Madame Rentz's Female Minstrels (later the **Rentz-Santley** troupe), he popularized burlesque performed by **women**.*† He moved easily into **legitimate*†** theater and formed a chain of theaters that became the prototype later imitated by the Theatrical Syndicate.† During his career, Leavitt worked with virtually every significant person in American show business, much of which is recounted in his magisterial memoir, *Fifty Years in Theatrical Management* (1912).

LED ASTRAY. **Dion Boucicault**'s† five-act play, loosely adapted from Octave Feuillet's *La Tentation*, opened at the **Union Square Theatre** on 6 December 1873 for 161 performances. Centered on marital infidelity, the play **starred*†** **Rose Eytinge†** as Armande, a young woman who marries a widower, played by **C. R. Thorne Jr.**, and has a daughter, acted by the teenaged **Kate Claxton**.† Armande truly loves the count, but when he dallies with another woman, an unhappy Armande is led into an affair of her own with a poet, played by **McKee Rankin**.† When the count discovers this, he duels with the poet, but misses his shot purposely and asks Armande's forgiveness, promising his future faithfulness. The play was produced successfully at London's Gaiety Theatre in 1874 and remained popular for decades, including an 1897 revival with Nance O'Neil† as Armande and Rankin repeating his original role. **George Odell†** subsequently described *Led Astray* as "one of the most famous dramas of its decade in America."

†**LEG BUSINESS.** The 1866 New York success of the **musical*†** **melodrama†** *The Black Crook*, often referred to as the prototype of the first musical, demonstrated that a huge paying audience was to be found for visual spectacle that included scantily clad **women**.*† The "leg business" was any endeavor that seemed to privilege the shape actress† and the female form over literary content. **Olive Logan†** emerged as a vociferous **critic*†** of what she viewed as a degradation of theater art.

†**LEGITIMATE THEATER.** The legitimate drama, stage, or theater, called "legit" in *Variety**† slang, meant straight plays without **musical*†** interpolations or variety, **vaudeville,†** **burlesque,*†** parodies, or travesties. The term originated when strict regulations during the 17th and 18th centuries were intended to protect the theaters that were licensed for the performance of plays. Nonlicensed theater groups would get around these restrictions by adding snatches of song or dance, which theoretically changed the piece into a different (unregulated) genre. By extension, the term "legitimate" ultimately came to imply works of serious purpose or literary merit.

LELAND, OLIVER S. (1834–1870). A native of Waltham, Massachusetts, and an 1854 Harvard graduate, Oliver Shepard Leland wrote prose and was a sometime drama **critic*†** for New York and Boston periodicals, including *Knickerbocker* magazine. He was also a **playwright,*†** scoring a notable success with *The Czarina* (revived in 1888 by **Mrs. D. P. Bowers**) and other works, including *Teverino: A Romance* (translated and adapted in 1855 from George Sand), *The Rights of Man* (1857), *Caprice; or, Lover and Husband* (also known as *Caprice; or, A Woman's Heart*, 1857), *Beatrice; or, The False and the True* (1857), and *Madame Pompadour* (1860). He was at work on another drama at the time of his sudden death from pneumonia.

LEMAN, WALTER M. (1810–1890). A native of Boston, Walter Moore Leman began his career as a journeyman **actor*†** at the **Tremont Theatre** at age 17. He appeared most frequently in his hometown, and on San Francisco and Philadelphia stages, and on **tour**.*† Leman wrote *Memories of an Old Actor* (1886), in which he chronicled his career and the notables with whom he acted. His colorful memories superseded any theories of acting or analysis of any particular role; he was typical of his peers in appearing in a wide range of contemporary and classic works. His memoirs are unfailingly warm about his colleagues, and his enthusiasm for his work is evident throughout, as when he records his youthful desires: "I read every play-book, good or bad, that I could lay my hands upon, and obtained access to the theatre by any and every means in my power."

LEON, FRANCIS (1844–after 1900). Born Francis Patrick Glassey in Fordham, New York, he performed as a boy soprano before developing into one of the most popular **blackface† minstrels†** and **female impersonators†** of the mid-19th century, adopting the stage name Francis Leon, though he preferred to bill himself as "Leon" or "The Only Leon." From the 1850s, he performed with a number of minstrel troupes, most notably **Hooley's** and **Christy's**. In 1864, Leon partnered with Edwin Kelly to establish Kelly and Leon's Minstrels, most acclaimed for their blackface parodies of popular comic operas, in which Leon played the prima donna roles. Usually working as a single after 1869, Leon continued as a **star*†** in minstrel shows, **vaudeville,†** and **musicals,*†** applauded for his comic skill, singing, and adept dancing. **Critics*†** of his day found Leon's comedy inoffensive and greatly admired his skill in drag roles.

LEONOR DE GUZMAN. **George H. Boker**'s five-act tragedy premiered at Philadelphia's **Walnut Street Theatre** on 3 October 1853 for six performances with **Julia Dean** in the title role of Guzman. Set in Castile, Spain, in 1350, the play depicts machinations for power in the wake of the battlefield death of King Alfonso II, whose devoted mistress, Leonor de Guzman (1310–1351), becomes the victim of the new king's mother, Queen Maria (played by Mrs. Duffield, formerly **Kate Wemyss**), who is consumed by jealousy of Leonor. Boker's play was praised for the complexity of its historical characters, but its popularity in Philadelphia was not matched in New York.

LEONORA; OR, THE WORLD'S OWN. **Julia Ward Howe**'s 1856 five-act blank verse **melodrama†** was written during a period in which this **women**'s*† rights advocate was frustrated by her own life in the domestic realm. The play was produced at **Wallack's Theatre**, where it opened on 16 March 1857 for a week, followed by a single performance in Boston. **Critics*†** admired the play's literary merits, but despite thunderous audience applause for Howe at the first night curtain, it was condemned for its weak dramaturgy and deemed indecent in its **sexualized*†** subject matter.

Leonora is a simple country girl enamored of a visiting count, who does not allow his marriage and children to stand in the way of a dalliance with Leonora. A young artist, Edward, who loves Leonora, tries to reveal the count's duplicity and, more significantly, Leonora's own culpability, noting that she has plunged from "passion into infamy." When the count abandons her, Leonora, awakened to her own sins, stabs herself with Edward's dagger, forgiving the count in her dying breath, as Edward mourns Leonora as "The wreck of all that's fair and excellent; / A thing of tears and tenderness forever!"

LEWIS, MRS. HENRY (d. 1855). Born in London as Bertha (?) Harvey, she appeared on English stages until 1835, when she and her husband, pantomimist Henry Lewis (1802?–1892), journeyed to New York, where she won approval as a graceful dancer and in **breeches roles,†** including the male leads in *Macbeth*, *Othello*, and *Richard III*, this last considered "her great part, and some old play-goers will even now declare that she was the equal of any of the tragedians in that role, an opinion that one will be justified in accepting only with liberal grains of salt," wrote Lyman Horace Weeks in *McBride's Magazine* in 1896. Mrs. Lewis divorced her husband in 1849 and spent most of her career **touring*†** the United States, while he played character roles and became a stage **director.*†**

†LEWIS, JAMES (1838–1896). Born in Troy, New York, this popular comedian, one of the "Big Four" of **Augustin Daly**'s† company (a group including **Ada Rehan,† Mrs. G. H. Gilbert,†** and **John Drew†**), began his theatrical apprenticeship in **Mrs. John Wood**'s troupe, performing in **burlesque*†** at the **Olympic Theatre**. Lewis made his debut in 1858 in a production of *The Writing on the Wall*, filling in for another **actor.*†** At the outbreak of the **Civil War**, Lewis was **touring*†** in the South and barely managed to return safely to the North by breaking through a blockade.

Lewis made his New York debut in 1866 in *Your Life's in Danger* and joined Daly in 1869, remaining in the **Fifth Avenue Theatre** company until his death. With Daly, he scored personal successes in a variety of classic and contemporary comedies, among which were roles in *Divorce* (1873), *Saratoga* (1874), *The Big Bonanza* (1875), *Pique* (1875), and a range of performances in **Shakespearean***† (*A Midsummer Night's Dream, As You Like It, Twelfth Night*) and 18th-century British (*She Stoops to Conquer, The School for Scandal*) comedies. At the time of Lewis's death, the *New York Times* noted that he was a quiet and private man offstage, but that onstage he "stood as the representative of wholesome merriment."

LIBERTY IN LOUISIANA. James Workman (d. 1832) wrote this comedy—his sole effort for the stage—in 1804, inspired, in part, by the comedies of **Richard Brinsley Sheridan** and with the intention of arousing Louisiana citizens to reject Spanish rule and presence in the territory, as well as to celebrate the Louisiana Purchase by the United States. Curiously, its first production was in Charleston at the **Charleston Theatre** on 4–5 April 1804 and 21 May 1804, two years before any play was produced in English in New Orleans or before Workman himself ever set foot in Louisiana.

John Hodgkinson played the lead, with the *Charleston Courier* applauding his "animated" performance as Phelim O'Flinn, a happy-go-lucky **Irish** adventurer courting a Spanish girl in New Orleans, with the backdrop of the machinations of various British, Scottish, and Spanish characters attempting to prevent the raising of the American flag over the city. Workman's satire is most boldly directed at Spanish authorities, particularly the Spanish legal system. Workman moved from Charleston to New Orleans in 1805, becoming judge of the county of Orleans. There were subsequent productions of the play in New York, Philadelphia, and Savannah, in 1805, but it soon disappeared from the stage canon.

LIFE IN BROOKLYN, ITS LIGHTS AND SHADES—VICES AND VIRTUES. This 1858 anonymous drama of New York City life in the middle of the 19th century was one of a series of such plays seen in the 50 years following the appearance of **Yankee**† characters and plays. **Melodramatic**† in nature, with an emphasis on spectacle, this and other such plays are of greater interest as a trend toward increasing realism,*† though comic actor **G. L. Fox**† appeared in the cast. Such contemporary plays depicted the turbulent lives of the lower classes; the problems and conditions of city life in a time (1820s–1860s) of rising nationalism and the arrival of growing numbers of immigrants, particularly the **Irish**, provide the major interest in such a play.

*†LIGHTING. Indoor theater lighting was at its most primitive during the period before electricity, consisting solely of candlelight, and this was often the condition in small-town halls in rural America even late in the 19th century. Barrett H. Schoberlin cites an instance in which only 12 candles served an entire facility—both stage and auditorium. Plays were written in acts that could be played before the candles burned down and had to be changed. Still, a smoking candle might require wick trimming or snuffing during a scene, to the frustration of players and audience members. Safety, convenience, and illumination all improved with the use of oil lamps, which first replaced candles in the **footlights**.†

According to *The Autobiography of Joseph Jefferson*,† during the first half of the 19th century in midwestern towns, "a second-class quality of sperm-oil was the height of any **manager**'s*† ambition." **Gas lighting**† was the norm for theaters in major cities during much of the 19th century, with steady improvements in equipment and the ability to control effects. The gas table allowed centralized control of the valves that regulated the gas lines to individual instruments. Gaslight required a backstage crew of gas men.

This was also the era of the **limelight**.† Toward the end of the 19th century, electric lighting began to replace gas in theaters. It was far safer, more economical, and easier to control. Similarly, the carbon arc† replaced the limelight. Yet many artists remained partial to gaslight and remembered it fondly long after it was no longer in use, and many turn-of-the-century theaters were built with both gas and electric lighting in compatible systems until the beginning of the 20th century. **Theater fires**,† such as the famous and most tragic one at Chicago's Iroquois Theatre† in 1903, finally forced changes that led to the permanent elimination of gas lighting.

†LIMELIGHT. Invented in England by Thomas Drummond in 1826, limelight (or calcium light†) was not regularly used in London theaters until much later. It was adopted by American **managers***† after the **Civil War**, but was gradually replaced by the cheaper carbon arc light.† The bright glow of limelight, directed through a lens, was produced by heating a block of limestone to incandescence with the spark of combined oxygen and hydrogen through hoses from their separate containers, allowing it to give off a misty white light. American theaters employed limelight during the latter half of the 19th century, mostly for spotlighting **star***† **actors**.*† The term "in the limelight" is frequently employed to suggest an actor at the center of attention.

LINCOLN, ABRAHAM (1809–1865). The 16th president of the United States was a regular theatergoer in adulthood, having developed a taste for dramatic art from his love of reading **Shakespeare**,*† whose plays he read and reread and could quote passages from at some length. Stories abound of Lincoln reading Shakespeare in his youth and carrying a copy of the plays with him while riding the midwestern judicial circuit as a young lawyer. His favorites among the plays were *Hamlet, Macbeth,* and *King Lear.*

Lincoln often attended performances without fanfare, so the complete record of his theater attendance is elusive, though it is known that he witnessed **James H. Hackett** as Falstaff in *Henry IV, Part 1* on 13 March 1863. The following year, Lincoln saw **Edwin Forrest** play Lear and is known to have seen **Edwin Booth**† play Shylock in *The Merchant of Venice.* On at least one chilling occasion, Lincoln saw his assassin, **John Wilkes Booth,**† in a production of *The Marble Heart* in Washington, DC, on 8 November 1863.

Lincoln's tastes were varied, however, and he enjoyed the lightest of contemporary comedies as well as the darkest of tragedies. Writing in *Abraham Lincoln: Redeemer President,* Allen C. Guelzo notes that "Once in Washington, Lincoln took every opportunity to be a regular theatergoer, attending the opera 19 times (for Bellini's *Norma* and Donizetti's *Fille du Régiment*), visiting **Leonard Grover**'s **National Theatre** on E Street 21 times, and **John Ford's Theatre** (itself a converted Baptist church, rebuilt after a **fire**† in 1863 as a 'magnificent new Thespian temple') on 10th Street at least 10 times during the presidency. There, without fear of serious interruption by office-seekers or generals, usually in the company of his secretaries or an invited politician or just his footman, Charles Forbes, Lincoln could indulge his passion for the stage."

The irony of Lincoln's assassination occurring in Ford's Theatre on 14 April 1865—and at the hands of sometime Shakespearean **actor***† and **matinee idol**† John Wilkes Booth—is tragically obvious. In the nearly 150 years since Lincoln's death, he has frequently appeared as a character in plays and, ultimately, films† and television programs, beginning with his addition as an iconic figure in some post-1865 stagings of *Uncle Tom's Cabin*† and continuing into the 21st century in movies, including such oddities as *Abraham Lincoln: Vampire Hunter* (2012) and the acclaimed, award-winning drama *Lincoln* (2012), directed by Steven Spielberg from a screenplay by Tony Kushner* that dramatized the last months of Lincoln's life. His frequent appearance in plays and films is only one indication of Lincoln's enduring significance to American life and culture.

LINCOLN'S ASSASSINATION. The bare facts of the assassination of the 16th United States president, **Abraham Lincoln**, are well-known, especially its occurrence in a theater and that Lincoln's assassin was an **actor**.*† On the evening of 14 April 1865, five days after Confederate General Robert E. Lee surrendered to Union General Ulysses S. Grant at Appomattox Courthouse, Virginia, effectively ending the catastrophic American **Civil War**, Lincoln, his wife, Mary, and two guests, Major Henry Rathbone and Rathbone's fiancée, Clara Harris, arrived at **Ford's Theatre** in Washington, DC. Late for the performance of **Tom Taylor**'s popular farce *Our American Cousin*, **starring*† Laura Keene**, Lincoln and his party made their way to a stage box draped in flag bunting and adorned with a portrait of **George Washington**. When Lincoln was spotted entering the box, the performance stopped as the orchestra played "Hail to the Chief," the audience cheering the president with gusto. Lincoln settled into a specially selected chair and held his wife's hand as the performance continued. During act 3, scene 2 of the comedy, a few audience members later reported noticing **actor*† John Wilkes Booth†** moving along the theater's wall toward the presidential box.

Shortly thereafter, actor **Harry Hawk**, in the comedic role of the "American cousin" Asa Trenchard, was left alone on the stage to speak the line, "Don't know the manners of good society, eh? Well, I guess I know enough to turn you inside out, old gal—you sockdologizing old man-trap!" As the audience laughed, Booth, having quietly gained entry to the stage box, fired a derringer at close range at the back of Lincoln's head. As the president slumped forward, Booth was set upon by Rathbone, who fell back in pain as Booth's dagger cut deeply into his shoulder. Booth then leapt from the box to the stage floor below, catching his foot in the flag bunting and breaking a bone in his ankle as he tumbled to the stage.

Rising in front of the audience and the stunned Hawk, Booth spoke, with some spectators, including Hawk, believing they heard him shout *"Sic semper tyrannis!"* before hobbling offstage through the wings, brushing past Keene, who recognized him, and out the stage door to a waiting horse. Chaos ensued in the theater with the realization that Lincoln had been shot, following Mary Lincoln's horrified scream as she noticed her husband slumped beside her and unresponsive. A young military doctor, Charles Leale, battled through the crowd to the president's box, as did Keene, who cradled the unconscious Lincoln's head in her lap. Determining that the wound would prove fatal, a decision was made to move Lincoln from the theater to a boardinghouse across the street, where, in a cramped room crowded with Lincoln's cabinet members and others, Lincoln died at 7:22 a.m. the following morning, 15 April 1865.

Booth, leader of a conspiracy that also involved planned murders of Vice President Andrew Johnson and Secretary of State William Seward, had previously failed to kidnap Lincoln in hopes of aiding the struggling Confederacy in the last months of the **war**.*† Frustrated, a few nights before the assassination and following Lee's surrender, Booth stood outside the White House as Lincoln gave an impromptu speech from a window in the White House. In this speech, which proved the last Lincoln ever gave, the president spoke of the possibility of freed **African American** slaves attaining voting rights, leading an infuriated Booth, a vicious racist, to alter his plan from kidnapping to murder. Of the hastily hatched plot, only Booth succeeded completely in his assignment, while coconspirator Lewis Powell managed to seriously injure Seward in a knife attack at the secretary of state's home (although Seward subsequently recovered). George Atzerodt, who was chosen to kill the vice president, failed to make the attempt after overindulging at a nearby bar. Booth, assuming that he would be hailed a hero in the Confederacy, was shocked while escaping south with coconspirator David Herold to read press accounts labeling him a coward and murderer, even in the South.

A few weeks after the assassination, Booth was cornered in a Virginia tobacco barn and shot to death by a Union soldier when he refused to surrender. Four of Booth's coconspirators (including Powell, Herald, Atzerodt, and Mrs. Mary Surratt, owner of the boardinghouse where the conspirators, including her son John, met to plan) were ultimately hanged and still others were jailed for various reasons relating to the assassination and for different periods of time. Theater owner **John T. Ford**, as well as Keene and other actors in *Our American Cousin*, were detained and questioned by police for a time, but ultimately cleared, though the careers of Ford and Keene never fully recovered from the night of tragedy.

Booth's brother, **Edwin Booth,**† widely considered America's greatest 19th-century actor and a loyal Unionist, was reported to be devastated by his brother's actions and, for a time, withdrew from the stage. Within a relatively short interlude, he was able to resume his career and to achieve greater heights in his art. He purportedly never spoke his brother's name again, although a photograph of the assassin hung on Booth's bedroom wall for the remainder of his life. Lincoln's youngest child, Thomas "Tad" Lincoln, was also attending a theater performance on the night of the assassination. Watching *Aladdin and His Wonderful Lamp* at Grover's Theatre, Tad became hysterical when the performance was interrupted with the announcement of the shooting.

Lincoln's assassination has been the subject of scores of books and documentaries, with depictions of the assassination and surrounding events in Hollywood films† for nearly one hundred years, from *The Birth of a Nation* (1915) to *Lincoln* (2012). The assassination neither enhanced the state of American theaters nor did it help theater personnel gain acceptance and respect, but few Americans blamed theater as an institution, reserving their resentment for Booth and his coconspirators.

LINDSAY, ADAM (late 18th century). In partnership with Thomas Wall, Adam Lindsay was cofounder, in 1781, of the Maryland Company of Comedians, the first theater company established in residence in Baltimore. In doing so, Lindsay and Wall defied a 1774 ban on theatrical entertainments† by the Continental Congress. Lindsay had previously operated a coffeehouse and returned to that profession in 1785. Little is otherwise known of his life or Wall's, although Wall built Baltimore's New Theatre, the first constructed in that city.

†**LINES OF BUSINESS.** From the 18th century until the rise of the **combination system**,† **actors***† were hired according to certain categories of roles that they would act throughout the repertory† of plays presented by that company. Apart from the **leading man**† and **leading woman**† roles, the usual **lines of business**† in any late 19th-century **touring***† company, presenting mostly **melodramas**† interspersed with comedies and **Shakespearean***† plays, were: **juvenile**,† **ingénue**,† **heavy man**† (or **villain**†), **eccentric**† (often ethnic types), light comedian,† **character actor**,† low comedian,† old man,† **walking gentleman**,† and **utility**.† There were, of course, **women***† counterparts to many of them, as well as endless variations, like the **Yankee**,† the **soubrette**,† and the respectable utility.

LINGARD, W. H. (1839–1927). Born William Horace Lingard in England, he gained success in music halls there before his New York debut in 1868 at the **Theatre Comique**. He appeared in plays and **musicals**,*† but his popularity in comedy derived almost exclusively from satiric sketches, songs, and impersonations he interpolated into many performances or added between acts. A *New York Times* review in 1872 stated that Lingard's "best performances are well known to the public, and his songs and personations still give great pleasure." Lingard's British-born wife, Alice Dunning (1847–1897), frequently performed with him, and he was **manager***† of several theaters. However, his lasting fame as one of the funniest entertainers† of his era resulted from his versatility in comedy and song, the most famous of which was the 1868 song "Captain Jinks of the Horse Marines," for which Lingard supplied lyrics to music by T. Maclagan. The song inspired Clyde Fitch*† to write a 1901 play with the same title, which provided the first **starring***† vehicle for Ethel Barrymore.*†

THE LION OF THE WEST; OR, A TRIP TO WASHINGTON. **James Kirke Paulding**'s four-act comedy, which introduced the beloved American character Nimrod Wildfire (played in its original production by **James H. Hackett**) to the theatergoing public, opened on 25 April 1831 at the **Park Theatre**. The winning play in a contest for a new comedy featuring a leading American character, *The Lion of the West* won Paulding $300 for what some considered a parody of legendary American hero Davy Crockett, though Paulding vehemently denied the notion. Despite the ultimate popularity of the Wildfire character, the play was not immediately successful, leading to a fairly significant rewrite by **John Augustus Stone**, with Paulding's blessing. Ultimately, *The Lion of the West* became the most popular American play prior to the runaway success of *Uncle Tom's Cabin* in 1852.

Basic plot elements from Paulding's version remained in Stone's three-act adaptation, with the plot focused on a flighty young woman who aims to marry a French aristocrat and move from America to Paris. A French count, played by **Peter Richings** in the play's original version, attempts to persuade her to elope even as two other suitors appear on the scene. Following multiple complicating situations and mistaken identities, the uneducated and bumptious Colonel Nimrod Wildfire, the girl's protective cousin, discovers that the count and another suitor are unfit, and he will only permit the third, Roebuck, to court her if he can prove he merits her attentions.

The name "Nimrod" refers to a fool, but Wildfire proved to be a depiction of Americanism audiences welcomed, with his coonskin cap, buckskin clothes, and blunt backwoods slang. The latter included such lines as, "You might as well try to scull a potash kettle up the falls of Niagara with a crowbar for an oar," or, when preparing for a duel with his opponent, "He'll come off as badly as a feller I once hit a sledge hammer lick over the head—a real sogdolloger. He disappeared altogether; all they could find of him was a little grease spot in one corner." Despite Paulding's (and Hackett's) protestations, the public saw Wildfire as Crockett, enhancing the **frontiersman's** legend and popularizing the play and several others in which the character appeared.

THE LITTLE CHURCH AROUND THE CORNER. Built and consecrated in 1849 by an Episcopal congregation established the year before, the Church of the Transfiguration, which came to be known as the Little Church Around the Corner, was constructed at 1 East 29th Street between Madison and Fifth Avenues. The name supposedly derived from an 1870 incident surrounding the funeral of **actor***† **George Holland**, who was denied a service at another Episcopal church because of his association with the theatrical profession.

Joseph Jefferson,† assisting Holland's son in arranging the services, was told that there was "a little church around the corner" more liberal in its attitudes thanks to the values of its pastor, Rev. George Hendric Houghton. Houghton's Christian values were of an inclusive variety—and he gave sanctuary to **African Americans***† targeted for violence during the 1863 draft riots during the **Civil War**. Houghton's openness to the theatrical community, often ostracized in religious communities during the 19th century, led theater professionals to its doors from that time to the present, while the church itself was immortalized in P. G. Wodehouse's libretto for the Jerome Kern-Guy Bolton **musical***† *Sally* in 1920. Wodehouse had been married there in 1914. In the early 1920s, the Episcopal Actors' Guild was formed there, with such luminaries as Tallulah Bankhead,*† Basil Rathbone,*† and others serving as officers.

LITTLE NELL AND THE MARCHIONESS. Inspired by **Charles Dickens**'s *The Old Curiosity Shop,* **John Brougham**'s four-act play **starring***† **Lotta Crabtree**† opened on 14 August 1867 at **Wallack's Theatre** for 28 performances. For Crabtree, the play became a lucrative vehicle in her **repertory***† despite its limited original run. The play was not particularly faithful to Dickens's novel, with excuses created for Crabtree's Nell to interpolate her skills at banjo playing, clog dancing, and **minstrel**†-style jigs. The plot centered on Nell and her grandfather, played by T. J. Hind, who are evicted from their old curiosity shop, by the **villain**† Quilp. After a nomadic existence leading the grandfather to employment in a small country church, his wealthy brother turns up to help retrieve the shop, though their difficult struggles culminate in Nell's death. A subplot provided a happier ending with Crabtree also playing a servant girl who falls in love with a nice young man, Dick Swiveller, who calls her "The Marchioness" and gratefully marries her after she nurses him through a near-fatal illness.

A LIVE WOMAN IN THE MINES; OR, PIKE COUNTY AHEAD!. **Alonzo Delano**'s "Local Play in Two Acts" written under the pseudonym "Old Block" was first performed and published in 1857. The rough-hewn play, written in what became known as "California Humor," depicted an "Amazonian" woman, High Betty Martin, working in male-dominated California gold mines beside the hero, Pike County Jess, during the gold rush. The play featured pithy dialogue Delano had drawn from visits to mining camps, including the exclamation, "Whoora! for a live woman in the mines. What'll the boys say? They'll peel out o' their skins for joy . . . Injins and grizzlies clar the track, or a young airthquake will swaller you." *A Live Woman in the Mines* found some success resulting from Delano's popularity as a humorist nearly equal to **Mark Twain** and **Bret Harte**, but most of his writing was published fiction or newspaper reportage outside of the theatrical realm.

LIVING MODELS. Otherwise known as **tableaux vivants**, living models were posed, stationary images providing an especially dramatic or artistic image, sometimes patriotic but often featuring either reproductions of famous historical moments or great works of art, a style begun in the late 1840s. Most famously, living models were nude or seminude women posed in artistic images, a style elevated by Florenz Ziegfeld Jr.† in his famous annual **musical***† **revue***† *The Ziegfeld Follies,* with new editions each year for two decades beginning in 1907. At various times, living models inspired moral protests over the nude element, and by the early 20th century, these tableaux were ultimately outlawed even though Ziegfeld's tasteful use of nudity had become famous.

LIVINGSTON, WILLIAM (c. 1675–1729). Born in New Kent County, Virginia, William Livingston (sometimes called Levingston), son of John Livingston and married to Susannah "Sukey" Rootes, was a merchant. In an arrangement with his indentured servants **Charles and Mary Stagg**, who were apparently dancers, Livingston built the first playhouse in America in Williamsburg, Virginia. A petition to build the playhouse was recorded on 19 November 1716. On a three-and-a-half-acre lot he built a dwelling house, kitchen, and stable. He also laid out a bowling alley and built a theater, the foundation remnants of which have been unearthed by archaeologists whose calculations indicate that the theater was 30 feet wide, 86.5 feet long, and at least two stories tall, similar to English provincial theaters of that era.

LOCKE, GEORGE E. (1817–1880). A native of Epsom, New Hampshire, George E. Locke debuted as an **actor*†** in Boston as Las Casas in *Pizarro*, followed by stints in Providence, Rhode Island, before his New York debut as Solomon Swap in *Jonathan in England* in 1858, followed by a **tour*†** of California in 1861. Locke established himself in **Yankee†** roles in comic plays written specifically for him, including such character names as Jedediah Homebred, Zedediah Short, and Moderation Easterbrook, winning for Locke the name "Yankee" Locke, firmly identifying him with this unique genre of comedy. He gained most of his fame in provincial theaters, only rarely playing in major cities.

LOGAN, CORNELIUS A. (1806–1852). Believed to have been born in Baltimore, Cornelius Ambrosius Logan was a painter and became an **actor*†** in the 1820s. As an actor, he found success in **Yankee†** roles in comedies and wrote several farces featuring this popular American **stock*†** character, including *Yankee Land; or, The Founding of the Apple Orchard* (1834), *The Wag of Maine* (1835), *The Vermont Wool Dealer* (1838), and *Chloroform; or, New York a Hundred Years Hence* (1849). Logan fathered three daughters, **Eliza**, Celia, and **Olive Logan**, all of whom followed him onto the stage and became successful.

LOGAN, ELIZA (1827–1872). Believed to be the eldest of the eight children of **Cornelius A. Logan**, Eliza Logan was born in Philadelphia and educated at an all-girls school in Lancaster, Pennsylvania, before making her stage debut in the **breeches role†** of Young Norval in *Douglas* at the **Walnut Street Theatre** on 28 January 1841. She found success playing Shakespeare's*† ingénues,† including Juliet and Ophelia, and in contemporary plays, including as Pauline in *The Lady of Lyons* in her 1850 New York debut at the **Bowery Theatre**. Though popular through the 1850s, compared with her sister **Olive Logan**,† she had a relatively brief career, retiring in 1859 when she married theater **manager*†** George Wood.

†**LOGAN, OLIVE (1836–1909).** Born in Elmira, New York, the activist **actress*†** and **playwright*†** grew up in a theatrical family, often as a **child*†** performer in her father's company. She made her adult debut in 1854 at the **Arch Street Theatre** in Philadelphia. From 1855 to 1863, she lived abroad, during which period she married the first of her three husbands. In 1864, she acted in her own play, *Evaleen*, at **Wallack's Theatre** in New York City and then **toured*†** it under the title *The Felon's Daughter*.

Having begun publishing essays in periodicals about her life in Paris while she lived there, Logan decided to pursue writing as a profession instead of acting. She wrote voluminously, not only about the theater, but also about **women**'s*† issues, on which she also lectured widely. Logan championed decency of behavior and dress for women, gaining national celebrity for the vehemence of her views. Her 1870 memoir, *Before the Footlights and Behind the Scenes*, colorfully evokes changes in theatrical customs during the post–**Civil War** years and recounts the controversy following publication of her famous essay on "the **leg business**,"† condemning scantily clad women onstage, in *Galaxy* magazine (summer 1867). Logan followed that book with another, *The Mimic World* (1871), and also began to see her plays produced in New York: *Surf* (1870), *A Business Woman* (1873), *A Will and a Way* (1874), her translation of *La Cigale* (1878), and *Newport* (1879).

LOGAN, THE LAST OF THE RACE OF SHIKELLEMUS, CHIEF OF THE CAYUGA NATION. **Joseph Doddridge**, a clergyman and historian, wrote this 1821 play about John (sometimes called James) Logan (c. 1725–1780), son of Cayuga chief Shikellemus in the Ohio Valley in the 1770s, who led calls for peace between **Native Americans*†** and whites. Shikellemus, also known as Shikellamy, was a French-Canadian raised by the Cayuga tribe, ultimately becoming an esteemed chief. His son, Tahgahhjute, whose mother was a full-blooded Cayuga woman, labored for peace between Indians and whites, earning him the name Logan after the secretary of the governor of Pennsylvania, his father's friend. However, Logan's views changed when his family was murdered by a party of land-hungry white men in what became known as the Yellow Creek Massacre. Logan thus became a force against peace—and led revenge parties to avenge the deaths.

LONDON ASSURANCE. **Dion Boucicault's**† enduring six-act comedy, originally titled *Out of Town*, premiered on 4 March 1841 at London's Theatre Royal, Covent Garden, before its American debut at the **Park Theatre** on 11 October 1841 for three continuous weeks of performances, the first long-run New York production. With a cast including **Charlotte Cushman** as adventurous horsewoman Lady Gay Spanker, the play centered on the machinations of Sir Harcourt Courtly, played by **Henry Placide**, a middle-aged fop attempting to woo much younger women, only to be foiled by his own grown son. The London production, staged by **Madame Vestris**, featured the innovation of the **box set**, which created fourth-wall realism.*† It caused something of a sensation when the same technique was used in the New York production of *London Assurance*, which was the first time American audiences experienced it.

The popularity of Boucicault's comedy was such that most of the **stars***† of the period performed in productions of it, including **Fanny Davenport**, **Rose Coghlan**, **Laura Keene**, **Ada Rehan**,† and others. Periodic New York revivals have kept the play before audiences into the 21st century, with occasional **stock***† and **touring***† productions, as well as frequent revivals in London, including a 2010 production of the play in an adaptation by Richard Bean featuring Fiona Shaw and Simon Russell Beale. Without question, this early play by the prolific Boucicault remains his most frequently produced work. Of a 1997 **Broadway***† revival starring Brian Bedford, *New York Times* **critic***† Peter Marks described Boucicault's play as "an 1841 prequel to the modern situation comedy" and a "witty confection" if "by no means a great play."

LONGFELLOW, HENRY WADSWORTH (1807–1882). Born in Portland, Maine, Henry Wadsworth Longfellow, a poet, novelist, and educator, studied at Bowdoin and Harvard Colleges and published his first collection of poetry in 1839. He subsequently became a prolific author of poems and novels, as well as the first English translation of Dante's *The Divine Comedy*. His own poems "Paul Revere's Ride," "The Song of Hiawatha," and "**Evangeline**" have secured his place in American letters of the 19th century, and *Evangeline*, in an 1860 stage adaptation by **Sidney Frances Cowell Bateman**, scored a success at New York's **Winter Garden**, with **Kate Bateman** achieving **stardom***† in the title role.

In 1842, Longfellow established himself as an abolitionist with the publication of *Poems on Slavery*. Though his fame rests on his poetry, Longfellow dabbled as a **playwright***† with such comparatively little-known plays as *The Spanish Student* (1843), *Giles Corey of the Salem Farms* (1868) and *John Endicott* (1868)—both part of his *The New England Tragedies*, and the five-act blank verse drama *Judas Maccabaeus* (1872). Some of his works inspired dramatic and **musical*†** treatments, but Longfellow was not directly involved in those efforts.

THE LOTOS CLUB. Founded in 1870 as a "gentlemen's club" with a name suggested by Alfred, Lord Tennyson's poem, "The Lotos-Eaters," it was established by an assortment of young writers, newspapermen, and **critics.*†** The Lotos Club, which still exists after nearly 150 years, was a kind of literary society expansive enough to include writers, artists, musicians, and celebrities. Though no longer housed in its original site at 2 Irving Place near 14th Street in New York, its aims were social and included a desire to support literature and the arts in the United States. Its most celebrated members included presidents (William Howard Taft) and major literary figures (**Mark Twain**) and most leading theatrical figures during its early years before various theatrical **clubs,†** including **The Lambs,†** were formed.

LOVE AND FRIENDSHIP; OR, YANKEE† NOTIONS. A. B. Lindsley's comedy, first produced at the **Park Theatre** during the 1807–1808 season (and published in 1809), features Brother Jonathan, a **Yankee** character, in vehement condemnation of the slave trade's Middle Passage. Lindsley, a member of **Thomas Abthorpe Cooper**'s company, was barely out of his teens when the play was produced.

LOVE IN '76: AN INCIDENT OF THE REVOLUTION. **Oliver Bell Bunce**'s two-act "comedietta" opened at **Laura Keene**'s Theatre on 27 February 1857 for 10 performances. The play was frequently produced during the second half of the 19th century. Set during the **American Revolution**, the romantic play focused on Rose Ellsworth, played by Keene, a daughter of a family of British loyalists who is harboring an American captain in the family home to prevent his capture by English soldiers. Rose loves Captain Armstrong, played by M. V. Lingham, but she is forced to pretend romantic interest in two British officers, particularly Major Cleveland, who agrees to protect Armstrong to please Rose. However, Cleveland, suspecting a trick, compels Armstrong to marry Rose's maid, Bridget, to clear his own path to Rose. However, Rose, in disguise, switches places with Bridget at the ceremony and is married to Armstrong. Cleveland is outraged, but Rose threatens to expose his traitorous promise to protect Armstrong if he goes back on his promise of protection. The play's romanticism is most evident in Rose's curtain speech, wherein she proclaims, "The heart of love is heroic in every age; and after all / What difference can we affix, / 'Twixt love to-day and Love in '76!"

LUCAS, SAM (1840?–1916). Born Samuel Milady to free black parents in Washington, Ohio, Sam Lucas became a popular **African American*†** actor,*† comic, and songwriter. After a time working as a barber, Lucas began his career in **minstrel†** companies, performing on **tour*†** and riverboats. He became well-known in pitiful comic characters, but he desired to branch out into serious drama, appearing in a **musical*†** drama about a freed slave, *Out of Bondage*, in 1875, and the following year he appeared with **Sprague's Georgia Minstrels** with other black minstrel greats **James A. Bland** and **Billy Kersands**.

Lucas had his best opportunity in serious drama when **Charles†** and **Gustave Frohman†** staged an 1878 production of *Uncle Tom's Cabin†* with Lucas as the first African American to play the title role. The production was not successful through no fault of Lucas's, and he returned to the minstrel stage to appear with Emma and Anna Hyer. In 1890, he appeared in Sam T. Jack's *The Creole Show*, considered among the first minstrel shows to begin breaking away from the white traditions in the form. In 1898, he was in the Boston cast of *A Trip to Coontown*, the first musical produced, written, and directed entirely by African Americans. After 1900, he worked in **vaudeville†** and played Uncle Tom again, this time in a 1915 **film†** version. In various sources, his birth year is given as 1840, 1848, and 1850.

LUDLOW, NOAH MILLER (1795–1886). Born in New York City, Noah Miller Ludlow spent some time in Albany, New York, after the early death of his father, where he made his debut as an **actor*†** in 1813. Two years later, Ludlow moved to the American **frontier**—then in the midwestern United States—and is credited with producing the first English-language plays staged in New Orleans. In 1816, Ludlow may have been a pioneer of **showboating;†** that year, along with several fellow actors, he bought a Mississippi River keelboat (nicknamed "Ludlow's ark") and traveled the Mississippi and Ohio Rivers giving performances along the shore wherever an audience could be found. Ludlow married Mary Maury Squires, a Louisville widow, in 1817, with whom he fathered eight children. In partnership with **Samuel Drake**, he operated theaters in Kentucky and organized the American Theatrical Commonwealth Company, which performed in various territories of the American frontier where little organized theater had been seen. Though he acted throughout his long career, excelling in comic roles, he was never regarded as the finest of actors, but his canny management skills kept him in the forefront of provincial American theater.

In 1828, **Thomas Abthorpe Cooper** offered Ludlow the management of New York's **Chatham Garden Theatre**, but it was not a good fit, and Ludlow returned to the frontier, where, in 1835, he partnered with **Sol Smith** to revitalize the American Theatrical Commonwealth Company. In 1843, Ludlow took over management of the Royal Street Theatre in Mobile, Alabama, where he also built other theaters and became a cultural fixture. In this era, his partnership with Smith ended in rancor. He retired from active participation in theatrical endeavors in 1853, but late in life, with the assistance of one of his daughters, Ludlow wrote his autobiography, *Dramatic Life as I Found It*. Published in 1880, it is considered one of the best of the 19th-century theatrical memoirs, providing a valuable record of the evolution of American theater as it moved west.

LYTTON, EDWARD BULWER- (1803–1873). Born in London, England, Edward Bulwer-Lytton vacillated between political and literary careers. As a writer, he composed poetry as a youth, but gained fame for his novels and plays. His influence in the American theater resulted from stage adaptations by others of his novels, including *Eugene Aram* (1832), and from three original plays, the **melodramas†** *The Lady of Lyons* (1837) and *Richelieu* (1839), and a comedy, *Money* (1840), all of which he wrote for **William Charles Macready** and all of which held the American and English stages throughout the 19th century, providing popular vehicles for some of the major stage **stars*†** of the era.

MACAULEY'S THEATRE. Built in 1873 at Walnut Street (between Third and Fourth Streets) in Louisville, by Bernard "Barney" Macauley (1837–1886), a leading Kentucky **actor**,*† this facility became Louisville's foremost theater during the remainder of the 19th century. When Macauley fell into debt in 1879, he sold the theater to his younger brother, Colonel John T. Macauley (1846–1915), who operated the theater successfully, luring leading **stars**,*† including **Edwin Booth**,† Lillie Langtry,† **Sarah Bernhardt**,† George M. Cohan,*† and numerous others, to perform there. Louisville's own **Mary Anderson** made her stage debut as Juliet at Macauley's in 1875. In the 1910s, Macauley's began showing films† as well as live theater, and following a performance of *The Naughty Wife*, it was torn down in 1925.

MACK, ANDREW (1863–1931). Born in Boston as William Andrew McAloon, he established himself as an **actor***† and singer (and wrote such popular songs as "Heart of My Heart") in **vaudeville**† under the name Andrew Williams before taking the name Andrew Mack. He became well-known playing romantic leads in **Irish** plays, including *Myles Aroon* (1895) and *The Last of the Rohans* (1899). He concluded his career stepping into the role of the Irish father in the long-running ethnic comedy *Abie's Irish Rose*† in the 1920s.

†MACKAYE, STEELE (1842–1894). James Morrison Steele MacKaye was born in Buffalo, New York, the son of a lawyer and art fancier who sent him to Paris to study art. MacKaye returned to join the Union Army during the **Civil War** and rose to the rank of major before illness ended his service. After recovering, MacKaye returned to Paris and in 1869 studied with François Delsarte. Returning to the United States, MacKaye lectured on Delsarte's theories and opened a school in New York in 1871 to teach Delsarte's techniques.

MacKaye launched himself as an **actor***† and **playwright***† with *Monaldi* (1872), co-authored by **Francis Durivage**, but it failed to find an audience. He played Hamlet in London's Crystal Palace in 1873, after which he scored

New York successes with two plays, *Rose Michel* (1875) and *Won at Last* (1877). MacKaye assumed management of the **Fifth Avenue Theatre** and refurbished it with a **lighting***† system designed by Thomas A. Edison and other state-of-the-art equipment, including an innovative elevator stage that permitted shifting of **scenery**.*† Renamed the **Madison Square Theatre,**† MacKaye opened it with his hit play *Hazel Kirke*† (1880), which achieved the longest run of a **nonmusical***† work in the history of the American theater to that time. Management problems led to his loss of the theater, so MacKaye designed another theater, in which he planned to include a hotel, but it was never built.

In 1885, MacKaye designed the Lyceum Theatre, which again incorporated technical innovations, including space for a drama school. Among MacKaye's later plays, *Paul Kauvar; or, Anarchy*† (1887), a French Revolution **melodrama,**† won favor, as did *The Drama of Civilization* (1887). MacKaye also designed a Spectatorium for the 1893 Chicago World's Fair in which he planned to present *The World Finder*, a **pageant**† of Columbus's life, but the elaborate plan had to be scaled back due to a national economic downturn. He was the father of playwright Percy MacKaye.†

MACREADY, WILLIAM CHARLES (1793–1873). Born in London, England, the son of a theater **manager,***† William Charles Macready was educated at Rugby and hoped to attend Oxford, but his father's financial affairs compelled him to step into the theatrical trade. As an **actor,***† he scored his first success playing Romeo in a provincial production in 1810, followed by other **Shakespearean***† roles and his London debut in *The Distressed Mother* in 1816. Equally successful in Shakespeare's plays and contemporary romantic dramas, Macready rose to **stardom***† by the mid-1820s, scoring a triumph in **James Sheridan Knowles**'s *William Tell* in 1825. A year later, he embarked on his first **tour***† of the United States.

Back in England, Macready developed a professional relationship with Edward Bulwer-Lytton, who wrote several plays for Macready, including *The Lady of Lyons* (1837), *Richelieu* (1838), and *Money* (1840). Successful tours of the United States followed, but during a visit in 1849, a rivalry with American tragedian **Edwin Forrest** ended in tragedy with the **Astor Place Opera House riot**, in which the local militia was called out to stop the rioting and 22 people were killed, with scores of others injured. Two years later, Macready retired from the stage.

†MADISON SQUARE THEATRE. This small theater located on 24th Street near **Broadway***† in New York was built in 1862 and operated under various **managements**† as the Fifth Avenue **Opera House, Brougham's Theatre**, and from 1869 until it burned in 1873, Daly's **Fifth Avenue Thea-**

tre. Rebuilt and redesigned by **Steele MacKaye**,† and renamed Madison Square Theatre, it opened in 1879 and earned renown for its air-conditioning (air circulated over tons of ice and blown into the auditorium) and for its unique elevator stage (two stages, one above the other, so that one was in view of the audience, while the other, above or below, could be undergoing a change of scenery, thus reducing the time between acts to less than a minute). Renamed Hoyt's Theatre in 1891, it continued in use until it was razed in 1908.

MAEDER, FREDERICK G. (1840–1891). The son of **actress***† **Clara Morris** and composer James Maeder, Frederick George Maeder was born in New York and made his stage debut as Bernardo in a Portland, Maine, production of *Hamlet*. As an **actor**,*† he was most appreciated as a light comedian and often performed and **toured***† with his wife, Rena. Maeder found success as a **playwright**,*† crafting minor vehicles to order for actors, including *Black Sheep* (1867), *Red Riding Hood; or, Wolf's at the Door* (1868), *Help* (1871), *Lola* (1871), *Buffalo Bill* (1872), *Life's Peril; or, The Drunkard's Wife* (1872; co-authored by E. Z. C. Judson, aka **Ned Buntline**), *Nip, the Pretty Flower* (1873), *Hazel Eye, the Girl Trapper; or, The Gold Hunters* (1873), *Captain Jack* (1877), *The Runaway Wife* (1888; co-authored with **McKee Rankin**†), and *Diavolo* (1891). He was occasionally inspired by Ned Buntline's stories, and his 1872 play *Buffalo Bill* helped to create the legend of **William F. Cody**.†

*†MAGIC/MAGICIANS. The trade of conjuring predates Europeans in America, with **Native Americans***† performing magic as part of rituals, but by the 17th century, Puritanical authorities outlawed conjurers. Itinerant performers still managed to eke out a living performing tricks in taverns and other public spaces for fascinated audiences. The first well-known American magician, Jacob Philadelphia (1735–1795?), whose real name, Meyer, was dropped in favor of his hometown (and, presumably, to obscure his Jewish heritage), scored success in America and Europe with magic lantern "ghosts" (for which the term "phantasmagoria" was coined), with sleight-of-hand tricks, and through various technological devices.

Mixed-race performer Richard Potter, in the early 19th century, won popularity with magic tricks and ventriloquism as part of his act, paving the way for such fellow magicians as John Wyman (1816–1881) and Jonathan Harrington (1809–1881). With the rise of the **vaudeville**† stage, performers increasingly endeavored to create unique acts, including in the magical realm. Sisters Margaret (1833–1893) and Kate (1837–1892) Fox capitalized on the popularity of Spiritualism in the 1840s by convincing audiences that strange noises they conjured were communications from the spirit realm when, in fact, they later acknowledged that the sounds were made by crack-ing their toe knuckles. This sham did not stop numerous other entertainers† from similarly capitalizing on Spiritualism and fascination with ghosts and other such phenomena.

Other prestidigitators of the mid-19th century included the **Davenport Brothers**, Erastus (1839–1911) and William Henry (1841–1877), who were expert escape artists and mind readers, an art developed by Stuart Cumber-land (1857–1922), J. Randall Brown (late 19th/early 20th century), and Washington Irving Bishop (1855–1889). Perhaps the most famous American magician of the late 19th century was **Alexander Herrmann** (1844–1896), a French-born performer whose presence was enhanced by formal wear and a goatee, establishing an image for magicians that pervaded the stage into the 20th century.

Following Herrmann's 1896 death, his wife, Adelaide Herrmann (1853–1922), stepped into the void to become the first successful **woman***† magician in an act she developed over a four-decade career. These 19th-century magicians and mentalists paved the way for such figures as Harry Kellar,† Harry Houdini,† and others who became major **stars***† in the early 20th century—and vaudeville stages were populated with magicians until the demise of the variety stage in the 1930s. With the advent of television varie-ty, magicians again reappeared, and many found solo fame well into the 21st century.

MAGUIRE, THOMAS (1820?–1896). Born in New York, presumably to poor parents, Thomas Maguire scrapped his way up from poverty through Tammany Hall connections and work as a cabbie in the theater district. In his 20s, he caught the gold fever of the '49ers and went to California, though his success came through running saloons. He ultimately became known as the "Napoleon of San Francisco Theater" through his operation of several thea-ters, beginning in 1850 with the Jenny Lind Theatre in the Parker House, a hotel he operated. In 1854, he built **Maguire's Opera House**, which became San Francisco's foremost theater for several decades. To enhance his mana-gerial success, he enticed **leading**† **actors***† from the East to perform in San Francisco, and he established the San Francisco **Minstrels**,† a popular enter-tainment† **attraction**† in the city. As his predominance declined in the 1870s, he moved to New York in 1878, hoping to become a force in theater there, but was unsuccessful and died in poverty.

MAGUIRE'S OPERA HOUSE. San Francisco's leading theater in the mid-19th century, it was built and operated by **Thomas Maguire** from 1854 to the mid-1870s. Built on Washington Street, between Kearny and Montgomery Streets, Maguire's ultimately attracted such **stars*†** as **Adah Isaacs Menken**, appearing in her scandalous *Mazeppa*, **Junius Brutus Booth Jr.**, and many others.

THE MAINE QUESTION. **Nathaniel H. Bannister**'s play opened at New York's Franklin Theatre on 19 February 1839, with Bannister himself playing Bob Buckeye, in this drama debating the northeastern boundary disputes leading to the Aroostock War with Great Britain and Canada. General Winfield Scott was a major character in this highly topical play.

MAJOR JACK DOWNING; OR, THE RETIRED POLITICIAN. This anonymous play opened at the **Park Theatre** on 10 May 1834 with **James H. Hackett** in the title role. This **Yankee†** play was based on the writings of humorist Seba Smith (1792–1868) and suited Hackett, who had attained fame in a series of such roles. Smith, who coined the phrase "there's more than one way to skin a cat," applied satire and vernacular language in his fiction, which greatly amused his readership. These techniques were emphasized in this play about his fictional New England hero, who first appears in his writings around 1830.

*†MANAGER. *See* *†ACTOR/MANAGER.

†MARBLE FAMILY. The Marbles are less known than other American **acting*†** dynasties like the **Booths†** or the **Barrymores*†** because the Marble family remained devoted to **repertory*†** in the Midwest. **Dan** and Anna (Warren) Marble ultimately had four children in the profession: William "Billy" (1840–1912), John (1844–1919), Edward (1846–1900), and Emma (1848–1930). Edward's daughter Anna (1880–1946) was a **playwright*†** and **press agent†** who married Channing Pollock.†

MARBLE, DAN (1810–1849). Born in East Windsor, Connecticut, Danforth Marble unfortunately had a short life and, as such, a short career, but despite this he was the patriarch of a dynasty of **actors.*†** With his wife, Anna Warren, he fathered four children: William, John, Edward (Edward's daughter Anna was a **playwright*†** and **press agent†** married to Channing Pollock†), and Emma. During the 10 years or so of his active career, Dan Marble was acclaimed as one of the best of the **Yankee† dialect** actors of the time.

Marble had actually begun his career as an apprentice silversmith and paid $20 for the opportunity of making his theatrical debut at the **Chatham Garden Theatre** in 1831. His vehicles were not in and of themselves notable, but provided ample opportunity for Marble to generate comedy, including in such plays as *The Forest Rose* (1825), *Yankee Land* (1834), **Sam Patch, or The Daring Yankee** (1836), **The Vermont Wool Dealer** (1838), **The Stage-Struck Yankee** (1845), and *The Backwoodsman; or, The Gamecock of the Wilderness* (1846). Marble's vehicles tended toward the romantic and had a Western environment, which, to some extent, accommodated Marble's rough, weather-beaten appearance.

THE MARBLE HEART; OR, THE SCULPTOR'S DREAM: A RO-MANCE OF REAL LIFE. Charles Selby's five-act drama adapted from a French play, *Les Filles De Marbre* by Barrière and Thiboust, was first produced at the **Laura Keene** Theatre in New York on 18 November 1856, **starring***† Keene in the role of Mlle. Marco, a ruthless, unfeeling woman willing to do anything or sacrifice anyone to become wealthy. She is, in fact, chiseled out of marble by a sculptor who carves her a marble heart; the sculptor loves his creation, but she rejects him. Keene scored a personal success in the role, and though other **actresses***† appeared in the part, none were seen by **critics***† to equal Keene's performance. **John Wilkes Booth**† appeared successfully in a production of the play in Washington, DC, and on 8 November 1863, President and Mrs. **Abraham Lincoln** saw his performance.

MARCO BOZZARIS; THE GRECIAN HERO. **Oliver Bell Bunce**'s three-act blank verse **melodrama**† opened on 10 June 1850 at the **Bowery Theatre**, with **James W. Wallack Jr.**, Mrs. Wallack (Ann Duff Sefton), and **John Gilbert**. Though there was a poem by Fitz-Greene Halleck that might well have supplied a dramatic outline for Bunce, he preferred to turn directly to historical accounts of the life and adventures of one of the Greeks' most beloved national heroes, Markos Botsaris (1788–1823), the Greek general and hero of the Greek **war***† of independence and captain of the Souliotes. The play was popular with Bowery audiences and ran the balance of the **repertory***† season.

MARKOE, PETER (1752–1792). West Indies–born, Peter Markoe moved to Philadelphia in 1783 following an education at Oxford. He remained in Philadelphia for the remainder of his short but productive life. He wrote an epistolary novel (*The Algerine Spy in Pennsylvania*), poetry, and two plays, **The Patriot Chief** (1784) and *The Reconciliation* (1790), with the latter being one of the first ballad operas composed in the United States. *The Patriot Chief* reflected on the problems of the aristocratic elements of society, and in 1788 he wrote a poem, "The Times," satirizing Philadelphia high society, clearly a recurring theme for Markoe.

†MARSDEN, FRED (1842–1888). Born William A. Sliver in Baltimore, Maryland, he gave up his law practice and changed his name to become an **actor**.*† However, it was his work as a writer of stage material for celebrities that made him a fortune. He wrote regularly for stage **Irishmen**, including Joe Murphy† (for whom Marsden wrote *Kerry Gow*, 1880), Roland Reed (*Cheek*, 1883), and William J. Scanlan† (*The Irish Minstrel*, 1884). Among his other plays produced in New York were *Zip, or Point Lynne Light* (1874), *Musette* (1876), and *Otto, a German* (1881). He committed suicide at the height of his success, and the event was immortalized in a poem by William Topaz McGonagall suggesting that estrangement from his daughter Blanche, who had become romantically involved with a married man, was the tragic cause of Marsden's death.

MARSH JUVENILE TROUPE. A traveling company of **child**† performers (also known as Marsh's **Juvenile**† Comedians), they **toured***† the United States from coast to coast and also Australia. Members of the troupe ultimately had careers as adult **actors**.*† Founded by R. G. Marsh, the troupe attained a surprisingly high level of popularity in the late 1850s, but the novelty of their programs of short plays (*Beauty and the Beast*, *The Rough Diamond*, and *The Loan of a Lover*) alternating with songs and dances wore out relatively quickly. A surviving full-length engraving of the troupe shows 16 girls and three boys. A tragedy befell the troupe in 1859, here as reported in "The Death of Little Mary Marsh," in the *Plain Dealer* (Ohio):

> Knowing how much interest you have always taken in our little children and especially in the pet of the company, "Little Mary," I thought I would let you know about the horrible accident which caused her death. On Wednesday night last, after the first act of the "Naiad Queen," Mary, in her blightsome glee ran tripping across the stage so near a candle that the flare of it caught the bottom of her fairy dress, and in a moment she was a mass of flame. Her mother and Georgiana were instantly by her side, but she was literally a ball of fire, and in their efforts to smother the flame were themselves badly burned. Poor little Mary screamed terrifically and the house was in frightful commotion. It was soon all over with her. She died the next afternoon.
>
> Her poor father and mother are almost distracted, but we are all comforted with the hope that she is where suffering and death are known no more. She died with the name of "Mother" on her lips, and with the prayers of all her little companions in her behalf.

Despite this tragedy—and the company's success—it was reported in its aftermath that "none of the Marsh Juveniles ever became **stars***† of more than common magnitude, and none of them are shining brilliantly on the stage to-day."

MARSTON, RICHARD (1847–1917). Born in Brighton, England, as the son of admired **Shakespearean***† **actor***† Henry Marston, he followed his father onto the stage as an actor. When he left England for the United States in 1867, he began to devote his energies almost exclusively to **scene design,***† and as he began he won the plum job of creating new scenery for the long-running **musical***† **melodrama***† *The Black Crook*, which has come to be viewed as the prototype of the first modern musical. When *The White Fawn*, the follow-up to *The Black Crook*, was produced in 1868, the **producers***† turned to Marston, but the production flopped.

He was a prolific designer, creating scenes for **John Brougham**'s plays and the **San Francisco Minstrels** and, ultimately, became house designer for the **Union Square Theatre**, where he designed *Rose Michel* (1875) and *A Parisian Romance* (1883). Later, Marston was house designer for the **Madison Square Theatre** and, increasingly, worked in musical theater, including such works as *The Devil's Deputy* (1894), *Fleur-de-Lis* (1895), *Half a King* (1896), and *A Little Bit of Everything* (1904). His occasional returns to straight plays were successes, including *The Great Diamond Robbery* (1895) and Richard Mansfield's† *Cyrano de Bergerac* (1898), which he designed in its first US production.

MARTIN, JOHN (1770–1807). William Dunlap referred to Martin as the first "native-born" American to become a professional **actor,***† but scholars believe that a Princeton student named Greville owns that honor. Martin did, however, have a long, active career, debuting as Young Norval in *Douglas* at the **John Street Theatre** in 1791. Despite Dunlap's error, Martin is undoubtedly the first "native-born" actor to achieve a busy and successful career, despite his early death. Dunlap records that Martin was essentially a **juvenile,**† but effective in both comedy and tragedy. He also played important roles in *The Duenna* (Mendoza), *Julius Caesar* (Octavius), and *Macbeth* (Malcolm), and was the first to play Ferdinand in *Tammany; or, The Indian Chief* (1794).

MASON, MRS. (1780–1835). The English-born **actress***† began her career in the British Isles, establishing popularity in comedy in Dublin and Edinburgh before leaving Europe for the United States in 1809, making her debut at the **Park Theatre** and, in short order, establishing that she was equally skilled in classics and contemporary plays. She married several times and so was, at various points, billed as Mrs. Entwistle and Mrs. Crooke. Her popularity won her large audiences for several seasons at Philadelphia's **Chestnut Street Theatre** and in New Orleans.

MATHEWS, CHARLES (1776–1835). Born in London, England, Charles Mathews was a bookseller's son and was educated at Merchant Taylors School in Lancashire. He became a celebrated comedian through his skills at parody and mimicry, and his quick wit, providing humor based on the culture of the moment and the celebrities of his time. He also provided memorable performances in virtually every classical comedy and many contemporary works. Mathews also succeeded as a theater **manager**.*

He became an **actor***† in the mid-1790s, appearing in the provinces and Dublin from 1794 prior to his 1803 London debut as Lingo in John O'Keefe's *The Agreeable Surprise*. It is believed he created no fewer than 400 characters and was a fixture of London's major theaters. He scored a major hit in Richard Brinsley Sheridan's *The Critic*, but it was only one among many such successes. The true versatility and skill of Mathews were displayed notably in his series of "At Home" performances, which allowed him the free range a single role denied him. The first of these, at the Lyceum Theatre in 1818, established Mathews as a singular talent. He was well-liked offstage by colleagues and well-known as a famous name even to those who had never seen him perform.

In 1822, Mathews made his first trip to the United States; his performances included many amusing observations of the country and were triumphant. He intended frequent visits to America and returned again in 1834–1835, offering his "At Home" performances and appearing as Samuel Coddle in *Married Life* and Andrew Steward in *The Lone House* shortly before his death. Poet Horace Smith wrote in the aftermath of Mathews's passing, "There was but one Charles Mathews in the world—there never can be such another! Mimics, buffoons, jesters, wags, and even admirable comedians we shall never want; but what are the best of them compared to him?"

Mathews's son, Charles Mathews Jr. (1803–1878), followed his father into theatrical life, but as a more conventional **actor**.*† He made his debut in 1835 at the **Olympic Theatre** and eventually married **Madame Vestris**, **manager***† of the Olympic. His first attempt at performing in America was not well received; however, following the death of Vestris in 1856 he again visited the United States and, beginning in 1861, scored success in a series of "At Home" performances in his father's style. He **toured***† many countries of the world, including three extended visits to the United States, making his last American appearance at **Wallack's Theatre** in 1872.

MATHEWS, CORNELIUS (1817–1889). A Port Chester, New York, native, Cornelius Mathews was an important figure in the formation of American literature from the 1830s. Along with Evert Duyckinck and William Gilmore Sims, he formed a literary group, Young America, with the goal of raising the quality of American literature in general. However, he first attended Columbia College, New York University, and passed the bar in 1837.

The general assumption in the early 19th century was that American literature was essentially inferior to British literature (as was true of theater as well), and the teaching of literature urged writers to follow English style and technique. Mathews and his Young America peers opposed the pro-British view, which was most vigorously espoused by Lewis Gaylord Clark, editor of *Knickerbocker* magazine. Mathews proposed Rabelais as a model, and for two years, with Duyckinck he edited *Arcturus*, in which they published works by such figures as **Nathaniel Hawthorne** and **Henry Wadsworth Longfellow**. Mathews was also in favor of strong copyright laws, but met with much opposition, including some notable writers.

Along with working on a number of periodicals, Mathews wrote six novels, three collections of poetry, and four plays, though the first, *The Politician* (1840), was never produced. His other plays included *Witchcraft; or, The Martyrs of Salem* (1846), *Jacob Leisler* (1848), and *False Pretenses; or, Both Sides of Good Society* (1855). He held no particular devotion to the stage, but simply seemed inclined to try his hand at every available form of literature.

†**MATINEE GIRL.** Since it was considered appropriate for women to attend the theater during daylight hours without male escort (it was deemed inappropriate at night), matinee audiences were predominantly women. Young ladies often attended in small groups on a regular basis, enjoying— perhaps as much as the plays—the freedom from male supervision as well as the justification for daytime wardrobe enhancement. The matinee girl made an obsession of her theatergoing and became a devoted fan of certain **actors***† known as **matinee idols**.† She would imitate an admired **actress**'s*† style of dress or manner of wearing a hat, for example, converting the actress into a model of fashion.

†**MATINEE IDOL.** A term applied to handsome **leading men**† who attracted large audiences of **women***† to matinee performances of popular **melodramas**† and comedies, it later applied to **film**† actors. Some historians describe **John Wilkes Booth**† as a matinee idol at the height of his career, from the late 1850s until his assassination of President **Abraham Lincoln** in 1865 ended his career. In the case of matinee idol John Barrymore,*† for example, the term applied to him at the height of his stage career (1910s–1920s) and on-screen (1920s–1930s).

†**MATTHEWS, BRANDER (1852–1929).** Born in New Orleans, the son of wealthy parents, James Brander Matthews moved to New York, where he attended Columbia University. He began law school in 1871, but when his family's fortunes collapsed he took a job writing for *The Nation* (1875–1895). Matthews also completed several plays, including *Margery's Lovers* (1878), *A Gold Mine* (1889), and *On Probation* (1889). He had a deep interest in French literature and theater, and this led to a position teaching literature at Columbia University in 1891. In 1902, Matthews became the first American academic called Professor of Dramatic Literature. Among his two dozen books on theater are *The French Dramatists of the Nineteenth Century* (1882), *Actors**† *and Actresses** *of Great Britain and the United States* (1886; a five-volume work co-authored with Laurence Hutton†), *Development of the Drama* (1903), *Principles of Playmaking* (1919), and two autobiographies, *These Many Years* (1917) and *Rip Van Winkle†* *Goes to the Play* (1926).

MAY-DAY IN TOWN; OR, NEW YORK IN AN UPROAR. **Royall Tyler**'s two-act **opéra bouffe** was performed on 19 May 1787 at the **John Street Theatre. Lewis Hallam Jr.** was in the cast, but it was deemed unsuccessful, and there were no further performances scheduled. It is believed that the farcical plot depicted the chaos caused in New York City on 1 May, a day established for both landlords and tenants for moving households. The play and its music are not known to survive.

MAYO, FRANK (1839–1896). Born in Boston as Frank Maguire Mayo, he moved to the other American coast—namely, San Francisco—in his late teens and, within a few years, was playing **supporting**† roles opposite **Edwin Booth**.† His parts grew in size, and he was appreciated in several classical characters, but Mayo won particular attention as Badger in **Dion Boucicault**'s† *The Streets of New York* in 1865. In New York, Mayo had his first major success as Ferdinand in *The Tempest* in 1869, which starred **E. L. Davenport** as Prospero. Despite skill in **Shakespeare,***† Mayo's greatest success came in the title role of **Frank H. Murdoch**'s *Davy Crockett* (1873)—and he was so popular in the part that he only rarely played anything else for the remainder of his career. Mayo said he patterned the character on two famous Americans: **Mark Twain** and Joe Goodman. In response to an 1879 performance, New York's *Spirit of the Times* wrote of Mayo's Crockett: "With a splendid presence, a rich voice, variety almost endless of facial and vocal expression, and also of picturesque attitude, he gave us a fresh, breezy picture of a new life, and was by turns friendless and vigorous, humorous and tender, always truthful."

†*MAZEPPA; OR, THE WILD HORSE OF TARTARY.* H. M. Milner's 1831 dramatization of Lord Byron's 1819 poem, based on the legend of Isaac Mazeppa, the 17th-century Ukrainian folk hero, was a popular success of significant proportions. At the climax of the three-act **melodrama,**† a youthful Mazeppa is stripped naked and tied to the back of a "fiery untamed steed" and sent galloping over mountainous terrain through torrential storms with thunder and lightning, followed by ravenous wolves while a vulture circles above. In some productions, the effect might be handled cheaply with a cardboard cutout horse and victim manipulated upstage, but more elaborate productions featured a treadmill with a moving **panorama**† to depict the ride through a hostile landscape. When a live horse was used for that scene, Mazeppa was often represented as a dummy strapped to its back, unless the **actor***† was also an accomplished **equestrian.**†

The turgid play got a second lease on life in 1861 when the **manager***† of the Green Street Theatre in Albany hit upon the idea of casting a **woman***† as Mazeppa and creating the illusion of **seminudity** by costuming the **actress***† in **fleshings**† under a flimsy bit of tunic. **Adah Isaacs Menken**† caused a sensation in the role, which launched her to international celebrity and inspired a slew of imitators. For the wilderness ride, she was strapped to a trained horse that negotiated a narrow, winding ramp on scaffolding camouflaged by painted **scenery.***† That production moved to **Broadway,*** and Menken subsequently **toured***† nationwide in the role. Other actresses closely associated with the role of Mazeppa were Kate Raymond at Donnelly's **Olympic Theatre**, Brooklyn, in 1869; Vernona Jarbeau on national tours in the 1880s; and **Leo Hudson**, who, along with her horse, died as a result of injuries suffered when her horse fell from the scaffolding.

MCCABE, JAMES D. (1842–1883). Born James Dabney McCabe Jr. in Richmond, Virginia, as the son of a journalist and Episcopal clergyman, McCabe was educated at the Virginia Military Institute, but during the **Civil War** he began writing an astonishing number of short stories, essays, poetry, and translations of a range of works, many written under various pseudonyms. He also wrote plays during that era (also under pseudonyms), including *The Guerillas; or, The War in Virginia* (1862), as well as a variety of writings about the war, including *The Life of Lieutenant General T. J. Jackson* (1863), *The Aide-de-Camp: A Romance of the War* (1863), *The Gray-Jackets* (1867), *The Secrets of the Great City* (1868), *The New Administration* (1869), and *Paris by Sunlight and Gaslight* (1870).

MCCLOSKEY, JAMES J. (1825–1913). Born in Canada, McCloskey was a '49er in California who first turned to the stage, working with most of the great **actors**† of the era before switching to **playwriting.***† Most of his plays were **melodramas**† and often recounted events from his time in California, including *Daring Dick* (1870), *Rory of the Hills* (1870), *The Far West* (1870), *The Trail of the Serpent* (1871), *Across the Continent; or Scenes from New York Life and the Pacific Railroad* (1871), *Poverty Flat* (1873), *For Lack of Gold* (1873), *Life or Death* (1874), *Arabs of New York* (1875), *Buff and Blue* (1876), *Nuggets* (1880), and *The Bowery Boys* (1881). Only *Across the Continent* was a major success, so McCloskey enhanced his income by working as a **manager***† at various times for the Marysville Theatre in California and the **Park Theatre** in Brooklyn. His last years were spent as a New York City court clerk.

†MCCULLOUGH, JOHN (1832–1885). Born John Edward McCullough in Coleraine, Ireland, he came to the United States at 15, learned his craft by performing with **amateur***† companies, and made his professional debut on 15 August 1857 in *The Belle's Stratagem* at the **Arch Street Theatre** in Philadelphia. During the 1860s, he **toured***† as second lead to **Edwin Forrest** and, following Forrest's death, scored successes in a few of Forrest's most famous roles, including *The Gladiator* and *Virginius*. McCullough also performed in support of **Edwin Booth**.† He subsequently turned to **management**,*† running the California Theatre in San Francisco in partnership with **Lawrence Barrett**;† Barrett departed in 1870, and McCullough continued.

In 1877, due to financial reverses, he was compelled to give up the theater and return to acting. McCullough's last decade was spent touring as a **star***† in historical **melodramas**† and **Shakespeare**.*† He was physically imposing and handsome, with a grand heroic style that was already seen as old-fashioned in the 1880s, when he suffered periods of mental instability resulting from paresis. The respect felt for McCullough by his fellow players is touchingly evoked in *Footlights and Spotlights* by **Otis Skinner**,† who called "Genial John" one of the "finest spirits" he ever met, and in *Fifty Years of Make-Believe* **Frederick Warde**† praised McCullough as "an honor to the profession that he so conspicuously adorned."

MCINTYRE, JAMES (1857–1937) and HEATH, THOMAS (1852–1938). This **minstrel**† duo won great popularity in **vaudeville**† during their long partnership. James McIntyre was born in Kenosha, Wisconsin, and went to work in his youth to help support his widowed mother. One of his jobs was to sell candy on trains, and if he felt the passengers were disinterested or bored, he would sing, dance, and tell jokes to win their interest. He learned clog dancing and other tricks of the theatrical trade before working in **circus***† and minstrel shows. At the height of his solo career, he claimed in an interview to have invented the buck-and-wing style of tap dancing.

In 1874, McIntyre met Thomas Kurton Heath, who was born in Philadelphia, and the two performers with complementary skills developed a **blackface†** tramp minstrel act in which McIntyre played Alexander Hambletonian and Heath was Henry Jones, a clever black entertainer† who often outsmarts Hambletonian. Their teaming lasted an astonishing 50 years, during which time they worked under two managers, **Tony Pastor†** and **B. F. Keith**, who booked the team in both vaudeville and on **Broadway**.*† Among their standout efforts, *The Ham Tree* was performed 90 times in 1905 at the New York Theatre (with a cast including W. C. Fields†); *In Hayti* was performed 56 times at the Circle Theatre in 1909; *Hello, Alexander* played 56 times at the 44 Street Theatre in 1919: and *Red Pepper* was performed 24 times at the Shubert Theatre in 1922.

MCVICKER, JAMES H. (1822–1896). New York–born **actor*†** and **manager*†** James H. McVicker began his career in New Orleans theaters and won kudos from audiences in his interpretation of **Yankee†** roles. Despite his success in New Orleans, McVicker moved to Chicago in 1857, where he opened his own theater, quickly emerging as the **leading†** actor and manager in the city. He managed theaters in other cities, most successfully New York's Lyceum Theatre, which he took over in 1876, opening with **Edwin Booth†** as Hamlet and McVicker as the First Gravedigger. Booth subsequently married McVicker's daughter, **Mary**.

MCVICKER, MARY. *See* BOOTH, MARY MCVICKER (1849–1881).

MCVICKER'S THEATRE. Located in Chicago at 25 W. Madison Street, McVicker's Theatre, named for its **star*†** **actor*†** and **manager,*†** **James H. McVicker**, opened its doors in 1857 at the cost of $85,000. The Great Chicago **Fire†** of 1871 completely destroyed the theater. The following year the theater was rebuilt on a grander scale, featuring **legitimate†** theater, opera, and **minstrel†** shows. In 1884–1885, the firm of Adler and Sullivan remodeled the building, but another fire in 1890 required them to return and redesign the theater. Louis Sullivan, who emerged as one of the great **architects** of his era, provided floral stencil-work decorations in the auditorium and other public spaces in the building. In 1922, McVicker's was torn down to build another structure, this time designed by the firm of Newhouse & Bernham to serve as a cinema. In 1960, McVicker's showed its first Cinerama film,† but finally turned to pornographic films in the 1970s, and the theater was torn down in 1985.

†**MCWADE, ROBERT (1835–1913).** The eminent **actor*†** was born in Long Sault Rapids, Canada, and made his stage debut at Detroit's Metropolitan **Opera House** following employment in a varnish factory. He joined the Union Army as a private at the outbreak of the **Civil War**, but was a full second lieutenant by the time he was given a disability discharge. He became an American citizen in 1889. His long career encompassed engagements with such luminaries as **Charlotte Cushman, Edwin Booth,†** and many others. His own version of *Rip Van Winkle†* was a mainstay of his career for 23 years and rivaled but did not eclipse the Rip of **Joseph Jefferson**.† He made several short silent films† in 1912–1913.

MEDICINE SHOWS. The origins of medicine shows are murky, but such shows clearly existed in Europe as early as the Middle Ages. In early America, medicine shows were first seen in the 18th century, and possibly earlier, but around the time of the **American Revolution** local laws either banned or restricted the excesses of medicine shows, which seemed, by that time, to be common and long-familiar activities. A typical American medicine show **toured*†** (most popularly in the western states and territories and the rural South) with wagons pulled by horses and alternated entertainments† with aggressive pitches for salesmen peddling "miracle elixirs" or "snake oil" "guaranteed" to cure virtually any ailment. The entertainments included songs and dances, comedy, flea **circuses,*† magic**, freak shows, animal acts, etc.

It seems increasingly probable, especially as medicine shows continued into the 20th century in rural areas, that audiences were well aware that the drugs for sale were harmless and probably fraudulent, but the entertainment was welcome, and the cheap price of the bottle of magic elixir was an acceptable expenditure for the fun. From the 18th to the 20th centuries, medicine shows slowly adapted to changes in the entertainment media and found their way into the new forms, from **vaudeville†** and **burlesque*†** to radio, films,† and television until essentially disappearing as electronic media offered so much advertisement that medicine show pitches were eclipsed.

MEDINA, LOUISA (1813?–1838). This Spanish American **playwright*†** was born Louisa Honor de Medina in Europe, and she arrived in the United States sometime between 1831 and 1833 after receiving a classical education. She was able to demonstrate her abilities as an adaptor and **dramatist*†** almost immediately and especially impressed **Thomas S. Hamblin, actor*†-manager*†** of the **Bowery Theatre**. It is perhaps not surprising that it took a **woman*†** dramatist to transform stage heroines from essentially passive beings to full participants within the complications of the plot.

Impressive among her adaptations were plays based on two novels by **Edward Bulwer-Lytton**, *The Last Days of Pompeii* (1835) and *Ernest Maltravers* (1838), and **Robert Montgomery Bird**'s *Nick of the Woods* (1838). They demonstrate the wide range of Medina's ability to adapt to the world of the particular source material in her dramatic adaptations; these are three distinctly different works in setting, time period, local color, etc., yet Medina seems to have mastered all three—and was particularly applauded for plays containing spectacle. *Nick of the Woods*, for example, depicts an **Indian** riding a flaming canoe over a waterfall.

Other Medina plays of the 34 credited to her (although only 11 have been verified) include *Wacousta; or, The Curse* (1833), *Norman Leslie* (1836), and *Rienzi* (1836). According to contemporary **critics**,*† the Medina-adapted **melodramas**† were produced with great spectacle and provided the Bowery with their first long-running successes. A *New York Mirror* critic, responding to the success of *Ernest Maltravers*, offered a short assessment of Medina's skills:

> Louisa H. Medina, who is [a] remarkably clever woman . . . Her power of composition is said to be astonishingly rapid. She is partial to startling and terrible catastrophes. Her knowledge of stage effect is very great and there is an impassioned ardour in her poetry, which enhances the thrilling interest of her pieces. It has been objected to them that their story departs from that of the novels on which some of them are based; and this objection, as we think, redounds to her praise, for it is evidence of the fertility of her invention—which is one of the highest attributes of true genius.

Medina and Hamblin, who had clearly evolved into effective artistic collaborators, were likely married, though Hamblin's romantic shenanigans are such that it is not clear when or if divorces or marriage occurred. Hamblin referred to Medina as Mrs. Hamblin, and they had a daughter together, Louisa Medina Hamblin.

MELMOTH, MRS. CHARLOTTE (1749–1823). The early life of **actress***† Mrs. Charlotte Melmoth is obscure, though she was the estranged wife of Courtney Melmoth (the pseudonym for Samuel Jackson Pratt). Melmoth was an **actor**,*† and as far as is known, she followed him onstage. They were close friends of Benjamin Franklin, but financial woes seem to have undermined their marriage. She made her stage debut at the Smock Alley Theatre in Dublin in May 1773 in a production of *The Orphan*. They established their own theater in Drogheda, but it quickly failed. She made her London debut in February 1774 in *The Fair Penitent*, and **critics***† admired her attractiveness and her well-interpreted performances as Calista. The Melmoths had both success and failure in England and Ireland, but developed solid reputations. They made their final appearance together at the Smock in Dublin, where they had begun, and their marriage ended.

Charlotte Melmoth arrived in New York in 1793 and won appreciative reviews giving recitations and readings from **Shakespeare**. Within months, she joined **John Hodgkinson**'s **American Company** at the **John Street Theatre**, where she debuted on 20 November 1793 in *The Grecian Daughter*. Over the subsequent five years, Melmoth specialized in a range of tragic roles, including Lady Macbeth, which had been one of her most acclaimed performances in England and Ireland. **William Dunlap** and leading critics praised Melmoth highly as the finest tragedienne of her generation. One setback came in 1794 when she refused to deliver the prologue to Ann Hatton's *Tammany*, objecting to its patriotic sentiments. There was a backlash in the press, with some calls for boycotting her performances, but in 1798 she was appearing successfully at the **Park Theatre** as its **leading woman**.†

Melmoth gained considerable weight and reluctantly gave up playing her specialty roles and instead performed **character**† parts and was seen as outstanding in such roles. Melmoth labored in the Park's company until 1805, when she joined the **Chestnut Street Theatre** in Philadelphia. In 1811, while traveling to fulfill an engagement† at New York's **Olympic Theatre**, she was in a serious carriage accident and suffered a bad fracture to her arm, which failed to heal. Reluctantly, she retired to run a seminary for girls and a dairy farm.

†MELODRAMA. The dominant dramatic genre on the American stage throughout the entire 19th century and beyond, melodrama began to lose its edge only in the 20th century when the influence of Henrik Ibsen† and a growing preference for plays of psychological realism*† relegated the popular appeals of melodrama first to the "ten-twenty-thirty"† theaters and then to silent films.†

Melodrama had taken hold in Europe by 1800 with the widespread translation and staging of German-language plays by **August von Kotzebue** and French plays by Guilbert de Pixérécourt, both of whom deployed gripping plots leavened by sentimentality and humor. American adaptations of their style came as early as **William Dunlap** and **Mordecai Noah**, who established the fairy-tale melodrama on the early 19th-century American stage, followed by romantic historical melodramas like those written for **Edwin Forrest**. By midcentury, **Thomas S. Hamblin**, **actor***†-**manager***† of New York's **Bowery Theatre**,† demonstrated the viability of maintaining a **stock***† company to perform blood-and-guts melodrama for working-class audiences.

A growing demand for spectacle spawned what Bruce McConachie terms "apocalyptic melodramas," featuring stage depictions of conflagrations, shipwrecks, natural disasters, street riots, and battlefield action. After the **Civil War** and the enduring example of the unprecedented popularity of the abolitionist melodrama *Uncle Tom's Cabin*, the form was often co-opted by social reformers, with **temperance**† plays as a prominent subcategory. While the spectacular effects of **sensation dramas**† continued to draw popular audiences throughout the modernist era, the genre also took a turn toward depicting the familiar realism of the lives of its patrons after 1870. Among the most successful authors of plays with sensational effects were **Augustin Daly**,† **Dion Boucicault**,† and later, Owen Davis.*† Those who kept their stories more grounded in everyday experience included **Bronson Howard**,† Clyde Fitch,† **Steele MacKaye**,† and **William Gillette**.†

While certain aspects of melodrama—clear distinctions between good and evil, suspenseful situations, spectacle, tight and logically structured linear action—will likely always have a place in drama, the genre itself gradually fell out of fashion as the film† industry siphoned off its customer base. By the early 20th century, the grand manner of **acting***† that was so effective in scenes of pathos or terror appeared to audiences as overwrought and even laughable. In the 21st century, 19th-century melodrama is often misunderstood and assumed to be something more like a parody of melodrama, but these plays were performed with the utmost seriousness and at their best thrilled audiences; the element of parody arises from pre-realism stage conventions employed in times in which these devices have been modernized and exceeded in other forms like film and television.

MELVILLE, EMILY (1850–1932). Born in Philadelphia, Emily (or Emilie or Emelie) Melville was a **child**† **actor***† equal to any prodigy. At five, she played the Duke of York to **Edwin Forrest**'s Richard III in Providence, Rhode Island. She was the major child **star***† of the western circuit and spent much of her time in Louisville, before moving to San Francisco in 1868, where, at 18, she made an official transition to adulthood. In San Francisco she spent a remarkable 60 years as one of the city's favorite **actresses**.*† She was remarkably versatile, moving easily from playing **ingénues**† and prima donnas of **opéra bouffe** to dramatic roles, including those in **Shakespeare**'s*† plays. In the 1920s, in her 70s, she played major older roles for the Alcazar Theatre's **stock***† company.

†MENKEN, ADAH ISAACS (1835–1868). A scandalous figure on the international stage of the mid-19th century, Adah Isaacs Menken obscured her actual origins in creating her short legendary career. At various times, she claimed her real name was Dolores Adios Los Fiertesorn or Marie Rachel

Adelaide de Vere Spencer, but she was in fact born either Ada C. McCord or Adah Bertha Theodore at Milneburg, Louisiana (near New Orleans), or Memphis, Tennessee. Such confusion only aided what must be assumed was a desire to either create mystery regarding her past or obscure humble or scandalous origins.

Menken is remembered mostly as an **equestrian actress**† who revived interest in the old H. M. Milner **melodrama**,† adapted from a poem by Lord Byron, *Mazeppa*† (1831), by **cross-dressing***† to play the title role, which calls for a suggestion of **nudity** via **fleshings**† and a scanty costume (the character is stripped of clothes in a climactic scene and strapped to a horse). Menken's acting ability was questionable, and both her acting and the play received decidedly mixed reviews, but more than many of her contemporaries she understood the power of **sexuality**,*† celebrity, and the means to hone them to her advantage.

Offstage, she converted to Judaism when she married Jewish musician Alexander Isaac Menken, though the marriage did not last. Her second husband, prizefighter John C. Heenan, was the cause of a scandal when she was accused of bigamy for marrying Heenan before attaining a legal divorce from Menken. There would ultimately be more husbands and affairs in the wake of her triumph in *Mazeppa* and a successful **tour***† of Europe, resulting in greater fame and friendship with some of the great literary and artistic figures of her age, though her dreams of becoming a great tragic actress went unfulfilled.

THE MERCENARY MATCH: A TRAGEDY. **Barnabas Bidwell**'s blank verse tragedy in five acts was produced in 1784 at Yale, and like several of his contemporaries, Bidwell was influenced by the previous generation of politically minded American **dramatists**.*† However, the influence seemed to have little impact on raising the play's quality or supplying new innovations to the form. The plot is constructed around the nefarious misdeeds of the **villainous**† Major Shapely, a seducer of innocent women and a casual murderer. Shapely is dallying with Mrs. Jensen, but when she learns Shapely has killed her husband, she dies from the shock, and in a moralistic ending typical of the tragedies of the period, Shapely is executed by hanging. Though **William Dunlap** reported that Bidwell's classmates seemed to enjoy the play, it was not an effective tragedy in that the audience laughed throughout at the wrong moments—at poorly constructed lines, **amateurish***† acting, and overwrought moralizing.

MERRY, MRS. ANNE (1769–1808). A native of Bristol, England, Ann Brunton was the daughter of **actor***† John Brunton, **manager***† of the Theatre Royal, Norwich. She made her debut in *The Grecian Daughter* in Bath in early 1785. Her London debut at the Covent Garden Theatre in late 1785 came as Horatio in *The Roman Father*, and she excelled in a variety of roles there, being favorably compared to Sarah Siddons. In 1792, she married Robert Merry, a **playwright***† and poet known by his pseudonym, Della Crusca. Merry had financial woes, but his wife quit the stage and joined him in Paris, though they were soon completely broke and she decided to return to the stage. London was not possible due to family strains, so she sought an offer from **Thomas Wignell** at Philadelphia's New Theatre.

The Merrys arrived in the United States in 1796, and Mrs. Merry debuted as Juliet to acclaim; the plaudits continued over the next nine years (1797 to 1808) as she **toured***† American cities. Her husband died in 1798, and five years later, in 1803, she married Wignell, though he died very soon after their marriage. In 1806, she married again, this time to actor **William Warren**. Mrs. Merry consistently met with stage success, whether in **Shakespeare***† or in more contemporary works, including *The Fair Penitent*, *Jane Shore*, *The Fatal Dowry*, and *The Orphan*. Scholars generally consider Mrs. Merry the first major talent to leave Europe for a permanent career in America, and there is little reason to believe she was bested by any **actress***† of her generation.

THE MESTAYER FAMILY. American theater has produced a number of family dynasties since virtually the beginning. The Mestayer family of the 19th century is less known than the **Booths**,† **Jeffersons**,† **Drews**,† or **Barrymores**,† but it is somewhat unique in the variety of talents within the family. The Mestayers are believed to have come from France to America before the **American Revolution** and had performed as traveling players in France. The Mestayer patriarch, John, and his wife won considerable success performing as comedians. Their children spread themselves around the United States and mastered different skills. Among their children, daughter Emily was a popular **actress***† on both coasts, Joseph was the longtime **leading man**† of the **Boston Museum**, Anna Maria married **actor***† **Charles R. Thorne**, and the others worked as journeymen actors, including Louis, Augustus, John, Harry, and Charles. A grandson, William (Emily's son), was also a successful actor and **playwright**.*† When he died in November 1896, the stage dynasty of the Mestayers more or less died with him.

METAMORA; OR, THE LAST OF THE WAMPANOAGS. **John Augustus Stone**'s five-act drama opened on 15 December 1829 at the **Park Theatre** in an **Edwin Forrest** production, with Forrest himself playing the title role. In 1828, Forrest, in an admirable attempt to inspire worthy American plays, announced a competition for a new American play featuring a **Native American** protagonist, offering a $500 prize for the winner. Stone's work was the winning effort and, at that point in time, a rare play featuring a Native American character in any fully dimensioned way. Forrest scored a major success as an **actor***† in the role and played it throughout his career, and it proved highly popular with audiences.

Other actors played the role, but after Forrest's death, the play disappeared from the canon of producible American drama. The play's leading character, the great Wampanoag chief, Metamora, decides to fight to preserve the land of his people, though he realizes he is fighting a battle he will inevitably lose. He confesses his fears to his wife, played by Mrs. Sharpe opposite Forrest, and in a subplot Metamora, despite his animosity toward whites, helps a young white couple overcome difficulties to be together. However, when the climactic battle comes, Metamora dies fighting for his people.

MET-A-MORA; OR, THE LAST OF THE POLLYWOGS. **John Brougham**'s two-act **burlesque***† of **John Augustus Stone**'s 1829 **melodrama**† *Metamora; or, The Last of the Wampanoags* opened on 19 November 1847 at Boston's Adelphi Theatre. Scholar Jill Lepore has written that "Brougham parodied more than a few elements of the stage Indian, and perhaps most powerfully, he resisted the vanishing-Indian theme prevalent in the nineteenth-century Indian drama by simply refusing to kill off his protagonist. In its final lines ('I will not die to please you'), Brougham's parody acknowledged the cultural importance of the dead stage Indian in placating whites' fears of real-life Indians. But while *The Last of the Pollywogs* mocked the convention of early Indian dramas, it also expressed bitter scorn for Indian peoples, an attitude that was becoming increasingly widespread at midcentury." Early published editions of the play spelled the last word of the play's title as "Pollywoogs," but most subsequent writings about the play drop one "o."

MEXICAN-AMERICAN WAR. This military conflict between the United States and the Centralist Republic of Mexico (which renewed the 1824 federal constitution during the **war,***† becoming the Second Federal Republic of Mexico) occurred in the aftermath of the annexation of Texas by the United States, which most Mexicans considered their territory despite prior events, including the 1836 Texas Revolution. The war was relatively brief, lasting from the spring of 1846 to the fall of 1847.

The war was controversial in the United States, and other American political issues, including the slavery question, were cited. Prior to the war itself, there was considerable strife within Mexico, and when American troops moved into Mexico, it was clear that the Mexicans were weary of the violence. The Mexican-American War was occasionally commented on in American plays in serious ways, stressing patriotism, celebrating heroes of the war (like Zachary Taylor or Winfield Scott), and commenting on success or disaster in particular battles or incidents. No plays of lasting significance emerged from the war—and few Americans know much about this particular war now except, perhaps, for a few famous leaders. Zachary Taylor became the next president of the United States in 1850 (though his time in office was short, he died within the first year of his term to be succeeded by Vice President Millard Fillmore).

MICHAEL BONHAM; OR, THE FALL OF BEXAR: A TALE OF TEX-AS. **William Gilmore Simms**'s five-act blank verse drama focused on the siege of San Antonio, the Alamo, and Texas's fight for independence. It was a relatively popular play and one of the most frequently produced on the subject of **Mexican-American** relations in the era. Simms balked at either publishing or producing the play, though he finally published it under a pseudonym (A. Southron) in the *Southern Literary Messenger* from February to June 1852. In July of that year, it was published as a pamphlet. The play was based on James Butler Bonham, a South Carolinian and lieutenant in the Texas calvary, who died at the Alamo in 1836. The play was finally produced at the New Charleston Theatre on 26 March 1855 for three performances. Local Charleston reviews were largely positive, but some pointed to weaknesses in plot and character development. Simms himself ultimately dismissed the play as one of his "trifles."

THE MIGHTY DOLLAR. **Benjamin E. Woolf**'s comedy (originally titled *The Almighty Dollar*) in four acts opened at the **Park Theatre** on 6 September 1875 for 104 performances. Crooked congressman, the Honorable Bardwell Slote, played by **William J. Florence** (for whom Woolf wrote the play), is just one of a small coterie of money-grubbing, ethically challenged, wealthy vulgarians who spend their leisure time at a Washington, DC, salon, Grabmoor, where their connections and interrelations help them in their endless search for "the mighty dollar." Other regulars include Mrs. General Gilflory, played by **Malvena Florence**, who, along with Slote, paused in her hunt for dollars to help a young bride, Clara Dart, played by **Maude Granger**, who is being harassed by a former paramour. Once that problem is solved, the money-grubbers return to their main occupation. **Critics***† were largely dismissive of the play, but audiences found it amusing and enjoyed the rich characterizations in what was the biggest hit the Florences had in their careers; in fact, within a decade, the Florences had performed the play no less than 2,500 times.

MILES, GEORGE HENRY (1824–1871). A native of Baltimore, George Henry Miles was educated for the law at Mount St. Mary's College in 1842. He practiced law, but it did not suit him, and he began to write for publication. Most momentously, in 1850, he won the $1,000 prize **Edwin Forrest** offered for a new play, *Mahommed.* In 1859, Miles had a significant success when his tragedy *De Soto* was staged at the **Broadway*† Theatre**. That same year, he demonstrated his versatility with the comedy *Mary's Birthday.* His *Señor Valiente* was performed in New York, Boston, and Baltimore on the same night in 1859. During the 1860–1861 season, Miles's play *Seven Sisters* was produced successfully at **Laura Keene**'s Theatre, exploring the timely topic of states seceding from the Union. Miles's subsequent plays were not as successful, and he worked for the government for a time when President Millard Fillmore sent him to Spain. He aimed to write an ambitious tragedy on Oliver Cromwell, but it went unfinished.

†MILLER, JOAQUIN (1839–1913). Born Cincinnatus Heine Miller in Liberty, Indiana (the date is given as 1837, 1839, and 1841 in a range of sources), the poet, journalist, and **playwright*†** spent formative years in the gold mining camps and among the **Native Americans*†** of the Pacific coast. His Western poetry earned him the epithets "poet of the Sierras" and "the Byron of the Rockies." He wrote the original story upon which the popular drama *The Danites; or, The Heart of the Sierras†* (1877) was based. The play was a triumph and provided a **star*†** part for **McKee Rankin,†** though its dramatization, long credited to Miller, was ultimately found to have been the work of a hired writer. Miller was rumored to have had an affair with **Adah Isaacs Menken,†** which may have hastened a divorce from his wife, Theresa Dyer.

MINER, HENRY C. (1842–1900). New York–born Henry Clay Miner, son of a New York civil engineer, attended public schools and studied medicine at the American Institute of Physicians and Surgeons. He was in the pharmaceutical business until he served in the Union Army during the **Civil War**. From the mid-1860s, he turned his attention to the stage and, in short order, owned five theaters in New York and Newark, New Jersey. He published the American Dramatic Directory, was president of the Actors Fund Association,† and served as a US representative from New York.

MINSHULL, JOHN (late 18th–early 19th centuries). Though born in England, John Minshull was part of a growing movement of **Irish dramatists*†** and performers as the era of Irish immigration to the United States expanded. Minshull's best-known work, *Rural Felicity* (1801), a comic opera in three acts, was eventually produced at the Grove Theatre in New York in

1805, and among other things, it celebrated Irish pride. Minshull's central character, Patrick, has loyalties to Ireland and to the king of England, but the character learns the value of American-style freedoms. The play also includes an early **Yankee†** character, Jonathan. Minshull also wrote *The Sprightly Widow with the Frolics of Youth, Or, a Speedy Way of Uniting the Sexes by Honorable Marriage* (1803); *He Stoops to Conquer, or, The Virgin Wife Triumphant: A comedy in three acts* (1804); and, *The Merry Dames, or, The Humorist's Triumph Over the Poet in Petticoats, and the gallant exploits of the knight of the comb: a comedy in three acts* (1805).

†MINSTRELS/MINSTREL SHOWS. Minstrel singing and **blackface†** performance can be traced back to the Middle Ages, but the origin of the American entertainment† known as minstrelsy is usually credited to **Thomas Dartmouth "Daddy" Rice**, who was performing a "**Jump Jim Crow**" song and dance in blackface (via the use of burned cork) by 1830. In 1843, the **Virginia Minstrels** began to set the pattern for minstrel shows as they would be seen throughout much of the 19th century and into the early 20th century. Songwriters responded to the unprecedented popularity of minstrel shows, with **Stephen C. Foster** emerging as a standout contributor, among many others. Many troupes in the mode of the Virginia Minstrels proliferated. One headed by **E. P. Christy**, whose **Christy Minstrels** were for a time dominant, set the tone, but scores of other companies formed and **toured*†** widely across the United States adding innovations.

After the **Civil War**, minstrelsy provided a ready foothold for **African Americans*†** who wished to find a way into show business as all-black or mixed minstrel troupes formed. The latter part of the century saw an increase in "genuine" Ethiopian minstrels. Yet the stylized production values called for exaggerated blackface makeup, even by black performers who were expected to exaggerate their facial characteristics like white performers did. The minstrel chorus would be brightly costumed in a caricature of fancy evening dress. They would sit in a semicircle, sometimes several rows deep, during the comic patter between the whiteface straight man called the Interlocutor and the two blackface end men, Tambo and Bones. The first part of the show would culminate in a cakewalk. The second part would include **olio** acts, often including **female impersonation.†**

By the early 20th century, minstrelsy fell into disfavor, although many of its traditions continued in **musicals,*†** **revues,*†** and **vaudeville†** well into the mid-20th century when blackface, in particular, came to be seen as an odious racial slur. The last first-rank entertainer to regularly perform in blackface, Al Jolson† mostly abandoned its use by the 1930s, but continued to sing the enduring songs written by Foster, as well as scores of Tin Pan Alley* American songwriters, inspired by minstrel show traditions.

†**MITCHELL, MAGGIE (1832–1918).** Margaret Julia Mitchell was born in New York City and began acting at 19, quickly developing a specialty in young boys' roles. For a quarter century, beginning in 1861, the tiny, energetic **actress*†** played the title role in *Fanchon, the Cricket*, a dramatization of a story by George Sand. Her portrayal of *Jane Eyre* (1885) was admired, and *Maggie the Midget* (1888) was created for her, but the public demanded *Fanchon* until Mitchell retired at 58. She was the mother of Julian Mitchell, a **musical*†** director with long association with Florenz Ziegfeld Jr.†

MITCHELL, WILLIAM (1798–1856). English-born **actor*†** and **manager,*†** William Mitchell arrived in the United States in 1836 before taking over management of the **Olympic Theatre** in 1839. **Charles Dickens** had admired Mitchell's acting in England and, as such, encouraged him to play the role of Sam Weller in *Pickwick Papers* and Squeers and Mr. Crummles in *Nicholas Nickleby* when those novels were adapted to the stage. By the 1840s, Mitchell had evolved into the **leading† producer*†** and performer in **burlesque.*†** He gave the Olympic an environment of absurdity that extended to posters, programs, and the silly titles of the shows, such as *Buy It Dear, 'Tis Made of Cashmere* (satirizing *Bayadère, or the Maid of Cashmere*). Mitchell was a gifted mimic and impersonated such diverse real and fictional figures as Hamlet, **Fanny Elssler**, and a range of characters from Dickens. He made the Olympic a popular center of entertainment,† but failing health forced an early retirement.

MITCHELL'S OLYMPIC. *See* OLYMPIC THEATRE.

M'LISS. **Clay Meredith Greene**'s four-act play, based on a **Bret Harte** story, opened on 23 September 1878 at **Niblo's Garden**. M'liss, played by Kate Mayhew, is an appealing and intelligent young hoyden, known as "the waif of the Sierras." She has largely had to look after herself since her drunken father, who works as a miner, ignores her on the rare occasions he is sober. Without losing her appeal, she has learned to be tough; for example, she beats off some toughs attempting to hurt the boy she loves, and she possesses the smarts to win his heart away from a citified sophisticate ("the pink and white thing").

　Star*† Kate Mayhew sought an injunction to halt a rival adaptation of Harte's story in which **actress*† Annie Pixley†** intended to appear. Mayhew won the injunction, but it was lifted in due course and Pixley's production ultimately became the popular version, enhanced by the fact that Pixley scored a personal success in the role. Pixley's version was usually titled *M'liss, the Child of the Sierras*. Of the Mayhew production, the *New York Clipper* pointed out weaknesses in the script and production, but also found

"*M'liss* is the most artistic picture of California life we have seen upon the stage." Many **critics*†** condemned the Pixley version of the play itself, but were enthusiastic in their praise of Pixley in a role that became indelibly associated with her.

MODERN HONOR; OR, THE VICTIM OF REVENGE. John Blake White's five-act tragedy performed in 1812 at **Charleston Theatre** centered on a duel and the ramifications of the resulting tragedy on survivors and their attendant desire for revenge.

MODERN INSANITY; OR, FASHION AND FORGERY. Thaddeus Mehan's 1857 drama was staged at the American Theatre. **E. L. Davenport** played Father Abraham in an exposé of the treatment of those dealing with mental illnesses. *The Spirit of the Times* described it as "a thing of the time, abounding in sharp and telling hits and illustrative of some of the dark phases of city life."

THE MODEST SOLDIER; OR, LOVE IN NEW YORK. William Dunlap's comedy of manners, inspired to some extent by **Royall Tyler**'s *The Contrast*, was his first play, though it was never produced. It was completed in late 1787, only months after *The Contrast*, which had scored an unparalleled success. Dunlap submitted it to **Lewis Hallam Jr.** and **John Henry** for the Old **American Company**, but despite some positive response, the play was not staged. Dunlap himself described the play as containing "a **Yankee†** servant, and old gentlemen and his two daughters, one of course lively, the other serious."

†MODJESKA, HELENA (1840–1909). Born Jadwiga Benda in Poland, she established herself as an **actress*†** there, first using the name Helena Opid, then Helena Modrzejewska. In 1876, Modjeska came to the United States with her second husband, Karol Chlapowski, Count Bozenta, and bought a ranch in California, where she worked on her English in preparation for restarting her career on the American stage; she hired young aspiring **dramatist*†** Sophie Treadwell† as her secretary. Modjeska made her English-language debut in San Francisco in 1877 and developed a **repertory*†** including 16 **Shakespearean*†** roles (notably Rosalind and Viola) as well as provocative characters in contemporary plays. Her memoirs, *Memories and Impressions* (1910), include vivid tales of her **tour*†** with **Edwin Booth†** in 1889.

MONTAGUE, HENRY JAMES (1844–1878). Born in England as Henry James Mann, he performed as an **amateur*†** **actor*†** before working with **Dion Boucicault†** in the mid-1860s. He gained his first success as an actor in T. W. Robertson's comedies and, in 1870, was a founder of London's **Vaudeville†** Theatre. His arrival in the United States almost instantly established him as a **matinee idol†** in 1874. As he was handsome, young, and elegant in his dress, the press viewed him as outshining other supposed matinee idols. Montague's successes came in a well-received production of Boucicault's *The Shaughraun*, and he also appeared to plaudits in *Caste*, *Diplomacy*, and *The Overland Route*. Montague gained significant popularity during the next four years, but collapsed onstage during a performance of *Diplomacy* in San Francisco in 1878 and died shortly thereafter.

MONTEZ, LOLA (1818–1861). Born in Limerick, Ireland (some sources give her birth year as 1821), Marie Dolores Eliza Rosanna Gilbert spent much of her **childhood†** in India, but was educated in the British Isles. She eloped in her late teens with Lieutenant Thomas James, but the marriage ended five years later, and she developed a career as a dancer. When it was revealed that she was Mrs. James and not "Lola Montez, Spanish dancer," a public uproar ensued, but thanks to her beauty and skill, she was able to reestablish (and, in fact, enhance, her career) on the European continent. She reputedly had liaisons with Franz Liszt and Alexandre Dumas, and she gained international fame (or infamy) through her affair with King Louis I (Ludwig I) of Bavaria. She was extremely influential with Louis (his cabinet, for example, became known as "Lolaministerium"), and she encouraged him toward liberal and anti-Jesuit policies. The public resisted, and in the revolution of 1848, Louis was compelled to abdicate in favor of his son while Montez escaped to London, where she married Lieutenant George Heald, although this was a further scandal in that she was never formally divorced from James.

In the early 1850s, Montez danced in theaters across the United States and married Patrick P. Hull in 1853, but the marriage was short-lived. She settled for a time in California and spent time coaching **Lotta Crabtree†** in performance techniques. Montez moved to New York in the mid-1850s before embarking on an unsuccessful **tour*†** of Australia, but she developed a secondary career as a lecturer of subjects of interest to **women,*†** including fashion and manners. She had a religious awakening and became a philanthropist, publishing an autobiography in 1858, as well as a few books on subjects she had addressed in her public lectures. Her early death only enhanced her legend, and she became the subject of literary works, performances, and dramatic characters.

MORANT, FANNY (1821–1900). English-born Fanny Morant debuted at the Drury Lane Theatre and had some stage experience before emigrating to the United States in 1853. Through most of the 1860s, Morant appeared with **Lester Wallack**'s company. In reporting a benefit for Morant given at **Wallack's Theatre** in 1862, the *New York Times* described her as a "painstaking and excellent" **actress.***† Her excellence provided the opportunity in 1868 to join **Augustin Daly**'s company, where she was able to demonstrate the diversity of her talents in such plays as *Fernande*, *Divorce*, *The Merry Wives of Windsor*, and *The School for Scandal*, among others. After a time with Daly, she switched to the **Union Square Company**, where she also won plaudits playing older **women***† as she aged. At the Union Square she appeared in the long-running hit *Rose Michel* by **Steele MacKaye**, which **starred***† **Rose Eytinge.**†

THE MORMONS; OR, LIFE AT SALT LAKE CITY. **Thomas Dunn English**'s farcical three-act play reflected the national fascination with and mistrust of the Mormon sect. Produced at **William Burton**'s Theatre beginning on 17 March 1858 for several performances, it was purported that English wrote the play in a mere 72 hours in an attempt to create a slice-of-life portrayal of Mormon ways ahead of other theaters. **Charles Fisher** portrayed Brigham Young, with Burton as Timothy Noggs, a New York alderman who has fled to Salt Lake City, where he takes it upon himself to instruct Young and his flock in the art of political manipulation, but ends up instead with 13 wives. **E. L. Davenport** and Fanny Vining (Mrs. Davenport) were also in the cast.

†**MORRIS, CLARA (1849–1925).** Born Clara LaMontagne in Toronto, Canada, she was raised by her mother in Cleveland. Their poverty meant that she received little formal schooling, but she was an avid reader. As a teen, she danced or played small parts in Cleveland's Academy of Music. An invitation to join **Augustin Daly**'s† **Fifth Avenue Theatre** company took her to New York, where she triumphed in her debut performance in *Man and Wife* (1870). During her three seasons with Daly, she established herself as the **leading**† **emotional**† **actress***† of her day. **Matinee girls**† in the 1880s flocked to weep with her as they watched the travails of her heroines. A *New York Times* review (6 January 1882) analyzed her art: "It is sometimes hard to believe that Miss Morris's presentments of sorrow and distress are, after all, mere artistic effects; there is about them a poignancy of truth which commands more than fictitious sympathy—an agony as black as that of life."

Morris **toured***† extensively into the 1890s, continuing to perform the old **melodramas**† in which she used exaggerated gestures and vocal intonations. Audiences were spellbound at the intensity of her mad scene in *Article 47,* the pathos of her "Camille" in *The Lady of the Camellius*, and the whispered suffering of her Mercy Merrick in *The New Magdalen*. Following her retirement from the stage, she wrote plays, novels, and memoirs.

MORRIS, MORRIS W. *See* MORRISON, LEWIS (1845–1906).

MORRIS, OWEN (1719?–1809). Owen Morris's early years are lost in obscurity until he made his 1759 debut with the **American Company**. He was known to specialize in comic old men roles, most notably Polonius and Oliver Surface in *The School for Scandal*. He retired in 1790. Morris was married twice and both wives were performers of distinction. The first Mrs. Morris (d. 1767) was America's first Ophelia and an early Lady Teazle in *The School for Scandal*. The second Mrs. Morris was a popular comedienne with audiences, but **critics***† seemed divided on her talents. She won plaudits as Beatrice in *Much Ado about Nothing* and also as Lady Teazle in *The School for Scandal*.

MORRISON, LEWIS (1845–1906). Born in Kingston, Jamaica, of African and Jewish heritage as Morris W. Morris (or Moritz W. Morris), he ultimately changed his name to Lewis Morrison. Living in Louisiana, he enlisted in the Confederate Army at the start of the **Civil War** in its first black military regiment, but when the state legislature outlawed blacks from serving, he joined the Union Army, becoming its first Jewish officer. Following the **war**,*† he went on the stage as an **actor***† in New Orleans, appearing in *The Loan of a Lover*. He acted in a secondary role with **Edwin Booth**† in Booth's production of *Richelieu*, after which he joined the **California Theatre** company for a few years.

Morrison subsequently appeared successfully at the **Park Theatre** in *The Legion of Honor* for **manager***† Henry E. Abbey. In that period, he had a hit in the title role of Henry Guy Carleton's 1885 play *Victor Durand*, which he **toured***† along with his second wife, Florence Roberts. During the 1880s, he acted at the **Walnut Street Theatre**, but scored his greatest success as Mephistopheles in *Faust* in 1889, a role he could never fully escape for the remainder of his career. Morrison was the grandfather of film† **actresses***† Constance and Joan Bennett.

MOSES, THOMAS G. (1856–1934). Painter and **scene designer***† of note, Thomas Gibbs Moses was born in England, but his family moved to the United States in the 1850s. The early loss of his mother, who had encouraged his artistic talents, was a difficult blow to overcome, but encouraged him to continue his painting, and he had several exhibits in major cities before the

1870s. He moved to Chicago in the immediate aftermath of the Great **Fire**† of 1871 and began scene painting for **McVicker's Theatre** while also studying at the Art Institute of Chicago.

In 1880, Moses became a member of the Sosman and Landis Scene Painting Studio, a concern that grew into the outstanding scenic studio in the Midwest. Moses was astonishingly productive, designing hundreds of productions, including settings for **Helena Modjeska**† in California and many New York productions, such as *The Magic Melody, At the Lower Harbor* (1900), *Florodora* (1900), *Under Southern Skies* (1901), *In Dahomey* (1903), *The Medal and the Maid* (1904), *The Pit* (1904), *Girls Will Be Gods* (1904), and others. It is perhaps not surprising that his scenic gifts were especially effective in creating landscapes and scenes of forests since his nonscenic paintings also demonstrated his flair in painting such scenes.

THE MOTLEY ASSEMBLY. **Mercy Otis Warren**'s one-act farce, "published for the entertainment† of the curious" in 1779, aimed her satire at Americans rather than the British. She is more often thought of as a pointed satirist of the British in the years of the **American Revolution**, but she switched to a little satire of America, pressing her desires for rights for **women**,*† including the vote. The play also reflects her view that Americans were becoming more concerned with personal ambitions than with public virtue.

THE MOUNTAIN TORRENT. **Samuel B. H. Judah**'s two-act **melodrama**† opened on 1 March 1820 at New York's **Park Theatre**. The plot involves a young woman compelled to marry a man she does not love to save her father from financial disaster. Judah's first produced play, *The Mountain Torrent* was well received and followed by *The Rose of Arragon* and *A Tale of Lexington*, after which Judah gave up writing for the stage.

MOWATT, ANNA CORA (1819–1870). Born Anna Cora Ogden in Bordeaux, France, the 10th of 14 children. Her father, Samuel Gouvenour Ogden, was a merchant, and her mother, Eliza Lewis Ogden, descended from a signer of the Declaration of Independence. The Ogdens returned to the United States around 1825, where she was mostly homeschooled, though she did attend a private school for a time. Her parents encouraged her interest in writing and the arts, and she proved especially drawn to the stage. At the age of 15, she eloped with James Mowatt, a well-to-do lawyer nearly 15 years her senior, and he encouraged her literary and artistic pursuits.

Mowatt published her first book in 1836, at the age of 17; wrote articles for periodicals; and composed a six-act play, *Gulzara*, which was published in the *New World* magazine. Using a pseudonym (Helen Berkley), she published two novels, *The Fortune Hunter* and *Evelyn*. To help with financial woes, she took up reading from her work in public in 1841 (**Edgar Allan Poe** was at her first reading). She was well received as a reader, but respiratory ailments ended her reading career shortly after it began, and her focus returned to her writing.

Mowatt's most acclaimed work, the satiric comedy of manners *Fashion* was published in 1845 and opened at the **Park Theatre** on 24 March 1845, scoring a major hit. Her respiratory problems in check, she debuted as an **actress***† on 13 June 1845 as Pauline in *The Lady of Lyons*, also to great acclaim. Although she continued to write, much of the rest of her career was devoted to acting. Mowatt published a play, *Armand, the Child of the People*, in 1847, but she was acting constantly, in **Shakespeare***† (*Cymbeline*), contemporary **melodramas**,† and her own plays. She **toured***† Europe and the United States for the remainder of her life, though she took some time off when her husband, James Mowatt, died in 1851. She married again, to William Foushee Ritchie, in 1853, with President Franklin Pierce and his cabinet in attendance, and while acting she continued to write. She also involved herself in the movement to save **George Washington**'s home, Mount Vernon. When her marriage ended in 1860, she moved to England in 1865 and lived there until her death in 1870.

THE MULLIGAN GUARDS' BALL. Actor,*† playwright,*† and **manager***† **Edward Harrigan**† wrote the libretto and lyrics for this comedy with music by David Braham. Harrigan **costarred***† for the first time with his longtime partner, **Tony Hart**,† and the results were joyous for happy audiences to the point that Harrigan wrote and, along with Hart, starred in several sequels, all of which were popular. In many respects, the Mulligan Guard shows were the prototypes of late 19th- and early 20th-century **musical***† comedy. *The Mulligan Guards' Ball* opened on 13 January 1879 at the **Theater Comique** for 138 performances.

An **Irish** American cohort called the Mulligan Guards is run by Dan Mulligan, played by Harrigan, who becomes concerned about his son Tommy, played by Hart, who is in love with a German girl, Katy. Dan disapproves of intermarriage between the Irish and Germans, but Dan's wife, Cordelia (played by **Annie Yeamans**), dislikes Katy's mother, which adds to the friction. The Mulligans are planning a ball, but discover that a "Negro" group, the Skidmores, have booked the same hall for the night they want. As expected, given the racial politics of the era, the Mulligans prevail when the Skidmores are forced to take a second-floor ballroom, but their dancing is so energetic that the roof collapses. In the melee, Tommy and Katy get away and elope. The lightweight plot, even reflecting the prejudices of the time, was rich with colorful characters and broad comedy, with a little romance added as well.

MUNFORD, COLONEL ROBERT (1737?–1783). A native of Wakefield, Maryland, Robert Munford III lost his father at a very young age. Despite this difficult start, by 1765 he entered the House of Burgesses (the same year as his good friend Patrick Henry). Munford had actually begun his adulthood with military experience, beginning in 1756, when he served under Colonel **George Washington** during the **French and Indian War** (1755–1763). Following the **war**,*† Munford was named county lieutenant of Mecklenburg County with the charge of defending the environs from slave uprisings. He himself owned slaves he had inherited from his father.

Munford was politically conservative in the decades prior to the **American Revolution**, but as tensions became increasingly inflamed between the colonies and Great Britain, he continued to oppose the war, though he commanded a militia during the war. In the years preceding the war, Munford began to write, including two plays, *The Candidates; or, the Humours of a Virginia Election* (c. 1770) and *The Patriots* (c. 1777), considered by scholars to be the first comedies written in America, both lightly satirical and highly topical, reflecting familiar characters, significant local color, and current events. It seems clear he enjoyed writing as a pleasurable activity, but that he had no plans to enter the theater professionally. Along with the plays, Munford wrote poems and did a partial translation of Ovid's *Metamorphoses*.

MURDOCH, FRANK H. (1843–1872). Born Frank Hitchcock, the son of a sister of **James E. Murdoch**, he took the name Murdoch to support his theatrical aspirations, which began when he was a teenager. His first play, *The Keeper of Lighthouse Cliff*, may have had a production in California in the 1870s and also may have influenced *Shore Acres*,† **James A. Herne's**† play (Herne was in Murdoch's cast).

Murdoch's most famous and enduring play, *Davy Crockett; or, Be Sure You're Right Then Go Ahead* (1872), scored two triumphs—one for the play itself and one for its **star**,*† **Frank Mayo**. Murdoch, who was seriously ill at the time of the play's premiere, seemed to accept Mayo's revisions of the play when he finally saw it during the over 2,000 performances of the role Mayo played. Murdoch also is credited with writing an anonymous play, *Bohemia; or, The Lottery of Art* (1872), a satire of drama **critics**,*† and a comedy, *Only a Jew* (1873).

†MURDOCH, JAMES E. (1811–1893). The eminent **actor-manager***† was born in Philadelphia, as James Edward Murdoch. He made his debut in 1829 at Philadelphia's **Arch Street Theatre** in a single performance of August von Kotzebue's play *Lover's Vow*, underwritten by his hesitant father. In 1836, he joined the company of the **Tremont Theatre** in Boston. His long slow rise in the profession culminated in **star*†** engagements† in the Union states during the **Civil War**. Murdoch played Hamlet at New York's **Park Theatre** in 1845, wrote a book about elocution in 1847, and appeared in **Shakespearean*†** plays as well as the standard works of mid-19th-century drama. He performed frequently in England, scoring a particular success there in a revival of **Edward Bulwer-Lytton**'s 1840 comedy *Money* in 1856. Murdoch's 1880 book *The Stage* recalls anecdotes from his 50 years in the theater.

MURDOCK, JOHN (1749–1834). Possibly a Philadelphian and a barber by trade, John Murdock either had some wealth or was particularly successful as he paid to publish his dramatic work at his own expense, including *The Triumphs of Love; or, Happy Reconciliation* (1795), a satire of contemporary events and the Quakers; *The Politicians; or, A State of Things* (1798), which called for strong government; and *The Beau Metamorphized* (1800), a farce.

MURRAY, JUDITH SARGENT (1751–1820). Born Judith Sargent in Gloucester, Massachusetts, early in her life she became aware of inequities between men and women in education, when her younger brother began studying the classics and her parents denied her the opportunity. She was largely self-educated and became particularly interested in history. Married twice, first to John Stevens and then to John Murray, she began writing under a variety of pseudonyms, including a man's name, Mr. Vigilius, feeling readers would accept her radical ideas about **women's*†** issues if they assumed she was a man.

Murray published a three-volume book of essays and plays called *The Gleaner* in 1798, and the book was a success, subscribed to by such prominent Americans as **George Washington**, John Adams, Henry Knox, and another female intellectual and **playwright,*† Mercy Otis Warren**. Among her many writings, her plays include *The Medium; or, Happy Tea-Party* (1795; also known as *The Medium; or, Virtue Triumphant*), *The Traveller Returned* (1796), and *The African* (1798), all of which feature her feminist views.

MURRAY, WALTER (mid-18th century). Along with **Thomas Kean**, Walter Murray opened New York's first theater, situated on Nassau Street in the mid-1700s. Kean and Murray produced **Shakespeare*†** and operas, presenting *Richard III* at the Theatre on Nassau Street on 5 March 1750, followed by performances of *The Beggar's Opera, Love for Love*, and *Cato*, perhaps among others. These appearances were met with controversy on religious grounds, and dogged with other problems, Kean and Murray left for Virginia, where they headed a company of **actors**.*†

*†MUSICAL THEATER. The origins of the American musical as it came into full focus in the 20th century are obscure at best. Music and drama have been inextricably linked since the dawn of theater in the ancient world, but the American musical undoubtedly emerged from a range of 19th-century cultural traditions, including folk music, **minstrels**,† **travesties**, **vaudeville**,† **burlesque**,*† European opera and **operetta**,† and sundry other entertainments.†

Many historians identify the 1866 production of the **melodrama**† *The Black Crook* as an inciting event, since the play, set in an enchanted forest, featured ballet sequences with dancers in **fleshings**† playing wood nymphs, providing musical interludes. The influence of English operettas by **W. S. Gilbert** and **Arthur Sullivan** had an impact after 1870, when audiences in the United States developed a taste for European-style operettas and, by the 1890s, musical entertainments with a more contemporary and American flavor.

This "Americanizing" was aided by the contributions of **actor***†-**manager***† George M. Cohan,*† who wrote, composed, and **starred***† in a series of musical comedies featuring simple plots about "**Broadway**"*† wise guys, **rubes**,† and one-dimensional **villains**,† all bundled together with mainstream values and the infectious patriotism typical of the varied ethnic groups crowding into the United States from the mid-19th through the 20th century.

MY PARTNER. **Bartley Campbell**'s **melodrama**† in four acts opened on 16 September 1879 at the **Union Square Theatre** for 39 performances. The play is set around two mining partners, Joe Saunders (played by **Louis Aldrich**) and Ned Singleton (played by Henry Crisp), one of whom is framed for killing the other during the last days of the California gold rush. Both men are in love with Mary Brandon (played by **Maude Granger**), and when Ned sexually assaults Mary, Joe demands that Ned marry her.

In the meantime, however, Ned is murdered by Josiah Scragg (played by J. W. Hague), who makes it appear that Joe is the killer. Joe goes on trial and is found guilty, but he and Mary, who are truly in love, agree to marry before his execution. At the 11th hour, Joe is saved by the broadly comic Chinaman, Wing Lee (played by **Charles T. Parsloe**), who is able to prove Scragg's guilt by revealing blood on his sleeve. Vindicated, Joe and his Mary are wed. The *New York Times* referred to the play as "a drama of unquestionable power [. . .] exceedingly fresh and unconventional." *My Partner* **toured*†** the United States, Berlin (1883), and London (1884), and remained popular for the remaining years of the 19th century.

THE MYSTERIES AND CRIMES OF NEW YORK AND BROOKLYN. **J. Burdette Howe**, an English **actor*†** and **playwright*†** who lived in America at this time and contributed to the stage, wrote this 1858 play in which a **villainous†** Italian (representing antiforeign influences) and his quadroon mistress work prodigiously to nearly eradicate all of the well-intentioned characters of the play.

N

NATIONAL THEATRE. Built in 1836 in the West End of Boston, the National Theatre, designed by William Washburn, was initially run by manager William Pelby. Its dominant mission was presenting original works performed by a small **stock***† company of mostly American **actors**,*† although standard works such as *Heir-at-Law* and *The Lady of Lyons*, as well as **Shakespeare**,*† were produced. Among its company at various times were **Edwin Adams**, Jean Margaret Davenport, **Julia Dean**, Jonathan Harrington, **William Henry Smith**, **Mrs. J. R. Vincent**, Billy Whitlock, and others. A **fire**† in 1852 destroyed the building. It was rebuilt, but razed in a fire again in 1863.

Another National Theatre in Boston opened in 1911. Washington, DC, also had a notable National Theatre built in 1835 by William Corcoran and other prominent Washingtonians who felt the capital city should have a major theater. Many US presidents attended plays there, beginning with President Andrew Jackson. It was later known as **Grover**'s National Theatre. President **Abraham Lincoln** attended plays there, and his son Tad was watching *Aladdin!; or, The Wonderful Lamp* there when Lincoln was assassinated by **John Wilkes Booth** at **Ford's Theatre** and the attack was announced at the National to a stunned audience. New York had **Purdy**'s National Theatre, which is where, among many other productions, the first New York City staging of *Uncle Tom's Cabin* appeared in 1852, with **Thomas Dartmouth "Daddy" Rice**. In the 19th century, Philadelphia also had the New National Theatre.

*†NATIVE AMERICANS. From the 18th century, Native Americans have been depicted in theatrical works, but the first to gain wide popular recognition was **John Augustus Stone**'s *Metamora; or, The Last of the Wampanoags* (1829), the winning entry in a playwriting competition established by **Edwin Forrest**, who played the title character in the original production. The play subsequently became a role strongly identified with him. Many 19th-century plays depicted Indians in mostly condescending ways, as **villains**† or tragically romantic figures. Tales like Stone's *Metamora; or, The Last of the*

Wampanoags led the way in romanticizing Native Americans as tragic figures, providing a portrait of a vanishing tribe and the last noble member of the tribe who hopes against all odds to save his people, but sees the sad reality of extinction looming. On the other end of the spectrum, **Louisa H. Medina**'s *Nick of the Woods; or, The Jibbenainosay* (1839) depicted the lone survivor of a white family slaughtered by Indians who becomes a jibbenainosay (avenging devil) and terrorizes the murderous Indians who killed his family and kidnapped his cousin.

Indians sometimes emerged as key elements in the plots of plays, for example, in **Dion Boucicault**'s† *The Octoroon* (1859), in which an Indian character unmasks the **villain**† as a murderer at the climax of the play. Variety entertainments from **minstrel shows**† and **circus***† to **musicals***† and **vaudeville**† tended to encourage familiar stereotypes. Stereotypical depictions continued throughout the 19th century and into the early 20th century in **Buffalo Bill Cody**'s† Wild West Show (and its competitors) and in plays like *Strongheart*† (1905) and *The Squaw Man*† (1905). Other dramatists, including **James A. Herne,**† **David Belasco,**† William C. deMille,† and Mary Austin,† sought to offer more accurate depictions of Native Americans, but white audiences seemingly preferred familiar stereotypes well into the 20th century, as films† made a genre of Western movies with Indians typically depicted in stereotypical ways, often as murderous savages. It was not until the post–World **War** II*† era that Native Americans would be depicted in more dimensioned and sympathetic ways in American theater and film.

NEAFIE, J. A. J. (1815–1892). Born John Andrew Jackson Neafie in New York, Neafie bought his way out of a blue-collar life in 1838 by paying $300 for the **Park Theatre** and company to support him in the role of Othello. He also appeared in *The Merchant of Venice* and *Richard III* before **touring***† with **Edwin Forrest** as the main supporting† **actor***† to the **star.***† He was **leading man**† of the **Bowery Theatre** for a time in the 1840s, but never attained the necessary popularity in New York to draw a sufficient audience to maintain his own company. However, he toured in the South and the western territories for the remainder of his career and was quite successful.

NEAL, JOHN (1793–1876). Son of Quakers, John Neal was born in Falmouth, Maine, where he was educated until he entered business at age 12, working as a clerk, miniature artist, and penmanship tutor, among other things. He studied law, supporting his study by writing for various periodicals and starting a literary society, The Delphian Club, and editing their journal. Within an astonishingly short time he wrote six novels (he claimed to have written one in a week) and two epic poems under a pseudonym, Jehu

O'Cataract. He spent some time living in London before returning to Portland, Maine, in 1827, where he lived and worked for the rest of his life. He wrote several plays, including *Otho: A Tragedy in Five Acts* (1819); as a literary **critic**,*† Neal wrote five essays for the *Yankee*† *and Boston Literary Gazette* in 1829.

NEIGHBOR JACKWOOD. **J. T. Trowbridge** dramatized in five acts his abolitionist novel of the same name. The play opened on 16 March 1857 at the **Boston Museum** under the direction of **William H. Smith** for a three-week run. Among other things, *Neighbor Jackwood* condemned the Fugitive Slave Law, and its abolitionist sentiments are unequivocal. Trowbridge innovated to a certain extent by avoiding the use of white **actors***† in **blackface**† playing **African American***† characters, which, to that point, had been typical in plays including black characters, dealing with the slave question, and even in support of abolition. Such characters would provide comedy as a rule, but Trowbridge chose instead to use **Yankee**† characters for comic purposes. Trowbridge was particularly appreciated for the uniqueness of his characters, and in *Neighbor Jackwood,* the title character, Bim, his dog Rove, Grandmother Rigglesty, and Enos Crumlett are the central characters illustrating life before the **Civil War**, particularly in relation to abolitionist sentiments.

NEILSON, ADELAIDE (1848–1880). Born in Leeds, England, out of wedlock to a strolling **actress**,*† Adelaide Neilson was first known as Elizabeth Anne Bland after her mother married Samuel Bland, a house decorator. Once she became a well-known actress, the stories of her birth and early years were glamorized, describing education in France and Italy, fluency in a multitude of languages, and such. She ran off to London at 15, and her physical beauty was essential in her obtaining of a position with a ballet troupe. Neilson married Philip Henry Lee in 1865, and after some study with **actor***† John Ryder, she acted at Sarah Thorne's Theatre Royal. Later, she played Julia in *The Hunchback* at the Theatre Royal Margate.

Up to 1871, Neilson played a variety of roles at a number of British theaters and developed a popular reputation, but she left for America in 1872, where she was extremely popular from the start, making her New York debut on 18 November 1872 at **Booth's Theatre** as Juliet. During the 1870s, she made several American **tours**.*† She played most of the heroines of **Shakespeare**'s*† romantic comedies, *As You Like It, Twelfth Night, Much Ado about Nothing*, and others, as well as many of the standard heroines in contemporary romantic plays. In 1877, Neilson divorced her husband, and she died suddenly in France in 1880, prematurely ending a career likely to have been one of the most acclaimed of the late 19th century.

THE NEW MAGDALEN. Wilkie Collins's novel was adapted by its author into a drama, which opened on 19 May 1873 at the **Olympic Theatre** in London. It had a number of continental productions, and Collins attended the American premiere in New York on 10 November 1873 at the **Broadway Theatre** in an **Augustin Daly** production. The plot involved two women, Mercy (Ada Cavendish) and Grace, who are friends, though quite different, but both caught up in the current **war***† between Germany and France. When a stray shell kills Grace, Mercy uses the tragedy as a chance to jettison her own persona as a "fallen woman" and takes on Grace's identity, moving to England in the process. **Clara Morris** appeared in an early 1880s revival.

NEW THEATRE. *See* PARK THEATRE.

A NEW WORLD PLANTED; OR, THE ADVENTURES OF THE FORE-FATHERS OF NEW ENGLAND WHO LANDED IN PLYMOUTH, DECEMBER 22d, 1620. Little is known about **playwright***† Joseph Croswell (1786–1857), author of this nationalistic play, which was performed in Boston in 1802. The history-based play's plot involved an Englishman and a **Native American***† girl, Pocahonte, falling in love.

NEW YORK AS IT IS. **Benjamin A. Baker**'s 1848 sequel to his own two-act "local drama," *A Glance at New York*, was written and produced earlier that year and was a triumphant success. The simple structure of a country bumpkin's visit to the big city was widely imitated, especially its main character, Mose, a Bowery **stock***† character whose language was riddled with contemporary slang, at that time a novelty on mid-19th-century stages. The play is little more than an extended sketch in which the **rube** in the big city is wised up after losing his watch and wallet to some city slickers.

   Frank S. Chanfrau scored a personal triumph as Mose, in *A Glance at New York*. A volunteer "fire laddie," Mose represented class differences in the rapidly changing cityscape in which the influx of immigrants added immeasurably to the culture. **Gallery**† audiences made Mose/Chanfrau their hero. *A Glance at New York* and *New York As It Is* established a vogue for localized plays and characters—and there were versions of the play set in other cities and usually written by other authors, though Baker crafted some successful sequels himself. This first sequel succeeded and two subsequent ones by Baker, *Three Years After* (1849) and *Mose in China* (1850), were also popular.

NEW YORK CLIPPER. See THE CLIPPER.

†*NEW YORK DRAMATIC MIRROR.* Founded as the *New York Mirror* in 1879, the trade paper of the theatrical profession added the word *Dramatic* to its official name in 1884, but was popularly known as *The Dramatic Mirror.* Editor (and for a time, sole proprietor) Harrison Grey Fiske† led it to an impressive circulation by including gossipy pieces of interest to a general readership, even as he used it in the fight against the power of the Theatrical Syndicate.† Fiske ended his association with the journal in 1911. After 1905, its fortunes steadily declined, with *Variety**† gaining ascendancy as the necessary publication in the profession, and in 1922, the *Dramatic Mirror* finally ceased publication. Fiske married **actress***† Minnie Maddern,† later known to audiences as Mrs. Fiske.

NIBLO, WILLIAM (1789–1878). Born in Ireland, William Niblo was an entrepreneur who began his career as a "victualler." From working as a tavern keeper in 1813, "Billy" Niblo established Sans Souci Park in 1828, a combination restaurant and garden with a 1,200-seat concert space. Beginning with Niblo, but under a variety of **managers,***† including **Charles Gilfert**, Joseph Sefton, and **James William Wallack**, it became **Niblo's Garden** and emerged as the home of **vaudeville**† and light entertainments, most often **musical.***† A decade after its establishment, Niblo oversaw the expansion of the Garden to also accommodate a typical theater space for musical events and plays.

Within another decade, Niblo took over the lease of the **Astor Place Opera House**, which he unfortunately held during the riot that year led by partisans of American **actor***† **Edwin Forrest** and British actor **William Charles Macready**. The Garden performance spaces reopened in 1849 with an emphasis on musical, dance, and pantomime entertainments† to conventional plays and extravaganzas. Niblo himself retired from management in 1861, but the Garden continued under other managers.

NIBLO'S GARDEN. Situated at **Broadway***† near Prince Street, Niblo's Garden was initially established in 1823 as Columbia Garden. Five years later it was renamed Sans Souci, but a few years after that it was appropriately named for its founder, **William Niblo**, as Niblo's Garden. A theater was built as part of the original garden, where refreshments had been served, but no organized entertainments.† A salon was set up on the grounds for **musical***† entertainments, and Niblo acquired more land adjacent to the garden to extend activities. Niblo built a Grand Saloon, and for a time it offered musical entertainments, but ultimately **vaudeville**† occupied the space.

In 1835, **P. T. Barnum** presented his first exhibitions at Niblo's, and other individuals and groups performed their acts there to growing and appreciative audiences. In 1837, Joseph Judson and Joseph Sefton established a vaudeville troupe at Niblo's, and farcical plays, including *Promotion of the General's Hat* and *Meg Young Wife and Old Umbrella*, were produced. Niblo's steadily gained a reputation as one of New York's most fashionable theaters. Unfortunately, on 18 September 1846 the theater at Niblo's burned to the ground.

The theater was redesigned and rebuilt, finally reopening in the summer of 1849 with the capacity for seating 3,200 patrons and equipped with state-of-the-art technology. Italian opera was produced in the theater along with the varied sorts of entertainments previously featured there. In this period, Niblo's became an important center of the finest of new plays and **actors**.*† Such **managers***† and **stars***† as **E. L. Davenport**, **William Wheatley**, Bennett Barrow, and **Maggie Mitchell**, among many others, appeared at Niblo's. Variety acts continued to be popular; for example, in 1855 Niblo brought **Charles Blondin**, the celebrated European tightrope walker, to appear in the Garden with great success. In 1850, Niblo's also presented the premiere of Verdi's opera *Macbeth.*

Following the **Civil War**, the economic boom boosted theater ticket sales, and Niblo's made the choice of offering more light entertainments. One momentous production was the *The Black Crook* (1866), which is deemed by many historians as the first modern musical comedy; that is, the first "book" musical. It was a runaway success and was followed by *The White Fawn* (1869), which was intended to duplicate the success of *The Black Crook*. Niblo himself had retired in 1861, and others took over management. In 1872, a **fire**† destroyed the theater, and a businessman, A. T. Stewart, rebuilt it. The theater was not as successful after the rebuilding as other theaters, and a proliferation of varied entertainments provided strong competition. Niblo's closed in 1895, and the building was torn down shortly thereafter.

NICK OF THE WOODS; OR, THE JIBBENAINOSAY. **Louisa H. Medina**'s three-act play, based on a novel by Robert A. Bird, was produced at the **New Bowery Theatre**, where it opened on 6 May 1839 for 12 performances. Reginald Ashburn (played by **Joseph Proctor**) is left as the only survivor of a family massacred by **Indians**, and to seek revenge against the killers of his family, he adopts the disguise of a pacifist Quaker. Eventually, he encounters a young white woman, Telie Doe (played by Mrs. Shaw), who has been kidnapped and raised by Indians. Telie turns out to be Reginald's long-lost cousin. In his acts of revenge, Reginald becomes known to the Indians by a number of names, including Nick of the Woods, Bloody Nathan, and *Jibbenainosay*, which means "devil avenger." He finally catches up with Wenonga, the chief who is responsible for the deaths of his family members and kills him. In this attack, however, Reginald and Telie are also killed. In many respects, this play countered the numerous works of this period (plays like

John Augustus Stone's heroically romantic *Metamora; or, The Last of the Wampanoags* [1829]) romanticizing **Native Americans**;*† in this case, the Indians are seen as murderous kidnappers, a racial stereotype that would continue for well over 100 years.

NOAH, MORDECAI MANUEL (1785–1851). Born in Philadelphia to a Portuguese Sephardic family, Mordecai Manuel Noah became the most prominent Jewish figure in the United States before the **Civil War**. He worked in business and became a lawyer, but when he moved to Charleston, he became engaged in politics. President James Madison appointed him consul to Riga, but Noah turned down the offer; in 1813, he was offered the same position in Tunis, where he won approval for saving Americans enslaved by Moroccans. Despite this success, President James Monroe removed him from the position because, in Monroe's view, Noah's religious faith made his success as a consul impossible. The situation set off outrage among both Jews and non-Jews. Jewish leaders, as well as three former presidents, John Adams, **Thomas Jefferson**, and James Madison, protested Monroe's action, but Noah was never able to receive a satisfactory explanation from the White House about the punitive and clearly anti-Semitic removal from his post.

Noah turned to journalism, founding *The National Advertiser* and several other newspapers he ultimately merged into the *New York Courier and Enquirer* and edited other papers. He also began writing plays, including the popular *She Would Be a Soldier; or, The Plains of the Chippewa* (1819). His plays reflected his intense patriotism; other works include *Fortress of Sorrento* (1808), *Paul and Alexis; or, The Orphans of the Rhine* (1812), *Siege of Tripoli* (1820; produced frequently under multiple titles), *Marion, or The Hero of Lake George* (1821), *The Grecian Captive* (1822), and *The Siege of Yorktown* (1824).

Almost single-handedly, Noah attempted to establish a Jewish "refuge" at Grand Island in the Niagara River in 1825. Noah shared a common belief among Jews that **Native Americans**ced*† were part of the Lost Tribes of Israel, which he wrote about in *Discourse on the Evidences of the American Indians being the Descendents of the Lost Tribes of Israel* (1837). He later followed this with *Discourse on the Restoration of the Jews* (1844). He wrote about the institution of slavery, but vacillated on it, sometimes supporting it as an economic necessity, other times condemning the human brutalities.

NORMAN MAURICE; OR, THE MAN OF THE PEOPLE. **William Gilmore Simms**'s five-act blank verse tragedy was written in 1851, though Simms had begun work on it in 1847. Though the play went into rehearsal in Nashville, Tennessee, in 1854, it was not produced despite the fact that

Simms hoped **Edwin Forrest** would appear in it. The play, set in Philadelphia and Missouri, focused on attempts by the enemies of Norman Maurice to ruin him, despite his role as a noble man defending the Constitution, making him something of a typical **melodramatic†** hero.

Considered by some to be Simms's best drama, its lack of production kept it in relative obscurity, though once it was published in 1853 for the first time (and multiple times since), it became a popular reading since Simms mixes current political concerns with vernacular language in the structure of Elizabethan tragedy. The contemporary concerns had to do with the Missouri Compromise and the Nullification crisis, but more generally with issues surrounding the institution of slavery. Setting the current events in a tragic framework rendered the issues potently moving and actively distressing to those concerned with the slave question and how it could be resolved.

NORTH POINT; OR, BALTIMORE DEFENDED. George **Washington Parke Custis**, the adopted son of President **George Washington**, was an orator and writer whose works included essays about his adoptive father. He also wrote plays, including this 1833 drama, first produced in Baltimore. This tale of the **War of 1812** battle takes on a little extra interest in that Custis fought in the actual battle. He had volunteered to help in the defense of Maryland's Fort McHenry when the British entered the state. Among Custis's other plays are *The Indian Prophecy; or, Visions of Glory* (1827), *The Rail Road* (1828), *Pocahontas; or, The Settlers of Virginia* (1830), *The Eighth of January, Hurra, for the Boys of the West* (c. 1830), and *Montgomerie; or, The Orphan of a Wreck* (1836).

†NUDITY IN THE AMERICAN THEATER. The earliest examples of nudity on the American stage were most likely a sham; that is, **actresses*†** dressed in **fleshings** (flesh-colored tights) provided fairly convincing images of nudity for the audience, as in **Adah Isaacs Menken**'s appearance as the title character in *Mazeppa*, who was billed as "The Naked Lady," though she made her famous ride lashed to a horse and supposedly nude, but wearing fleshings. This did not deter audiences, who viewed her as perhaps the theater's first sex symbol; Menken and the play won scandalous reputations and filled box office coffers. Audiences were simultaneously titillated and scandalized by the ballet dancers of the work considered the first modern **musical,*† *The Black Crook*** (1866), who wore fleshings to suggest nudity.

Genuine nudity found its way slowly to American stages in September 1831 with **tableaux vivants,†** a form of living pictures with the one unchangeable rule that forbade a nude or seminude actress from moving. As such, the tableaux became living pictures, with the first introduced by Ada Adams Barrymore illustrating a painting, *The Soldier's Widow*. This well-intentioned live re-creation of a serious artwork sans nudity was shown again by **Laura Keene** 25 years later, and such recreations of paintings have been seen in musicals and plays since.

"Living Models" first appeared in 1847 when a Dr. Collyer introduced them as what were ostensibly living re-creations of classical sculpture. Male and female forms—nude or seminude—re-created everything from biblical scenes and classical art to prizefighters, prostitutes, and other nudes that could be somehow justified as artistic, though much of this sort of thing was seen in taverns, dime museums, and night cellars, and often raided by police and assailed by moralists. But the opportunity to exhibit nude or scantily clad young women (and men) was lucrative enough that by the late 1840s these establishments were willing to risk the legal penalties. Much later, from the mid-1890s to the mid-1920s, tableaux vivants depicted nudity in chorines appearing in musical revues of the most artistic type, such as Florenz Ziegfeld's† *Follies*,† to lesser imitators.

†OAKLEY, ANNIE (1860–1926). Annie Oakley was born Phoebe Ann Moses in North Star, Ohio, of Quaker descent; her father, a **War of 1812** veteran, died when she was young, and her family fell into poverty. She learned to shoot and trap to help feed the family and sold game to local hotels and restaurants. When, in 1875, traveling sharpshooter Frank Butler performed in the area, he made a bet with an Ohio hotel owner that he could beat any local sharpshooter. Oakley at age 15 defeated Butler, who was charmed by her, and they married in 1876.

Butler and Oakley joined Buffalo Bill's† Wild West Show in 1885, leading to world fame and the nickname "Little Sure Shot," given to her by Sitting Bull, who was also an attraction† in the show. Oakley was internationally popular as a result of a European **tour**,*† in which she performed before Queen Victoria and famously shot a cigarette out of the mouth of Kaiser Wilhelm II. Her life was the subject of films† and plays, most notably a 1946 **musical**,*† *Annie Get Your Gun*.

OATES, ALICE (1849–1887). Born in Nashville, Tennessee, as Alice Merritt, she trained in preparation for an operatic career. However, after marrying an **actor**,*† James A. Oates of Wood's Theatre in Cincinnati, Ohio, Oates played **supporting roles**.† In the wake of the popular success of **Lydia Thompson†** and her British Blondes in the late 1860s, Oates established a **burlesque*** troupe ultimately named the Alice Oates New English Opera Company, performing French **opéra bouffe** in English. Her company **toured***† mostly in the midwestern and western parts of the United States. She admired the **operettas†** of **Gilbert and Sullivan** and staged their *H.M.S. Pinafore* before its New York premiere.

OCTAVIA BRAGALDI; OR, THE CONFESSION. Considered the finest of **Charlotte Mary Sanford Barnes**'s plays, this five-act blank verse tragedy opened on 8 November 1837 at New York's **National Theatre**, and Barnes appeared, along with her husband, E. S. Connor, in the play. *Octavia Bragaldi* was popular until well past the middle of the 19th century. Though it was based on a true incident in Frankfort, Kentucky, in 1825, in which one soldier killed another for the premarital seduction of his wife, Barnes moved the story to Milan in the 15th century, where Octavia deceives her father and runs off with Count Castelli, who tricks the virtuous young woman with a sham marriage. Castelli deserts Octavia and five years later she marries Bragaldi. When Castelli reemerges and slanders Octavia, Bragaldi challenges him to a duel. Castelli refuses, so Octavia, driven to revenge her seduction and abandonment by him, confronts Bragaldi and insists he kill Castelli. He does so and commits suicide before he can be imprisoned. Left to face her own culpability, Octavia takes poison.

THE OCTOROON; OR, LIFE IN LOUISIANA. **Dion Boucicault**'s† romantic **melodrama**,† adapted from the 1856 Thomas Mayne Reid novel *The Quadroon*, opened on 6 December 1859 at the **Winter Garden Theatre** for 48 performances. In the over 150 years since its premiere, this play has inspired scholarly debate over its history and themes, especially in regard to its depictions of race issues and the once-explosive issue of miscegenation.

The original production of *The Octoroon* opened just days after John Brown's execution for his violent raid on Harper's Ferry, an inciting event in the coming **Civil War**, and, as such, the play, like **George L. Aiken**'s adaptation of Harriet Beecher Stowe's popular novel *Uncle Tom's Cabin*, is often discussed as inflaming abolitionist sentiments. However, the play's content seems comparatively ambivalent on the subject of race, depicting the tragic results of love between the races, and does not seem to take a decisive stand on the institution of slavery. Boucicault, a consummate commercial theater man, may have chosen to avoid obvious polemics in order for the play to find an audience even in the slave-owning Southern states. Little more than a month after the play's opening in New York, and immediately following its closing, Boucicault felt compelled to defend his position in a 17 January 1860 letter to the *New Orleans Picayune*, which was reprinted in the *New York Times*:

> GENTLEMEN: My work, "The Octoroon; or, Life in Louisiana," has been attacked by the Press here—some alleging that it is a rank pro-slavery drama, others that it is an Abolition play in disguise, and others that it is neither.
>
> As for my political persuasion, I am a Democrat, and a Southern Democrat, but do not mix myself up with politics in any way; still when I found myself under an imputation of writing anything with the smallest tendency against my convictions, I withdrew the work not because I disowned it—I withdrew it to send it down South that you might see for yourselves whether even inadvertently I could prostitute my abilities, my convictions and my feelings.

> It is not probable that I shall ever visit the South again, so I am doubly anxious to retain the good opinion of the friends I made and left there. And I have no more honest, straight, and manly course to pursue than to send on the work as I do now, and prove by its representation that I am not unworthy to retain your kind remembrance.

Boucicault sent a similar letter to the governor of Louisiana. The play found some acceptance in the South, but Boucicault's diplomacy did little to silence its proslavery **critics***† before the Civil War. After the **war**,*† the play was more popular, tapping in to increasingly sentimental views of the prewar years.

The plot of *The Octoroon* begins with George Peyton's return from Europe to discover that Terrebonne, his aunt's plantation, is in financial jeopardy despite the efforts of **Yankee**† Salem Scudder (played by **Joseph Jefferson**,† in one of his most popular roles), who was the business associate of his late uncle, Judge Peyton. The nefarious Jacob McClosky, who ruined the Peytons' fortunes, informs George that the plantation is up for sale and its slaves will be sold off. Dora Sunnyside, a wealthy Southern girl, is enamored of George, but he is in love with the octoroon (one-eighth black) Zoe, the daughter of his late uncle and a slave, played by **Agnes Robertson**.†

McClosky desires Zoe and plots to buy her to be his mistress, since she has rebuffed his amorous advances. Using a tomahawk, McClosky murders Paul, a slave boy, who is delivering mail with news of a plan to save Terrebonne. The murder is accidentally captured in a photograph and observed by a **Native American**,*† Wahnotee. However, since he cannot speak English, he is unable to share the evidence. Zoe loves George, but rejects his marriage proposal believing that her racial heritage will ruin his life. George persists, promising to take her away from Louisiana, but Zoe stands firm. Scudder explains to George that Terrebonne could be saved if he would marry Dora. George nearly proposes to her, but his feelings for Zoe prevent it, and he tells Dora the truth. When the slave auction begins, Zoe is put on the block when McClosky is able to prove that Judge Peyton never officially freed her, as he had clearly intended. To help George and Zoe, Dora attempts to outbid McClosky for Zoe, but he succeeds in buying her. When Paul's body is discovered, the slave buyers accuse Wahnotee of killing him, and McClosky calls for a lynching of the Indian. Scudder intervenes, and Wahnotee is instead arrested, but another slave arrives with the photographic proof of McClosky's guilt. Scudder prevents a lynching of McClosky, who subsequently escapes and sets fire to a steamship populated with the Terrebonne slaves. Wahnotee catches up to McClosky and kills him. Zoe, realizing she and George cannot possibly be together, takes poison before the news arrives that Terrebonne has been saved. Zoe dies in George's arms as the play ends.

In its English premiere, the play's tragic ending was changed to a happy one with the lovers united, but in 1859 the subject of miscegenation was deemed unacceptable to many in the American audience and the only possible outcome was the death of Zoe. This device of a tragic ending underscoring traditional mainstream values permitted playwrights like Boucicault to flirt with controversial subjects, but leave his audience with the opportunity of accepting the meaning of the ending in their own way. Among the few American plays from the mid-19th century still produced, including **Broadway***† revivals in 1929 and 1969, and several Off-Broadway* revivals, including in 2006 at the Metropolitan Theatre and in 2010 at the Performance Space 122, the once-taboo theme is, perhaps, the main reason for its enduring producibility, though Boucicault strives to take no particular stand on slavery or to explore racial matters in any depth (though from a contemporary point of view, the play seems to express abolitionist sentiments).

Some **critics***† at the time of its original production chided him for this, though the play remained popular with audiences for decades, including in Southern states, especially after the Civil War. Stories, real or apocryphal, abound of powerfully emotional audience reactions to the slave auction scene in which Zoe, the play's sympathetic heroine, is sold. The realism*† of the scene, by mid-19th-century standards, apparently made this scene especially shocking. To a contemporary sensibility, the depiction of **African Americans***† and Native Americans seems stereotypical, but compared with much popular entertainment in that era, these characters are uncommonly three dimensional and, as such, the travails and tragedies they suffer disturbed audiences.

ODELL, GEORGE (1866–1949). A native of Newburgh, New York, George Clinton Densmore Odell graduated from Columbia University, where he succeeded **Brander Matthews** on the faculty in 1924. Though Odell's work as a theater historian was done after 1880, his importance has much to do with the research he began in 1894 chronicling the New York theater from its origins through the late 19th century. This resulted in the 15-volume *Annals of the New York Stage*, published between 1927 and 1949 (the year of his death). This extraordinary compendium is, for theater scholars, a definitive resource on early American theater.

OLD LOVE LETTERS. **Bronson Howard**'s† one-act, two-character comedy was first performed on 31 August 1878 at Abbey's Theatre starring **Agnes Booth**, for whom Howard wrote the play, and Joseph Whiting. It proved a popular vehicle for Booth, in which she played a sentimental widow reliving the past through love letters from a former beau, and she performed it often.

OLDMIXON, MRS. JOHN (1763?–1836). Born in England as Georgina Sidus, she made her stage debut as Miss George at the Haymarket Theatre in 1783 and, later, at the Drury Lane Theatre. She appeared in London for a decade before traveling to the United States shortly after her marriage to John Oldmixon. She appeared at the **Chestnut Street Theatre** in Philadelphia, under the management of **Thomas Wignell**, where in time she became the theater's highest-paid **actor**.*† Mrs. Oldmixon also appeared frequently at New York's **Park Theatre**, though most of her career was spent in Philadelphia. Her range included **Shakespearean***† roles and contemporary comedies, but she was much admired for her singing voice and gave concert performances even after she retired from acting around 1814. **William Dunlap** wrote that she possessed "great vivacity and force; in the later years of her stage history, she frequently played the old woman of comedy, and with peculiar effect."

OLIO. This term generally refers to a miscellaneous mixture of elements, and in its theatrical sense it was essentially just that, usually referring to songs, dances, etc., inserted in front of a curtain, often to cover a scene change in **melodramas**† or **vaudeville**.† On the stage, the term might also refer to a large canvas drop painted either with a scene or, during the vaudeville years, with advertisements for local businesses. These drops could provide a solo performer or act with use of the front part of the stage while another scene could be set up behind it.

OLYMPIC THEATRE. Not to be confused with London's Olympic Theatre, run by **Madame Vestris** at its height, New York's Olympic Theatre (which was also designed by **architect**† Calvin Pollard), was built at 444 **Broadway**ardway*† in place of the **National Theatre**, which was destroyed by **fire**† in September 1839. The Olympic was taken on by **manager***† and **star***† **William Mitchell** at its height (1839–1850), with specialties in **burlesques**,*† parodies of celebrities and fictional characters, and plays drawn from popular literature. Mitchell specialized in the works of **Charles Dickens** and also staged the early Mose plays about the Bowery b'hoys starring **Frank S. Chanfrau**. Mitchell's ill health ended his management in 1850, and the Olympic became a German-language theater and **minstrel**† hall. It did not succeed, and the Olympic closed in 1852 and was torn down in 1854.

ONE THOUSAND MILLINERS WANTED FOR THE GOLD DIGGINS IN CALIFORNIA. Joseph Stirling Coyne's *One Thousand Spirited Milliners Wanted for the Gold Diggings in Australia* first opened in London in October 1852 at the Royal Olympic Theatre as a one-act afterpiece. Americanized with a shortened title, it opened at **Burton's Theatre** in New

York on 8 November 1852, and its broad shenanigans involved a law clerk, Baggs (played in the original production by **William Burton**), and his medical student friend, Tipton, who trick girls into coming to the law office to interview with Baggs's boss, Singleton, offering promises of high-paying work in gold-rush country. The machinations involve the two young men dressing as old women in hopes of getting close to the girls while Singleton is away. The girls outsmart them, tying Baggs and Tipton to chairs at just the moment Singleton returns. To avoid trouble, Singleton is persuaded to throw a party to placate the girls.

The play's central conceit of two men in drag is a device that would be used to greater effect a generation later in English **playwright***† Brandon Thomas's farce *Charley's Aunt* (1892) and numerous other works, though Coyne's play was highly popular for decades (sometimes with a shortened title), especially when **Ben De Bar** took on the role of Baggs as one of his most popular vehicles.

†**O'NEILL, JAMES (1846–1920).** Born in County Kilkenny, Ireland, James O'Neill was brought to America in his youth by his family; they settled in Buffalo, New York. The family lived in **Dickensian** poverty and constant hunger, which formed his lifelong habit of penny-pinching, ultimately dramatized by his son, Eugene O'Neill,*† in the semi-autobiographical drama *Long Day's Journey into Night** (1939). O'Neill's stage career began by accident in 1865 when he was paid to go on as an extra† in Cincinnati and discovered his inclination.

Blessed with a good voice and attractive appearance, O'Neill worked hard to learn the craft of an **actor**.*† By 1870 he obtained a **leading man**† engagement† with a Cleveland **stock***† company. In 1872, O'Neill became leading man at **McVicker's Theatre**† in Chicago. For a month during his two seasons there, he alternated the roles of Othello and Iago with **Edwin Booth**,† an experience he regarded as a highlight of his career. At various times, he also appeared with **Edwin Forrest, Charlotte Cushman**, and **Adelaide Neilson**.

O'Neill scored a particular success in the title role in *The Count of Monte Cristo* in 1883, and its popularity was such that O'Neill became closely identified with the title role of Edmund Dantès. Though he saw himself as a **Shakespearean***† actor, ultimately audiences wanted him only in the popular **melodramas**† of the time. He eventually felt trapped in the role he played over 6,000 times, and although it served him well financially, to some extent it frustrated his artistic ambitions, a situation depicted by his son in *Long Day's Journey into Night*.

†**OPERA HOUSE.** Before the 1880s, the word "theater" often carried unsavory connotations of cheap variety performances or immorality. Thus the grand 2000-seat playhouses constructed in major cities were most often labeled "opera houses" in an attempt to achieve dignity and respectability, even though the fare at so-called opera houses often included **musical*†** theater, **minstrel†** companies, lectures, **burlesque,*†** and **legitimate†** drama.

OPÉRA BOUFFE. The popularity of this form in France arrived in the United States with productions of Jacques Offenbach's **operettas,†** *La Grande Duchesse de Gérolstein* and *La Belle Hélène* in 1867. Appreciated by American audiences for the music, style, and spectacle, and not the content (since the earliest were performed in French and satirized aspects of France's cultural landscape), these and other opera bouffe works caused some controversy. The controversy, which emerged when these works were first performed in English, resulted from what some **critics*†** and audiences saw as violations of Victorian values. However, there was an enduring popularity for these works on American stages well into the 20th century.

†**OPERETTA.** The term "operetta" derives from French, German, and Italian sources, but in common usage it suggests a small or light opera, something between opera and **musical*†** comedy. In America, operetta gained popularity when Jacques Offenbach's **opéra bouffe** works first appeared in the 1860s and, in part, even more so through the popularity of the English operettas of **W. S. Gilbert** and **Arthur Sullivan**, beginning with a highly successful New York run of *The Pirates of Penzance* in 1879. American operetta emerged in the same period with the triumph of *The Black Crook* (1866), which is often considered the first musical and, if something less than that, a prototype for many musicals following it. *Erminie* (1886), an operetta with music by Edward Jakobowski, scored a great success, playing over 1,250 performances, after which operettas filled stages in the United States well into the 20th century. In the first decade of sound films,† operettas achieved some popularity on-screen.

ORALOOSA; OR, THE LAST OF THE INCAS. **Robert Montgomery Bird**'s five-act blank verse tragedy (sometimes titled *Oraloosa, Son of the Incas*) opened on 10 October 1832 for five performances at the **Arch Street Theatre** in Philadelphia, **starring*†** **Edwin Forrest** in the title role. Spanish conquistador Francisco Pizarro takes power in Peru following his defeat of Incan leader Atahualpa. However, Atahualpa's son, Oraloosa, slays Pizarro with the goading of ambitious Diego de Almagro (played by **John R. Scott**), who then betrays Oraloosa, who is murdered while his sister, Orallie, is buried alive. Almagro does not realize his ambitions for power, since his actions are discovered, leading to a sentence of death by a new Spanish viceroy, Vaca de Castro. Bird's dramas, including this one, were acknowledged in play competitions sponsored by Forrest, who, in this period, was attempting to actively encourage the writing and production of new American plays. Bird was one of the first **dramatists***† in the United States to establish a career as a full-time professional **playwright**.*†

ORDWAY, JOHN (1824–1880). A native of Salem, Massachusetts, John Pond Ordway was educated at Harvard, becoming a doctor and one of the first of his profession to volunteer for service with the Union Army at the outbreak of the **Civil War**. Before the **war**,*† he was also a composer and performer and owned a music shop in Boston. In 1849, he organized **Ordway's Aeolians**, a **touring***† **minstrel**† troupe, and he composed songs, several of which became popular, including "Dreaming of Home and Mother" (1851), "Going Home" (1855), and "Twinkling Stars Are Laughing, Love" (1855).

Other composers wrote songs for Ordway's Aeolians, and the company introduced "Jingle Bells," written by James Lord Pierpont, who dedicated the enduring holiday song to Ordway. In 1852, Ordway opened and served as **manager***† of Ordway Hall, where his troupe performed and which specialized in **blackface**† minstrelsy. The entertainers in his company included a young **Dan Emmett**. The hall was seriously damaged by **fire***† in 1864, after which it was rebuilt as an office building. After Ordway's service during the Civil War, which included tending the wounded following the Battle of Gettysburg, he became a politician and educator in Massachusetts, where he was a vigorous opponent of corporal punishment in schools. At the time of his death, his obituaries barely mentioned his prior popularity as a composer and minstrel.

ORDWAY'S AEOLIANS. This **blackface**† **minstrel**† troupe, established by composer and performer **John B. Ordway** in 1849, became popular, especially in Boston, where, in 1852, Ordway opened and served as **manager***† of Ordway Hall, where the Aeolians performed songs by Ordway and others in the evolving minstrel tradition. Historians credit the Aeolians with creating the tradition of a street parade announcing the minstrel troupe's arrival in a town, a device they employed in occasional **tours***† by the Aeolians around the United States, as well as with making use of lavish scenic and costume spectacle and with attempting to popularize whiteface minstrelsy.

OREGON; OR, THE DISPUTED TERRITORY. **Joseph M. Field**'s 1846 topical and satirical allegory dramatized the complex conflict between the United States and England over the Northwest Territory in **melodramatic†** fashion. President James K. Polk sought to add Oregon, Texas, and California to the United States, which is portrayed in a play that is something like a masque.

OROLOSA; OR, DEAD SHOT OF THE SIERRA NEVADAS. Produced by Dan Shelby as part of an evening with an acrobatic troupe, the Zitella Family, at St. James Hall in Auburn, New York, on 21 February 1873, this "dramatic sensation," as it was billed in local newspapers, featured a cast of 25.

OSSAWATTOMIE BROWN; OR, THE INSURRECTION AT HARPER'S FERRY. This three-act drama by Mrs. J. C. Swayze (Kate Edwards), opened on 16 December 1859 at the **Bowery Theatre**, with **G. C. Boniface** in the role of abolitionist firebrand John Brown, and was produced a mere two weeks following Brown's execution. The **melodramatic†** play freely fictionalized Brown's family life before and after his assault on Harper's Ferry, one of the inciting events of the **Civil War**, and contributed to shaping public sentiments, if not about Brown, then about his cause.

At one point, Brown's widowed daughter-in-law attempts to persuade an abolitionist from using Brown to his ends since, as she sees it, "under his [Brown's] great trials, his mind has warped and cramped until he can see nothing but through the glass of his revenge, and lives but to redress his wrongs." Kate Edwards Swayze (1833–1862) was born in England and came to the United States in 1846 and acted small parts in several New York theaters prior to marriage to a printer, J. Clarke Swayze, in 1856. *Ossawattomie Brown* may have been her only play—and may or may not have reflected her own political views—for she placed dramatic emphasis more on sensation, Brown family dynamics (including a near rape of Brown's daughter), and melodrama than on the complexities of racial or abolitionist issues. Swayze moved with her husband to Georgia in 1860, where he was briefly jailed as a Northern sympathizer after the war began.

OTHO: A TRAGEDY IN FIVE ACTS. **John Neal**'s five-act poetic tragedy was written in 1819 for **Thomas Abthorpe Cooper**, though Cooper never appeared in it. In fact, though it was published that year, it was never performed. In a lengthy preface to the printed play, Neal acknowledges the borrowing of elements from Charles Robert Maturin's *Bertram*, Lord Byron's *Corsair* and *Manfred*, and **Shakespeare**'s*† *Macbeth*. Neal claims this play as an "American tragedy," perhaps the first of its kind, but it seems more a manifestation of a kind of literary nationalism. The character of Otho is a bastard and revolutionary ultimately murdered by his foe, Duke Alva, and dies calling for the father he never knew.

OUR AMERICAN COUSIN. English **playwright*† Tom Taylor**'s three-act farce, a popular work in its time, would likely have been forgotten out of its era save for the fact that in the midst of a 14 April 1865 performance at Washington, DC's **Ford's Theatre**, **John Wilkes Booth†** assassinated President **Abraham Lincoln**, who was sitting in a stage box watching as **actor*† Harry Hawk**, playing Asa Trenchard, delivered the last words Lincoln heard: "Don't know the manners of good society, eh? Well, I guess I know enough to turn you inside out, old gal—you sockdologizing old man-trap." Booth chose this particular laugh line, one of the biggest and most reliable in the play, knowing that the audience response would at least partially cover the sound of his derringer firing at close range at the back of Lincoln's head, permitting him at least a momentary advantage in escaping after leaping from the stage box to the stage and out of the theater through the wings, brushing past the play's **star*†** and **manager,*† Laura Keene**, who had just exited the scene onstage moments before the shot was fired.

Hawk played the role originated by **Joseph Jefferson†** when the play premiered at Laura Keene's Theatre in New York on 15 October 1858, scoring a major success and becoming a permanent fixture in Keene's repertoire. Keene played Florence, the daughter of an English baron, who hosts the "American cousin," Asa, a **Yankee†** character lacking manners and graces, but who rescues the fortunes of his high society English family. Cast members also included **C. W. Couldock†** and **Effie Germon**, but the play was made a hit by **E. A. Sothern** in the role of Lord Dundreary, a lisping British fop, who expanded his comparatively small role with ad-libs that not only pleased the New York audience, but ultimately became part of the play's acting text. In fact, the term "Dundrearyisms" was coined to describe the sort of one-liners supplied by Sothern. Sothern was not in the Ford's Theatre cast; E. A. Emerson played Dundreary on that tragic night. The Dundreary character spawned spin-off plays by other authors, with **Charles Gayler** penning *Our American Cousin at Home; or, Lord Dundreary Abroad* (1860). Other Dundreary plays include H. J. Byron's *Dundreary Married and Done For* (1862) and John Oxenford's *Brother Sam* (1862).

OUR BOARDING HOUSE. **Leonard Grover**'s four-act comedy opened 29 January 1877 at the **Park Theatre** for 104 performances. Beatrice Manheim is informed by her brother-in-law, Joseph Fioretti (**W. E. Sheridan**), that her marriage to her late husband was not legal, leading other boarders in the rooming house in which she lives to overreact, with one clique insisting on her eviction on moral grounds and others supporting her. Most of the play's comedy centered on the eccentric behaviors of the boardinghouse residents, especially Professor Gregarious Gillypod (**Stuart Robson†**), the inventor of a flying machine, and Colonel M. T. Elevator (**W. H. Crane†**), a speculator in grain. Ultimately, Beatrice learns that her marriage was, in fact, legal—and that she has also inherited great wealth. This first teaming of Robson and Crane led to a long association. Robson later wrote in an *Everybody's Magazine* article that the parts of Gillypod and Elevator were originally small, but that the chemistry between himself and Crane was "a profitable and pleasant partnership of 12 years—and a partnership which one might say was formed by the public."

OWENS, JOHN E. (1823–1886). Born in Liverpool, England, John Edward (or Edmond) Owens immigrated to the United States with his family, who established themselves in Philadelphia, where he joined the company of **William Burton** as an **actor*†** in 1841. In 1850, **John Brougham** provided Owens with his first opportunities in New York, where he became a popular stage comedian in a range of character roles, including as Dr. Pangloss in *Heir-at-Law*, Caleb Plummer in a stage version of **Charles Dickens**'s *The Cricket on the Hearth*, and the old man in *Esmeralda*, in which he made his final appearance.

Owens reached the pinnacle of his popular success playing the **Yankee†** character (and title role) in the **Joseph S. Jones** comedy *Solon Shingle* (1842) in 1856, a play also known as *The People's Lawyer*. As a **manager,*†** Owens effectively marketed this play, performing it over 2,000 times in theaters around the country and amassing significant wealth. After his death, Owens's wife, Mary C. Stevens, wrote a memoir of his career, and of his performance as Shingle, she noted, it was

> a finished piece of character acting, perfect in detail, and yet free from exaggeration. The power of the artist is prominent from the fact that this great success evolved from a mere sketch, which his own genius elaborated and clothed with vitality. This marvellous [sic] portrayal has formed the basis for many rural dramas, wherein the central figure is a palpable imitation of Owens's *original* conception and manner of playing *Solon Shingle*; but their light is a borrowed one, relatively as bright as the moon compared to the sun.

PADDY THE PIPER. James **Pilgrim**'s **Irish**-themed one-act comic-drama was performed in 1850 at the **Broadway Theatre**—and was just one of many works about Irish culture and heritage written by Pilgrim and popular with Irish immigrant audiences, and one of a series of so-called Paddy comedies. In the play, an archetypal young Irishman acclimating to life in the United States clings to aspects of his Irish heritage. Other than **Dion Boucicault,†** Pilgrim was perhaps the most successful of antebellum **playwrights*†** exploring Irish culture and a forerunner of Irish-themed plays and **musicals*†** to appear for decades after the **Civil War.***

THE PADLOCK. Isaac Bickerstaffe's two-act comic opera, with music by Charles Dibdin, borrowed plot elements from Miguel de Cervantes's novel *The Jealous Husband.* First performed in 1768 at the Drury Lane Theatre in London, it became especially popular in the United States and was regularly performed into the 1840s. Dibdin, in **blackface,†** played the central character of a servant from the West Indies, Mungo, in the original London production, but the role was later performed by **Lewis Hallam Jr.** in its first American performances—and later still by **African American*† actor*† Ira Aldridge**.

Mungo provides the comic elements in *The Padlock*, and he is depicted as a boozing, greedy caricature, with an exaggerated West Indies accent. Dibdin and Hallam were believed to be among the first **actors*†** to perform in blackface, which subsequently became an American stage tradition (ultimately recognized as an odious racial stereotype) in the early 19th century and continuing well into the 20th century, especially through **minstrel†** shows and, later, **vaudeville,† musicals,*†** and early films.**†**

In 1787, Dibdin began to perform a **one-man*** show inspired by the Mungo character, but Aldridge won acclaim in the role when he gave the character a more realistic persona. Dibdin's score was influenced by Italian opera, including Mungo's songs, which did not reflect the African rhythms that would profoundly influence American popular music. The simple plot of *The*

339

Padlock centers on an elderly miser keeping his intended young bride locked up to prevent encounters with other men, possibly influenced by Molière's *The School for Wives*.

†**PALMER, A. M. (1838–1905).** North Stonington, Connecticut–born Albert Marshman Palmer studied law at New York University. Instead of law, he chose to pursue political opportunity through a friendship with New York's collector of internal revenue, **Sheridan Shook**, who ultimately made Palmer **manager*†** of the **Union Square Theatre,†** where he produced *Rose Michel* (1870) and *The Two Orphans* (1874). The theater failed at **vaudeville,†** so Palmer established a **repertory*†** company to rival those headed by **Lester Wallack** and **Augustin Daly**.† The company scored successes with several new plays, but a falling-out with Shook terminated the experiment, and Palmer retired from the venture in 1883.

Palmer then took over the **Madison Square Theatre,†** building a reputation for high-quality productions of both American and European plays, the most successful of which included *Dr. Jekyll and Mr. Hyde* (1887), *Partners* (1888), *Beau Brummel†* (1890), *Alabama†* (1891), *Lady Windermere's Fan* (1893), and *Trilby†* (1895). Palmer also served as president of the Actors Fund of America† from 1885 to 1897.

PALMER, MINNIE (1857–1936). A native of Philadelphia, Minnie Palmer spent part of her childhood in a convent, after which she studied singing in Vienna. She became an **actress*†** in America in 1874, appearing in Baltimore and at **Booth's Theatre** in *Dan'l Druce*. She was considered a great beauty in her time and scored a hit in *My Sweetheart* (1882), playing Tina, a virtuous girl who ultimately eludes the interference of a corrupt woman. Palmer appeared in this role in England and America with significant success—and she spent much of her career in Europe.

In 1890, while in New York, Palmer was nearly killed by her possessive husband, John P. Rogers, who was also her **manager,*†** when he attacked her with a knife. He only injured her slightly, though a considerable amount of publicity resulted in the tabloid press. Palmer made her final New York appearance in the long-running hit *Lightnin',†* written by Winchell Smith† and Frank Bacon,† playing the character role Mrs. Jordan.

†**PANORAMA.** Although panoramas cannot exactly be called a form of theater, they had an important impact on **scene design*†** for both the **legitimate†** and **musical*†** stages, and they were marketed to the public, along with live theater and dime museums, under the category of **amusements**.†

After paying admission, a patron would climb a spiral staircase to a viewing platform from which one could contemplate an encircling painted vista of a city or a battlefield, with three-dimensional elements in the foreground.

Panoramas were novelties in Europe around 1800, but enjoyed a second surge of worldwide popularity in the mid- to late 19th century. A mid-19th-century variation was the moving panorama; this involved scrolling across the stage a huge canvas depicting the changes of scenery over a vast distance. When **actors***† or horse-drawn chariots (as in *Ben-Hur*†) moved in the opposite direction on a treadmill in front of the spooling canvas, the illusion of a journey past changing scenery was created and was, by all accounts, impressive.

In theatrical circumstances, panoramas often addressed historical events, such as famous battles from **wars***† as recent as the **Civil War**, but also back to the dawn of history. Also, well-known personages, past and present, and the worlds in which they lived were often the subject of a panorama. One of the most acclaimed of these, created by **Imre Kiralfy**, *Nero, of the Destruction of Rome* (1889) was a great success as part of **P. T. Barnum's**† **Circus***† in London.

Current events were frequent topics, including Henry Box Brown's *Mirror of Slavery*, a panorama illuminating his life in slavery and his daring escape. Brown had famously shipped himself out of a slave state by hiding in a crate delivered to an abolitionist in Philadelphia. The story made considerable news, and Brown became an instant celebrity in the Northern states, narrating the story of his experience in tandem with the panorama. Another **African American, playwright***† **William Wells Brown** also offered a slave narrative with his *Original Panoramic Views of the Scenes in the Life of an American Slave, From His Birth in Slavery to his Death or His Escape to His First Home on British Soil* (1850). Not surprisingly, these slave narratives and other subjects related to race exploited in panoramas were somewhat popular imagery in the United States—and more so in England—capturing the sentiments of the time, pro and con, on the institution of slavery, depicting for many what they could only otherwise learn about from books and fictional plays. The best of the panoramas were exciting experiences for audiences, and the form was particularly popular in the decades prior to the Civil War.

PARK THEATRE. Though first known as the **New Theatre**, Lewis Hallam Jr. and **John Hodgkinson** opened the Park Theatre in 1798 as a replacement for the **John Street Theatre**, and it was the predominant New York theater for a quarter of a century (for a long time, it was the only one). It remained an important center of theatrical activity until a **fire**† destroyed it in 1848. Located at Park Row east of Ann Street and the back of Theatre Alley, the first architectural plan for the theater was designed by French architect

Marc Isambard Brunel; however, money problems led to the elimination of most of Brunel's elaborate exterior embellishments. As such, the building was more austere in appearance than originally intended, though embellishments added by English **architect John Joseph Holland** in 1807 included the installation of **gas lighting.**†

Most important American plays in the first half of the 19th century were performed at the Park Theatre under a string of important **managers***† of the era, including **William Dunlap, Thomas Abthorpe Cooper, Stephen Price, Edmund Shaw Simpson**, and **Thomas Hamblin**, who had just commenced his management of the theater when it burned. The Park had a resident **stock***† company (made up of members of the Old **American Company**) performing a **repertory***† of plays during its early years. Under Price's management, however, it employed noted European **actors***† and encouraged the **star***† system, leading to the decline of the stock/repertory system in New York.

William Dunlap's *André* (1798) premiered there as one of the Park's first productions. Among major plays produced in the last decade of the Park Theatre was **Dion Boucicault**'s† first major success, *London Assurance* (1841), which gave New York its first long-running hit, followed by a triumph of the first American play to have a similar success, **Anna Cora Mowatt**'s satiric comedy of manners, *Fashion* (1845). Other theaters named the Park Theatre were built in Brooklyn, New York, in 1863, and in Boston in 1879.

PARKE, JOHN (1754–1789). Born in Dover, Delaware, John Parke studied at the College of Philadelphia and translated Greek and Latin poetry before, during, and after he served as a lieutenant-colonel in the Continental Army during the **American Revolution**. His 1776 commission had been recommended to General **George Washington** by Thomas McKean, under whom Parke had studied for the legal profession, and Caesar Rodney, both of whom were signers of the Declaration of Independence. Parke served at Valley Forge under brutal winter conditions before leaving military service in 1778.

After the **war**,*† Parke anonymously published *The Lyric Works of Horace* in 1786, adapting Horace's poems to American subjects. Parke also wrote a play, *Virginia, A Pastoral Drama on the Birth-Day of an Illustrious Personage and the Return of Peace, February 11, 1784*, which honored Washington, under whom Parke had served during the Revolution. The play was probably never professionally produced and was more likely performed in **amateur***† circumstances. It is believed Parke also wrote satires, but none of these survive.

THE PARLOR CAR. **William Dean Howells's**† 1876 one-act comedy is a charming little romance in which a teary young woman, Lucy Galbraith, attempting to flee her fiancé, Allen Richards, encounters him unexpectedly in a train car when he comes to her service in dealing with a broken window. Allen ultimately wears down her proud resistance, and they resolve their differences, leaving the car reunited, and with a happy Lucy proclaiming, "Only think, Allen! If this car hadn't broken *its* engagement, we might never have mended ours."

Howells's plays in general, especially in the characters and dialogue, were appreciated for their wit and fidelity to reality, all evident in *The Parlor Car*, one of his earliest dramatic works. In a 23 August 1876 letter to Howells, his friend **Mark Twain** commented that the play "is wonderfully bright and delicious, and must make a hit. You read it to me, and it was mighty good; I read it last night and it was better; I read it aloud to the household this morning and it was better than ever. So it would be worth going a long way to see it well played; for without any question an **actor***† of genius always adds a little something to any man's work that none but the writer knew was there before."

PARSLOE, CHARLES THOMAS, JR. (1836–1898). Born in New York, the son of Charles Thomas Parsloe, a well-known **actor,***† he began his career as callboy† at **William E. Burton**'s Chambers Street Theatre in 1850. Six years later, he began playing small roles with Burton's **stock***† company and became a popular **juvenile,**† though after he joined the company of **Lester Wallack** in 1857, he began to develop a highly successful career in character roles and, ultimately, as **manager***† of his own **touring***† company. Parsloe won **critical***† claim in a series of Asian roles, including *Under the Gaslight* (1867), *The Danites*† (1877), *Ah Sin* (1877), and *My Partner* (1879). He played over 1,300 performances in the latter, earning a fortune, before he lost it in the stock market and was reduced to poverty. His last years were spent as a beneficiary of the Actors Fund of America.† His obituary in the *New York Times* described him as "once an actor."

THE PASSION PLAY. Jewish writer Salmi Morse crafted this play, which, at its full length was 24 acts, sometimes known as *The Passion*. Based on events in the New Testament, it was produced in San Francisco at **Tom Maguire**'s Theatre in 1879 in an elaborate staging by **David Belasco**† with the role of Christ played by **James O'Neill**.† Local Protestant clergy brought charges against Maguire, Belasco, and the cast for violating a local ordinance against stage depictions of Jesus Christ, while most **critics***† were mixed about the play. *The Passion Play* was staged in New York in a six-act version (that ran nearly four hours) in 1883, but met with similar attempts at censorship. When interviewed by the *New York Times*, an agitated Morse felt he deserved a license to stage the play and that "I would like to have the *Passion* played for the sake of mankind." The New York production failed, and Morse committed suicide by jumping into the Hudson River shortly after the production closed.

†**PASTOR, TONY (1837–1908).** Antonio Pastor was born in New York and began performing as a **child*†** on the **temperance†** circuit and at **P. T. Barnum**'s **American Museum** in 1846. He also worked in **minstrel†** shows and as a **circus*†** performer. Pastor established himself as a songwriter at Robert Butler's American Music Hall and opened his first theater in New York, Tony Pastor's **Opera House**, in the Bowery in 1865 with the goal of making the variety stage more family-friendly.

In 1874, Pastor took over **M. B. Leavitt**'s theater prior to moving to the **Germania Theatre** on **Fourteenth Street†** in 1881, which he developed as a home for what he billed as **vaudeville†** entertainment, a field in which he became known as a premiere **manager.*†** Pastor served as a participating master of ceremonies and was a significant force in nurturing performers, including George M. Cohan,*† Emma Carus, **Maggie Cline**, **Nat C. Goodwin,†** **Lillian Russell,†** and Joe Weber and Lew Fields, among many others. At his death, the *New York Times* reported that over 2,000 people attended his funeral; most of the leading lights of turn-of-the-century New York theater were present to acknowledge "the manager who 'made' more **stars*†** than any other in the business, and many of the first names of the stage were first heard of in his theaters."

THE PATRIOT CHIEF. **Peter Markoe**'s 1784 tragedy, *The Patriot Chief*, the first of his two plays, dramatizes a revolution against a Lydian king. The play's overall theme emphasizes the dangers behind the power of the aristocracy. Markoe's other play, *The Reconciliation* (1790), was a comic opera (one of the first ballad operas written in America). Neither of Markoe's plays were staged during his lifetime, but referring to *The Patriot Chief* as "meritorious," historian Perley Isaac Reed described it as "the best play of the epoch. Although treating a foreign fable, its theme is particularly pertinent, being to show the dangers that often threaten a state from within at the hands of traitors, and the certain triumph over all perfidy when devoted Patriots are aroused."

THE PATRIOTS. During his lifetime, military figure and government official Colonel **Robert Munford** wrote two plays, as well as poetry and other forms of writing, most of which were little known during his life, though they were published after his 1783 death. *The Patriots*, a five-act comedy written circa 1777 and published in 1798, like Munford's other play, *The Candidates* (written circa 1779), is highly topical, depicting life in contemporary Virginia, and believed by historians to be among the first comedies written in America.

The Patriots is set during the **American Revolution** and focuses on tensions between the Tories, those remaining loyal to England, and the Whigs, those in favor of independence from Great Britain, and a third group, those who preferred to remain neutral during the conflict. Munford points to confusions among these groups and depicts violent acts directed against Virginians considered to have less pro-independence patriotism than the Whigs wished.

PAULDING, JAMES KIRKE (1778–1860). Born in Dutchess County, New York, James Kirke Paulding wrote plays and novels, but his distinction in these areas emerged from his use of American themes and background in his literature (and his advocating that other writers in the United States do the same). Around 1796, Paulding moved to New York City, where he became close friends with **Washington Irving** and Irving's brother, William. Together, they founded *Salmagundi* (1807–1808), a publication that emphasized satires of local and topical subjects. When mounting hostilities with Great Britain broke out into the **War of 1812**, Paulding demonstrated his nationalistic fervor in his writings. He parodied England's treatment of America during the **war***† in *The Diverting History of John Bull and Brother Jonathan* (1812); *The Secret of Uncle Sam and His Boys* (1835), widely regarded as an inferior sequel; and *The Lay of the Scottish Fiddle: A Tale of Havre de Grace* (1813), the latter a **burlesque***† treatment of the work of Sir Walter Scott. After the war's end, Paulding did not temper his attitudes about England.

Paulding's most popular play, *The Lion of the West* (1831), a farce written for **actor***† **James H. Hackett**, brought **frontier** humor to the stage with a character, Nimrod Wildfire, patterned on Davy Crockett. Despite the comedy, the play contributed significantly to building Crockett's enduring legend. Though Paulding spent most of his later years in government service, he did continue to write, including *The Bucktails; or, American in England*, a comedy of manners with a sharp satiric edge, as a young American girl is for a time enamored of caricatured English courtiers before she realizes she truly loves her American lover.

THE PAXTON BOYS. This anonymous 1764 play explored the uprising of Presbyterian frontier settlers against **Native American***† tribes. The play's action centers on the political factionalism of Pennsylvania, where the Penn family had caused controversy with the Walking Purchase, which was essentially a land grab of territory occupied by Delaware tribal groups. Pennsylvanians became defensive over the controversy, and *The Paxton Boys* depicts the formation of a militia to do battle with the Conestoga tribe, a destructive act since prior to this time Pennsylvanians had developed a positive and peaceful relationship and mutually constructive economic relations with the Indians. The march led to the killing of 20 tribe members, and the militia marched on to Philadelphia to confront the Quaker-dominated state assembly.

The play's emphasis is on this latter portion of this situation and pays little attention to the deaths of the Indians, adopting a farcical quality satirizing the positions of all factions in the state, especially mocking the unwillingness of Quakers to take up arms. *The Paxton Boys* was published in pamphlet form, as many plays with political content were in these times.

PAYNE, JOHN HOWARD (1791–1852). New York–born eldest son of a teacher with nine children, John Howard Payne was an infant when his parents moved the family to Boston, where his father headed a school. He began writing plays in **childhood***† and was considered something of a prodigy. Payne's father placed him as an apprentice in an accountants' business, but he did not find this an appealing career choice. At the mere age of 14, he published *The Thespian Mirror*, a journal of theatrical **criticism**,*† and wrote his first major play, *Julia; or, The Wanderer*, a comedy in five acts. The play's common vernacular language, considered too racy for the stage of the time, caused its premature closing. A rich New Yorker named John E. Seaman appreciated Payne's talents and offered to pay for his education at Union College. Payne created a college newspaper, *Pastime*, but his college time was cut short by the death of his mother and the failure of his father's business.

Payne determined to go onstage in order to help his family's sudden reversal of fortunes. He debuted on 24 February 1809 as Young Norval in *Douglas* at the **Park Theatre**. He scored a significant success and **toured***† to other cities with the role. During this time, Payne also founded the Athenaeum, a circulating library. English tragedian **George Frederick Cooke**, touring in America, saw Payne's work and took an interest in him, inviting him to appear in *King Lear* with Cooke. He traveled to England with Cooke and appeared at the Covent Garden Theatre and Drury Lane Theatre. He also spent time in Paris seeing theater and translated several French plays into English for production there.

Payne wrote and staged plays at Sadler's Wells Theatre, where he served as **manager***† for a time, and in 1818 wrote **Brutus; or, The Fall of Tarquin**, a drama that gained some popularity. In 1823, Charles Kemble commissioned a play from Payne as part of several Payne works Kemble purchased. He sold Kemble an opera, **Clari: The Maid of Milan** (1823), which included the enduring ballad "Home Sweet Home." The song (with music by

Sir Henry Bishop based on an Italian folk song) made a fortune for Payne, but he was a poor manager of money. He became romantically interested in Mary Shelley, author of *Frankenstein*, but she did not return his interest, and Payne never married.

After many years in England, Payne finally returned to the United States in 1832. He became intensely involved in **Native American*†** issues, particularly the fate of the Cherokee Indians, who were part of the so-called Five Civilized Tribes and who were fighting against being removed from Georgia. Following considerable research, Payne determined that the Cherokees were part of the Ten Lost Tribes of Israel. President John Tyler appointed Payne American Consul in Tunis, where Payne died in 1852, but his fame continued. Payne's "Home Sweet Home" had revived popularity during the **Civil War**, and it was known to be a favorite of President **Abraham Lincoln**.

PEARMAN, MR. (1792–1829?). Very little is known about this singer and **actor,*†** except that Pearman was born in England and made his stage debut some time before 1817. His first appearance in the United States was in *The Devil's Bridge* in 1823 and was a triumph. He also appeared in the American premiere of **John Howard Payne**'s *Clari: The Maid of Milan* that same year. Pearman went back to England after *Clari* and did not return to the United States until 1828, only briefly, prior to traveling to the West Indies where, apparently, he died.

THE PEOPLE'S LAWYER. First performed in Boston in 1839, this **Joseph S. Jones** two-act comedy, also known to audiences as *Solon Shingle*, was first performed on 12 December 1842 at the **Park Theatre starring*†** **George H. Hill** as Solon Shingle. This **Yankee†** character was a major reason for the play's initial success—and enduring popularity when played by **John E. Owens** from the 1850s. In the play, Charles Otis, an honest clerk, is framed for theft by his merchant boss, Winslow, when he refuses to commit perjury for Winslow's sake. Otis is defended by Robert Howard, known as "The People's Lawyer," who also happens to be in love with Otis's sister. Howard calls Solon Shingle as a defense witness, but the well-meaning bumpkin is confused since he thinks he has been called to solve the case of his lost barrel of "apple-sarse." Ultimately, the truth comes out, and Otis is exonerated. Hill found lucrative success playing Shingle, as did **Charles Burke** and, after 1857, Owens, who beefed up the part and **toured*†** it widely. **Joseph Jefferson** also played Solon, as did several lesser comic **actors.*†**

PERIL; OR, LOVE AT LONG BRANCH. **Bartley Campbell**'s second play, a social comedy, was written for **actor*†-manager*†** **E. L. Davenport**, who produced it for his daughter, **Fanny Davenport**. *Peril* opened at the Pittsburgh Playhouse on 23 October 1871 for a well-received run thanks in large measure to Davenport's popularity. The New York production opened in 1872 at the **Union Square Theatre** featuring **McKee Rankin** as the hero, Dick Rothly, and **Maude Granger** in Davenport's role. The play was also performed in April 1873 at **Hooley's Opera House** in Chicago. Described as "A view of the city by the sea," the play set the usual romantic entanglements at the popular New Jersey resort town, summer home to the wealthy and famous, including United States presidents, during the latter half of the 19th century.

The play managed only a two-week run in New York, with one **critic*†** noting, "There is some good dialogue, and the situations are sufficiently inspiring to draw applause from the audience, but there is a want of motive, or rather a lack of dignity of motive in the working out of the plot which prevents any active exercise of sympathy." Despite the brief original run and critical apathy, the play was popular with audiences for the rest of the 19th century, often under the title *Matrimony*, an 1880 version rewritten by Campbell for a run at the Standard Theatre, and, as one *Pittsburgh Post-Gazette* journalist wrote in 1911, *Peril; or, Love at Long Branch* "proved to be Bartley Campbell's first step on his long journey to the heights of successful dramatic authorship."

THE PERSECUTED DUTCHMAN; OR, THE ORIGINAL JOHN SCHMIDT. Summerfield Barry's one-act farce was first produced at the **Bowery Theatre** on 10 November 1854 with S. W. Glenn, who specialized in Dutch (or German) roles, in the title character, and author Barry in a secondary character, Honorable Augustus Clearstarch. The play was performed again in 1857 at **Brougham**'s **Bowery Theatre** with Barry in the lead this time. The mid-19th century saw innumerable "Dutch" plays, from the most famous, **Dion Boucicault**'s† stage adaptation of **Washington Irving**'s *Rip Van Winkle*† starring*† **Joseph Jefferson**,† to many short farcical pieces, like *The Persecuted Dutchman*, appealing to the influx of German immigrants arriving in New York in the mid- to late 19th century.

PFAFF'S. As **Walt Whitman** stated of this notable "trysting place," "The vault at Pfaffs where the drinkers and laughers meet to eat and drink and carouse," is a reasonable statement of the purpose and popularity of Pfaff's, a beer cellar in lower Manhattan established by Charles Pfaff around 1858. Pfaff's became the popular meeting place of artists, writers, and theatrical personages in New York, Whitman among them, and such notables as **Adah**

Isaacs Menken, Edwin Booth,† John Brougham, Henry Clapp, William Dean Howells, Augustin Daly,† Thomas Blades de Walden, Ralph Waldo Emerson, Rose Eytinge, Stephen Ryder Fiske, Charles Gayler, Matilda Heron, Joseph Jefferson,† Laura Keene, Lola Montez, Thomas Nast, Edgar Allan Poe, Mark Twain, Lester Wallack, William Winter,† Elihu Vedder, and Horatio Alger, among many others. Pfaff's was particularly notable for attracting the mid- to late-19th-century avant-garde and controversial figures, as well as those with strong political or aesthetic convictions for after-hours libation and conversation.

PHILADELPHIA SCHOOL OF DRAMATISTS. During the first half of the 19th century, a number of diverse, active **playwrights*†** dominated American stages in one of the country's largest cities—and one with an active artistic community. **Edwin Forrest**, residing in Philadelphia, actively encouraged new dramatists, especially those writing on American subjects. Those writers, particularly working in the tragic vein, and considered part of the Philadelphia School of Dramatists, included **Robert Montgomery Bird**, **George H. Boker**, **Robert T. Conrad**, **Robert Penn Smith**, **John Augustus Stone**, and others.

PHOTOGRAPHERS. The first photographs captured by a camera date from the early 1820s, but by the mid-1840s photography had become relatively commonplace, partly through Louis Daguerre and his daguerreotype, and some photographers began specializing in theater. Undoubtedly, the most famous of these was **Napoleon Sarony**, who founded a studio on **Broadway*†** in 1866 and endeavored to photograph in and out of costume every noted **actor*†** and **actress*†** working on the New York stage over a period of 30 years.

Other individual photographers and studios followed in Sarony's footsteps, including Charles D. Fredericks (1823–1894) and Jeremiah Gurney (1812–1886). Matthew Brady (c. 1822–1896), who, in his early days, associated himself with the E. & H. T. Anthony Studio, built a reputation photographing celebrated individuals, including President **Abraham Lincoln**, and is now most remembered for his **Civil War**–era photographs from the battlefields, where he recorded the horrors of **war*†** with graphic detail previously unseen by the public. All of these photographers were established in New York.

Washington Lafayette Germon (1822–1877), a Philadelphia photographer, emphasized actors in that city and those passing through. *Cartes-de-visite* photographs, which were small card-like images, became popular with the public. For theater historians, those photographers interested in capturing stage personalities provide an invaluable collection of images of both the great and forgotten performers of the days from the beginning of photography to the present. Photographs of play scenes in the actual theaters did not regularly occur until late in the 19th century because stage **lighting***† was usually not adequate in the **gaslight** era.

PILGRIM, JAMES (1825–1879). Born in England, James Pilgrim found success as an **actor***† in America and also writing a series of short comedies and full-length plays dealing with **Irish** characters and culture. These included *Paddy the Piper* (1850), *Ireland and America* (1851), *Robert Emmet* (1853), *Irish Assurance and Yankee*† *Modesty* (1853), and *Katy O'Shiel* (1857), among many others.

One of Pilgrim's best-known plays, *Harry Burnham* (1851), was set during the **American Revolution** to inspire patriotism during the era of the **Mexican-American War**. Pilgrim was one among a few successful **dramatists**,*† led by **Dion Boucicault**,† focusing on Irish history and life in America in the antebellum era, but his work was a forerunner of the many Irish plays and **musicals***† to appear after the **Civil War** and well into the 20th century, all of which would influence the Irish American **playwright***† Eugene O'Neill,*† among others.

PIQUE. **Augustin Daly**'s five-act play opened on 14 December 1875 at the **Fifth Avenue Theatre**, where it played for an impressive 237 performances. Billed as a "play of today," the first three acts of the plot were based on Florence Lean's novel, *Her Lord and Master.*

The play centers on a young woman, Mabel Renfrew, played by **Fanny Davenport**, who breaks off her relationship with her fiancé, Raymond, played by **Maurice Barrymore**, to instead marry Captain Arthur Standish (played by D. H. Hawkins), son of a rigid moralizing man, Matthew Standish (played by **Charles Fisher**). The young couple goes to live with the unyielding Standish, where Arthur concludes that Mabel is not in love with him. When Arthur and Mabel's **child***† is kidnapped, the frantic search for the child brings the couple together, and old Standish proves his mettle as well. In the meantime, Raymond marries Mabel's widowed stepmother, the child is saved, and Mabel comes to the conclusion that her initial decision, made "in pique," has turned out to bring happiness to all.

Critics*† were mixed on the play's artistic merits and themes, but audiences were largely positive and a **road***† company of the play, one of the first such **tours**,*† was hurriedly prepared and sent on the road.

†**PITOU, AUGUSTUS (1843–1915).** Born in New York, Augustus Pitou began as an **actor***† in a small role in **Edwin Booth**'s† *Hamlet* in 1867 and continued in Booth's company for a few seasons. He was a member of the

inaugural company at Kansas City's Coates Opera House during the 1870–1871 season. Then Pitou settled in New York as **manager,***† at various times, of **Booth's Theatre,**† the **Fifth Avenue Theatre**, the **Fourteenth Street Theatre**, and the Grand **Opera House**. He also managed several **stars,***† including Robert B. Mantell,† **Rose Coghlan,**† William Scanlan,† and Chauncey Olcott,† and served as Olcott's **agent***† as well as producing and writing librettos for romantic **musical***† dramas for the **Irish** tenor. His 1914 memoir is titled *Masters of the Show*.

†**PIXLEY, ANNIE (1858–1893).** Brooklyn, New York–born Annie Shea spent her youth in San Francisco playing supporting† roles to **touring***† **stars***† **Joseph Jefferson**† in *Rip Van Winkle*† and **McKee Rankin**† in *The Danites*† in the 1870s, taking her stepfather's surname as her stage name. Pixley made her eastern debut in Philadelphia in the **W. S. Gilbert** and **Arthur Sullivan operetta**† *H.M.S. Pinafore*, but gained fame (and favorable comparisons with **Lotta Crabtree**†) as an **Irish soubrette**† in a series of operettas and light comedies (with **musical***† sequences) such as *M'liss* (1878), *Eily* (1885), *The Deacon's Daughter* (1887), and *Kate* (1890). At her premature death, the *New York Times*, referring to her acting, described its central enhancement to be "the profound tenderness of her humanity."

PIZARRO IN PERU. **William Dunlap**'s adaptation of **Richard Brinsley Sheridan**'s *Pizarro*, set in Peru during the Spanish conquest, opened at the **Park Theatre** on 26 March 1800 as a sequel to *The Virgin of the Sun*, Dunlap's adaptation of August von Kotzebue's *Die Sonnenjungfrau*. Like *The Virgin of the Sun, Pizarro in Peru* made significant use of music and altered the original work to suit American tastes, which, at the time, inclined more toward action and **melodrama**.†

PLACIDE, ALEXANDRE (1750–1812). Born in Paris as Alexandre Bussart Placide to a theatrical family, he gained a range of skills as an acrobat, **rope dancer**, and pantomimist in France and then in England after 1777. With a **child**† performer, Suzanne Théodore Valliande (b. c. 1777), Placide spent three years performing in Santo Domingo before working in the eastern cities of the United States, most notably Charleston, where he built a significant operation, offering operas, ballets, and French plays.

Billed as Madame Placide, Suzanne gave birth to two of Placide's children despite the fact that he had left a wife behind in France. When Suzanne eloped with a singer, Placide remarried to a teenage girl, Charlotte Sophia Wrighten, a Charleston **actress***† and daughter of an English actress. This marriage brought Placide six more children: John Alexander (1794–1812), Caroline (1798–1881), **Jane** (1804–1835), Eliza (d. 1874), Thomas

(1809–1877), and **Henry** (1799–1870). All succeeded at various levels in some form of performance, and the name of Placide became indelibly associated with American theater.

PLACIDE, HENRY (1799–1870). The son of noted French **actor*†** **Alexandre Placide**, Henry Placide was born in Charleston. He made his debut at the age of eight in Augusta, Georgia, and made his adult debut in New York in 1823, developing a reputation as one of the theater's greatest comedians. Placide performed in both Europe and the United States and, for a time, appeared at and served as **manager*†** of the **Park Theatre**. Placide's obituary included a story about Park Theatre actor **Tyrone Power**'s planned trip to Europe. Placide was to accompany him, but changed plans at the last minute at the request of **Edwin Forrest**. The ship, the *President*, sank, and Power was lost.

Placide retired briefly in 1843, but returned to performing and continued on for over 20 more years, appearing in most New York theaters as well as on **tour**.*† Historians record that at the time of his retirement in 1865, Placide had played over 500 roles in almost all genres and periods, from **Shakespeare*†** and opera to contemporary comedies and **melodramas,†** a remarkable level of achievement, especially given that most **critics*†** felt his immersion in each individual character was total.

PLACIDE, JANE (1804–1835). The daughter of **actor*†** **Alexandre Placide**, Jane Placide went on the stage in 1820 in Norfolk, Virginia, prior to her 1823 debut in New Orleans, where she became the most celebrated **actress*†** in that city, appearing notably in **Shakespearean*†** tragic roles as well as comedy, and became particularly well-known for her beauty and the refinement of her acting. In contemporary drama, Placide scored a singular success at **James H. Caldwell**'s American Theatre in **James H. Kennicott**'s romantic tragedy *Irma; or, The Prediction* in 1830.

Supposedly, both Caldwell and a young **Edwin Forrest** were in love with her, with Forrest challenging Caldwell to a duel, though it apparently never occurred. Placide went to England in 1833, but shortly after her return to New Orleans, she became ill and died. Following her death, *The Dramatic Mirror* referred to her performance as Lady Macbeth as "a fearfully grand performance" and said of her style that in each performance "the sublimity of genius is rendered evident."

*†PLAYWRIGHTS. One of the standard clichés of American theater history is that no significant playwrights emerged in the United States prior to World **War** I,*† and that the appearance of Eugene O'Neill*† and his generation transformed **Broadway*†** drama after 1920 from solely a marketplace of frivolous entertainments† to a center of drama of serious purpose and social significance. Though it may well be true that few **dramatists***† of truly lasting international significance appeared in the 18th or 19th centuries, several generations of diverse and challenging playwrights filled American stages with intriguing dramas, **melodramas,**† and comedies from the end of the **American Revolution** to World War I, when O'Neill and his contemporaries established themselves. In fact, the period beginning with the end of the Revolution to the mid-19th century was one in which American dramatists slowly but steadily turned away from European, especially English, models and developed distinctly American stylistic and structural form and content relating directly to national concerns.

In the first half of the 19th century, the outstanding literary figures of the age—**Nathaniel Hawthorne, Herman Melville, Washington Irving, Edgar Allan Poe**—generally avoided playwriting (although all attempted playwriting and/or dramatic **criticism***† at one time or another) perhaps because theater was generally—and somewhat inexplicably—considered an inferior literary form. This situation may also result from the fact that much serious drama in America was imported from Europe, or more significantly, plays were adapted from foreign and other sources (novels, short stories), tasks frequently taken on by lesser writers or **actor***†**-managers***† and often diluting the edgier thematic content. It was also a moralizing and sentimentalizing era for the theater filled with **melodramas,**† and audiences resisted certain taboo subjects such as **sexuality***† and **gender***† difference and **women's***† rights—and demanded that misbehaving characters receive punishments in the stories at least equal to their offenses. As such, these plays often seem one-dimensional and unrealistic, though filled with action and sensations.

At mid-19th century little had changed, although there was considerably more dramatic activity and a few dramatists, particularly **Irish** American playwright **Dion Boucicault,**† demonstrating uncommon skill in a range of genres. The most celebrated and commercially successful play of the era, *Uncle Tom's Cabin*, was adapted from Harriet Beecher Stowe's novel by **George L. Aiken**, a little-known actor-manager. Aiken's effort was essentially a hack job intended to as quickly as possible exploit the source's unprecedented popularity before other adaptors could provide their own versions of the novel, as many did.

Dramatists adapted popular novels into melodramatic form or were compelled to create tailor-made vehicles to showcase the particular skills of **leading actors**.† Few could expect to make a comfortable living as a playwright (**Bronson Howard**† was widely considered, whether true or false, as the first American playwright to fully make his living as a dramatist, one hundred years after the American Revolution), which may account for the fact that many dramatists of the era also worked as actors or managers—or at some nontheatrical profession.

As the first tremors of modernism were felt in the United States in the 1870s, American dramatists tentatively broke away from the grip of melodrama to explore new European developments in drama, particularly the much-vaunted rise of **realism***† and, more importantly, the greater seriousness of purpose inherent in it. Bronson Howard, for example, scored a major success with *The Henrietta*† (1887), a comic assault on Wall Street speculation, and other writers looked to the tragedies of the **Civil War** and its aftermath for potent subject matter. In post–Civil War America, successful novelists and short story writers like **Mark Twain** and **Bret Harte** either wrote plays, adapted them from their own nondramatic works (or the works of others), and/or saw their writings adapted by others. By the end of the 19th century, the stage was literally set for an O'Neill to raise the bar, as the generation preceding him, including **James A. Herne**,† Edward Sheldon,† Clyde Fitch,† **William Gillette**,† and others, tentatively experimented with elements of those European playwrights perfecting realism.

†**PLYMPTON, EBEN (1853–1915).** Born in Boston, Eben Plympton worked as a bookkeeper before migrating to California. He began as an **actor***† in Stockton, California, in 1871, after which his robust masculinity and confidence won him a place in **Lester Wallack**'s company. A few years of apprenticeship led to **leading man**† roles in *Rose Michel* (1875) and *Our Boarding House* (1878), and he won plaudits as Romeo in 1877. Plympton scored back-to-back triumphs in *Hazel Kirke*† (1880) and *Esmeralda*† (1881), after which he **starred***† opposite **Mary Anderson**† and played Laertes to **Edwin Booth**'s† Hamlet. Between 1894 and 1914, he continued to appear reliably in a range of classic and contemporary plays.

PO-CA-HON-TAS; OR, THE GENTLE SAVAGE. **John Brougham**'s two-act **burlesque***† with music by James G. Maeger, which opened 24 December 1855 at **Wallack's Theatre**, was, at the height of popularity of the burlesque era, one of the most enduring and popular works intended to be shown as an afterpiece for **minstrel**† shows. Subtitled "An Original Aboriginal Erratic Operatic Semi-civilized and Demi-savage Extravaganza," the absurd and pun-laden text finds Captain John Smith (originally played by **Charles M. Walcot**) in Tuscarora discovering Pocahontas (played by Georgina Hodson) at the "Tuscarora Finishing School of Emancipated Maidens" and they fall deeply in love. Smith approaches her father, King H. J. Powhatan (played by Brougham), for permission to marry Pocahontas, but the king has promised her to a Dutchman, Mynheer Rolff (played by Charles Peters), so they play cards to decide the situation, and Smith wins his Pocahontas. The prolific Brougham, aside from all of his **Irish**-themed works, had previously crafted the burlesque of the **Native American***†–themed *Meta-mora; or, The Last of the Wampanoags* (1829) retitled *Met-a-mora; or, The Last of the Pollywogs* (1847).

POCAHONTAS. Socialist reformer Robert Dale Owen's (1801–1877) five-act "historical drama" from 1837 recounts the familiar myth of the encounter of Captain John Smith and the Powhatan princess Pocahontas, emphasizing, among other things, her recognition that her own people are savages, which is one key reason she is drawn to Smith. This vision of **Native Americans**,*† evident in many plays on this subject—and others—in the first half of the 19th century, hardened into a "historical" depiction that required nearly two centuries to correct.

As the century drew closer to the **Civil War**, plays with mixed-race relationships as subject matter switched to **African Americans**,*† but as with this play, the black characters tend to recognize, whether they believe it or not, that they are considered inferior. This formula reasserted itself with almost every immigrant "other" arriving in large numbers in the United States during the second half of the 19th century and well into the 20th century.

POE, EDGAR ALLAN (1809–1849). The Boston-born second child of two **actors**,*† Edgar Poe (he later added the middle name "Allan") became one of the great American writers of the first half of the 19th century. Considered by most **critics***† as part of the Romantic movement, Poe made his reputation with Gothic mysteries, tales of the macabre, and the creation of detective fiction, and some credit him with also contributing to the evolving genre of science fiction. He was particularly effective writing in short story style, which had been comparatively rare until he became a master of it, simultaneously popularizing the form.

Poe wrote poetry and prose, but also made an attempt at drama with a play, *Politian*, written in 1835, but never completed. The play was suggested by a real event referred to as the "Kentucky Tragedy," which was an 1825 murder of one Solomon P. Sharp by Jereboam O. Beauchamp. This murder had been much written about, but Poe chose to set the basic events in a decadent image of 16th-century Rome. Poe began publishing the play in installments in late 1835, but after the second installment appeared in January 1836, Poe essentially abandoned the play, probably because it had not been well received critically.

Poe also wrote dramatic criticism on occasion for the **Broadway*†** *Journal*, which he subsequently purchased, and in his writing on theater tended to condemn what he deemed works of superficial quality or content and championed American plays that, in his view, raised the bar of quality. For example, he praised **Anna Cora Mowatt**'s *Fashion* as a superior work.

†**POINTS.** When **melodrama†** ruled the stage during the 19th century, "points" were the **actor's*†** stock-in-trade. **Edwin Booth†** was among the first **star*†** actors to eschew points for a more natural style. Playing for points was a way of underscoring certain lines, poses, or dramatic moments to get a reaction from the audience. Actors who knew how to perform that kind of flourish still trod the boards even into the modernist era, but by then **critic*†** John Mason Brown† noted that "'points' are more or less looked down on by the moderns."

THE POLITICIAN OUT-WITTED. Billed as written by "An American" (Samuel Low) and published in 1789, this five-act play is an early example of an American play reflecting the political outlook of its times, at least in a lighthearted manner. The elderly, cantankerous Loveyet insists his Constitution is better than the one recently written for the United States. His friend Trueman is a devout Federalist and differs in his opinion on the Constitution. Their relationship suffers and interferes with Loveyet's son Charles and Trueman's daughter Harriet, whose love affair is also undermined by the **villainous†** Worthnought. Eventually, the old friends mend their relationship, Worthnought is foiled, and Charles and Harriet are united. When or if the play was actually produced cannot be determined, and little is known about Low's life except that he was very probably well off financially and wrote and published poetry.

THE POLITICIANS. **Cornelius Mathews**'s first play, a five-act 1840 comedy, went unproduced but is an interesting example of works emphasizing New York politics of the time and surprisingly relevant to 21st-century concerns as two essentially unscrupulous politicians battle each other ruthlessly, employing dubious tactics to win an alderman's seat. Mathews frequently repeated these themes in his works, and the play is otherwise a model of literature making strong use of local color techniques.

†**POLYGLOT PRODUCTIONS.** In the era of international **touring*†** **stars*†** visiting America with regularity, audiences craved celebrity performers like **Helena Modjeska†** or **Sarah Bernhardt†** despite even those with an inability to perform in English. This posed little problem since audi-

ences knew their **Shakespeare***† in ways contemporary audiences do not, and other works of the standard 19th-century **repertory***† were also essentially well-known.

If the star did not travel with a company performing in the same language, American **actors***† might be hired to support the star. Thus the lines would be given and cues picked up in two different languages, or sometimes even three. For example, the Polish-born actor Bogomil Dawison (1818–1872) performed in German opposite **Edwin Booth**† in 1866. Among other polyglot productions, Booth played Iago to the Italian-speaking Othello of **Tommaso Salvini**† in 1886, although he referred to the production as "a terrible mess of Shakespeare and macaroni."

PONISI, ELIZABETH (1818–1899). Born Elizabeth Hansom in England, she went on the stage in her teen years and married James Ponisi. She debuted in America in Philadelphia in 1850 as Lady Teazle in *The School for Scandal*. She divorced Ponisi in 1856 and married again, in 1859, to Samuel Wallis. Ponisi consistently triumphed with audiences and was engaged as **leading lady**† at the **Walnut Street Theatre**, debuting in *The Wife*, and despite playing the usual female roles, she also appeared in male roles with success (although she never played Hamlet, as some scholars suggest), including Edward Ardent in *The Morning Call*, as well as Faustus, Romeo, and others.

Ponisi was particularly acclaimed as Mrs. Malaprop, and **Edwin Forrest** declared her Lady Macbeth the best on the contemporary stage (she also played Desdemona and Cordelia opposite Forrest). In 1855 she created the role of *Francesca da Rimini,* and Ponisi joined **Wallack**'s company in 1871 as the leading portrayer of old women, including Mrs. Malaprop and Mrs. Hardcastle in *She Stoops to Conquer*, but she did not shy away from creating new roles, including Widow O'Kelly in *The Shaughraun* (1874). She made her farewell appearance on 6 April 1893 at the Academy of Music.

PONTEACH; OR, THE SAVAGES OF AMERICA: A TRAGEDY. Major Robert Rogers composed this play in 1766 while in England, based in part on his own experiences at **war***† as an Indian fighter in the war against Ponteach (also known as Pontiac), in which Rogers's Rangers played a key role. The play is something of a rarity in depicting **Native American***† characters in a dimensioned and sympathetic, if not downright positive light. Most of Rogers's writings were well received, but **critics***† largely condemned *Ponteach; or, The Savages of America*, which did not encourage authors to offer positive images of Native Americans.

THE POOR OF NEW YORK. **Dion Boucicault**'s† five-act socially conscious **melodrama**† was adapted from the French play, *Les Pauvres de Paris*
by Edouard-Louis-Alexandre Brisbane and Eugene Nus. Also sometimes
called *The Streets of New York*, the play opened on 8 December 1857
presented by **James W. Wallack** at Wallack's Lyceum Theatre for 42 performances. Though its original run was short, *The Poor of New York* is one of
the iconic plays of the 19th century. Facing the financial panic of 1857 (with
some background reflecting the panic of 1837), a middle-class family is
ruined in the current panic and struggles to survive despite the intensely
hostile efforts of a **villainous**† banker.

In the first act, it is 1837, and a banker, Gideon Bloodgood (played by W.
H. Norton), is planning to flee to England as he can see from stock market
returns that the bank will surely fail. Badger (played by **Lester Wallack**), a
bank clerk, is blackmailing Bloodgood since he kept detailed records of
Bloodgood's operations. Captain Fairweather (played by W. R. Blake) arrives and, counter to the situation, deposits his life savings with Bloodgood
personally. He departs with his receipt, but returns shortly demanding his
money back as his colleagues in the ship-building business have informed
him of the shaky state of Bloodgood's bank. Bloodgood refuses and argues
with the captain, who collapses and dies of a heart attack. Badger agrees to
help Bloodgood dispose of the captain's body and takes the deposit slip.

Act two jumps to the present, in the midst of the panic of 1857, and
presents the ramifications of the financial collapse on a series of characters.
A recently impoverished man, Livingstone, and a baker named Puffy are in a
park near Tammany Hall, and Bloodgood arrives to demand Puffy's rent,
inspiring Livingstone to give an impassioned speech explaining that the poor
of New York are the newly poor middle class. Bloodgood's daughter, Alida
(played by **Mrs. Hoey**), unsuccessfully demands money from her father to
cover her lover's gambling debts, and at the same time, Mrs. Fairweather, the
captain's widow, who is not aware that Bloodgood has saved his bank with
her husband's money, has given Puffy a note to cover her rent, which Puffy
gives Bloodgood to cover his.

At the start of act three, Alida sees a newspaper story describing her father
as a financial vulture and worries about her hopes to reenter high society.
Livingstone comes to Bloodgood asking for help in saving himself financially. Bloodgood refuses to help, but Alida pressures him to do so in hopes
Livingstone will propose to her. Badger arrives to extort money from Bloodgood, reminding him that he possesses the incriminating Fairweather receipt.
Paul Fairweather, the captain's son, arrives to plead for more time for his
mother's debt. Badger realizes that Paul is the true Fairweather heir, and
Alida, who overhears all this, tells Lucy (played Mrs. J. H. Allen), Paul's
sister, about the situation. Lucy tries to leave, but encounters Livingstone,
who has returned to get his loan from Bloodgood. Livingstone reveals that he

loves Lucy, but also that Alida has been his benefactress, saving him from his gambling debts, and that he had contemplated suicide. Badger is arrested, but has left Bloodgood exposed since the receipt remains hidden in his lodgings.

The fourth act is set in Union Square, where Puffy and some of the others share their tales of woe regarding their lost resources. Mrs. Puffy arrives with some dinner and decides they should share it with Paul, who is asleep in a building's corner on the street. Everyone seems in desperate straits, including Mrs. Fairweather, who is prepared to sell her wedding ring to feed her children. Bloodgood enters, and he and Badger recognize each other, leading to a threatening confrontation, with Bloodgood drawing a gun and Badger a knife. Badger further extorts money from Bloodgood with a threat of revealing the receipt to the authorities. Paul learns that his mother and Lucy are broke and have failed to raise any money, even on Mrs. Fairweather's wedding ring. Paul sends them home, promising to bring food. In adjoining rooms in the Five Points neighborhood, Mrs. Fairweather and Lucy make a pact to commit suicide in one room, while Badger greedily imagines the money he will be getting from Bloodgood. Mrs. Fairweather and Lucy have stopped up windows and doors and turned up the **gas,** hoping for asphyxiation, but Paul arrives in time to save them, though Badger is seriously injured by the gas and realizes he is dying and hides the receipt. Badger recognizes Paul and tells him of Bloodgood's duplicity and that he has proof, but collapses before he can retrieve it.

In the final act, the Fairweathers are restored to their home in Brooklyn Heights, with the Puffys working for them, and Lucy is recovering from the near suicide. Badger has survived and is now cooperating with an anticrime unit of the police. Livingstone and Lucy are reunited, but all learn of a **fire†** in the building where Badger lived, and the assumption is made that Bloodgood has set the building on fire to destroy the incriminating receipt. In fact, it is true; Bloodgood is revealed setting fires in the building, and Badger, trying to get the receipt, is nearly killed in the fire. In the final scene, Bloodgood returns home, triumphant in his belief that he has destroyed the receipt. Livingstone informs Alida that he is marrying Lucy, and Alida flees in despair. The Fairweathers arrive, demanding restitution of the captain's funds. Bloodgood, confronted by Badger, who arrives with the police, is cornered, but Paul asks only for the return of his father's money. Bloodgood rushes away to find the distraught Alida. The Puffys join the Fairweathers in marveling at the Bloodgood mansion, and the Fairweathers, in a final gesture, appeal to the audience to extend their help to the poor.

Despite its comparatively short run, the play was much-discussed and written about; **critics***† were positive; and Boucicault, in changing its title to *The Streets of New York*, emphasized the opportunity for other cities to change the title to specifically localize the play to their city and, as such, to make the play more immediately involving for its audience.

†POPE, CHARLES (1832–1899). Born in Germany, not far from Weimar, Charles Pope was brought to the United States before his first birthday. From his youth he was attracted to the stage and soon found employment as an **actor***† with various theaters in New York City. From 1854 he played major roles with **Benedict De Bar**'s† company in New Orleans and St. Louis. He served as **manager***† of the inaugural season of Kansas City's first **opera house**† (1870–1871), after which he **toured***† for a time as a **leading man**.† His career peaked at his own theater, Pope's Theatre, in St. Louis.

POTTER, JOHN S. (1809–1869). Born in Philadelphia, John S. Potter began his career as an **actor***† while still a teenager. He ultimately became a theater **manager**,*† but was not a typical one. His tendency was to move to a midsized city and build what was often its first theater. Typically not elegant facilities, they were wooden structures and before long would be replaced by other managers with more elaborate facilities. He built theaters in cities in all regions of the country and had a significant impact on the proliferation of theater facilities across the country in the middle of the 19th century.

POTTER, RICHARD (1783–1835). A native of Hopkinton, Massachusetts, Richard Potter was of mixed race. His father was an English tax collector and his mother an **African American***† servant. Potter developed his skills as a **magician**, working at first in New England. He gained such popularity that he played up and down the East Coast, including into the South. In Mobile, Alabama, he ran into a virulent case of prejudice, but despite this, he made considerable sums of money with his act and became known historically as the first African American magician and the first to gain fame in his own country. When he retired, Potter moved to New Hampshire, buying a large tract of land, and it was ultimately named Potter Place.

POWELL, CHARLES STUART (1748–1811). A native of Wales, Charles Stuart Powell arrived in America following some modest success as an **actor***† in England. In 1792, he presented a one-man show in Boston, after which he joined Joseph Harper's Boston company. He became **manager***† of the **Federal Street Theatre** for two seasons and opened the Haymarket

Theatre in December 1796, but went bankrupt. For a couple of seasons he returned to acting, after which he ran a theater for 12 years in Nova Scotia, interrupted briefly by a Boston appearance.

POWER, TYRONE (1795–1841). The patriarch of the Power theatrical dynasty, Tyrone Power was born in Ireland and played a range of stage **Irishmen** in England before his arrival in the United States in 1833. He became greatly popular in both America and England, but was lost at sea traveling between the United States and England. His sons, Maurice (d. 1849) and Harold, became **actors**.*† Harold was the father of Frederick Tyrone Edmond Power (1869–1931), a popular **leading man**† and major member of **Augustin Daly**'s company who eventually worked with Minnie Maddern Fiske*† and in revivals of **Shakespeare**.*† Frederick's son, Tyrone Power (1914–1958), started his career onstage, working with Katharine Cornell,*† but in the early 1930s Power became a major film† **star***† under contract for much of his career to Twentieth Century-Fox until his early death. His son, Tyrone Power Jr. (b. 1959), also became a movie actor.

PRICE, FANNY B. (1847–1897). Born Fanny Bayard Price in Vicksburg, Mississippi, she was a niece of **William Warren** and made her debut as an **actress***† in Chicago while a small **child**,† playing "The Child" with **James E. Murdoch** as Rolla in *Pizarro*. She became a **leading lady**† in **stock***† in Louisville in 1864 and **toured***† for most of her career with **star***† status, playing many of the heroines of contemporary dramas and comedies.

PRICE, STEPHEN (1783–1840). Born in New York as the son of a farmer, Stephen Price became a lawyer in 1804 and practiced for four years until he emerged as a groundbreaking theater **manager**.*† For example, he was the first manager who was neither an **actor***† nor a **playwright**,*† but the first in America to focus exclusively on management. He rose to an opportunity in 1808 when the **Park Theatre** was in financial trouble, and he purchased shares until he was able to amass a controlling interest.

Price introduced several large and small changes to get the theater in the black, with his notion of bringing in celebrated English **stars**,*† including **George Frederick Cooke** and **Edmund Kean**, and audiences seized the opportunity to turn out to see these acclaimed figures. He also staged shows with visual spectacle, which his audience preferred, and Price's long run as the Park's manager coincided with its greatest success.

PRIMROSE AND WEST. George Primrose and William H. "Billy" West were a song-and-dance team in the **blackface**† **minstrel**† tradition. They began working with **J. H. Haverly**'s **United Mastodon Minstrels** in 1877, but the arrangement ended quickly when they could not come to agreement with Haverly on pay. Their response was to transition their popularity as a team into their own minstrel company, Primrose and West's Big Minstrels, a large company borrowing on Haverly's style with an emphasis on spectacle and elaborate **scene design**.*†

Within a couple of years, they proved to be perhaps the most successful minstrel troupe in the United States. In 1881, Primrose and West saw Sam Hague's British Minstrels, who were **touring***† the United States, and found the refined qualities of the Hague company appealing in its omission of low comedy and **African American***† songs, which they replaced with ballet sequences and a large orchestra performing pseudoclassical music. Blackface, with the exception of end men, was essentially replaced by evening clothes and powdered wigs. The novelty of these changes proved popular with American audiences, and the Primrose and West troupe became known as "The Millionaires of Minstrelsy."

For some minstrel traditionalists, the changes made by Primrose and West were too much; one competitor, Lew Dockstader, commented that they had "refined all the fun out" of minstrelsy. More significantly, blackface minstrelsy was in slow decline in national popularity, and many of the best performers after the 1890s found work in the great variety possible in **vaudeville**,† even if some performers maintained the use of blackface in vaudeville and, later, other forms, including films.†

PRINCE DEUKALION. **Bayard Taylor**'s 1878 lyrical drama adopts high-flown verse and the form of allegory and symbolic characters. That same year, Taylor produced his most praised work, a metrical translation into English of Goethe's *Faust*. The profoundly philosophical *Prince Deukalion* is clearly inspired by classical literature and characters and attempts to depict the central aspects of life's experiences in the most poetic vein.

Taylor died shortly after completing *Prince Deukalion* and never saw it produced in a theater. In fact, he barely lived long enough to see the entire text in proofs for its imminent publication. Though some **critics***† questioned how large a reading or theatergoing public would exist for a work like *Prince Deukalion*, the critic writing in the *Atlantic Monthly* in January 1879 wrote that Taylor's play "is a sustained adventurous effort, definite in purpose and careful in design. The poet has bestowed upon it, as if with intent to produce a masterpiece, all his natural resources enhanced by lifelong practice,—the ripest thought and imagination of his prime."

THE PRINCE OF PARTHIA. Philadelphia poet **Thomas Godfrey** wrote the five-act tragedy, *The Prince of Parthia*, his only play, but it was not produced until three years after his early death. Staged on 24 April 1767 for one performance at the **Southwark Theatre** by the **American Company**, it was constructed in the style of **Shakespearean*†** tragedy.

The Prince of Parthia is ignited by an intense sibling rivalry, when Vardanes, who resents his brother Arsaces's success in **war,*†** concocts a plan to turn his father, King Artabanus, against him. Vardanes's resentment also encompasses the success Arsaces has had with Evanthe, a comely prisoner, whom both the king and Vardanes also desire. Vardanes persuades the king to jail Arsaces, but a third brother, Gotarzes, calls up an army to free his brother. A battle ensues during which Evanthe, who has fallen in love with Arsaces, hears that Arsaces has been killed. She is distraught at this news and takes poison. However, Arsaces is alive, and when he hears of Evanthe's dire condition, he rushes to her side as she dies. Devastated, Arsaces kills himself, and as the battle subsides, Gotarzes takes command and brings new order to his country.

The cast of *The Prince of Parthia* featured **David Douglass** as King Artabanus, **Miss Cheer** as Evanthe, **Lewis Hallam Jr.** as Arsaces, and Mr. Tomlinson as Vardanes. Despite its historical significance, *The Prince of Parthia* was rarely produced in its own time or since.

PROCTOR, JOSEPH (1816–1897). Born in Philadelphia, Joseph Proctor became a noted **actor*†** in **Shakespearean*†** roles, scoring successes in *Macbeth*, playing opposite **Charlotte Cushman**, and in other Shakespearean tragic roles and contemporary dramas. Like a number of other **star*†** actors of the 19th century, Proctor played a role he became significantly associated with, in this particular case the title role of *Nick of the Woods; or, the Jibbenainosay* (1839), adapted by **Louisa H. Medina** from **Robert Montgomery Bird**'s novel. Much like **Joseph Jefferson†** with *Rip Van Winkle* or **James O'Neill†** with *The Count of Monte Cristo*, Proctor spent a large portion of his long career amassing a fortune playing his most popular role frequently on extended **tours*†** across the country.

†PRODUCER. This term typically refers to an individual or an organization providing financial and organizational support for the production of a play. Prior to the 20th century, plays were often produced by **actor*†-managers*** and **star*†** actors who were also managers of a **repertory*†**-style company and, in many cases, owned and operated their own theaters. Producers often sprang from the ranks of theater workers; some were box office or publicity managers while others, increasingly, were actors and/or **playwrights**.*† To protect their interests, **dramatists***† created several organizations to produce plays.

The system was essentially inspired by the English theater dating back to Colley Cibber and was perfected by such actor-managers as Henry Irving in the late 19th century. Even prior to the use of the terminology, English-speaking actors in England and America, the leaders of troupes of actors such as **Lewis Hallam Jr., David Douglass**, and others, essentially functioned as actor-managers. These actor-managers in America in the 17th century and beyond controlled the company's play selection, casting of roles, **tour***† schedules, finances, etc., while also dominating each production, playing major roles.

In the 18th century, this process continued, but it was actually in the early 19th century when the true actor-manager emerged in the person of **Edwin Forrest**, almost certainly America's foremost tragedian of the pre–**Civil War** era. While Forrest's acting style—and some of his personal behaviors—could certainly be subject to **criticism**,*† he worked intensely not only to elevate the quality of his company of actors, but to challenge the tastes of his audience and encourage playwrights to write on American subjects and develop a national style. In this sense, he was a model actor-manager, and many outstanding actors of the next generation followed suit, most obviously **Edwin Booth**,† **Laura Keene**, **Augustin Daly**, **William Gillette**,† and numerous others of equal or lesser quality.

†**PROTEAN COMIC. Lotta Crabtree**† and **Sol Smith Russell**† were protean comics; that is, they could switch rapidly among very different characterizations. The term "protean" came to mean generally versatile, but because of the theatricality of the technique, most opportunities for protean displays occurred in comedy.

†**PUFF.** This term, which dates back to the 17th century, refers to excessive hype in advertisements, publicity, and reviews of a theatrical production. Richard Brinsley Sheridan immortalized the word when he used it as the name of his flamboyant Mr. Puff in *The Critic**† (1779), but in the United States "puff" became prevalent as theater **managers***† sought any means to win the battle for audience attention.

†**PUPPETRY.** Puppets, inanimate figures manipulated by a puppeteer, have been seen by audiences since the beginning of recorded history. Whether hand puppets or marionettes (puppets manipulated by strings), these iconic human symbols are found in multiple cultures and date, in many areas, to the dawn of theatrical history. Spanish puppeteers first performed in North

America as early as the 16th century, and **Native Americans***† were known to use puppets in ritual performances. English puppet shows were frequently seen during the 18th century, with the earliest documented performance in Barbados in 1708. Chinese shadow puppets were seen in America in this era, as were puppet performances from Central and South America, France, Italy, and elsewhere. Puppets were popular with American **children***† from the early 18th century, and many shops sold puppet stages and puppets to youngsters.

PURDY, ALEXANDER H. (c. 1815–1862). Not much is known about Alexander H. Purdy's life beyond his service as **manager***† of New York's **National Theatre** (also known as Purdy's National Theatre) for the decade of the 1850s, an undeniably extraordinary era of American theater and the nation's history. Purdy had an eye for top talent. He introduced the anarchic clown **George L. Fox**; produced the Howard family in a production of *Uncle Tom's Cabin* in 1852 that ran for 325 consecutive performances; staged the popular and enduring **melodrama**† *Ten Nights in a Bar-Room* (1858); introduced and popularized holiday morning and afternoon matinee performances; established segregated sections of the audience for **African Americans**;*† produced innumerable **Yankee**† plays with the most popular **stars***† of the form such as **Frank S. Chanfrau**, **Thomas Dartmouth "Daddy" Rice** (in his **Jump Jim Crow** persona), and such major stars as **Junius Brutus Booth** and **James W. Wallack**. Troubles with the facilities itself, requiring frequent repairs, subsequently bankrupted Purdy, and the theater was torn down in 1862, the same year as his death.

PURDY'S NATIONAL THEATRE. *See* NATIONAL THEATRE.

PUTNAM, THE IRON SON OF '76. **Nathaniel H. Bannister**'s only major success as a **playwright**,*† a patriotic three-act **melodrama**† with comic elements, opened at the **Bowery Theatre** in 1844 and racked up a solid 78 performances, with subsequent revivals for several decades. The play is based on events in the life of General Israel Putnam (1718–1790), a genuine hero at Bunker Hill during the **American Revolution**, and earlier during the **French and Indian War**. Putnam had famously escaped British imprisonment on horseback, an event Bannister dramatizes with live horses onstage (an early example of the taste for **equestrian** spectacle) and adds a rescue of a **Native American***† **child**† for good measure.

R

†**RACE ON THE AMERICAN STAGE.** *See* *†AFRICAN AMERICAN THEATER.

†**RANKIN, ARTHUR MCKEE (1844–1914).** Born in Sandwich, Canada, Arthur McKee Rankin debuted as an **actor***† in 1861 under the stage name George Henley in Rochester, New York. After a few seasons in England, Rankin made his first New York appearance in *A Regular Fix* in 1866 before joining the **Union Square Theatre**† in 1872. There he appeared in major roles before finding enduring popularity as miner Alexander McGee in *The Danites*† (1877) opposite his wife, **Kitty Blanchard**. Initial success as a **manager,***† and frequent revivals of *The Danites* (later opposite Nance O'Neill†), kept him in the public eye, but various personal troubles and managerial failings led to bankruptcy in 1904. In attempts to find another vehicle as popular as *The Danites*, Rankin appeared with modest success in *'49* (1881) and *The Canuck* (1891). Rankin's daughters, Gladys and Doris, married actors Sidney Drew and Lionel Barrymore,† respectively.

RAVEL FAMILY. Four generations of the French Ravel family of **circus***† and variety performers were trained in Italy, based in Paris, and **toured***† the United States with some frequency. Gabriel Ravel was the patriarch, but the act seemed to truly form under the oversight of his son, Jean (1797–1868). Jean's children were the major elements of the act, including Gabriel (1810–1882), Antoine (1812–1872), Angelique (1813–1895), Jerome (1814–1890), and Françoise (1823–1881). Their specialties included rope dancing, acrobatics, ballet, wire walking, tumbling, and pantomime.

The company added to its ranks with nonfamily members, the most celebrated being **Charles Blondin**, who famously crossed Niagara Falls on a tightrope, and also Leon Javelli (1821–1854), who performed with the Ravels during an engagement† at **Niblo's Garden**. Following Jean's retirement, Gabriel headed the company. Subsequently, Angelique's children, Charles, a celebrated clown, and Marietta (who became a member of the **Hanlon** troupe), were variety **stars**.*† The Ravels made their first American appearance in 1825.

†**RAYMOND, JOHN T. (1836–1887).** Born John O'Brien in Buffalo, New York, the **actor***† had a distinguished career as a comic **character actor**† from his debut in 1853 in a Rochester, New York, production of *The Honeymoon*. In 1858, he scored a success in **E. A. Sothern**'s production of **Tom Taylor**'s *Our American Cousin*. His New York debut in 1861 was as part of **Laura Keene**'s company, taking over comic roles formerly played by **Joseph Jefferson**.† Late in his career, Raymond was known primarily as Colonel Sellers in the stage adaptation of **Mark Twain**'s novel *The Gilded Age* (1874), which remained the role with which he was most identified until his death.

†**RECALL.** To be called back by the audience after the usual curtain call was a sign of genuine appreciation. Newspapers often reported when a **star***† got one or more recalls. Scholar Eleanor Ruggles recounts a joke made by **Edwin Booth**† at the funeral of **actor***†/**playwright***† **John Brougham**, a very large man. His coffin was partially lowered into the grave, but had to be laboriously raised again so the grave could be widened, at which Booth noted that it was Brougham's "last recall."

THE RED MAZEPPA; OR, THE MADMAN OF THE PLAINS. Albert W. Aiken, brother of **George L. Aiken**, **actor***† and author of the most produced adaptation of **Harriet Beecher Stowe**'s *Uncle Tom's Cabin*, and cousin of the anarchic clown **George L. Fox**, wrote this "Grand Romantic Drama" played in New York for the first time on 17 June 1870. Attempting to capitalize on the popularity of *Mazeppa; or, The Wild Horse of Tartary*, which became a legendary success starring **Adah Isaacs Menken** a few years earlier, *The Red Mazeppa* also capitalized on the growing number of plays dealing with **Native Americans**,*† but unfortunately in one-dimensional and stereotypical ways. It was also billed under the title *The Red Mazeppa; or, The Wild Horse of Tartary.*

Five years later, under the title *The Prairie Mazeppa; or, The Madman of the Plains* (1875), it was sold as a twenty-cent novel. Three years later, again retitled as *The Indian Mazeppa; or, The Madman of the Plains* (1878), it was published as a dime novel, Aiken's specialty. The play (and novels) in which Mazeppa is transformed into an Indian maiden features Davy Crockett as a major character and is set in Texas with Mexicans, **Indians**, and gringos in the Sabinal and Rio Sego districts of Texas in early times.

THE RED SCARF. **Augustin Daly**'s spectacular five-act **melodrama†** opened on 10 June 1868 at the **Bowery Theatre**. The play, which played a subsequent engagement† at Conway's Theatre in Brooklyn in 1869, would almost certainly be completely forgotten were it not for the fact that it includes one of the classic cliché climaxes of melodrama. A man bound to a log entering a sawmill on a conveyor belt is rescued from being cut in two by the revolving saw blade. Curiously, contemporary depictions of this melodramatic cliché usually show the hero rescuing a woman tied to the log—Daly's version made the hero the victim. Daly's large output of melodramas featured similar devices, but often in stronger plays than this slight effort, though the excitement of its spectacle and emotional intensity pleased audiences.

REES, JAMES (1802–1885). A native of Norristown, Pennsylvania, James Rees worked as a salesman and a clerk in Philadelphia's US Post Office branch before becoming editor for several publications including ***The Dramatic Mirror†*** in 1842, among others. He wrote several plays, but without much success. These included ***The Headsman***, ***Washington*** *at Valley Forge*, *Changes*, *Marion*, *Pat Lyon*, and *Anthony Wayne*, and he wrote several books, including *The Dramatic Authors of America* (1842), *The Life of Edwin Forrest* (1874), and ***Shakespeare****† *and the Bible* (1875).

†REHAN, ADA (1860–1916). Born Ada Delia Crehan in Limerick, Ireland, this **actress***† came to America with her family at age five. Her two older sisters and a brother became **actors**,*† and she unexpectedly followed them into the profession as a last-minute replacement. A typesetter's error, listing her as Ada C. Rehan in a program, created her stage name. She made her little-noticed New York debut in 1873 in her brother-in-law **Oliver Doud Byron**'s *Across the Continent*. Rehan performed for two seasons at Philadelphia's **Arch Street Theatre** with **Mrs. John Drew**, followed by **tours**.*†

Most of Rehan's career was associated with **manager***† **Augustin Daly,†** whose company she joined in 1879. As his **leading lady†** for 20 years, Rehan excelled in light comedy, especially in **Shakespeare**'s*† plays. She was tall, graceful, and energetic, with an apparent spontaneity that worked well in the superficial fare of her first decade with Daly. In the late 1880s, he began featuring her in Shakespeare, and she won particular acclaim as Kate in *The Taming of the Shrew*. However, she became emotionally as well as artistically dependent upon Daly, and his death in 1899 was a devastating setback to her. After an absence from the stage, she **toured***† with **Otis Skinner,†** but never recovered the spirit of her Daly years. **William Winter†** wrote that Rehan's acting "if closely scrutinized, was seen to have been studied; yet it always seemed spontaneous; her handsome, ingenuous, winning countenance informed it with sympathy, while her voice—copious, tender, and wonderfully **musical***†—filled it with emotion, speaking always from the heart."

†**REIGNOLDS, KATE (1836–1911).** Born Catherine Mary Reignolds near London, England, she immigrated to the United States in 1850 with her mother and sisters, settling in Chicago, where they performed for **manager***† **John B. Rice**. As Kate Reignolds, she made her New York debut opposite **actor***† **Edwin Forrest** in 1855. Among the companies with which she subsequently performed were those of **Laura Keene**, **John Brougham**, **Benedict De Bar**,† and **Charlotte Cushman**, all of whom are described in her 1887 memoir, *Yesterdays with Actors*. Reignolds's five years with the **Boston Museum stock***† company included a stint playing opposite **John Wilkes Booth**,† whom she regarded as "an irresponsible person, . . . this sad-faced, handsome, passionate boy." She spent the later years of her career giving dramatic readings and elocution lessons.

REINAGLE, ALEXANDER (1756–1809). Raised in Portsmouth, England, where he was born, Alexander Reinagle was the son of an Austrian musician and studied with Raynor Taylor in Edinburgh. Reinagle arrived in the United States in 1786 and resided in Philadelphia. **George Washington** admired Reinagle's work, and Reinagle composed a choral piece to celebrate Washington's stop in Trenton, New Jersey, on his way to his 1789 inauguration. Following Washington's 1799 death, Reinagle composed *Monody on the Death of George Washington*.

By 1791, Reinagle gained a major reputation as a composer and teacher, while also working in Philadelphia and Baltimore theaters with the New Company. He partnered with **actor***† **Thomas Wignell** to build the **Chestnut Street Theatre**, which opened in 1794 and which he actively managed with Wignell. In regard to creative achievement, Reinagle adapted English ballad operas for local tastes, composed music for various plays, and wrote scores for several light operas, including *The Sicilian Romance* (1795). When Wignell died in 1803, Reinagle moved to Baltimore and worked with the **Holliday Street Theatre**.

†**RELIGIOUS DRAMA.** The Christian church's resistance to theatrical activity in early America had the effect of keeping overt religious drama to a minimum. However, throughout the 19th century Judeo-Christian values were the unquestioned foundation of most plays, as obviously exemplified by **temperance dramas**,† but also in the basic depiction of admirable societal values. Plays drawn from biblical sources and other aspects of religious history did not appear with any regularity until the turn of the century, al-

though ministers (and the occasional rabbi) appeared as secondary characters, often to permit the dramatist to make points about religious values, typically of the Judeo-Christian tradition.

Occasionally, dramatists focused on religious issues or figures. For example, **Edward Bulwer-Lytton**'s *Richelieu* (1839), an English play popular with American audiences, portrayed the title character, but did not deeply explore religious issues. Other British plays such as Henry Arthur Jones's *Saints and Sinners* (1895) and Jerome K. Jerome's *The Passing of the Third Floor Back* (1909) won some acceptance for religious drama, but when **playwright*†** Salmi Morse offered *The Passion Play* (1879), a retelling of Christ's final hours, some Christian clergy fought to suppress it because Morse was a Jew.

The 19th century concluded with William Young's† stage adaptation of General Lew Wallace's novel *Ben-Hur†* (1899), which became one of the most popular plays of the time, perhaps more for its **melodramatic†** components and onstage chariot race than for its religious story. Non-Christian religions, particularly America's first significant homegrown sect, the Mormons, became the concern of some **dramatists**.† Among numerous plays about Mormons, many of which condemned the religion, **Joaquin Miller**'s *The Danites; or, The Heart of the Sierras* (1877) became a **star*†**-making vehicle for **McKee Rankin,†** who performed the play for the remainder of his career.

REMOVING THE DEPOSITS. Inspired by President Andrew Jackson's political battle with the United States Bank, *Removing the Deposits* focused on the moment in 1833 when Jackson announced he would make no deposits of US funds in the bank. Comic **actor*†** Henry J. Finn wrote a farce on the topical subject. When it opened on 7 September 1835 at the **Bowery Theatre**, working-class audiences were entertained by a simplified and satirized version of Jackson's economic theories and his hatred of the bank as a government entity.

RENTZ-SANTLEY NOVELTY AND BURLESQUE COMPANY. Manager*† **Michael B. Leavitt** borrowed aspects of both the popular act of **Lydia Thompson** and her British Blondes and **blackface†** **minstrel†** shows to create a form of **burlesque*†** emphasizing **women.*†** Minstrel shows were populated with male performers (sometimes in drag), so in 1870, Leavitt introduced the first burlesque show featuring women and promising to deliver images of the gay life of Paris, which, it became clear, was code for informing audiences that women's bodies would be a significant element.

A riot occurred in San Francisco when Mabel Santley, the show's **star**,*† lifted her dress to expose her ankle. The shock was brief, and before long the emphasis was more obviously placed on women's bodies. Leavitt renamed the company Mme. Rentz and Her Female Minstrels to underscore the obvious. The taste of audiences tended toward heavy women, which in the 19th century was the gold standard of **sexual***† attractiveness. Something of a competition emerged among shows imitating Leavitt's version of burlesque—and extending beyond it. For example, Billy Watson's Beef Trust advertised the fact that all of his female performers were over 200 pounds, and the press printed stories of the lengths some women in the company went to in order to meet and maintain the weight minimum. Over the decades into the 20th century, burlesque became increasingly a mix of low comedy and scantily clad or nude (where legally possible) women of more modest proportions.

*†REPERTORY. From the 18th into the 19th centuries, many **actor***†-**managers*** adopted the repertory structure, hiring a corps of actors to appear in a season of plays. By the early 19th century, actors were cast according to **lines of business,**† playing the same size and type of role in each play presented. Performing in repertory not only challenges an actor's abilities at line memorization, but also stretches an actor as insights are transferred from one role to another. The system was economically feasible in the days of large companies and before strict union regulation. The repertory model was revived during the 1960s, the first decade of newly booming regional resident companies around the United States, but the labor costs of **scenery**† changeovers quickly took a toll, and most theaters abandoned the repertory structure.

THE RETURN FROM A CRUISE. This anonymous play (also called *Returned from a Cruise*) was performed at Philadelphia's **Chestnut Street Theatre** on 11 December 1812. A mere three days after the event on which the play is based—8 December 1812—the theater put together a tribute to the victory of the USS *United States* over the HMS *Macedonian* with a central character based on the victorious Captain Stephen Decatur.

*†REVUE. Though the golden age of **musical***† revues did not develop until the early 20th century, aspects of the revue—a type of variety program of music, dance, and sketches (sometimes all thematically connected)—were evident in 19th-century entertainments,† including **minstrel**† show **olios**, which provided the structure of the great revues popular in the United States and England between **World War I** and the 1950s.

†**THE RIALTO.** Borrowing the name from the famous Venetian district, New York's theatrical intelligentsia of the 1870s began referring to that part of the city filled with theaters between Union and Madison Squares as "The Rialto." After New York's theater district became known as **Broadway*†** in the later 19th century (and particularly after theaters appeared in Longacre Square, ultimately known as Times Square*†), the term continued to be used among the many names for the area well into the mid-20th century.

†**RICE, DAN (1823–1900).** A **circus*†** clown who became a major icon of mid-19th-century American popular culture, Rice, who was born in New York as Daniel McLaren, spent his early years living in frontier towns and working, at various times, as a jockey, **minstrel†** man, and **agent*†** for **Mormon** leader Joseph Smith. Choosing a life in the circus, where he became lionized as "The American Grimaldi," Rice merged his lowbrow comedy with that of British clown William F. Wallett (1806–1892), his sometime rival.

In 1848, Rice and Wallett began performing together, with Wallett imitating noted **Shakespearean*†** actors of the day, while Rice offered rowdy parodies entitled *Dan Rice's Version of Othello* or *Dan Rice's Multifarious Account of Hamlet.* His uniquely American humor and mocking of the powerful, while dressed in a red-and-white-striped "Uncle Sam" costume, endeared him to audiences, including President **Abraham Lincoln**.

Audiences were particularly amused when Rice ran a semiserious campaign for the United States presidency in 1868. Despite frequent bouts with alcohol, Rice ultimately moderated his drinking and **toured*†** giving **temperance†** lectures. He became one of the most popular entertainers† of his day, making his last one-ring circus appearances in New York in the early 1890s before retiring to Long Branch, New Jersey.

RICE, E. E. (1847–1924). Born Edward Everett Rice in poverty in Brighton, Massachusetts, E. E. Rice was working as a clerk for a steamship company in the early 1870s when he saw a British production of *The Black Crook* and found inspiration to create a **musical*†** entertainment.† The result, in 1874, was *Evangeline*, a **burlesque*†** spectacle Rice composed with **John Cheever Goodwin** that was the first to be billed as a musical comedy. Into the early 20th century, Rice composed nearly 20 musicals, including *Adonis* (1884), the first musical to achieve a run of more than 500 performances, and on the roof of the Casino Theatre, he presented *The Origin of the Cake Walk; or, Clorindy* (1898), the first musical written by **African Americans*†** with an all-black cast to run on **Broadway*†** for predominantly white audiences.

One of Rice's talents was recognizing emerging **stars**.*† He was a key force in the rise to success of Lillian Russell,† Henry E. Dixey, Fay Templeton,† Julian Eltinge,† and Jerome Kern.

RICE, JOHN BLAKE (1809–1874). A native of Easton, Maryland, John Blake Rice made his debut as an **actor***† in Annapolis in an 1829 production of *The London Merchant*. He gathered significant experience **touring***† the eastern United States and the West Indies. Rice married Mary Ann Warren of a Philadelphia theater family and resided there and then in Buffalo, New York, working as **manager***† of theaters in Buffalo and Albany. He moved to Chicago in 1847 to work as an actor, providing entertainment† at political events. He founded his own theater, Rice's, but in 1850 during a performance of an opera, a **fire**† destroyed the theater. He moved to Milwaukee before returning to Chicago in 1851 to build another theater, this time of brick, and hired **James McVicker** to manage it. Rice worked in theater until 1857, when he entered Chicago politics. He was elected mayor on a conservative ticket, eventually losing in the face of charges of corruption.

RICE, THOMAS DARTMOUTH "DADDY" (1806–1860). Born Thomas Dartmouth Rice in New York City, he received some education, but in his teens worked as an apprentice woodcarver. He turned to performing in the 1820s, becoming a frequently employed **stock***† **actor***† and **touring***† in the American **frontier** and in the South. **Stardom***† came to Rice with the creation of his **Jim Crow** character. The origins of the character are subject to several conflicting legends, but a dominant account is that Rice saw a partially disabled **African American***† singing and performing an eccentric dance, punctuating each chorus with a jump, while entertaining some children. Rice's resulting song, "**Jump Jim Crow**," and his apparent interest in African American performers, encouraged his use of **blackface**.†

Rice perfected the routine, performing in the South before playing at the **Park Theatre**, frequently adding new stanzas to the song. His routine caught on with the audience and encouraged the evolution of **minstrel**† performance, which, from that time into the early 20th century, was a highly popular form of **musical***† entertainment.† Unfortunately, it also encouraged the tradition of white performers performing in blackface and developing racial stereotypes. From the early 1830s to the mid-1840s, Rice was greeted with sold-out audiences virtually everywhere he performed. He toured England in 1836, popularizing minstrelsy there. By the late 1840s, illness in the form of a type of paralysis hindered his performing until he had to quit. Jim Crow, Rice's character and its dance, became in the 1950s–1960s a symbol of racial segregation in the South.

RICHELIEU; OR, THE CONSPIRACY. **Edward Bulwer-Lytton**'s five-act play centered on the character of 17th-century French Cardinal Richelieu, depicted as a manipulative figure using spies and his own cleverness to outwit assassins trying to kill him. Lytton first penned the famous line "the pen is mightier than the sword" in this play. *Richelieu* had premiered in England, but its first American production opened on 4 September 1839 at the **National Theatre starring*†** **Edwin Forrest** in the title role, a character he frequently returned to playing along with his other best-known roles. **Edwin Booth** revived the play at the **Winter Garden†** in February 1866 and included it among his frequently performed characterizations for the remainder of his career. Robert B. Mantell† made the play central to his repertoire, and later, E. H. Sothern† and Walter Hampden*† both had **Broadway*†** successes in the role.

RICHINGS, CAROLINE (1827–1882). Born Mary Caroline Reynoldson in England and orphaned, Caroline Richings became the adopted daughter of **Peter Richings** and was brought to the United States. She was trained as a pianist and opera singer, performing the role of Marie in *The Daughter of the Regiment* and scoring a major success in 1852, and generally thrived in both areas. She was also a **manager*†** and **director,*†** as was her adoptive father, and following his retirement, she continued his work for a time.

RICHINGS, PETER (1797–1871). Born in Kensington, England, as Peter Puget, the son of a navy captain, he studied law at Oxford University. When he decided to pursue a theatrical career instead, the friction with his father encouraged his departure for the United States in 1821 and the change of his name. He debuted at the **Park Theatre** in the drama *Guy Mannering*, but soon developed a celebrated reputation as a first-rank comic **actor,*†** especially appreciated as fops and other outrageous characters. He also proved to be a fine **manager*†** of theater, including the **National Theatre, Walnut Street Theatre**, and **Chestnut Street Theatre** in Philadelphia in the 1840s, and Baltimore's **Holliday Street Theatre**. He retired in 1868.

RICKETTS, JOHN BILL (1760?–1799). English-born **equestrian†** and **circus*†** performer, John Bill Ricketts brought the first of modern circuses to America in 1792 after a decade of perfecting his work with the Hughes Royal Circus in London during the 1780s. He founded his first circus in Philadelphia in the year of his arrival, constructing a circus building, giving riding lessons, and training horses to perform. On 3 April 1793 he offered America's first circus performance and presented it two or three times per week. His success was so great that he built a second arena and **toured*†** New

England and Canada. Unfortunately, both of his circus structures were destroyed by **fire**,† and he departed for England, but died when the ship on which he was traveling sank.

***THE RIGHTS OF MAN*. Oliver S. Leland**'s two-act comedy opened at **Wallack's Theatre** in 1857, followed by a production at the **Howard Athenaeum** that same year. Set into a romantic plot, the play features a heroine, Helen, with advanced ideas on the role of **women**,*† stating the need she had to reconcile herself to "play the part of the silly slave which nature seems to have given to my sex." The girl's father has traditional attitudes, but her friend, a widow named Aurora, explains that marriage is "large, heavy and difficult to move" and that love is "the small pocket edition, women take wherever they go." Repelled by what she believes are the dominant rights of man, she later concludes that men have no God-given rights and, as a male character intones as the curtain falls, "Women will rule, despite the 'Rights of Man.'"

RIGL, EMILY (19th century). For an **actress***† as celebrated as Emily Rigl at the height of her career, surprisingly little is known about her early and offstage life. It is believed she was born either in Holland or Austria and trained in ballet, which her father taught. She arrived in the United States with her sister Betty to dance in the chorus of ballerinas in the historic production of *The Black Crook* (1866) at **Niblo's Garden**. After two years of performing in *The Black Crook*, Rigl left the show to study acting, and in 1874 joined **Augustin Daly**'s company. She appeared in numerous **Broadway***† hits, including *Humpty Dumpty* (1868) with **George L. Fox**, *What Should She Do?* (1874), *The Big Bonanza* (1875), *Saratoga* (1875), *Pique* (1875), *The Galley Slave* (1879), *Mr. Barnes of New York* (1888), *Devil's Island* (1898), and a revival of *Uncle Tom's Cabin* (1901). Though Rigl mostly appeared in contemporary plays, she also successfully played Olivia in *Twelfth Night*.

†*RIP VAN WINKLE*. The play and character that remain so indelibly identified with the beloved comic **actor***† **Joseph Jefferson**† were based upon the 1819 story, published in *The Sketchbook*, by **Washington Irving**, in which the kindly, hard-drinking Dutchman Rip Van Winkle leaves his New England colonial village to go hunting in the Catskills (and to escape his nagging wife), encounters Henry Hudson's men, and, as the result of sharing their drink, falls asleep for 20 years. He awakes thinking he has only been asleep for a few hours, but he slowly discovers that his little village has turned into an American town and that he has been forgotten.

Prior versions include many adaptations, including an anonymous 1828 version; *Rip Van Winkle; or, The Demons of the Catskill Mountains!! A National Drama* (1829) by John Kerr, which was produced at the **Park Theatre** with **James H. Hackett** on 22 April 1830; and *Rip Van Winkle, A Legend of the Catskills, A Romantic Drama* (1850) by and **starring*†** **Charles Burke**, Jefferson's brother-in-law. There was also a **musical*†** version, with libretto by J. Howard Wainwright and music by George F. Bristow, offered for a brief run at **Niblo's Garden** from 27 September to 23 October 1855. A **burlesque*†** version entitled *Rip Van Winkle; or, a 20 Year's Snooze*, written, directed, and starring James Barnes, opened at Wood's Museum and Metropolitan on 3 October 1870 for 10 performances.

There had also been Jefferson's own 1859 version, cobbled together from parts of the earlier adaptations and Jefferson's own ideas. He continued to work on his version, but to little effect. It was this version, revised in 1865 by **Dion Boucicault,†** that held the stage during four decades and made Jefferson a stage legend. First performed in London on 5 September 1865 at the Adelphia Theatre, it was a huge hit, delivering 170 performances. Jefferson brought it to New York, where it played at the **Olympic Theatre** on 3 September 1866 starring himself. It was revived at **Booth's Theatre** on 15 August 1870, but Jefferson played the role continually for the remaining 35 years of his career.

Despite productions and varied versions of *Rip Van Winkle* with other actors, audiences overwhelmingly preferred Jefferson, who even appeared in an 1896 silent film† of scenes from the play. Benjamin Arthur wrote in his book *The Man Who Was Rip Van Winkle: Joseph Jefferson and the Nineteenth-Century American Theatre* that Jefferson's genius in the role so long associated with him resulted from Jefferson's discovery through his career "that humor mixed with pathos produced a potent blend." Some contemporary **critics*†** wagged fingers at the play's tolerance for Rip's drinking, but all acclaimed the realism*† of Jefferson's performance, as the critic for *The Nation* wrote, noting that "all is as natural as if there were no **footlights**, no audience, no orchestra, no **scenery**,*† and no **prompter**.† He seems unaware of the audience's presence." Jefferson's son, Thomas (1856–1932), revived the play unsuccessfully in 1905 following his father's death.

RISTORI, ADELAIDE (1822–1906). The Italian-born tragic **actress*†** was regarded by some **critics*†** as the greatest international tragedienne of her generation. The first of her American **tours*†** was in 1866, playing Medea, and during her visit she impressed critics with her range of classic and contemporary roles, including Mary Stuart, Phèdre, Adrienne Lecouvreur, **Francesca da Rimini**, and Lady Macbeth. In the United States, Ristori seemed to top all of her great performances playing the title role in Paolo

Giacometti's *Queen Elizabeth*. She periodically toured America until her last tour in 1884–1885 and attempted, for the first time, to perform in English, but audiences were disappointed.

*†THE ROAD. "The road" generally refers to the vast web of **legitimate†** and **vaudeville†** theaters across the United States. **Opera houses** and theaters of various size in cities and towns across America presented a steady flow of performances for the local public, while providing employment for **actors,*†** stage technicians, and musicians, many of whom spent their careers on the road. Going on the road, or **touring,*†** was corollary to any career, for residing and working steadily in any given large city was rarely possible. Even the top **stars*†** needed to maintain their aura of stardom by appearing before live audiences all across America. Some actors, plays, and **playwrights*†** found little success in New York, but garnered a vast following on the road. Relying on **railroad†** connections, the road flourished until World **War** I.***†**

ROBERT EMMET, THE MARTYR OF IRISH LIBERTY. James **Pilgrim**'s three-act drama had its first performances at the **St. Charles Theatre** in 1853 (with Pilgrim himself in the cast); in 1854, it had productions at the **Chestnut Street Theatre** and the **Bowery Theatre**, and in 1856 at the **National Theatre**. The play, based on the life of the great **Irish** patriot Robert Emmet (1778–1803), was, not surprisingly, popular with the growing Irish population in northeastern theaters. Pilgrim's approach was to mix joyous Irish jigs, to establish the environment, together with serious political speeches on the issues Emmet faced and general statements of Irish patriotism. The play ends as Emmet is executed, but it is clear that as tragically as the story of Emmet can be shaped, Pilgrim kept his play within the confines of his audience's expectations of **melodrama.†**

ROBERTS, JAMES (1835–1892). A native of Bath, England, James Roberts worked in London theater learning the skills of a **scene designer*†** prior to traveling to the United States in 1860. In 1869, he became chief designer for **Augustin Daly†** and was much praised for his realistic interiors, which effectively served many of the domestic plays Daly produced in that era. These happened to be some of his most memorable works, including *Man and Wife* (1870), *Saratoga* (1870), *The Merry Wives of Windsor* in 1872, and *Diplomacy* (1878). Roberts was injured when the **Fifth Avenue Theatre** burned in a **fire,†** damaging his hearing and weakening his overall health. He continued to work, but in a much-reduced schedule, typically designing no more than two settings per production.

ROBERTS, J. B. (1818–1901). Born James Booth Roberts in Newcastle, Delaware, he became an **actor*†** in his late teens, making his debut at Philadelphia's **Walnut Street Theatre** as Richmond to **Junius Brutus Booth**'s Richard III, and received positive response from **critics*†** who found his acting style natural. He was never able to achieve much success in New York, but he was a **star*†** on the **road,***† appearing effectively in most of the major tragic roles of **Shakespeare**'s† plays.

ROBERTSON, AGNES (1833–1916). A native of Edinburgh, Agnes Kelly Robertson became the ward of **actor*†** Charles Kean and debuted at age 13, amassing considerable experience prior to marrying **Dion Boucicault** (his second wife) and making her American debut with him as Maria in *The Young Actress*, a Boucicault play.

Robertson typically appeared in Boucicault plays, either new works or revivals. She appeared in several revivals of Boucicault's 1841 comedy, *London Assurance*, *Violet* (1856), *Jessie Brown; or, The Siege of Lucknow* (1858), *Cricket on the Hearth* (1859), *The Octoroon* (1859), *The Colleen Bawn* (1860), and *The Trial of Effie Deans* (1863), after which she returned to England, only rarely returning to the United States to perform. In 1888, Boucicault claimed they were never legally wed, and he married Louise Thorndyke, a young **actress*†** 44 years his junior, causing a front-page scandal. Despite this, Robertson continued to appear in Boucicault plays and gave her last performance in London in *The Colleen Bawn* in 1896.

ROBINSON, DAVID G. (b. c. 1807). Born in East Monmouth, Maine, little else is known about David G. Robinson's early life, though it is believed he attended Yale and graduated with a medical degree sometime in the 1830s. Exactly when he began his theatrical career is not known, but Robinson, who bore the nicknames "Doc" or "**Yankee,**"† **toured*†** in a **temperance play**, *A Reformed Drunkard*, with his family before he settled in San Francisco around 1847 working as a doctor and opening a pharmacy.

Robinson built the Dramatic Museum on California Street in San Francisco around 1850, one of the first theaters in that city. He offered **burlesque*†** entertainments,† including those he wrote himself, such as *Seeing the Elephant*, a satiric caricature of gold-rush prospectors, and *Who's Got the Countess?*, a spoof of **Lola Montez** and her amorous adventures. He also parodied local politics, and in an ironic twist, he was elected an alderman. The Museum was ultimately destroyed by **fire,**† but he built and served as **manager*†** of other theaters. His career wound down in the 1850s, although he aided his young daughter, Sue, who had a brief career as a **child**† prodigy.

Some historians posit that Robinson died of a fever in Mobile, Alabama, in 1856, while others believe he lived (in poverty) into the 1870s, but neither scenario has been proven.

ROBINSON, FAYETTE LODAWICK (1818–1884). Born in Avon Mineral Springs, New York, and nicknamed **"Yankee"**† Robinson (not to be confused with **David G. Robinson**, who also bore this nickname), his start in theater was inauspicious when, in 1835, he joined a small **touring***† tent show. Robinson found success by establishing his own tent show called Robinson's Athenaeum, producing familiar **temperance melodramas**† like *The Drunkard*, which were vastly popular with rural audiences. He also founded a **circus,***† which also won success with small-town patrons.

†**ROBSON, STUART (1836–1903).** Born Henry Robson Stuart in Annapolis, Maryland, Stuart Robson made his debut as an **actor***† in the Baltimore Museum's 1852 parody *Uncle Tom's Cabin As It Is*. He also appeared with **Rose Eytinge**† in **Steele MacKaye**'s *Rose Michel* at the **Union Square Theatre**. During the 1860s and 1870s, he appeared in the companies of **Laura Keene, Mrs. John Drew,**† and **William Warren** before teaming with actor **W. H. Crane**† in the farcical hit *Our Boarding House* (1877). They appeared together in a variety of plays including *Our Bachelors* (1878), *The Comedy of Errors* (1878), *Sharps and Flats* (1880), and, most notably, **Bronson Howard**'s† *The Henrietta*† (1887), which the **playwright***† is purported to have written with Robson and Crane in mind.

Robson's partnership with Crane ended amicably in 1889, and Robson bought Crane's share in *The Henrietta* and continued to play Bertie. **Augustus Pitou**† quoted Robson's wistful observation about his own talent: "I have the soul of a tragedian with the high squeaky voice of a low comedian."

ROGERS, ROBERT (1731–1795). Born in Methuen, Massachusetts, Robert Rogers formed a militia of 600 New England **frontiersman**, Rogers's Rangers, whom he led in battle during the **French and Indian War** at Lake George in 1758 and the capture of Quebec in 1759. He was involved in relieving Detroit during Pontiac's rebellion. He spent some time in London, where he published his journals of the adventures of Rogers's Rangers and wrote a play, *Ponteach; or, The Savages of America* (1766), an early American play, noted especially for its uncommonly sympathetic portrayals of **Native Americans.***† When the **American Revolution** began, accusations of treason were made against Rogers, and **George Washington** had him arrested for spying in 1776. This led to Rogers becoming a loyalist, and he left America for London in 1780.

ROPE DANCING. An early way of describing aerial acrobatics or tightrope walking; a rope dancer walked across or performed acrobatics on a rope stretched tightly at some distance above the floor or ground. This form of entertainment† dates to the dawn of theatrical activity and was popular in American theaters.

ROSE MICHEL. **Steele MacKaye** adapted Ernest Blum's French play into a five-act romantic **melodrama**.† It opened at the **Union Square Theatre** on 23 November 1875 for 122 performances. *Rose Michel* proved to be one of the biggest hits of the decade in its tense story of a woman's dilemma: Should she reveal that her husband is a murderer and thus destroy the imminent marital plans of her daughter? **Rose Eytinge**† scored a personal success in the title role, and the cast also included **Charles Thorne, Stuart Robson,** and **Fanny Morant**.

In her memoirs, Eytinge, who played the title role, wrote of friction with MacKaye over the interpretation of the character and his persistent interruptions of her during rehearsals. She finally walked out of a rehearsal, but they discussed the matter, and MacKaye agreed to give her notes after rehearsals instead of interrupting her. And he did so. Following the first performance, as she writes, he met her in the wings, took her hands, and said, "'Can you ever forgive me for ever having presumed to offer you a suggestion?' I tell this incident," Eytinge writes, "not in order that I may vindicate my claim to a better understanding of the character of Rose Michel than his had been, but as a tribute to the nobility and generosity of Steele MacKaye's nature."

ROSEDALE; OR, THE RIFLE BALL. **Lester Wallack**'s dense five-act **melodrama**† opened at **Wallack's Theatre** on 30 September 1863 for 125 performances. The play was one of Wallack's most popular and frequently performed works, revived on **Broadway***† on 12 March 1894 at the **Star Theatre** with Joseph Haworth and on 13 April 1913 in a William A. Brady† production **starring***† Robert Warwick and Jobyna Howland for 23 performances.

The late husband of widow Florence May (played in the original production by **Mrs. Hoey**) stipulated in his will that she would require the permission of her late husband's uncle, Colonel Cavendish May (played by H. F. Daly), to remarry and in regard to whom she could remarry, or she would forfeit her inheritance. Her inheritance would then be divided between the colonel and her young son.

The colonel wants all of the money and plots to murder the **child**† and manipulate Florence into marrying without his permission. With his henchman, Miles (played by **John Gilbert**), he plots to do her out of the inheritance. Florence has two suitors, one of whom is Elliot Grey (played by

Wallack), who became a soldier of fortune after Florence's initial rejection, though he still cares for her deeply. The other suitor, Matthew Leigh (played by **Charles Fisher**), a doctor, also loves Florence. Years earlier, Matthew's baby brother was kidnapped by gypsies. When the colonel and Miles attempt to kidnap Florence's child, Elliot reveals that he is Matthew's long-lost brother. The colonel and Miles are foiled, and Florence and Matthew wed.

A ROW AT THE LYCEUM; OR, GREEN ROOM SECRETS. **John Brougham**'s one-act farce opened on 26 April 1851 at the **Lyceum Theatre** for 21 performances. In this uniquely structured piece, the audience enters the theater to find the **actors***† rehearsing a tragedy, *Horror on Horror's Head; or, The Liar and the Slave,* when one of the **actresses,***† played by **Mrs. Brougham**, expresses her annoyance about the size of her role. Her complaint rouses a man in the audience (played by Brougham), who rises from his seat and claims she is his wife and insists she leave the stage. A fireman in the gallery (played by **W. J. Florence**) shouts that he will beat up the husband if he touches his wife. Mayhem interrupts the rehearsal as the husband and fireman run onstage and are apprehended by policemen. The entire cast then turns to the audience as one of them delivers an epilogue explaining that the row at the Lyceum was all just a joke.

ROWE, GEORGE FAWCETT (1834–1889). The early years of George Fawcett Rowe are obscure, though he was most likely English and worked as an **actor***† in England and Australia before making his New York debut as Sir Charles Coldstream in *Used Up* at the **Olympic Theatre** in 1866. A typical journeyman actor of his times, Rowe made a mark in both comic and serious roles, and he also had some success as a **playwright**.*† He appeared in *Two Roses* (1872), *Little Em'ly* (1874), *Brass* (1876), and as the title character in his own adaptation of *Leatherstocking: The Last of the Mohicans* (1874). He wrote **burlesque***† sketches for **Lydia Thompson**, including *Mephisto and the Four Sensations* (1873), and a **melodrama,**† *The Sphinx,* for **Clara Morris**.

ROWSON, SUSANNA HASWELL (1762–1824). She was born into a naval family in Portsmouth, England, as Susanna Haswell, but her mother died within days of her birth and her father was stationed in Boston. When the **American Revolution** began, her father was placed under house arrest and they were eventually compelled to live in Nova Scotia in poverty. Her education and intelligence made it possible for her to work as a governess to assist in her family's support, and she began to write in a wide range of genres, including a novel, a **musical***† farce lampooning the Whiskey Rebellion called *The Volunteers*, an opera, and a poetical tribute to soldiers. **Critics***† noted her liberal attitudes, particularly regarding issues of **gender**,*† and she was rejected by William Cobbett, who called her "our American Sappho."

In 1786, she married William Rowson, but when his business failed, the Rowsons turned to the stage, working for **Thomas Wignell**, and she appeared in no fewer than 57 roles onstage within two seasons. The Rowsons moved to Boston in 1796 and acted for the **Federal Street Theatre**. In 1797, Rowson quit acting and established a boarding school for girls, which was a success for over 10 years and, during that time and after, she continued writing.

Regarding her writing, Rowson continued to work in multiple genres. She scored a major success with her novel *Charlotte Temple* (1790, originally titled *Charlotte: A Tale of Truth*); it was so successful that she ultimately wrote a sequel, *Charlotte's Daughter; or, The Three Orphans* (1828). Along with novels and poetry, Rowson wrote school texts, from spelling dictionaries to geography books, and she wrote six plays, among the earliest by a woman **playwright***† in America. These plays were *Slaves in Algiers; or, A Struggle for Freedom* (1794; the particular work attacked so vehemently by William Cobbett), *The Female Patriot* (1795), *The Volunteers* (1795), *Americans in England* (1797; retitled *Columbian Daughters* in 1800), *The American Tar* (1796), and *Hearts of Oak* (1811).

†**RUBE.** Originally a rube was a farmer character in a play. Later the term came to refer to any character belonging to a rural setting or atmosphere. The term was frequently employed, for example, by George M. Cohan,*† who used the term in his song lyrics and shows in which he dropped a **Broadway***† type into a rural environment, as in his hit **musical**,*† *Forty-Five Minutes from Broadway* (1906), among others.

Actors*† specialized in rube roles. **Denman Thompson**, for example, developed a **vaudeville**† sketch in 1875 about the definitive "**rube**,"† a good-natured New England farmer, and the character proved so popular that Thompson wrote a play about him called *Joshua Whitcomb* (1878), then collaborated with George W. Ryer on a second Whitcomb play, *The Old Homestead*† (1887), which achieved 160 performances at New York's **Fourteenth Street Theatre**,† phenomenal success on the **road**,*† and occasional returns to New York in 1899, 1904, 1907, and 1908.

THE RULING PASSION. **John Brougham** wrote this six-act comedy for the opening of the 1859 season at **Wallack's Theatre**. The title referred to Brougham's idea of giving each character a passion for something he chose for them, and he made an effort to fit the passions to the personas of the **actors***† for whom he wrote the roles. Some of the "all-stars" appearing were **Lester Wallack**, W. R. Walcot, John Dyott, **Mrs. Hoey**, **Mary Gannon**, **Mrs. Vernon**, and Mrs. Walcot, among others. **Critics*†** were mixed and regarded this as a slight work by a talented **dramatist.*†**

RURAL FELICITY: WITH THE HUMOUR OF PATRICK, AND MARRIAGE OF SHELTY. **John Minshull**'s three-act **opéra bouffe** was published in 1801, but not produced until Minshull staged it in January 1805 at the Grove Theatre. The piece dealt with the growing **Irish** immigration to the United States. Patrick works as a laborer and is loyal to both the English king and to Ireland, and the play's debate centers on challenges facing Patrick, including by his boss, Clover, who sees him as faithless to both. Patrick does not agree and intends to defend himself to prove "that an Irishman has a heart corresponding with a noble disposition." His proof wins him a wife and the ultimate respect of his boss.

†RUSSELL, ANNIE (1864–1936). English-born **actress*†** Annie Russell spent her youth in Canada, making her stage debut as a **child†** in a Montreal production of *Miss Multon* (1872), **starring*†** **Rose Eytinge,†** after which Russell made her first New York appearance in the **operetta†** *H.M.S. Pinafore* (1879), the first **W. S. Gilbert** and **Arthur Sullivan** piece performed in the United States. She spent some years on arduous **tours*†** to South America and Australia, but returned to New York to score a personal triumph in the title role of Frances Hodgson Burnett† and **William Gillette's†** *Esmeralda†* (1881). **Critics*†** and audiences appreciated her in important roles in *Elaine* (1887), **Bret Harte**'s *Sue* (1896), and Clyde Fitch's† *The Girl and the Judge†* (1901). Later in her career, Russell appeared in Edward Sheldon's† controversial drama *The Nigger†* (1909) and Henrik Ibsen's† *Brand* in 1910, before she retired from the stage in 1918.

†RUSSELL, SOL SMITH (1848–1902). A native of Brunswick, Missouri, Sol Smith Russell debuted as a **child†** during the **Civil War** but won enduring popularity as a monologist and comedian, particularly with the Berger family of bell ringers and in the **stock*†** company of **Ben De Bar.†** Russell joined **Augustin Daly's†** **Fifth Avenue Theatre** company in 1874, first appearing there in *What Could She Do?; or, Jealousy.* He subsequently appeared in Daly productions of *The School for Scandal* and *Masks and Faces.* Russell achieved his greatest success as a **rube†** in J. E. Brown's ***Edgewood Folks*** (1880), a role he is reported to have played in excess of 1,500 times. Similar roles followed in *A Poor Relation* (1889) and *A Bachelor's Romance* (1897), among others, all of which won Russell a large following on the **road.*†**

Russell's recollections of his beginnings, published in Lewis Clinton Strang's *Famous Actors**† *of the Day in America*, provides a glimpse at the struggles facing a rookie actor in the mid-19th century:

> My first theatrical engagement† was at the Defiance Theatre, Cairo, Illinois, in 1862, at the magnificent salary of six dollars a week. For this recompense I sang between the acts and played and drummed in the orchestra. I had for a bed the stage lounge, and counted myself lucky to have even so good a place to sleep as that. The **manager***† of the theater, Mr. Holland, was very kind to me. He took me to his home and gave me free access to his excellent theatrical library, and during such spare time as I had, I read. My first acting was in a play called *The Hidden Hand*, and my part was that of a negro girl. I made quite a success of it.

RYAN, DENNIS (d. 1786). Little is known about this early **actor***†-**manager***† who, with his wife, appeared in New York in 1783, after which he was manager of a company in Baltimore and **toured***† throughout the South. Like many of his peers, Ryan played classical and contemporary roles, including **Shakespeare***† and Oliver Goldsmith.

S

ST. CHARLES STREET THEATRE. Located at 426 St. Charles, New Orleans, the St. Charles Street Theatre was built in 1835 from a neo-Renaissance design by **architect** A. Mondelli and opened on 30 November 1835. When the theater opened, **James H. Caldwell** served as **manager*†** and ran it as a **legitimate†** theater. It is believed that the theater could seat as many as 4,000 and, at the time, was considered one of the most elaborate theaters in the South. Unfortunately, it was totally destroyed in an 1842 **fire.†** A year later, the theater was rebuilt, although smaller and less extravagant in its facade, while the interior was elaborate (designed by Dr. George King Pratt).

This second version of the theater offered performances from the cream of the theatrical trade, including legendary figures such as **Edwin Booth†** and Jenny Lind. The theater survived almost 55 years, but was again destroyed by fire in 1899. A third version of the St. Charles was designed in 1902 by Favrot & Livaudais to service the burgeoning **vaudeville†** circuit, and its name was changed to the Orpheum Theatre. When, in 1924, another Orpheum Theatre was constructed nearby, the old theater was sold to the Saenger circuit and its original name restored. This time it became a **film†** theater and live stage shows were also offered. In 1932, the theater was remodeled and became exclusively a movie theater and continued as such until it was closed and torn down in 1965.

ST. EMANUEL STREET THEATRE. Built and opened on 30 November 1835 by **actor*†-managers*†** **Noah Ludlow** and **Sol Smith** in Mobile, Alabama, the St. Emanuel Street Theatre was destroyed by a **fire†** in 1838. Ludlow and Smith had not purchased insurance, so the loss was total: $30,000.

ST. PHILIP STREET THEATRE. This New Orleans theater began its life as a ballroom, and during difficult economic times, the facility would return to its ballroom status. It was the first such space in New Orleans to be used for a quadroon ball for **African Americans.*†** Built in 1808, the theater did not come into full flower until 1820 when **manager*†** **James H. Caldwell** established a theater company there and ushered in English-speaking theater in New Orleans with a play called *The Honey Moon*.

THE SACK OF ROME. Mercy Otis Warren's blank verse tragedy in five acts was published in 1790. The thematic emphasis in this historically based play focused on former republics undermined by the lack of civic virtue in their own citizens. The play encouraged citizens to contribute to and influence national politics. Warren also **criticized*†** the rise of an American aristocracy, which she viewed as a danger to democracy, and posited a greater involvement in national politics by **women.*†**

SALT LAKE THEATRE. Built during 1861–1862 in Salt Lake City, the Salt Lake Theatre cost $100,000. Brigham Young donated more than half of the needed amount because he believed his flock needed a theater for the sake of recreation and as a device for establishing great unity in his community. The scandalous reputation of theater in some religious arenas arose among Young's followers, some of whom resisted the idea of the theater. However, at its dedication, Young stressed the importance of moral theater.

The theater could seat 1,500, and **architecturally** it was regarded as one of the outstanding buildings in mid-19th-century Salt Lake City. The greatest of American **actors†** appeared at the theater, including **Julia Dean, E. L. Davenport**, and **John McCullough**, among others. As the building aged, it was sold in 1928 and torn down for a commercial office building to replace it.

†SALVINI, TOMMASO (1829–1915). The great Italian tragedian, born in Milan, Italy, was a **star*†** long before the first of his five American **tours,*†** in 1873–1874, when he performed with **Edwin Booth†** in a **polyglot production.†** On that and subsequent tours (1880–1881, 1882–1883, 1885–1886, 1889–1890), Salvini performed in Italian. He never learned much English, though he came to love America and was highly appreciated by audiences across the United States. Salvini was best known to Americans for the unbridled passion of his Othello, which proved daunting to **actresses*†** playing Desdemona's death scene opposite him.

SAM PATCH; OR, THE DARING †YANKEE. E. H. Thompson's 1836 play about the leap into Niagara Falls by Sam Patch (1799–1829), known as the "**Yankee** Leaper," opened first in the Buffalo Theatre in Buffalo, New York, and on 1 May 1837 at the **Bowery Theatre. Starring*† Dan Marble** as Patch, the first widely known American daredevil, Thompson crafted the role specifically for Marble, acknowledging his expertise playing Yankee roles. Marble played Patch in theaters across the eastern and southern United

States, and it permanently endeared him to American audiences. In fact, Marble was so popular in the role that a series of sequels were written, including *Sam Patch at Home*, *Sam Patch in France*, and *Sam Patch the Jumper* during the 1830s. President Andrew Jackson was so taken with Patch's stunt he named his horse after Patch.

SAMSON. **William Dean Howells**'s first play, a five-act tragedy written and first produced on **tour*†** in 1874, is a translation and adaptation of Ippolito Tito D'Aste's *Sansone*, which **starred*† Tommaso Salvini** in the tragedy about the mythological strongman. Howells's version was written as a vehicle for **actor*† Charles Pope** and remained popular on American stages for a quarter of a century. The play was well received by audiences, and Howells's close friend, **Mark Twain**, commented on the play's "enthusiastic" reception in a letter to Howells dated 24 October 1874. The first New York production was in October 1889.

*†SAMUEL FRENCH, INC. Samuel French,† a publisher of inexpensive editions of various literary works, also published plays via his French's American Drama series. From this he raised enough capital to buy out his major competitor, William Taylor and Company, in 1854. The company bearing French's name provided all manner of theatrical services from its beginnings, but by the end of the 19th century its management settled on publication of acting editions of plays and licensing stage works for performance. Along with Dramatists Play Service, Inc.,***†** it remains the most important company serving this purpose for professional and **amateur*†** theaters.

SAN FRANCISCO MINSTRELS. Founded in the 1850s, the San Francisco Minstrels were a **blackface† minstrel†** troupe that found two decades of success following the **Civil War**. The company was led by three well-established minstrel greats, **Billy Birch**, **Charlie Backus**, and David Wambold, performers whose special skills helped shape the troupe's style, with a mix of physical slapstick, wittiness, and improvisational spontaneity. This mix brought them considerable popularity, and they became the highest-paid minstrels in the country.

Unlike most minstrel troupes, the San Francisco Minstrels did not **tour,*†** but spent 19 years in residence in New York—an astonishing length of time—perhaps, in part, because the troupe made a point of incorporating all of the legendary elements of minstrelsy, from **Jim Crow** to Bones and Tambo; unfortunately, these characters were interpreted as **childlike†** and of inferior intelligence, adding to negative stereotypical stage images of **African Americans.*†**

The San Francisco Minstrels were Mark Twain's favorites, and he marveled at their success in 1867: "Our old San Francisco Minstrels have made their mark here, most unquestionably. . . . Every night of their lives they play to packed houses—every single seat full and dozens of people standing up. I have good reason to know, because I have been there pretty often, have always paid my way but once, and I had to buy a box the last time I went."

SANFORD, SAM S. (1821–1905). Born Samuel Sanguin Sanford, he became a **minstrel†** show **manager*†** and performer. In 1853, he built the first theater in Philadelphia constructed strictly for the purpose of minstrel performances. He was a masterful showman and marketer, distributing toys to **children† (African American*†** and white) at Christmas and 5,000 loaves of bread to the poor population of the city. These stunts helped win attention for his troupe, though the idea of tossing the gifts and food from the roof of the theater to a crowd below caused some consternation. Sanford also marketed the company with publications of "Sanford's Songs," collections of favorites performed by the troupe (he published 36 of these), and other show souvenirs. Though the national popularity of minstrels began to decline by the 1880s, Sanford's troupe continued for years after in Philadelphia, a theater town that enjoyed a wide range of entertainments,† including minstrels.

SANFORD'S MINSTRELS. Sanford's Theatre, built by **Sam S. Sanford** in 1853 as Philadelphia's first theater devoted exclusively to **minstrel†** shows, was destroyed by **fire†** within months of its opening and had to be rebuilt. The company renamed itself Sanford's Opera Troupe the same year it was founded and began a seven-year run at the Eleventh Street **Opera House**. One of its most popular sketches was *Happy Uncle Tom*, a spoof of *Uncle Tom's Cabin*,† which showed how happy **African Americans*** were in the South in slavery in a broadly ironic tone. The troupe innovated and began staging **tableaux** (often patriotic) that were clearly forerunners of **tableaux vivants**, which would become popular in **revues*†** in several decades.

SANS SOUCI, ALIAS, FREE AND EASY, OR, AN EVENING'S PEEP INTO A POLITICAL CIRCLE. Though possibly authored by **Mercy Otis Warren** in 1785, her authorship of this three-act satire is disputed, and in fact, she denied writing it, saying, "I hope I shall never write anything I should be so much ashamed to avow as that little indigested farrago." A Sans Souci Club was formed in 1785. Warren, who had written several plays, became antitheater in the aftermath of the **American Revolution**. She perhaps feared that in an anti-Republican era frivolous use would be made of public playhouses. In any event, in the play, allegorical characters reveal the elite Sans Souci, a weekly club in which tea and cards occupy its members. The author attacked citizens for the moral corruption resulting from the emergence of fashionable society, a subject that would interest several authors until the mid-19th century, especially **women*†** writers.

SARATOGA; OR, PISTOLS FOR SEVEN. **Bronson Howard**'s five-act farce was produced by **Augustin Daly** at the **Fifth Avenue Theatre** on 21 December 1870 for 101 performances. An estimable success for Howard, Daly, and Daly's troupe, *Saratoga* was one of the first American plays to find international popularity.

The plot is simple, though crowded with colorful characters. A young gentleman, Bob Sackett (played by **James Lewis**), has recently become engaged to Effie Remington (played by **Fanny Davenport**), but he is a practiced philanderer and has, in one way or another, attached himself to a widow (played by **Fanny Morant**), a newlywed (played by **Clara Morris**), and a flirt (played by Linda Dietz). Unable to balance his lies and promises, Bob heads to Saratoga to hide out, but all four women follow him there, also followed by the newlywed's furiously angry husband (played by J. Burnett) and the flirt's parents, the Vanderpools (played by **William Davidge** and **Mrs. Gilbert**).

Theater scholar **Brander Matthews** wrote that *Saratoga* owed its popularity to "the brisk ingenuity of its intrigue, to the unflagging virtuosity of its adroit situations and to the humorous felicity of its dialogue."

SARDOU, VICTORIEN (1831–1908). In childhood, Parisian-born Victorien Sardou survived the traumatic experience of watching his family go from prosperity in the country raising olives to poverty when a frost destroyed their crop. The family moved to Paris, and Sardou gained an education, read voraciously, and began to write.

Between 1854 and 1898, Sardou wrote 70 plays, many popular with French audiences, but also in international theaters. Many of his works were adapted into operas and some by **playwrights;*†** for example **Augustin Daly** translated and adapted Sardou's *La Papillonne* (1864) as *Taming of a Butterfly*. International **stars*† touring*†** in America, **Sarah Bernhardt†** paramount among them, performed Sardou's plays and contributed to popularizing them in America. Not everyone admired Sardou's plays; George Bernard Shaw,† for example, referred to them as "Sardoodledum."

SARGENT, EPES (1813–1880). Born in Gloucester, Massachusetts, Epes Sargent was educated in Boston's Latin School and traveled to Russia for six months with his father before attending Harvard University. In 1831, he became a newspaperman in Boston, writing on politics and befriending such distinguished figures as Henry Clay, Daniel Webster, and John C. Calhoun. He wrote his first play, *The Bride of Genoa*, in 1836, produced at New York's **Park Theatre starring*† Charlotte Cushman**. He followed up with *Velasco* (1837), a fictionalized treatment of events in the life of El Cid, which was first produced at Boston's **Tremont Theatre** with **Ellen Tree**, after which it had runs at other American theaters and in London.

Sargent's other plays include a five-act blank verse tragedy, *The Priestess* (1854), and some minor comedies, *The Candid Critic*,*† *The Lampoon*, and *Change Makes Change*, all written in 1845. Sargent moved to New York in 1839 and worked for several newspapers, using the pen name Chicot, and authored a biography of Henry Clay, as well as poetry and novels. He wrote school texts on speaking and reading and also edited *The Modern Standard Drama* (1846), a seven-volume collection of plays. A member of the Knickerbocker group of writers and artists, including **Washington Irving, James Kirke Paulding, Nathaniel Parker Willis**, and others, Sargent was also a close friend of **Anna Cora Mowatt**, whose stage career and popular comedy *Fashion* he encouraged.

SARONY, NAPOLEON (1821–1896). Born in Quebec, Napoleon Sarony moved with his family to New York sometime around 1836. He found employment as an illustrator for Currier & Ives before partnering with James Major in 1843 to found his own lithography business. Sarony left their company in 1867 and set up a photography studio at 37 Union Square in New York, just as celebrity photography was becoming nationally popular, and Sarony further popularized it.

Photographers like Sarony would pay their subjects to sit for the camera, and once having done so, the photographer would retain the rights to reproduce and sell the photographs. Fees varied, but Sarony supposedly paid **Sarah Bernhardt** $1,500 to sit for him; at the time, it was well beyond top dollar. Sarony photographed noted historical and political individuals, writers and artists, and theatrical personnel. He also helped popularize *carte de visite* photographs—small card-like pictures people could purchase of favorite celebrities. From 1867 to the end of his life—nearly 30 years—Sarony captured memorable images of the famous, especially those of the theater.

SAUNDERS, CHARLES H. (1818–1856). Little is known about the early life of Charles H. Saunders, who was an **actor*†** and **playwright*†** of more than 50 **melodramas**.† His best-known work was his adaptation of the novel *Rosina Meadows* for the stage, and it played at the **National Theatre** in 1849 for two continuous months, then at **Barnum**'s **American Museum** in 1851, and also in Boston. When the play was published several years after its performances, Saunders acknowledged that it was no literary masterpiece, which could be said of his entire dramatic output that, as he saw it, was an "effective acting piece," and that seemed to be all he was aiming for in his playwriting.

THE SAW-MILL; OR, A YANKEE†   TRICK. **Micah Hawkins**'s (1777–1825) 1824 comic opera in two acts featured orchestral arrangements by **James Hewitt**. It opened on 29 November 1824 at the **Chatham Garden Theatre**, with **scene designs*†** by Hugh Reinagle, the son of **Alexander Reinagle**. The plot involved the rich Baron Schafferdwal, who offers 100 acres of land to anyone who will build a sawmill on nearby Oneida Creek. Bloom and Herman, two young men, devise a scheme to claim the baron's land and win the hands of the girls they love by disguising themselves as **Yankees.†** After a variety of machinations, all works out for them; the score is overloaded with 28 **musical*†** numbers and a great deal of local color and Dutch dialects.

*†**SCENE DESIGN/SCENERY.** The earliest American publication on scene painting, according to Warren C. Lounsbury, was *A Practical Guide to Scene Painting and Painting in Distemper* (c. 1883) by F. Lloyds, who described techniques, equipment, and scenic elements. Most colors had to be purchased as lumps to be crushed or else ground down with a palette knife in water. Some form of glue or "size" had to be mixed with the water as a binder. However, scene design and scene painting was prevalent in theaters in the United States from nearly its beginnings and especially once permanent theaters and some rudimentary technologies were available.

A good summary of the art of the scene painter appears in Claude Bragdon's† *More Lives Than One*:

> First, the linen- or canvas-covered flats are arranged vertically on the paint-frame, a gigantic easel, sliding up and down through a slit running the entire length of the floor. The design is then drawn in charcoal, enlarged from the scenic designer's sketch. The paint (opaque water-color with an admixture of liquid glue) is laid on rapidly with broad, flat brushes. To give tone, texture, "life," the painted surfaces are either spattered with a brush, stippled with a sponge, or rolled with a tightly twisted damp cloth. Sometimes the flats are laid out horizontally, free of the floor, and drenched with dashed-on pails of water, or paint of a different colour, causing the pigments to mingle and deposit themselves in delightful, sometimes unpremeditated ways. Silver or bronze powder, sparingly sprinkled on the still wet canvas, relieves the deadness of dark hues. For curtains and cycloramas dye is used instead of paint, which would stiffen the canvas and flake off. Effects of extraordinary richness are obtained by the use of so-called broken colour, where the mixing takes place in the eye of the beholder, instead of on the surface seen.

Wing-and-drop† settings were still common, as was the use of **stock*†** scenery, throughout the 19th century despite advances. The rise of the **combination†** system meant that many companies traveled with their own scenery specific to the show, usually **box sets†** with practical elements. For transport by railroad,† scenic units had to fit through the door of a boxcar, and all professional designers knew that five-foot-nine-inch measurement.

SCOTT, JOHN R. (1808–1856). Philadelphia-born John R. Scott was drawn to **amateur†** theatrics in his youth, but by adulthood he made his professional debut as Malcolm opposite **Junius Brutus Booth**'s Macbeth in 1829. He was able to parlay his career into a two-city success, becoming popular in both New York at the **Bowery Theatre** and Philadelphia at the **Arch Street Theatre**. He played leads in **Shakespeare**'s*† tragedies and in romantic roles in contemporary popular **melodramas.†** He never quite achieved first-rank status, but was popular with audiences in the two decades before the **Civil War**.

THE SCOUTS; OR, THE PLAINS OF MANASSAS. **John Hill Hewitt**, the **manager*†** of the Richmond Theatre, known as the "Bard of the Stars and Bars," was the most successful songwriter of the **Civil War** in sympathy with the Confederate States of America. He also wrote plays, including this 1861 **melodrama†** celebrating the first major Southern victory of the war, emphasizing the contribution of guerilla soldiers at Manassas.

THE SCOUTS OF THE PRAIRIE. **Ned Buntline**, a journalist and dime novelist, wrote this **sensation melodrama†** as a vehicle for the popular American hero **William F. "Buffalo Bill" Cody**. The shoddily written play, which Buntline, with assistance, may have written in as little as four hours, opened in Chicago at Nixon's Amphitheatre on 18 December 1873. It was advertised as featuring "The real Buffalo Bill, Texas Jack and ten Sioux and Pawnee chiefs in Ned Buntline's great drama *Buffalo Bill*." Obviously, the title changed, possibly because it had not yet been written when the ad appeared.

Buntline appeared in a supporting† role, and when Cody came on, he struggled with his lines, so Buntline began asking questions, allowing Cody to respond without having to stick to prewritten speeches. As Cody recounted himself:

> [I] proceeded to relate in detail the particulars of the affair. I succeeded in making it rather funny, and I was frequently interrupted by rounds of applause. Whenever I began to "weaken," Buntline would give me a fresh start by asking some question. In this way I took up fifteen minutes, without once speaking a word of my part; nor did I speak a word of it

during the whole evening. The prompter,† who was standing between the wings, attempted to prompt me, but it did no good; for while I was on the stage I "chipped in" anything I thought of.

The many deficiencies and shoddiness of *The Scouts of the Prairie* does not obscure the fact that it may well be considered the first "Western" and provided the impetus for more such plays featuring Cody and, ultimately, his legendary "Wild West Show," which would not only enhance his legend, but make legends of **Annie Oakley,**† Sitting Bull, and others.

SCRIBE, EUGÈNE (1791–1861). Born Augustin Eugène Scribe, this French **dramatist***† turned away from the improbable **melodramas**† of his time to "invent" the well-made play, which was essentially a carefully and neatly contrived realistic plot focusing on the domestic problems of the middle class and rejecting the inflated, pseudopoetic language employed in many melodramatic plays, turning instead to the ordinary colloquial speech of everyday life. In essence, he provided a structural prototype for the socially conscious plays of the late 19th century mastered by Henrik Ibsen,† George Bernard Shaw,† and others.

Slowly, American playwrights moved toward Scribe's model, though well behind European dramatists, who at first borrowed Scribe's techniques before more importantly following Ibsen's lead toward realism*† in plays focusing on contemporary social problems. Scribe's own plays mostly met with a mixed reaction from American audiences, though his *Adrienne Lecouvreur* was often performed, but typically by the great international **actresses***† who made frequent **tours***† of America, especially **Sarah Bernhardt,**† **Helena Modjeska,**† and others.

SEA OF ICE; OR, A MOTHER'S PRAYER. Though first performed in Baltimore a few months earlier, **Laura Keene** staged this improbable five-act **melodrama**† by **Adolphe-Philippe D'Ennery** and F. Dugue at her New York theater during the economic panic of 1857. Produced in November and playing over a month, until 19 December, the play defied expectations and helped restore the empty coffers of Keene's company. The implausible plot emphasized the contrast between Old World (European) society and the freer but "half-savage" New World (America). It was one of many such plays stressing the contrast between the Old and New Worlds, but with a strong cast, effective **scene design,***† and lowered ticket prices, Keene had a success.

†SECOND. Like the second in a duel, the second lead could step in to cover for the **leading man,**† but otherwise played a strong supporting† role. In every **line of business**† for which two or more **actors***† were employed, the second deferred to the principal. A **stock***† company might include a second **heavy**,† a second low comedian, a second old man, and (perhaps doubling as a low comedienne) a second old woman.

SELF. This three-act comedy by Mrs. **Sidney Bateman** opened on 27 October 1856 for 18 performances at **William Burton**'s Chamber Theatre. Inspired to an extent by the spirit and satire of **Anna Cora Mowatt**'s *Fashion*, *Self* depicts a family with varied levels of responsibility about money. Mrs. Apex and her son, Charles, live well beyond their means, and when Charles discovers that his frugal sister, Mary, has saved up $15,000, he forges a check for that amount and takes her money. When Mary later writes a check to her father, Mr. Apex (played by **Charles Fisher**), the check bounces, setting off a family battle exacerbated by Mary's unwillingness to have her brother arrested. Eventually, a wise and friendly banker, John Unit (played by Burton), helps the family to alter their ways and to understand his rueful philosophy that all human interactions are driven by one consideration: "Self!" Burton scored a personal success, and after a time, **John E. Owens** played the role of Unit successfully on **tour**.*†

†**SENSATION DRAMA.** A play designed to arouse strong sensations in the spectator—either by suspense and surprising twists of plot or by amazing scenic effects—could be touted for its "sensations." Most of these plays were **melodramas**,† but not all melodramas were sensational. Prominent among the sensation dramas that were widely produced during the 19th century were H. M. Milner's *Mazeppa*† (1831), in which an apparently naked youth is tied to the back of a wild horse that gallops through a craggy landscape; **Dion Boucicault**'s† *The Octoroon* (1859), in which the heroine is put on the slave auction block and in which a steamboat explodes and a new-fangled camera captures an image of a murder; and **Augustin Daly**'s† *Under the Gaslight* (1867), featuring a man tied to the railroad tracks who is rescued by a woman just in time before a locomotive roars onto the stage.

THE SERIOUS FAMILY. The comedy in three acts adapted by Morris Barnett from the French comedy *Un Mari en Champaigne* was first staged by **William E. Burton** in 1849 and was one of his major hits. Burton played a comic character full of pious sentiments named Aminadab Sleek, but he is ultimately saved from his own self-indulgences by love. Burton played the role for the remainder of his career, after which **William Davidge** had success with it.

SERTORIUS; OR, THE ROMAN PATRIOT. Lawyer and Pennsylvania Supreme Court justice **David Paul Brown** adopted elements of **Shakespeare**'s*† style and structure for this five-act historical tragedy, which was first performed at the **Chestnut Street Theatre** in Philadelphia on 14 December 1830 with **Junius Brutus Booth** in the title role. Brown's play drew on Plutarch's life of Quintus Sertorius (c. 126–73 BC), who rebelled against Sulla's rise in Rome by establishing a base in Spain. Though he never betrayed Roman concerns and refused attempts to engage him in attacks on Rome, Sertorius fell victim to his patriotism, assassinated by his officers. In the climactic assassination scene, Sertorius proclaims, "Death to me—To me, alone, is but repose from toil: 'Tis only for the living that I fear."

Some scholars believe that the historical Sertorius, as well as Brown's fictional character, influenced the thinking of **John Wilkes Booth**† as he planned to assassinate President **Abraham Lincoln**. Arthur Hobson Quinn† said *Sertorius* possessed "fine passages but lacks action," but the senior Booth kept it in his repertoire, appearing in it again on 6 February 1832 at the **Arch Street Theatre**.

*†**SEXUALITY.** The depiction of sexuality on American stages has always been fraught with controversy, challenging **playwrights**,*† **managers**,*† and **censors**,*† not to mention audiences. By the middle of the 19th century, attention was focused on the revelation of the female form as most vividly exemplified by **Adah Isaacs Menken**'s† illusion of **nudity** in *Mazeppa*† (1861), which simultaneously scandalized and titillated audiences. Other **shape actresses**,† from Menken to **Lydia Thompson**, proved audience interest in the female form, despite backlashes from censors and puritanical theatergoers on rural stages.

In serious plays of the 18th and 19th century, sexuality was rarely overtly present, though idealized or betrayed love was often at the center of romantic or **melodramatic**† works. Virtue—that is, the virtue of presumably innocent **women***† (**ingénues**†) was often at risk. Women might be threatened with undesired marriages or assignations by various **villainous**† figures while heroic young men often prevented any compromising of virtue. Such dynamics often fueled the motion of 19th-century melodramas, with diverse plays, from farces to the most serious of dramas, making use of love stories as major plot devices, but sex generally went unmentioned though implied.

Marriage, both happy and unhappy, might also figure prominently in 19th-century plays, whether set in the present day or in some earlier or exotic environment. Playwrights generally honored the accepted values that marriage was the appropriate place for sexuality, but the stage was not. Again, sex was implied but rarely mentioned in overt ways.

From 1880 to 1930, the focus shifted from **nudity** (it was generally not permitted, although **musical*†** comedies and **burlesque*†** featured scantily clad chorus girls throughout this period) to frank discussions of life's realities, including sexuality, in the plays of Henrik Ibsen,† George Bernard Shaw,† and a few of their contemporaries. The earliest productions of these plays in American theaters inspired considerable controversy, mostly over depictions of marital infidelity, divorce, unwed mothers, social disease, prostitution, etc. US **dramatists*†** were slow to step into such areas except in the most moralizing or romanticized ways. **James A. Herne**'s† *Margaret Fleming†* (1890), which dealt with a faithless husband forced to bring his out-of-wedlock child to his wife's care, including her breast-feeding of the child, appeared in this period and was a rare exception, although it was not widely seen.

Homosexuality was not seen or discussed overtly in any play of the 18th and 19th century in America, though fops and other dandies implied gay life as existing under a mask (or in a closet) of usually comic proportions, as can still be seen in early 20th-century silent films† and theater.

†SEYMOUR, WILLIAM (1851–1933). Born in New Orleans, William Seymour began a successful career as an **actor,*†** **director,*†** and stage **manager*†** as a **child†** actor. In 1865, he became a callboy† at **Booth's Theatre†** and acted with **Edwin Booth,†** **Joseph Jefferson,†** **Charlotte Cushman**, and **Edwin Forrest**, after which he managed several theaters, including the **Union Square Theatre,†** the **Madison Square Theatre,†** the Metropolitan **Opera House**, and the Empire Theatre. His directorial credits include Clyde Fitch's† *Barbara Freitchie†* (1899) and an **all-star*†** revival of *Trelawny of the "Wells"* in 1925. Seymour also managed the **Boston Museum** from 1879 to 1888 and was married to **E. L. Davenport**'s daughter, May.

*†SHAKESPEARE IN AMERICA. The plays of William Shakespeare (1564–1616) were frequently produced in North America from the time of the earliest settlements of Europeans. Prior to American independence, and well into the 19th century, English troupes or British-trained **actors*†** included Shakespeare's plays centrally in their repertoires.

The first performance of Shakespeare in New York is believed to have been a production of *Richard III*, staged in 1750 by **Thomas Kean**, though he used Colley Cibber's bowdlerization of Shakespeare for his text. Though Shakespeare's plays were always popular on American stages through the 19th century, resistance to English players in America came to a violent head in the **Astor Place Opera House riot** in 1849, pitting supporters of stage rivals **William Charles Macready**, an English actor, and **Edwin Forrest**, America's greatest tragedian to date, against each other in rival productions of *Macbeth*.

African American*† actors and **managers*†** made their first theatrical inroads when the **African Grove Theatre** launched careers for black Shakespeareans **James Hewlett** and **Ira Aldridge**. By the mid-19th century, **Edwin Booth†** emerged as the premiere American Shakespearean, scoring a major triumph in *Hamlet*, which ran for 100 consecutive performances in 1865, a record that held until the 1920s when John Barrymore† played the role for 101 performances. Shakespeare was central to the repertoires of Booth and other **touring*†** stars: **Thomas W. Keene,† Lawrence Barrett,† Frederick Warde,† Louis James,† Marie Wainwright,† E. L. Davenport,† Emma Waller, John McCullough,†** and **Helena Modjeska.†** As European immigrants poured into New York beginning in the 1890s, foreign language productions of Shakespeare were frequently seen, including notable **Yiddish Theater†** performances by Jacob Adler† in *The Merchant of Venice* and *King Lear*.

SHANDY MAGUIRE; OR, THE BOULD BOY OF THE MOUNTAIN. **James Pilgrim**'s two-act **Irish** romantic drama opened on 15 August 1851 at the **Bowery Theatre**. The Bowery run was preceded by performances of the play in Philadelphia at the **Arch Street Theatre** in 1851 with **Barney Williams** as Shandy. Typical of Pilgrim's plays is the featuring of the central comic Irishman, here Shandy Maguire, who is jailed on trumped-up charges of an English romantic rival for the heart of Mary Connor. Shillelagh in hand, in the final analysis, Shandy's good heart and courage exceed those of his rival, and he clears up his legal obstacle and wins Mary's hand. Such Irish plays, and there were many from the early 1840s on, were, not surprisingly, highly popular in New York, Boston, and Philadelphia, all cities with high concentrations of Irish immigrants.

†SHAPE ACTRESS. This slang term for an **actress*†** who revealed the contours of her body, often by cross-dressing to play male roles, was mildly pejorative in that it implied a reliance on flaunting one's physical attributes as opposed to genuine artistry. In their individual ways, **Adah Isaacs Menken†** and **Lydia Thompson†** established this vogue; and in **musical*†** works, such as *The Black Crook†* (1866), featuring a chorus of ballerinas in pink **fleshings,†** the female form became a lucrative **attraction.†** In this period, feminine attractiveness seemed to be led by large **women,*†** though some of the 19th-century actresses most known as beauties were not heavy.

In her book *Performing Mazeppa*,† Renée M. Sentilles discusses the mid-19th-century trend of women in **breeches roles** as a social phenomenon related to the **Civil War** and as one of many appeals to novelty seekers. However, it is important to note that heroines of **Shakespeare**,*† like Rosalind and Viola, who disguise themselves as boys during much of the action, were handled with considerable modesty by serious actresses like **Helena Modjeska**† and Julia Marlowe.† Indeed, Modjeska announced in 1893 (when she was 53) that she was dropping Rosalind from her repertoire "because she cannot consent any more to wear the costume."

SHARPS AND FLATS. A four-act farce by **Clay Meredith Greene** and Slauson Thompson, *Sharps and Flats* opened on 8 November 1880 at Standard Theatre. **Starring***† the comedy team of **Stuart Robson** and **William H. Crane**, it was, as **critics***† reported, "intended to caricature the speculative spirit of the age." Indeed, the convoluted plot revolves around stock speculators, **amateur***† and professional, and mistaken identities, love interests, and extended opportunities for the comedians to demonstrate what one reviewer called their "exquisite skill."

The critic for *The Spirit of the Times*, wrote in the 20 November 1880 issue: "Robson everybody knows as a trick comedian, with a queer voice and quaint manner, at whom it is impossible not to laugh, although his voice and manner become monotonous. But W. H. Crane is a genuine comedian, of the best school, who makes all his effects legitimately. Often when the audience think they are laughing at what Robson says, or at the way he says it, Mr. Crane is supplying the real fun by the manner in which he receives Robson's remarks and by the constant by-play with which he emphasizes every point and strengthens every scene."

THE SHAUGHRAUN. One of **Dion Boucicault**'s most iconic **Irish** plays, a three-act romantic **melodrama**,† *The Shaughraun* opened on 14 November 1874 for 143 performances at **Wallack's Theatre**. Boucicault himself appeared in the role of Conn O'Kelly in the original production.

The plot revolves around Robert Ffolliott, who is engaged to Arte O'Neil and returns to Ireland from Australia, where he was sent because he was considered a Fenian fugitive. It becomes clear that Robert is actually not involved with the Fenians and is completely innocent of everything he has been tricked into agreeing to be part of, though a country squire, Kinchela, who loves Arte, arranges Robert's betrayal to clear his path to Arte. In attempting to clear his name, Robert is aided by Conn, a shaughraun (wanderer), and they find themselves in numerous melodramatically dangerous circumstances. Robert's sister, Claire, is married to an English soldier hunting Fenians and struggling to understand the local culture of rural Ireland. As Robert is cleared, the Fenians are given a general amnesty and Conn provides much humor, Robert and Arte marry, and the **villain**† Kinchela is arrested.

Widely considered Boucicault's finest Irish play—and his own performance as Conn one of his best—*The Shaughraun* was a huge success and earned over half a million dollars. It was frequently revived during the 19th century and occasionally in the 20th and 21st.

SHE WOULD BE A SOLDIER; OR, THE PLAINS OF CHIPPEWA.
Mordecai M. Noah's play was first performed on 21 June 1819 at the **Park Theatre**, where it ran in **repertory**.*† Noah wrote the play with **actress***† Catharine Leesugg in mind, and she played the role of Christine, who disguises herself as a man and runs away from home to avoid an arranged marriage to a slow-witted country bumpkin, which her father has planned for her. She is actually in love with Lenox (played by James Pritchard), who is in the army during the **War of 1812**. She poses as a soldier to be with him, but is arrested as a spy and condemned to death. When she is in front of a firing squad, Lenox recognizes her and halts the execution. The bumpkin arrives, having followed her, but comes to the realization that her love for Lenox is real and states, "Miss Crissy, you look very pretty in pantaloons, and make a fine solger, but after all, I'm glad to have escaped a wife who wears the breeches before marriage."

The **breeches role** and the general romantic plot were nothing new, and in fact, the plot seems suggested (or directly borrowed) from Thomas Shadwell's *The Woman Captain* (1680) and Frederick Pilon's *He Would Be a Soldier* (1786). The play is considered by many scholars to be one of the best early American romantic **melodramas**.†

SHERIDAN, RICHARD BRINSLEY (1751–1816). A native of Dublin, Ireland, Richard Brinsley Sheridan was one of the most popular comic **dramatists***† of his era. He spent most of his career working in London theater, and though he never visited the United States, his plays were enormously popular with Americans. This was the obvious result of most visiting British **actors***† having included Sheridan's most popular plays, *The Rivals* (1775) and *The School for Scandal* (1777), among their offerings.

These plays, and others by Sheridan, presented good comic roles for actors, but **actresses***† were particularly drawn to the role of Lady Teazle in *The School for Scandal*, and in a sense, it was a role that was a test of the comic skill of 18th- and early 19th-century actresses. These plays, as well as those by Sheridan's peers in the British theater, were frequent offerings in American theaters even during those periods of cultural friction between America and England.

SHERIDAN, W. E. (1840–1887). Boston-born William Edward Sheridan made his 1858 debut as an **actor*†** in *Town and Country* at the **Howard Athenaeum** where, as he would throughout his career, Sheridan specialized in portraying **villains†** and tragic victims. Sheridan appeared for two years (1859–1861) at Pike's **Opera House** in Cincinnati. He signed up with the Sixth Ohio Volunteers at the start of the **Civil War** and was in uniform for over three years. Wounded at the Battle of Resaca, Georgia, he nearly lost his right arm. Following his service, Sheridan returned to Pike's as **leading man†** in 1865–1866. After that time, he worked more as a journeyman actor, playing in all of the major theater cities, including New York, Boston, Philadelphia, New Orleans, and others.

SHOOK, SHERIDAN (1828–1899). A native of Red Hook, New York, Sheridan "Shed" Shook, began his working life as a clerk for a produce merchant, but ultimately became involved in politics, becoming an active member of the Whig Party before joining the Republican Party to support **Abraham Lincoln**'s candidacy for president of the United States. He became collector for internal revenue in New York City, and following **Lincoln's assassination**, supported President Andrew Johnson through his 1868 impeachment trial.

In 1871, Shook became involved in theatrical endeavors when he built the **Union Square Theatre,†** which he opened with a **vaudeville†** bill including the **Vokes** family of English comedians. He became a **manager*†** in partnership with **A. M. Palmer.†** They also ran the **Brooklyn Theatre** at the time of its tragic **fire†** in December 1876. When Palmer retired in 1883, Shook continued to successfully manage the Union Square Theatre until 1885. At the time of his death, he had been divorced from his wife, who married his former partner, Palmer.

†SHOWBOATS. Floating theaters were operating downriver on the Mississippi and Ohio Rivers before the **Civil War**, but the heyday of showboating came after midcentury (and after the catastrophic interruption of the Civil War) as steam power allowed them to operate both up- and downriver. Steamboats pulled separate boats fitted out as theaters. Eventually, some— including **circus*†** boats—became quite elaborate.

From the Civil War to the 1930s as many as 75 showboats operated on major American rivers. One of the leading showboat owners, Augustus Byron French (1832–1902), operated five showboats (advertising some as "floating palaces") between 1878 and 1901, pioneering the use of marching bands put ashore to attract the local community to the theater. Another important **manager***† in this period, E. A. Price, developed numerous publicity devices, including calliopes and billboards, to call attention to the arrival of his theaters.

The showboats featured all manner of entertainments,† from **minstrels**† and variety acts to dramatic works, including the perennial **melodrama**† *Uncle Tom's Cabin*. Some operators sought to produce **Shakespeare***† and other prestigious dramas, while others focused on "moral amusements"† including lectures. E. E. Eisenbarth's "Temple of Amusement" was renamed the "Cotton Blossom," and under Ralph Emerson's management, it presented **Broadway***† hits and popular melodramas until 1931.

Showboats inspired the Edna Ferber*† novel *Show Boat* (1926) and the subsequent Broadway **musical***† *Show Boat* (1927) based on it, both presenting an epic story of a theatrical family set on a Mississippi River showboat from the 1880s to the 1920s. The Great Depression and the arrival of sound films† significantly undermined the survival of the showboat phenomenon, which had truly thrived during the last decades of the 19th century, although some operated as late as the 1940s.

THE SIEGE OF ALGIERS; OR, THE DOWNFALL OF HADGI-ALI-BASHAW, A POLITICAL, HISTORICAL AND SENTIMENTAL TRAGI-COMEDY. Jonathan S. Smith's 1823 five-act play was published by J. Maxwell in Philadelphia the year it was written, and the author explained, "In this drama will be strongly exemplified the great contrast between the government, customs, and manners of unlettered despotism, and those of the most free and enlightened nations." A Barbary Coast pirate play, it was one of a number of such works believed largely inspired by **Susanna Haswell Rowson**'s *Charlotte Temple* (1793), which was an unprecedentedly popular novel **dramatists***† attempted to imitate.

THE SIEGE OF TRIPOLI. **Mordecai M. Noah**'s play was first performed at the **Park Theatre** on 15 May 1820 and again in Philadelphia in 1822. One of about a dozen plays in this period about Barbary Coast pirates and related issues of America's national problems with the piracy on the high seas, Noah's play, like **Susanna Haswell Rowson**'s *Slaves in Algiers* (1794) and Jonathan S. Smith's *The Siege of Algiers* (1823), was frequently staged (sometimes under variant titles) and the depictions of pirates seemed to attract audiences. Noah's national service as consul to Tunis provided him actual encounters with pirates, which may have enhanced his play with levels of verisimilitude not evident in other works on this subject.

SILSBEE, JOSHUA (1813–1855). The early life of Joshua Silsbee is quite obscure, with historians debating whether he was born in Connecticut or New York, and little else is known until he became an **actor***† in 1839, making his debut in Natchez, Mississippi. He developed a reputation as a comedian, specializing in **juveniles**† and dandies, but did not really find success until he turned to playing **Yankee**† characters in the mold of **George H. Hill** and **Dan Marble**. Silsbee debuted in New York in 1843 with his Jonathan Ploughboy and other such characters serving as his drawing cards. He found success **touring***† in England in Yankee roles in 1850. He went on tour in America when he returned in 1853, but became ill in California and died there in 1855.

THE SILVER SPOON. **Joseph Stevens Jones**'s four-act comedy opened on 26 February 1852 at the **Boston Museum**, where it played in **repertory**.*† A comedy with **melodramatic**† embellishments, *The Silver Spoon* deals with the election of Jefferson S. Batkins (played by **William Warren**), who has been elected to the assembly to support his area, Cranberry Center, which he intends to fight for against big city interests. He stays with Ezra Austin (played by **W. H. Smith**), whose Aunt Hannah is a former sweetheart of Batkins, and he hopes to court her once again.

In the meantime, Glandon King returns from Europe for the reading of his father's will. To his shock, Glandon learns that his father left him only a silver spoon (making the point that Glandon has already received all of life's benefits) and that his money has gone to establishing a college. A crooked lawyer attempts to pass off his clerk (played by **C. H. Saunders**) as a second son of the late Mr. King in hopes of breaking the will. His plot is foiled, and a genuine second will is discovered, which indicates that if Glandon has made no attempt to break the first will he inherits the entire estate, allowing him to marry the girl he loves, while Aunt Hannah agrees to marry Batkins.

The play was a popular one, especially in **stock**,*† and despite the convoluted plot, much of the comedy centered on Batkins and his bumbling.

SIMMS, WILLIAM GILMORE (1806–1870). Born in Charleston, William Gilmore Simms lost his mother early, and his father became an **Indian** fighter, so he lived with his grandmother. He studied law and passed the bar, but he did not find it a satisfactory profession and gave it up to try his hand as an art **critic***† and writer. His work became closely associated with the South in his poetry and novels, eight of which are set in South Carolina during the **American Revolution**.

Simms strongly supported the institution of slavery, which is evident in his writing, especially *The Sword and the Distaff*, which opposed the abolitionist viewpoints of *Uncle Tom's Cabin*. He wrote some plays, most notably *Nor-*

man Maurice; or, The Man of the People. An American Drama (1853). This play, despite its Southern sympathies, raises the slavery issue in ways that have an impact on a range of characters. The play was published but rarely performed.

SIMPSON, EDMUND SHAW (1784–1848). English-born Edmund Shaw Simpson made his debut as an **actor*†** in 1806 in *The Stranger* at Towchester. He was seen acting in Dublin in 1809, and **Thomas Abthorpe Cooper** and **Stephen Price** signed him to act at the **Park Theatre**. He debuted in America in *The Road to Ruin* in 1809, was well received, and developed a reputation as a versatile performer. In 1812, he was appointed acting **manager*†** of the Park, and he and Price became partners three years later.

As manager of the Park, Simpson traveled to England to sign up actors, and his published diary provides fascinating encounters with some of the most celebrated actors and literary figures of the time, including **Washington Irving**, **Edmund Kean**, Charles Kean, **Junius Brutus Booth**, **John Howard Payne**, Charles Lamb, **William Charles Macready**, John Philip Kemble, Joseph Grimaldi, etc. Simpson was seriously injured in an accident at the theater in 1828, leaving him permanently disabled, though he continued to act until 1833. When Price died in 1840, Simpson continued running the Park alone, though the theater fell on hard times despite decisive successes with the premieres of *London Assurance* and *Fashion*, and he sold it to **Thomas Hamblin**.

SINN, COLONEL WILLIAM E. (1834?–1899). Born in Washington, DC, William E. Sinn worked as a traveling salesman before partnering with his brother-in-law, **Leonard B. Grover**, in 1861. As **managers,*†** they took over several DC-area theaters, as well as others in Cincinnati. On his own, Sinn managed Philadelphia's **Chestnut Street Theatre** in 1864 and the **Front Street Theatre** in Baltimore in 1869. He did not serve in the military, but the Confederate States of America made him an honorary colonel for helping to recruit rebel soldiers during the **Civil War**. Despite his prior successes, his greatest triumph as a manager came in 1875 when he took over the **Park Theatre** and made it New York's leading house.

*†SKINNER, OTIS (1858–1942). Born in Cambridge, Massachusetts, where his father was a local minister, Otis Skinner began his long career at the Philadelphia Museum in 1877, followed by two seasons at the **Walnut Street Theatre** and small roles in productions starring† **Edwin Booth,**† **Lawrence Barrett,**† and **Joseph Jefferson.**† Skinner joined **Augustin Daly's**† company for four years, after which he appeared with Booth and **Helena Modjeska**† in a series of **Shakespeare*†** productions.

In 1894, Skinner achieved **star***† status in *His Grace de Grammont*, followed by notable—and many **critics***† felt flamboyant—performances in a 1901 revival of *Francesca da Rimini*, *The Taming of the Shrew* (1904), *Kismet*† (1911), *Blood and Sand* (1921), *A Hundred Years Old* (1929), and his final New York performance in the title role of a 1933 revival of *Uncle Tom's Cabin*. With his wife, Maud, he authored several books, and he was the father of **actress***†-**playwright***† Cornelia Otis Skinner.*†

SLAVES IN ALGIERS; OR, A STRUGGLE FOR FREEDOM. **Susanna Haswell Rowson**'s play was first produced at the **Federal Street Theatre** in 1794. Despite its exotic setting in Barbary, ostensibly a land on the Mediterranean coast of North Africa (and more precisely in Algiers), the drama is truly about the American love of the concept of freedom.

The plot is simple: several American slaves, held against their will in Barbary, are avidly plotting their escape with a longing to regain their freedom, not just from their enslavement, but from an uncivilized place where the notion of freedom is unknown. Barbary is portrayed as exotic, but to the American, civilization equals freedom. This subject, in different guises, is central to Rowson's thematic foundation. There is an anti-Semitic aspect to the play in its character of Ben Hassan, a slave trader, who is depicted as lacking any understanding of American or Christian values, apparently meant to indicate that Jews fail to understand the tenets of freedom and fundamental human values.

SMITH, DR. ELIHU HUBBARD (1771–1798). This native of Litchfield, Connecticut, a doctor and writer, Elihu Hubbard Smith wrote one of the first American comic operas, *Edwin and Angelina; or, The Banditti* (1796), adapted from Oliver Goldsmith's *The Hermit*. He also won appreciation for some prologues, but his career ended abruptly when he died of yellow fever while treating patients suffering with it.

SMITH, RICHARD PENN (1799–1854). Philadelphia-born son of a minister and grandson of the first provost of the College of Philadelphia, Richard Penn Smith studied for the law, but instead he purchased a small newspaper, *The Aurora*, which he edited from 1822 to 1827. He also began to write plays, beginning with *Quite Correct* (1828), which was produced at the **Chestnut Street Theatre**. Within less than a decade, he had written more than 13 plays, concluding with *Davy Crockett's Journal*, which was a hoax in that it claimed to be Crockett's genuine diary found by a Mexican general in the Alamo after the famous battle.

Considered part of the Philadelphia School of Dramatists, Smith was considered an able craftsman, most of whose plays were based on earlier works. These included *The Eighth of January* (1829), *The Disowned: or The Prodigals* (1829), *A Wife at a Venture* (1829), *The Sentinels; or, The Two Sergeants* (1829), **William Penn** (1829), *The Bombardment of Algiers* (1829), **The Triumph of Plattsburgh** (1830), **The Deformed; or, Woman's Trial** (1830), *The Water Witch* (1830), **Caius Marius** (1831), *Is She a Brigand?* (1833), *The Daughter* (1836), *The Actress*†* of Padua (1836), and *The Last Man; or, The Cock of the Village* (n.d.).

SMITH, SAMUEL MORGAN (1832–1882). Born in Philadelphia, Samuel Morgan Smith, an **African American,*†** married and moved to England with his wife and **child†** in May 1866 and began a career as an **actor*†** on provincial stages and then in London. He played Othello at the **Olympic Theatre**, off the Strand, in London beginning on 25 August 1866, billed as "the Coloured American Tragedian, Mr. S. Morgan Smith."

Tragedy struck when his young wife, Mary Eliza Smith, died on 6 October 1867, though Smith later remarried to an English **actress.*†** Smith worked to develop a range of **Shakespearean*†** and contemporary roles and **toured*†** British stages from 1866 until his death in 1882, with the *London Morning Post* noting that Smith "was little known in London, but popular in the provinces." Not unlike **Ira Aldridge**, this African American actor was compelled to work in European theaters more open to seeing black actors on stages in serious roles.

SMITH, SARAH POGSON (1774–1870). Believed to have been born Sarah Pogson in Essex, England, the essayist, novelist, and **playwright*†** moved to Charleston sometime between 1788 and 1793. Little is known about her life other than that she married New York judge Peter Smith. A contemporary biography of Smith indicates that the marriage took place in 1818 after the death of his first wife, but that the marriage was short and ended acrimoniously. There is reason to believe she was widowed, lost a son to illness, and was faced with her eldest daughter's serious illness when she published *Essays Religious, Moral, Dramatic, and Poetical* (1818), which contains three of her plays, if the hints published in the collection's preface are to be believed.

Smith's work as a **dramatist*†** has otherwise been obscured because her work has been mistakenly credited to Maria Pinckney and because she published under the pseudonym "A Lady." Her dramatic output includes the plays **The Female Enthusiast** (1807), a verse drama about the murder of Jean Paul Marat by Charlotte Corday; **The Young Carolinians; or, Americans in Algiers** (1818), dealing with the capture of American sailors by Barbary pirates; *The Tyrant's Victims* (1818), a tale of Agathocles, the despotic king of Syracuse; and, *The Orphans* (1818), about three young women swindled of their inheritance by their guardian. Smith's novels include *Daughters of Eve* (1826), *Zerah, the Believing Jew* (1837), and *The Arabians* (1844).

SMITH, SOL (1801–1869). Born Solomon Franklin Smith in Norwich, New York, he moved west in the 1820s, studied for the legal profession, and became a theater **manager*†** and **actor*** in Cincinnati in 1823. Smith set up his own company, but it financially failed four years later and he joined **James H. Caldwell**'s company, appearing in plays along the Mississippi River. He subsequently formed a partnership with **Noah Ludlow** that lasted from 1835 to 1853. They built a theater in St. Louis and performed plays up and down the Mississippi as he had with Caldwell.

Known as "Old Sol" to audiences, partly because he typically played old men and partly affectionately, he became a singular Southwestern Humorist and, along with his acting—specializing in low comedy—published collections of humor, and, with Ludlow, works on theater management. Politically, Smith was a supporter of President Andrew Jackson and opposed slavery. After retiring from theater, he practiced law in St. Louis. Smith's son, Mark (1829–1874), became an actor and like his father played old men.

SMITH, WILLIAM T. RUSSELL (1812–1896). Born William Thompson Russell in Glasgow, Scotland, he arrived in western Pennsylvania in 1819 with his family. In 1827, he became an **actor*†** and painted scenery for a local **amateur*†** theater in Pittsburgh. He served as curator and took painting lessons at the Lambdin Museum with its founder, artist James Reid Lambdin.

In 1833, he was appointed **scene designer*†** for the **Pittsburgh Theatre** founded by **Francis Courtney Wemyss**. In 1835, he moved with Wemyss to Philadelphia to work at the **Walnut Street Theatre**, and that year he also began landscape painting and became a romantic-realist painter in the style of the Hudson River School.

As a designer, he occasionally worked out of Philadelphia—for example, designing for **Dion Boucicault†** and **Mrs. John Wood**—but in Philadelphia he designed all manner of scenery and decorations for the Walnut Street Theatre, the **Chestnut Street Theatre** under **manager*† William Wood**, the **Arch Street Theatre** under **Mrs. John Drew**, and for the Academy of Music. His landscape paintings led to particularly atmospheric exterior drops for the theaters, but all of his work met with high praise from audiences and **critics.*†**

SMITH, W. H. (1806–1872). Born William Henry Sedley Smith in Wales, he became an **actor*†** and **toured*†** the English provinces for many years. In 1827, he arrived in the United States and debuted in a production of *Raising the Wind* at the **Walnut Street Theatre** in Philadelphia. He was a competent journeyman actor, but switched to the job of **stage† manager*†** for the **Boston Museum**, holding that position from 1843 to 1860. In 1869, he became stage manager of the **California Theatre**, where he worked until his death.

†SNOW. The deadheads in a theater audience were "snow."

SOLON SHINGLE. See *THE PEOPLE'S LAWYER*.

SOTHERN, E. A. (1826–1881). Born Edward Askew Sothern in Liverpool, England, he was the son of a storekeeper. Sothern studied medicine and considered becoming a minister, instead working as a clerk in the 1840s before he married Fannie Stewart. In 1848, his work as an **actor*†** began in **amateur†** theatricals using the stage name Douglas Stewart. He debuted professionally in 1849 in a production of ***The Lady of Lyons*** in Jersey. For most of the 1850s, he played in various cities in the English provinces.

Sothern's first American performances came in 1852 in *The Heir-at-Law* in Boston at the **National Theatre**, as well as at the **Howard Athenaeum** and **Barnum**'s **American Museum**. He joined **Wallack's Theatre** company in 1854 and began using his own name in 1856 and joined **Laura Keene**'s company. Also working with Wallack, he scored his first major success as Armand in ***Camille***, but romantic roles would eventually give way to broad character parts.

Working with Keene, he found an even greater triumph in 1858 as the comic Lord Dundreary in her production of **Tom Taylor**'s ***Our American Cousin***. His foppish, eccentric performance brought rave reviews and frequent appearances in the role, including in plays written especially to showcase the character, such as *Our American Cousin at Home; or, Lord Dundreary Abroad* (1860), *Dundreary Married and Done For* (1861), and *Brother Sam* (1862), a play about Dundreary's brother. In the role, Sothern wore long, drooping side-whiskers that became known as "Dundrearys." He took what was essentially a secondary role and built it through broad comic business and eccentric ad-libs (called "Dundrearyisms") into the comic sensation of the production (legend has it that he balked at playing the role because it was small and confessed his fears to **Joseph Jefferson**, who was also in the production, inspiring Jefferson to supposedly state the famous line: "There are no small parts, only small actors.").

Though Sothern played a range of roles through the 1860s and 1870s, he ran into the problem many noted actors of his time did: audiences wanted him in one role, and for Sothern it was Dundreary or, if not that, a role giving him a similar type of character. He went to England for a time in the mid-1870s and appeared successfully, but returned to America in 1876. Whatever the role, he was typically admired for the eccentricity and details of his performances, and even if a play was not well received, Sothern's performance typically was praised. He returned to England in 1879 to perform in a play written for him by **W. S. Gilbert**, but he eventually became ill and never appeared in it. He died in 1881. Sothern and his wife had four children, one of whom, **Edward Hugh Sothern**, as E. H. Sothern, had a notable American career as an actor.

†**SOUBRETTE.** The French term refers to an **actress***† playing a saucy or coquettish character (often a maidservant) in neoclassical comedy or opera, but the term has been freely used to describe secondary comic female characters in **melodramas,**† comedies, **musicals,***† and **operettas.**†

SOUTHWARK THEATRE. Philadelphia's Southwark Theatre, built on the corner of what is now South and Leithgow Streets, was opened on 14 November 1766 by **David Douglass** and his **American Company** with a production of **Isaac Bickerstaffe**'s 1760 play *Thomas and Sally.* The theater was later run by Douglass's successors **Lewis Hallam Jr.** and **John Henry**. In 1767, the Southwark housed the first performance of a professionally produced play by an American author, **Thomas Godfrey**'s *The Prince of Parthia*.

The presence of the theater and company began to regularize theatrical offerings in Philadelphia, which had been quite irregular, with **touring***† troupes and **actors***† performing in temporary or converted spaces. A permanent structure devoted to theater performance made the Southwark the center of late 18th-century theatrical life, despite conservative resistance to the stage in the city. Conservative resistance became more vocal and organized, but the American Company held sway.

The theater operated successfully until the **American Revolution**, when the Continental Congress outlawed theatrical activity, though the British produced performances in the theater in 1777–1778 when they occupied Philadelphia. During the 1780s, the Southwark offered plays marketed as lectures to get around the ban that continued for a few years after the **war**.*† The ban was officially lifted in 1789, but within a short period of time the **Chestnut Street Theatre** was built (1794), featuring a larger stage and audience capacity and greater ornamentation. The Southwark continued, but was no longer the preeminent theater in the city, and when it was destroyed in a **fire** in

1823,† it was replaced by a distillery, ending its run as a pioneering theater space in what became a major theater city in the mid-18th and -19th centuries.

SOUTHWORTH, E. D. E. N. (1819–1899). Born Emma Dorothy Eliza Nevitte, at the request of her dying father (and to honor his request), she used the acronym E.D.E.N. for the rest of her life. She was educated at her stepfather's academy, and in 1835 she graduated and began teaching school, which she did for five years before marrying inventor Frederick Southworth, with whom she moved to Wisconsin. In 1844, while she was pregnant with their second **child,†** Southworth abandoned her, so she returned to Washington, DC, to continue her teaching career.

Southworth began to write sentimental, **melodramatic†** novels set in the American South. Her novels adapted effectively to stage versions, and during the 1850s they were quite popular and often featured heroines who defied Victorian conventions and the expectations of the domestic realm as the place for **women**.*† She spent the first two years of the **Civil War** in Europe, but returned as a vocal supporter of the Union and volunteered as a nurse. Her novels adapted to the stage include the most popular, *The Hidden Hand* (1859), as well as *The Bride of Evening* (1858), *The Doom of Deville* (1859), and *Rose Elmer; or, A Divided Heart* (1860).

THE SPANISH STUDENT. **Henry Wadsworth Longfellow**'s 1843 play in five acts was, in its time, popular since it emphasized sentimental morality, which audiences appreciated in that era. The play is considered by scholars as a reflection of Longfellow's time in Spain during the 1820s and his resulting immersion in Spanish literature. It was printed in *Graham's Magazine*, but Longfellow significantly revised it after its appearance there. **Edgar Allan Poe** accused Longfellow of stealing parts of *The Spanish Student* from his as yet unpublished play, *Politian*.

THE SPARKLING CUP. Thomas Stewart Denison's five-act **temperance** drama was published in 1877. **Critical***† response was mixed, and even the compliments were dismissive, such as *The Anvil*'s (Washington, DC) statement that, "It is just the thing for dramatic **clubs**."*† One of the many temperance-themed plays of the 19th century, its theme was the same as many, expressing the damage alcoholism does to family and working lives.

†**SPECULATION.** The practice presently known as "scalping" was earlier called "speculation." In towns and cities where a **star*†** was booked for a limited engagement† of only a few performances, tickets could sell out quickly, and the demand for tickets meant that they could be resold at inflated prices. Even more perniciously, bogus tickets might be sold on the street.

THE SPIRIT OF THE TIMES. In 1831, this weekly periodical, *The Spirit of the Times*, was established by William T. Porter and his brothers. With the goal of reaching an upper-class readership, its full title explains its mission: *A Chronicle of the Turf, Agriculture, Field Sports, Literature and the Stage.* News on each of these areas made up the paper, with theater news being central. In the beginning, *The Spirit of the Times* made it its business to report on all theatrical goings-on in New York, though it mostly covered the **Park Theatre** because it was aiming at an upper-class readership. Coverage of the working-class theaters, the **Bowery Theatre** and the **Chatham Garden Theatre**, for example, tended to be negative. Porter himself frequently wrote about the theater scene and, when being **critical,*†** tended to use humor.

THE SPY; A TALE OF THE NEUTRAL GROUND. **Charles Powell Clinch** adapted James Fenimore Cooper's popular novel to the stage, where it opened as a three-act play on 1 March 1822 at the **Park Theatre**, running in **repertory.*†** Cooper's novel was the first in America to find such widespread popularity and, as many **critics*†** have noted, established an American form of romanticism that was popular until the mid-19th century—and after.

The Spy is also regarded as the first stage adaptation of a novel to find success. During the **American Revolution**, a peddler named Harvey Birch is viewed suspiciously by both sides. Many consider him a loyalist, but in fact he is working for General **George Washington**, spying on the British. Birch recognizes the true tragedy of the **war,*†** that it divides friends and neighbors—and despite the fierce hostility between the Americans and the English, he performs acts of kindness and decency in dealing with individuals, regardless of their political sympathies. He even helps a British captain scheduled for execution to escape. However, Birch is arrested on suspicion of being a British spy by the Americans and executed, though after the fact a letter from Washington is found on his body making clear that Birch was a true patriot.

STADT THEATRE. Across the street from the **Bowery Theatre**, the Bowery Amphitheatre was used in multiple ways by different **managers*†** and groups—and under different names, more often than not, unsuccessfully. The amphitheater was used for **minstrel**† shows, **circuses,***† menageries, and a roller rink, as well as for other uses, but in the summer of 1854, German Seigrist and Otto Hoym leased the amphitheater and rebuilt it.

As the Stadt Theatre, it opened on 20 October 1854 with the goal of specializing in German-language productions, but also presented American and English works. Several managers operated the Stadt similarly until 1863–1864, when the theater moved to 45 Bowery, where it operated for eight years before returning to the Bowery Amphitheatre. In 1871, the Stadt was the venue for the first American performances of Richard Wagner's opera *Lohengrin.*

When the Stadt returned to the Bowery Amphitheatre in 1872, it continued its emphasis on German-language material. The Stadt presented the first American performances of Johann Strauss's *Die Fledermaus* in German when it opened on 21 November 1874. The theater's name was changed to the Windsor Theatre in 1880, but it was destroyed by fire in 1883. The theater was rebuilt, but the German-language emphasis ended, and the building was used as a roller rink.

†STAGE-DOOR JOHNNY. *See* †JOHNNY.

THE STAGE-STRUCK †*YANKEE.* **Oliver E. Durivage**'s one-act **Yankee** farce is one among the many such plays written in the 19th century. It opened at the **Eagle Theatre** in Boston in March 1845, with Durivage himself as Captain Chunk, the title character, subsequently playing at Boston's **Lyceum Theatre** in 1850, New York's **National Theatre** in 1853, and the **Federal Street Theatre** in Boston in 1857. The play spoofs theater practices and rural New England life in its depiction of a theater company rolling into a New England town to perform *Richard III.* A local bumpkin falls in love with the **leading woman**† of the company, but she is ultimately rescued from this unwanted suitor by a Yankee girl.

STAGG, CHARLES and MARY (early 18th century). Charles and Mary Stagg are named as **actors,***† though they were more likely dancers, on a 1716 petition document requesting permission to build a theater in Williamsburg, Virginia. If, in fact, they were professionals and performed in America a decade after **Anthony Aston**, they were among the earliest actors working in the colonies. The Staggs were **William Livingston**'s indentured servants, who had apparently agreed to perform in the theater he built in Williamsburg. It is believed that Charles died in 1735 in Williamsburg and that Mary later supported herself by arranging "dancing assemblies." Little else is known about them.

STAR THEATRE. Built by **James W. Wallack Sr.** in 1861 at **Broadway***† and 13th Street, it was designed in the German Romanesque "Rundbogenstil" style, a hulking brick building that dominated its neighborhood. The auditorium sat 1,600 people and was decorated in gold and red embellishments. Its stage measured 48 by 45 feet. **Lester Wallack** took over as **manager***† in 1864, and under his leadership, the theater featured some of the leading **actors***† in the country, including **John Gilbert**, **Rose Eytinge**, **Maud Granger**, and **Maurice Barrymore,**† among others.

In 1867, exploiting **Charles Dickens**'s visit to the United States, Wallack staged an **all-star***† production of *Oliver Twist*, just one of many productions that brought the theater a reputation for excellence. In 1874, Wallack had his biggest hit with the original production of **Dion Boucicault**'s† **Irish** drama, *The Shaughraun*. Not long after, Wallack built a new theater further uptown and leased the old theater to the **Germania Theatre** for eight years. However, that company overestimated their audience interest, and the theater proved too large and closed in 1883.

Wallack's longtime partner, Theodore Moss, took over management and redecorated the theater, renaming it the Star Theatre. English stars Henry Irving and Ellen Terry made their first American appearances at the Star. In 1887, more redecoration was done and the theater could then seat 1,750. Despite these efforts and continued fine productions, the Star's day had passed. The press began reporting its imminent demise in 1901, and it was actually torn down in 1902. American Mutoscope & Biograph Co. filmed† an extraordinary time-lapse short subject showing the Star Theatre being torn down in stages.

STETSON, JOHN B. (1836–1896). Born in Charlestown, Massachusetts, John B. Stetson was a talented athlete who was able to support himself doing acrobatics and other athletic activities. He then took over editing a Boston periodical before becoming involved in theater. Stetson served as **manager***† of Boston (**Howard Athenaeum**, **Olympic**, **Globe**, and **Park**) and New York (**Globe**, **Booth's**, **Fifth Avenue**, **Standard**, **Star**) theaters at various times. Stetson worked in close partnership with **Edward Harrigan** and **Tony Hart**, managing them for a time at the height of their fame, and produced some of the early productions of **Gilbert and Sullivan operettas**† performed in the United States. He also managed **stars,***† including such luminaries as **Tommaso Salvini**, **Lily Langtry**, **Helena Modjeska**, and **James O'Neill**. Stetson died wealthy, and it is clear that during his multiple careers, he was always successful.

*†STOCK/STOCK COMPANY/STOCK CHARACTER. A stock company is an ensemble of **actors,***† led by a **manager***† and/or **director,***† performing a season of plays in sequence (or in **repertory***†) during a residence at a theater or in a town; it was an important form of theater, despite its economic vicissitudes. The essence of stock companies was that the same actors, employed according to **lines of business,**† worked together for an extended period. During the 1870s, before the rise of the **road,***† a city's resident stock company would have to perform a different play almost every night, and thus, the early stock companies performed what amounted to rotating repertory.

During the heyday of **touring***† companies presenting several plays in repertory in the 1880s, stock companies disappeared except in the biggest population centers, such as New York, Boston, and San Francisco. With the rise of the **combination**† system in the 1890s, stock companies once again found audiences that relished the old familiar warhorses of dramatic literature, occasionally with rising or falling **stars***† appearing to bolster audience attendance. Typically, the **leading**† player dominated (and often managed) the company, but in some cases—as with **Augustin Daly**'s† company—the ensemble as a whole was more important than any single player. The word "stock" may also apply to standard **scenery***† or properties that are reused by a theater as needed to save money or it may be used to refer to a kind of **character***† type (**villain,**† **ingénue,**† **soubrette,**† **rube,**† etc.).

STODDART, J. H. (1827–1907). Born James Henry Stoddart in Yorkshire, England, J. H. Stoddart was the son of an **actor,***† and he began his own career acting **children**'s† roles opposite his father. In adulthood, Stoddart acted in Scotland and the English provinces before making his debut in the United States at **Wallack's Theatre** in *A Phenomenon in a Frock Smock* in 1854. This comedy established him as a popular comic actor, and he appeared in such plays as *The Critic,**† winning plaudits.

Stoddart's demonstrations of temperament offstage caused him to leave Wallack's after two years, and he joined **Laura Keene**'s company, working with the equally tempestuous **actress***† for 10 years. He returned to Wallack's for a time, and in 1875 Stoddart joined **A. M. Palmer** at the **Union Square Theatre**. He was highly praised in **villainous**† roles in **Steele MacKaye**'s *Rose Michel* (1875), and this reception led him to abandon comic roles for villains. He continued to work despite temperamental outbursts, but his career ended abruptly when he was struck by a train and killed.

STONE, JOHN AUGUSTUS (1801–1834). Born in Concord, Massachusetts, John Augustus Stone worked in theater as an **actor***† and **playwright.***† His stage debut, in 1822 in New York, was the first of many performances, but he also won a $500 prize and the box office take of the third performance offered by **Edwin Forrest** for a new American play—*Metamora; or, The Last of the Wampanoags*—which became a frequently performed vehicle for Forrest for the remainder of his career.

Stone also wrote nearly a dozen other plays, including *Montrano; or, Who's the Traitor* (1822), first performed in Philadelphia; *Restoration; or, The Diamond Cross* (1824), which debuted at the **Chatham Garden Theatre**; *Tancred; or, The Siege of Antioch* (1827); *La Roque; A Regicide*, first performed in Charleston; *Fauntleroy; or, The Fatal Forgery*, first performed in Charleston; *Touretoun; Banker of Rouen; Tancred, King of Sicily* (1831); *The Demoniac* (1831); *The Ancient Briton* (1833); and, *The Knight of the Golden Fleece; or, The Yankee† in Spain* (1834), the last a vehicle for Yankee actor **G. H. Hill**. Stone suffered bouts of insanity, and his life ended prematurely when he committed suicide by drowning himself in the Schuylkill River.

THE STRANGER. William Dunlap's first adaptation from several plays by August von Kotzebue, in this case *Menschenhass und Reue*, opened on 10 December 1798 at the **Park Theatre**. The play was significant in making Kotzebue's work popular with American audiences, in part because its melancholic atmosphere was the introduction to theatrical romanticism in the United States.

The Stranger focuses on the heroic actions of a stranger (originally played by **Thomas Abthorpe Cooper**) who turns up at a castle where Mrs. Haller is staying. Separated from her husband because she was unfaithful, Mrs. Haller is courted by a baron. She resists his proposal and those of others. It is ultimately revealed that the stranger is Mrs. Haller's husband, who is at first reluctant to be reunited with her, but the efforts of the Haller children change his mind. A frequently revived work until the **Civil War** era, most notable actors*† played the role of the stranger, including **James W. Wallack**, **Thomas Barry**, and **James Murdoch**, among others.

THE STREETS OF NEW YORK. See THE POOR OF NEW YORK.

STUDLEY, J. B. (1831–1910). The Boston-born **actor*†** John B. Studley made his stage debut in Charleston in 1848, and its success launched him into a career as a **leading man†** with a host of theaters. He became leading man for **Charlotte Cushman** and won praise playing Bill Sykes in **Charles Dickens**'s *Oliver Twist*. He also had particular success as the **villain†** Byke in *Under the Gaslight* (1867) and the alcoholic Wolf in *Horizon* (1871). As the **melodramatic** style of acting, at which Studley was expert, faded from popularity, he found himself increasingly playing secondary roles in New York productions and leading parts on the **road**.*† In late 1876, while appearing in a production of *Two Orphans,* Studley was trapped in a **theater fire**† along with a crowd of audience members. After several attempts to get out of the building—and receiving some minor injuries—Studley finally broke through a door that permitted the patrons to escape along with him.

†**SUPERNUMERARY/SUPER/SUPE/SUPING.** A supernumerary, referred to slangily as a "super" or "supe," served as an extra in crowd scenes of a production. Locally hired extras were also known as "jobbers." Sometimes the **gallery gods**† would call out "Supe! Supe!" when they recognized the awkwardness of the **amateur***† amid professional actors. During the last quarter of the 19th century, when **touring***† companies presented **Shakespeare***† or other historical dramas, they regularly engaged local amateurs as supernumeraries, or extras, to fill in the crowd scenes. Because they often swelled the ranks of an army for battle scenes, supes were sometimes pejoratively referred to as "spear-carriers." As many as 200 supes might be hired for a spectacle like Richard Mansfield's† production of *Henry V,* but 15 usually sufficed for **melodramas**† of the period.

SUPERSTITION; OR, THE FANATIC FATHER. **James Nelson Barker**'s five-act tragedy was produced by **William Wood** on 12 March 1824 at Philadelphia's **Chestnut Street Theatre**, running in **repertory**.*† Scholars have come to consider *Superstition* as the outstanding American drama of the first quarter of the 19th century in its seamless revelation of what may seem an improbable plot.

A duel between George Egerton (originally played by **F. C. Wemyss**) and Charles Fitzroy (played by **Wood**) in defense of the honor of Mary Ravensworth (played by **Mary Ann Duff**) leaves Egerton wounded, while Fitzroy is uninjured. Rev. Ravensworth (played by Mr. Darley) is not pleased by the duel, feeling that Charles and his mother, Isabella (played by **Mrs. Wood**), have not shown his clerical role due respect. In the meantime, an **Indian** attack threatens the village and Charles and a stranger, The Unknown (played by **Mr. Duff**), leads the attack against the Indians and win unharmed. Charles and his mother fall under suspicion as devils and are put on trial, with Ravensworth testifying against them. Charles is convicted and executed and his mother dies from shock and grief. The Unknown turns out to be William Goffe, one of those who sentenced King Charles I to death and is also Isabella's father and Charles's grandfather. The play concludes with Mary denouncing her father for his cruelty.

Critics*† refer to the play as an attack on Puritan excesses in colonial New England, and its mixture of the execution of Charles I with elements of psychology, witchcraft, and religious intolerance attracted audiences to it. *Superstition* was Barker's last play, and widely considered his best, after which he devoted his energies to public service posts.

T

†**TABLEAU/TABLEAUX VIVANTS.** This generic term refers to a scene (usually short) establishing location, atmosphere, or period, but a "tableau" is usually thought of as a picture or image presenting something like a living fresco. The term relates to a more specific term, "tableaux vivants," which involves performers frozen in decorous positions like a living painting. These were particularly popular in **musicals*†** and **revues*†** between the mid-19th and early 20th centuries. The expression "hold picture," which literally indicates the idea of freezing action into an appealing image, is often used interchangeably with "tableau."

TAKE CARE OF LITTLE CHARLEY. **John Brougham**'s one-act **Irish** farce was first performed at **Wallack's Theatre** on 26 November 1858, with Brougham as Mickey Fogarty, Viola Plunkett as Little Charley, **Mary Gannon** as Susan Sly, **C. T. Parsloe Jr.** as Bunkers, and Mrs. Sloan as Mrs. T. Sawyer. With a typical mix of sentiment and farcical humor, Brougham provided himself an opportunity for broad comedy with strong support from Gannon and Parsloe, as **critics*†** noted.

A TALE OF LEXINGTON: A NATIONAL COMEDY FOUNDED ON THE OPENING OF THE REVOLUTION. **Samuel B. Judah**'s three-act prose drama was first performed in New York in 1822. This historical comedy set in the era of the **American Revolution** was Judah's last play written before he devoted his career to practicing law. The play was reviewed by England's *Literary Gazette* when it was published, and a play dealing with the Battle of Lexington as a momentous American event seemed lost on the **critic,*†** who clearly resented the treatment of British soldiers in the play, sarcastically describing Judah as the "popular founder of dramatic poetry in the New World" and found his work "a new world it is in this species of writing."

TAMMANY; OR, THE INDIAN CHIEF. **Anne Kemble Hatton** wrote the libretto for this **musical*†** drama, with music supplied by **James Hewitt**. It opened on 3 March 1794 at the **John Street Theatre**, where it ran in **repertory**.*† **John Hodgkinson** played the **Indian** chief Tammany, who loves an Indian girl (played by Mrs. Hodgkinson), who is kidnapped by the invading Spanish under their leader Ferdinand (played by **John Martin**). Tammany manages to rescue her, and they hide out in a deserted cabin where they are tracked down by Ferdinand and the Spanish, who set fire to the cabin, killing the lovers. *Tammany; or, The Indian Chief* was the first known work in America to focus on **Native American*†** characters.

TAYLEURE, CLIFTON W. (1830–1887). Born in South Carolina, Clifton W. Tayleure began his theatrical career as an **actor**.*† Tayleure spent much of his early career at Baltimore's **Holliday Street Theatre**, where he also ultimately served as house **dramatist*†** after he quit acting in 1856. Tayleure served as **manager*†** of several **Broadway*†** theaters, including the **Olympic Theatre** and the Grand **Opera House**. He also wrote **melodramas,†** including *Horseshoe Robinson* (1856), *A Woman's Wrongs* (1874), *Rube; or, The Wall Street Undertow* (1875), *Parted* (1876), and *Won Back* (1892). Though none of these plays won much success, Tayleure's adaptation of **Mrs. Henry Wood**'s novel *East Lynne* (1863) became one of the most popular and most produced plays of the second half of the 19th century. The story focuses on an unfaithful woman, in a disguise as a governess, who uses this mask to return to her family, wanting to repent and hoping for forgiveness.

TAYLOR, BAYARD (1825–1878). Born in Kennett Square, Pennsylvania, he became a romantic poet, and his success led to a career as correspondent for the *New York Tribune*. He traveled the world and used the experience to write novels, lectures, and travel guides. His most ambitious work for the theater was his translation into metrical English of Goethe's *Faust* in 1870–1871.

TAYLOR, MARY (1836–1866). Born Mary Cecilia Taylor in New York, where her father played in the orchestra of the **Park Theatre**, "Our Mary," as she became known, was a popular **child† actress**.*† She made her debut in *Zazezizozu* at the **National Theatre**. By the time she was barely in her teens, Taylor was a highly popular performer at the **Olympic Theatre** and the **Bowery Theatre**. She made notable appearances in *The Magic Arrow* (1844) and *A Glance at New York* (1848). Taylor married in 1851 and retired. She clearly had talent, but audiences were mixed about her—and her retirement, at the end of her childhood, was perhaps a wise decision. For a time, however, she had a huge following.

TAYLOR, RAYNOR (1747–1825). Born in Soho, Westminster, England, he began singing in a boy choir at the Chapel Royal, including singing at Handel's funeral. He studied aspects of music and ultimately became resident composer and **musical*†   director*†** for Sadler's Wells Theatre and Marylebone Gardens, holding those positions for a quarter of a century.

In 1792, Taylor arrived in the United States at the encouragement of a former student, **Alexander Reinagle**. He established himself in Baltimore, where he taught music and staged musical extravaganzas with a particularly **burlesque*†** flair. He moved to Philadelphia in 1795 and within a short time became perhaps the most important figure on the musical scene in Philadelphia, writing and performing serious music as well as comic theater songs. Only one of his theater scores survives, *The Aethiop; or, The Child of the Desert* (1814), based on William Dimon's oriental drama.

TAYLOR, TOM (1817–1880). This English-born **dramatist*†** proved to be a master of two genres: domestic comedy/farce and **melodrama**.† He was a rarity in that he won equal popularity in his own country and in the United States. Among his many plays, the most popular in the United States were *Masks and Faces* (1852), *Still Waters Run Deep* (1855), ***Our American Cousin*** (1858), *The Contested Election* (1859), *The Overland Route* (1860), ***The Ticket-of-Leave Man*** (1865), *Mary Warner* (1869), ***The Fool's Revenge*** (1869), and *Anne Boleyn* (1875).

Taylor was also a **critic**,*† biographer, and editor of *Punch*. His best plays had relatively long stage lives, but by the early 20th century they slowly disappeared from the canon of produced works, and *Our American Cousin* remains the best-known Taylor play due to its association with the assassination of President **Abraham Lincoln**, who was enjoying the play at **Ford's Theatre** when he was shot by **actor*†** and Confederate sympathizer **John Wilkes Booth**.

TEARS AND SMILES. **James Nelson Barker**'s three-act comedy influenced by **Royall Tyler**'s *The Contrast* opened on 4 March 1807 at Philadelphia's **Chestnut Street Theatre**, where it ran in **repertory**.*† The Tyler influence is seen most vividly in the foppish character, Fluttermore, who believes whatever is French is superior to anything else, though he is wooing American Louisa Compton. Louisa is also loved by Sydney Osbert, who returns home to Philadelphia as something of a hero after vanquishing a band of pirates. Sydney eventually wins Louisa's hand with the assistance of friends, American patriot Nathan Yank (obviously, a **Yankee†** character) and Widow Freegrace (who herself is busily trying to win the affections of Nathan's master, Rangely). Much of the humor of the play, Barker's first, is centered on satirizing American fascination with French fashions, which was prevalent at that time.

*†TECHNOLOGICAL DEVELOPMENTS. Theater technology was somewhat limited until the early 19th century in America, but in the wake of the Industrial Revolution, theatrical technologies in Europe and America evolved rapidly. The major development between the 17th and the early 19th centuries was a move from makeshift, temporary theater spaces to permanent brick buildings and, ultimately, to elaborate and large facilities meant to be permanent showplaces in the major cities. Though this is not exactly a technological change, as the theaters became more permanent and more expensively outfitted, technology became a greater concern.

The shift from candles and **gas*†** to electrical **lighting,*†** for example, was a significant innovation, though audiences and practitioners during that century both applauded and lamented the changes, as each kind of lighting offered distinctly different environments and advantages. Most particularly, many who had begun their theatergoing in the days of gas lighting lamented its disappearance. The end of **limelight†** and the decline in the use of **footlights†** were especially troubling to old-timers in the late 19th century. Use of electric lighting began in some urban American theaters as early as the 1880s, but the slow transition from gas to electric lighting was accelerated in 1903 following the catastrophic Iroquois Theatre† **fire†** in Chicago, which resulted in the deaths of over 600 people.

Painted flat profile scenery† slowly gave way to three-dimensional realism*† by the mid-19th century, as the **box set** approach became more prevalent. Improvements in stage machinery, stage elevators, and other innovations made scene shifting and special effects more efficient and effective, although until the early 20th century a style that might be described as painted realism dominated. Stage effects grew more impressive after the **Civil War,** as **melodramas†** attempted to draw audiences with spectacular scenes of train wrecks, fires, waterfalls, etc., in **sensation dramas**.†

TECUMSEH; OR, THE BATTLE OF THE THAMES. Richard Emmons's "national drama, in five acts," first performed in Baltimore in 1834, opened in New York and Philadelphia in 1836, and was published that same year. The play was a re-creation of how Richard M. Johnson purportedly killed the Shawnee **Indian** leader, who, in Emmons's **melodramatic†** prose, fell dying with the proclamation: "The Red man's course is run; I die—the last of all my race." *Tecumseh* was intended to help Johnson in his campaign for vice president as Martin Van Buren's running mate and supplied a campaign slogan: "Rumpsey Dumpsey, Rumpsey Dumpsey, Colonel Johnson killed Tecumseh!"

TELL THE TRUTH AND SHAME THE DEVIL.* William Dunlap**'s two-act farce was produced in New York by the **Old American Company** in January 1797 (published that year as well) and in London in 1799. Dunlap's play was adapted from a French one-act—*Jerome Pointu*—and depicts spirited and moral young protagonists, in this case a young man, Tom, who exposes the corruption and folly of unrighteous elders, in this case, Semblance, Tom's guardian. When the play was produced in London, a British **critic† wrote, "America bids fair to equal us in the productions of wit, as well as in science, in arms, and in commerce."

†TEMPERANCE PLAYS. Plays (mostly **melodramas**†) illustrating the evils of drink were written during a period of reformist zeal in early to mid-19th-century America (although temperance sentiments can be found in some late 18th-century plays and across the 19th century and well into the 20th) and yet they proved surprisingly enduring, continuing to the instituting of Prohibition after World **War** I.*† Thus, *The Drunkard* (1844) and *Ten Nights in a Bar-Room* (1858) were still finding audiences in rural theaters in the 1920s and beyond.

THE TEMPERANCE DOCTOR.* Harry Seymour**'s "moral drama in two acts," also known as *Aunt Dinah's Pledge: A **Temperance** Doctor* (this title did not appear until 1888, so may suggest a revision of the play), was published by **Samuel French† in 1880; it was dramatized from a story published in the National Temperance Society and Publication House dealing with a doctor who treats alcoholic patients.

***TEMPTATION; OR, THE IRISH EMIGRANT.* See *THE IRISH EMIGRANT*.**

***TEN NIGHTS IN A BAR-ROOM.* William W.** Pratt adapted his five-act **melodrama**† from Timothy S. Arthur's 1854 **temperance** novel *Ten Nights in a Bar-Room and What I Saw There*. It opened at New York's **National Theatre** on 23 August 1858 for 7 performances. Never popular in big cities, *Ten Nights in a Bar-Room* was a tremendously successful play on the **road**,*† especially in rural areas, where only *Uncle Tom's Cabin*† bested it in pulling in audiences.

The play's protagonist, Joe Morgan, is a basically decent but weak man known as the town drunk. Simon Slade, the owner of the Sickle and Sheaf Hotel & Bar, where Joe spends much of his time, encourages Joe's bad habits. Slade is a **villainous**† figure, manipulative and corrupt, as even his own family views him. When Joe's little daughter, Mary, comes to the bar to plead with Joe in the play's most famous line—"Father, dear father, come home . . ."—he does, but not for long. When Mary tries again to get him to leave the bar, she is accidentally struck by a glass thrown at Joe. Her injury so upsets Joe that he vows to give up drink and reform. Meanwhile, the nefarious Slade is killed by his own son, and the local townspeople agree to close the bar, which is depicted as a den of evil.

Ten Nights in a Bar-Room was a play frequently performed in **stock***† and **amateur***† theater as well as by professional **touring***† productions. A 1931 film version, produced by the Women's Christian Temperance Union, was not well received; it seemed antiquated and melodramatic to **critics**.*† A **Broadway***† revival, directed by Billy Bryant, opened at the John Golden† Theatre on 20 January 1932 with a cast of unknowns and lasted for a mere 37 performances.

†TENT SHOWS. A popular entertainment† tradition in the midwestern United States in the 1850s, tent shows featured plays and variety shows staged inside canvas tents in the **circus***† style. **Touring***† tent shows, carrying performers and **scenery***† for as much as a week of entertainments, spread across the country during the 19th century. Major **stars**,*† including Minnie Maddern Fiske† and **Sarah Bernhardt**,† appeared in tent shows during the late 19th century when they battled the oppressive control of the Theatrical Syndicate,† and they essentially, over time, prevailed over monopolizing **producers**.*†

THALIA THEATRE. First named the **New York Theatre**, it opened in October 1826 with a production of *The Road to Ruin*. The theater stood at 46 Bowery in New York. A name change to the **Bowery Theatre** in 1828 opened up the most active and rowdy era for this theater, with the working-class audiences packing the theater vocal in their responses, pro and con, to the fare on the stage. Interestingly enough, despite this, the theater presented its most diverse fare during the Bowery era, including **Shakespeare**.†

Fires† destroyed the Thalia Theatre, which was rebuilt a total of four times in the 19th century, in the years 1828, 1836, 1838, and 1845. (The name Thalia Theatre was applied in 1879 to somewhat elevate the tone of the theater, but in 1929 the name changed to Fay's Bowery Theatre and, presumably to reflect the theater's glory days, opened with a revival of **Augustin Daly**'s **melodrama**† *Under the Gaslight*. A June 1929 fire closed the theater permanently.

THAYER, MRS. EDWARD (c. 1800–1873). Born Agnes Diamond in England, she was in Kentucky by 1820, where she debuted under the name Mrs. Palmer Fisher. She moved to Philadelphia, where she married Edward Thayer (1798–1870) and took his name as her stage name. She was greatly appreciated by Philadelphia audiences, especially at the **Chestnut Street Theatre** and **Arch Street Theatre**, but she rarely appeared in New York. Mrs. Thayer was most acclaimed in comedy and played opposite her husband throughout their careers. She retired in 1865.

†THEATER COMIQUE. This was a popular name used for variety theaters across the nation in the 1870s. Generally regarded as the breeding ground for the **vaudeville**† theaters that later sprang up, the Comiques also launched the careers of some legitimate† theater performers and writers. For example, **J. K. Emmet**,† later renowned for his "Fritz" character, got his start at Philadelphia's Comique, and Eddie Foy† performed in a "two act" at Kansas City's Theater Comique. Though most of the entertainment† was of the "free and easy" variety, full-fledged plays frequently got thrown into the mix. Out West, cowboys tended to refer to the "The-ay-ter Com-ee-cue."

†THEATER FIRES. From the time of the earliest permanent playhouses in the United States in the early 18th century to the early 20th century, theater fires were a continual danger. Mostly due to dangerous candle or **gas lighting***† and highly flammable materials used in theatrical production, there were well over 100 major theater fires between the first serious one at Boston's **Federal Street Theatre** in 1798 to a tragedy at the Brooklyn Theatre in 1876 during a performance of *The Two Orphans* when 197 people were killed. The greatest disaster occurred on 30 December 1903 when Chicago's Iroquois Theatre† burned during a performance of the **musical***† *Mr. Bluebeard* **starring***† Eddie Foy.† Despite Foy's heroic efforts to calm the panicked audience, over 600 people were killed. The tragedy led to the end of gas-lit theaters and to comparatively stringent laws to prevent future fires.

†THEATRICAL CLUBS. The first known theatrical club in the United States is believed to be the Actors' Order of Friendship, which was established in 1849 in Philadelphia. In 1868, the Benevolent and Protective Order of Elks provided charitable efforts on behalf of performers. Within a short time, its work was taken over by a New York lodge, set up in 1888, devoted to charitable efforts for members of the profession. This lodge, in turn, was supplanted by the Actors Fund of America,† which quickly became the main source of assistance to indigent theatrical workers.

The Lambs' Club,† a purely social organization for theatricals, was started in 1874, but was rivaled by The Players,† the most prestigious theater club of the era, established in 1888 by **Edwin Booth**.† Along with theater professionals, membership included celebrated literary and political figures such as **Mark Twain** and **Civil War** hero General William T. Sherman. Because of its all-male membership (until 1992), **actresses**ized*† founded the Twelfth Night Club in 1891 and the Professional **Womens'***† League in 1892. In 1907, the **Charlotte Cushman** Club was founded in Philadelphia to provide housing for actresses and to preserve Cushman's papers.

THEATRICAL COMMONWEALTH. Following **William Dunlap**'s financial ruin in 1805, **actors***† and other theater workers associated to protect their opportunities to secure a living, calling themselves the Theatrical Commonwealth. When Dunlap's fortunes improved and the **Park Theatre** reopened, the group broke up. Seven years later, some Philadelphia actors who had built up frustrations with theatrical conditions there revived the name to stage their own productions, but without success.

In 1813 in New York, the situation repeated itself when actors complaining about policies and conditions at the Park were joined by actors who could not find work there and adopted the name. In an abandoned **circus***† building converted into a theater, they began offering productions in late 1813. For a brief period, the Theatrical Commonwealth challenged the Park, but with the death of Mrs. Twaits, one of the group's lead **actresses***† and the wife of its **manager**,*† the group disbanded.

THÉRÈSE, THE ORPHAN OF GENEVA. **John Howard Payne** freely translated and adapted this three-act **melodrama**† from Victor Ducange's *Thérèse, ou L'orpheline de Genève*. The first production opened in London at the Drury Lane Theatre on 2 February 1821, followed by a production at New York's Anthony Street Theatre later that year. Also that same year Thomas Longworth published the play.

The plot follows an evil man, Carwin (played by **Edwin Forrest**), who tries to murder an apparently illegitimate girl (played by Louisa Lane, later known as **Mrs. John Drew**) so that he might keep her inheritance. When he learns that he has accidentally killed the wrong woman, he is shattered and confesses to the murder. Forrest was well received as Carwin, as was **James W. Wallack**, who played the role in the London production of the play. Payne wrote *Thérèse* while incarcerated in the London Fleet debtors' prison. It is worth noting that Payne is an oddity among American dramatists—most of his plays were written and first produced in London, often followed by productions in the United States, and the influences on Payne's work were often British or French writers.

THE THESPIAN ORACLE. Founded in 1798, *The Thespian Oracle* was among the first American periodicals to devote considerable attention to theatrical matters. The Puritan foundation of much of colonial America's attitudes tended to reject and even condemn theatrical art, but by the end of the 18th century, particularly in the cities along the Eastern seaboard, an audience was growing for theater (and theater itself was becoming more prevalent, organized, and marketed in more and more permanent theater structures) and audiences hungered for guidance and opinions on the quality of what they found on American stages. *The Thespian Oracle* was meant to satisfy the growing interest of urban Americans in theater. Other similar publications in that era include *Theatrical Censor* (1805), *Thespian Mirror* (1805), and *Mirror of Taste and Dramatic Censor* (1810).

THOMAS À BECKET. *See HENRY II; OR, THE DEATH OF THOMAS À BECKET.*

†THOMPSON, DENMAN (1833–1911). Girard, Pennsylvania–born Denman Thompson grew up in New England and performed in **circus*†**and **stock*†** without gaining much attention. When, in 1875, he developed a **vaudeville†** sketch about the definitive "**rube**,"† a good-natured New England farmer, the character proved so popular that Thompson wrote a play about him called *Joshua Whitcomb* (1878), which did well on **tour.*†** Thompson then collaborated with George W. Ryer on a second Whitcomb play, *The Old Homestead†* (1887), which achieved 160 performances at New York's **Fourteenth Street Theatre,†** phenomenal success on the **road,*†** and returns to New York in 1899, 1904, 1907, and 1908.

Despite his attempts at other roles, Thompson's audience demanded Joshua Whitcomb, and he played the iconic character for the rest of his career. With Ryer, Thompson also wrote *The Sunshine of Paradise Alley* (1896) and *Our New Minister* (1903). At Thompson's death in 1911, his obituary in the *New York Times* noted his long association with the Whitcomb character, acknowledging that although "**Joseph Jefferson†** was quite as faithful to **Rip Van Winkle†** and Lewis Morrison to Mephistopheles," neither "conceived the characters which they for so long interpreted or lived so much amid the scenes they portrayed."

†**THOMPSON, LYDIA (1836–1908).** London-born Lydia Thompson **toured***† to New York in 1868 with her British Blondes and generated significant excitement with a series of **burlesque***† **musicals,***† including *Ixion* (1868), *Ernani* (1868), *The Forty Thieves* (1869), and *Sinbad the Sailor* (1869), in which Thompson, a **shape actress,**† played the **breeches role**† to show off her well-contoured figure. Some **critics***† found her performances scandalous, while others commented favorably on her beauty and skill at comedy. The popularity of Thompson's entertainments† led to American imitators, and she toured frequently to the United States, making her last New York appearance in *The Crust of Society* (1894).

THORNE, CHARLES R. (1814?–1893). Born Charles Robert Thorne in New York, the son of a merchant, he debuted as an **actor***† at the **Park Theatre** in 1829. He was an effective **manager***† and, at various times, managed the **Chatham Garden Theatre** and the **National Theatre** in New York, as well as the **Baldwin Theatre** in San Francisco. He **toured***† with his wife, Ann Maria **Mestayer** Thorne, through Central and South America. His troupe also played along the area around the Erie Canal. Thorne's career lasted 50 years, and he and his wife had a son who became an actor, **Charles Robert Thorne Jr.**

THORNE, CHARLES R., JR. (1840–1883). Born Charles Robert Thorne Jr. to **actors***† **Charles R. Thorne** and Ann Maria **Mestayer** Thorne, he went onstage as a **child**† acting with his parents at age 12. He spent a season at the **Boston Museum** in 1859–1860 and worked his way up in **stock***† companies. By his 20s, he developed as a handsome, dashing figure onstage and was cast in such roles in established plays including *The Ticket-of-Leave Man* in 1873, *Camille* opposite **Clara Morris** in 1875, and *The Marble Heart* in 1877.

Thorne also created the roles of Chevalier de Vaudrey in *The Two Orphans* (1874), John Strebelow in *The Banker's Daughter* (1880), and the title character of **Victorien Sardou**'s *Daniel Rochat* (1880), of which the *New York Times* **critic***† wrote, "Mr. Thorne did full justice to the strong and broadly dramatic effects of his part, and his acting was robust and pathetic in the last act, but he missed most of the subtle beauties of the part, and he failed almost wholly to suggest the youthful and intense enthusiasm of Rochat's temperament, its absorbed spirituality." Despite the critic's view, *Daniel Rochat* was Thorne's most popular role. Thorne traveled to China and built a theater in Shanghai prior to a world **tour.***† At the height of his success, illness forced him to quit acting, and he died shortly thereafter.

THUMB, TOM (1838–1883). Born Charles Sherwood Stratton in Bridge-port, Connecticut, he was thoroughly normal until about the age of one, when his parents noticed that he had neither grown nor gained weight in the previous six months. He was 25 inches tall and weighed 15 pounds. Stratton's distant relative, **P. T. Barnum**, heard about Stratton and took him under his wing, training him in singing, dancing, mimicry, and mime. At age five, Stratton made his first **tour***† of America, known as Tom Thumb, and was such a success that the tour was lengthened.

Barnum built on the American success by taking Stratton to Europe, where he twice appeared before Queen Victoria, and as had been the case in the United States, Stratton was a great success. In 1847, he started to grow again, and by 1862, he was two feet 11 inches tall. Thumb's marriage to another little person was a national news story despite the competition of **Civil War** news; he married Lavinia Warren on 20 February 1863 in a New York ceremony with 10,000 guests. A honeymoon reception for Tom Thumb and his fiancée at the White House, at which President and Mrs. **Abraham Lincoln** met the Thumbs, only heightened the newsworthiness of the marriage and Thumb as a major **attraction**.† The sensational success of Thumb's act and marriage under Barnum's management made him wealthy, and the Thumbs lived a lavish lifestyle until his sudden death of a stroke at age 45.

THE TICKET-OF-LEAVE MAN. This much-revived **sensation**† **drama**† by English **dramatist***† **Tom Taylor** made its debut at London's **Olympic Theatre** on 27 March 1863 and at New York's **Winter Garden** on 30 November 1863 with **W. J. Florence** in the role of Robert Brierly, who is imprisoned when framed by a coworker who fancies Robert's fiancée. Convicted in London in 1860 for passing forged bank notes, he is sentenced to four years, but released for good behavior on a "ticket-of-leave," which meant he was free but subject to a return to prison if he associated with criminals. Brierly, with no means of support, struggles with the difficulties of life as a ticket-of-leave man. Through various misadventures, Brierly tries to walk the straight and narrow and, in the final analysis, states, "You would not trust me. But you see there may be some good in a ticket-of-leave man after all." The play became a **film**† in England in 1918.

THE TIMES; OR, LIFE IN NEW YORK. Written by "a gentleman of this city" as a vehicle for **James H. Hackett**, this three-act comedy opened on 10 December 1829 at the **Park Theatre**, where it ran in **repertory**.*† Seen as a forerunner of *A Glance at New York*, this lost play provided Hackett, who acted the character Industrious Doolittle, and his fellow players the opportunity of portraying a series of character types likely to be seen in the New York of that era.

TIVOLI OPERA HOUSE. Joseph Kreling converted an old San Francisco mansion into a beer garden providing **musical*†** entertainments† between 1872 and 1875. The success of this venture led to the building of a large theater and café in 1878, with Kreling changing the name from the Tivoli Beer Garden to the Tivoli Opera House. Since its main floor remained essentially a restaurant and bar, the Tivoli could not technically be considered the first legitimate theater designed exclusively for the performance of musical events (New York's Casino Theatre was the first). From 1878 until 1906, when the Tivoli was destroyed by the great San Francisco earthquake and **fire,†** it was the center of musical activity west of the Mississippi River. The Tivoli presented original musical works created in San Francisco and established works from the New York theater.

TOM AND JERRY; OR, LIFE IN LONDON. W. T. Moncrieff's adaptation of Pierce Egan's story in a **musical*†** work opened in 1823 at the **Park Theatre**. In a series of loosely constructed scenes interspersed with songs and dances, the two title characters are seen taking a **tour*†** of the high spots of London.

†TOMMERS. Tommers were **actors*†** who made a career of appearing in the innumerable productions of *Uncle Tom's Cabin* that **toured*†** the United States from its first performances in Troy, New York, in 1852 well into the 1930s. These productions, often referred to as "Tom Shows," were enduringly popular, but being called a "tommer" was tantamount to being called a **ham.†**

THE TOODLES. **William E. Burton**'s two-act comedy opened on 2 October 1848 at Burton's Chambers Street Theatre, where it ran in **repertory*†** with Burton himself in the lead role of Timothy Toodle, a mild-mannered man with an eccentric wife, played by **Mrs. Vernon**. Mrs. Toodle is something of a hoarder, buying objects at auctions that she does not really need, but believes she might have use for someday. Rising above his gentle nature, Toodle goes to an auction, bids on a coffin, and wins. He brings the coffin home with the explanation that it might come in handy if his wife dies before he does. The shock of his comment cures her of her compulsion.

Burton borrowed the subplot of an old play, *The Broken Heart; or, The Farmer's Daughter* (1832), for this piece. As both **playwright*†** and **actor,*†** Burton had the outstanding success of his career with *The Toodles*, and **actor*† John Sleeper Clarke** also found success with it. In reviewing a book about Burton by William L. Keese, a *New York Times* **critic*†** noted that a photograph of Burton in the role of Toodle could only "faintly suggest the personality of the actor and the rich humor of his impersonations."

TORTESA, THE USURER. **Nathaniel Parker Willis**'s five-act tragedy opened on 8 April 1839 at the **National Theatre** for six performances. Willis wrote the play for **James W. Wallack** in the title character, and the play and Wallack's performance were well received. In August 1839, Wallack repeated the role at the Surrey Theatre in London and often included it in his repertoire. Wallack's son, **Lester Wallack**, made his stage debut in *Tortesa, The Usurer* playing the character of Angelo. **Critics***† saw the influence of **Shakespeare**'s† *Romeo and Juliet* and *The Winter's Tale* in the play, in which a young woman, Isabella, is in love with Angelo. She feigns death to avoid marriage to Tortesa, the Usurer, who has tried bribing her father, Count Falcone, to win her hand in marriage. Her faked death impresses Tortesa, who relinquishes his claim on her in favor of Angelo.

*†TOUR/TOURING. The practice of a theatrical production, act, or **actor***† traveling to various theaters in various cities and towns. Despite the inherent hardships, during the 18th century—and increasingly during the 19th century—productions and actors took to the **road***† as the United States expanded westward. Many performers spent most of their careers on the road, some finding a level of success there that eluded them in New York or the other large cities.

See also †TRAVEL.

†TOWSE, J. RANKEN (1845–1933). Born in Streatham, England, as John Ranken Towse, he came to the United States in 1869 and made his career in New York without ever becoming an American citizen; he later died in England. After four years in various positions at the *New York Post*, he became drama **critic***† in 1874 and continued until 1927, when he retired. He was highly conservative in his tastes and resisted the modernist tide of interest in realism*† and social problem plays, as made evident in his autobiography, *Sixty Years of the Theatre* (1916).

TOY THEATER. Essentially small-scale model theaters (variant in size and materials used—often heavy paper or light wood), these miniature theaters became prevalent in the early 19th century, and over the course of the century, materials were sold to allow **children**† or adults to build legitimate, **vaudeville,**† and **Shakespearean***†-era theaters (the kits sold often were of vintage theaters from the Renaissance to the 18th century), as well as **opera houses, puppet** stages, etc. With the arrival of stage realism*† in the late 19th century, toy theaters decreased in popularity and more so with the emergence of films† and, later, television.

†**TRANSFORMATION SCENE.** The visual effect of one spectacular scene fading into another constituted a basic appeal of the fairy extravaganza,† a type of production in which scenic effects trumped coherent narrative. Beginning with *The Black Crook* in 1866, transformation scenes found their way into **burlesque,***† pantomime spectacles, and **musical***† **revue***† productions for three decades or more.

†**TRAVEL.** From its beginnings, theater in America seemed situated exclusively in a few East Coast cities, but as the United States expanded westward, **actors***† and productions took to the **road***† with great frequency. By the mid-1800s, the nation was honeycombed by producing chains operating theaters in even the smallest towns (for example, by 1915 over 5,000 **vaudeville**† houses were to be found across the country). **Legitimate**† theater productions, vaudeville, **burlesque,***† **circus,***† and virtually every form of entertainment† traveled to cities, towns, and even the most unsettled territories.

In the 18th and much of the 19th centuries, traveling was often arduous and dangerous, particularly as performers and productions ventured farther away from major cities. For example, on **tour***† **Junius Brutus Booth** drank contaminated water while riding on a steamboat, leading to his death from typhus. By the mid-19th century, the growing network of **railroads**† supported tours, and **stars***† were frequently indulged with private railroad cars.†

Circuses made use of entire trains to transport performers, equipment, and animals. Despite the relative comfort of rail travel, touring was a tremendous strain, but even major **stars***† were obliged to tour. Young actors as yet unknown built reputations on tour, while a "name" performer whose popularity was on the wane could extend a career by spending the last years touring. When touring near major bodies of water, riverboats carried performers from one town to the next until well into the 20th century, while the popularity of **showboats**†—floating theaters—on the Mississippi River and others also continued until the 1930s. The Florenz Ziegfeld†–produced **musical***† drama *Show Boat* (1927) offered a theatrical valentine to this era of touring by boat just as the tradition was dying away.

See also *†TOUR/TOURING.

TRAVESTIES. Basically, a travesty in theatrical terms is similar to the actual definition of the word. It is an absurd or grotesque misrepresentation; a parody; a heavily styled imitation; or an elaborately inferior imitation. Many popular travesties filled theaters in the 19th century, and they are barely distinguishable from **burlesque***† parodies, which satirize familiar and usually serious source material. An example: **John Augustus Stone**'s *Metamo-*

ra; or, The Last of the Wampanoags (1829), **Edwin Forrest**'s popular dramatic vehicle about a **Native American**,*† was travestied or burlesqued as **John Brougham**'s *Met-a-mora; or, The Last of the Pollywogs* (1847).

TREMONT THEATRE. Built at 88 Tremont Street in Boston in 1827, the Tremont Theatre was backed by several rich Bostonians and designed by Isaiah Rogers. Opened on 24 September 1827, the Tremont became only the second theater in Boston, following the **Federal Street Theatre**. The Tremont struggled for financial survival because the city's population was too small to support two major theaters, though the Tremont tried to prevail by booking major **stars***† including **Junius Brutus Booth**, **Charlotte Cushman**, **Edwin Forrest**, **Fanny Elssler**, **Thomas Dartmouth "Daddy" Rice**, and many others. On 28 December 1843, the eternally struggling theater was sold to Free Church Baptists who renamed it the Tremont Temple for religious events, though it was occasionally used for public activities.

THE TRIAL OF ATTICUS BEFORE JUSTICE BEAU, FOR A RAPE. This anonymous play was published in 1771 and depicts a fictional rape trial in which Mrs. Chuckle charges that her neighbor Atticus sat on a bed with her two years before. Her accusation balloons up to a rape trial with Atticus's enemies fueling the hysteria. The justice of the peace is insulted by Atticus's attitude; and a greedy lawyer, Rattle, as well as long-standing unpleasantness between Atticus and the Chuckle family leave Atticus in a difficult position. Mrs. Chuckle is coached to embellish her story to include a violent rape against her will and to say that she told her husband about it at once. The play seems intended as a condemnation of corruption among officials of law enforcement, the medical profession, merchants, and religious figures, who, as the author sees it, are able to subvert the justice system to their own ends.

TRIMBLE, JOHN M. (1815–1867). Born John Montague Trimble in New York, he became a builder and ultimately a theater **architect**, responsible for the design and construction of many of New York's theaters built in the era of his lifetime, including that of **Barnum's Museum**, a redesign of the **Bowery Theatre** after a **fire**,† and a remodel of the **Park Theatre** and **Laura Keene's Theatre**; he also worked as a **scene designer***† for the **National Theatre**, among others. Trimble also built theaters in Buffalo, Richmond, and Charleston. Near the end of his life he lost his sight, ending his career.

A TRIP TO NIAGARA; OR, TRAVELLERS IN AMERICA. Late in his theatrical career, **William Dunlap** wrote this 1828 play staged at the **Bowery Theatre**. It won for him the greatest popularity of any of his stage works during his lifetime. This patriotic play featured English tourists traveling on a steamboat up the Hudson River, and its content lampooned British fashions and manners at one of several peaks in anti-British sentiment in the United States. The American characters are bluntly assertive figures, including an **African American***† servant on the boat who, when thought to be a slave, replies abruptly, "I am my own master." The scenery featured a **panorama** of over 25,000 feet of canvas rolled up on giant spools, unwound to depict scenes along the Hudson River shore as the boat glides by, creating a memorable effect and providing the boat's passengers (and the audience) with the "wonders of the Hudson."

THE TRIUMPH AT PLATTSBURG. **Richard Penn Smith**'s comedy-drama opened on 8 January 1830 at Philadelphia's **Chestnut Street Theatre**, where it ran in **repertory**.*† To track down his missing daughter, Elinor, and escape capture by the British forces during the **War of 1812**, Major McCrea disguises himself as André Macklegraith and poses as the slow-witted son of Mrs. Macklegraith. Elinor has married British captain Stanley and believes he has deserted her. Her situation puts her father in danger, but he is able to elude the British. Stanley reappears and proves his love for Elinor. All of this is set against the defeat of the British fleet at Plattsburg. Scenes of great spectacle showing historical moments from the war enhanced the short play.

THE TRIUMPHS OF LOVE; OR, HAPPY RECONCILIATION. **John Murdock**'s comedy opened on 22 May 1795 at Philadelphia's **New Theatre**, where it ran in **repertory**.*† The play satirized the "in breeding" of the Quakers and is set against the background of the Whiskey Rebellion and the tensions with Algiers. The play is a minor effort, but happens to be the first American play to feature Quaker characters and the first to have an **African American***† character, who was performed, as became a long tradition, by a white **actor***† in **blackface**.†

TROWBRIDGE, J. T. (1827–1916). Born John Townsend Trowbridge in Ogden, New York, in a log cabin built by his father, he taught school and worked on a farm before moving to New York City. There he wrote for newspapers and periodicals. While editing, Trowbridge began writing fiction, with the novels *Neighbor Jackwood* (1857), *The Old Battle-Ground* (1859), *Cudjo's Cave* (1864), *The Three Scouts* (1865), *Lucy Arlyn* (1866), *Neighbors' Wives* (1867), and *Coupon Bonds and Other Stories* (1873), among others.

Trowbridge also wrote works under the pseudonym Paul Creyton. He wrote little for the theater, but scored a success with his five-act dramatization of his novel *Neighbor Jackwood*, an abolitionist work. It played at the

Boston Museum for three weeks in 1857, condemning in its themes the Fugitive Slave Law, and although he dealt with race issues, Trowbridge avoided using the common practice of **blackface.†**

TUCKER, ST. GEORGE (1752–1827). Born in Bermuda, St. George Tucker became a much-admired jurist whose plays reflect the Federal versus Republican attitudes of the time, as well as the rise of nationalistic fervor following the **War of 1812**. He wrote four plays, but had little luck getting them produced. His Republican beliefs are stressed in the first two of the plays, *Up and Rise; or, The Borough of Brooklyn: A Farce* (1789), which satirized John Adams, and *The Wheel of Fortune* (1796–1797), in which he complains about the lack of American drama and mines humor from the anti-British sentiments after the **American Revolution**. His other two plays are *The Times; or, The Patriot Rous'd* (1811), which assailed the British impressment of American sailors into their navy, and *The Patriot Cooled* (c. 1815), completed after the War of 1812, which celebrates Andrew Jackson's victory at the Battle of New Orleans. While he was also a poet, Tucker's dramatic output generated little interest, but the plays are reflective of his times.

TWAIN, MARK (1835–1910). Born Samuel Langhorne Clemens in Hannibal, Missouri, under the pseudonym Mark Twain he became a legendary American writer and humorist, perhaps the most famous and beloved public figure of the late 19th century. His fictional output was unfailingly popular, with two novels, *The Adventures of Tom Sawyer* (1876) and *The Adventures of Huckleberry Finn* (1885), emerging as essential American literary works, and only two among many that he wrote. Twain also dabbled in theater, and many of his works have been dramatized and **musicalized*†** by others. However, he wrote the original farcical play, *Is He Dead?* (1898). The play was not particularly popular in Twain's time, but David Ives's 2007 adaptation has won popularity for the play 100 years late. Twain's works also reflect inspirations from the stage and comments about it—and his comic novel, *A Connecticut Yankee in King Arthur's Court* (1889), capitalized on the **stock*†** character of the **Yankee**, a figure that had a healthy stage life from the 18th century. Not exactly a drama **critic,*†** Twain often commented in his writings on contemporary drama, usually humorously.

TWO MEN OF SANDY BAR. **Bret Harte**'s three-act play opened on 17 July 1876 at Chicago's **Hooley Theatre** featuring members of the **Union Square Theatre** Company. The play was adapted from Harte's story, "A Passage in the Life of Mr. John Oakhurst," a romantic tale set in old California of a love affair between Jovita, a Mexican girl, and Jack Oakhurst, an

American adventurer. Harte satirized the notions of chivalry and honor in recounting his tale. **Charles R. Thorne Jr.** played Oakhurst and **J. H. Stoddart** played his friend, Sandy Morton, in the original production.

†*THE TWO ORPHANS.* N. Hart Jackson's 1874 play, featuring four acts and seven **tableaux,**† was adapted from the French play *Les Deus Orphelines* by Eugène Cormon and **Adolphe-Philippe D'Ennery**. It focuses on two sisters—one blind—caught up in the French Revolution. There were several English-language versions, though Jackson's became one of the most frequently performed **melodramas**† of the last decades of the 19th century.

The Two Orphans, first staged by **A. M. Palmer**† at the **Union Square Theatre,**† opened on 21 December 1874 with a cast including **Kitty Blanchard, Kate Claxton,**† **Rose Eytinge,**† and **Charles R. Thorne Jr**. On 28 March 1904, producer **George Tyler**† revived the old warhorse with an **all-star***† cast including **James O'Neill,**† **Louis James,**† Grace George,† **Clara Morris,**† Thomas Meighan,† Kyrle Bellew,† Sarah Cowell Lemoyne,† and Sarah Truex.† It ran for 56 performances and was a last sentimental revisiting of the already moribund genre, although *The Two Orphans* was revived on **Broadway***† again on 5 April 1926 for 32 performances with a cast including Fay Bainter,† Henrietta Crosman,† **Henry E. Dixey,**† Wilton Lackaye,† May Robson, and Mrs. Thomas Whiffen.† In the days of silent films,† *The Two Orphans* inspired several movie versions, including D. W. Griffith's 1921 classic, renamed *Orphans of the Storm*, starring Lillian† and Dorothy Gish.†

TYLER, ROYALL (1757–1826). Born in Boston, and educated at Harvard, where he graduated in 1776, Royall Tyler practiced law for a time and served in the Continental Army during the **American Revolution**, and, later, helped repress Shay's Rebellion (1786–1787). While on a visit to New York, Tyler saw a production of **Richard Brinsley Sheridan**'s comedy of manners *The School for Scandal* and within three weeks he wrote *The Contrast* (1787), a social comedy contrasting the homespun American **Yankee** character with the alien and decadent foppery of the British.

The Contrast is the second play and the first comedy written by a United States citizen. Within a month of *The Contrast*'s first production, Tyler presented a two-act comic opera, *May-Day in Town; or New York in an Uproar*, which has not survived and is known only to have been a satire on contemporary manners, concerned with the confusion caused by spring housecleaning and moving. Another comedy, *Georgia Spec; or, Land in the Moon* (1797), is also lost, but is known to have ridiculed the Yazoo frauds, in which Georgia governors sold large tracts of Georgia land to insiders at ridiculously low prices.

In addition to these plays, Tyler wrote four unproduced and unpublished plays: *The Island of Barrataria*, a farce based on *Don Quixote*; and *The Origin of the Feast of Purim, Joseph and His Brethren*, and *The Judgment of Solomon*, blank verse biblical dramas. Having moved from Boston to Vermont in 1790 to pursue his legal career, Tyler eventually became chief justice of the state supreme court from 1807 to 1813 and professor of jurisprudence at the University of Vermont from 1811 to 1814.

Tyler met Joseph Dennie in this period, with whom he collaborated on writing satirical verses and light essays under the pseudonym Spondee (while Dennie called himself Colon). The essays feature a bias toward the Federalist Party and were published in the *Farmer's Weekly Museum* and other publications. In addition, a long poem, *The Chestnut Tree*, written by Tyler in 1824, is a work depicting contemporary rural life but imagines the rise of industrialism. Tyler also wrote a picaresque novel, *The Algerine Captive* (1797), and **Yankey in London** (1809), a series of letters supposedly written by an American resident in England. His previously uncollected *Verse* and *Prose* appeared in print, respectively, in 1968 and 1972.

UNCLE TOM'S CABIN. Harriet Beecher Stowe's 1852 novel *Uncle Tom's Cabin; or, Life Among the Lowly* captured the mid-19th-century American zeitgeist, particularly in regard to race and the institution of slavery, the most explosive national issue in the decades leading up to the **Civil War**. The novel's astonishing popularity led almost immediately to stage adaptations (all unauthorized by Stowe), with the first significant version, written by **C. W. Taylor**, performed at **Purdy's National Theatre** in 1852. Another version, which ultimately became the standard stage text, was adapted by **actor*† George L. Aiken** into a six-act play that debuted in Troy, New York, for an impressive 100 performances in September 1852. It then moved to Purdy's, where it opened on 18 July 1853 for an astonishing 325-performance run. **H. J. Conway** also adapted a noted version of *Uncle Tom's Cabin* for the **Boston Museum**—and it opened in November 1852, two months following Aiken's version. Conway's version was popular and ran over 200 performances. In November 1853, Conway's *Uncle Tom's Cabin* was presented at **P. T. Barnum's American Museum**.

However popular other versions were in the first year or so after the novel appeared, the Aiken adaptation found permanent favor. The plot of Aiken's *Uncle Tom's Cabin*, which is mostly taken from the first half of Stowe's novel, begins with slave George Harris (played in the Troy, New York, production by Aiken, though he was replaced by S. Siple for the run at Purdy's) about to escape to Canada with hopes of earning enough money to buy his wife, Eliza, and their infant son from their master. After George's escape, Eliza finds out that she and her child are to be sold, so she turns to the kindly elderly slave Uncle Tom, in whom she confides her plan to escape and join George. She is pursued across the frozen Ohio River, but is ultimately reunited with George.

St. Clare, a decent slave owner with alcoholic tendencies, promises Uncle Tom that he will free him for saving the life of an angelic child, Little Eva. Cared for by a slave girl, Topsy, who is chided for her laziness ("Oh, I'se so Wicked!"), Eva forms a close bond with Tom before she dies in a highly sentimental death scene. Tom attempts to keep St. Clare sober, but St.

Clare's drinking leads to an opportunity for St. Clare's cruel wife to sell Tom to brutal slave owner Simon Legree, who appears to get away with murdering St. Clare. When Tom refuses to inform on some escaped slaves, Legree orders his overseers to savagely beat him. Tom's deep faith allows him to forgive Legree and the overseers as he dies. Legree is ultimately killed resisting arrest when it is revealed that he is St. Clare's murderer.

In Aiken's hands, the **melodramatic†** and sentimental elements of the novel are brought into full focus, with the opposing views over slavery vividly delineated in pure melodramatic style, with abolitionists and **African American*†** characters seen heroically (or sentimentally) and slave owners as **villains,†** as in the case of Simon Legree, a brutal slaveholder and one of the most unyielding villains of 19th-century melodrama. The character of George is given by Aiken (via Stowe) a bold statement of the life of the slave: "Yes, Eliza, it's all misery! misery! The very life is burning out of me! I'm a poor, miserable, forlorn drudge! I shall only drag you down with me, that's all! What's the use of our trying to do anything—trying to know anything—trying to be anything? I wish I was dead!"

Aiken's play, other versions of the play, sequels, **musical*†** adaptations, **vaudeville†** acts, songs, and **minstrel†** shows all drew on the play's unparalleled popularity, rendering questions of literary or aesthetic quality moot as the combination of the novel and its stage manifestations burrowed deeply into the American consciousness for several generations. The play's popularity continued unabated after the **Civil War,†** and revivals and **tours†** were continuous until the 1930s (some historians believe that the play was being performed somewhere in America every day between 1852 and 1932), spawning a class of actors known as **"tommers"†** for their frequent appearances in the play or in **blackface†** roles. Mrs. George C. Howard, who originated the role of Topsy in Aiken's play, appeared in the role throughout her long career, and her daughter, **Cordelia Howard**, was a memorable Little Eva, according to contemporary **critics,*†** though she gave up acting in her teens.

By the dawn of the 20th century, *Uncle Tom's Cabin* began to seem old-fashioned and as belonging to the previous century. After 1930, the play's stereotypical racial elements and moralizing sentimentality more fully fell out of favor. Though the play exhibits strong abolitionist sentiments, it in fact ultimately created as many racial stereotypes as those it sought to expunge. In addition, stage practices of the time underscored this problem; for example, the play's African American characters were played by whites wearing blackface makeup for decades. Over the years, black actors took on some or all of the slave roles, but a few white actors specializing in blackface, including Mrs. G. C. Howard, played these roles well into the 20th century. **Film†** versions go back to the dawn of the movie industry, with a short version in 1903. The play is frequently anthologized, and Stowe's novel has remained in print since its initial publication.

UNDER THE GASLIGHT; OR, LIFE AND LOVE IN THESE TIMES.

Augustin Daly's† five-act **melodrama**† opened at the **New York Theatre** on 13 August 1867 for 47 performances starring **Rose Eytinge†** as Laura Courtland, one of her most celebrated roles. A revival in December of that year at the Worrell Sisters Theatre ran for 100 performances, and it returned again in 1869. Daly's bold mixture of elements of realism*† and social commentary with the play's undeniably melodramatic and **sensational†** effects pleased audiences for decades. In this, he succeeded in his oft-stated primary mission: to entertain audiences.

In a picturesque work that moves from **Delmonico's Restaurant** to the slums of New York, emphasizing the different worlds of rich and poor, the angelic young heroine Laura, an heiress, learns that she has been adopted by the Courtlands. She is informed that she was instead a **child†** of poverty and not wealthy. Her happy life and romance with Captain Ray Trafford are put at risk by these lies, which are spouted by a malicious **villain,†** William Byke (played in the original production by **J. B. Studley**), who claims she is his daughter for mercenary reasons.

Byke is granted legal custody of Laura, but Trafford and a one-armed **Civil War** veteran, Snorkey, track his machinations as he attempts to take Laura away and, as importantly, to take her money away. In a confrontation, Byke hurls Laura into a river, but she proves her resilience and survives to return to the Courtlands, leading Byke to conceive a plan to rob the Courtland estate. When Snorkey gets wind of the plot, Byke ties him to a railroad† track to prevent his intervention. Laura arrives in time to rescue Snorkey, untying him just before the train arrives. Byke is subsequently foiled, and Laura returns to the Courtlands and her plan to marry Trafford.

The device of the villain tying a character to the tracks is a well-worn cliché of melodramas, but in this case instead of the heroine being the victim, she is the rescuer. This sensational effect proved to be the play's highlight, and Daly attempted to patent it; however, Eytinge's lauded portrayal of the feisty Laura was the play's strongest appeal, with the strong-willed, courageous character a precursor to feminist counterparts in the dramas of realism in the late 19th century.

Under the Gaslight was filmed† in 1914 and revived (unsuccessfully) on **Broadway*†** in 1929. It remains a standout exemplar of American melodrama and one of the few 19th-century American plays occasionally revived, including a well-received 2009 production at the Metropolitan Playhouse, where **critic*†** Anita Gates, writing in the *New York Times*, noted that "Clearly, 142-year-old melodrama can still be fun."

UNDER THE YOKE; OR, BOUND AND FREE. **African American***† **actor***† and **playwright***† **John S. Ladue** wrote this play (the title of which is sometimes given, almost certainly erroneously, as *Under the Yoke; or, Bond and Free*), referred to as a companion piece to *Uncle Tom's Cabin*, and it was first performed on 2 July 1877 at the Third Avenue Theatre by the Louisiana Colored Troupe, and subsequently performed in New Haven, Connecticut, and, in May 1888, at the Brooklyn Grand **Opera House**, and again in New York in 1890. With a cast of 60 actors (black and white), this plantation play featured music and centered on a black character, played by **J. A. Arneaux**† in his debut role as Tom Walcott, a Southern planter. A New York **critic***† dismissed Ladue's play as "a mass of meaningless phrases."

THE UNION SPY; OR, THE BATTLE OF WELDON RAILROAD. L. W. Osgood's 1871 **melodrama**,† billed as a military drama in five acts, featured a mix of fictional and historical characters (the final **tableaux** depicts Confederate general Robert E. Lee's surrender to Union general Ulysses S. Grant). The play is set during the **Civil War** and is typical of a range of run-of-the-mill works adding weight to their melodramatic machinations with historical events and characters; it is only one of many melodramas set during the Civil War.

†**UNION SQUARE THEATRE.** In 1871, **Sheridan Shook**, owner of the Union Place Hotel, opened a theater in the hotel and acted as **manager***† in partnership with **A. M. Palmer**† from the following year until Palmer's retirement in 1883. In the theater, Palmer staged a series of successful romantic **melodramas**,† mostly with French origins, including *Agnes*, *The Lady of the Camellias (Camille)*, and *The Two Orphans*. Destroyed by fire† in 1888, the theater was rebuilt and operated by the B. F. Keith–E. F. Albee† **vaudeville**† circuit until 1893, after which it continued as a **burlesque***† house before becoming a film† theater.

UNITED MASTODON MINSTRELS. J. H. Haverly founded this **blackface**† **minstrel**† troupe in 1877 through a merger of four smaller **touring***† troupes. With this troupe, Haverly reinvented the minstrel show through advertising in the style of **P. T. Barnum**'s brand of bombastic hucksterism and by stressing the size of the company. This was accomplished, in part, through the device of parading the company and a brass band through each town in which the troupe appeared, much like a **circus***† parade.

Managed by Charles Frohman,† the United Mastodon Minstrels were provided elaborate **scene designs**,*† a departure from other comparatively modestly appointed minstrel shows, and the finale featured acrobats, animals, and clowns, with some of the performers dressed as elephants. In a sense, the

UMM, despite its success and longevity, and its influence on other troupes, signaled the beginning of the end for minstrelsy, as small troupes could not hope to equal the production values and size of the UMM, and many folded. Changing tastes, especially regarding demeaning racial stereotyping and blackface, further undermined minstrel shows in the early 20th century, and the form mostly disappeared by the 1930s.

THE UPPER TEN AND THE LOWER TWENTY. **Thomas Blades de Walden**'s **melodrama†** opened on 16 November 1854 at **Burton's Theatre** for 21 performances. Spanning 14 years, the play centers on Christopher Crookpath (played by **William E. Burton**), a good husband abandoned by his faithless wife and former friend, who seduces her. He falls into alcoholism and a dissolute life, as his only **child†** dies of poverty and neglect on the mean streets of New York. Vengefully, Crookpath kidnaps the son of his wife and her seducer and sends the boy into the streets as his accomplice in a life of crime. When Crookpath ultimately sobers up and reclaims his life, he sets about to bring his former wife and ex-friend to justice for their actions and as repentance for his own. **Critics*†** were resistant to the play, despite its **temperance** message and the fact that it pleased audiences.

UPTON, ROBERT (mid-18th century). Little is known about the life of this English-born mid-18th-century **manager*†** sent to America in 1751 by **Lewis Hallam** to advertise the forthcoming appearance by Hallam's company. He did arrive in America, but set up his own company with himself and his wife in **leading†** roles. They performed in New York during 1751–1752, offering *Othello* in what is believed to be its first American production, as well as *Venice Preserved, Richard III,* and *The Provoked Husband.* The season was unsuccessful, and Upton returned to England in 1752.

THE USURPER. **Irish**-born novelist James McHenry's first play, this five-act blank verse tragedy was produced on 26 December 1827 at the **Chestnut Street Theatre** in Philadelphia, where the play was published in 1829. Considered among the earliest plays in America to draw on Irish mythology (and, to most **critics,*†** its only distinction), *The Usurper* is set in Druidical times, and its themes emphasize the pitfalls of ambition, which turns to murder in the play. McHenry (1785–1845), who was a doctor, was better known for his writings in other genres, particularly novels.

†UTILITY. An "all-purpose" **actor*†** in a **stock*†** company was expected to be capable of playing all types of small parts. This **line of business†** was low in the company hierarchy, and the salary was correspondingly modest.

V

THE VAMPIRE: A PHANTASM IN THREE DRAMAS. This play was first produced at the Princess's Theatre in London on 14 June 1852, with **Dion Boucicault†** in the lead (his debut as a **leading man†**), though he had written it for Charles Kean. Boucicault's **melodrama†** was also produced, again with Boucicault in the lead, at **Wallack's Theatre** with a cast including **Rose Eytinge** and **Agnes Robertson** (Robertson and Boucicault became romantically involved during rehearsals for this play, and she remained his common-law wife for many years). The play received mixed reviews and was not commercially successful.

The main **actors*†** all playing dual roles in a Welsh family are seen through a period of 100 years, with the descendants of the older characters recounting the story, in part by the characters, as portraits, coming to life in a dream. *The Vampire*, as would become a tradition, needed to drink blood to survive, and in this case seeks the blood of a virgin, played by Robertson. Boucicault was particularly praised for his performance, encouraging him to continue to play important roles in his own works throughout his career. Boucicault published the play in 1857 and revised it as *The Phantom*, eliminating the portraits coming to life and making the overall play more realistic, but it remained one of his minor works despite the fact that it was significant in creating the conception of vampires, contributing to their becoming popular characters in 19th-century literature and theater.

VAN AMBURGH, ISAAC A. (1811–1865). Born in Fishkill, New York, Isaac A. Van Amburgh, of **Native American*†** heritage (his grandfather was Iroquois), began his career working at the Zoological Institute of New York, which was actually a small traveling menagerie. He became an animal trainer and ultimately developed his skills, stepping into cages of tigers, lions, and panthers, who, according to spectators (including Nathaniel Hawthorne at an 1828 performance), became astonishingly tame in his presence.

Van Amburgh **toured*†** Europe, where he debuted in England at the Drury Lane Theatre in 1839 and performed for Queen Victoria, who was impressed enough to see several performances. Despite success, Van Amburgh was **criticized***† for animal brutality and by religious figures opposed to **circus***† performers in general. Van Amburgh responded to these complaints by citing Bible passages arguing human domain over animals. He became wealthy and was immortalized in the popular song, "The Menagerie." Long after his death, the Ringling Brothers circus purchased rights to his name, which for 19th-century audiences was synonymous with animal acts.

VAN DAM, RIP (1660?–1749). Born in Holland, Rip Van Dam, the acting governor of New York City from 1731 to 1732, is believed to be the first **manager***† of a theater in New York, the **New Theatre**, near Pearl Street and Maiden Lane, where he staged *The Recruiting Officer* on 6 December 1732, possibly performed by English **actors**.*†

VANDENHOFF, GEORGE (1820–1885). Born in England, and son of tragedian **John M. Vandenhoff**, George Vandenhoff made his English debut on 14 October 1839 in *Rule a Wife and Have a Wife* at the Covent Garden Theatre. His American debut came in 1842 playing Hamlet at the **Park Theatre**. In America, he was admired in **Shakespearean***† roles as well as contemporary plays until he left the stage in 1856, after which he studied law and was admitted to the bar in 1858. He also wrote several books about acting, stage life in the United States and England, and elocution, as well as poetry.

VANDENHOFF, JOHN M. (1790–1861). An English-born tragedian, John M. Vandenhoff debuted in America at **Wallack's Theatre** in *Coriolanus* in 1837, where some **critics***† recognized him as an equal of **William Charles Macready**. Most frequently appearing in **Shakespearean***† tragic roles, Vandenhoff was appreciated for his strong presence and powerful voice, though some critics felt he overemphasized his effects. He was popular with American audiences from the time of his debut until his last appearance in the United States in 1844. He was the father of **actor***† **George Vandenhoff**.

VARIETIES THEATRE. This theater, which opened in New Orleans in 1849, was situated on Gravier Street, between Baronne and Carondelet, and it was operated by **manager***† and **actor***† Thomas Placide. Partially destroyed by **fire**† in 1854, the theater needed significant rebuilding and was renamed the Gaiety Theatre in 1855 under **Dion Boucicault**'s† management. Placide returned as manager in 1858 and introduced a **stock***† company to the venue. Shortly thereafter, **John E. Owens** took over as manager. The theater operated until 1870, when it was totally destroyed in another fire. Again rebuilt, it was renamed the Grand **Opera House**.

†**VAUDEVILLE.** American "vaudeville" has little relation to the original French usage of the word, but **managers*†** borrowed the term to give a classy aura to bills of short variety acts, thus distinguishing them from the risqué variety acts presented in concert saloons. The word appears in American theater as early as 1840, but the quintessential American vaudeville style was established by **Tony Pastor,†** whose **Fourteenth Street Theatre†** opened in 1881 and perfected a style of family-oriented variety **amusements†** of the highest quality.

Pastor's success spurred other variety producers to elevate the quality of their work and to dispense with the more vulgar acts offensive to family audiences. B. F. Keith† and his associate E. F. Albee† attempted a "store-show" at the Gaiety Theatre in Boston, and it was so successful that they expanded their operations to various entertainments† in several theaters before opening their first exclusively vaudeville theater in Boston in 1894. Other producers, including F. F. Proctor, Martin Beck,† and Oscar Hammerstein I,† followed suit.

VELASCO. A five-act tragedy by **Epes Sargent**, it was first produced on 20 November 1837 at the **Tremont Theatre** in Boston, with **James E. Murdoch** in the title role and **Ellen Tree** as Izidora, in a historical fiction set in Burgos, Spain, in 1046. Published in 1838, the text includes a statement from Sargent explaining that he has fictionalized events in the life of Rodrigo Diaz (El Cid), stressing that "its scenes and situations are purely imaginary. All that may seem strange or unnatural in the conduct of the drama is in strict accordance with popular tradition." With *Velasco* emphasizing the themes of love and honor, **critics*†** pointed to the influence of **Shakespearean*†** tragedy in the play's style and structure. **Edgar Allan Poe** wrote that *Velasco* "compared with American tragedies generally, is a good tragedy—indeed, an excellent one, but positively considered, its merits are very inconsiderable." The play was well received by the public and produced successfully in New York in 1838 and London in 1849.

THE VERMONT WOOL DEALER. This one-act farce was written by **Cornelius A. Logan** in 1838 and centered on the **Yankee†** character Deuteronomy Dutiful, played by **Dan Marble** in his London debut in 1840. The simple plot, providing ample comic opportunities for the Dutiful character, revolves around Amanda, Dutiful's young ward, who uses him to make her suitor, Captain Oakley, jealous. All ends well when Dutiful promises to pay for the wedding celebration.

VERNON, MRS. (1796–1869). Born in Brighton, England, as Jane Marchant Fisher, she debuted at London's Drury Lane Theatre in 1817, working with her future husband, George Vernon. Ten years later, she made her American debut at New York's **Bowery Theatre** in *The Heir-at-Law*. Her siblings, John Aubrey Fisher and **Clara Fisher**, also found success in the same period. Following the death of Vernon in 1830, Fisher, billed as Mrs. Vernon, achieved great popularity in diverse roles, but with particular acclaim in comedy at the Bowery and the **Park Theatre**, where she remained in the company for 17 years.

Mrs. Vernon excelled at old women roles and, as her contemporaries noted, in parts calling for spirit, charm, and intelligence. Some believed she quietly provided behind-the-scenes directing tips in the production of plays in which she acted. Mrs. Vernon acted until shortly before her death, making her last appearance as part of the **stock***† company at **Wallack's Theatre** in *School* (1869).

THE VERY AGE!. Edward Sherman Gould's five-act comedy of manners, written in 1850, drew most of its humor from the character of a young dandy, Alfred Spooney, who attempts to impress New York society after a six-week European **tour**.*† Gould mocks the state of fashionable follies, duties, and occupations of those adhering to society's strictures. A **critic**,*† writing in *The Knickerbocker*, called it "a clever comedy."

VESTRIS, MADAME (1797–1856). Born in London, Lucia Eliza Bartolozzi won success as an opera singer and **actress***† from her debut in 1815. She appeared in numerous operas for 15 years, but ultimately turned to theater. Her lasting fame came after she leased London's **Olympic Theatre** in 1830, staging popular **burlesques***† and extravaganzas,† as well as contemporary plays by James Planché. Vestris appeared as Oberon in *A Midsummer Night's Dream*, inaugurating a tradition of women playing that role, and staged other **Shakespearean***† works.

The staging innovations of Madame Vestris, including introduction of the **box set** in a production of **Dion Boucicault's**† *London Assurance* in 1841, were among the first steps leading toward greater realism*† in theater production and were, as such, highly influential. She made her United States debut in 1838 in *The Loan of a Lover*, but she was not popular, partly due to some ill-considered public **criticisms***† she made of American **actors**.*†

THE VIGILANTES; OR, THE HEART OF THE SIERRAS. See *HOW WOMEN LOVE: A DRAMA IN SEVEN ACTS.*

†**VILLAIN.** The villains of **melodrama,**† as well as those of **Shakespeare,***† provide some of the juiciest roles for an **actor.***† Indeed, many great actors, like Robert Mantell,† **John McCullough,**† and **Thomas W. Keene,**† made a specialty of the title role in *Richard III*, one of the great villains from Shakespeare's pen. In **lines of business,**† it was normally the heavy† who was cast in villain roles, but Richard III always went to the **leading man**† instead of the heavy.† Similarly, Othello's malignant antagonist Iago was considered by many to be **Edwin Booth**'s† best role, and other Shakespearean actors followed Booth's path in playing this decidedly secondary role.

William A. Brady's† recollection of a basic technique for playing the villain in melodrama is worth quoting:

> The small fry in the Old **Bowery gallery**† had strict theories of how the villain ought to die, when the hero did him in in the final scene. The old melodrama villains had a specialized technique for kicking the bucket—elbows stiff, spine rigid, then fall over backward square on the back of your head. It took skill to do it right and not kill yourself in good earnest. We all practiced it—I've spent hours bruising myself to a pulp practicing a villain's fall. And we valued villains in direct proportion to the stiffness of their falls. When **J. B. Studley**, a fine old-time actor, started doing villains at the Old Bowery and tried dying like a human being—a natural sprawling collapse—the whole house came right over the **footlights**† at him with hisses and cat-calls and roars of protest—they wanted a real fall. It wasn't till Studley had learned to stiffen up and crash in the conventional way—and he got to be one of the best fallers in the business—that they'd tolerate him at all.

Ample evidence suggests that 19th-century audiences enjoyed booing and hissing villains in melodramas—especially such memorable ones as Simon Legree, the brutal slave owner in the perennial ***Uncle Tom's Cabin***.

VINCENT, MRS. J. R. (1818–1887). Born Mary Ann Farley in Portsmouth, England, she debuted in the role of a maid in Cowes, on the Isle of Wight, in 1835. She married J. R. Vincent, a comic **actor***† nearly 20 years older, that same year, and they appeared throughout England and Scotland. In 1845, they joined the company of the Queen's Theatre in Dublin, where Mrs. Vincent played the Nurse to Helen Faucit's Juliet with success, despite being too young for the role. For their American debuts, the Vincents appeared at Boston's **National Theatre** in November 1846 in *Popping the Question*, remaining in the National company for several years, appearing at times with **Charlotte Cushman**, **James E. Murdoch**,† **James W. Wallack**, and **Mrs. John Drew**,† among others.

Two years following Vincent's death in 1850, Mrs. Vincent joined the **Boston Museum** company, remaining with them for the rest of her career, apart from a **tour*†** in 1861–1862 with **Edwin Forrest**, appearing in *The Lady of Lyons*. At the Boston Museum, she was credited with appearing in an astonishing 444 different characters, including everything from **Shakespeare*†** to contemporary plays, and she appeared with most of the noted actors of the era, including **E. L. Davenport**, **Agnes Robertson**,† **Eliza Logan**, **C. W. Couldock**,† **Lucille Western**, **John McCullough**,† **Helena Modjeska**,† **Lawrence Barrett**,† and **John Wilkes Booth**,† among others. Mrs. Vincent's *New York Times* obituary referred to her as Boston's favorite **actress*†** and credited her "character and virtues" with counteracting "the prejudices against actresses in the minds of many worthy people."

THE VIRGIN OF THE SUN. **William Dunlap**'s five-act adaptation of August von Kotzebue's play about Peruvian Incas in the era of Spanish conquest won greater popularity than at least three other English versions of Kotzebue's original, *Die Sonnenjungfrau.* Dunlap incorporated music and enhanced the play's **melodramatic†** elements, aiming at the prevailing taste of American audiences. Produced at the **Park Theatre** on 12 March 1800, it was immediately followed at the Park on 26 March by Dunlap's *Pizarro in Peru*, adapted from **Richard Brinsley Sheridan**'s play, with both works winning approval from audiences.

VIRGINIA MINSTRELS. Also known as the Virginia Serenaders, the Virginia **Minstrels†** are considered the oldest and most iconic **blackface†** minstrel show, founded in 1843 by **Dan Emmett**, Frank Brower, R. W. Pelham, and Billy Whitlock. They are believed to have performed first at the Branch Hotel in the **Bowery** district in early 1843, followed by performances at the **Chatham Garden Theatre** on 31 January 1843 and at New York's Bowery Amphitheatre on 6 February 1843, but when they gave an "Ethiopian Concert" at the Masonic Temple in Boston, on 7 March 1843, their act had been honed into a full-fledged production.

The Virginia Minstrels essentially created the prototype for subsequent minstrel shows as the form became phenomenally popular in the mid-19th century. Later troupes were significantly larger, with as many as 50 or more performers, but the four wore what became characteristic costumes and mixed songs and comedy, each playing musical instruments. The troupe is credited with popularizing the songs "Jimmy Crack Corn," "Polly Wolly Doodle," and "Old Dan Tucker," among many others.

The Virginia Minstrels' use of blackface and humor depending on grotesque racial stereotypes set the tone first established by **Thomas Dartmouth "Daddy" Rice**'s "**Jump Jim Crow**" routine, which continued through the history of American minstrelsy well into the 20th century. However, the Virginia Minstrels' great popularity ended early as the result of disputes among the four performers. Despite a successful **tour*†** in England, the company disbanded by July 1843, though Emmett, especially, had a long career in the form, performing with other minstrel troupes and in **circuses**.*†

THE VIRGINIA VETERAN. Billed as a military drama in four acts, Thomas F. Power's 1874 play, written and published as a benefit for veteran organizations, centered on Colonel Robert Blunt, an aging veteran of the **Mexican War** living as a Virginia planter during the **Civil War** who wishes he could draw the sword he wielded at the Battle of Buena Vista and participate in the new conflict. Blunt's son, Henry, a Union soldier, must ultimately save his father from Confederate guerillas who accuse the defiant old man of treason for supporting the Union cause. At curtain's fall, the old colonel, disappointed to be left on the sidelines of the current **war**,*† speaks of peace:

> Let us all pray this cruel war may cease;
> And when 'tis over, may we peaceful live,
> A reunited family of states,—
> All hate dispelled beneath the starry flag
> I've followed,—even from my boyhood's days.

The Virginia Veteran is rife with stereotypes of **African American*** characters and full of **melodramatic†** flourishes and patriotic speeches.

VIRGINIUS. Written for English **actor*† Edmund Kean** in 1820, *Virginius*, by **James Sheridan Knowles**, became an early 19th-century stage staple in America. **William Charles Macready** popularized the five-act tragedy at the Covent Garden Theatre in 1824 and at New York's **Park Theatre** in 1842, appearing opposite **Charlotte Cushman**. In a preface to the published version, Knowles writes, "This Play was written in great haste, and, no doubt, abounds in defects," though audiences kept it on the boards for decades, in part as a result of Macready's performance.

Inspired, in part, by plot elements from **Shakespeare**'s*† *Titus Andronicus* and *Othello*, the tragedy centers on the death of Virginia, daughter of Virginius, at the hands of the dictator Appius Claudius. It is, as the prologue notes, "a tale—made beautiful by years—Of pure, old, Roman sorrow—old in tears! And those who shed o'er it in childhood, may Still fall—and fall— for sweet Virginia!"

VOEGTLIN, WILLIAM T. (b. 1835). Swiss-born **scene designer*†** William T. Voegtlin arrived in the United States in 1850 and found stage work in New Orleans painting scenery. He worked there and in San Francisco before moving to New York in 1870, where he designed scenery for the first revival of *The Black Crook* that same year. His reputation was built on elaborate scenery, but he designed all manner of plays at **Niblo's Garden** and **Booth's Theatre**, among others, including *Heartsease* (1870), *Innisfallen* (1870), *Kit, The Arkansas Traveler* (1871), *Connie Soogah* (1875), *Hiawatha* (1880), *The Beggar Student* (1883), and *Romeo and Juliet* in 1885. His son, Arthur Voegtlin (1858?–1948), was also a successful scene designer prior to World **War** I.*†

VOKES, ROSINA (1854–1894). Born in England to a costumer, Rosina Vokes became a popular favorite as an **actress*†** in America on visits, first with her brother, Fred, and two sisters, Jessie and Victoria. They debuted in New York at the **Union Square Theatre** in *The Belles of the Kitchen* in 1872, a comedy with music sometimes described as a forerunning work in the history of **musical*†** comedy. Over the next couple of years, the family visited the United States and presented shows along similar lines, including *The Right Man in the Wrong Place* and *Fun in a Fog*, and revived *The Belles in the Kitchen*. In all cases, Vokes was seen as the standout performer and returned to America in 1885 with her own troupe. Praised for her dancing skills and charm, when she left New York for England in 1893 due to ill health, the *New York Times* reported that the stage would be deprived of "one of its very brightest ornaments."

WACOUSTA; OR, THE CURSE. **Louisa Medina** adapted this **melodrama†** from John Richardson's 1832 Colonial Gothic novel *Wacousta; or, The Prophecy: A Tale of the Canadas*. The play opened on 30 December 1833 at the **Bowery Street Theatre** where David Ingersoll played the title role of a **Native American**.*† Set in Detroit in the period of conflicts between British soldiers and Chief Pontiac, the play dramatized the various clashes in melodramatic terms.

†WAINWRIGHT, MARIE (1853–1923). The Philadelphia-born **actress*†** was the daughter of Commodore J. M. and Marie Wainwright. A privileged background permitted her education in France, after which she was accepted for training with the **Boston Museum stock*†** company. She quickly moved into roles in **Shakespeare*†** opposite **Edwin Booth,†** **Tommaso Salvini,†** and **Lawrence Barrett**.† Later she **toured*†** with her second husband, **Louis James**.† Best known for playing Viola in *Twelfth Night*, she acted that role over 1,000 times. Wainwright's melodious voice and delicate gestures enhanced her wistful, poetic characterization of Viola in contrast to the more coquettish approach of other actresses. Before her retirement, Wainwright appeared in a few silent films.*†

WALCOT, CHARLES MELTON, SR. (1815–1868). This London-born comic **actor*†** initially studied for a career as an architect, but that work did not interest him so he traveled to the United States in 1837. Marriage to an **actress*†** drew him toward the theater, and he debuted in 1842 prior to joining the company of **William Mitchell** at the **Olympic Theatre**. He appeared successfully in contemporary comedies and scored a hit writing a two-act parody of **Henry Wadsworth Longfellow**'s poem "Hiawatha," which Walcot called *Hi-A-Wa-Tha; or, Ardent Spirits and Laughing Water* (1856).

Walcot's son, Charles M. Walcot Jr. (1840–1921), who performed under the name Charles Brown, was a popular **leading man**† in romantic plays at Philadelphia's **Walnut Street Theatre**. He ended his career along with his wife, Isabella Nickinson (1847–1906), playing comic roles for **producer***† Daniel Frohman.†

†WALKING GENTLEMAN/LADY. These 19th-century **lines of business**† were considered a step above **supernumerary**† in that the characters that fell to these **actors***† might occasionally speak lines. In his 1880 memoir *The Stage*, **James E. Murdoch**† notes that a walking gentleman would play a character who is "essential to the progress and development of the plot," but who has "a merely mechanical part in the dialogue." These parts, like Rosencrantz and Guildenstern in *Hamlet*, were useful for giving young actors the opportunity to observe the techniques of their betters at close range.

WALL STREET. **Thomas Blades de Walden**'s scathing satire of the stock exchange opened in May 1857 at **Burton's Old Chamber Street Theatre**. With a cast of characters including Knickerbocker Van Dorn, Alfred Highbred, Mrs. Uptown, and Quicksnap, De Walden offered a cynical view of Wall Street as essentially a rigged gaming table where those in the know cannot lose and anyone else is sure to lose. All of the characters, great and small, are afflicted with the disease of speculation, which in the play represents a route to easy, unearned money if a person is fortunate enough to learn how to play the game. **Lawrence Barrett starred***† as Reynolds in the original production. In theaters during the financial Panic of 1857, audiences found De Walden's slanted view of the financial game apropos.

WALL, THOMAS (mid-18th century). An **actor***† and **manager***† who established himself as a member of **David Douglass**'s **American Company** in 1766, Wall promoted himself as a successful British actor from the Theatre Royal and Haymarket. He appeared with the **American Company** in Charleston, as well as at Philadelphia's **Southwark Theatre** and New York's **John Street Theatre**. With **Adam Lindsay**, Wall established the Maryland Company of Comedians in 1781 in Baltimore, where he appeared as Richard III, among other roles. Wall, who also built Baltimore's first permanent theater, the **New Theatre**, may have also appeared under the name of John Wall.

WALLACK, HENRY JOHN (1790–1870). Born in London to parents in the theatrical profession who were popular comedians, Henry John Wallack was the brother of **James William Wallack**. He performed without much notice in America beginning around 1821, but returned to acting in England for much of the 1820s, including playing Julius Caesar to his brother's Marc Antony. He returned to the United States, but never became a **star**,*† though he was well received as Hamlet and in various productions of 18th-century English comedies. He married an **actress**,*† Miss Turpin, and had two daughters, one of whom became a singer and the other an actress.

WALLACK, JAMES WILLIAM (1794–1864). London-born **actor***† and **manager**,*† and son of provincial comedians, James William Wallack was also the brother of actor **Henry John Wallack**. He debuted as a **child**† at London's Surrey Theatre, after which he moved up to **juvenile**† roles at the Drury Lane Theatre, and at 18 he made his adult debut as Laertes in *Hamlet.* He became the Drury Lane's stage manager in 1824 and moved up to supporting† roles. Wallack also served as stage manager at the Princess's Theatre.

Wallack's first performance in the United States was in *Macbeth* at the **Park Theatre**. He also performed several other **Shakespearean***† roles, but made little impression on **critics***† or audiences. In more contemporary works, including *The Stranger*, *Pizarro*, and *The Gamester*, he was better liked. Wallack trouped the United States from 1818 to 1845, well received in Shakespeare's most sophisticated comedies and the leading roles in *The Brigand, The Rent-Day, The Wonder, Don Cassar de Bazan*, and *Wild Oats.*

Beginning in 1837, Wallack ran the **National Theatre**, presenting a well-respected **repertory***† of great English-language plays performed by a strong company that Wallack assembled over time. In 1852, he took on management of **Brougham**'s Lyceum, renaming it Wallack's Lyceum, and in 1861 he built a new structure called **Wallack's Theatre**. He was the father of actor and manager **Lester Wallack**.

WALLACK, JAMES WILLIAM, JR. (1818–1873). Though his name might suggest otherwise, James William Wallack Jr. was the son of **Henry John Wallack** and went onstage as a **child**.*† He made his adult debut in *Pizarro* at Philadelphia's **Chestnut Street Theatre** in 1822. It took another decade before he made his New York debut in *Hofer, The "Tell" of the Tyrol.* He worked with his uncle at the **National Theatre** and was judged by **critics***† as at his best in **Shakespearean***† tragedy. He debuted in London in 1851 as Othello, one of his strongest characterizations. Back in America, he scored as Fagin in a production of *Oliver!* and Mathais in *The Bells*, Henry Irving's iconic role. Unlike the other Wallacks, his New York appearances were comparatively rare; he was most often on **tour***† across the United States.

WALLACK, LESTER (1820–1888). Born in New York as John Johnstone Wallack, the son of **James William Wallack**, he changed his name to John Lester Wallack for theatrical purposes and ultimately shortened that to Lester Wallack. He considered a military career for a time, but like the rest of his family, he went on the stage. Wallack debuted in Dublin around 1844, and in 1846 he appeared at the Haymarket Theatre. He was seen there by an American **manager**'s*† agent*† who hired him to come to the United States and appear at the **Broadway***† **Theatre**, which he did in 1847 in **Dion Boucicault**'s† *Used Up*, playing Sir Charles Coldstream.

Over the subsequent decades, Wallack appeared at various times in all of New York's major theaters, including the **Bowery Theatre**, **Burton's Theatre**, **Niblo's Garden**, **Brougham**'s Lyceum, and others. He became manager of the second **Wallack's Theatre** (the first had been run by his father) in 1861, and after operating there for over 20 years, he opened the third Wallack's Theatre at 30th Street and Broadway. Another theater was named after him in 1924. Wallack tended to be most applauded in comic and romantic roles in **Shakespeare**† and in 18th-century British plays, though he had a few successes in contemporary plays, including *Diplomacy* (1878) and his own **melodramatic**† adaptation of *Rosedale* (1863).

WALLACK'S THEATRE. Beginning in 1850, New York had a Wallack's Theatre—there were ultimately four, and the first three are essential to the history of 19th-century American theater. **Playwright**,*† **actor**,*† and **manager*** **John Brougham** opened Brougham's Lyceum at 485 **Broadway***† on 23 December 1850, the theater having been built and designed by **architect John M. Trimble**.

Under Brougham's management, the theater reflected his specialties, **Irish** farces and **burlesques**,*† but after two years his management failed, and he leased the theater to **James W. Wallack**, who renamed it for himself. Wallack extensively renovated the theater, elevating the décor to a more elegant style, and reopened it on 8 September 1852. His sons, Charles and **Lester Wallack**, served in various capacities at the theater. Theodore Moss, who worked with the Wallacks for many years, signed on as assistant treasurer, though he was to hold many positions with the Wallacks over the years.

In 1861, Wallack's moved to a theater at 844 Broadway at 13th Street, and it, like the earlier Wallack's, was generally highly praised for presenting quality productions and great actors, including such figures as **Charles Fisher**, **E. L. Davenport**, **J. H. Stoddart**, **Charles Mathews**, **Steele MacKaye**, **Mrs. Hoey**, **Mary Gannon**, **Rose Eytinge**, and many others. Lester Wallack took over as manager in this period with a mix of classics and contemporary works, which, over time, built a large and loyal following. In 1874, **Dion**

Boucicault's† *The Shaughraun* ran for 143 performances at Wallack's, proving to be the theater's biggest hit. Around 1881, diminishing audiences caused Wallack to consider a new location north.

In February 1881, Wallack leased the corner of 30th Street and Broadway and sold his lease on 844 Broadway to Adolph Neuendorff for the **Germania Theatre**, a German-language company. The Germania was not successful, and Neuendorff sold the property back to Wallack, who renamed it the **Star Theatre** and reopened in March with a company headed by Dion Boucicault. As far as Wallack's was concerned, in the summer of 1881, Wallack announced that the space would be used exclusively for **touring***† companies, beginning with **Lawrence Barrett**'s, while Henry Irving and Ellen Terry began their first American **tour***† at the Star Theatre.

For the next several years, the leading American and English actors, among occasional international companies and **stars**,*† appeared at the Star and at Wallack's. The list of actors is a who's who of the era: **Edwin Booth**,† **Joseph Jefferson**,† **E. H. Sothern**, **Fanny Janauschek**, **Helena Modjeska**,† **Maurice Barrymore**, **Sarah Bernhardt**,† **Fanny Davenport**, **Rose Coghlan**, and many more. Renovation was done, enlarging the stage in 1889, as well as introducing electric **lighting**.*† Moss took over management of the Star Theatre from 1889 to 1895. In 1890, a cooling system was installed. After financial difficulties and other problems, the Star Theatre closed in 1901, and an early film made by American Mutoscope and Biograph Company made a time-lapse recording of the building's demolition.

Lester Wallack built a new theater at 30th Street and Broadway in 1881, and it opened on 4 December 1881. The first production was an acclaimed revival of **Richard Brinsley Sheridan**'s *The School for Scandal*, but Wallack's health was declining. He carried on for six more seasons, but retired as manager in 1887, and others leased the theater into the second decade of the 20th century, finally closing for good on 1 May 1915. In 1924, a new Wallack's Theatre was built and dedicated to the memory of the Wallack legacy.

WALLER, EMMA (1819?–1899). The English-born **actress***† made her 1856 London debut at the Drury Lane Theatre as Pauline in *The Lady of Lyons*, although there is evidence that she appeared in Melbourne, Australia, the year before. A year later, in 1857, Waller debuted at Philadelphia's **Walnut Street Theatre** as Ophelia, and she appeared the following year, acting with her husband, D. W. Waller, in *The Duchess of Malfi*. She **toured***† America as a **star***† for several years, but in 1869 she scored a hit as Meg Merrilies in a revival of *Guy Mannering* in New York, and this became one of her favored roles, as were Lady Macbeth and the Duchess of Malfi. She spent much of her career on tour playing these roles. Waller also won plaudits playing male roles, including Hamlet and Iago, partly supported by what **critics*†** identified as her dignified presence, which led them to consider her the logical successor of **Charlotte Cushman**.

WALNUT STREET THEATRE. This storied theater is the oldest continually operating English-speaking theater in the world. Built at 825 Walnut Street in Philadelphia in 1809 by the **Circus*†** of Pepin and Breschard, it was originally called the New Circus. In 1811, **architect** William Strickland added a stage and orchestra pit, and the theater's name was changed, this time to the **Olympic Theatre**. There is clearly confusion about the theater's ultimate name. It was apparently called the Walnut Street Theatre in 1820 when a very young **Edwin Forrest** made his debut there, but it was called the Olympic again in 1822, and finally, permanently, the Walnut Street Theatre in 1828. In the middle of the 19th century, it was also referred to as the **American Theatre**. Most leading American **actors*†** of the 19th and 20th century have, at some time, appeared at the Walnut Street Theatre, including Forrest, **Edwin Booth,† Edmund Kean**, the **Drew†** and **Barrymore*†** families, George M. Cohan,*† Will Rogers,† the Marx Brothers,† Helen Hayes,*† Henry Fonda,* Katharine Hepburn,* Marlon Brando,* Jessica Tandy,* Ethel Waters,* Audrey Hepburn,* Sidney Poitier,* Lauren Bacall,* George C. Scott,* Julie Harris,* and numerous others.

The Walnut Street Theatre was renovated by architect John Haviland in 1828 and was the first in the United States to install **gas† footlights†** in 1837; in 1855 it was the first to make use of air-conditioning. In 1892, the Walnut Street Theatre was an early theater to employ electric **lighting**.*† The first play produced at the theater, in 1812, was a production of **Richard Brinsley Sheridan**'s *The Rivals*, and President Thomas Jefferson and the Marquis de Lafayette were in the audience.

Edwin Booth partnered with his brother-in-law **John Sleeper Clarke†** to buy the theater in 1865. In 1941, the Walnut Street Theatre became a possession of the Shubert*† Organization—and many **Broadway*†** plays of that era had out-of-town tryouts at the Walnut Street Theatre, including the original productions of *A Streetcar Named Desire,† Mister Roberts,† Gigi,† The Diary of Anne Frank,† A Raisin in the Sun,†* etc. In 1966, the theater was designated a National Historical Landmark. In the 19th century, Cincinnati also had a Walnut Street Theatre built by **John H. Havlin**.

*†WAR. War, or more particularly, the impact of war on individual ordinary lives, has been a source for American **playwrights**,*† and their attention has usually been focused on those conflicts in which America participated directly. Military conflicts were depicted from the beginnings of theater in North America to the end of the 19th century. Beginning in the eras of the actual declared conflicts, the wars most often represented on the stage were the **American Revolution**, the **War of 1812**, the **Mexican War**, and the **Civil War**, though there is not much contemporary drama dealing with the **French and Indian War**, which was fought in a formative era for American theater.

The American Revolution was dramatized in plays dealing with the tensions among the rebellious colonists and the British loyalists. **Mercy Otis Warren**, a close friend of John and Abigail Adams, satirized British works and attitudes during the conflict—and her plays and those by others dramatized events of the war and/or used the historical events as a backdrop for otherwise fictional stories. *The Adulateur* (1772), *The Defeat* (1773), *The Group* (1775), *The Blockheads* (1776), and *The Motley Assembly* (1779), all by Warren (though the latter two were published anonymously), were more pamphlet plays than dramatically feasible works, but they did their part to fuel patriotic fervor, and other works, such as **John Leacock**'s *The Fall of British Tyranny; or, Liberty Triumphant* (1776), were more theatrical, in Leacock's case with a title that leaves little chance of misunderstanding its author's intent. Like Leacock's work, many Revolutionary plays took a strongly patriotic stance, attempting to explain the desire for American independence and placing blame on various British political and military actions for this desire.

When the war ended and the United States of America was established, the war was viewed with some nostalgia—and reminders of the war as well as the major personages of the war featured in American plays in every genre, from satiric farces to tragedy, including the anonymous *The Battle of Brooklyn* (1776), which appeared very shortly after the battle. American patriots, led by **George Washington** (a sometime theatergoer), were subject to dramatic treatment, while traitors, including the most famous, Benedict Arnold and Major John André, were also depicted. André, particularly, was a popular character—and his actions and ultimate execution were the subject of several plays, most notably in **William Dunlap**'s *André* (1798) and **William Hill Brown**'s *West Point Preserved; or, The Treason of Arnold* (1797). While English forces held Boston in late 1775 and early 1776, British general John Burgoyne wrote *The Blockade of Boston*, satirizing George Washington and the American forces. The play was produced in Boston at Faneuil Hall on 8 January 1776, with the performance interrupted by a British soldier running onstage to announce that the Americans were attacking English forces.

Up to the Civil War, more than 50 American plays depicted aspects of the Revolution. Many are lost, but among the surviving works, *Briar Cliff* (1828), *Putnam, the Iron Son of '76* (1844), *Love in '76* (1844), and *Horseshoe Robinson* (1858) are standout works. After the Civil War, aspects of the Revolution continued to be dramatized in such works as **James A. Herne**'s† *The Minute Men of 1774–75*† (1886) as well as Clyde Fitch's† *Nathan Hale*

(1898) and *Major André* (1903). Herbert Fields, Richard Rodgers, and Lorenz Hart's **musical*†** comedy *Dearest Enemy* (1925) was praised for its colorful Revolutionary War background. However, it was not until the 1930s that this period received a worthy stage depiction in Maxwell Anderson's† *Valley Forge†* (1934). As late as 1969, the musical *1776*, depicting the debate in the Continental Congress over a declaration of independence from England, won critical and popular acclaim.

The **War of 1812** (1812–1815) inspired a few plays in the early 19th century, most notably **Robert Penn Smith**'s *The Eighth of January* (1829) and *The Triumph at Plattsburgh* (1830), and some plays celebrating Andrew Jackson's victory at the Battle of New Orleans, including C. E. Grice's *The Battle of New Orleans; or, Glory, Love and Loyalty* (1816). The **Mexican War** (1846–1848) made a national hero of General Zachary Taylor, who was elected president of the United States in 1850, but little drama arose except in regard to the tragic struggle at the Alamo and the life of Davy Crockett and other American icons (Jim Bowie) who died there. An anonymous work, *The Battle of Buena Vista* (1858), celebrated Taylor's triumph.

The most tragic of American conflicts was the Civil War (1861–1865), which produced numerous plays on various aspects of the conflict and the national tensions leading up to the outbreak of war, most particularly over slavery. Prewar, *Uncle Tom's Cabin* (1852), a runaway hit stage play adapted by **George L. Aiken** from Harriet Beecher Stowe's abolitionist novel of the same name, inspired considerable discussion over the slave question (Aiken was only one among several adaptors of Stowe's novel), as did **Dion Boucicault**'s† more noncommital **melodrama†** *The Octoroon* (1859), which depicted tragic outcomes of race conflict. Politically inspired works on the slave question and race issues were somewhat less prevalent in this age of melodrama than plays depicting the separation of families and the brother-versus-brother conflicts of the time. Few dramas equaled the real one when mere days after Confederate general Robert E. Lee's surrender to Union general Ulysses S. Grant, the Southern-sympathizing actor, **John Wilkes Booth†** assassinated President **Abraham Lincoln** as he watched **Tom Taylor**'s comedy *Our American Cousin* at **Ford's Theatre** on 14 April 1865.

After the Civil War, Boucicault's *Belle Lamar* (1874) was one among many melodramas using the war as its backdrop during the late 19th century. Some of these include David Belasco's† *May Blossom* (1884) and *The Heart of Maryland†* (1895), William Gillette's† *Held by the Enemy†* (1886) and *Secret Service†* (1895), **Bronson Howard**'s† *Shenandoah†* (1889), James A. Herne's *The Reverend Griffith Davenport* (1899), Clyde Fitch's *Barbara Freitchie†* (1899; and the 1927 Sigmund Romberg **operetta†** *My Maryland* based on it), the Julian Edwards and Stanislaus Stange† musical *When Johnny Comes Marching Home* (1902), William C. deMille's† *The Warrens of Virginia†* (1907), and Augustus Thomas's† *The Copperhead†* (1918). Some plays focused on the Reconstruction era following the war, including Thomas's *Alabama*† (1891) and Joseph R. Grismer† and **Clay Greene's**† *The New South*† (1893).

WAR OF 1812. The 32-month conflict between the United States and Great Britain was, in essence, resolving unresolved issues untended to in the Treaty of Paris in 1783, which officially ended the **American Revolution**. **War***† was declared on 18 June 1812, and peace was restored when the Treaty of Ghent was signed on 24 December 1814, though military and naval conflict continued into June 1815, including the Battle of New Orleans, where General Andrew Jackson won a decisive victory that made him a national hero despite the fact that the war had officially ended two weeks before the battle. Among the plays that focused on the War of 1812 was **C. E. Grice's** *The Battle of New Orleans; or, Glory, Love and Loyalty* (1816). Much of the conflict had to do with America's continuing struggle to gain economic independence from England.

France and England were in conflict, and prior to the start of the war this gave an advantage to the United States, who, from a neutral position, were able to trade with both sides. The British practice of impressing American merchant sailors into their service was a central conflict that brought the United States to war with England. The war, however, was often punishing for America. Though the USS *Constitution* won some naval battles, the British captured Washington, DC, and burned the White House and Capitol, with President James Madison and his wife, Dolley, managing to escape only shortly before the arrival of the British. Dolley Madison won praise for her courage, in part for saving a copy of the Declaration of Independence and the famous Gilbert Stuart portrait of **George Washington** on her quick departure from the White House. In 1814, Francis Scott Key wrote "The Star-Spangled Banner" while watching the British bombardment of Fort McHenry in Baltimore Harbor.

There is ample reason to believe that the resolution of the War of 1812 only fueled American desire to gain full independence from Europe, but most particularly from a dependence on England for economic and cultural success. In theater, romantic **melodramas**† depicted the conflict on personal levels: lovers were separated by conflicting interests, families were disrupted, and trust among neighbors disturbed, etc. However, what built up over time was a resistance of American audiences to foreign (particularly English) plays and performers. The worst case was an ongoing conflict between American tragedian **Edwin Forrest** and visiting British tragedian **William Charles Macready**, which exploded into New York's **Astor Place Opera House riot** on 10 May 1849, killing no less than 22 people and injuring over 100 others. *See also* *†WAR.

†WARDE, FREDERICK (1851–1935). Born Frederick Barkham Warde in Oxfordshire, England, he gave up a law career to become an **actor**.*† Following his 1867 British stage debut, he arrived in the United States in 1874 and worked with **John McCullough,† Charlotte Cushman**, **Edwin Booth,† Lawrence Barrett,†** and others before establishing his own company in 1881. He acted in **Shakespeare***† and 19th century chestnuts including *The Gladiator*, *The Lady of Lyons*, and *Virginius*, but he also played a few contemporary characters, including the **leading†** role in Percy MacKaye's† *A Thousand Years Ago* (1914) late in his career. Following his 1919 retirement, Warde frequently lectured on theater and wrote books, including *The Fools of Shakespeare* (1913) and his memoir *Fifty Years of Make-Believe* (1920).

†WARDROBE. Throughout much of the early 19th century, designing and constructing costumes for a specific production was seldom done. An **actor***† was typically expected to furnish his or her own theatrical wardrobe, and the ability to do so was a major factor in one's employability. On the **road**,*† actors spent much of their discretionary time plying the needle to keep their stage garments in good repair. In those days, when most people owned only the clothes they wore every day, investment in a stage wardrobe was a major expense, especially for **Shakespearean***† actors.

Indeed, when Walker Whiteside† lost his entire wardrobe in a **theater fire†** in 1901, he could not afford to replace it, and thus he changed the course of his career from Shakespearean acting to **character†** roles in contemporary plays. **Frank S. Chanfrau** recalled that in his early days at the **Chatham Garden Theatre** in New York, he was cast as the apothecary in *Romeo and Juliet* to **Charlotte Cushman**'s Romeo. The apothecary role required a pair of black tights. However, on a utility man's† 65-cents-a-week salary, Chanfrau could not afford to buy them. He sought out the stage **manager***† and asked for help, but was told to find himself some tights or another actor would be hired as utility. In despair, Chanfrau combed through the theater's wardrobe in search of anything that might serve the purpose. In a pile of moth-eaten royal robes, he found a rusty black domino. For the performance, he thrust his legs through the sleeves of the domino and wound the rest of the garment around his body. He succeeded in making his entrance without having been seen by the stage manager, but the audience roared with laughter at his appearance. This caused Chanfrau to forget his lines, so he rushed out of his shop, leaving Romeo to get his own poison. He expected to be discharged, but Cushman learned the circumstances, interceded for him, and presented him with a pair of black tights, which he wore to success the following night.

Gladys Hurlbut's entertainingly informative memoir provides a view of the circumstances faced by actors regarding wardrobe: "When the **direc-tor***† said to me, 'You're poor for the first two acts,' that was great good news, for the 'Rags to Riches' plays took less wardrobe. Clothes were a terrific problem to **stock***† **actresses***†. . . . A **leading**† woman averaged four changes a week and often more. The higher salary we got, the better we were expected to dress. I always spent most of my wages on clothes." Indeed, Hurlbut worked out a plan with several other **leading women,***† whereby each would stay with a **stock***† company in a given city long enough to use their wardrobes, which could be stretched over three or four months. Then they would give notice and exchange jobs.

WARREN, MERCY OTIS (1728–1814). Born in West Barnstable, Massachusetts, Mercy Otis was the third of 13 children of James and Mary Otis; her father was elected to the Massachusetts House of Representatives in 1745. She had no formal education, but along with her brother James was tutored. As she moved into adulthood, her political beliefs were strongly opposed to English monarchic rule and the various taxes and harsh policies levied against the colonies.

Otis read voraciously, including **Shakespeare,***† Pope, and others, and resolved to use her literary interests and ability in service of the movement toward American independence. Her revolutionary friends included John and Abigail Adams, and Otis married James Warren, a member of the Massachusetts House of Representatives, who, like her, was outspoken in opposition to the English monarch. There is no question that Mercy Otis Warren was a rarity among **women***† in her time, both in her literary pursuits and in her political activism, particularly between 1765 and 1789.

Warren's 1788 pamphlet, "Observations on the New Constitution," played a role in the making of and support for the Bill of Rights. She wrote letters and poems, and a series of satirical plays, *The Adulateur* (1772), *The Defeat* (1773), and *The Group* (1775), that are considered the first written by an American woman (though she published them under a male pseudonym). The anonymously published *The Blockheads* (1776) and *The Motley Assembly* (1779) are credited to her as well. It is doubtful that Warren regarded herself as an artist; more likely, she merely employed dramatic technique, as well as other literary forms, to serve her revolutionary and sociopolitical purposes.

WARREN, WILLIAM (1767–1832). Born in Bath, England, he debuted as Young Norval in *Douglas* before leaving his homeland for the United States shortly thereafter. He made his American debut in Baltimore as the apothecary in *Romeo and Juliet*. In 1805, he returned to England serving as an agent*† for the Philadelphia Theatre with the goal of hiring a corps of comedians. While there, Warren met and married **Mrs. Anne Merry**, a celebrated **actress**.*† Upon his return to the United States, he became **manager***† of the **Chestnut Street Theatre**, where he made his last appearance in 1829 in *Poor Gentleman*. He was the father of comic **actor***† **William Warren Jr.**

WARREN, WILLIAM, JR. (1812–1888). Son of **actor***† **William Warren**, he was born in Philadelphia and made his stage debut at age 20 as Young Norval in *Douglas* (coincidentally, the same role that provided his father's debut) at Philadelphia's **Arch Street Theatre**. For 14 years he was an intrepid **touring***† actor, playing many cities in the United States, including New York, and he also appeared in London. Many of Warren's contemporaries considered him the greatest American comedian of his time. He settled in Boston in 1846, weary of the touring life, and acted at the **Howard Athenaeum** for a year before joining the **Boston Museum** company, where he became **leading**† comedian and continued in that position until his retirement in 1882.

During Warren's time at the Boston Museum, it is believed he gave some 13,000 performances in nearly 600 plays, an astonishing feat that so closely identified him with the Boston Museum that audiences of the era thought them synonymous. His range within the comic realm was extraordinary—he could play Polonius in *Hamlet* and other **Shakespearean***† comic characters and appear as well in contemporary farces such as *The Silver Spoon*. His death brought an outpouring of affection from the Boston public.

WASHINGTON, GEORGE (1732–1799). One of the most iconic American personalities, George Washington was born in Westmoreland County, Virginia, and ultimately became the commander in chief of the Continental Army during the **American Revolution**, following service during the **French and Indian War**, and the first president of the United States. He presided over the convention that drafted the US Constitution and was widely referred to as the "Father of His Country." Even in his own time, Washington was a legendary, larger-than-life figure, and his peers looked to him to set the tone for the way the new American government would function. The most obvious example is that he chose to step aside after two four-year terms as president, when he could have served for as long as he wished. His modest approach to his job underscored his innate humanity and was, in every sense, a repudiation of the monarchical style of England.

Washington enjoyed attending theater; in fact, his frequent attendance may have done a great deal to convince his fellow Americans of the worth of theater. Puritanical voices rejected theater and other forms of entertainment,† but if Washington appreciated theater, it became more acceptable. Though theater was banned by the Continental Congress during the Revolution, following the war theater burgeoned in the major East Coast cities and **actors*†** **toured*†** with regularity in both urban and rural settings. Throughout the 1760s and 1770s, Washington is known to have frequently attended theater in Williamsburg and elsewhere. Specifically, Washington attended a performance of **William Dunlap**'s *Darby's Return* and saw such works as *The Beggar's Opera*, *Douglas*, *The Recruiting Officer*, *Hamlet*, *The Tempest*, and *Julius Caesar*. Philadelphia's **Southwark Theatre** had a presidential box decorated with patriotic bunting and other appropriate décor for Washington's comfort. It is also known that Washington enjoyed reading plays, including **Royall Tyler**'s *The Contrast*, and he quoted from **Shakespeare's†** plays in various letters.

WATKINS, HARRY (1825–1894). A little-known **actor,*†** **playwright,*†** and theater **manager*†** mostly remembered for the diary he kept from 1845 to 1863, Harry Watkins acted in theaters around the United States and occasionally in New York. He never achieved fame, and his informative, fascinating diary grows in bitter feelings as his career goes nowhere, despite his frequent opportunities to work with some of the greats, including **P. T. Barnum**, **Junius Brutus Booth**, and **Edwin Forrest**, though it is a valuable document of theater in the mid-19th century. It was first published in 1938 as *One Man in His Time* and is the only known theatrical diary covering the decade prior to the **Civil War**.

WEMYSS, FRANCIS COURTNEY (1797–1859). London-born and the son of a naval officer and an American mother, Francis Courtney Wemyss arrived in the United States in 1822 after working as an **actor*†** on English stages, including the Adelphi Theatre, for several years. He debuted at New York's **Chatham Garden Theatre**, then joined Philadelphia's **Chestnut Street Theatre** and played comic roles, mostly, beginning with the character of Vapid in *The Dramatist*, and he **toured*†** the major cities of the United States. Wemyss happened to be playing Duncan to **William Charles Macready**'s Macbeth on the night of the **Astor Place Opera House riot** in 1849. Eventually, Wemyss took over as **manager*†** of the Chestnut Street Theatre and, later, as manager of a series of theaters in Pittsburgh, Baltimore, Delaware, West Virginia, Washington, and New York, including **P. T. Barnum**'s **American Museum**. Wemyss served as secretary of the Dramatic Fund beginning in 1852 and continued until his death. He also authored *Twenty-Six Years of the Life of an Actor and Manager* (1847) and edited a series of collections of early American plays, *Acting American Theatre*.

WEMYSS, KATE (b. 1821). Born Catherine Bertha Mahon, Kate Wemyss, later known onstage as Mrs. Duffield, debuted in 1847 in the city of her birth, Philadelphia, at the **Arch Street Theatre** in *The Lady of Lyons* playing opposite **James E. Murdoch**. The following year, she made her New York debut at the **Bowery Theatre** in the same play and returned to Philadelphia as the **leading**† **actress***† of the **Walnut Street Theatre** before her marriage to a US naval officer, Captain Duffield, after which she retired from the stage. Of her performance playing Queen Katharine to **Charlotte Cushman**'s Cardinal Wolsey in **Shakespeare**'s*† *Henry VIII* on 2 November 1860, the *New York Times* said that "she sustained the part well, and deservedly met with much applause."

WEST, THOMAS WADE (1745–1799). Born in England, Thomas Wade West was a comedian, and he married Margaretta Shepherd in 1774, the daughter of **Irish** theater **manager***† Charles Shepherd. She was apparently an **actress**,*† and they **toured***† the provinces between 1774 and 1788. They also appeared in London at the Haymarket Theatre and China Hall Theatre from 1775 to 1778. The Wests moved to the United States and ultimately became naturalized citizens in 1792. They founded and built theaters in several towns in Virginia and the Carolinas between the years 1788 and 1799. West fell to his death while building a theater in Alexandria, Virginia. Until her death in 1810, Margaretta managed theaters.

WEST POINT PRESERVED; OR, THE TREASON OF ARNOLD. **William Hill Brown**'s 1797 tragedy about Major John André, Benedict Arnold, and the **American Revolution** was not performed until after his death, but it received five professional productions and won plaudits from **critics**.*† The text of the play is believed lost.

WESTERN, LUCILLE (1843–1877). Born in New Orleans as Pauline Lucille Western, she was the **child**† of **actors**.*† Her father had a theater in Washington, DC, where Western and her sister, Helen (1844–1868), debuted as change artists, after which they **toured***† the United States as the "Star Sisters," gaining popularity in *Three Fast Men*, which they also performed at the **Bowery Theatre**. Helen was at one time romantically involved with **John Wilkes Booth**.† Lucille appeared in 1860 at Baltimore's **Holliday Street Theatre** in *East Lynne*, scoring a major personal success in one of the most popular plays of the era.

During the **Civil War**, Western toured with **E. L. Davenport** and **James W. Wallack Jr.**, with Western playing the role of Nancy in *Oliver Twist*. Western appeared in theaters throughout the United States in a range of contemporary plays and died while engaged at Brooklyn's New **Park Thea-**

tre appearing in *Oliver Twist*. Western's *New York Times* obituary described the intensity of her acting, stressing that "in spite of **critical*†** disapproval of her methods—realistic almost to brutality—the impression of these performances will not be easily effaced."

WHEATLEY, SARAH (1790–1872). Born in Nova Scotia as Sarah Ross, she married an **Irish actor*†** and made her stage debut in 1805 at the **Park Theatre**. She was not a beauty and won success playing older women, including the Nurse in *Romeo and Juliet* and Mrs. Malaprop in **Richard Brinsley Sheridan**'s *The Rivals*. Claiming she did not care for acting, Wheatley retired in 1842.

WHEATLEY, WILLIAM (1816–1876). The son of **Sarah Wheatley**, William Wheatley was born in New York and debuted as a **child†** playing opposite **William Charles Macready**. He spent much of his early career as an **actor*†** in Philadelphia at the **Walnut Street Theatre** and the **Chestnut Street Theatre** prior to becoming **manager*†** of the **Arch Street Theatre**, first in partnership with **John Drew,†** then on his own. He managed **Niblo's Garden** in New York beginning in 1862 and was in charge when *The Black Crook* (1866) opened there and caused a sensation. As its nominal **producer,*†** he made a fortune, and it allowed him to retire in 1868.

†WHEELER, ANDREW CARPENTER (1832–1903). Born in New York City, this drama **critic,*** whose writing appeared under the pen name Nym Crinkle, began his career as a reporter for the *New York Times* in 1857, but resigned to seek adventure on the western **frontier**. After serving as a correspondent during the **Civil War**, he returned to New York and wrote under the pseudonym Trinculo for *The Weekly Leader*. As Nym Crinkle, he wrote for *The World*, *The Sun*, and even the front page of the *New York Dramatic Mirror†* (1886–1889), to all of which he brought an acerbic wit and an impressive knowledge of dramatic literature and stagecraft. After 1892, he used the pen name J. P. Mowbray, which coincided with a more embracing critical outlook.

WHIGS AND DEMOCRATS; OR, LOVE OF NO POLITICS. This 1839 three-act comedy, attributed to **J. E. Heath**, is typical of a number of plays written in the period, focusing on the conflicts between the major political parties. In this case, the play satirizes a rural election and the shenanigans that transpire during the run-up to the vote. *Whigs and Democrats* was first performed in Philadelphia.

WHITE, JOHN BLAKE (1781–1859). A lawyer, painter, and **dramatist,***† John Blake White was born near Eutaw Springs, South Carolina, and studied painting in London. He returned to the United States in 1804, and attempted to set himself up as a painter in Boston. White spent two decades as a lawyer in Charleston, was elected to the South Carolina legislature in 1818, and ran a paper mill. He became a **playwright***† with *Foscari; or, The Venetian Empire*, a Gothic blank verse tragedy staged at the **Charleston Theatre** in 1806. That same year, White's *The Mysteries of the Castle* was also produced at the Charleston Theatre and similarly demonstrated a Gothic environment. White's last three plays made a major shift to contemporary issues: *Modern Honor* (1812), a condemnation of the tradition of dueling; *The Forgers* (1837), in praise of **temperance**; and *The Triumph of Liberty* (1819), which went unproduced despite its patriotic title. Later in life, White returned to painting and found more appreciation of his work at this point than at the beginning of his career.

WHITE, RICHARD GRANT (1822–1885). Born in New York, Richard Grant White was a leading **Shakespearean***† scholar and literary and music **critic,***† perhaps the most noted of his time. He was the brother of the celebrated **architect** Stanford White. He attended Bristol College and New York University, studying both medicine and law, and he practiced law for a time. Among his many accomplishments and publications, he edited a 12-volume edition of **Shakespeare***† (1857–1865). White also wrote several books about Shakespeare.

WHITMAN, WALT (1819–1892). Born on Long Island as Walter Whitman, he became one of the most inspiring and important American poets, one whose humanism was something of a transition between transcendentalism and the rise of realism*† in the mid- to late 19th century. He was also known as the father of free verse and was a cultural **critic***† of a sort in an extraordinary American era. He nursed wounded Union soldiers during the **Civil War** and was deeply interested in politics.

Whitman's most admired work, *Leaves of Grass* (1855), is central to the canon of American literature. Though he never wrote for the stage, he was a regular theatergoer and avidly opinionated about the authorship of **Shakespeare's***† plays, denying that Shakespeare was the actual author. As a teenager in the 1830s, he anonymously attended theater and opera performances regularly. In his early theatergoing, he was most fascinated with Shakespeare's plays—admiring **Junius Brutus Booth**'s performance as Richard III—and he saw other greats of the era, including **William Charles Macready** and **Edwin Forrest**. He wrote dramatic criticism for publication as a young man, usually anonymously, and remained a lifelong theatergoer.

†*WIDOW BEDOTT; OR, A HUNT FOR A HUSBAND.* In 1879, humorist David Ross Locke, whose writings were much admired by President **Abraham Lincoln**, freely adapted humorist Frances M. Whitcher's collected stories, *The Widow Bedott Papers.* The play was first published in 1856 as a four-act comedy at the behest of **female impersonator†** **Neil Burgess,†** who found in the title character a perfect vehicle. The original production opened on 15 March 1880 for 56 performances at **Haverly's Fourteenth Street Theatre**, but Burgess revived it frequently over the subsequent decade on **tour.*†**

The simple plot provided Burgess ample opportunity for comedy as a gossipy meddler and "widdy woman," Widow Bedott, who sets her cap for remarriage with Elder Shadrack Sniffles (played by George Stoddart), despite interference from her rival, Widow Jenkins. The play was also known as *Vim; or, A Visit to Puffy Farm.* In 1880, at the time of its original production, a **critic*†** for the *New York Mirror* wrote of Burgess's characterization that "No one seeing him on the stage as the garrulous Widow would suspect for a moment that it was a man masquerading in women's clothes, were it not so announced. There is not a movement, gesture, motion or action that is not thoroughly and perfectly feminine. To Mr. Burgess' credit be it said, he never oversteps the proprieties. No matter how strong the temptation, he is only the woman, without the slightest approach to indelicacy. No **actor*†** on the stage is more thoroughly conscientious in this particular."

THE WIDOW'S SON; OR, WHICH IS THE TRAITOR?. **Samuel Woodworth**'s three-act tragedy opened at the **Park Theatre** on 25 November 1825, where it ran in **repertory.*†** In the play, set during the **American Revolution**, Captain William Darby is angered at being called a traitor, and his mother, Margaret Darby, is suspected of being a witch. In fact, Captain Darby is so angry that he assists the British in taking Fort Montgomery. Margaret is deeply shamed by her son's treasonous actions and volunteers to spy on the British forces for General **George Washington**, at which she proves most successful. She subsequently learns of her son's death, but she takes some cold comfort in the fact that he has been killed by English and not American forces, which she sees as a kind of redemption.

THE WIFE'S APPEAL. Mrs. L. D. Shears's six-act **temperance** drama written in 1878 was another potboiler of its kind, perhaps only of particular interest because it was written by a **woman*†** and is rich with the sort of **melodramatic†** dialogue found in temperance plays, including the final accusation: "'twas you who placed the fatal cup to his lisping lips before he knew the danger."

WIGNELL, THOMAS (1753–1803). English-born, Thomas Wignell arrived in America in 1774 with his cousin **Lewis Hallam** and other **actors,***† then because of the frictions leading up to the **American Revolution**, he departed with Hallam for Jamaica. Back in America in 1785, Wignell was a member of the Old **American Company** at the **John Street Theatre** in New York, the Philadelphia Company and with **Alexander Reinagle** at the **Chestnut Street Theatre**, and the **Holliday Street Theatre** in Baltimore.

With the American Company, Wignell became a well-known and popular character actor, both in **Shakespearean***† plays (Laertes in *Hamlet*, Prospero in *The Tempest*) and in contemporary English comedies. However, he was more successful in the role of a **manager***† than as an actor. It is believed that Wignell persuaded **Royall Tyler** to write *The Contrast* (1787), and he played Jonathan, the **Yankee**† character. With Reinagle, he is considered the force that built the Chestnut Street Theatre into the leading theater in the country at the time. He married the **actress***† **Mrs. Merry** not long before his death.

WILKINS, EDWARD G. P. (1829–1861). Born in Boston, Edward G. P. "Ned" Wilkins developed careers as a drama **critic,***† **playwright,***† and journalist. With encouragement from noted critic **William Winter,**† who brought him to the attention of publisher **J. Gordon Bennett**, Wilkins wrote for the *New York Herald*, becoming their theater critic. He also wrote dramatic and literary criticism for the *Saturday Press* in a column titled "Dramatic Feuilleton."

In this period, Wilkins emerged as an early admirer of poet **Walt Whitman**, who said of Wilkins, "I never heard Ned say a foolish thing." Wilkins was a regular among the bohemian artists and intellectuals meeting at **Pfaff's** in the 1850s. During that period, he wrote the comedies *Young New York* (1856) and the one-act *My Wife's Mirror* (1856), both first staged by **Laura Keene** and published by **Samuel French**. Wilkins also adapted **Victorien Sardou**'s *Les Pattes des Mouche* at **Wallack's Theatre**, produced under the title *Henriette*.

As a critic, Wilkins commented on many **leading**† players and **managers,***† including providing an early positive assessment of **Edwin Booth**'s† promise and an assault on what he considered the avarice of Keene's management in frequent revivals of *Our American Cousin*, as well as a condemnation of her 1859 adaptation of *A Midsummer Night's Dream*, which he felt relegated **Shakespeare***† to the position of a minor contributor. Wilkins also commented on **international***† performers appearing in the United States and assailed the practice of passing off plagiarized scripts as original. His early death abruptly ended a promising playwriting and critical career.

WILLIAM PENN; OR, THE ELM TREE. **Richard Penn Smith**'s three-act **melodrama**,† billed as a "historical play," opened on 25 December 1829 at Philadelphia's **Walnut Street Theatre** and was well received by the public, holding the stage for two decades. Set in colonial times, Smith focuses on one central event in Penn's life, his intervention in the life of Tammany, the **Indian** chief, whose life he hoped to save, and the reconciliation of rival Indian tribes. Penn's centrality in resolving the crisis is the core of the play.

WILLIAMS, BARNEY (1823–1876). Bernard O'Flaherty was born in Cork, Ireland, and, as a youth, moved to the United States with his family in 1831, where his father became a New York City cop. In his youth, he worked several odd jobs before appearing at the Franklin Theatre as a **supernumerary**.† In 1836, he played his first speaking role in *The Ice Witch*, replacing an ailing **actor**.*† Having changed his name to Barney Williams, he became a member of the theater's company and began accumulating experience onstage. He scored a major hit in the play *The Omnibus*, written by **Tyrone Power**, who guided Williams's career. Williams's wife, Maria Pray (1828–1911), taking the stage name of Mrs. Barney Williams, appeared at the **Chatham Theatre** in a **burlesque***† called *New York Assurance*, a parody of **Dion Boucicault**'s† acclaimed comedy, ***London Assurance.***

Williams had appeared in **blackface**† **minstrelsy**† for a time, but when he partnered with his wife, he found his most notable successes. They appeared together at New York's **National Theatre** in *The Irish Boy and Yankee*† *Girl* in 1850 and in 1853 appeared in *Ireland As It Is* at **Niblo's Garden**. Steadily, their specialty became Irish-themed entertainments,† which, in the mid-19th century, were especially popular. They became significant players at San Francisco's Metropolitan Theatre and **toured***† in the western United States before a visit to England in 1855, where they performed at London's Adelphi Theatre, and Ireland, where they were well received.

Back in the United States, the Williamses **toured***† in the eastern states, and Williams became **manager***† of **Wallack's Theatre** in 1867. In the 1860s and 1870s, they continued to perform comedies and romantic works in the Irish vein until Barney was felled by a stroke and died. He was well-liked by his peers, and his pallbearers included **star***† actors such as **Lester Wallack** and **John Brougham**, as well as celebrated public figures. Maria acted for another year, but retired in 1877.

WILLIAMS, PERCY (1857–1923). Born in Baltimore, Percy G. Williams was the son of a doctor and newspaper editor, and he, too, studied medicine at Baltimore College. However, Williams soon turned to a stage career at Colonel **William E. Sinn**'s Theatre in Baltimore. In 1875, Williams joined Brooklyn's **Park Theatre** company but returned to Baltimore in 1877 as the lead comedian at the **Holliday Street Theatre**. Apparent disappointments in his career as an **actor*†** led him to give it up for business, first in electrical goods and then in real estate. This led him back to theater, where he became a major **manager*†** and theater owner, first with the Brooklyn Music Hall. The **vaudeville†** bill he produced there was successful, and he continued to build a vaudeville empire, being particularly known for bringing **international*†** variety stars to his theaters, including Vesta Victoria, Vesta Tilley, and Alice and Marie Lloyd. When he retired and sold his empire to E. F. Albee,† he was a multimillionaire.

WILLIS, NATHANIEL PARKER (1806–1867). A native of Portland, Maine, Nathaniel Parker Willis was born into a family prominent in the publishing business. While attending Yale, Willis became interested in literature and ultimately worked with major American writers including **Henry Wadsworth Longfellow** and **Edgar Allan Poe**. After some time as a correspondent in Europe, he returned to New York, where he steadily grew in stature as a writer, mostly as a novelist, though he wrote two well-received plays, the five-act tragedy *Bianca Visconti; or, The Heart Overtasked* (1839) and *Tortesa; or, The Usurer* (1839). Some of his novels were often successfully dramatized by others. Willis devoted relatively little effort to theater, but his two plays were part of the pre–**Civil War** canon of popular plays.

†WILSON, FRANCIS (1854–1935). Born in Philadelphia, this comedian and **playwright*†** began his stage career in a **minstrel†** troupe, but joined a **stock*†** company in 1877. Thereafter, he balanced the **legitimate†** stage with **opéra bouffe**. He was also a prolific writer, authoring two memoirs as well as books on fellow **actors,*†** including **Joseph Jefferson,†** with whom he performed in an **all-star*†** revival of **Richard Brinsley Sheridan**'s *The Rivals* in 1896. Among Wilson's plays are *The Bachelor's Baby* (1909) and *The Spiritualist* (1913). He was the first president of the Actors' Equity Association.*†

†WINTER, WILLIAM (1836–1917). Born in Gloucester, Massachusetts, William Winter was educated for law at Harvard, but gave it up when he was inspired by **Henry Wadsworth Longfellow** to become a writer. Winter wrote poetry and became literary editor of the *Saturday Press* in 1859 before joining the staff of the *Albion* as its drama **critic*†** in 1861. He was appointed the *New York Tribune*'s drama editor in 1865 and remained there until he retired in 1909. His penchant for writing florid memorial tributes to deceased **actors*†** and his affection for 19th-century romanticism earned him the nickname "Weeping Willie."

Winter was well-respected in his early years. However, with the emergence of Henrik Ibsen's† social problem plays, Winter became a vocal opponent of the modernist movement toward realism,*† believing that a clear and positive moral outcome to a play was all-important. He found the new drama, and Ibsen's plays in particular, "unhealthful and injurious," seeing them as inherently pessimistic. In response, he vigorously upheld old standards.

Of the purpose of the stage, Winter wrote, "The province of art, and especially dramatic art, is beauty, not deformity; the need of the world is to be cheered, not depressed; and the author who avows, as Ibsen did, that he goes down into the sewers,—whatever be the purpose of his descent into those insalubrious regions,—should be left to the enjoyment of them." Along with regular criticism published in the *Tribune*, Winter wrote for numerous other publications and authored several books, including *Other Days* (1908), *Old Friends* (1909), and *The Wallet of Time* (1913), along with biographies of notable theater artists, including **Edwin Booth†** (1893), **Ada Rehan†** (1898), Richard Mansfield† (1910), **Joseph Jefferson†** (1913), **Tyrone Power†** (1913), and **David Belasco†** (1918, two volumes).

WINTER GARDEN THEATRE. Built in 1850 at 667 Broadway, this large theater offered diverse genres of theatrical fare, from extravaganzas† to **Shakespeare.***† First named Tripler's Hall or Metropolitan Hall, it was destroyed by **fire†** in 1854 and was immediately rebuilt with the name New York Theatre. In 1855, **Laura Keene** reopened the theater as Laura Keene's Varieties, appearing in *Old Heads and Young Hearts.* Unfortunately, the economic Panic of 1857 sent the theater into bankruptcy. In 1859, **Dion Boucicault†** took over management, and his controversial production of his play *The Octoroon* focused the attention of theatergoers on the evils of slavery and the tragedies inherent in prejudice against mixed-race relationships.

The facility suffered several fires, but it was rebuilt and varied **managers***† ran the theater, steadily developing it into one of the finest showcases in New York City. Most of the legendary names of mid-19th-century theater appeared there at one time or another, including all three Booth brothers, **Junius Brutus Booth Jr.,†** **Edwin Booth,†** and **John Wilkes Booth,†** all of whom appeared together in a 25 November 1864 benefit of **Shakespeare's***† *Julius Caesar* to build a fund to create a statue of Shakespeare for Central Park. This was a mere four months before John Wilkes Booth shot President **Abraham Lincoln** at **Ford's Theatre** in Washington, DC. During the performance of *Julius Caesar*, fire alarms were heard outside the theater as Confederate sympathizers attempted to ignite fires to destroy the city as the **Civil War** moved toward its conclusion. Edwin Booth was compelled to calm the audience so the performance could continue.

Edwin Booth, with his partner and brother-in-law **John Sleeper Clarke**, took over management of the Winter Garden and moved the fare from **musicals***† and variety entertainments† to classical drama. Booth also performed his record-setting 100 consecutive performances of *Hamlet* at the Winter Garden. He planned a series of classical revivals, but his brother's murder of Lincoln compelled Booth to retire from the stage until February 1866, when he returned in a production of *Richelieu* and, in January 1867, a spectacularly staged production of *The Merchant of Venice*, restoring his career.

The theater burned again on 23 March 1867, and Booth decided not to rebuild and instead built Booth's Theatre uptown in a tonier neighborhood. Another Winter Garden was constructed in 1911 by the **Shubert***† Brothers, and for its first two decades became the **Broadway***† home of the major **musical***† theater **star***† Al Jolson.† Most shows at this Winter Garden, to the present, have been large-scale musicals.

WITCHCRAFT; OR, THE MARTYRS OF SALEM. **Cornelius Mathews**'s blank verse tragedy opened on 17 May 1847 at the **Bowery Theatre** for five performances after a successful run at Philadelphia's **Walnut Street Theatre**, where it was highly successful, as it was in other cities despite its brief run in New York. Set against the background of the historic Salem, Massachusetts, witch hunts, **James E. Murdoch** played Gideon Bodish, who must defend his strange, mysterious mother, Ambla, when she is accused of witchcraft. The main witness in court against Ambla is Susanna Peache, who believes the old woman is somehow using mystical powers to interfere with her love for Gideon. Ambla is convicted and executed, but Susanna realizes it has cost her the love of Gideon, and she kills herself. Jarvis Dane, played by **J. A. J. Neafie**, a rival suitor of Susanna's, kills Gideon to avenge Susanna's suicide.

†WITHAM, CHARLES W. (1842–1926). Born in Portland, Maine, Charles W. Witham studied art and became a landscape painter, but quickly moved into theater when he was hired in the 1860s as Gaspard Maeder's **scene design***† assistant at **Niblo's Garden** in New York. In 1863, as chief designer at the **Boston Theatre**, Witham painted scenery for **Edwin Forrest**. Then he joined **Edwin Booth**'s† staff of designers and exercised considerable influence on the construction of **Booth's Theatre**.† His renderings of that theater, which opened in 1869, provide an important iconographic record. For a decade, Witham designed the scenery for Booth's **Shakespeare***† productions, overlapping with his work for **Augustin Daly**,† beginning in 1873. During the 1880s, Witham also designed site-specific New York settings for the ethnic comedies at **Edward Harrigan**'s† theater. After 1890, he was a freelance designer until he retired in 1909.

WITHIN AN INCH OF HIS LIFE. **James A. Herne†** and **David Belasco†**
collaborated on this **melodrama†** dramatized and adapted from Emile Gabo-
riau's novel *La Corde au Cou*. It opened on 17 February 1879 at San Francisco's Grand **Opera House**. Belasco and Herne later disagreed over the authorship of the play, with each claiming full credit, but clearly both had
assistance since neither could read French. The play centers on a man attempting to end an illicit affair before his marriage and is replete with melodramatic embellishments, from plot twists to a major reversal of action at the
climax and an onstage **fire.†** **James O'Neill†** appeared in the **leading†** role
of the play, which won some approval from audiences and cynicism from
critics,*† who found it replete with typical clichés of melodrama. Herne
himself and Katherine Corcoran, who became Herne's wife, were also in the
cast.

†WOMEN IN THE THEATER PROFESSION. The modern era was one
of great change for women in general and more particularly for those working in the theatrical profession. From the beginnings of American theater,
women had been vividly present as **actresses,*†** and, by the mid-19th century, as **managers,*†** but other opportunities seemed closed. Despite this,
women **playwrights*†** made inroads. **Mercy Otis Warren** is often thought
of as the first woman dramatist in America; a devout patriot for the cause of
American independence, Warren wrote several plays satirizing the British
and their policies toward the colonies. Other pre–**Civil War** American wom-
en playwrights include **Sarah Pogson Smith**, **Mary Carr Clarke**, **Judith
Sargent Murray**, **Susanna Haswell Rowson**, **Charlotte Mary Sanford
Barnes**, **Frances Wright**, **Louisa Medina**, and perhaps above all, **Anna
Cora Mowatt**, whose *Fashion* (1845) is generally considered the finest play
by an American woman writer of the era. Mowatt wrote other plays, but
generally preferred acting, perhaps because it provided a consistent living
wage when playwriting, even successfully, did not. Virtually no one, male or
female, could make a living as a playwright alone prior to the late 19th
century.

In the mid-19th century, as actresses more frequently managed their own
companies, liberation from traditional roles for women both onstage and off
began to take place, beginning with more overt displays of women's issues
and **sexuality.*†** **Charlotte Cushman** and others performed **breeches
roles,†** while **Adah Isaacs Menken†** and **Lydia Thompson's†** British
Blondes scandalized some audiences with displays of the feminine form.
Women managers were often successful, though they suffered from the same
struggles as male managers—rising and falling fortunes, **theater fires,†** etc.
Few women managers were as effective or successful as **Laura Keene**, who
for a time had her own theater in New York and maintained a relatively long
career despite the tragic setback of leading the cast of one of her hits, **Tom**

Taylor's comedy *Our American Cousin*, at Washington, DC's **Ford's Theatre** on 14 April 1865 when **John Wilkes Booth**† assassinated President **Abraham Lincoln**, who was sitting in a theater box enjoying the performance. Keene's career never fully recovered from this, though she intrepidly continued on for several more years.

From the 1870s, European plays, particularly those by Henrik Ibsen† and, later, George Bernard Shaw,† offered deeper, more complex women characters than was typical in frequently stereotypical **melodramas**† in which women tended to be seen only in the traditional roles of wife, mother, an object of male desire, or a "fallen woman," though some dramatists managed in plays set in the past to depict more varied images of women. The emergence of realism*† via Ibsen's plays allowed American actresses such as Minnie Maddern Fiske† and Mary Shaw,† and later Alla Nazimova*† and Eva Le Gallienne,*† to address inequities faced by women in contemporary life. The last decades of the 19th century saw a remarkable flourishing of women dramatists, including Edith Ellis,† Marion Fairfax,† Harriet Ford,† Eleanor Gates, Georgia Douglas Johnson,† Margaret Mayo,† Marguerite Merington,† Martha Morton,† Lottie Blair Parker,† Josephine Preston Peabody,† Mary Roberts Rinehart,† Madeline Lucette Ryley,† and Rida Johnson Young.† Some of these, notably Ellis and Morton, staged their own works, though women **directors***† were comparatively rare until the mid-20th century, as were women **critics**.*† Given that there existed many strictures regarding women's attending and participating in theater, the earliest known woman critic billed herself with the pseudonym Arabella Sly, for her contributions to the *Virginia Gazette* in the 1750s. Her expressed concern was whether in a comic scene in *The Beaux Stratagem* a woman should shield her face with a fan. Around the same time, under another pseudonym, Clarinda, a woman critic for the *Maryland Gazette* chastised the comedians in a production of *Hamlet* who did not know their lines and ad-libbed vulgarities. How many other women critics wrote under pseudonyms has never been fully assessed, but women critics writing under their own names did not appear until the late 19th century.

WON AT LAST. **Steele MacKaye**'s five-act comedy-drama, along with his play **Rose Michel** (1875), brought him his first great successes in the United States. *Won at Last* opened on 10 December 1877 at **Wallack's Theatre**. **Rose Coghlan** and **John Gilbert** appeared in what **critic***† **William Winter** called an "analysis of the passions and affections" of its characters. Winter described the play and production as "a brilliant success" and commented that it "was set in costly and handsome scenery, acted with extraordinary felicity of talent, and received with a warmth of public favor such as seldom finds manifestation in this decorous theatre." However, despite Winter's approval, MacKaye was disappointed in Wallack's production, and he revised the play, renaming it *Aftermath; or, Won at Last*, and produced it on 23 April 1879 at his own **Madison Square Theatre**, emphasizing the play's comedy. *Won at Last* had a long stage life in **stock**.*†

WOOD, MRS. HENRY (1814–1887). Born Ellen Price in Worcester, England, she married Henry Wood in 1836 and lived with him in the South of France, where his banking and shipping interests kept him. When Wood's business interests subsequently failed, the couple moved to London, where Mrs. Henry Wood began writing. She wrote 30 novels, of which several were uncommonly popular, especially *East Lynne* (1861), which was adapted for the **melodramatic†** stage and became a major and enduring hit. There were competing stage adaptations of *East Lynne*, but the version written by **Clifton W. Tayleure** for **actress*† Lucille Western** was the most popular and is viewed as the definitive treatment. Wood's husband died in 1866, and she continued to write and edit periodicals until shortly before her death.

WOOD, MRS. JOHN (1831–1915). Born in Liverpool, England, as Matilda Charlotte Vining into a family of **actors**,*† she **toured*†** the provinces and developed her skills, especially in comedy. She married English actor John Wood in 1854, and they moved to Boston, where she made her American debut in *A Loan of a Lover* in 1854. They performed in Boston for three years prior to joining **Wallack's Theatre** in New York, where her talents began to exceed those of her husband. In the summer of 1857 they moved to San Francisco and appeared at **Maguire's Opera House** in comedies and **burlesques**.*† The Woods separated in 1859, and she moved back to New York to join **Dion Boucicault's†** company at the **Winter Garden Theatre**.

In April 1861, 10 days before the outbreak of the **Civil War**, Mrs. Wood sang "Dixie" in the final scene of the burlesque *Po-ca-hon-tas*, winning popularity for the song that the Confederate States of America would make their national anthem. She subsequently became **manager*†** of the **Olympic Theatre** in 1863, emphasizing burlesques and comedies as the theater's major fare. In 1866, she left for England and performed there until 1872, when she returned to the United States for that year's season, but subsequently returned to England permanently, managing a number of British theaters and appearing in **W. S. Gilbert**'s *Foggerty's Fairy* (1881).

WOOD, MR. JOSEPH (1801–1890), and MRS. JOSEPH WOOD (1802–1863). Born in Great Britain, Joseph Wood built a reputation as one of the **leading†** singing **actors*†** in both England and America. He married and partnered onstage with Mary Ann Paton. They visited the United States in 1833, but their initial success was marred by a public squabble with the editor of the *New York Courier and Inquirer* that concluded in a riot at the

Park Theatre. On another visit, they refused to appear at a benefit and were excoriated with bad publicity. After 1841, they no longer **toured***† America and ended their careers in England.

WOOD, WILLIAM BURKE (1779–1861). Born in Montreal, Canada, he moved with his family to New York and, as a young adult, worked as a clerk. He left for Annapolis, Maryland, to begin a theater career, and a family friend, **Thomas Wignell**, helped him achieve his aspirations as an **actor***† and **manager.***† Under the pseudonym George Barnwell, he made his first appearance in Annapolis in 1798, after which he acted in Philadelphia in *Secrets Worth Knowing*. In 1804, he married English **actress***† Juliana Westray, and she appeared with him in the theaters he managed.

In 1809, Wood bought into a management partnership with **William Warren**, who owned theaters in Philadelphia, Baltimore, and Washington, DC. From 1812 to 1820, he managed in Baltimore prior to taking the same position at Philadelphia's **Chestnut Street Theatre**. When the theater was destroyed by **fire,**† uninsured, he switched to the **Walnut Street Theatre**. As a **child**† actor, **Edwin Forrest** made his first appearance in *Douglas* with Wood. The Chestnut Street Theatre was rebuilt, and Wood appeared in the first production, **Richard Brinsley Sheridan**'s *The School for Scandal*, in 1822. In 1826, Wood and Warren ended their partnership, and Wood took on managing the **Arch Street Theatre**, but was unsuccessful there. The remainder of his career, until his retirement in 1846, was spent acting at various theaters in Philadelphia. In retirement, Wood observed the rise of the **star***† system and lamented its "degradation of the stage."

WOOD'S MINSTRELS. Established by legendary **minstrel***† man **E. P. Christy** sometime around 1842, Wood's Minstrels were a **touring***† company performing in **blackface.**† Success on tour led to New York, where they renamed themselves the Ethiopian Minstrel Band and performed at the American **Opera House**. In the early 1850s, the troupe fell apart and Christy retired, leading to the formation of another troupe, George Christy and Wood's Minstrels, led by Henry Wood, who included both male and female performers and various variety acts. Under Wood, the company moved from some minstrel traditions to performing lengthy **burlesque***† sketches satirizing popular plays and events.

A theater, Henry Wood's Marble Hall, opened in 1857 with an auditorium seating 1,000 patrons and was immediately successful with the public. Located on **Broadway***† near Prince Street, it operated until it was destroyed by fire in 1877. Meanwhile, Wood's Minstrels purchased an old synagogue in 1862 and converted it into a theater capable of seating 2,000. Wood retired in 1863, with the company taken over by George Wood, manager of the **Broad-**

way*† Theatre. A fire in 1868 seriously damaged the building, but it was renovated and reconstructed, and for the next 13 years it changed hands and names multiple times.

WOODWORTH, SAMUEL (1784–1842). Born in Scituate, Massachusetts, to a veteran of the **American Revolution**, he subsequently was apprenticed to the editor of a periodical, *Columbian Sentinel.* When Woodworth moved to New Haven, Connecticut, he worked briefly as publisher of the *Belles-Lettres Repository*, a weekly publication. Most of his fame came from poetry, but he wrote a novel, opera librettos, and plays, the latter including ***Bunker-Hill; or, The Death of General Warren*** (1817), *La Fayette; or, The Castle of Olmutz* (1824), ***The Widow's Son; or, Which is the Traitor?*** (1825), and *King Bridge Cottage* (1826). Most of his work featured characters and background related to the **American Revolution**, but he was best-known as lyricist of "The Old Oaken Bucket."

WOOLF, BENJAMIN E. (1836–1901). London-born Benjamin Edward Woolf came to America with his family as a youth. Woolf's father, an orchestra leader, conducted orchestras in numerous American cities, finally settling in New York, where he became a leading conductor. The senior Woolf trained his son on the violin and helped him get experience playing in theater orchestras. He became first violinist at the **Boston Museum** and moved from there to serving as music editor of the *Boston Saturday Evening Gazette.*

Woolf worked for the *Gazette* for 23 years and served for a time as its editor. When he left the *Gazette*, he became music editor for the *Boston Herald* and remained in that job until his death. For the theater, Woolf's major accomplishment was in writing 62 plays, including ***The Mighty Dollar*** (1875), which was written for **actor***† **William J. Florence**. Others included *Lawn Tennis* (1880) and *Westward Ho* (1894), among many **opéra bouffe** works. Woolf married Josephine Orton (1841?–1926), who was **leading†** **actress***† at the Boston Museum for a time and appeared in **Dion Boucicault's†** plays *Arrah-na-Pogue†* and *The Colleen Bawn*.

WRIGHT, FRANCES (1795–1852). Fanny Wright, as she was widely known, was born in Dundee, Scotland, to a wealthy family. Through her politically active father, she got to know important people, including Adam Smith and the Marquis de Lafayette. She was orphaned when both of her parents died young, and she eventually left Scotland for a two-year **tour***† of the United States in 1818.

For her time, Wright had what were considered radical ideas about the equality of **women***† and men, believing that women should be educated. Wright's feminism, which included a belief in birth control and **sexual***† freedom, was matched by her devotion to the abolition of slavery and free public education. She expressed the view that progress for women was essential for society's progress. Wright established several publications to share her views, but was mocked for giving public lectures in the late 1820s when it was deemed controversial and inappropriate for women to speak in public.

Wright accompanied Lafayette on his famed tour of the United States and was a controversial advocate for her political beliefs. She wrote one play, *Altorf* (1819), a tragedy about Swiss independence, which was produced by **James W. Wallack**, but closed after a mere three performances. Wright, who became an American citizen in 1825, is not known to have written any other plays, but she produced numerous controversial political and social tracts.

WYNDHAM, CHARLES (1837–1919). Born Charles Culverwell in Liverpool, England, Charles Wyndham studied both religion and medicine, but he became involved in **amateur**† theatricals and moved into the profession and, ultimately, to the United States. During the American **Civil War**, Wyndham used his medical skills to serve as a doctor for the Confederate Army. He acted during the **war***† as well, but with little success and returned to England until 1869, when back in America he was well received as a member of **Wallack's Theatre** company. He subsequently set up his own troupe, but returned to England in 1873. In London, he became a major **actor***† and **manager,***† winning great fame and an ultimate knighthood. He returned to America for several brief **tours***† prior to the end of his career.

†YANKEE CHARACTER/PLAYS. Characters† from New England or otherwise identified as "Yankee" date to the 18th century, including "Jonathan" of the first American comedy, **Royall Tyler**'s *The Contrast*. The first true exemplar of the character as he would be seen in much 19th-century American theater, particularly comedy, appeared in the 1820s. Such figures of New England origin, and with a personality combining a variety of attributes, including sentiment, patriotic fervor, simple good-heartedness, rustic hominess (with a critical eye for urban and European opposites), an inclination toward frugality, and a penchant for storytelling, were prevalent after that time and were usually comically heroic, though there were exceptions.

The character in his most familiar guise was often named Jonathan, although he appeared under other names (including, for example, Hiram Dodge of Morris Barnett's 1841 one-act farce, *Yankee Peddler; or, Old Times in Virginia*). Perfected by a series of **actors*†** beginning with Englishman **Charles Mathews**, the character was taken on by American actors including **James H. Hackett, George Handel "Yankee" Hill, Danforth Marble**, and Joshua Pilsee, all before the mid-19th century. The character became a **stock*†** figure in American drama and can be seen in a range of "rustic" characters or "**rubes**,"† as George M. Cohan*† subsequently labeled them in his plays and **musicals*†** as late as the early 20th century. Such later guises of these characters, from **James A. Herne**'s† New Englander "Captain Dan Marble" in *Sag Harbor†* (1900) to the numerous midwestern variations populating numerous comedies and **musicals*†** from the 1910s to the 1930s, continued the tradition.

†*YANKEE CHRONOLOGY; OR, HUZZA FOR THE CONSTITUTION!.*
William Dunlap's 1812 patriotic play with music was much applauded during the **War of 1812**. Only days after the actual event, the 31 August 1812 sea battle between the American ship *Constitution* and the British *Guerriere*, the battle is recounted by sailor Ben Bundle, Dunlap's fictional participant in the battle. Among the one-act play's embellishments is a song remembering the **American Revolution**, an embellishment that enhanced the nationalistic

background of the play, as did "Yankee Chronology," a song Dunlap had written for the previous Fourth of July and included in the play, along with the addition of an extra stanza celebrating the victory of the *Constitution*. The play opened on 7 September 1812 at the **Park Theatre**.

†*YANKEE PEDDLER; OR, OLD TIMES IN VIRGINIA*. British **actor*†** and **playwright*†** Morris Barnett's one-act farce published by **Samuel French*†** in 1841 and performed that same year in St. Louis, with subsequent productions in Louisville in 1845 and Chicago in 1853, was one of many popular British-made comedies on American stages in the mid-19th century. It focused on Hiram Dodge, played in its original production by **Dan Marble**, a peddler in the tradition of the American Yankee **stock*†** **character,†** who is an underhanded parasite without the usual affection for liberty and independence typical of his ilk. Much humor was generated by Dodge's language, which was rife with contemporary slang (and prejudices), as when he brags, "Oh, you can scrape me to death if I ain't the slickest white man about these diggin's. But, squire, you must confess I'm some pumpkins on speculations."

THE *YANKEY IN ENGLAND*. This comedy by **American Revolutionary** soldier and diplomat David Humphreys is perhaps the first to transplant the familiar **Yankee†** **character†** from the United States to foreign settings. The play is believed to have been performed only once, in **amateur*†** circumstances in 1814, when the boys employed in Humphreys's mill played the roles. *The Yankey in England* has a convoluted plot in which an American Whig and a Tory meet in London, where they encounter a French count and his wife, who is an adventuress with a "Yankey" servant, Doolittle, a sometimes clever bungler. When the countess considers taking poison when her romantic misadventures go amiss, another Yankee, Newman, saves the day.

YE BARE AND YE CUBB [YE BEAR AND YE CUBB]. Written by Cornelius Watkinson, Philip Howard, and William Darby, this first play in English staged in America was presented in Fowkes Tavern in Accomack County, Virginia, on 27 August 1665. The performance met with puritanical resistance, and Watkinson, Howard, and Darby were compelled to reproduce the performance in court, where they were exonerated of the charge of licentiousness. Only Darby was arrested. The text does not survive, although it is believed that its content was political in nature, but little else is known about the play or its staging.

YEAMANS, ANNIE (1835–1912). Born Annie Griffiths on the Isle of Man, she was the daughter of **actors***† who took her with them to perform in Australia when she was a **child**.† From her teens, she performed in **circuses***† as an **equestrian**† and traveled the world performing. She married Edward Yeamans, a clown, and gave birth to three daughters, before they moved to San Francisco. When Edward Yeamans died suddenly shortly after their arrival, and with no recourse to support her children, Yeamans moved to New York and became an **actress***† particularly skilled in comedy, although she performed in all manner of plays.

Yeamans acted opposite **G. L. Fox** in an 1871 revival of *Humpty Dumpty* and also in revivals of *Uncle Tom's Cabin*† and *Under the Gaslight*, among many others. Yeamans first performed with **Edward Harrigan**† in 1877 and continued as his **leading lady**† for 18 years, originating the role of Cordelia in the Mulligan Guard plays with Harrigan and **Tony Hart**.† After her years with Harrigan, she appeared in several **musicals***† (including her last, *The Echo*, in 1910), as well as *The Great Train Robbery* (1895), *Why Smith Left Home* (1899), and *Under Cover*† (1903), the latter with Harrigan. Her daughters all went on the stage, and one, Jennie Yeamans (1862–1906), had considerable success, occasionally appearing with her mother. Known in her youth for beauty and her **Irish** charm, when Yeamans died her *New York Times* obituary celebrated her 66-year-long career, calling her an "old actress, who had seemed for so many years one of the young actresses."

*†YIDDISH THEATER. Yiddish theater, which emerged in Europe in the early 18th century, flourished in European capitals and in America, particularly New York City, from the late 19th century. Focused on dramas by Jews written and performed in Yiddish, the language of the Eastern European Ashkenazic Jewish community, Yiddish theater became known for its diversity, including plays in every theatrical genre as well as **operetta**† and **musical***† comedy, **revues**,*† and variety entertainments. In the United States, Yiddish theater also encompassed a wide array of classic and contemporary plays from other cultures translated into the Yiddish language and cultural idiom.

Avrom Goldfaden† is generally regarded as the founder of the first professional Yiddish theater troupe in Romania, after which he moved it to Bucharest and ultimately performed in New York. Initially an all-male company, Goldfaden's troupe eventually included **women**,*† sometimes in male roles, as when Molly Picon*† became popular in the **stock***† role of Schmendrick, a comic type that was one of many stereotypical roles featured in every early Yiddish play. While Goldfaden and others had long careers in Eastern Europe, the Russian ban on Yiddish theater of 1883 pushed the entire industry to Western Europe and the United States. The popularity of Yiddish theater in American continued into the mid-20th century.

YORICK'S LOVE. Written by **William Dean Howells**† and first produced by **Lawrence Barrett**† (playing the **leading**† role) at Cincinnati's Grand **Opera House** on 11 October 1877, the play found some favor with cultivated audiences and remained in Barrett's repertoire† for some years, including a much-publicized engagement† at the **Star Theatre** on 13 February 1885 with **Louis James**† and **Marie Wainwright**† in support. A *New York Times* critic*† applauded the **actors**,*† but found the play "a constant strain upon the sympathies" of an audience, while other **critics***† were somewhat more appreciative.

    Mark Twain, who attended a 10 March 1880 performance of the play, wrote to Howells that the "magnificence of it is beyond praise. The language is so beautiful, the passion so fine, the plot so ingenious, the whole thing so stirring, so charming, so pathetic!" Adapted from Manuel Tamayo y Baus's 1867 play *Un drama Nuevo*, the **melodrama**,† which was inspired by characters from **Shakespeare**,*† was also performed at times under the title *A New Play* and focuses on a jealous husband racked with doubts about his wife's faithfulness.

THE YOUNG CAROLINIANS; OR, AMERICANS IN ALGIERS. **Sarah Pogson Smith**'s 1818 drama depicts a true event, the 1785 capture of American sailors by Barbary pirates and their subsequent imprisonment in Algiers. Pogson presents the events as a test of a new nation's resolve to defend its commitment to liberty. For many years, *The Young Carolinians*, which may never have been produced, was misattributed to Maria Pinckney. Doreen Alvarez Saar has called the play "an important feminist transcription of the ideas of the **American Revolution**."

Z

ZIP; OR, POINT LYNNE LIGHT. **Fred Marsden**'s play about a lively girl, Zip, played notably by **Lotta Crabtree**,† opened at the **Booth Theatre**† on 20 March 1874. Zip lives with a lighthouse keeper she believes to be her father. When some unscrupulous men murder him and disable the light in an attempt to sink a ship, Zip improbably saves the day. A passenger on the ship turns out to be Zip's real mother, who takes her to England to claim a major inheritance. Despite a plot to steal her newfound fortune, Zip again overcomes all difficulties and finds love in the process. Crabtree scored a major success and found one of her most enduring vehicles in Marsden's play, which provided ample opportunities for showcasing her charm and **musical***† talents.

Bibliography

CONTENTS

Introduction	487
Bibliographies and General Reference Works	488
Historical and Critical Studies	491
General Theater Studies	492
Cultural and Regional Studies	494
Acting and Actors	498
Playwriting and Playwrights	499
Producing, Directing, Management, and Scenography	499
Critics and Criticism	500
Theaters and Architecture	500
Melodrama	501
African Americans	502
Jewish Americans	503
Native Americans	503
Other Ethnic Groups	504
Minstrels, Vaudeville, Burlesques, Musicals, and Popular Fare	504
Women	508
Biographies and Memoirs of Theater Artists	509
General	509
Actors and Actresses	509
Playwrights	516
Critics	519
Producers, Directors, Managers, and Scenographers	520
Plays and Anthologies of Plays	520
Theater Practice, Management, Technology, and Terminology	523

INTRODUCTION

The era of early American theater can be a bibliophile's delight, though locating published copies of plays prior to the mid-19th century is a challenge. However, it is possible to collect many volumes with gilt-encrusted covers, lavish illustrations, and abundant anecdotes that were published, particularly from the late 18th century. Though there was little interest prior to the mid-19th century, the theatergoing public became avid for books that afforded glimpses of theatrical life and published plays, as well as memoirs by theatrical personalities. Not only actors, but managers, playwrights, and critics all published autobiographies or retrospective memoirs of one kind or another. Increasingly during the first half of the 19th century, writers produced a steady flow of books offering collective coverage of a selection of artists.

While the books published during the 19th century were aimed at a general readership and tended to anecdotal coverage of mainstream theater, recent studies by contemporary scholars have more often focused on placing early American theater history in its cultural, economic, and sociological context while embracing a broader range of theatrical activities, including ethnic and popular entertainments outside traditional venues. There has also been a major surge of scholarly interest in vaudeville, burlesque, minstrel shows, and showboats, among other popular forms. Current scholars have also turned their attention to overlooked groups—women, African Americans, Native Americans, Jewish Americans—producing significant scholarship on artists and works little known out of their time and now more fully understood within the context of American history and culture. On the whole, however, the quaint charm of the Revolutionary War–era theater, the rise of melodrama, and the evolution of a range of popular entertainments offer critics and historians a rich period for study. Most of the bibliographies and general reference works listed here are not specific to the early American period (though centrally include it), but instead cover a wider swath.

The breakdown of the bibliography into categories is somewhat problematic. For example, the decision whether to place a collection of short biographies of actors under historical studies of actors or under biographies and memoirs of actors was resolved by considering where the reader would be most likely to look for it: under historical studies of actors. Only in very few instances have there been duplicated listings under more than one category.

BIBLIOGRAPHIES AND GENERAL REFERENCE WORKS

The standard ready references for American theater that reside on every theater person's bookshelf are Bordman's *Oxford Companion to American Theatre* and Wilmeth and Miller's *Cambridge Guide to American Theatre.* Although comparable in format, each has distinctive features. Bordman inclines toward the commercial theater and takes an anecdotal approach. Wilmeth and Miller are more comprehensive, including more extensive coverage of ethnic theaters, written with an economy of words. Kennedy's essay-style entries in the *Oxford Encyclopedia of Theatre & Performance* encompass American as well as international theater. Sherman's labor of love is interesting for its inclusion of many otherwise neglected figures, but his spelling of names and other data need to be checked against other sources. For more details about performers, one turns to Bryan's *Stage Lives* and Moyer's *American Actors, 1861–1910.*

A range of Internet sources are readily available online to supply production specifics about plays; the Internet Broadway database is a particularly useful quick resource for plays produced in New York in the late 19th century, credits, dates, and production personnel; however, prior to 1880, such information included tends to be incomplete or unavailable.

Bordman, Gerald. *American Theatre: A Chronicle of Comedy and Drama, 1869–1914.* New York: Oxford University, 1994.

———. *The Oxford Companion to American Theatre*, 2nd edition. New York: Oxford University, 1992.

Bordman, Gerald, and Thomas S. Hischak. *The Oxford Companion to American Theatre*, 3rd edition. New York: Oxford University, 2004.

Brown, T. Allston. *History of the American Stage: Biographical Sketches of Nearly Every Member of the Profession That Has Appeared on the American Stage, from 1733 to 1870.* New York: Burt Franklin, 1870.

Bryan, George B. *American Theatrical Regulation 1607–1900: Conspectus and Texts.* Metuchen, NJ: Scarecrow Press, 1993.

———. *Stage Deaths: A Biographical Guide to International Theatre Obituaries, 1850–1990*, 2 vols. Westport, CT: Greenwood, 1991.

———. *Stage Lives: A Bibliography and Index to Theatrical Biographies in English.* Westport, CT: Greenwood, 1985.

Bryer, Jackson R., ed. *The Facts on File Companion to American Drama.* New York: Facts on File, 2004.

Cassell Companion to Theatre. London: Cassell, 1997.

Durham, Weldon B., ed. *American Theatre Companies, 1749–1887.* Westport, CT: Greenwood, 1986.

Fisher, James. *The Historical Dictionary of Contemporary American Theater: 1930–2010.* Lanham, MD: Scarecrow Press, 2011.

Fisher, James, and Felicia Hardison Londré. *The Historical Dictionary of American Theater: Modernism: 1880–1930.* Lanham, MD: Scarecrow, 2008.

Gassner, John, and Edward Quinn, eds. *The Reader's Encyclopedia of World Drama.* New York: Crowell, 1969.

Griffiths, Trevor R. *The Ivan R. Dee Guide to Plays and Playwrights.* Chicago: Ivan R. Dee, 2003.

Hewitt, Barnard. *Theatre U.S.A., 1665–1957.* New York: McGraw-Hill, 1959.

Hixon, Don L., and Don A. Hennessee. *Nineteenth-Century American Drama: A Finding Guide*. Metuchen, NJ: Scarecrow Press, 1977.

Hodge, Francis Richard. *Yankee Theatre: The Image of America on the Stage, 1825–1850*. Austin: University of Texas, 1965.

Hughes, Glenn. *A History of the American Theatre, 1700–1950*. New York: Samuel French, 1951.

———. *The Story of the Theatre*. New York: Samuel French, 1954.

Hutton, Laurence. *Curiosities of the American Stage*. New York: Harper & Brothers, 1891.

Ireland, Joseph N. *Records of the New York Stage*, 2 vols. New York: Burt Franklin, 1968.

Johnson, Odai, and William J. Burling, eds. *The Colonial American Stage, 1665–1784: A Documentary Calendar*. Madison, NJ: Fairleigh Dickinson, 2002.

Kennedy, Dennis, ed. *The Oxford Encyclopedia of Theatre & Performance*, 2 vols. New York: Oxford University, 2003.

Lauter, Paul, ed. *A Companion to American Literature and Culture*. Oxford: Wiley-Blackwell, 2010.

Mainiero, Lina, ed. *American Women Writers*, 4 vols. New York: Ungar, 1979.

McGill, Raymond D. *Notable Names in the American Theatre*. Clifton, NJ: James T. White, 1976.

Meserve, Walter J. *American Drama to 1900: A Guide to Information Sources*. Detroit, MI: Gale, 1980.

———. *An Outline History of American Drama*. New York: Feedback Books & Prospero Press, 1994.

———. *Heralds of Promise: The Drama of the American People during the Age of Jackson, 1829–1949*. Westport, CT: Greenwood, 1986.

Moody, Richard. *America Takes the Stage*. Bloomington: Indiana University, 1955.

Moses, Montrose J., and John Mason Brown, eds. *The American Theatre As Seen by Its Critics, 1752–1934*. New York: W. W. Norton, 1934.

Moyer, Ronald L. *American Actors, 1861–1910: An Annotated Bibliography of Books Published in the United States in English from 1861 through 1976*. Troy, NY: Whitson, 1979.

Nelson, Emmanuel S., ed. *African American Dramatists: An A-to-Z Guide*. Westport, CT: Greenwood, 2004.

New York Times Theater Reviews, 1870–1930, 8 vols. New York: The New York Times & Arno Press, 1971–1975.

New York Times Theater Reviews Index 1870–1919. New York: The New York Times & Arno Press, 1975.

Odell, George C. D. *Annals of the New York Stage*, 15 vols. New York: Columbia University, 1927–1949.

Patterson, Michael. *The Oxford Dictionary of Plays*. New York: Oxford University, 2005.

Pavis, Patrice. *Dictionary of the Theatre: Terms, Concepts, and Analysis.* Toronto: University of Toronto, 1998.

Perkins, George, Barbara Perkins, and Phillip Leininger, eds. *Benét's Reader's Encyclopedia of American Literature*. New York: HarperCollins, 1991.

Peterson, Bernard L., Jr. *The African American Theatre Directory, 1816–1960: A Comprehensive Guide to Early Black Theatre Organizations, Companies, Theatres, and Performing Groups*. Foreword by Errol Hill. Westport, CT: Greenwood, 1997.

Robinson, Alice M., Vera Mowry Roberts, and Milly S. Barranger, eds. *Notable Women in the American Theatre: A Biographical Dictionary*. Westport, CT: Greenwood, 1989.

Seilhamer, George O. *History of the American Theatre*, 3 vols. Philadelphia, PA: Globe Printing House, 1888–1891.

Sherman, Robert L. *Actors and Authors: With Composers and Managers Who Helped Make Them Famous: A Chronological Record and Brief Biography of Theatrical Celebrities from 1750 to 1950*. Chicago: Robert L. Sherman, 1951.

Wilmeth, Don B. *The American Stage to World War I: A Guide to Information Sources*. Detroit, MI: Gale, 1978.

———. *The Language of American Popular Entertainment: A Glossary of Argot, Slang, and Terminology*. Westport, CT: Greenwood, 1981.

Wilmeth, Don B., and Tice Miller. *Cambridge Guide to American Theatre*. New York: Cambridge University, 1993.

Witham, Barry, ed. *Theatre in the United States, Vol. 1: 1750–1915, Theatre in the Colonies and the United States: A Documentary History*. Cambridge: Cambridge University, 2009.

HISTORICAL AND CRITICAL STUDIES

For histories of the American stage prior to 1880, such works as Dunlap's *A History of the American Theatre from Its Origins to 1832* is essential, as is Odell's towering 15-volume *Annals of the New York Stage*. Bernheim's economic history of American theater remains invaluable and is long overdue to be reprinted. For general histories, volume 1 of Wilmeth and Bigsby's three-volume *Cambridge History of American Theatre* and Londré and Watermeier's *History of North American Theater* complement each other nicely. Earlier surveys include those by Coad and Mims, Hewitt, Hughes, Morris, and Wilson. Among regional theater histories, Schoberlin's 1941 study of Colorado theater remains particularly engaging. Londré's research for *The Enchanted Years of the Stage* generated some information about Kansas City theater in the mid-19th century that proved useful. Shattuck's *Shakespeare on the American Stage* is a fascinating text embellished by a wealth of illustrations. Mary Henderson's book on New York City's theaters contributes greatly to our understanding of the architecture and changing urban landscape there. Among a rapidly growing list of resources on African American theater, Hill and Hatch's *History of African American Theatre* merits particular attention.

General Theater Studies

Bassham, Ben L. *The Theatrical Photographs of Napoleon Sarony*. Kent, OH: Kent State University, 1995.

Bernheim, Alfred L. *The Business of the Theatre: An Economic History of the American Theatre, 1750–1932*. New York: Benjamin Blom, 1962 (reprint of 1932 edition).

Brown, Jared. *The Theatre in America during the Revolution*. New York: Cambridge University, 2007.

Bryer, Jackson, and Mary C. Hartig. *The Facts on File Companion to American Drama*. New York: Facts on File, 2003.

Chinoy, Helen Krich, and Linda Walsh Jenkins. *Women in American Theatre*. New York: Crown, 1981.

Cliff, Nigel. *The Shakespeare Riots: Revenge, Drama, and Death in Nineteenth-Century America*. New York: Random House, 2007.

Coad, Oral Sumner, and Edwin Mims Jr. *The American Stage*. New Haven, CT: Yale University, 1929.

Conolly, L. W., ed. *Theatrical Touring and Founding in North America*. Westport, CT: Greenwood, 1982.

Csida, Joseph, and June Bundy Csida. *American Entertainment: A Unique History of Popular Show Business*. New York: Watson-Guptill, 1978.

Dunlap, William. *A History of the American Theatre*. New York: J. J. Harper, 1832.

Fields, Armond, and L. M. Fields. *From the Bowery to Broadway: Lew Fields and the Roots of American Popular Theater*. New York: Oxford University, 1993.

Graham, Philip. *Showboats: The History of an American Institution*. Austin: University of Texas, 1951.

Hewitt, Barnard. *Theatre U.S.A. 1665–1957*. New York: McGraw-Hill, 1959.

Hischak, Thomas S. *The Theatregoer's Almanac: A Collection of Lists, People, History, and Commentary on the American Theatre*. Westport, CT: Greenwood, 1997.

Hixon, Donald L., and Don A. Hennessee. *Nineteenth-Century American Drama: A Finding Guide*. Metuchen, NJ: Scarecrow, 1977.

Hornblow, Arthur. *A History of the Theatre in America*. Vol. 1. Philadelphia: J. B. Lippincott, 1919.

Hughes, Glenn. *A History of the American Theatre, 1700–1950*. New York: Samuel French, 1951.

Johnson, Claudia D., and Vernon E. Johnson. *Nineteenth-Century Theatrical Memoirs*. Westport, CT: Greenwood, 1982.

Johnson, Odai. *Absence and Memory in Colonial American Theatre: Fiorelli's Plaster*. New York: Palgrave Macmillan, 2006.

Kierner, Cynthia A. *The Contrast: Manners, Morals, and Authority in the Early American Republic*. New York: New York University, 2007.

Lindfors, Bernth, ed. *Africans on Stage: Studies in Ethnological Show Business*. Bloomington: Indiana University, 2000.

Londré, Felicia Hardison. *The Enchanted Years of the Stage: Kansas City at the Crossroads of American Theater, 1870–1930*. Columbia: University of Missouri, 2007.

Londré, Felicia Hardison, and Daniel J. Watermeier. *The History of North American Theater: The United States, Canada, and Mexico from Pre-Columbian Times to the Present*. New York: Continuum, 1998.

Mayorga, Margaret G. *A Short History of the American Drama*. New York: Dodd, Mead, 1932.

McArthur, Benjamin. "Theatrical Clubs of the Nineteenth Century: Tradition versus Assimilation in the Acting Community," *Theatre Survey* 23 (November 1982), 197–212.

Meserve, Walter J. *An Emerging Entertainment: The Drama of the American People to 1828*. Bloomington: Indiana University, 1977.

———. *An Outline History of American Drama*. Totowa, NJ: Littlefield Adams, 1965.

Miller, Tice L. *Entertaining the Nation: American Drama in the Eighteenth and Nineteenth Centuries*. Carbondale: Southern Illinois, 2007.

Morris, Lloyd. *Curtain Time: The Story of the American Theater*. New York: Random House, 1953.

Nathans, Heather. *Early American Theatre from the Revolution to Thomas Jefferson: Into the Hands of the People*. Cambridge: Cambridge University, 2003.

Orr, John. *Tragic Drama and Modern Society: Studies in the Social and Literary Theory of Drama from 1870 to the Present*. New York: Macmillan, 1981.

Paul, Joel Richard. *Unlikely Allies: How a Merchant, a Playwright, and a Spy Saved the American Revolution*. New York: Riverhead, 2009.

Quinn, Arthur Hobson. *A History of American Drama, from the Beginning to the Civil War*. New York: Appleton-Century-Crofts, 1943.

———. *A History of American Drama, from the Civil War to the Present Day*. New York: F. S. Crofts, 1936.

Rankin, Hugh F. *The Theatre in Colonial America*. Chapel Hill: University of North Carolina, 1965.

Reiss, Benjamin. *Theaters of Madness: Insane Asylums and Nineteenth-Century American Culture*. Chicago: University of Chicago, 2008.

Richards, Jeffrey H. *Theater Enough: American Culture and the Metaphor of the World Stage, 1607–1789*. Durham, NC: Duke University, 1991.

Richardson, Gary A. *American Drama from the Colonial Period through World War I: A Critical History*. New York: Twayne, 1993.

Ruyter, Nancy Lee Chalfa. *The Cultivation of Body and Mind in Nineteenth-Century American Delsartism*. Westport, CT: Praeger, 1999.

Shaffer, Jason. *Performing Patriotism: National Identity in the Colonial and Revolutionary American Theater*. Philadelphia: University of Pennsylvania, 2007.

Shattuck, Charles H. *Shakespeare on the American Stage: From the Hallams to Edwin Booth*. Washington, DC: Folger Shakespeare Library, 1978.

Unger, Harlow Giles. *Improbable Patriot: The Secret History of Monsieur de Beaumarchais, the French Playwright Who Saved the American Revolution*. Hanover, NH: University Press of New England, 2011.

Wilmeth, Don B., and Christopher Bigsby, eds. *The Cambridge History of American Theatre, Volume I: Beginnings to 1870*. Cambridge: Cambridge University, 1998.

Wilmeth, Don B., and Christopher Bigsby, eds. *The Cambridge History of American Theatre, Volume II: 1870–1945*. Cambridge: Cambridge University, 1999.

Wilson, Garff B. *Three Hundred Years of American Drama and Theatre, from Ye Bare and Ye Cubb to Chorus Line*. Englewood Cliffs, NJ: Prentice-Hall, 1973.

Cultural and Regional Studies

Ackerman, Alan L. *The Portable Theater: American Literature and the Nineteenth-Century Stage*. Baltimore, MD: Johns Hopkins University, 2002.

Aleandri, Emelise. *The Italian-American Immigrant Theatre of New York City, 1746–1899*. Lewiston, NY: Edwin Mellen, 2012.

Altschuler, Bruce E. *Acting Presidents: 100 Years of Plays about the Presidents*. New York: Palgrave Macmillan, 2010.

Anderson, John. *The American Theater in New York*. New York: Dial, 1938.

Ashby, LeRoy. *With Amusement for All: A History of American Popular Culture since 1830*. Lexington: University Press of Kentucky, 2006.

Baker, Meredith Henne. *The Richmond Theater Fire: Early America's First Great Disaster*. Baton Rogue: Louisiana State University, 2012.

Bank, Rosemarie K. *Theatre Culture in America, 1825–1860*. Cambridge: Cambridge University, 2007.

Barrett, Daniel, and Beth R. Barrett. *High Drama: Colorado's Historic Theatres*. Lake City, CO: Western Reflections, 2005.

Bogar, Thomas A. *American Presidents Attend the Theatre: The Playgoing Experiences of Each Chief Executive*. Jefferson, NC: McFarland, 2009.

Brown, T. A. *A History of the New York Stage from the First Performance in 1732 to 1901*, 3 vols. New York: Dodd, Mead, 1903.

Butsch, Richard. *The Making of American Audiences: From Stage to Television, 1750–1990*. Cambridge: Cambridge University, 2000.

Caldwell, Howard. *The Golden Age of Indianapolis Theaters*. Bloomington, IN: Quarry, 2010.

Carson, William G. *Managers in Distress: The St. Louis Stage, 1840–1844*. New York: Ayer, 1949.

Casto, Marilyn. *Actors, Audiences, and Historic Theaters of Kentucky*. Lexington: University Press of Kentucky, 2000.

Clapp, W. W., Jr. *A Record of the Boston Stage*. Boston: J. Munroe, 1853.

Cliff, Nigel. *The Shakespeare Riots: Revenge, Drama, and Death in Nineteenth-Century America*. New York: Random House, 2007.

Collins, Thomas P. *Stage-Struck Settlers in the Sun-Kissed Land: The Amateur Theatre in Territorial Prescott, 1868–1903*. Tuscon, AZ: Wheatmark, 2007.

Conner, Lynn. *Pittsburgh in Stages: Two Hundred Years of Theater*. Pittsburgh, PA: University of Pittsburgh, 2007.

Daniels, Bruce C. *Puritans at Plays: Leisure and Recreation in Colonial New England*. New York: Palgrave Macmillan, 1996.

Demastes, William W., and Iris Smith Fischer, eds. *Interrogating America through Theatre and Performance*. New York: Palgrave Macmillan, 2007.

Dormon, James H., Jr. *Theater in the Antebellum South*. Chapel Hill: University of North Carolina, 2011.

Ellis, Joseph J. *After the Revolution: Profile of Early American Culture*. New York: Norton, 1979.

Fichtelberg, Joseph. *Risk Culture: Performance and Danger in Early America*. Ann Arbor: University of Michigan, 2010.

Freedman, Morris. *American Drama in Social Context*. Carbondale: Southern Illinois University, 1971.

Gallegly, Joseph. *Footlights on the Border: The Galveston and Houston Stage before 1900*. The Hague, Netherlands: Mouton, 1962.

Glenn, George D., and Richard L. Poole. *The Opera Houses of Iowa*. Ames: Iowa State University, 1993.

Goodall, Jane. *Performance and Evolution in the Age of Darwin: Out of the Natural Order*. New York: Routledge, 2002.

Hall, Roger A. *Performing the American Frontier, 1870–1906*. Cambridge: Cambridge University, 2001.

Hartman, John Geoffrey. *The Development of American Social Comedy from 1787 to 1936*. Philadelphia: University of Pennsylvania, 1939.

Hill, West T. *The Theatre in Kentucky: 1790–1820*. Lexington: University of Kentucky, 2009.

Hodge, Francis. *Yankee Theatre: The Image of America on the Stage, 1825–1850*. Austin: University of Texas, 1965.

Hughes, Amy E. *Spectacles of Reform: Theater and Activism in Nineteenth-Century America*. Ann Arbor: University of Michigan, 2014.

Ireland, Joseph Norton. *Records of the New York Stage, from 1750 to 1860*, 2 vols. New York: T. H. Morrell, 1866–1867.

James, Henry. *The Scenic Art: Notes on Acting and the Drama*. Edited by Allen Wade. New Brunswick, NJ: Rutgers University, 1948.

Jones, Jan. *Renegades, Showmen & Angels: A Theatrical History of Fort Worth, 1873–2001*. Fort Worth: Texas Christian University, 2006.

Kendall, John S. *The Golden Age of the New Orleans Theatre*. New York: Greenwood, 1968.

King, Donald C. *Theatres of Boston: A Stage and Screen History*. Jefferson, NC: McFarland, 2008.

Kippola, Karl M. *Acts of Manhood: The Performance of Masculinity on the American Stage, 1828–1865*. New York: Palgrave Macmillan, 2012.

Koon, Helene Wickham. *How Shakespeare Won the West: Players and Performances in America's Gold Rush, 1849–1865*. Jefferson, NC: McFarland, 1989.

Levine, Lawrence. *Highbrow/Lowbrow: The Emergence of Cultural Hierarchy in America*. Cambridge, MA: Harvard University, 1990.

Lindenberger, Herbert. *Historical Drama: The Relation of Literature and Reality*. Chicago: University of Chicago, 1975.

Londré, Felicia Hardison. *Much Ado about Shakespeare on Midwestern Frontier Stages*. Lincoln: University of Nebraska-Lincoln: The Geske Lectures, 2005.

McDonald, Nancy. *If You Can Play Scranton: A Theatrical History: 1871–2010*. Archbald, PA: TB, 2011.

MacMinn, George R. *The Theater of the Golden Era in California*. Caldwell, ID: Caxton, 1941.

McNamara, Brooks. *Step Right Up*. Jackson: University Press of Mississippi, 1996.

Meserve, Walter J. *Heralds of Promise: The Drama of the American People during the Age of Jackson, 1829–1849*. New York: Greenwood, 1986.

Murphy, Brenda. *American Realism and American Drama, 1880–1940*. New York: Cambridge University, 1987.

Nemerov, Alexander. *Acting in the Night: Macbeth and the Places of the Civil War*. Berkeley: University of California, 2010.

Parrington, Vernon L. *The Beginnings of Critical Realism in America, 1860–1920*. New York: Harcourt, Brace, and World, 1930.

Pizer, Donald. *Realism and Naturalism in Nineteenth-Century American Literature*, rev. ed. Carbondale: Southern Illinois University, 1984.

Poggi, Jack. *Theater in America: The Impact of Economic Forces, 1870–1967*. Ithaca, NY: Cornell University, 1968.

Pollock, Thomas C. *The Philadelphia Theatre in the Eighteenth Century*. Philadelphia: University of Pennsylvania, 1933.

Rebhorn, Matthew. *Pioneer Performances: Staging the Frontier*. New York: Oxford University, 2012.

Reed, Peter P. *Rogue Performances: Staging the Underclasses in Early American Theatre Culture*. New York: Palgrave Macmillan, 2009.

Reiss, Benjamin. *Theaters of Madness: Insane Asylums and Nineteenth-Century American Culture*. Chicago: University of Chicago, 2008.

Schnitzspahn, Karen L. *Stars of the Jersey Shore: A Theatrical History 1860s–1930s*. Atglen, PA: Schiffer, 2007.

Schoberlin, Melvin. *From Candles to Footlights: A Biography of Pike's Peak Theatre, 1859–1876*. Denver, CO: Old West, 1941.

Segrave, Kerry. *Ticket Scalping: An American History, 1850–2005*. Jefferson, NC: McFarland, 2006.

Smith, Gay. *Lady Macbeth in America: From the Stage to the White House*. New York: Palgrave Macmillan, 2010.

Sova, Dawn B. *Banned Plays: Censorship Histories of 125 Stage Dramas*. New York: Facts on File, 2004.

Springhall, John. *The Genesis of Mass Culture: Show Business Live in America, 1840 to 1940*. New York: Palgrave Macmillan, 2008.

Teague, Frances. *Shakespeare and the American Popular Stage*. New York: Cambridge University, 2006.

Tenneriello, Susan. *Spectacle Culture and American Identity, 1815–1940*. New York: Palgrave Macmillan, 2013.

Westgate, J. Chris. *Staging the Slums, Slumming the Stage: Class, Poverty, Ethnicity, and Sexuality in American Theatre, 1890–1916*. New York: Palgrave Macmillan, 2014.

Wetmore, Kevin J. *Portrayals of Americans on the World Stage: Critical Essays*. Jefferson, NC: McFarland, 2009.

Acting and Actors

Blum, Daniel. *Great Stars of the American Stage: A Pictorial Record.* New York: Greenberg, 1952.

———. *A Pictorial History of the American Theatre 1860–1970.* New, 3rd ed., enlarged and revised by John Willis. New York: Crown, 1972.

———. *A Pictorial History of the American Theatre 1860–1985.* New, 6th ed., updated and enlarged by John Willis. New York: Crown, 1986.

Burge, James C. *Lines of Business: Casting Practice and Policy in the American Theatre 1752–1899.* New York: Peter Lang, 1986.

Cohen-Stratyner, Barbara Naomi, ed. *Performing Arts Resources, Volume Thirteen: The Drews and the Barrymores: A Dynasty of Actors.* New York: Theatre Library Association, 1988.

Fisher, Judith L., and Stephen Watts, eds. *When They Weren't Doing Shakespeare: Essays on Nineteenth-Century British and American Theatre.* Athens: University of Georgia, 1989.

Hanners, John. *"It Was Play or Starve": Acting in the Nineteenth-Century American Popular Theatre.* Bowling Green, OH: Bowling Green State, 1993.

Hutton, Laurence. *Curiosities of the American Stage.* New York: Classic, 1891.

The Illustrated American Stage: A Pictorial Review of the Most Notable Recent Theatrical Successes, Together with Many Drawings and Portraits of Celebrated Players. New York: R. H. Russell, 1901.

Johnson, Claudia. *American Actress: Perspectives on the Nineteenth Century.* Chicago: Nelson-Hall, 1984.

Marra, Kim. *Strange Duets: Impresarios and Actresses in the American Theatre, 1865–1914.* Ames: University of Iowa, 2006.

Moses, Montrose J. *Famous Actor Families in America.* New York: Crowell, 1906.

Mullin, Donald. *Victorian Actors and Actresses in Review: A Dictionary of Contemporary Views of Representative British and American Actors and Actresses, 1837–1901.* Westport, CT; Greenwood, 1983.

Paul, Howard, and George Gebbie, eds. *The Stage and Its Stars, Past and Present,* 2 vols. Philadelphia: Gebbie, n. d. [1898?].

Shattuck, Charles H. *Shakespeare on the American Stage: From Booth and Barrett to Sothern and Marlowe.* Washington, DC: Folger, 1987.

Strang, Lewis C. *Famous Actors of the Day in America.* Boston: L. C. Page, 1900.

———. *Famous Actresses of the Day in America.* Boston: L. C. Page, 1899.

———. *Players and Plays of the Last Quarter Century,* 2 vols. Boston: L. C. Page, 1903.

Young, William C. *Famous Actors and Actresses on the American Stage: Documents of American Theater History*, 2 vols. New York: R. R. Bowker, 1975.

Playwriting and Playwrights

Andreach, Robert J. *Tragedy in the Contemporary American Theatre*. Lanham, MD: University Press of America, 2014.

Anthony, M. Susan. *Gothic Plays and American Society, 1794–1830*. Jefferson City, NC: McFarland, 2008.

Birdoff, Harry. *The World's Greatest Hit:* Uncle Tom's Cabin. New York: S. F. Vanni, 1947.

Davies, Kate. *Catharine Macauley and Mercy Otis Warren: The Revolutionary Atlantic and the Politics of Gender*. New York: Oxford University, 2005.

Eis, Joel. *A Full Investigation of the Historic Perfomance of the First Play in English in the New World: The Case of Ye Bare & Ye Cubbe, 1665*. Lewiston, NY: Edwin Mellen, 2004.

Foley, P. K. *American Authors 1795–1895: A Bibliography of First and Notable Editions*. New York: Milford, 1969.

Meserve, Walter J. *Heralds of Promise: The Drama of the American People during the Age of Jackson, 1829–1849*. Westport, CT: Greenwood, 1986.

Miller, Jordan Y. *American Dramatic Literature*. New York: McGraw-Hill, 1961.

Montrose, Moses J. *The American Dramatist*. Boston: Little, Brown, 1925.

Pressley, Nelson. *American Playwriting and the Anti-Political Prejudice: Twentieth and Twenty-First Century Perspectives*. New York: Palgrave Macmillan, 2014.

Robinson, Marc. *The American Play: 1787–2000*. New Haven, CT: Yale University, 2010.

Vaughan, Alden T., and Virginia Mason Vaughan. *Shakespeare in America*. New York: Oxford University, 2012.

Vaughn, Jack A. *Early American Dramatists: From the Beginnings to 1900*. New York: Ungar, 1981.

Producing, Directing, Management, and Scenography

Bost, James S. *Monarchs of the Mimic World; or, The American Theatre of the Eighteenth Century through the Managers—the Men Who Made It*. Orono: University of Maine, 1977.

Curry, J. K. *Nineteenth-Century American Women Managers*. Westport, CT: Greenwood, 1994.

Donohue, Joseph W., Jr., ed. *The Theatrical Manager in England and America: Player of a Perilous Game*. Princeton, NJ: Princeton University, 1971.

Durham, Weldon B., ed. *American Theatre Companies, 1749–1887*. New York: Greenwood, 1986.

Marker, Lise-Lone. *David Belasco: Naturalism in the American Theatre*. Princeton, NJ: Princeton University, 1975.

Marra, Kim. *Strange Duets: Impresarios and Actresses in the American Theatre, 1865–1914*. Ames: University of Iowa, 2006.

Critics and Criticism

Bennett, Alma J. *American Women Theatre Critics: Biographies and Selected Writings of Twelve Reviewers, 1753–1919*. Jefferson, NC: McFarland, 2010.

Downer, Alan S., ed. *American Drama and Its Critics*. Chicago: University of Chicago, 1967.

Londré, Felicia Hardison. *The Enchanted Years of the Stage: Kansas City at the Crossroads of American Theater, 1870–1930*. Columbia: University of Missouri, 2007.

Miller, Tice L. *Bohemians and Critics: American Theatre Criticism in the Nineteenth Century*. Metuchen, NJ: Scarecrow, 1981.

Moses, Montrose J., and John Mason Brown, eds. *The American Theatre as Seen by Its Critics, 1752–1934*. New York: W. W. Norton, 1934.

Palmer, Helen H. *American Drama Criticism*. Hamden, CT: Shoe String Press, 1967.

Scharnhorst, Gary. *Kate Field: The Many Lives of a Nineteenth-Century American Journalist*. Syracuse, NY: Syracuse University, 2008.

Seilhamer, George O. *An Interviewer's Album: Comprising a Series of Chats with Eminent Players and Playwrights*. New York: A. Perry, 1881.

Senelick, Laurence, ed. *The American Stage: Writing on Theater from Washington Irving to Tony Kushner*. New York: Library of America, 2010.

Slout, William L. *Life upon the Wicked Stage: A Visit to the American Theatre of the 1860s, 1870s, and 1880s as Seen in the Pages of the New York Clipper*. San Bernardino, CA: Borgo, 1996.

Wolter, Jürgen, ed. *The Dawning of American Drama: American Dramatic Criticism, 1746–1915*. Westport, CT: Greenwood, 1993.

Theaters and Architecture

Bruns, Roger A. *Desert Honkytonk: The Story of Tombstone's Bird Cage Theatre*. Golden, CO: Fulcrum, 2000.

Davis, Andrew. *America's Longest Run: A History of the Walnut Street Theatre*. University Park: Pennsylvania State University, 2010.

Durham, Weldon B., ed. *American Theatre Companies, 1749–1887*. New York: Greenwood, 1986.

Frick, John W. *New York's First Theatrical Center: The Rialto at Union Square*. Ann Arbor: UMI Research, 1985.

Frick, John W., and Carlton Ward, eds. *Directory of Historic American Theatres*. Westport, CT: Greenwood, 1987.

Graham, Philip. Showboats: *The History of an American Institution*. Austin: University of Texas, 1951.

Henderson, Mary C. *The City and the Theatre: The History of New York Playhouses: A 250 Year Journey from Bowling Green to Times Square*. Foreword by Gerald Schoenfeld. New York: Back Stage, 2004.

Morrison, William. *Broadway Theatres: History and Architecture*. New York: Dover, 1998.

Naylor, David, and Joan Dillon. *American Theaters: Performance Halls of the Nineteenth Century*. Atglen, PA: Schiffer, 2006.

Van Hoogstraten, Nicholas. *Lost Broadway Theatres*. Princeton, NJ: Princeton Architectural, 1997.

Melodrama

Grinsted, David. *Melodrama Unveiled, American Theatre and Culture, 1800–1850*. Chicago: University of Chicago, 1968.

Hays, Michael, and Anastasia Nikolopoulou. *Melodrama: The Cultural Emergence of a Genre*. New York: Palgrave Macmillan, 1999.

Jones, Megan Sanborn. *Performing American Identity in Anti-Mormon Melodrama*. New York: Routledge, 2009.

Mason, Jeffrey D. *Melodrama and the Myth of America*. Bloomington: Indiana University, 1993.

McConachie, Bruce A. *Melodramatic Formations: American Theatre & Society, 1820–1870*. Iowa City: University of Iowa, 1992.

Morgan, Jo-Ann. Uncle Tom's Cabin *as Visual Culture*. Columbia: University of Missouri, 2007.

Pisani, Michael V. *Music for the Melodramatic Theatre in Nineteenth-Century London and New York*. Iowa City: University of Iowa, 2014.

Rahill, Frank. *The World of Melodrama*. University Park: Pennsylvania State University, 1967.

Singer, Ben. *Melodrama and Modernity*. New York: Columbia University, 2001.

Smith, James L. *Melodrama*. London: Methuen, 1973.

Williams, Linda. *Playing the Race Card: Melodramas of Black and White from* Uncle Tom's Cabin *to O. J. Simpson.* Princeton, NJ: Princeton University, 2002.

African Americans

Afro-American Poetry and Drama, 1760–1975: A Guide to Information Resources. Detroit, MI: Gale, 1979.

Allen, Carol D. *Peculiar Passages: Black Women Playwrights, 1875 to 2000.* New York: Peter Lang, 2005.

Bernstein, Robin. *Racial Innocence: Performing American Childhood from Slavery to Civil Rights.* New York: New York University, 2011.

Bey, B. A. *Early African-American Writers: Their Place in American Society.* Heath Springs, SC: CreateSpace, 2011.

Boskin, Joseph. *Sambo: The Rise & Demise of an American Jester.* New York: Oxford University, 1988.

Brooks, Daphne A. *Bodies in Dissent: Spectacular Performances of Race and Freedom, 1850–1910.* Durham, NC: Duke University, 2006.

Cima, Gay Gibson. *Performing Anti-Slavery: Activist Women on Antebellum Stages.* New York: Cambridge University, 2014.

Curtis, Susan. *The First Black Actors on the Great White Way.* Columbia: University of Missouri, 1998.

Dicker/sun, Glenda. *African American Theater: A Cultural Companion.* Cambridge: Polity, 2008.

Elam, Harry J., and David Krasner, eds. *African American Performance and Theater History: A Critical Reader.* New York: Oxford University, 2001.

Engle, Ron, and Tice L. Miller, eds. *The American Stage.* Cambridge: Cambridge University, 1993.

Hay, Samuel A. *African American Theatre. A Historical and Critical Analysis.* Cambridge: Cambridge University, 1994.

Hill, Anthony D., and Douglas Q. Barnett. *The Historical Dictionary of African American Theater.* Lanham, MD: Scarecrow, 2008.

Hill, Errol G., and James V. Hatch. *A History of African American Theatre.* Cambridge: Cambridge University, 2003.

Jones, Douglas A. *The Captive Stage: Performance and the Proslavery Imagination of the Antebellum North.* Ann Arbor: University of Michigan, 2014.

McAllister, Marvin. *Whiting Up: Whiteface Minstrels and Stage Europeans in African American Performance.* Chapel Hill: University of North Carolina, 2014.

Molette, Carlton W., and Barbara J. Molette. *Black Theatre: Premise and Presentation.* Bristol, IN: Wyndham Hall, 1986.

Nathans, Heather. *Slavery and Sentiment on the American Stage, 1787–1861: Lifting the Veil of Black.* Cambridge: Cambridge University, 2009.

Nelson, Emmanuel S. *African American Dramatists: An A-to-Z Guide.* Westport, CT: Greenwood, 2004.

Paskman, Dailey. *"Gentlemen, Be Seated!": A Parade of American Minstrels.* New York: Clarkson Potter, 1976.

Peterson, Bernard L. *Profiles of African American Stage Performers and Theatre People, 1816–1960.* Westport, CT: Greenwood, 2000.

Sampson, Henry T. *The Ghost Walks: A Chronological History of Blacks in Show Business, 1865–1910.* Metuchen, NJ: Scarecrow, 1988.

Sanders, Leslie Catherine. *The Development of Black Theatre in America: From Shadows to Selves.* Baton Rouge: Louisiana State University, 1988.

Thompson, George A., Jr. *A Documentary History of the African Theatre.* Evanston, IL: Northwestern University, 1998.

Waters, Hazel. *Racism on the Victorian Stage: Representation of Slavery and the Black Character.* Cambridge: Cambridge University, 2009.

White, Shane, and Graham White. *Stylin': African American Expressive Culture from Its Beginnings to the Zoot Suit.* Ithaca, NY: Cornell University, 1998.

Jewish Americans

Erdman, Harley. *Staging the Jew: The Performance of an American Ethnicity, 1860–1920.* New Brunswick, NJ: Rutgers University, 1997.

Fisher, James. "Jews in American Drama." In *Jews and American Popular Culture*, 3 volumes, edited by Paul Buhle, vol. 2, 49–75. Westport, CT: Praeger, 2007.

Kanfer, Stefan. *Stardust Lost: The Triumph, Tragedy, and Mishugas of the Yiddish Theater in America.* New York: Alfred A. Knopf, 2006.

Lifson, David S. *The Yiddish Theatre in America.* New York: Thomas Yoseloff, 1965.

Mitchell, Lofton. *Black Drama: The Story of the American Negro in the Theatre.* New York: Hawthorn, 1967.

Novick, Julius. *Beyond the Golden Door: Jewish American Drama and Jewish American Experience.* New York: Palgrave Macmillan, 2009.

Native Americans

Bellin, Joshua David, Laura L. Mielke, and Philip J. Deloria. *Native Acts: Indian Performance, 1603–1832.* Lincoln: University of Nebraska, 2012.

Jones, Eugene H. *Native Americans as Shown on the Stage, 1753–1916*. Metuchen, NJ: Scarecrow, 1988.

Sears, Priscilla. *A Pillar of Fire to Follow: American Indian Dramas, 1808–1859*. Bowling Green, OH: Bowling Green University, 1982.

Wilmer, S. E., ed. *Native American Performance and Representation*. Tucson: University of Arizona, 2011.

Other Ethnic Groups

Aleandri, Emelise. *The Italian-American Immigrant Theatre of New York City 1746–1899: The Trickle before the Flood, 1871*. Lewiston, NY: Edwin Mellen, 2014.

Grene, Nicholas. *The Politics of Irish Drama: Plays in Context from Boucicault to Friel*. Cambridge: Cambridge University, 2000.

Harrington, John P. *The Irish Play on the New York Stage, 1874–1966*. Lexington: University Press of Kentucky, 1997.

———, ed. *Irish Theater in America: Essays on Irish Theatrical Diaspora*. Syracuse, NY: Syracuse University, 2008.

Kanellos, Nicholas. *A History of Hispanic Theatre in the United States*. Austin: University of Texas, 1990.

Koegel, John. *Music in German Immigrant Theater: New York City, 1840–1940*. Rochester, NY: University of Rochester, 2009.

Lee, Esther Kim. *A History of Asian American Theatre*. Cambridge: Cambridge University, 2006.

Lee, Robert G. *Orientals: Asian Americans in Popular Culture*. Philadelphia: Temple University, 1999.

Moon, Krystan R. *Yellowface: Creating the Chinese in American Popular Music and Performance, 1850s–1920s*. New Brunswick, NJ: Rutgers University, 2004.

Williams, William H. *'Twas Only an Irishman's Dream: The Image of Ireland and the Irish in American Popular Song Lyrics, 1800–1920*. Urbana: University of Illinois, 1996.

Minstrels, Vaudeville, Burlesques, Musicals, and Popular Fare

Agnew, Jeremy. *Entertainment in the Old West: Theater, Music, Circuses, Medicine Shows, Prizefighting and Other Popular Amusements*. Jefferson, NC: McFarland, 2011.

Allen, R. C. *Horrible Prettiness: Burlesque and American Culture*. Chapel Hill: University of North Carolina, 1991.

Anderson, Ann. *Snake Oil, Hustlers and Hambones: The American Medicine Show*. Jefferson, NC: McFarland, 2004.

Ashby, LeRoy. *With Amusement for All: A History of American Popular Culture since 1830.* Lexington: University Press of Kentucky, 2006.

Bean, Annemarie, James V. Hatch, and Brooks McNamara, eds. *Inside the Minstrel Mask: Readings in Nineteenth-Century Blackface Minstrelsy.* Hanover, NH: Wesleyan, 1996.

Blackstone, Sarah J. *Buckskins, Bullets, and Business: A History of Buffalo Bill's Wild West.* Westport, CT: Greenwood, 1986.

Bordman, Gerald. *American Musical Theater: A Chronicle.* New York: Oxford University, 2001.

Canning, Charlotte M. *The Most American Thing in America: Circuit Chautauqua as Performance.* Iowa City: University of Iowa, 2005.

Cockrell, Dale. *Demons of Disorder: Early Blackface Minstrels and Their World.* Cambridge: Cambridge University, 1997.

Cook, James W. *The Arts of Deception: Playing with Fraud in the Age of Barnum.* Cambridge, MA: Harvard University, 2001.

Cosden, Mark. *The Hanlon Brothers: From Daredevil Acrobatics to Spectacle Pantomime, 1833–1931.* Carbondale: Southern Illinois University, 2010.

Davis, Janet M. *The Circus Age: Culture and Society under the American Big Top.* Chapel Hill: University of North Carolina, 2002.

Dennett, Andrea. *Weird and Wonderful: The Dime Museum in America.* New York: New York University, 1997.

DesRochers, Rick. *The New Humor in the Progressive Era: Americanization and the Vaudeville Comedian.* New York: Palgrave Macmillan, 2014.

Di Meglio, John E. *Vaudeville, U.S.A.* Bowling Green, OH: Bowling Green University, 1973.

Dobbins, Washington R., Jr. *Tambourines, Bone Castanets, and Banjos Meet Jump Jim Crow: A History of Blackfaced Minstrelsy in American from 1828 to 1898: A Forgotten Heirloom in American Entertainment.* Parker, CO: Outskirts, 2011.

Emeljanow, Victor, and Gillian Arrighi. *Entertaining Children: The Participation of Youth in the Entertainment Industry.* New York: Palgrave Macmillan, 2014.

Fields, Armond. *Women Vaudeville Stars: Eighty Biographical Profiles.* Jefferson, NC: McFarland, 2006.

Gibbs, Jenna M. *Performing the Temple of Liberty: Slavery, Theater, and Popular Culture in London and Philadelphia, 1760–1850 (Early America: History, Context, Culture).* Baltimore: John Hopkins University, 2014.

Gilbert, Douglas. *American Vaudeville.* New York: Dover, 1963.

Graham, Philip. *Showboats: The History of an American Institution.* Austin: University of Texas, 1951.

Green, Abel, and Laurie, Joe, Jr. *Show Biz from Vaude to Video.* New York: Holt, 1950.

Hartzman, Marc. *American Sideshow*. New York: Tarcher, 2006.

Hoyt, Harlowe. *Town Hall Tonight*. Englewood Cliffs, NJ: Prentice-Hall, 1955.

Jennings, John J. *Theatrical and Circus Life*. Brandon, VT: Sidney M. Southard, 1884.

Johnson, Stephen, ed. *Burnt Cork: Traditions and Legacies of Blackface Minstrelsy*. Amherst: University of Massachusetts, 2012.

Jones, John Bush. *Our Musicals, Ourselves: A Social History of the American Musical Theatre*. Lebanon, NH: University Press of New England, 2004.

Kantor, Michael, and Laurence Maslon. *Broadway: The American Musical*. New York: Bullfinch, 2004.

Kasson, Joy S. *Buffalo Bill's Wild West: Celebrity, Memory, and Popular History*. New York: Hill and Wang, 2001.

Kattwinkel, Susan. *Tony Pastor Presents: Afterpieces from the Vaudeville Stage*. Westport, CT: Greenwood, 1988.

Kislan, Richard. *The Musical: A Look at the American Musical Theatre*. New York: Applause, 2000.

Kotar, S. L., and J. E. Gessler. *The Rise of the American Circus, 1716–1899*. Jefferson, NC: McFarland, 2011.

Kunzog, John C. *The One-Horse Show; The Life and Times of Dan Rice, Circus Jester and Philanthropist*. Jamestown, NY: n.p., 1962.

Laurie, Joe, Jr. *Vaudeville: From the Honky-Tonks to the Palace*. Port Washington, NY: Kennikat, 1953.

Lewis, Robert M., ed. *From Traveling Show to Vaudeville: Theatrical Spectacle in America, 1830–1910*. Baltimore, MD: Johns Hopkins University, 2007.

Lhamon, W. T., Jr. *Raising Cain: Blackface Performance from Jim Crow to Hip Hop*. Cambridge, MA: Harvard University, 2000.

Lott, Eric. *Love & Theft: Blackface Minstrelsy and the American Working Class*. New York: Oxford University, 1995.

Mahar, William J. *Behind the Burnt Cork Mask: Early Blackface Minstrelsy and Antebellum American Popular Culture*. Urbana: University of Illinois, 1998.

Marston, William Moulton, and John Henry Feller. *F. F. Proctor, Vaudeville Pioneer*. New York: Smith, 1943.

Matlaw, Myron, ed. *American Popular Entertainment*. Westport, CT: Greenwood, 1979.

McAllister, Marvin. *White People Do Not Know How to Behave at Entertainments Designed for Ladies and Gentlemen of Colour: William Brown's African and American Theater*. Chapel Hill: University of North Carolina, 2002.

————. *Whiting Up: Whiteface Minstrels & Stage Europeans in African American Performance*. Chapel Hill: University of North Carolina, 2011.

McKinven, John A. *The Hanlon Brothers: Their Amazing Acrobatics, Pantomimes and Stage Spectacles*. Glenwood, IL: David Meyer, 1998.

McMurty, Larry. *The Colonel and Little Missie: Buffalo Bill, Annie Oakley, and the Beginnings of Superstardom in America*. New York: Simon & Schuster, 2006.

McNamara, Brooks, ed. *American Popular Entertainments: A Collection of Jokes, Monologues & Comedy Routines*. New York: PAJ, 1983.

————. *The New York Concert Saloon: The Devil's Own Nights*. Cambridge: Cambridge University, 2002.

Meer, Sarah. *Uncle Tom Mania: Slavery, Minstrelsy, and Transatlantic Culture in the 1850s*. Athens: University of Georgia, 2005.

Ogden, Tom. *Two Hundred Years of the American Circus: From Aba-Daba to the Zoppe-Zavatta Troupe*. New York: Facts on File, 1993.

Paskman, Dailey. *Gentlemen, Be Seated!: A Parade of the American Minstrels*. New York: Clarkson N. Potter, 1976.

Pisani, Michael V. *Music for the Melodramatic Theatre in Nineteenth-Century London and New York*. Iowa City: University of Iowa, 2014.

Porter, Susan L. *With an Air Debonair: Musical Theatre in America, 1785–1815*. Washington, DC: Smithsonian, 1991.

Rodger, Gillian. *Champagne Charlie and Pretty Jemima: Variety Theater in the Nineteenth Century*. Urbana: University of Illinois, 2010.

Schwartz, Michael. *Class Divisions on the Broadway Stage: The Staging and Taming of the I.W.W. Theatre and Performance History*. New York: Palgrave Macmillan, 2014.

Slout, William L. *Clowns and Cannons: The American Circus during the Civil War*. San Bernardino, CA: Borgo, 2009.

————. *Olympians of the Sawdust Circle: A Biographical Dictionary of the Nineteenth Century American Circus*. San Bernardino, CA: Borgo, 2010.

Smith, Cecil, and Glenn Litton. *Musical Comedy in America: From* The Black Crook *to* South Pacific, *From* The King & I *to* Sweeney Todd. New York: Routledge, 1987.

Stempel, Larry. *Showtime: A History of the Broadway Musical Theater*. New York: W. W. Norton, 2010.

Stone, Harry. *Stage Effect Sensations: An Astounding History Revealing Amazing Mechanical Devices*. UK: AuthorHouse, 2011.

Strausbaugh, John. *Black Like You: Blackface, Whiteface, Insult & Imitation in American Popular Culture*. New York: Tarcher, 2006.

Streeby, Shelley. *American Sensations: Class, Empire, and the Production of Popular Culture*. Berkeley: University of California, 2002.

Sweet, Frank W. *A History of the Medicine Show*. Palm Coast, FL: Backintyme, 2000.

Taylor, Yuval, and Jane Austen. *Darkest America: Black Minstrelsy from Slavery to Hip-Hop*. New York: W. W. Norton, 2012.

Toll, Robert. *Behind the Blackface: Minstrel Men and Minstrel Myths*. New York: American Heritage, 1978.

———. *Blacking Up. The Minstrel Show in Nineteenth-Century America*. New York: Oxford University, 1974.

Traubner, Richard. *Operetta. A Theatrical History*. Garden City, NY: Doubleday, 1983.

Watkins, Mel. *On the Real Side: A History of African American Comedy*. Chicago: Lawrence Hill, 1999.

Wittke, Carl. *Tambo and Bones*. Durham, NC: Duke University, 1930.

Wyatt III, Robert Lee. *The History of the Haverstock Tent Show*. Carbondale: Southern Illinois University, 1997.

Women

Bennett, Alma J. *American Women Theatre Critics: Biographies and Selected Writings of Twelve Reviewers, 1753–1919*. Jefferson, NC: McFarland, 2010.

Chinoy, Helen Krich, and Linda Walsh Jenkins. *Women in American Theatre*. New York: Theatre Communications Group, 1987.

Cima, Gay Gibson. *Performing Anti-Slavery: Activist Women on Antebellum Stages*. Lewiston, NY: Edwin Mellen, 2014.

Curry, Jane Kathleen. *Nineteenth-Century American Women Theatre Managers*. Westport, CT: Praeger, 1994.

Desti-Demanti, Zoe. *Early American Women Dramatists, 1780–1860*. New York: Routledge, 1998.

Dudden, Fay E. *Women in the American Theatre: Actresses and Audiences 1790–1870*. New Haven, CT: Yale University, 1994.

Fields, Armond. *Women Vaudeville Stars: Eighty Biographical Profiles*. Jefferson, NC: McFarland, 2012.

Johnson, Claudia D. *American Actress: Perspective on the Nineteenth Century*. Chicago: Nelson-Hall, 1984.

Schofield, Mary A., and Christine Macheski, eds. *Curtain Calls: British and American Women and the Theater, 1660–1820*. Athens: Ohio University Press, 1991.

BIOGRAPHIES AND MEMOIRS OF THEATER ARTISTS

The theatrical memoir (autobiography), a popular genre of literature during the 19th century, often provides a colorful, if somewhat imperfect (and often inaccurate in detail), portrait of American theatrical life, particularly between the American Revolution and World War I. Certainly, the top theater personages of the present day become the subjects of biographies, but they only infrequently write their own accounts. Browsing in some of the memoirs listed here will make it clear how crucial that form is to knowledge of the premodern era. Despite the artists' faulty memories and inevitable omissions, there is an immediacy, authenticity, and color to personal recollections that no biographer or historian can fully capture. The autobiography of Joseph Jefferson, for example, is one among many such documents that not only provides specific insights into one career, but captures the spirit of the times. In Jefferson's case, his recollections cover much of the hurly-burly of the 19th-century stage. In the most fascinating memoirs, the artist does not simply chronicle her or his own career, but also reminisces about friendships and influences in the profession.

While the lives of actors, understandably, most readily attract interest, the memoirs and biographies of playwrights and other artists are also compelling. Special mention must be made of published recollections of managers, for they necessarily had extensive interconnections with many artists as well as prodigious memories for people.

General

Bogar, Thomas A. *Backstage at the Lincoln Assassination: The Untold Story of the Actors and Stagehands at Ford's Theatre.* Washington, DC: Regnery History, 2013.

Edwards, Anne. *The DeMilles: An American Family.* New York: Harry N. Abrams, 1988.

Horton, Judge. *About Stage Folks.* Detroit: Free Press, 1902.

Hurlbut, Gladys. *Next Week* East Lynne*!* New York: E. P. Dutton, 1950.

Logan, Olive. *Before the Footlights and Behind the Scenes.* Philadelphia, PA: Parmelee, 1870.

Actors and Actresses

Alford, Terry, ed. *The Unlocked Book: A Memoir of John Wilkes Booth by His Sister, Asia Booth Clarke.* Jackson: University Press of Mississippi, 1999.

Alger, William Rounseville. *Life of Edwin Forrest, the American Tragedian.* New York: B. Blom, 1972.

Anonymous. *Memoirs of Junius Brutus Booth.* London: Chapple et al., 1817.

Archer, Stephen M. *Junius Brutus Booth: Theatrical Prometheus.* Carbondale: Southern Illinois University, 1992.

Archer, William. *William Charles Macready.* London: K. Paul, Trench, Trubner, 1890.

Barrett, Lawrence. *Edwin Forrest.* Boston: J. R. Osgood, 1881.

Beasley, David. *McKee Rankin and the Heyday of American Theatre.* Waterloo, Ontario: Wilfrid Laurier University, 2002.

Bloom, Arthur. *Edwin Booth: A Biography and Performance History.* Jefferson, NC: McFarland, 2013.

―――. *Joseph Jefferson: Dean of the American Theatre.* Savannah: Frederic C. Beil, 2000.

Bradley, Marshell. *The Brothers Booth.* Bloomington, IN: AuthorHouse, 2004.

Brooks, Lynn Matluck. *John Durang: Man of the American Stage.* Amherst, NY: Cambria, 2011.

Butler, Mildred Allen. *Actress in Spite of Herself: The Life of Anna Cora Mowatt.* New York: Funk & Wagnalls, 1966.

Carlyon, David, and Ken Emerson. *Dan Rice: The Most Famous Man You've Never Heard Of.* New York: Public Affairs, 2001.

Carson, William G. B., ed. *Letters of Mr. and Mrs. Charles Kean Relating to Their American Tours.* St. Louis, MO: n. p., 1945.

Carter, Robert A. *Buffalo Bill Cody: The Man behind the Legend.* New York: John Wiley, 2002.

Christianson, Frank, ed. *The Life of Hon. William F. Cody, Known as Buffalo Bill.* Lincoln: University of Nebraska, 2011.

Clarke, Asia Booth. *The Elder and the Younger Booth.* Boston: J. R. Osgood, 1882.

―――. *Junius Brutus Booth.* New York: Carleton, 1865.

Clinton, Catherine. *Fanny Kemble's Civil Wars.* New York: Oxford University, 2001.

―――, ed. *Fanny Kemble's Journals.* Cambridge, MA: Harvard University, 2000.

Clinton, Craig. *Cora Urquhart Potter: The Victorian Actress as Provocateur.* Jefferson, NC: McFarland, 2010.

Coleman, Marion Moore. *Fair Rosalind: The American Career of Helena Modjeska.* Cheshire, CT: Cherry Hill, 1969.

Cook, Doris E. *Sherlock Holmes and Much More: or Some of the Facts about William Gillette.* Hartford: The Connecticut Historical Society, 1970.

Copeland, Charles Townsend. *Edwin Booth.* Boston: Small, Maynard, 1901.

Cowell, Joe. *Thirty Years Passed Among the Players in England and America*. New York: Harper, 1844.

Darling, Amanda. *Lola Montez*. New York: Stein & Day, 1972.

David, Deirdre. *Fanny Kemble: A Performed Life*. University Park: University of Pennsylvania, 2007.

Dempsey, David, and Raymond P. Baldwin. *The Triumphs and Trials of Lotta Crabtree*. New York: William Morrow, 1968.

Dithmar, Edward Augustus. *John Drew*. New York: F. A. Stokes, c. 1900.

Downer, Alan S., ed. *The Autobiography of Joseph Jefferson*. Cambridge, MA: Harvard University, 1964.

Downer, Alan S. *The Eminent Tragedian: William Charles Macready*. Cambridge, MA: Harvard University, 1966.

Drew, John. *My Years on the Stage*. New York: E. P. Dutton, 1922.

Drew, Louisa. *Autobiographical Sketch of Mrs. John Drew with an Introduction by Her Son John Drew with Biographical Notes by Douglas Taylor*. New York: Scribner's, 1899.

Drew, Mrs. John. *Autobiographical Sketch of Mrs. John Drew*. New York: C. Scribners's, 1899.

Dunlap, William. *Memoirs of the Life of George Frederick Cooke, Esquire: Late of the Theatre Royal, Covent Garden*. London: D. Longworth, 1813.

Ellsler, John E. *Stage Memoirs*. Cleveland, OH: The Rowfant Club, 1950.

Emerson, Ken. *Doo-dah!: Stephen Foster and the Rise of American Popular Culture*. New York: Da Capo, 1998.

Eytinge, Rose. *The Memories of Rose Eytinge: Being Recollections and Observations of Men, Women, and Events during Half a Century*. New York: F. A. Stokes, 1905.

Fawkes, Richard. *Dion Boucicault*. London: Quartet, 1979.

Fields, Armond. *Eddie Foy: A Biography of the Early Popular Stage Comedian*. Jefferson, NC: McFarland, 1999.

———. *Lillian Russell: A Biography of 'America's Beauty.'* Jefferson, NC: McFarland, 1999.

Ford, George D. *These Were Actors*. New York: Library Publishers, 1955.

Foster, Michael, and Barbara Foster. *A Dangerous Woman: The Life, Loves, and Scandals of Ada Isaacs Menken, 1835–1868*. Guilford, CT: Lyons, 2011.

Foy, Eddie. *Clowning through Life*, with Alvin F. Harlow. New York: E. P. Dutton, 1928.

Ganzl, Kurt. *Lydia Thompson: Queen of Burlesque*. New York: Routledge, 2002.

———. *William B. Gill: From the Goldfields to Broadway*. New York: Routlege, 2002.

Giblin, James. *Good Brother, Bad Brother: The Story of Edwin Booth and John Wilkes Booth*. New York: Clarion, 2005.

Gilbert, Anne Hartley. *Stage Reminiscences.* New York: Charles Scribner's Sons, 1901.

Goodale, Katherine. *Behind the Scenes with Edwin Booth.* Boston: Houghton Mifflin, 1931.

Goodwin, Nat C. *Nat Goodwin's Book.* Boston: R. G. Badger, 1914.

Gould, Thomas R. *The Tragedian.* New York: Hurd and Houghton, 1868.

Grossman, Barbara Wallace. *A Spectacle of Suffering: Clara Morris on the American Stage.* Carbondale: Southern Illinois University, 2009.

Grossman, Edwina Booth. *Edwin Booth: Recollections by His Daughter Edwina Booth Grossman.* New York: Century, 1894.

Grove, Frederick Philip. *Fanny Elssler.* Ottawa: Oberon, 1984.

Guest, Ivor Forbes. *Fanny Elssler.* Middletown, CT: Wesleyan University, 1970.

Harris, Neil. *Humbug: The Art of P. T. Barnum.* Chicago: University of Chicago, 1981.

Hoffman, Carol Stein. *The Barrymores Hollywood's First Family.* Lexington: University Press of Kentucky, 2001.

Hogan, Robert Goode. *Dion Boucicault.* New York: Twayne, 1969.

Holmgren, Beth. *Starring Madame Modjeska: On Tour in Poland and America.* Bloomington: Indiana University, 2011.

Howells, William Dean. *Literary Friends and Acquaintances.* New York: Harper & Brothers, 1902.

Hoyles, Martin. *Ira Aldridge: Celebrated 19th Century Actor.* Hertfordshire, UK: Hamsib, 2008.

Hutton, Laurence. *Edwin Booth.* New York: Harper & Brothers, 1893.

Ireland, Joseph Norton. *A Memoir of the Professional Life of Thomas Abthorpe Cooper.* New York: Dunlap Society, 1888.

———. *Mrs. Duff.* Boston: J. R. Osgood, 1882.

Jefferson, Joseph. *The Autobiography of Joseph Jefferson.* New York: Century Company, 1890.

Kahn, E. J., Jr. *The Merry Partners: The Age and Stage of Harrigan and Hart.* New York: Random House, 1955.

Kauffman, Michael W. *American Brutus: John Wilkes Booth and the Lincoln Conspiracies.* New York: Random House, 2004.

Keese, William L. *William E. Burton: Actor, Author, and Manager: A Sketch of His Career with Recollections of His Performances.* New York: G. P. Putnam's Sons, 1885.

Kotsilibas-Davis, James. *Great Times, Good Times: The Odyssey of Maurice Barrymore.* New York: Doubleday, 1977.

Leman, Walter M. *Memories of an Old Actor.* San Francisco, CA: A. Roman Company, 1886.

Lindfors, Bernth. *Ira Aldridge: American Roscius.* Rochester, NY: University of Rochester, 2007.

————. *Ira Aldridge: The Early Years, 1807–1833*. Rochester, NY: University of Rochester, 2011.

————. *Ira Aldridge: The Vagabond Years, 1833–1852*. Rochester, NY: University of Rochester, 2011.

Lockridge, Richard. *Darling of Misfortune: Edwin Booth: 1833–1893*. New York: Century Company, 1932.

Loux, Arthur F. *John Wilkes Booth: Day by Day*. Jefferson, NC: McFarland, 2014.

Maginnes, F. Arant. *Thomas Abthorpe Cooper: Father of the American Stage, 1775–1849*. Jefferson, NC: McFarland, 2004.

Malone, Mary, and Eros Keith. *Actor in Exile: The Life of Ira Aldridge*. New York: Crowell, 1969.

Mankowitz, Wolf. *Mazeppa: The Lives, Loves, and Legends of Adah Isaacs Menken: A Biographical Quest*. New York: Stein & Day, 1982.

Margaret. *Theatrical Sketches: Here and There with Prominent Actors*. New York: The Merriam, 1894.

Marks, Patricia. *Sarah Bernhardt's First American Theatrical Tour, 1880–1881*. Jefferson, NC: McFarland, 2003.

Marshall, Herbert. *Ira Aldridge: Negro Tragedian*. Washington. DC: Howard University, 1993.

Mathews, Brander. *The Life and Art of Edwin Booth and His Contemporaries*. Boston: L. C. Page, 1906.

Mathews, Brander, and Laurence Hutton, eds. *Kean and Booth and Their Contemporaries*. Boston: L. C. Page, 1886.

McArthur, Benjamin. *The Man Who Was Rip Van Winkle: Joseph Jefferson and Nineteenth-Century American Theatre*. New Haven, CT: Yale University, 2007.

McFeely, Deirdre. *Dion Boucicault: Irish Identity on Stage*. Cambridge: Cambridge University, 2012.

McKay, Frederic Edward, and Charles E. L. Wingate, eds. *Famous American Actors of To-day*. New York: Crowell, 1896.

McVicker, James Hubert. *The Press, The Pulpit, and the Stage: A Lecture Delivered at Central Music Hall, Chicago, November 28, 1882*. Chicago: Western News, 1883.

Merrill, Lisa. *When Romeo Was a Woman: Charlotte Cushman and Her Circle of Female Spectators*. Ann Arbor: University of Michigan, 1999.

Miller, Darlis A. *Captain Jack Crawford: Buckskin Poet, Scout, and Showman*. Albuquerque: University of New Mexico, 2012.

Modjeska, Helena. *Memories and Impressions*. New York: Macmillan, 1910.

Moody, Richard. *Edwin Forrest, First Star of the American Stage*. New York: Knopf, 1960.

————. *Ned Harrigan: From Corlear's Hook to Herald Square*. Chicago: Nelson-Hall, 1980.

Morris, Clara. *Life on the Stage*. New York: S. S. McClure, Phillips, 1901.

———. *Some Recollections of John Wilkes Booth*. New York: S. S. McClure, 1901.

———. *Stage Confidences*. Boston: Lothrop, 1902.

Moses, Montrose J. *Famous Actor Families in America*. New York: Crowell, 1906.

Mowatt, Anna Cora. *Autobiography of an Actress or Eight Years on the Stage*. Boston: Ticknor, Reed, and Fields, 1854.

Murdoch, James E. *The Stage: Recollections of Actors and Acting from an Experience of Fifty Years*. Philadelphia, PA: J. M. Stoddart, 1880.

Oggel, L. Terry. *Edwin Booth: A Bio-Bibliography*. Westport, CT: Greenwood, 1992.

———. *The Letters and Notebooks of Mary Devlin Booth*. New York: Greenwood, 1987.

Overmyer, Grace. *America's First Hamlet*. Westport, CT: Greenwood, 1975.

Pitou, Augustus. *Masters of the Show*. New York: Neale, 1914.

Peters, Margot. *The House of Barrymore*. New York: Random House, 1993.

Reignolds-Winslow, Catherine Mary. *Yesterdays with Actors*. Boston: Cupples and Hurd, 1887.

Rhodehamel, John, and Louis Taper, eds. *Right or Wrong, God Judge Me: The Writings of John Wilkes Booth*. Champaign: University of Illinois, 1997.

Rice, Dan. *Memoirs of Dan Rice*. Long Branch, NJ: n.p., 1901.

Rinear, David L. *Stage, Page, Scandals, & Vandals: William E. Burton and Nineteenth-Century American Theatre*. Carbondale: Southern Illinois University, 2004.

Robins, Edward. *Twelve Great Actors*. New York: G. P. Putnam's Sons, 1900.

Rourke, Constance. *Troupers of the Gold Coast, Or the Rise of Lotta Crabtree*. New York: Harcourt, Brace, 1928.

Royle, Edwin Milton. *Edwin Booth as I Knew Him*. New York: The Players, 1933.

Ruggles, Eleanor. *Prince of Players: Edwin Booth*. New York: W. W. Norton, 1953.

Sagala, Sandra K. *Buffalo Bill on Stage*. Albuquerque: University of New Mexico, 2008.

Samples, Gordon. *Lust for Fame: The Stage Career of John Wilkes Booth*. Jefferson, NC: McFarland, 1998.

Saxon, Arthur H. *P. T. Barnum: The Legend and the Man*. New York: Columbia University, 1995.

Schanke, Robert A., and Kim Marra, eds. *Passing Performances: Queer Readings of Leading Players in American Theater History*. Ann Arbor: University of Michigan, 1998.

Schoch, Richard W. *Macready, Booth, Irving, Terry: Great Shakespeareans*. New York: Continuum, 2011.

―――. *Shakespeare's Victorian Stage: Performing History in the Theatre of Charles Kean*. Cambridge: Cambridge University, 2006.

Scott, John A., ed. *Journal of a Residence on a Georgian Plantation in 1838–1839*. Athens: University of Georgia, 1984.

Sentilles, Renée M. *Performing Menken: Adah Isaacs Menken and the Birth of American Celebrity*. New York: Cambridge University, 2003.

Seymour, Bruce. *Lola Montez: A Life*. New Haven, CT: Yale University, 1998.

Shattuck, Charles H. *The Hamlet of Edwin Booth*. Urbana: University of Illinois, 1969.

Shaw, Dale. *Titans of the American Stage: Edwin Forrest, the Booths, the O'Neills*. London: Westminster, 1971.

Skinner, Otis. *Footlights and Spotlights: Recollections of My Life on the Stage*. Indianapolis: Bobbs-Merrill, 1924.

―――. *The Last Tragedian*. New York: Dodd, Mead, 1939.

Smith, Geddeth. *Thomas Abthorpe Cooper: America's Premier Tragedian*. Madison, NJ: Fairleigh Dickinson University, 1996.

Smith, Gene. *American Gothic: The Story of America's Legendary Theatrical Family—Junius, Edwin, and John Wilkes Booth*. New York: Simon & Schuster, 1992.

Stebbins, Emma. *Charlotte Cushman: Her Letters and Memories of Her Life*. Boston: Houghton, Osgood and Company, 1878.

Strang, Lewis C. *Famous Actors of the Day in America*. Boston: L. C. Page, 1900.

―――. *Famous Actresses of the Day in America*. Boston. L. C. Page, 1899.

―――. *Players and Plays of the Last Quarter Century*, 2 vols. Boston: L. C. Page, 1893.

Titone, Nora. *My Thoughts Be Bloody: The Bitter Rivalry between Edwin and John Wilkes Booth That Led to an American Tragedy*. New York: Free Press, 2010.

Trewin, J. C., ed. *The Journal of William Charles Macready*. Carbondale: Southern Illinois University, 2009.

Wallack, Lester. *Memories of Fifty Years*. New York: Charles Scribner's Sons, 1889.

Walter, Mrs. Dr. *Reminiscences of the Life of the World-Renowned Charlotte Cushman*. Boston: W. P. Tenny, 1876.

Warde, Frederick. *Fifty Years of Make-Believe*. New York: International Press Syndicate, 1920.

Watermeier, Daniel J. *Edwin Booth's Performances: The Mary Isabella Stone Commentaries*. Ann Arbor, MI: UMI Research Press, 1990.

Waters, Clara. *Charlotte Cushman*. Boston: J. R. Osgood, 1882.

Werner, Morris Robert. *P. T. Barnum*. London: J. Cape, 1923.

Whiffen, Mrs. Thomas. *Keeping Off the Shelf*. New York: E. P. Dutton, 1928.

Williamson, Jane. *Charles Kemble*. Lincoln: University of Nebraska, 1970.

Wilmeth, Don B. *George Frederick Cooke: Machiavel of the Stage*. Westport, CT: Greenwood, 1980.

Wilson, Francis. *Joseph Jefferson*. New York: Charles Scribner's Sons, 1897.

———. *John Wilkes Booth*. Boston: Houghton Mifflin, 1929.

Wilstach, Paul. *Richard Mansfield*. New York: Charles Scribner's, 1908.

Wingate, Charles E. L., and F. E. McKay, eds. *Famous American Actors of Today*. New York: Crowell, 1896.

Winslow, Catherine. *Yesterdays with Actors*. Boston: Cupples and Hurd, 1887.

Winter, William. *The Jeffersons*. Boston: J. R. Osgood, 1881.

———. *Life and Art of Edwin Booth*. New York and London: Macmillan, 1883.

———. *Life and Art of Joseph Jefferson; Together with Some Account of His Ancestry and of the Jefferson Family of Actors*. New York: Macmillan, 1893.

———. *Life and Art of Richard Mansfield; with Selections from His Letters*. New York: Moffat, Yard, 1910.

———. *Other Days*. New York: Moffatt, Yard, 1908.

———. *Tyrone Power*. New York: Moffat, Yard, 1913.

———. *Vagrant Memories*. New York: George H. Doran, 1915.

Zecher, Henry. *William Gillette, America's Sherlock Holmes*. n.c.: Xlibris, 2011.

Playwrights

Aderman, Ralph M., and Wayne R. Kime. *Advocate for America: The Life of James Kirke Paulding*. Selinsgrove, PA: Susquehanna University, 2003.

Andrews, William R., ed. *From Fugitive Slave to Free Man: The Autobiography of William Wells Brown*. Columbia: University of Missouri, 2003.

Anthony, Katharine. *First Lady of the Revolution: The Life of Mercy Otis Warren*. Garden City, NY: Doubleday, 1958.

Arms, George, Mary Bess Whidden, and Gary Scharnhorst. *Staging Howells: Plays and Correspondence with Lawrence Barrett*. Albuquerque: University of New Mexico, 1994.

Baine, Rodney M. *Robert Munford*. Athens: University of Georgia, 1967.

Banham, Martin, ed. *Plays by Tom Taylor*. Cambridge: Cambridge University, 1985.

Barnes, Eric. *The Lady of Fashion*. New York: Charles Scribner's Sons, 1954.

Belasco, David. *The Theatre through Its Stage Door*. Edited by Louis V. Defoe. New York and London: Harper & Brothers, 1919.

Bradley, Edward Sculley. *George Henry Boker, Poet and Patriot*. Philadelphia: University of Pennsylvania, 1927.

Brown, Alice. *Mercy Warren*. New York: C. Scribner's Sons, 1896.

Canary, Robert H. *William Dunlap*. New York: Twayne, 1970.

Carson, Ada Lou, and Herbert L. Carson. *Royall Tyler*. Boston: Twayne, 1979.

Carter, Everett. *Howells and the Age of Realism*. Philadelphia, PA: Lippincott, 1950.

Chiles, Rosa Pendleton. *John Howard Payne*. New York: Columbia Historical Society, 1930.

Claeren, Wayne H. *Bartley Campbell: Playwright of the Gilded Age*. Pittsburgh, PA: University of Pittsburgh, 1975.

Clarke, Henry V. *John Howard Payne*. New York: Munsey's Magazine, 1892.

Coad, Oral Sumner. *William Dunlap: A Study of His Life and Works*. New York: Dunlap Society, 1917.

Dahl, Curtis. *Robert Montgomery Bird*. New York: Twayne, 1963.

Daly, Joseph Francis. *The Life of Augustin Daly*. New York: Macmillan, 1917.

Davis, Ronald J. *Augustus Thomas*. Boston: Twayne, 1984.

Edwards, Herbert J., and Julia A. Herne. *James A. Herne: The Rise of Realism in the American Drama*. Orono: University of Maine, 1964.

Evans, Oliver H. *George Henry Boker*. Boston: Twayne, 1984.

Farrison, William Edward. *William Wells Brown: Author & Reformer*. Chicago: University of Chicago, 1969.

Fawkes, Richard. *Dion Boucicault: A Biography*. London: Quartet, 1979, 2011.

Felheim, Marvin. *The Theater of Augustin Daly; An Account of the Late Nineteenth Century American Stage*. Cambridge, MA: Harvard University, 1956.

Foust, Clement. *The Life and Dramatic Works of Robert Montgomery Bird*. New York: Knickerbocker, 1919.

Frerer, Lloyd Anton. *Bronson Howard, Dean of American Dramatists*. Lewiston, NY: Edwin Mellen, 2001.

Frost, O. W. *Joaquin Miller*. New York: Twayne, 1967.

Gelb, Arthur, and Barbara Gelb. *O'Neill: Life with Monte Cristo*. New York: Applause, 2000.

Goodman, Susan, and Carl Dawson. *William Dean Howells: A Writer's Life*. Berkeley: University of California, 2005.

Greenspan, Ezra, ed. *William Wells Brown: A Reader*. Athens: University of Georgia, 2008.

Harrison, Gabriel. *John Howard Payne, Dramatist, Poet, Actor and Author of "Home, Sweet Home"; His Life and Writing*. Philadelphia: J. B. Lippincott, 1885.

Herold, Amos L. *James Kirke Paulding, Versatile American*. New York: Columbia University, 1926.

Hogan, Robert. *Dion Boucicault*. New York: Twayne, 1969.

Karp, Abraham J. *Mordecai Manuel Noah: The First American Jew*. New York: Yeshiva University Museum, 1987.

Kirk, Rudolf, and Clara M. Kirk. *William Dean Howells*. New York: Twayne, 1962.

Kitts, Thomas M. *The Theatrical Life of George Henry Boker*. New York: Peter Lang, 1994.

Kleinfeld, Daniel, and Michaek Schuldiner. *The Selected Writings of Mordecai Noah*. Westport, CT: Praeger, 1999.

Knowles, James Sheridan. *The Dramatic Works of James Sheridan Knowles*. London: Routledge, Warnes & Routledge, 1859.

Knowles, Richard Brinsley. *The Life of James Sheridan Knowles*. London: James McHenry, 1872.

Lawson, Benjamin S. *Joaquin Miller*. Boise, ID: Boise State University, 1980.

Lyons, Maura. *William Dunlap and the Construction of an American Art History*. Amherst: University of Massachusetts, 2005.

Makover, A. B. *Mordecai M. Noah, His Life and Work from the Jewish Viewpoint*. New York: Bloch, 1917.

Molin, Sven Eric, and Robin Goodfellow, eds. *Dion Boucicault: A Documentary Life*. Newark, DE: Proscenium, 1979.

Mowatt, Anna Cora. *Plays by Anna Cora Mowatt*. Boston: Ticknor and Fields, 1855.

Musser, Paul H. *James Nelson Barker, with a Reprint of His Comedy* Tears and Smiles. Philadelphia: University of Pennsylvania, 1929.

Nason, Elias. *A Memoir of Mrs. Susanna Rowson, With Elegant and Illustrative Extracts from Her Writing in Prose and Poetry*. Albany, NY: J. Munsell, 1870.

Parker, Patricia L. *Susanna Rowson*. Boston: Twayne 1986.

Payne, John Howard. *Memoirs of John Howard Payne, The American Roscius: With Criticisms on His Acting, In the Various Theatres of America, England, and Ireland. Compiled from Authentic Documents*. London: J. Miller, 1815.

Perry, John. *James A. Herne: The American Ibsen*. Chicago: Nelson-Hall, 1978.

Peterson, Martin Severin. *Joaquin Miller, Literary Frontiersman.* Stanford, CA: Stanford University, 1937.

Reynolds, Larry J. *James Kirke Paulding.* New York: Twayne, 1984.

Richards, Jeffrey. *Mercy Otis Warren.* New York: Twayne, 1995.

Richards, Jeffrey, and Sharon M. Harris, eds. *Mercy Otis Warren: Selected Letters.* Athens: University of Georgia, 2009.

Rust, Marion. *Prodigal Daughters: Susanna Rowson's Early American Women.* Chapel Hill: University of North Carolina, 2008.

Sarna, Jonathan D. *Jacksonian Jew: The Two Worlds of Mordecai Noah.* Teaneck, NJ: Holmes & Meier, 1981.

Scharnhorst, Gary. *Bret Harte: Opening the American Literary West.* Norman: University of Oklahoma, 2000.

Stuart, Nancy Rubin. *The Muse of the Revolution: The Secret Pen of Mercy Otis Warren and the Founding of a Nation.* Boston: Beacon, 2008.

Tanselle, G. Thomas. *Royall Tyler.* Cambridge, MA: Harvard University, 1967.

Tasch, Peter A. *The Dramatic Cobbler: The Life and Works of Isaac Bickerstaff.* Lewisburg, PA: Bucknell University, 1975.

Temple, Charlotte. *Susanna Rowson.* New York: Oxford University, 1986.

Tolles, Winton. *Tom Taylor and the Victorian Drama.* New York: Columbia University, 1940.

Tyler, Royall. *Four Plays by Royall Tyler.* Princeton, NJ: Princeton University, 1941.

Walsh, Townsend. *The Career of Dion Boucicault.* New York: Dunlap Society, 1915.

Whelchel, L. H. *My Chains Fell Off: William Wells Brown, Fugitive Abolitionist.* Lanham, MD: University Press of America, 1985.

Winter, William, ed. *Life, Stories and Poems of John Brougham.* Boston: James R. Osgood, 1881.

Zagarri, Rosemarie. *A Woman's Dilemma: Mercy Otis Warren and the American Revolution.* Wheeling, IL: Harlan Davidson, 1995.

Critics

Crouthamel, James L. *Bennett's New York Herald and the Rise of the Popular Press.* Syracuse, NY: Syracuse University, 1989.

Leslie, Amy. *Some Players: Personal Sketches.* Chicago: Herbert S. Stone, 1901.

Seitz, Don C. *James Gordon Bennett.* Boston: Bobbs-Merrill, 1928.

Watermeier, Daniel J. *Between Actor and Critic: Selected Letter of Edwin Booth and William Winter.* Princeton, NJ: Princeton University, 1972.

Whiting, Lilian. *Kate Field: A Record.* Boston: Little, Brown, 1900.

Producers, Directors, Managers, and Scenographers

Blumenthal, George. *My Sixty Years in Show Business: A Chronicle of the American Theatre, 1874–1934*, as told to Arthur H. Menkin. New York: Frederick C. Osberg, 1936.

Curry, Jane Kathleen. *Nineteenth-Century American Women Theatre Managers*. Westport, CT: Greenwood, 1994.

Grau, Robert. *The Business Man in the Amusement World*. New York: Broadway, 1910.

———. *Forty Years of Observation of Music and the Drama*. New York: Broadway, 1909.

Kunhardt, Philip B., Jr., Philip B. Kunhardt III, and Peter W. Kunhardt. *P. T. Barnum: America's Greatest Showman*. New York: Knopf, 1995.

Leavitt, M. B. *Fifty Years in Theatrical Management*. New York: Broadway, 1912.

Marker, Lise-Lone. *David Belasco: Naturalism in the American Theatre*. Princeton, NJ: Princeton University, 1974.

Pitou, Augustus. *Masters of the Show*. New York: Neale, 1914.

Sokalski, J. A. *Pictorial Illusionism: The Theatre of Steele Mackaye*. Montreal, Canada: McGill-Queens University, 2007.

Timberlake, Craig. *The Life & Work of David Belasco, the Bishop of Broadway*. New York: Library Publishers, 1954.

Winter, William. *The Life of David Belasco*, 2 vols. New York: Moffat, Yard, 1918.

Zellers, Parker. *Tony Pastor: Dean of the Vaudeville Stage*. Ypsilanti: Eastern Michigan University, 1971.

PLAYS AND ANTHOLOGIES OF PLAYS

This listing of plays and anthologies of plays must be highly selective, considering the thousands of plays published during the era. Hixon and Hennessee's finding guide to *Nineteenth-Century Drama* (see bibliographies and reference works) is helpful in this regard. Fortunately, many libraries still house a plethora of single-play editions published during the 1910s and 1920s. Plays that did not get published may often be found in manuscripts in the Billy Rose Theatre Collection at Lincoln Center Library for the Performing Arts or in other theater archives.

America's Lost Plays, Vols. 1–21 (bound in 11 volumes). Princeton, NJ: Princeton University Press, 1941/Bloomington: Indiana University, 1963.

Armour, Robert A. *The Plays of Robert Munford*. Tucson, AZ: American Eagle, 1992.

Barlow, Judith E. *Plays by American Women: The Early Years*. New York: Avon, 1981.

Booth, Michael, ed. *Hiss the Villain*. New York: B. Blom, 1964.

Boucicault, Dion. *British and American Playwrights: Plays by Dion Boucicault*. Cambridge: Cambridge University, 1984.

Clark, Barrett H., ed. *America's Lost Plays*, 20 vols. Princeton, NJ: Princeton University, 1940–1941.

———. *Favorite American Plays of the Nineteenth Century*. Princeton, NJ: Princeton University, 1943.

Coyle, William, and Harry G. Damaser, eds. *Six Early American Plays, 1798–1900*. Columbus, OH: Charles E. Merrill, 1968.

Downer, Alan A. *American Drama*. New York: Crowell, 1960.

Engle, Gary D. *Grotesque Essence: Plays from the American Minstrel Stage*. Baton Rouge: Louisiana State University, 1978.

Frick, John W. *Uncle Tom's Cabin on the American Stage and Screen*. New York: Palgrave Macmillan, 2012.

Gardner, Eric, ed. *Major Voices: The Drama of Slavery*. New Milford, CT: Toby, 2005.

Gassner, John, and Molly Gassner, eds. *Best Plays of the Early American Theatre, 1787–1911*. New York: Crown, 1967.

Gates, Henry Louis, Jr., and Hollis Robbins, eds. *The Annotated Uncle Tom's Cabin*. New York: W. W. Norton, 2006.

Gerould, Daniel C., ed. *American Melodrama*. New York: PAJ, 1983.

Gillette, William. *Plays by William Hooker Gillette*. Edited by Rosemary Cullen and Don B. Wilmeth. Cambridge: Cambridge University, 1983.

Halline, Allan G., ed. *American Plays*. New York: American, 1935.

Hamalian, Leo, ed. *The Roots of African American Drama: An Anthology of Early Plays, 1858–1938*. Detroit, MI: Wayne State University, 1991.

Hatch, James V., and Ted Shine, eds. *Black Theatre U.S.A.: Plays by African Americans, The Early Period, 1847–1938*. New York: Free Press, 1996.

Jacobus, Lee A., ed. *Longman Anthology of American Drama*. New York: Longman, 1982.

Knowles, James Sheridan. *The Dramatic Works of James Sheridan Knowles*. London: E. Moxon, 1841.

Kritzer, Amelia H., ed. *Plays by Early American Women, 1775–1850*. Ann Arbor: University of Michigan, 1995.

Lhamon, W. T., Jr. *Jump Jim Crow: Lost Plays, Lyrics, and Street Prose of the First Atlantic Popular Culture*. Cambridge, MA: Harvard University, 2003.

Loney, Glenn, ed. *California Gold-Rush Plays*. New York: PAJ, 1983.

Mackin, Dorothy, ed. *Famous Victorian Melodramas*. New York: Sterling.

Matlaw, Myron, ed. *The Black Crook and Other Nineteenth-Century American Plays*. New York: E. P. Dutton, 1967.

———. *Nineteenth-Century American Plays*. New York: Applause, 1967.

Meserve, Walter J., ed. *The Complete Plays of W. D. Howells*. New York: New York University, 1960.

———. *On Stage, America!: A Selection of Distinctly American Plays*. New York: Feedback Theatrebooks & Prospero, 1996.

Meserve, Walter J., and Mollie A. Meserve, eds. *When Conscience Trod the Stage: American Plays of Social Awareness*. New York: Feedback Theatrebooks & Prospero, 1998.

Moody, Richard, ed. *Dramas from the American Theatre, 1762–1909*. Cleveland, OH: World, 1966.

Moses, Montrose J., ed. *Representative American Drama, National and Local*. Boston: Little, Brown, 1925.

———. *Representative Plays by American Dramatists*. New York: Dutton, 1918–1921.

Parkin, Andrew, ed. *Selected Plays by Dion Boucicault*. Washington, DC: Catholic University of America, 1987.

Philbrick, Norman, ed. *Trumpets Sounding: Propaganda Plays of the American Revolution*. New York: B. Blom, 1972.

Quinn, Arthur Hobson. *Representative American Plays, From 1767 to the Present Day*. New York: Century, 1930.

Reynolds, David S. *Mightier Than the Sword:* Uncle Tom's Cabin *and the Battle for America*. New York: W. W. Norton, 2011.

Richards, Jeffrey H., ed. *Early American Drama*. New York: Viking Penguin, 1997.

Richardson, Dorothy B. *Moving Diorama in Play: William Dunlap's Comedy* A Trip to Niagara *(1828)*. Amherst, NY: Teneo, 2010.

Rogers, Robert. *Ponteach, or the Savages of America: A Tragedy*. Edited by Tiffany Potter. Toronto: University of Toronto, 2010.

Stierstorfer, Klaus, ed. London Assurance *and Other Victorian Comedies*. London: Oxford University, 2001.

Warren, Mercy Otis. *Poems, Dramatic and Miscellaneous*. Boston: I. Thomas and E. T. Andrews, 1790.

Wilmeth, Don. B., ed. *Staging the Nation: Plays from the American Theater, 1787–1909*. Boston: Bedford, 1998.

Wilmeth, Don. B., and Rosemary Cullen, eds. *Plays by Augustin Daly*. New York: Cambridge University, 1984.

———. *Plays by William Hooker Gillette*. New York: Cambridge University, 1983.

THEATER PRACTICE, MANAGEMENT, TECHNOLOGY, AND TERMINOLOGY

Practical manuals of theatrical techniques and technology have never been abundant, partly due to the limited market and partly due to the speed with which they become outdated as new production methodologies are discovered. In addition to the works listed here, one may find nuggets in biographies of artists like David Belasco, as well as of designers. Similarly, there are not many resources on theatrical terminology, although much can be gleaned from memoirs and histories written in or about the period.

Ackerman, Alan J., Jr. *The Portable Theater: American Literature and the Nineteenth Century Stage*. Baltimore, MD. Johns Hopkins University, 2002.

Bernheim, Alfred L. *The Business of the Theatre: An Economic History of the American Theatre, 1750–1932*. New York: Benjamin Blom, 1964 (originally published 1932).

Bowman, Walter Parker, and Robert Hamilton Ball. *Theatre Language: A Dictionary of Terms in English*. New York: Theatre Arts, 1961.

Fay, W. G. *A Short Glossary of Theatrical Terms*. London: Samuel French, 1930.

Granville, Wilfred. *The Theater Dictionary: British and American Terms in the Drama, Opera, and Ballet*. New York: Philosophical Library, 1952.

Lewis, Robert M., ed. *From Traveling Show to Vaudeville: Theatrical Spectacle in America, 1830–1910*. Baltimore, MD: Johns Hopkins University, 2003.

Lounsbury, Warren C. *Theatre Backstage from A to Z*, rev. ed. Seattle: University of Washington, 1972.

Pavis, Patrice. *Dictionary of the Theatre: Terms, Concepts, and Analysis*. Translated by Christine Shantz. Toronto: University of Toronto, 1999.

Sokalski, J. A. "The Madison Square Theatre: Stage Practice and Technology in Transition," *Theatre History Studies* XXI (2001), 105–131.

Trapido, Joel, Edward A. Langhans, James Brandon, June V. Gibson, eds. *An International Dictionary of Theatre Language*. Westport, CT: Greenwood, 1985.

White, R. Kerry. *An Annotated Dictionary of Technical, Historical, and Stylistic Terms Related to Theatre and Drama: A Handbook of Dramaturgy*. Lewiston, NY: Edwin Mellen, 1995.

About the Author

James Fisher is professor of theater and former head of the Department of Theatre at the University of North Carolina at Greensboro, where he received an MFA in acting/directing in 1976. He has written several books, including the two-volume *Historical Dictionary of Contemporary American Theater: 1930–2010* (Scarecrow, 2011), *Understanding Tony Kushner* (2008), and *Historical Dictionary of American Theater: Modernism* (coauthored with Felicia Hardison Londré; Scarecrow, 2007).

Fisher's other books include *The Theatre of Tony Kushner: Living Past Hope* (2001); *The Theatre of Yesterday and Tomorrow: Commedia dell'arte on the Modern Stage* (1992); four "In an Hour" books on Eugene O'Neill (2010), Thornton Wilder (2010), Arthur Miller (2010), and Tony Kushner (2011); and biobibliographies of Spencer Tracy (1994), Al Jolson (1994), and Eddie Cantor (1997). Fisher has contributed book chapters and essays to a wide range of publications on theater and film. He has also edited *To Have or Have Not: Essays on Commerce and Capital in Modernist Theatre* (2011), *"We Will Be Citizens": New Essays on Gay and Lesbian Theatre* (2008), *Tony Kushner: New Essays on the Art and Politics of His Plays* (2006), six volumes of *The Puppetry Yearbook,* and two special issues of the *Journal of American Drama and Theatre* (2012 and 2013).

Fisher's many credits as a director include *The Metal Children, Stage Door, Angels in America, Holiday, Pinocchio, The 25th Annual Putnam County Spelling Bee, Chapter Two, Mere Mortals, 1776, The Illusion, The Complete Works of William Shakespeare (Abridged), Glengarry Glen Ross, Mister Roberts, The Notebook of Trigorin, Tartuffe, Accidental Death of an Anarchist, True West, Bus Stop, The School for Wives, Mrs. Warren's Profession,* his own adaptation of Plautus's *The Braggart Soldier,* and his own original play, *The Bogus Bride.* Also an actor, Fisher most recently played Sheridan Whiteside in *The Man Who Came to Dinner* and has also acted in *Ah, Wilderness!, The Prisoner of Second Avenue, God's Favorite, Hughie, Talley's Folly, California Suite,* and many others.

Fisher was elected to the National Theatre Conference in 2010 and received the Betty Jean Jones Award for Excellence in the Teaching of American Theatre from the American Theatre and Drama Society in 2007. He taught at Wabash College from 1978 to 2007, where he was twice named McLain-McTurnan-Arnold Research Scholar and where he chaired the Theater Department for many years.